CIVICS

Responsibilities and Citizenship

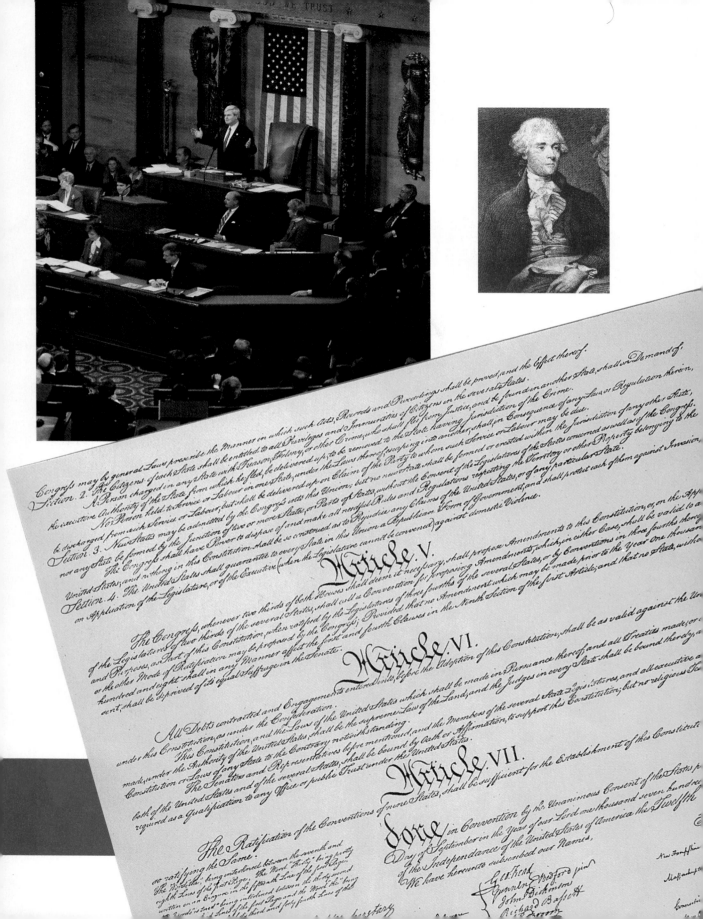

Includes Multimedia Activities

CIVICS

Responsibilities and Citizenship

David C. Saffell, Ph.D.
Chair, Department of History and Political Science
Ohio Northern University

**Glencoe
McGraw-Hill**

New York, New York   Columbus, Ohio   Woodland Hills, California   Peoria, Illinois

★ ABOUT THE AUTHOR ★

David C. Saffell teaches courses in national, state, and local government and politics at Ohio Northern University where he is also chair of the Social Sciences Division.
He is a graduate of Baldwin-Wallace College and holds master's and doctoral degrees in political science from the University of Minnesota. Professor Saffell has taught for more than 25 years at various colleges in Minnesota and Ohio. Among his various publications are *Essentials of American Government, Change and Continuity,* and *State and Local Government: Politics and Public Policy.*

★ CONSULTANTS ★

BANKING CONSULTANT

Ms. Veronica Micklin
Chicago, Illinois

ECONOMICS CONSULTANT

Dr. Gary E. Clayton
Professor of Economics
Northern Kentucky University
Highland Heights, Kentucky

GOVERNMENT CONSULTANT

Dr. Richard C. Remy
Associate Director
The Mershon Center for Research
    and Education
The Ohio State University
Columbus, Ohio

Glencoe/McGraw-Hill

A Division of The **McGraw·Hill** *Companies*

Send all inquiries to:
Glencoe/McGraw-Hill
936 Eastwind Drive
Westerville, OH 43081-3374

ISBN 0-02-821913-9 (Student Edition)   ISBN 0-02-821914-7 (Teacher's Wraparound Edition)

Printed in the United States of America

5 6 7 8 9 10 11 12 13 14 15   003/046   03 02 01 00 99 98

★ TABLE OF CONTENTS ★

★ FEATURES ★

Exploring ISSUES

Supreme Court Case Studies

★CITIZENSHIP SKILLS★

Great American Documents

CLOSEUP

American Profiles

Careers

DID YOU KNOW?

★ MAPS, GRAPHS, AND CHARTS ★

CHART STUDY

UNIT 1

Foundations of American Citizenship

YOUR ROLE AS A CITIZEN

For more than 200 years, the United States has flourished. As citizens we enjoy the rewards of our system of government, but we also have certain responsibilities. Through our participation, this system will continue to provide the blessings of life, liberty, and the pursuit of happiness.

In Unit 1, you will learn about the citizens of the United States and how our democratic system of government evolved. ■

CHAPTERS IN THIS UNIT

CHAPTER 1

What Is Civics?

CIVIC PARTICIPATION

The celebration of our nation's birthday on July 4 is a good occasion to think about what government does for us. It protects our rights and provides us with many benefits in return for certain responsibilities. These responsibilities include becoming informed on how government works, how it affects our lives, and how we can make it better. Contact the offices of your local government and find out what issues officials are dealing with now and how you can help.

Working in Your Community

After you have obtained the information, ask neighbors how they would deal with these community issues. Encourage them to become actively involved in community affairs. ■

Your Civics Journal

For the next week, look for things you and your family do every day that the government affects in some way. For example, if your parents drive, they need a license and must obey speed limits. Keep a list of the things you observe and note how government is involved.

Fourth of July parade ➤

Government of the People, by the People, for the People

FOCUS

TERMS TO KNOW

civics, citizen, government, dictatorship, democracy, representative democracy

OBJECTIVES

- Discuss the basic **purposes of government.**

- Identify various **levels of government.**

- Explain the difference between **dictatorship and democracy.**

- Describe **two kinds of democracy.**

- Discuss **how citizens influence government.**

Civics is the study of citizenship and government. The word comes from the Latin word *civis,* meaning "citizen." In ancient Rome, where the word was first used, only wealthy landowners were allowed to be citizens. As such, they enjoyed special privileges that the common people did not share. Today the word *citizen*—a member of a community with a government and

laws—applies to most people. Wealth and property are no longer requirements for citizenship.

Being a citizen means much more than just living in a country. American citizens who live abroad are still citizens of the United States. Similarly, many foreigners living in this country remain citizens of their own countries.

Being a citizen means being a part of a country or community. Citizens usually share a common history, common customs, and common values. They agree to abide by a set of rules and to accept the government's authority.

The Purposes of Government

Government, the power or authority that rules a country, is an essential part of every nation and of many communities. It provides the stability that makes many things we take for granted possible. A government makes laws, provides services, and keeps order.

Citizenship   A new citizen recites the Pledge of Allegiance for the first time.   *What rights do you think a citizen has?*

The Need for Government

To understand why having a government is important, imagine living without one. Without government, how would disagreements between individuals, groups, or nations be settled? Disputes between individuals, for example, might be settled by fighting or arguing. The stronger or smarter person—not necessarily the "right" person—would most likely win. Rules help protect us from others, bring order to our lives, and help us live together peacefully.

Without government, imagine how much more difficult your life would be in other ways. Traveling would be difficult because there would be few roads. Those that did exist would be owned by people who could afford to build them.

The Earliest Governments

Every society needs rules and some form of government. It is likely that people learned this lesson very early. The earliest writings known—from the ancient Sumerians—show that people had set up formal governments more than 5,000 years ago.

What Governments Do

Ancient governments served much the same purposes that modern governments serve today. The most important purpose of a government is to provide laws, or rules of conduct. These laws help prevent conflicts between individuals, groups, or nations and help settle any conflicts that do occur. By using laws, a government establishes order and provides security for its citizens.

Governments not only make laws, but also make sure that people obey the laws. Almost every country in history,

Roles of Government   Training young men and women, like these West Point cadets, to serve in the armed forces is one role of government.   *What are some of its other roles?*

for example, has had laws against stealing. When people know they will be punished if they take someone else's property, they are less likely to steal.

In general, judges and courts, which are a part of government, settle conflicts. If one person accuses another of stealing, but the accused person denies the charge, a court determines who is telling the truth. Then, the judge orders an appropriate punishment, if necessary.

In addition to providing and enforcing laws, governments serve many other purposes. They set up armed services, police forces, and fire departments to protect their citizens. They provide services such as education, health facilities, and road construction that most individuals would not be able to provide for themselves. Governments also plan for the future of their country by setting goals, making budgets, and cooperating with other governments.

Levels of Government

Many levels of government exist, each representing a particular collection of people. Each of the 50 states in the United States has its own government; so do most counties, cities, and towns. The students in your school may have their own student government.

National Government

Although each of these is a government, when most people talk about "the government" they are talking about the *national* government—the government of an entire country. A national government is different from other levels of government in two important ways.

First, a national government has the highest level of authority over its citizens. A city or state government, for example, cannot make any laws that would go against the laws of the national government. The national government, however, has the power to make whatever laws it feels would benefit the country. Second, a national government provides the basic framework for citizenship.

Citizenship

Being a citizen of a nation means that you share a history and a set of beliefs with the rest of the country's citizens. Americans, for example, share the ideals of individual rights and equality of opportunity. These ideals are expressed in many of our nation's most important documents, and time and again Americans have fought when necessary to uphold these ideals. The shared beliefs and history are a part of the heritage of all American citizens, whether they were born here or became citizens after settling here.

Dictatorship and Democracy

Nearly 200 countries exist in the world today. Each has its own history and beliefs and its own form of government. In many countries, the power of the national government is in the hands of a very small group of people—or sometimes of just a single person.

A government that one person or a small group of people controls is called a **dictatorship.** The leader or leaders of a dictatorship have complete control over the laws and government of the country, and thus over the lives of its citizens. Often, the citizens are told where to live, what kind of work to do, and what political beliefs to have. They may not be allowed to travel to other countries.

Throughout the ages, there have been many dictatorships. Kings, conquerors, and other powerful leaders have controlled their countries completely and often ruled by force. More than 2,000 years ago in ancient Greece, however, the citizens of the city of Athens established

Dictatorship   Adolf Hitler ruled Germany as a dictator from 1933 to 1945.   *Why do you think dictators need large armies?*

Careers

Teaching

Preschool teacher

Have you ever thought about what it is like to be a teacher? A teacher's job is to help students learn about different subjects and learn to think and express themselves clearly. In elementary school, teachers spend all day with the same group of students, teaching them several subjects. In junior high and high school, teachers do just the opposite. They teach the same subject—social studies, for example—to different groups of students all day long. Teachers who work in colleges and universities also specialize in one subject.

Vocational teachers are another type of teacher. They often work for vocational schools or labor unions, teaching students how to perform a specific skill, such as repairing cars or operating a computer.

Outside Work

Teachers spend a great deal of time working outside the classroom. They prepare lesson plans, grade exams and papers, take courses, and attend meetings. They also confer with parents or help with after-school activities.

Qualifications

To become a teacher, you usually must be a college graduate. Many schools also require advanced degrees. You must like young people and have a great deal of patience.

School TO WORK

To learn more about teaching as a career, volunteer to serve as a teacher's aide either in your school or in a school nearby. Use your experience to find out what particular training teachers must have.

---

a different type of government called democracy. In a **democracy,** the citizens hold the power to rule and to make the laws.

Two Kinds of Democracy

The government the ancient Athenians set up was a "direct democracy," in which every adult male citizen participated directly. When laws needed to be made or leaders chosen, the citizens would meet to debate and vote on every issue.

Because modern countries are generally much larger than ancient Athens, direct democracy is no longer a practical way to run a national government. Instead, in many countries, including the United States, citizens elect representatives to govern on their behalf. In a **representative democracy,** the citizens' representatives carry on the work of government.

Democracy in Action Town meetings in New England give local residents a chance to express their views on community issues. *How else do citizens express their views?*

In large modern nations, a government of elected representatives can work more efficiently than a direct democracy. Nevertheless, the power to govern still comes from the citizens. In a representative democracy, the citizens are the final source of authority.

How Citizens Influence Government

The United States government is one of the oldest democracies in the world. For more than 200 years, the people of the United States have used their power and authority to influence their government. They have done this in various ways.

Each American citizen has the right to elect representatives to the national government, including senators, members of the House of Representatives, a President, and a Vice President. As representatives of the people, these leaders have the responsibility to listen to the opinions of voters, whether expressed in person, by mail, by phone, or through public opinion polls.

Americans also have other ways to make themselves heard and influence their government. By joining a political party, they can help decide who will run for office and help plan for the country's future. By joining with other citizens who share similar viewpoints about a particular issue, they can get the government and other Americans to listen.

Abraham Lincoln, America's sixteenth President, described the United States as a "government of the people, by the people, for the people." Lincoln's words make three important points about American democracy. First, the power of the government comes from the people. Second, the American people themselves, acting through their representatives, run their government. Third, the purpose of the government is to make the United States a better place for the people who live there.

★ **SECTION 1 REVIEW** ★

UNDERSTANDING VOCABULARY
Define civics, citizen, government, dictatorship, democracy, representative democracy.

REVIEWING OBJECTIVES
1 What are the basic purposes of government?

2 What are some of the different levels of government?

3 What is the difference between a dictatorship and democracy?

4 What are two kinds of democracy?

5 How can American citizens influence their government?

Exploring ISSUES

Schenck, Skokie, and Free Speech

Americans generally agree that the limits of free speech must be very broad to ensure liberty and democracy. Situations sometimes arise that test where the courts and the people feel that the boundaries should be.

The Schenck Case

Schenck v. *United States* (1919) is one of the nation's most famous free speech cases. Charles Schenck was convicted of violating the Espionage Act of 1917 by passing out leaflets to young men urging them to resist the military draft. His attorneys claimed that his conviction was unconstitutional because it violated the free-speech protections of the First Amendment.

In a landmark opinion, the Supreme Court upheld Schenck's conviction. Justice Oliver Wendell Holmes said that the leaflets posed a "clear and present danger" of causing a criminal action (draft resistance).

The Skokie Case

The Skokie case began in 1976 when a small neo-Nazi organization, the National Socialist Party of America (NSPA), was not allowed to hold a rally in Chicago. The group, which preached hatred of Jews and other groups, decided to hold its rally in Skokie, a Chicago suburb with a large Jewish population that included survivors of the Nazi Holocaust.

The idea of neo-Nazis parading caused a furor in Skokie. The town passed laws

Protest rally

banning military uniforms, "symbols offensive to the community," and literature containing false charges against any group. The American Civil Liberties Union (ACLU), a legal organization that defends constitutional rights, supported the right of the neo-Nazis to exercise free speech, no matter how offensive their message.

The courts decided in favor of the NSPA, ruling that Skokie's laws were unconstitutional violations of free speech. Although it won the right to parade, the NSPA decided to hold its rally elsewhere.

DEVELOPING A POINT OF VIEW

1 How were the Schenck and Skokie cases different?

2 Do you think the ACLU was right to defend the neo-Nazis? Why or why not?

★ SECTION 2 ★

We the People

FOCUS

TERMS TO KNOW
alien, immigrant, deport, naturalization

OBJECTIVES

- List ways in which people can become United States **citizens by birth.**

- Compare the status and rights of **illegal and legal aliens.**

- Describe the process of **naturalization.**

The Constitution of the United States, the document that set up the government we have today, begins with the phrase "We, the people." With those words, the people of the original 13 American states took on the rights and responsibilities of citizens.

In 1787, the year the Constitution was signed, there were fewer than 4 million people in the United States. By 1800—less than 13 years later—there were already 4 new states, and the population of the country was well over 5 million. This remarkable growth has continued ever since. Today, our 50 states contain about 265 million people.

Which of these people are United States citizens? How can someone who is not a citizen become one? These have been important questions throughout the nation's history. The answers have af-

fected the way our country is today and will also affect our future.

Established customs—unwritten rules all nations observe—have determined some of the answers. Others have come from specific laws. Although the answers have changed over the years, the essential question—Who is a citizen?—remains important. United States citizenship is a prize that many seek, but only a few receive.

Citizens by Birth

With very few exceptions, anyone born within the borders of the United States automatically becomes an American citizen. For purposes of citizenship, "the United States" includes not only the 50 states and the District of Columbia, but also American territories such as Guam and Puerto Rico.

If citizens of another country give birth to a child while they are in the United States, that child is considered a citizen. (The citizenship of the parent does not change, however.)

An exception to this rule is made for children born to official representatives

Legal Aliens   Legal aliens must live in the United States for a certain period of time before they can apply for citizenship.   *What is the first step for immigrants who want to settle here?*

Diversity The people of the United States come from many different ethnic and cultural backgrounds. *How do you think this has influenced our country?*

of a foreign government living in the United States. Those children are considered citizens of their parents' country, even though they are born in the United States.

A child whose parents are both United States citizens is automatically a United States citizen, wherever he or she is born. The issue is more complicated, however, if only one parent is a United States citizen and the child is born outside the United States. Such children are usually considered citizens of the country where they were born. A child in this situation is said to have *dual citizenship*—citizenship in two countries.

Illegal and Legal Aliens

Many people in the United States have come here from other countries. Those who have not become citizens are referred to as **aliens,** or noncitizens.

Some aliens come to the United States for a short period of time, perhaps as tourists or students. Some aliens, however, come to the United States with the intention of living here permanently. These people, known as **immigrants,** must apply to the United States government for permission to settle in this country.

Restrictions on Immigrants

The United States government restricts the number of immigrants who can enter the country each year. Millions of people apply, but only a few hundred thousand are granted permission to immigrate. People who fall into special categories—for example, relatives of United States citizens or people with special talents and job skills—receive preference.

The Legal Immigration Revision Act of 1990 made major changes in immigration policy. The law increased the number of immigrants allowed to enter the United States each year. It granted special consideration to people with needed

Ellis Island Wave after wave of immigrants to this country came through Ellis Island in New York harbor in the early 1900s. *What rights do legal aliens have?*

job skills or with money to invest in our economy. It increased the number of people allowed to immigrate from Europe and from nations that were disadvantaged under past laws. It also eased restrictions that were based on political beliefs.

Illegal Aliens

Despite government restrictions, a large number of aliens are living in this country illegally. Some are people who were refused permission to immigrate; others never applied for permission because they knew they would be turned down.

These illegal aliens come to the United States in a variety of ways. A few enter the country as temporary visitors, but then fail to leave. Others risk capture and arrest by sneaking across the borders of the United States. Although no one knows exactly how many illegal aliens there are in this country, some experts believe the number may be as high as 10 million.

Illegal aliens often have a difficult time in the United States. Many have no friends or family here, no place to live, and no sure way to earn money. It is against the law to hire illegal aliens. For all of them, even those with family or friends, each day is spent fearing that government officials will discover them. Any aliens found to be here illegally are **deported,** or sent back to their own country.

Legal Aliens

Aliens who have entered the United States legally have a much easier time. Their lives, in fact, are not very different from the lives of United States citizens. Legal aliens may hold jobs, own property, attend school, and travel throughout the United States. They must obey the laws of the United States and pay taxes, just as United States citizens must.

American Profiles

Carl Schurz: An Immigrant Patriot

Carl Schurz came to the United States from Germany in 1852. Like many immigrants, he quickly learned English and became an American citizen.

Schurz became a United States senator, a secretary of the interior, and a journalist. In all he did, Schurz was ahead of his time, and his ideas helped shape American political thought.

Soon after coming to America, Schurz took up the antislavery cause. While reporting on conditions after the Civil War, he advocated giving formerly enslaved persons the right to vote.

As a senator, and later as a journalist, he was always a tireless crusader against political corruption. As secretary of the interior, he worked for better treatment for Native Americans. He also hired and promoted employees on the basis of merit long before civil service reform, and he favored the creation of a national park system to protect federal lands.

Schurz's courage and vision place him in the front ranks of immigrants who helped make this country great.

PROFILE REVIEW

1 What government posts did Schurz hold? What were some contributions he made while serving in them?

2 Identify at least two other immigrants to the United States, and describe their contributions to American life.

There are, however, some things that aliens are not permitted to do. They may not vote in any political elections or run for political office. They may not work in most government jobs. The laws of some states also prohibit them from working in certain jobs such as public school teaching. Unlike United States citizens, aliens must carry identification cards at all times.

Some immigrants to the United States live their entire lives here as aliens, remaining citizens of their homeland. Others, however, decide to change their citizenship and become United States citizens.

Naturalization

The process by which aliens become citizens is called **naturalization.** It involves several years and many steps. Aliens who have entered the United States legally may become naturalized citizens.

Beginning Naturalization

The first step toward naturalization is to file a Declaration of Intention with the immigration authorities. An immigrant may do this any time after entering the United States. The Declaration states that the immigrant intends to become a United States citizen.

Most immigrants must live in the United States for five years before they can take the next step toward naturaliza-

Learning English   Many immigrants to the United States attend English classes.   *What does learning English suggest about an immigrant's interest in this country?*

tion. (There are exceptions to this rule; for example, those who are married to United States citizens must wait only three years.) During this time, many immigrants take special classes to prepare for citizenship. They study the English language, American history, and civics. To become citizens, they must demonstrate basic knowledge in all three areas.

After the waiting period, an immigrant may file an application for naturalization. Applicants must be at least 18 years old. A government agency called the Immigration and Naturalization Service reviews this application to make sure the information on it is true and complete. This review process often takes several months.

The Final Steps

If the application is approved, the immigrant will be given an appointment to meet with an immigration examiner. The examiner's job is to decide whether the immigrant is qualified to become a United States citizen. The examiner determines this by asking a series of questions about American history, American government, and his or her reasons for wanting to become an American citizen. The immigrant must answer these questions correctly, in simple English.

If the examiner is satisfied that the immigrant is ready to become a citizen, the final step is a brief court appearance. In court, the immigrant is asked to take an oath of loyalty to the United States. After taking the oath, the immigrant is officially declared a United States citizen, with all the rights and responsibilities that go along with citizenship. If the immigrant has children under 18, those children automatically become naturalized citizens as well.

Oath of Allegiance to the United States

I hereby declare, on oath, that I absolutely and entirely renounce and abjure all allegiance and fidelity to any foreign prince, potentate, state, or sovereignty, to whom or which I have heretofore been a subject or citizen; that I will support and defend the Constitution and laws of the United States of America against all enemies, foreign and domestic; that I will bear true faith and allegiance to the same; that I will bear arms on behalf of the United States when required by law; that I will perform noncombatant service in the armed forces of the United States when required by law; that I will perform work of national importance under civilian direction when required by law; and that I take this obligation freely without any mental reservation or purpose of evasion; so help me God.

Citizenship Oath   All citizenship applicants must take the citizenship oath. *What step in the naturalization process comes just before taking the citizenship oath?*

Loss of Citizenship

American citizens, whether by birth or by naturalization, are United States citizens for life. Even if they move to another country, they remain citizens of the United States.

Virtually the only way to lose United States citizenship is to become a naturalized citizen of another country. This is because the United States does not want its citizens to divide their loyalty between two governments. (An exception is made for those who were born into dual citizenship, since they were not given a choice.)

In the past, people sometimes lost their citizenship for other reasons, such as threatening to overthrow the United States government or serving in the armed forces of a foreign country. Later court decisions cast a doubt on the legality of taking away citizenship for reasons like these. Therefore, no matter what

crimes they commit, or how disloyal they may seem to be, most United States citizens can count on keeping their citizenship forever.

★ SECTION 2 REVIEW ★

UNDERSTANDING VOCABULARY
Define alien, immigrant, deport, naturalization.

REVIEWING OBJECTIVES

1 In what ways can a person become a United States citizen by birth?

2 What differences are there between legal and illegal aliens?

3 What steps are involved in the process of naturalization?

TECHNOLOGY SKILLS

Using a Computerized Card Catalog

Using a computerized card catalog makes it easy to find any information you need for a term paper or research project.

Learning the Skill

Computerized card catalogs vary from library to library, so you may want to look for specific directions or ask the librarian for help if you have a problem. The following guidelines will help you get started in your search for information.

Using the Catalog Type in the subject you want to research or the name of an author whose work might be helpful to you. If you are looking for a specific book you may enter the title.

Suppose you want to find information about American citizenship. You could search by entering **s** (for **subject**)/citizenship, American.

What You Will See First, you will see a list of titles. Select one of these, and a "card" will appear on the screen. This shows important information about the book.

Practicing the Skill

Use the following steps in a search for information about the German-born immigrant Albert Einstein:

- Type s/Einstein, Albert

- Choose a title from the list that appears. You might see the screen below.

- From the description on the screen, determine whether the book will give you the information you need, and then determine the book's availability.

- Remember to follow the directions at the bottom of the screen. These will enable you to change screens or find additional information about the book.

APPLYING THE SKILL

Using a computerized card catalog, compile a list of 10 sources you might use to write an essay about Albert Einstein.

```
CALL NO:        B. EINSTEIN, ALBERT
AUTHOR:         Highfield, Roger.
MAIN TITLE:     The Private Lives of Albert Einstein/Roger Highfield and Paul Carter.
PUBLISHER:      New York: St. Martin's Press, 1994


LOCATION                STATUS                          UNITS


1. ADULT BIOGRAPHY      Available


PS ...............Previous screen     CA...........Longer description
/HELP........General help             HELP......About this screen        ........Any command
```

Who Are Americans?

FOCUS

TERMS TO KNOW

census, quota, refugee, migration

OBJECTIVES

- Discuss **changes in immigration** from the 1500s to the present.

- Identify reasons for the rapid **growth of United States population.**

- Describe **shifts in American population.**

One of the duties of the United States government, as specified in the Constitution, is to keep an accurate count of the people living here. This includes both citizens and noncitizens. To do this, the government set up a process for counting population called the **census.** The government agency that does this job is called the Census Bureau. Since the first United States census, taken in 1790, the Census Bureau has counted the nation's population every 10 years.

From the very beginning, the government's census takers have done more than simply count people. They have also asked a variety of questions—in person or by mail—to get more information about the people who make up our country. These questions are concerned with people's place of residence, their work, their income, and many other things. After reviewing the answers to these questions, the Census Bureau can provide a snapshot—a group portrait—of what America looks like every 10 years. Not surprisingly, the portrait has gone through many changes.

Changes in Immigration

The Latin phrase *E pluribus unum* is found on the backs of all American coins. The meaning of this phrase, "Out of many, one," reminds us that the United States is a nation made up of many kinds of people—people with different backgrounds, beliefs, and cultures.

Because of its heritage, the United States is often called "a nation of immigrants." Every American, even those born here, is descended from someone

Early Settlements Towns like Bethlehem, Pennsylvania, sprang up as German immigrants settled in America. *Why is the United States called "a nation of immigrants"?*

who came to this country from some-where else.

Even the first Americans—the Native Americans—were immigrants. There is evidence that they came to America from Asia many thousands of years ago. They made the journey on foot, traveling over a land bridge between Siberia and Alaska that no longer exists.

Early European Settlers

The first Europeans to settle perma-nently in North America were from Spain. Throughout the 1500s, the search for gold and riches brought Spanish ex-plorers and adventurers. Spanish influ-ence is still evident in states such as Florida, Texas, and California.

Beginning in the 1600s, people from France and England started to come here. The French settled primarily in Canada, but they also occupied a large area around the Mississippi River. Much later, a group of French settlers moved from Canada to the state of Louisiana, where their language and culture still thrive in the area around New Orleans.

English immigrants settled mainly along the east coast of North America, where their settlements formed the back-bone of the original 13 colonies. During the late 1600s and the 1700s, immigrants from Germany, the Netherlands, Ireland, Scotland, and Sweden joined these En-glish settlers.

Other Immigrants

Another group of immigrants who arrived during this time were black Africans. Unlike other immigrant groups, however, these people did not come willingly. Hundreds of thousands of black Africans were forced to come here as slaves. Once here, they lived and worked on plantations in the present-day southern United States.

By 1776, when the 13 English colonies officially became the United States of America, only 60 percent of the citizens in those states were of English descent. Cultures of many different lands influenced the way these early United States citizens ate, dressed, spoke, and led their lives. Over the next 75 years, as the United States expanded to the west,

DID YOU KNOW?

The First Census

When the United States became a nation in 1787, it was the first government to require that its population be counted every 10 years. The first counting, or census, took place in 1790 and was very difficult.

Although the United States consisted of only 13 states at that time, its people were scat-tered from what is now Maine to Georgia and as far west as present-day Kentucky. Few roads existed, and people lived far apart. United States marshals were assigned to ride from farm to farm taking the census.

The marshals made many mistakes in their handwritten records and did not find everyone. They did manage to count 3.9 million Amer-icans. The first census cost the nation about $45,000—or about one cent per person that was counted.

Census taker

Keep the Foreigners Out These wealthy American business leaders do not want to share this land of opportunity with immigrants. *How do you suppose these men came to be Americans?*

the cultures of the continent's earlier inhabitants—Spanish, French, and Native American—entered the mix.

The Great Immigration

As the young nation grew, it became known throughout Europe as a land of promise. Poor and oppressed people from Germany, England, and Ireland flocked to the United States in search of freedom and opportunity. The flood of immigrants grew from 600,000 in the 1830s to more than 2 million in the 1850s. Between 1860 and 1890, more than 10 million Europeans—many of them from Norway, Sweden, and Denmark—came to this country.

In the early days, most Americans had welcomed the new arrivals. There was plenty of space and much work to be done. By the mid-1800s, however, many Americans began to worry that immigrants were taking away their land and jobs. As a result, in 1882 the United States government passed the first of several laws to restrict immigration.

Despite restrictions, another flood of immigrants began just a few years later. Between 1890 and 1930, about 22 million people entered the United States. Most of them came from central and eastern Europe, from countries such as Greece, Poland, and Russia. This immigration slowed only after the government passed new laws in the 1920s. For the first time, these laws set **quotas,** or numerical limits, on the number of people who could enter the United States each year.

Immigration Today

Although immigration laws have changed since the 1920s, the quotas still exist. According to current quotas, only 675,000 immigrants are allowed to enter the United States each year. In most cases, only 27,000 of those people may come from any one country.

The major exception to this rule involves **refugees**—people who have lost their homes because of war, famine, or political oppression. The United States has opened its doors to refugees many times during this century. One large group of refugees has come from Southeast Asia, particularly from Vietnam and Cambodia. More recently, hundreds of thousands of refugees have poured in from the troubled countries of Central America and the Caribbean.

For many years, the United States was referred to as a "melting pot." This meant a place where people from many backgrounds and cultures blended into a new kind of person—an American. Today, however, most people realize that there is no such thing as a typical American. Americans come in all shapes, colors, and sizes. They hold a variety of views and beliefs, and they all have something special to contribute to the country.

Growth of United States Population

The growth of America's population was not due entirely to immigration. Even before the first great flood of immigrants began, the number of Americans

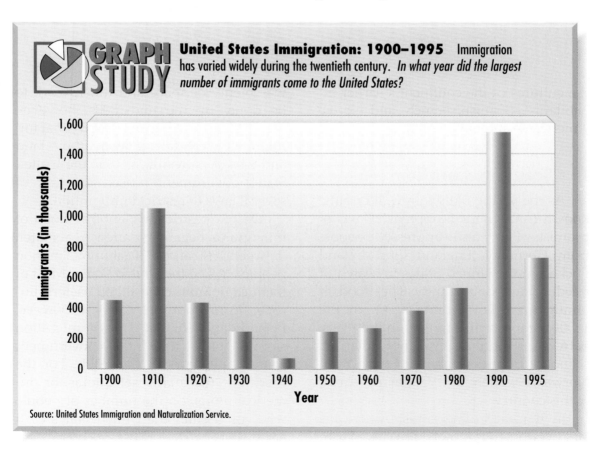

GRAPH STUDY **United States Immigration: 1900–1995** Immigration has varied widely during the twentieth century. *In what year did the largest number of immigrants come to the United States?*

Source: United States Immigration and Naturalization Service.

Urban Growth   In the mid-1800s, Americans began to move from rural areas to cities.   *How was this change related to technological advances?*

had increased from nearly 4 million in 1790 to more than 12 million in 1830. Much of this growth was simply the result of Americans having many children.

In the 100 years between 1830 and 1930, the nation's population grew almost 10 times larger, from about 12 million people to about 120 million. Surprisingly, fewer than 40 million of these new Americans were immigrants. Instead, the great leap in population was once again due primarily to a natural increase. Immigrant Americans, like the Americans who were here before them, tended to have large families. With more Americans having large families, the birthrate was high and the population grew rapidly.

One reason for this high birthrate is quite simple: During our country's earlier years, American families needed as much help as possible to survive. This was especially true on farms, where much of the American population lived. In the days before modern machines and appliances, the work of maintaining a home and family and earning a living was difficult and time-consuming. Children were needed to do household chores, work on family farms, and bring in additional money from outside jobs.

As modern life became more automated, and fewer people lived on farms, having large families became less important. As a result, America's birthrate has dropped steadily throughout the 1900s. From 1930 to 1996, the country's population increased from 123 million to 265 million. Although the population more than doubled in those 66 years, the rate of increase was the slowest in our nation's history.

Shifts in American Population

As the American population has grown, it has also moved around a number of times during our history. The first great shift in population came in the mid-1800s, when Americans began to move from rural areas to cities. The main reason for the move was employment—in the cities, jobs could easily be found in manufacturing, transportation, sales, and services. Also, as cities began to grow, they became exciting centers of art, music, and fashion. For more than 100 years, small towns throughout rural America steadily became smaller as cities became larger.

Shortly after this first shift in population began, another started. Freed from slavery after the Civil War, African Americans were seeking jobs, respect, and a new way of life. Like many other Americans, they also headed for the cities, most of which were in the North. The result was a **migration,** or mass movement, of African Americans from the South to the North. This migration began in the late 1800s and lasted well into this century.

Shift to the Sunbelt

Another important population shift in the United States began in the 1970s with a migration to the western and southern parts of the country. These regions have grown quite rapidly while most of the older, industrial areas in the North and East have grown more slowly or even lost population. Many people have left the crowded, industrial Northeast for warmer, more spacious parts of the country. States such as Arizona, Nevada, New Mexico, Georgia, and Florida have grown tremendously. For many years, the state with the largest population was New York. That honor now belongs to California, and Texas is the second largest state.

Urban Shifts

The population of cities has also changed. Some of the nation's older cities have lost population while younger cities have grown. Residential areas of New York, Chicago, Detroit, and other cities of the Northeast or Midwest have deteriorated as a result. In many cities, it is often difficult to find decent housing at affordable prices. For many years, people have been moving from the centers of cities to the surrounding areas, or suburbs. These suburbs, in turn, have spread out in ever-larger rings around the cities. In the Northeast, this suburban growth

Suburban Growth Population in suburban areas continues to grow as people move away from urban neighborhoods. *What are some other population trends?*

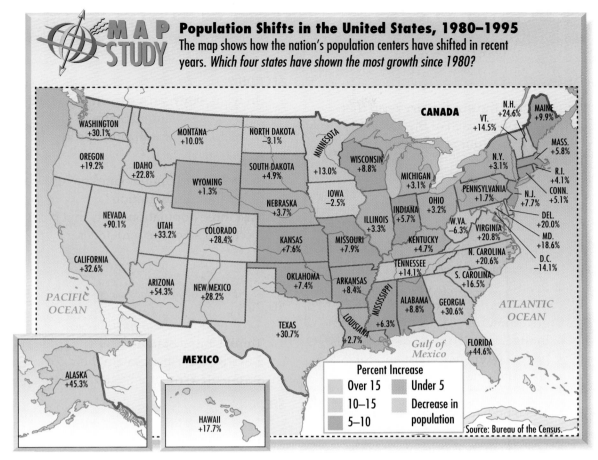

MAP STUDY

Population Shifts in the United States, 1980–1995

The map shows how the nation's population centers have shifted in recent years. *Which four states have shown the most growth since 1980?*

CANADA

WASHINGTON +30.1%
MONTANA +10.0%
NORTH DAKOTA –3.1%
N.H. +24.6%
MAINE +9.9%
VT. +14.5%

OREGON +19.2%
IDAHO +22.8%
SOUTH DAKOTA +4.9%
WISCONSIN +8.8%
MINNESOTA
MASS. +5.8%
N.Y. +3.1%
R.I. +4.1%

WYOMING +1.3%
NEBRASKA +3.7%
IOWA –2.5%
MICHIGAN +3.1%
PENNSYLVANIA +1.7%
CONN. +5.1%
N.J. +7.7%

NEVADA +90.1%
UTAH +33.2%
COLORADO +28.4%
KANSAS +7.6%
MISSOURI +7.9%
ILLINOIS +3.3%
INDIANA +5.7%
OHIO +3.2%
W.VA. –6.3%
VIRGINIA +20.8%
DEL. +20.0%
MD. +18.6%
KENTUCKY +4.7%
N. CAROLINA +20.6%
D.C. –14.1%

CALIFORNIA +32.6%
TENNESSEE +14.1%
S. CAROLINA +16.5%

ARIZONA +54.3%
NEW MEXICO +28.2%
OKLAHOMA +7.4%
ARKANSAS +8.4%
MISSISSIPPI +6.3%
ALABAMA +8.8%
GEORGIA +30.6%

PACIFIC OCEAN

TEXAS +30.7%
LOUISIANA +2.7%
FLORIDA +44.6%

ATLANTIC OCEAN

Gulf of Mexico

MEXICO

ALASKA +45.3%

HAWAII +17.7%

Percent Increase
Over 15
10–15
5–10
Under 5
Decrease in population

Source: Bureau of the Census.

has changed much of the region into a single, large, dense metropolitan—or city and suburbs—area.

A Changing Nation

Census Bureau information has revealed other ways in which the nation's population is changing. Because most Americans are living longer than they used to, there are more elderly and retired Americans than ever before. More women are taking jobs outside the home, and women now own 30 percent of all businesses.

The picture we see is of a growing, changing United States. It is a country where people refuse to stand still and where new ideas constantly come into view. As we move toward the census in the year 2000, Americans will continue to look for new challenges, find new roles, and search for better ways of living.

★ **SECTION 3 REVIEW** ★

UNDERSTANDING VOCABULARY
Define census, quota, refugee, migration.

REVIEWING OBJECTIVES

1 How has immigration to America changed since the 1500s?

2 What were the reasons for the rapid growth of America's population?

3 What shifts in United States population have occurred since the 1800s?

Identifying Key Terms

Choose the vocabulary term that best completes each of the sentences below. Write your answers on a separate sheet of paper.

dictatorship   representative democracy
alien   immigrant   naturalization   census
refugee

1. Anyone who lives in this country but is not a citizen is a(n) _____ .
2. In a(n) _____ , people chosen by the citizens carry on the work of government.
3. In the _____ , the leader ruled his people with an iron fist and tolerated absolutely no opposition to his authority.
4. The man had fled a civil war in his country and was considered a(n) _____ in this country.
5. The government takes a(n) _____ every 10 years to count the population.
6. Because the woman had arrived in the country legally to become a citizen, she was considered a(n) _____ .
7. _____ is the process by which a person not born a citizen can become one.

Reviewing the Main Ideas

SECTION 1
1. Explain why governments are necessary.
2. What is the difference between a direct democracy and a representative democracy?

SECTION 2
3. In what ways can a person become a citizen of the United States?
4. Explain the naturalization process.

SECTION 3
5. How did the United States government limit immigration?
6. List three population shifts that have occurred since the mid-1800s.

Critical Thinking

SECTION 1
1. **Evaluating Information**   Do you think United States citizens should have a more direct say in their government? Why or why not?

SECTION 2
2. **Synthesizing Information**   How might feelings about citizenship differ among people who are born citizens and others who are naturalized citizens?

SECTION 3
3. **Analyzing Information**   The character of the United States is based, in part, on its multicultural heritage. How do you think the country would be different without this heritage?

Reinforcing Citizenship Skills

Find a recent newspaper or magazine photograph that shows immigrants entering this country. Look at the photo carefully. Write a description of what you see and your impressions. Then write a few sentences explaining what you think the photographer was trying to say.

Immigration to the United States

SOURCE	1891–1910	1911–1930	1931–1950	1951–1970	1971–1995
Europe	11,611,392	6,785,081	968,713	2,449,219	2,316,661
Asia	398,405	359,295	53,623	580,891	5,919,221
Latin America	218,323	993,687	236,596	1,922,056	7,676,322
Africa	7,718	14,729	9,117	43,046	410,621
Canada	182,537	1,666,700	278,245	791,262	405,177

Source: United States Immigration and Naturalization Service.

Focusing on Your Community

Investigate the different groups of people in your community. What immigrant groups originally settled there? How has the character of the population changed over the years? Have there been any significant population shifts? Interview some elderly citizens about the changes they have observed in the community. Prepare an informal report for your class on the character of your community and how it has changed.

Technology Activity

Using the Internet

Search the Internet to find the home page for the Immigration and Naturalization Service. You may want to use the following key words to focus your search: **immigration, naturalization, citizenship.** Once you reach the home page, search through the sites referenced to find the most recent statistics on immigration to the United States. List the five countries that sent the most immigrants to the United States and the number each sent.

Cooperative Learning

In groups of four, find out the location of the nearest immigration office. Call the office and ask for information on becoming a naturalized citizen. Try to find out what types of questions an immigrant will be asked during the application and interview processes. If possible, ask a naturalized citizen to speak to your class about his or her experiences in becoming a United States citizen.

Analyzing Visuals

Immigration to this country has changed a great deal during the nation's history. The table above shows the numbers of immigrants who have come from Europe, Asia, Africa, and the Americas in the past 100 years. Use this table to help you answer the following questions.

1. Which immigrant groups have declined since 1970?
2. Which immigrant groups have grown in size since 1970?
3. During which period did the largest number of immigrants come to the United States?

CHAPTER 2

Roots of American Democracy

CIVIC PARTICIPATION

When this nation's Founders met in Philadelphia to establish a new government, they drew inspiration from ancient Greece and Rome and from the democratic institutions of Great Britain. Using these ideas and others, they created a democracy well suited to the needs of generations of Americans. Contact a local historical society to learn about your community's history. Collect information about its founders, charter, and history.

Working in Your Community

Interview people in your neighborhood to learn about their roots in the community. Find out when their families first settled there. Write a history of the community, and give a copy of it to the historical society. ■

Your Civics Journal

Imagine that you are living in the 1770s on the eve of the American Revolution. Record your observations and feelings about such events as the writing of the Declaration of Independence. Include your feelings about independence and how people opposed to it might feel.

Visiting Independence Hall ➤

Our English Heritage

During the rule of King John, the king made large grants of land to nobles, who pledged to obey him and serve him faithfully. This meant supplying armies and equipment and paying taxes to help King John support his wars. Nobles who failed in their duties were punished severely. In 1215, the nobles rebelled. They felt the king did not respect their rights as nobles and his taxes were making them poor. They forced him to sign an agreement, called the Magna Carta (or Great Charter). An important part of this document was a list of the nobles' rights.

The document established a principle that had far-reaching effects. In signing it, the king admitted that his power had certain limits and that he, too, had to obey the laws.

The Development of Parliament

Henry III, the king who followed John on the throne, met on a fairly regular basis with a group of nobles and church officials. They advised the king and helped govern the realm. The group's meetings were called parliaments, from the French word *parler,* meaning "to talk." Over the years, this advisory group grew in size and power.

By the late 1300s, **Parliament** had developed into a legislature. A **legislature** is a group of people who make laws for a state or country. The king still ruled England, but the English Parliament had taken over most of the day-to-day work of governing.

Although Parliament began as a single group, it eventually split into two

Nobles' Rights The English nobles forced King John to sign the Magna Carta. *Why did the nobles draw up the Magna Carta?*

parts, or houses. The upper house, called the House of Lords, grew out of the group of nobles who had once advised King Henry. The lower house, called the House of Commons, was made up of representatives of towns and counties. This arrangement divided the governing power between the two houses of the English Parliament.

The Glorious Revolution

The role of Parliament changed again in the late 1600s, with an event called the Glorious Revolution. During the rule of King James II, England went through a period of great unrest. In 1688 Parliament removed King James from power and offered his throne to a new pair of rulers, William and Mary.

In doing so, Parliament demonstrated that its power was now greater than that of the monarch. The idea of government in England had changed. No longer did Parliament's right to govern come directly from a monarch. From that time on, Parliament's power would come from English citizens, and no ruler's power could be greater than that of the legislature.

To make sure that no monarch would ever question the legislature's right to govern, Parliament drew up a bill of rights in 1689. This English Bill of Rights gave Parliament the sole power to make laws, raise taxes, and control the nation's army. It also set up a system for parliamentary elections.

Unwritten Constitution

As you will discover in Chapter 3, the Framers of the United States Constitution carefully planned the government of the United States. They spent many days discussing the way the government would be organized and how it would work. After reaching agreement, they put the plan in writing as a guide for future generations of Americans.

The government of England was never planned in this way, and its rules were never written down. There were, of course, many written documents that helped to shape the government—among them, the Magna Carta and the English Bill of Rights. No one document, however, contained a master plan for government. For this reason, England is said to have an unwritten constitution.

Common Law

Just as a constitution can be unwritten, the day-to-day laws people live by also can be unwritten. If enough people follow a certain "law," then that law exists, even if it is not written down.

In its earliest days, England had no laws as we know them today. The monarch could make and change rules at will. The monarch also had the power to punish citizens for breaking laws.

Development

Over the centuries, however, a system of courts developed, and the courts' decisions became the basis of a system of law. When early judges were asked to decide a case, they would look for a **precedent**—a ruling in an earlier case that was similar. If someone was accused of breaking a contract, for example, the judge would try to find out whether anyone had ever been accused of breaking a similar contract. The judge would then find out whether that person had been found guilty, and, if so, what the punishment had been. The judge would then make a similar ruling in the current case.

This system of law, based on precedent, is known as **common law.** An important aspect of common law was that it was consistent. That meant that in simi-lar circumstances, the law would produce similar results.

American Common Law

Like England's system of government, the system of common law came about without being planned. Because it worked well, it remained in place for many centuries. Today our laws about property, contracts, and personal injury are based on English common law.

This, then, was the English citizen's heritage. It included the idea that the ruler is not above the law, that people should have a voice in their government, and that citizens have basic rights protected by law. This heritage also included a consistent system of common law and a legislature made up of representatives of different groups of English citizens. These ideas took root in a new land when the English established colonies in America.

★ **SECTION 1 REVIEW** ★

UNDERSTANDING VOCABULARY
Define Parliament, legislature, precedent, common law.

REVIEWING OBJECTIVES
1 How did the English Parliament develop?

2 How did the government of England change after the Glorious Revolution?

3 What is meant by an unwritten constitution?

4 What is English common law?

How to Volunteer for Community Service

A volunteer is someone who provides a service to the community without getting paid. Perhaps you have helped out with a school food drive or worked with students in the library. If so, you already have some volunteer experience.

Volunteer Opportunities

Opportunities to do volunteer work exist all around you.

- **Local hospitals.** In most hospitals, volunteers visit patients and perform services to make their stay more pleasant. Some hospitals have volunteer programs for teens. This enables students to become familiar with hospital work to see if they want to pursue a medical career.

- **Volunteer fire departments and rescue squads.** Volunteers usually start in their mid- or late teens to learn the skills they need to become firefighters. Being a volunteer firefighter is an important job you can do for your community.

- **Libraries.** Public libraries often use teenage volunteers to help shelve books, work with students, and help at the circulation desk.

- **Nursing homes and daycare centers.** Like hospitals, these are two very good places to learn care-giving skills you can use in careers such as medicine, nursing, and child care. Many elderly people in nursing homes have no family to visit them.

Student volunteer at nursing home

By volunteering you can help brighten their days.

- **Schools.** Many schools have programs in which older students tutor younger ones. If you are very good at one or two subjects, check with your school office to see if you can tutor someone else in those subjects.

To volunteer for any of these jobs, look up the organization in your telephone directory, and call. If one agency cannot use your help, try another. There is always a need for volunteers.

CITIZENSHIP IN ACTION

1 Why do you think volunteer work is an important way to practice good citizenship?

2 What kind of volunteer work would you like to do? Why?

SECTION 2 ★

The Colonial Experience

FOCUS

TERMS TO KNOW
colony, colonists, compact, town meeting

OBJECTIVES

- Explain the importance of **the House of Burgesses.**

- Discuss the importance of **the Mayflower Compact.**

- Describe the similarities among **English colonial governments.**

- Explain why the colonists began to develop **a new sense of identity** as Americans.

A **colony** is a group of people in one place who are ruled by the government of another place. When English citizens left their own country to settle in America, they became **colonists.** They lived in America, but they were still under the rule of Parliament.

For most practical purposes, however, the colonists were beyond the reach of their home government. If colonists committed crimes, there were no English police to arrest them and no English courts to try them. If Parliament was considering a new law, there was no easy

way for American colonists to express their opinion about it.

England was, after all, about 3,000 miles away. Airplanes, telephones, and radios did not exist. The only way to send messages between America and England was by ship. Making that trip across the Atlantic could take as long as two months.

For these reasons, the English colonists in America could not depend on Parliament to meet their needs. They had to learn to govern themselves.

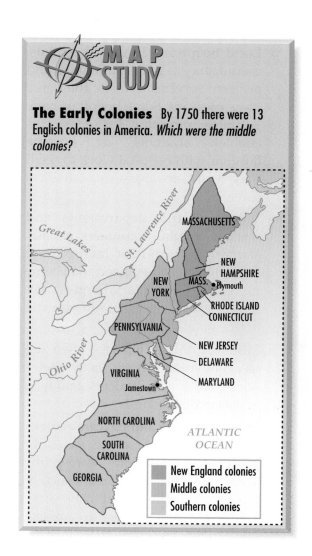

MAP STUDY

The Early Colonies By 1750 there were 13 English colonies in America. *Which were the middle colonies?*

New England colonies
Middle colonies
Southern colonies

The House of Burgesses

In 1607 a group of English colonists arrived in what is now the state of Virginia. They founded Jamestown, which became the first permanent English settlement in North America. These early colonists had to struggle to survive in a strange land. They tried raising a variety of crops, often without success. They suffered from hunger and from various diseases, including malaria. At the same time, they had to fight off attacks by Native Americans, on whose lands they had built Jamestown.

In 1619 the people of Jamestown took steps to deal with these pressing problems. Colonists from each town or plantation chose two representatives (called burgesses) to meet with the colony's governor. These 22 representatives formed the Jamestown House of Burgesses. It had very little power and solved few of Jamestown's problems. This early attempt at representative government, however, became the first legislature in colonial America.

The Mayflower Compact

In 1620 shortly after the House of Burgesses was formed, a new group of colonists arrived in America. They came ashore hundreds of miles north of Virginia and built a settlement called Plymouth. Today, this area is in the state of Massachusetts, part of New England.

Unlike the colonists of Jamestown, the Plymouth settlers drew up a plan for government to direct the colony. Even before their ship, the *Mayflower,* reached America, 41 of its passengers wrote and signed a document called the Mayflower Compact.

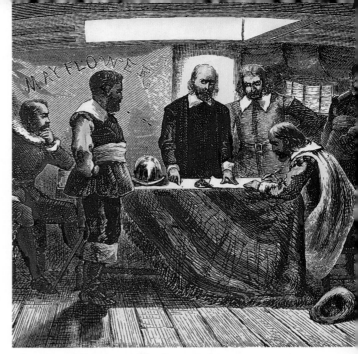

Signing the Mayflower Compact
This agreement established a democratic form of government among the settlers of Plymouth. *On what basis were the laws of the colony to be made?*

A **compact** is an agreement, or contract, made among a group of people. The Mayflower Compact said that the government would make "just and equal laws" for the good of the community. The signers pledged to obey those laws. The compact set up a direct democracy, in which all men would vote and the majority would rule. (As was true almost everywhere at this time, only adult males were allowed to vote.)

The Mayflower Compact established a tradition of direct democracy that remained strong in New England. Throughout the colonial period, many communities in New England held town meetings, and many still do. At **town meetings,** the local citizens gathered to discuss and vote on important issues.

Jamestown House of Burgesses

Following the example of Jamestown, each new colony set up its own government. *What was the model for most colonial legislatures?*

English Colonial Governments

The success of Jamestown and Plymouth led to the formation of other English settlements in America. By 1733 these settlements had grown into 13 colonies, from Massachusetts in the North to Georgia in the South. Following the examples of the House of Burgesses and the Mayflower Compact, each new colony set up its own government.

Although there were differences among the colonial governments, there were many similarities as well. Each colony had a governor, who was either elected by the colonists or appointed by the English king.

Each colony also had a legislature. Many of the colonial legislatures were modeled after the English Parliament, with an upper house and a lower house. The governor appointed the members of most of the upper houses, but colonists usually elected the members of the lower houses.

A New Sense of Identity

As years passed, the colonial governments took on more power and responsibility. Although Parliament paid little attention to America, the colonists continued to think of themselves as British citizens. (Their home country was renamed Great Britain in 1707.)

Although officially British, the colonists lived as Americans. They built towns and roads; they organized their own churches, schools, hospitals, and fire departments. They built a thriving economy and learned they could solve their own problems without help from Britain.

At first, the British government left the colonists alone. As the colonies became more successful, however, Great Britain saw them as a possible source of great wealth. In the mid-1700s, the actions of Parliament made some colonists see themselves, for the first time, as Americans.

★ SECTION 2 REVIEW ★

UNDERSTANDING VOCABULARY

Define colony, colonists, compact, town meeting.

REVIEWING OBJECTIVES

1 What was the House of Burgesses and why was it important?

2 Why was the Mayflower Compact an important document?

3 How were the governments of English colonies similar?

4 Why did the colonists begin to develop a sense of identity as Americans?

Great American Documents

Washington's Letter to the Newport Congregation

Throughout their history, Jews have suffered persecution because of their beliefs. They have been tortured, exiled, killed, or forced to adopt other religions. Newport, Rhode Island, must have seemed like a paradise to the first few Jewish settlers who arrived there in the 1650s. It was a place where they could practice their own religion openly, without fear of prosecution.

Think About It

As you read the following excerpt, think about why toleration and a respect for others is important in a democracy.

Religious Toleration in Rhode Island

Roger Williams founded Rhode Island in 1635 to escape the religious intolerance of the Puritans in the Massachusetts Bay Colony. The laws of Rhode Island decreed freedom of religion for all. Newport's Jewish community thrived and contributed to the town's social, business, and cultural life. In 1759 the Jewish residents laid the cornerstone for the Touro Synagogue, now the oldest synagogue in the United States.

During the Revolutionary War, Newport's Jewish citizens supported the colonial cause wholeheartedly. After the war the members of the synagogue sent President Washington a letter. It expressed their gratitude for living under a government in which people from all religious and national backgrounds had equal rights.

Washington Replies

President Washington agreed with the Jewish congregation. In a reply to them, he wrote that in the United States:

All possess alike liberty of conscience and immunities [protection] *of citizenship. It is now no more that toleration* [allowing other people's beliefs] *is spoken of, as if it was the indulgence* [favor] *of one class of people, that another enjoyed the exercise of their inherent natural rights. For happily, the Government of the United States, which gives to bigotry* [intolerance] *no sanction* [approval], *to persecution no assistance requires only that they who live under its protection should demean* [conduct] *themselves as good citizens.*

Washington was saying that in the United States all citizens enjoyed certain basic rights. These rights did not depend on the goodwill of one group. They were unconditional, and the government would protect them.

INTERPRETING SOURCES

1 Why did Jewish colonists settle in Newport, Rhode Island?

2 Compare Washington's letter with the First Amendment to the Constitution. Do they deal with the same questions?

Toward Independence

FOCUS

TERMS TO KNOW

mercantilism, boycott, repeal, delegate, congress, independence

OBJECTIVES

■ Discuss the American colonists' reaction to **British taxes.**

■ Discuss the roles of the First Continental Congress and the Second Continental Congress in the **movement toward independence.**

■ Explain the basic ideas found in **the Declaration of Independence.**

During the 1600s and 1700s, Great Britain followed a policy called mercantilism. **Mercantilism** is the theory that a country should sell more goods to other countries than it buys. The British believed that this policy would make them wealthy. This wealth would be used to develop the nation's industries and its navy.

For mercantilism to be successful, Britain needed a source of cheap raw materials. It viewed America, with its fertile farmland and abundant minerals, as a good source. After ignoring the American colonies for many years, the British began to realize how valuable those colonies could be.

British Taxes

After 1760, when George III took the throne, British policy was to squeeze as much wealth as possible out of America. Parliament required the American colonies to sell raw materials, such as cotton and lumber, to Britain at low prices. The colonists also had to buy British products at high prices. As a result, colonial businesses suffered.

The situation worsened after 1763. Britain had fought a long, expensive war with France and had gone into debt. As the victor, Britain won France's North American territory. To pay its debts, Britain levied heavy taxes on the American colonies. In 1765, for example, Parliament passed the Stamp Act, which required colonists to attach expensive tax stamps to all newspapers and legal documents.

Colonial Tax Stamps   Colonists had to pay a tax on every sheet of paper they used. When the tax was paid, a stamp was attached to the paper.   *Why did England tax the colonists so heavily?*

Careers

Librarian

You probably think librarians have dull jobs shuffling dusty books all day. Not true. Look around your own public library. The reference librarian is helping a high school student find information for a report on ancient Mesopotamia, while workers at the circulation desk are helping people check out books, records, and videotapes.

Types of Librarians

If you want to become a librarian, you can choose among many library specialties. School librarians teach children how to use the library. Special collections librarians work in libraries devoted to a specific field, such as medicine. Classifiers and catalogers work primarily with books—numbering, cataloging, and shelving them. Audiovisual librarians handle films, videotapes, slides, and the equipment used to show these materials.

Whatever their specialty, all librarians must graduate from col-

Librarian at work

lege and take a year or more of graduate courses in library science. Enjoying working with the public is also a plus.

School TO WORK

Volunteer to serve as an aide in your school or public library. Some public libraries also provide part-time paid positions to interested students. Use your experience to learn more about the qualifications and the type of work involved in being a librarian.

The colonists resented the British taxes. Because the colonists could not send representatives to Parliament—as people living in Great Britain could—they felt Parliament had no right to tax them. They summed up their feelings with the slogan "No taxation without representation!"

Besides protesting, many colonists **boycotted,** or refused to buy, British goods. Rebellious colonists proudly wore clothing made entirely of American cloth.

The boycott had its intended effect; Parliament **repealed,** or canceled, the Stamp Act and other tax laws. The situation soon worsened, however. To show that it was still in control, Parliament passed new laws, which Americans called the Intolerable Acts. These laws restricted the colonists' rights, including the right to trial by jury. The Intolerable Acts also allowed British soldiers to search, and even to move into, colonists' homes.

Movement Toward Independence

The colonial governments banded together to fight the Intolerable Acts. In September 1774, 12 of the colonies sent **delegates,** or representatives, to a meeting in Philadelphia. The meeting became known as the First Continental Congress. (A **congress** is a formal meeting at which delegates discuss matters of common concern.)

The First Continental Congress

The First Continental Congress lasted seven weeks. During that time, the delegates sent a document to King George III demanding that the rights of the colonists be restored. They also made plans to extend the boycott of British goods. When the Congress ended, the delegates vowed to hold another meeting if King George did not meet their demands by the following year.

Not only did King George refuse to meet their demands, but he also decided to use force against the colonists. In 1775, two battles between British and colonial soldiers took place in Massachusetts, at Lexington and Concord.

Until this time, most colonists still thought of themselves as loyal citizens of Great Britain. Now, with British soldiers shooting at Americans, many colonists began to question their attachment to Britain. Many people began talking about **independence**—self-reliance and freedom from outside control.

The Second Continental Congress

Faced with the king's refusal to meet their demands, colonial leaders formed the Second Continental Congress, which met in Philadelphia in May 1775. Not every member of the Congress favored independence. Some believed the colonists could never win a war with Great Britain. Others were still loyal to their home country. The Congress spent many months debating independence.

By 1776, however, more than half the delegates had been persuaded that the colonies must become independent.

Declaration of Independence   The Second Continental Congress appointed a committee to draft a declaration of independence.   *Which British actions made independence a popular idea?*

The Congress appointed a committee to write a document officially announcing America's independence.

The Declaration of Independence

Although a committee was assigned to write the document, one man—Thomas Jefferson—did almost all the work. His Declaration of Independence was a passionate explanation of why Americans had the *right* to be independent. The second paragraph of the Declaration began this way:

"We hold these truths to be self-evident, that all men are created equal, that they are endowed by their Creator with certain unalienable Rights, that among these are Life, Liberty, and the pursuit of Happiness."

Ideas Behind the Declaration

Most of these ideas did not originate with Jefferson. The idea that all people are equal came from a French philosopher named Jean-Jacques Rousseau.

The idea that people have certain natural rights came from an English philosopher named John Locke. Locke also said that all governments were based on a social compact, an agreement between the people and the rulers. In return for the government protecting their lives, property, and rights, the people gave up some of their freedom.

An Uncertain Future

The Declaration of Independence argued that the British government did not look after the interests of the colonists or protect their rights. For this reason, the British government was no longer the rightful government of the colonies.

Thomas Jefferson In the Declaration Jefferson argued that the British had broken the social compact. *What was the social compact?*

Congress approved the Declaration of Independence on July 4, 1776. The American colonies were now independent states—at least in theory. Their war with Great Britain, however, had just begun, and they would not be truly independent until the fighting ended.

★ SECTION 3 REVIEW ★

UNDERSTANDING VOCABULARY
Define mercantilism, boycott, repeal, delegate, congress, independence.

REVIEWING OBJECTIVES

1 How did American colonists react to British taxes?

2 What roles did the First Continental Congress and the Second Continental Congress play in the movement toward independence?

3 What are the basic ideas found in the Declaration of Independence?

The First Amendment protects the right to speak and write freely on public issues. Over time, judicial opinion has extended this right to cover freedom of expression, which has included protest signs, advertising, clothing, and even obscenity. In *Tinker* v. *Des Moines Independent Community School District* (1969), the Supreme Court ruled that freedom of speech also applies to symbols and that the right to free speech belongs to children as well as adults.

The Case

The Tinker case began in 1965, when a group of students in Des Moines, Iowa, wore black armbands to school to protest the Vietnam War. The school board learned of this and voted to ban the armbands and suspend students who wore them on the school grounds. Five students were suspended. Three of them,

The Tinkers

Mary Beth Tinker, her brother John, and Christopher Eckhart, took the school board to court. They charged that it had violated their right to free speech.

When the case reached the Supreme Court, the students' lawyers argued that the armbands were a form of "symbolic speech," similar to symbols, such as political campaign buttons, which were allowed. The school board's lawyer countered that the school had the right to make rules to ensure discipline and order. The board feared the armbands would disrupt classes and lead to fights between pro- and antiwar students.

The Court's Decision

The Supreme Court ruled in favor of the students, deciding that the armbands were a form of protected speech. On the issue of whether free speech applied to children, Justice Abe Fortas said: "It can hardly be argued that either students or teachers shed their constitutional rights to freedom of speech or expression at the schoolhouse gate."

REVIEWING THE CASE

1 Why did the students' lawyers argue that the armbands were protected by the First Amendment?

2 Do you think you enjoy freedom of speech in your school? Why or why not?

The Nation's First Governments

FOCUS

TERMS TO KNOW

interpret, confederation, ratify, amend

OBJECTIVES

- Explain the basic provisions of **early state constitutions.**

- Identify the major weaknesses of the **confederation** formed under the Articles of Confederation.

- Discuss the significance of **Shays's Rebellion.**

When the Continental Congress approved the Declaration of Independence, it took a giant step into the unknown. Once the colonies had thrown off the British government, how would they be governed?

The Declaration of Independence did not declare America to be a single country. The 13 colonies, in fact, became 13 separate countries, each with its own government and laws. They called themselves "states."

At the time, the idea of separate, independent states appealed to most Americans. The citizens of South Carolina, for example, felt they had little in common with the citizens of Connecticut. A few Americans, however, wanted to create a large central government of their own.

Early State Constitutions

Each new American state immediately confirmed its independence from Britain (and from the other states) by writing its own constitution. Unlike Britain's constitution, which was unwritten and largely unplanned, these state constitutions were detailed, written documents.

Each state's constitution set up a government similar to the colonial government that had come before it. Each state had a legislature, and most of these legislatures had two houses. The legislature would pass laws for the state. Each state also had a governor, who was either chosen by the legislature or elected by the citizens. The governor's job was to carry out the laws. Finally, each state had courts to **interpret** the laws—to decide what the laws meant and how they applied to each new situation.

Many state constitutions included a bill of rights, guaranteeing certain basic freedoms to the state's citizens. Many of

Patrick Henry   A strong supporter of the movement for independence, Patrick Henry became the first governor of the state of Virginia. *At what point did Virginia become a state?*

these rights, such as trial by jury and protection of personal property, can be traced back to the Magna Carta.

Confederation

Although each state was well prepared and eager to govern itself, a state could not do some things on its own. It could not raise and maintain a large army, for example. The war against Great Britain could never have been won by 13 small state armies. A single, strong army under central control was necessary.

For this and other reasons, the Second Continental Congress made plans for "a firm league of friendship" among the states. In 1777 the Congress detailed these plans in a document called the Articles of Confederation.

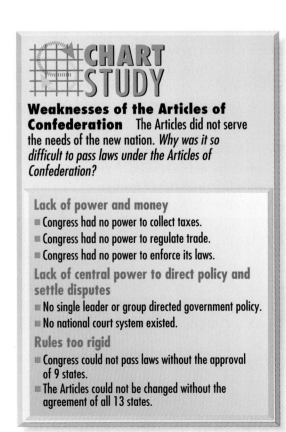

CHART STUDY

Weaknesses of the Articles of Confederation   The Articles did not serve the needs of the new nation. *Why was it so difficult to pass laws under the Articles of Confederation?*

Lack of power and money
- Congress had no power to collect taxes.
- Congress had no power to regulate trade.
- Congress had no power to enforce its laws.

Lack of central power to direct policy and settle disputes
- No single leader or group directed government policy.
- No national court system existed.

Rules too rigid
- Congress could not pass laws without the approval of 9 states.
- The Articles could not be changed without the agreement of all 13 states.

The Articles of Confederation

A **confederation** is a group of individuals (or, in this case, individual governments) who band together for a common purpose. The Articles of Confederation did not unite the states into a single country. Instead, they established a system for cooperation among independent states.

The Articles set up a one-house legislature in which each state had one vote. This Congress had a few limited powers. Among these was the power to control the army and to deal with foreign countries on behalf of the states.

Because of their bad experiences with the British government, the states refused to let the Congress have two important powers. It had no power to tax and no power to enforce its laws. The Articles allowed the Congress to ask the states for money, but not to demand it. The Congress could not, in fact, require the states to do anything.

Weaknesses of the Articles

By 1781 all 13 states had **ratified,** or approved, the Articles of Confederation. Within the next few years, however, it became clear that the Articles had serious problems.

To begin with, the Congress could not pass a law unless 9 states voted in favor of it. Any attempt to **amend,** or change, the Articles required a unanimous vote of all 13 states. These strict voting requirements made it difficult for the Congress to accomplish anything.

Even when the Congress managed to pass laws, it could not enforce them. Unlike the state constitutions, the Articles did not provide for a governor or for courts. If a state decided to ignore a law, the Congress could do nothing.

The Articles' weaknesses had severe consequences. Unable to collect taxes, the Congress had to borrow money to pay for the war against Britain. It accumulated a debt that would take years to repay.

The Congress also allowed the states to fall into debt. Conducting business was difficult during the war against Britain. To make up for lost income, each state placed heavy taxes on goods from other states and countries. Some foreign countries refused to trade with the American states. The Congress could do nothing to remedy the problem.

Shays's Rebellion

The burden of taxes again fell on American citizens, as it had before independence. In 1786 a Massachusetts citizen named Daniel Shays finally decided he had had enough.

Shays was a farmer who, like many other Americans, had fallen into debt because of heavy state taxes. Now the Massachusetts courts were threatening to take his farm away as payment for his debts. Shays felt the state had no right to punish him for a problem the state had created. Many other people in Shays's situation agreed.

A group of 1,200 farmers, led by Shays, marched on the federal arsenal in Springfield. Fearing a riot, the governor ordered state troops to break up the march. Shays and his followers were defeated, but word of the rebellion spread. Americans began to fear that more violent incidents would follow.

It had been clear for some time that the states needed a stronger central government. Now they had a reason to act. In 1787, 12 of the states sent delegates to

Tax Debts   Daniel Shays led a rebellion against high taxes that forced farmers into debt. *What need did the rebellion make clear to the states?*

a meeting in Philadelphia. Their purpose was to change the Articles of Confederation. At the time, no one realized how sweeping those changes would be.

★ SECTION 4 REVIEW ★

UNDERSTANDING VOCABULARY
Define interpret, confederation, ratify, amend.

REVIEWING OBJECTIVES
1 What were the basic provisions of early state constitutions?

2 What were the major weaknesses of the Confederation formed under the Articles?

3 What was the significance of Shays's Rebellion?

July 4, 1776

DELEGATES AT THE SECOND CONTINENTAL Congress faced an enormous task. The war against Great Britain had begun, but to many colonists the purpose for fighting was unclear. As sentiment increased for a complete break with Britain, Congress decided to act. A committee was appointed to prepare a document that declared the 13 colonies free and independent from Britain. The result was the Declaration of Independence.

To aid in comprehension, selected words and their definitions appear in the side margin, along with other explanatory notes.

impel *force*

endowed *provided*

People create governments to ensure that their natural rights are protected.

If a government does not serve its purpose, the people have a right to abolish it.

IN CONGRESS, JULY 4, 1776. The unanimous Declaration of the thirteen united States of America,

When in the Course of human events, it becomes necessary for one people to dissolve the political bands which have connected them with another, and to assume among the powers of the earth, the separate and equal station to which the Laws of Nature and Nature's God entitle them, a decent respect to the opinions of mankind requires that they should declare the causes which impel them to the separation.—

We hold these truths to be self-evident, that all men are created equal, that they are endowed by their Creator with certain unalienable Rights, that among these are Life, Liberty, and the pursuit of Happiness.—

That to secure these rights, Governments are instituted among Men, deriving their just powers from the consent of the governed,—

That whenever any Form of Government becomes destructive of these ends, it is the Right of the People to alter or to abolish it, and to institute new Government, laying its foundation on such principles and organizing its powers in such form, as to them shall seem most likely to effect their Safety and Happiness. Prudence, indeed, will dictate that Governments long established should not be changed for light and transient causes; and accordingly all experience hath shewn, that mankind are more disposed to suffer, while evils are sufferable, than to right themselves by abolishing the forms to which they are accustomed. But when a long train of abuses and usurpations, pursuing invariably the same Object evinces a design to reduce them under absolute Despotism, it is their right, it is their duty, to throw off such Government, and to provide new Guards for their future security.—

Such has been the patient sufferance of these Colonies; and such is now the necessity which constrains them to alter their former Systems of Government. The history of the present King of Great Britain is a history of repeated injuries and usurpations, all having in direct object the establishment of an absolute Tyranny over these States. To prove this, let Facts be submitted to a candid world.—

He has refused his Assent to Laws, the most wholesome and necessary for the public good.—

He has forbidden his Governors to pass Laws of immediate and pressing importance, unless suspended in their operation till his Assent should be obtained; and when so suspended, he has utterly neglected to attend to them.—

He has refused to pass other Laws for the accommodation of large districts of people, unless those people would relinquish the right of Representation in the Legislature, a right inestimable to them and formidable to tyrants only.—

He has called together legislative bodies at places unusual, uncomfortable, and distant from the depository of their public Records, for the sole purpose of fatiguing them into compliance with his measures.—

He has dissolved Representative Houses repeatedly, for opposing with manly firmness his invasions on the rights of the people.—

He has refused for a long time, after such dissolutions, to cause others to be elected; whereby the Legislative powers, incapable of Annihilation, have returned to the People at large for their exercise; the State remaining in the meantime exposed to all the dangers of invasion from without, and convulsions within.—

He has endeavoured to prevent the population of these States; for that purpose obstructing the Laws for Naturalization of Foreigners; refusing to pass others to encourage their migrations hither, and raising the conditions of new Appropriations of Lands.—

He has obstructed the Administration of Justice, by refusing his Assent to Laws for establishing Judiciary powers.—

He has made Judges dependent on his Will alone, for the tenure of their offices, and the amount and payment of their salaries.—

He has erected a multitude of New Offices, and sent hither swarms of Officers to harass our people, and eat out their substance.—

Then the people have the right and duty to create a new government that will safeguard their security.

Despotism   *unlimited power*

usurpations   *unjust uses of power*

Each paragraph lists alleged injustices of George III.

relinquish   *give up*
inestimable   *priceless*

Annihilation   *destruction*

convulsions   *violent disturbances*
Naturalization of Foreigners *process by which foreign-born persons become citizens*

tenure   *term*

Refers to the British troops sent to the colonies after the French and Indian War.

He has kept among us, in times of peace, Standing Armies without the Consent of our legislatures.—

He has affected to render the Military independent of and superior to the Civil power.—

He has combined with others to subject us to a jurisdiction foreign to our constitution, and unacknowledged by our laws; giving his Assent to their Acts of pretended Legislation:—

quartering *lodging*

For quartering large bodies of troops among us:—

For protecting them, by a mock Trial, from punishment for any Murders which they should commit on the Inhabitants of these States:—

For cutting off our Trade with all parts of the world:—

For imposing Taxes on us without our Consent:—

For depriving us in many cases, of the benefits of Trial by Jury:—

For transporting us beyond Seas to be tried for pretended offences:—

Refers to the 1774 Quebec Act.

For abolishing the free System of English Laws in a neighbouring Province, establishing therein an Arbitrary government, and enlarging its Boundaries so as to render it at once an example and fit instrument for introducing the same absolute rule into these Colonies:—

render *make*

For taking away our Charters, abolishing our most valuable Laws, and altering fundamentally the Forms of our Governments:—

For suspending our own Legislatures, and declaring themselves invested with power to legislate for us in all cases whatsoever.—

abdicated *given up*

He has abdicated Government here, by declaring us out of his Protection and waging War against us.—

He has plundered our seas, ravaged our Coasts, burnt our towns, and destroyed the Lives of our people.—

He is at this time transporting large Armies of foreign Mercenaries to compleat the works of death, desolation and tyranny, already begun with circumstances of Cruelty & perfidy scarcely paralleled in the most barbarous ages, and totally unworthy the Head of a civilized nation.—

perfidy *violation of trust*

He has constrained our fellow Citizens taken Captive on the high Seas to bear Arms against their Country, to become the executioners of their friends and Brethren, or to fall themselves by their Hands.—

insurrections *rebellions*

He has excited domestic insurrections amongst us, and has endeavoured to bring on the inhabitants of our frontiers, the merciless Indian Savages, whose known rule of warfare, is an undistinguished destruction of all ages, sexes and conditions.

Petitioned for Redress *asked formally for a correction of wrongs*

In every stage of these Oppressions We have Petitioned for Redress in the most humble terms: Our repeated Petitions have been answered only by repeated injury. A Prince, whose character is thus marked by every act which may define a Tyrant, is unfit to be the ruler of a free people.

Nor have We been wanting in attentions to our British brethren. We have warned them from time to time of attempts by their legislature to extend an unwarrantable jurisdiction over us. We have reminded them of the circumstances of our emigration and settlement here. We have appealed to their native justice and magnanimity, and we have conjured them by the ties of our common kindred to disavow these usurpations, which would inevitably interrupt our connections and correspondence. They too have been deaf to the voice of justice and of consanguinity. We must, therefore, acquiesce in the necessity, which denounces our Separation, and hold them, as we hold the rest of mankind, Enemies in War, in Peace Friends.—

We, therefore, the Representatives of the united States of America, in General Congress, Assembled, appealing to the Supreme Judge of the world for the rectitude of our intentions, do, in the Name, and by Authority of the good People of these Colonies, solemnly publish and declare, That these United Colonies are, and of Right ought to be Free and Independent States; that they are Absolved from all Allegiance to the British Crown, and that all political connection between them and the State of Great Britain, is and ought to be totally dissolved; and that as Free and Independent States, they have full Power to levy War, conclude Peace, contract Alliances, establish Commerce, and to do all other Acts and Things which Independent States may of right do.—

And for the support of this Declaration, with a firm reliance on the protection of divine Providence, we mutually pledge to each other our Lives, our Fortunes and our sacred Honour.

unwarrantable jurisdiction *unjustified authority*

consanguinity *originating from the same ancestor*

rectitude *rightness*

The signers, as representatives of the American people, declared the colonies independent from Great Britain. Most members signed the document on August 2, 1776.

John Hancock
  President from
  Massachusetts

Georgia
Button Gwinnett
Lyman Hall
George Walton

North Carolina
William Hooper
Joseph Hewes
John Penn

South Carolina
Edward Rutledge
Thomas Heyward, Jr.
Thomas Lynch, Jr.
Arthur Middleton

Maryland
Samuel Chase

William Paca
Thomas Stone
Charles Carroll
  of Carrollton

Virginia
George Wythe
Richard Henry Lee
Thomas Jefferson
Benjamin Harrison
Thomas Nelson Jr.
Francis Lightfoot Lee
Carter Braxton

Pennsylvania
Robert Morris
Benjamin Rush
Benjamin Franklin
John Morton
George Clymer

James Smith
George Taylor
James Wilson
George Ross

Delaware
Caesar Rodney
George Read
Thomas McKean

New York
William Floyd
Philip Livingston
Francis Lewis
Lewis Morris

New Jersey
Richard Stockton
John Witherspoon
Francis Hopkinson
John Hart

Abraham Clark

New Hampshire
Josiah Bartlett
William Whipple
Matthew Thornton

Massachusetts
Samuel Adams
John Adams
Robert Treat Paine
Elbridge Gerry

Rhode Island
Stephen Hopkins
William Ellery

Connecticut
Samuel Huntington
William Williams
Oliver Wolcott
Roger Sherman

Identifying Key Terms

Choose the vocabulary term that best completes each of the sentences below. Write your answers on a separate sheet of paper.

delegate   common law   boycott   repeal
Parliament   confederation

1. The club members chose a(n) _____ to represent them at the annual meeting.
2. The legislature voted to _____ the tax because the citizens felt it was unfair.
3. To protest unfair taxation, angry colonists decided to _____ British goods.
4. _____ has two houses, the House of Commons and the House of Lords.
5. _____ is based on precedent and is often unwritten.
6. In 1777 state delegates in Philadelphia voted to form a union or _____.

Reviewing the Main Ideas

SECTION 1
1. Name some aspects of our system of government that can be traced back to America's English heritage.
2. Explain what common law is.

SECTION 2
3. Give two reasons why the colonists could not depend on Parliament to meet their needs.
4. In what ways were the governments of the 13 colonies similar? In what ways were they different?

SECTION 3
5. How did Britain's mercantilist policy affect the American colonies?

6. Why and how did American colonists protest against British taxes?

SECTION 4
7. What were the main weaknesses of the Articles of Confederation?
8. What was Shays's Rebellion?

Critical Thinking

SECTION 1
1. **Analyzing Information**   Why do you think the colonists based their governments on written laws rather than on English common law?

SECTION 2
2. **Analyzing Information**   How did the problems of colonial governments differ from those of state governments today?

SECTION 3
3. **Evaluating Information**   Do you think the colonists could have settled their differences with the British in 1776? Explain your answer.

SECTION 4
4. **Analyzing Information**   The Articles of Confederation denied Congress the power to collect taxes. Could a government survive without this power? Why or why not?

Reinforcing Citizenship Skills

Make a list of places in your community that need the services of volunteers, such as libraries, nursing homes, and daycare centers. Call each place and ask what the volunteers do, what times of the day and week they are needed, and how a volunteer can get started. Share your findings with the class. Then volunteer some of your time at one of the places you contacted.

Focusing on Your Community

Investigate the early history of your community. Find out when and why it was founded. Who were the first settlers and early leaders? How did the government change over the years? Prepare a talk for your class about what you have discovered.

Cooperative Learning

Work with a partner to research the contributions one of the following patriots made to the struggle for independence: Thomas Paine, Patrick Henry, Samuel Adams, Benjamin Franklin, or Thomas Jefferson. Select some of the most persuasive things this patriot said and share them with your class. Discuss the power that the written and spoken word can have in gaining support for political causes.

Technology Activity

Using a Spreadsheet

Find information in your local or school library about the constitutions of the original 13 states. Use the information to create a spreadsheet with the following headings: State, Date of First Constitution, Date of Current Constitution, Number of Constitutions, Number of Amendments.

Analyzing Visuals

American painters and cartoonists in the late 1700s used symbols to represent the new nation. This early painting shows a number of symbols. Study the painting and answer the questions.

1. The concept of liberty was often portrayed as a young woman. What is Miss Liberty stepping on? What is she holding in her right hand? What is the painter trying to show with these symbols?
2. Explain why this flag has 1 large star and 13 small ones.
3. Why do you suppose an eagle was chosen to represent the United States?
4. What are other symbols in the painting?

CLOSEUP
THE AMERICAN FLAG

For Americans, the flag has always had a special meaning. It is a symbol of our nation's freedom and democracy.

The First Flag

The Continental Congress adopted the earliest version of the American flag on June 14, 1777. In 1916, June 14 was designated as Flag Day, a day of national observance. Flag Day became a national holiday in 1949.

Rules and Customs

Over the years, Americans have developed rules and customs concerning the use and display of the flag. One of the most important things every American should remember is to treat the flag with respect:

- The flag should be displayed from sunrise to sunset. It should not be flown at night except on special occasions or in certain places.

- The flag should not be flown in bad weather.

- No flag should be flown above the American flag or to the right of it at the same height.

- The flag may be flown at half-mast to mourn the death of public officials.

- The flag should never touch the ground or floor beneath it.

- The flag may be flown upside down only to signal distress.

- When the flag becomes old and tattered, it should be destroyed by burning.

The American flag

CLOSEUP REVIEW

1 When was the first American flag adopted, and how has that day been honored?

2 What is the basic purpose of the rules and customs concerning the use and display of the American flag?

Multimedia Activities

Surfing the "Net"

How to Become A Citizen

Some people who live in the United States are not citizens. These people are called *aliens*. The process by which aliens can become citizens is called *naturalization*. To learn more about this process look on the Internet.

Getting There

Follow the steps below to gather information about the naturalization process.

1. Go to your favorite search engine.
2. Type in the word *naturalization*. Following the word *naturalization*, enter words like the ones shown below to focus your search:

> immigration
> INS
> citizenship skills
> alien

The search engine should provide you with a number of links to follow. Links are pointers to different sites on the Internet and commonly appear as blue underlined words.

What to Do When You Are There

1. Click on the links to navigate through the pages of information.
2. Gather your findings.
3. Using a word processor, create an information pamphlet on how to become a citizen through the naturalization process. Include sample questions asked of immigrants by immigration examiners. These questions determine their knowledge about the United States.

Focus on Government

Citizenship in Our Lives

Even though the Constitution was written more than 200 years ago, the Framers used language that was broad enough to apply to the twentieth century. The **Focus on Government** programs referenced below provide a tour of the building where the Constitution was written and show how activities of our everyday lives are affected by the Constitution.

Setting Up the Video

Using a bar code reader or an electronic keypad, work with a group of your classmates to view these video segments of the videodisc **Focus on Government:**

Side 1, Chapter 1
Electronic Field Trip:
Independence Hall

Side 1, Chapter 2
Lecture Launcher:
Government and Our Lives

Hands-On Activity

Use ideas from the video programs to design a group bulletin board display on the role the Constitution plays in our daily lives. Clip photographs from magazines that show people going about their everyday activities. Create captions that identify and describe which parts of the Constitution apply to each activity displayed in the photographs.

UNIT 2

Blueprint for a New Nation

The Constitution and the Bill of Rights are the basis of our democratic government. The strength of these documents comes from the American people. Our government works because we support it. By working with our government, we can ensure that our democratic system will endure.

In Unit 2 you will study the Constitution and the Bill of Rights and learn the basic principles of these documents. ■

CHAPTERS IN THIS UNIT

The Jefferson Memorial ➤

The Constitution

CIVIC PARTICIPATION

The Constitution is the nation's most important document. Written in 1787, it set up a system of government that has weathered crisis and change for more than 200 years. Its priceless heritage is its ability to adapt while preserving the basic form of American government. Contact the National Archives in Washington, D.C., for information about the Constitution. Find out how many pages the document is, how it is stored, and when it can be viewed. Also research the writers and signers of the Constitution.

Working in Your Community

Prepare a brief report on what you learned about the Constitution. Include some of the Constitution's key provisions. Present the report to your family and friends. ■

Your Civics Journal

As you study the Constitution, observe how its basic democratic principles are reflected in government actions and policies. Note also how these principles affect the daily life of Americans. Write down specific examples of your observations.

Constitution on display ➤

The Road to the Constitution

FOCUS

TERMS TO KNOW

federal system, compromise, export, Electoral College, Anti-Federalist, Federalist

OBJECTIVES

- Discuss the key decisions and proposals made at **the Constitutional Convention.**

- Identify three **constitutional compromises** the convention delegates made.

- Identify **the Electoral College** and explain why it was created.

- Compare the positions of the Federalists and Anti-Federalists in regard to **ratification of the Constitution.**

Ten years of living under the Articles of Confederation had shown Americans that the loose association of 13 independent states was not working. Many Americans became convinced that they needed a stronger central government. Few, however, agreed on how that government should be set up or what powers it should have.

Some people thought the 13 states should be combined into one large state with one central government. Others felt the states should keep as much power as possible for themselves. These people favored a **federal system,** in which the power to govern would be divided between a national government and the states.

The Constitutional Convention

On May 25, 1787, 55 delegates from 12 states met in Philadelphia. Rhode Island, the thirteenth state, opposed a stronger central government and did not participate. The delegates had assembled to revise the Articles of Confederation. Within a few days, however, they agreed that the Articles were not worth saving.

Instead, the delegates decided to write a new document—a constitution—that would set up an entirely new central government. As a result of that decision,

Articles of Confederation Representatives of 12 states set out to change this document but soon decided that an entirely new document was needed. *What took its place?*

Constitutional Convention   The delegates to the convention had to make many compromises before working out a plan for a government acceptable to all.   *What two important qualities made the delegates well suited to write a constitution?*

the meeting in Philadelphia became known as the Constitutional Convention.

The delegates to the Constitutional Convention were not a typical group of American citizens. Although America's population included people of many backgrounds, occupations, and ages, the delegates were all very similar. To begin with, all were white men. Although most Americans were farmers and laborers, all the delegates were professionals and businesspeople. They were also unusually young—more than half were under age 40.

The delegates, however, had two important qualities that made them well suited for writing a constitution: education and experience. At a time when few Americans had any formal schooling, the delegates were well read in politics, philosophy, and economics. About half of the delegates were college graduates. Most of the delegates also had experi-

ence in government. Many had been active in their state governments, and more than half had been members of Congress under the Articles of Confederation.

Several delegates, such as Benjamin Franklin and Alexander Hamilton, had been active in the fight for independence. (Thomas Jefferson, author of the Declaration of Independence, could not attend the Constitutional Convention because he was overseas, serving as America's ambassador to France.) George Washington, who had led the American army to victory against Great Britain, was a delegate from Virginia. When the convention began, the delegates unanimously chose Washington to preside over the meeting.

Key Decisions

At the very start of the convention, the delegates made several important decisions. They agreed that each state

Careers

Journalism

Television reporter

Journalists are people who gather information about important events and report it through newspapers, magazines, and radio and television news.

Journalism is hard work. Some reporters go to accidents or fires to gather information. Others sit through hours of meetings so that they can report on them. Reporters are always under pressure to get the news to the public as quickly as possible.

Despite these drawbacks, journalism can be very rewarding. Through their work, journalists reach many people. Their names, or bylines, appear on articles they write; or they are seen or heard on TV or radio. Reporters may also influence events by exposing wrongdoing or airing important issues.

Jobs in Journalism

Reporting and newscasting are only two of the positions available in journalism. There are also jobs for copy editors, film editors, columnists or editorial writers, and radio and TV producers. All these jobs require a thorough knowledge of grammar and the ability to write clearly. For most jobs, you need a bachelor's degree in liberal arts or journalism. Most journalists start at low-level positions and work their way up.

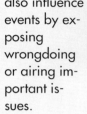

School TO WORK

An excellent way to learn more about journalism would be to volunteer to work on your school newspaper or yearbook staff. Such experience will help you find out about the many jobs available in journalism.

would have one vote, no matter how many delegates represented that state. They also agreed that a simple majority —in this case seven votes—would decide any issue.

The delegates decided to keep the work of the convention secret. After all, the task they had taken on was controversial—they were supposed to revise the Articles of Confederation, not replace them. The delegates knew that public pressure could make it difficult for them to complete their work. A policy of secrecy would remove that pressure. It would allow the delegates to speak freely and to make deals with one another, without having to consider how people in their home states would react to various proposals.

Because of this secrecy, we have virtually no written records of the convention. The only details we have came from a notebook James Madison, a delegate from Virginia, kept.

Two Plans of Government

Shortly after the convention began, the Virginia delegates proposed a plan for the new government. James Madison had designed most of the plan.

The Virginia Plan, as it came to be known, described a federal government very similar to the one we have today. It included a president, courts, and a congress with two houses. Representation in each house of congress would be based on each state's population. Large states would have more votes than smaller states.

Delegates from the smaller states disliked the Virginia Plan. They feared that the large states would control congress, leaving them with little or no power. After two weeks of angry discussion, delegates from the smaller states submitted their own plan. Because William Paterson of New Jersey presented the plan, it was called the New Jersey Plan.

The New Jersey Plan called for a government similar to the one under the Articles of Confederation. It included a one-house congress in which states would have equal representation and therefore equal votes.

Naturally, the large states would not accept the New Jersey Plan. They thought larger states should have more power than smaller states. The delegates argued about the two plans for weeks, but neither side was willing to give in.

Constitutional Compromises

Finally, the Connecticut delegates suggested a way to satisfy both sides. They proposed that the new Congress should have two houses. In one house, each state would have equal representation. In the other house, representation would be based on each state's population.

Both sides agreed to this suggestion, which became known as the Connecticut Compromise, or the Great Compromise. (A **compromise** is an agreement in which each side agrees to give up something to get something more important.)

Three-Fifths Compromise

Other compromises made at the convention involved slavery. The southern states wanted enslaved people counted as part of their populations. In this way, they hoped to increase their voting power in Congress. Most of the northern states, which had few enslaved people, opposed the idea. Eventually, both sides reached a compromise. In the Three-Fifths Compromise, delegates agreed that enslaved persons would count as

---

Benjamin Franklin   A man of many accomplishments, Franklin helped frame the Constitution.   *Which delegate kept written records of the proceedings?*

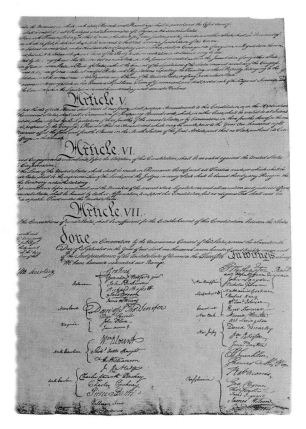

Law of the Land The delegates signed the Constitution about four months after they convened. *What requirement had to be met before the Constitution became law?*

three-fifths of other persons. This number would be used to determine both representation and taxes.

The Slave Trade

Another compromise between the North and the South was the Commerce and Slave Trade Compromise. The northern states felt that Congress should be able to regulate trade with other countries. The southern states, however, feared that Congress would use this power to tax **exports,** that is, goods sold to other countries. They also feared that

Congress might interfere with trading enslaved people.

After some discussion, another compromise was reached. The South agreed that Congress could regulate trade between the states, as well as with other countries. In exchange, the North agreed that Congress could not interfere with the slave trade for 20 years or tax exports.

The Electoral College

Another important compromise dealt with how the President would be selected. Some delegates thought members of Congress should choose the President. Other delegates believed the people should elect the President.

The convention delegates settled on a system in which each state legislature would choose a number of electors. These electors, known as the **Electoral College,** would select the President and Vice President. The Electoral College system is still used today, except that voters now choose electors directly.

After weeks of debate and compromise, the delegates were ready to put their ideas down on paper. A style committee, headed by a delegate named Gouverneur Morris, wrote the document that we call the Constitution. The delegates signed the Constitution on September 17, 1787.

Ratification of the Constitution

The delegates had decided that the Constitution would become law when 9 of the 13 states ratified it. They did not realize, however, how difficult that process would be.

Alexander Hamilton *The Federalist* helped convince Americans that the Constitution was important to the nation's survival. *Who were the authors of* The Federalist?

Anti-Federalists

One group, the **Anti-Federalists,** openly opposed the Constitution. They felt it gave too much power to the national government and took too much away from the states. The Anti-Federalists also opposed the Constitution because it lacked a bill of rights. They thought it failed to provide for certain basic liberties, such as freedom of speech or religion.

The Federalists

The group that supported the new Constitution, the **Federalists,** included many of the delegates who had helped write the document. They argued that the nation would not survive without a strong national government and pointed to the failure of the Articles of Confederation to support their view. In a series of essays known as *The Federalist*, James Madison, Alexander Hamilton, and John Jay defended the Constitution.

The Federalists agreed with the Anti-Federalists that a bill of rights was a good idea. They promised that if the Constitution was adopted, the new government would add a bill of rights.

That promise helped turn the tide for the Constitution. On June 21, 1788, New Hampshire became the ninth state to ratify, and the Constitution became law. In time, the other four states ratified the Constitution. The last state, Rhode Island, ratified it in 1790. The 13 independent states were now one nation, the United States of America.

★ SECTION 1 REVIEW ★

UNDERSTANDING VOCABULARY
Define federal system, compromise, export, Electoral College, Anti-Federalist, Federalist.

REVIEWING OBJECTIVES

1 What key decisions and proposals were made at the Constitutional Convention?

2 What three constitutional compromises did convention delegates make?

3 What is the Electoral College, and why was it created?

4 How did the positions of the Federalists and Anti-Federalists differ in regard to ratification of the Constitution?

Great American Documents

The Federalist, No. 51

The Framers of the Constitution faced two formidable tasks in 1787. The first, of course, was to create a new national government. The second was to convince the people to accept it. The second task may have been the more difficult. Most Americans were jealous of their liberties, and they feared that a strong national government might take away the rights they had won.

Think About It

As you read the following excerpts, think about why the protection of individual rights is so important in our society.

Federalist Writers

The supporters of the new Constitution, the Federalists, wrote a series of articles and pamphlets explaining how it would work. These essays, written by James Madison, Alexander Hamilton, and John Jay, were later published in *The Federalist*. The following passages are drawn from *The Federalist*, No. 51, by James Madison. In this first excerpt, Madison discusses the nature of society and government:

If men were angels, no government would be necessary. If angels were to govern man, neither internal nor external controls on government would be necessary. In framing a government which is to be administered by men over men, the great difficulty lies in this: you must first enable the government to control the governed; and in the next place oblige it to control itself.

Minority Rights

This second excerpt reveals Madison's thoughts about protecting individuals and groups against the will of the majority:

It is of great importance in a republic not only to guard the society against the oppression of its rulers, but to guard one part of the society against the injustice of the other part. Different interests necessarily exist in different classes of citizens. If a majority be united by a common interest, the rights of the minority will be insecure. . . . In the federal republic of the United States . . . the society itself will be broken into so many parts, interests, and classes of citizens, that the rights of individuals, or the minority, will be in little danger from interested combinations of the majority.

People still consult *The Federalist* today whenever there is a disagreement over the meaning of a particular article or clause in the Constitution. It is the best guide we have for understanding the intentions of the nation's Founders.

INTERPRETING SOURCES

1 What was the purpose of *The Federalist*?

2 What did Madison mean when he wrote that it was necessary "to guard one part of the society against the injustice of the other part"? How did he think that would happen?

The Constitution

The Constitution is the basic law of the United States. Although it is a relatively short document, it manages to accomplish a great deal in very few words.

The Constitution's most obvious purpose was to provide a framework for the United States government. The Constitution does more than outline the structure of our government, however. As the highest authority of the nation, it has legal and political force. The power of all the branches of government and of all elected officials, even the President, comes from the Constitution.

Beyond everything else, the Constitution—like the American flag—is a symbol. It stands for our system of government and for our basic beliefs and ideals, such as liberty and freedom.

Every American President takes an oath to "preserve, protect, and defend the Constitution of the United States." In taking this oath, the President is not pledging loyalty to a piece of paper. He or she is promising to protect what the Constitution stands for—America's ideals and beliefs.

The Preamble

The Constitution begins with an introduction, or **Preamble.** The Preamble identifies certain ideas that the government of the United States should stand for and also states the purpose of the Constitution.

Oath of Office   At his second inauguration in 1985, President Ronald Reagan once again took the oath to "preserve, protect, and defend the Constitution."   *What is the President really pledging to protect?*

The Ideas

The Preamble is only a single sentence. The beginning and end of this sentence say: "We the People of the United States . . . do ordain and establish this Constitution for the United States of America."

This statement expresses the most important idea behind our government: The people of the United States have the right and the power to govern themselves. They have chosen to place this power in the hands of a government set up by the Constitution. The government depends on the people for its power and exists to serve them.

The Goals

The middle of the Preamble lists these six goals for the United States government:

1. To "form a more perfect Union"—to allow the states to operate as a single country, for the benefit of all

2. To "establish Justice"—to make certain that all citizens are treated fairly and equally

3. To "insure domestic tranquility"—to keep peace among the people

4. To "provide for the common defence"—to maintain armed forces to protect the country and its citizens from attack

5. To "promote the general Welfare"—to ensure, as much as possible, that citizens will be free from poverty, hunger, and disease

6. To "secure the Blessings of Liberty to ourselves and our Posterity"—to guarantee that no American's basic rights will be taken away, now or in the future (*Posterity* means generations not yet born.)

DID YOU KNOW?

The First Inaugural

George Washington became the first President of the United States on April 30, 1789. His inaugural, or swearing in, took place on the balcony of Federal Hall in New York City, which was then the nation's capital. A large crowd escorted the new President from his lodgings while bands played, cannons roared, and flags waved from nearly every house in the city.

As the large, joyful crowd looked on from the street below, Washington stood proud and tall on the second-floor balcony. Wearing knee breeches, an American-made coat, and a ceremonial sword, he placed his hand on a Bible and solemnly took the oath of office.

Today, each new President takes the same oath, and the ceremony and celebration of Inauguration Day are much the same as they were for Washington.

The presidential oath

Checks and Balances

To meet the goals listed in the Preamble, the writers of the Constitution divided the national government into three parts, or branches. The **legislative** branch—Congress—makes the laws. The **executive** branch—the President, the Vice President, and their assistants—makes sure those laws are carried out. The **judicial** branch—the court system, including the Supreme Court—decides how the laws should be applied in individual cases.

To keep any one of these three branches of government from becoming too powerful, the Constitution also set up a system of **checks and balances.** Under this system each branch of government is able to check, or limit, the power of the others. The system of checks and balances helps maintain a balance between the three branches.

The President, for example, has an important check on the power of Congress. The President can **veto,** or reject, a bill Congress proposes and keep it from becoming a law.

Congress can also check the Chief Executive's power. It has the power to **override,** or defeat, the President's veto. To do so, however, requires a vote by two-thirds of the members of both houses of Congress.

The judicial branch can check the power of both the legislative and executive branches. The Supreme Court has the power to decide the meaning of laws and to declare that a law goes against the Constitution. In this way, it can overrule laws the President and Congress propose.

The Articles

Following the Preamble, the Constitution is broken into seven parts, or "articles." The first three articles describe the powers and responsibilities of the three branches of government.

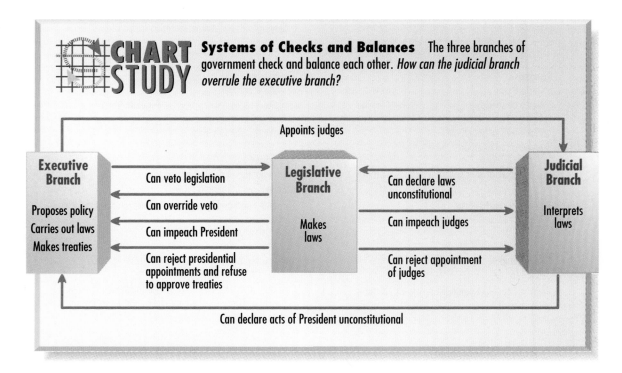

CHART STUDY **Systems of Checks and Balances** The three branches of government check and balance each other. *How can the judicial branch overrule the executive branch?*

Appoints judges

Executive Branch

Proposes policy
Carries out laws
Makes treaties

Can veto legislation
Can override veto
Can impeach President
Can reject presidential appointments and refuse to approve treaties

Legislative Branch

Makes laws

Can declare laws unconstitutional
Can impeach judges
Can reject appointment of judges

Judicial Branch

Interprets laws

Can declare acts of President unconstitutional

Article I

Article I states that a Congress made up of two houses—the Senate and the House of Representatives—will carry out the legislative duties of government. The article then describes how each house will be organized and how its members will be chosen.

The article also lists the powers given to Congress, including the power to tax, to regulate trade, to coin money, and to declare war. Following this list is another that tells what powers are denied to Congress. This second list includes the power to tax exports.

Article II

Article II deals with the executive branch and provides for a President and Vice President to carry out the duties of this branch. The article explains how these two leaders are to be chosen. It then goes on to list the President's powers, including the power to command the

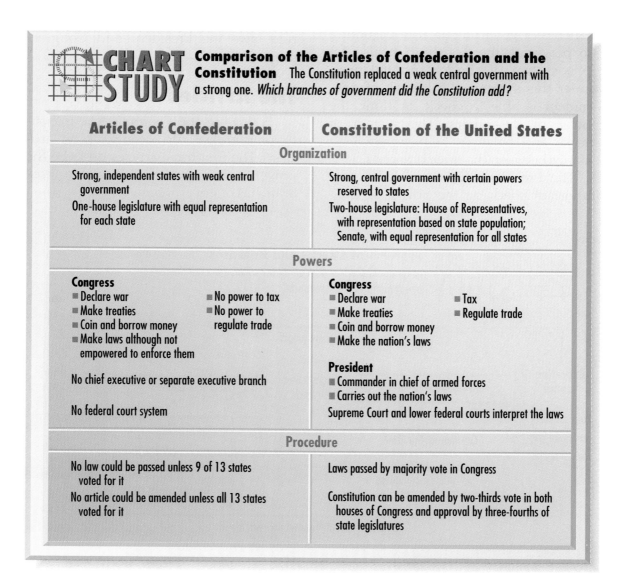

CHART STUDY **Comparison of the Articles of Confederation and the Constitution** The Constitution replaced a weak central government with a strong one. *Which branches of government did the Constitution add?*

Articles of Confederation	Constitution of the United States
Organization	
Strong, independent states with weak central government One-house legislature with equal representation for each state	Strong, central government with certain powers reserved to states Two-house legislature: House of Representatives, with representation based on state population; Senate, with equal representation for all states
Powers	
Congress ■ Declare war ■ No power to tax ■ Make treaties ■ No power to ■ Coin and borrow money regulate trade ■ Make laws although not empowered to enforce them No chief executive or separate executive branch No federal court system	**Congress** ■ Declare war ■ Tax ■ Make treaties ■ Regulate trade ■ Coin and borrow money ■ Make the nation's laws **President** ■ Commander in chief of armed forces ■ Carries out the nation's laws Supreme Court and lower federal courts interpret the laws
Procedure	
No law could be passed unless 9 of 13 states voted for it No article could be amended unless all 13 states voted for it	Laws passed by majority vote in Congress Constitution can be amended by two-thirds vote in both houses of Congress and approval by three-fourths of state legislatures

State of the Union Address   The executive and legislative branches of government must work together to govern the nation.   *Which branch has the power to declare war?*

armed forces, to make treaties with other nations, and to pardon criminals. The President also has the power to appoint certain government officials. Under the system of checks and balances, however, the Senate must approve these appointments.

Article III

Article III gives the judicial powers of government to a Supreme Court and other federal courts. The President appoints the judges of these courts. These judges serve for life or, in the words of the Constitution, "during good behavior." Article III states that the courts will have the power to judge "all cases . . . arising under this Constitution." This statement allows the Supreme Court to prevent the other branches from violating the Constitution.

Articles IV–VII

Article IV explains the relationship between the states and the national government. Article V specifies how the Constitution can be changed. Article VI discusses general provisions about the government. Article VII states that the Constitution will go into effect after nine states ratify it.

★ **SECTION 2 REVIEW** ★

UNDERSTANDING VOCABULARY
Define Preamble, legislative, executive, judicial, checks and balances, veto, override.

REVIEWING OBJECTIVES

1 What are the six goals of government listed in the Preamble to the Constitution?

2 How do the three branches of government provide checks and balances to each other?

3 What are some powers the first three articles of the Constitution give Congress, the President, and the Supreme Court?

★ THE CONSTITUTION OF THE UNITED STATES ★

THE CONSTITUTION THE FRAMERS WROTE created a representative legislature, the office of President, a system of courts, and a process for adding amendments. For more than 200 years, the flexibility and strength of the Constitution has guided the nation's political leaders. The document has become a symbol of pride and a force for national unity.

For easier study of the Constitution, those passages that have been set aside or changed by the adoption of amendments are printed in blue. Also included are explanatory notes that will help clarify the meaning of each article and section.

The Preamble introduces the Constitution and sets forth the general purposes for which the government was established. The preamble also declares that the power of the government comes from the people.

ARTICLE I. THE LEGISLATIVE BRANCH

Section 1. Congress

The power to make laws is given to a Congress made up of two chambers: the Senate and the House of Representatives.

Section 2. House of Representatives

1. Election and Term of Office Every two years the voters choose new Congress members to serve in the House of Representatives.

2. Qualifications Representatives must be 25 years old, citizens of the United States for 7 years, and residents of the state they represent.

3. Division of Representatives Among the States The number of representatives from each state is based on the size of the state's population. Each state is entitled to at least

PREAMBLE

We, the people of the United States, in Order to form a more perfect Union, establish Justice, insure domestic Tranquility, provide for the common defence, promote the general Welfare, and secure the Blessings of Liberty to ourselves and our Posterity, do ordain and establish this Constitution for the United States of America.

ARTICLE I

Section 1

All legislative Powers herein granted shall be vested in a Congress of the United States, which shall consist of a Senate and House of Representatives.

Section 2

1. The House of Representatives shall be composed of Members chosen every second Year by the People of the several States, and the Electors in each State shall have the Qualifications requisite for Electors of the most numerous Branch of the State Legislature.

2. No Person shall be a Representative who shall not have attained to the Age of twenty-five Years, and been seven Years a Citizen of the United States, and who shall not, when elected, be an Inhabitant of that State in which he shall be chosen.

3. Representatives and direct Taxes shall be apportioned among the several states which may be included within this Union, according to the respective Numbers, which shall be determined by adding to the whole Number of free Persons, including those bound to Service for a Term of Years, and excluding Indians not taxed, three-fifths of all other Persons. The actual Enumeration shall be made within three Years after the first Meeting of the Congress of the United States, and within every subsequent Term of ten Years, in such Manner as they shall by Law direct. The Number of Representatives shall not exceed one for every thirty Thousand, but each state shall have at Least one Representative; and until such enumeration shall be made, the State of New Hampshire shall be entitled

to chuse three; Massachusetts eight, Rhode Island and Providence Plantations one, Connecticut five, New York six, New Jersey four, Pennsylvania eight, Delaware one, Maryland six, Virginia ten; North Carolina five, South Carolina five, and Georgia three.

4. When vacancies happen in the Representation from any State, the Executive Authority thereof shall issue Writs of Election to fill such Vacancies.

5. The House of Representatives shall chuse their Speaker and other Officers; and shall have the sole Power of Impeachment.

Section 3

1. The Senate of the United States shall be composed of two Senators from each State, chosen by the Legislature thereof; for six Years; and each Senator shall have one Vote.

2. Immediately after they shall be assembled in Consequence of the first Election, they shall be divided as equally as may be into three Classes. The Seats of the Senators of the first Class shall be vacated at the Expiration of the second Year, of the second Class at the Expiration of the fourth Year, and of the third Class at the Expiration of the sixth Year, so that one-third may be chosen every second Year; and if Vacancies happen by Resignations, or otherwise, during the Recess of the Legislature of any State, the Executive thereof may make temporary Appointments until the next Meeting of the Legislature, which shall then fill such Vacancies.

3. No person shall be a Senator who shall not have attained the Age of thirty Years, and been nine Years a Citizen of the United States, and who shall not, when elected, be an Inhabitant of that State in which he shall be chosen.

4. The Vice President of the United States shall be President of the Senate, but shall have no vote, unless they be equally divided.

5. The Senate shall chuse their Officers, and also a President pro tempore, in the absence of the Vice-President or when he shall exercise the Office of the President of the United States.

6. The Senate shall have the sole Power to try all impeachments. When sitting for that purpose they shall be on Oath or Affirmation. When the President of the United States is tried, the Chief Justice shall preside: And no person shall be convicted without the Concurrence of two-thirds of the Members present.

7. Judgment in Cases of Impeachment shall not extend further than to removal from Office, and disqualification to hold and enjoy any Office of Honor, Trust or Profit under the United States: but the Party convicted shall nevertheless be liable and subject to Indictment, Trial, Judgment and Punishment, according to Law.

one representative.

The "enumeration" referred to is the census, the population count taken every 10 years since 1790.

4. Vacancies Vacancies in the House are filled through special elections called by the state's governor.

5. Officers The speaker is the leader of the majority party in the House and is responsible for choosing the heads of various House committees. "Impeachment" means indictment, or bringing charges against an official.

Section 3. The Senate

1. Number of Members, Terms of Office, and Voting Procedure Originally, senators were chosen by the state legislators of their own states. The 17th Amendment changed this, so that senators are now elected directly by the people. There are 100 senators, 2 from each state.

2. Staggered Elections; Vacancies One-third of the Senate is elected every two years. The 17th Amendment changed the method of filling vacancies in the Senate.

3. Qualifications Senators must be at least 30 years old and they must have been citizens of the United States for at least 9 years.

4. President of the Senate The Vice President presides over the Senate and votes if there is a tie.

5. Other Officers The Senate selects its other officers, including a presiding officer (president pro tempore) who serves when the Vice President is absent.

6. Trial of Impeachments The Senate tries impeachment cases. The Chief Justice acts as the judge, and the Senate acts as the jury. A two-thirds vote of the members present is necessary to convict.

7. Penalty for Conviction If the Senate convicts an official, it may only remove the official from office and prevent that person from holding another federal position. The convicted official may still be tried in a regular court of law.

Section 4. Elections and Meetings

1. Holding Elections Each state legislature determines its own rules for congressional elections. Congress, however, can overrule state election laws.

2. Meetings The 20th Amendment changed the date of the opening of the regular session of Congress to January 3.

Section 5. Organization and Rules of Procedure

1. Organization The Supreme Court has ruled that Congress cannot legally exclude victorious candidates who meet all the requirements listed in Article I, Section 2. A "quorum" is the minimum number of members that must be present for the House or Senate to conduct sessions.

2. Rules Each house sets its own rules.

3. Journals A complete official record of everything said on the floor is available in the *Congressional Record*.

4. Adjournment Neither house may adjourn for more than three days or move to another location without the approval of the other house.

Section 6. Privileges and Restrictions

1. Pay and Privileges Congressional salaries are paid by the United States Treasury rather than by members' respective states.

Members cannot be sued or be prosecuted for anything they say in Congress. They cannot be arrested while Congress is in session, except for treason, major crimes, or breaking the peace.

2. Restrictions The purpose of this clause is to prevent members of Congress from passing laws that would benefit them personally.

Section 4

1. The Times, Places, and Manner of holding Elections for Senators and Representatives, shall be prescribed in each state by the Legislature thereof; but the Congress may at any time by Law make or alter such Regulations, except as to the Places of Chusing Senators.

2. The Congress shall assemble at least once in every Year, and such Meeting shall be on the first Monday in December, unless they shall by Law appoint a different Day.

Section 5

1. Each House shall be the Judge of the Elections, Returns and Qualifications of its own Members, and a Majority of each shall constitute a Quorum to do Business; but a smaller Number may adjourn from day to day, and may be authorized to compel the Attendance of absent Members, in such Manner, and under such Penalties as each House may provide.

2. Each House may determine the Rules of its Proceedings, punish its Members for disorderly Behaviour, and, with the Concurrence of two-thirds, expel a Member.

3. Each House shall keep a Journal of its Proceedings, and from time to time publish the same, excepting such Parts as may in their Judgment require Secrecy; and the Yeas and Nays of the Members of either House on any question shall, at the desire of one-fifth of those Present, be entered on the Journal.

4. Neither House during the Session of Congress, shall, without the Consent of the other, adjourn for more than three days, nor to any other Place than that in which the two Houses shall be sitting.

Section 6

1. The Senators and Representatives shall receive a Compensation for their Services, to be ascertained by Law, and paid out of the Treasury of the United States. They shall in all Cases, except Treason, Felony and Breach of the Peace be privileged from Arrest during their attendance at the Session of their respective Houses, and in going to and returning from the same; and for any Speech or Debate in either House, they shall not be questioned in any other place.

2. No Senator or Representative shall, during the Time for which he was elected, be appointed to any civil Office under the Authority of the United States, which shall have been created, or the Emoluments whereof shall have been encreased, during such time; and no Person holding any Office under the United States, shall be a Member of either House during his continuance in Office.

Section 7

1. All Bills for raising Revenue shall originate in the House of Representatives; but the Senate may propose or concur with Amendments as on other bills.

2. Every Bill which shall have passed the House of Representatives and the Senate, shall, before it become a Law, be presented to the President of the United States; If he approve he shall sign it, but if not he shall return it, with his Objections, to that House in which it shall have originated, who shall enter the Objections at large on their Journal, and proceed to reconsider it. If after such Reconsideration two-thirds of that House shall agree to pass the bill, it shall be sent, together with the objections, to the other House, by which it shall likewise be reconsidered, and if approved by two-thirds of that House, it shall become a Law. But in all such Cases the Votes of both Houses shall be determined by Yeas and Nays, and the Names of the Persons voting for and against the Bill shall be entered on the Journal of each House respectively. If any Bill shall not be returned by the President within ten Days (Sundays excepted) after it shall have been presented to him, the Same shall be a Law, in like Manner as if he had signed it, unless the Congress by their Adjournment prevent its Return, in which Case it shall not be a Law.

3. Every Order, Resolution, or Vote to which the Concurrence of the Senate and House of Representatives may be necessary (except on a question of Adjournment) shall be presented to the President of the United States; and before the Same shall take Effect, shall be approved by him, or, being disapproved by him, shall be repassed by two-thirds of the Senate and House of Representatives, according to the Rules and Limitations prescribed in the case of a Bill.

Section 8

The Congress shall have the Power

1. To lay and collect Taxes, Duties, Imposts and Excises, to pay the Debts and provide for the common Defence and general Welfare of the United States; but all Duties, Imposts and Excises shall be uniform throughout the United States;

2. To borrow money on the credit of the United States;

3. To regulate Commerce with foreign Nations, and among the several States, and with the Indian Tribes;

4. To establish an uniform Rule of Naturalization, and uniform Laws on the subject of Bankruptcies throughout the United States.

5. To coin Money, regulate the Value thereof, and of foreign Coin, and fix the Standard of Weights and Measures;

6. To provide for the Punishment of counterfeiting the Securities and current Coin of the United States;

7. To establish Post Offices and post Roads;

8. To promote the Progress of Science and useful Arts, by securing for limited Times to Authors and Inventors the exclusive Right to their respective Writings and Discoveries;

9. To constitute Tribunals inferior to the Supreme Court;

10. To define and punish Piracies and Felonies committed on the high Seas, and Offenses against the Law of Nations.

11. To declare War, grant Letters of Marque and Reprisal, and make Rules concerning Captures on Land and Water;

12. To raise and support Armies, but no Appropriation of Money to that Use shall be for a longer Term than two Years;

Section 7. Passing Laws

1. Revenue Bills All tax laws must originate in the House of Representatives.

2. How Bills Become Laws A bill may become a law only by passing both houses of Congress and by being signed by the President. If the President disapproves, or vetoes, the bill, it is returned to the house where it originated, along with a written statement of the President's objections. If two-thirds of each house approves the bill after the President has vetoed it, it becomes law. If the President does not sign or veto a bill within 10 days (excluding Sundays), it becomes law. However, if Congress has adjourned during this 10-day period, the bill does not become law. This is known as a "pocket veto."

3. Presidential Approval or Veto The Framers included this paragraph to prevent Congress from passing joint resolutions instead of bills to avoid the possibility of a presidential veto.

Section 8. Powers Granted to Congress

1. Revenue Taxes must be levied at the same rate throughout the nation.

2. Borrowing The federal government borrows money by issuing bonds.

3. Commerce Congress regulates foreign and interstate commerce.

4. Naturalization and Bankruptcy "Naturalization" refers to the procedure by which a citizen of a foreign nation becomes a citizen of the United States.

5. Currency Control over money is an exclusive federal power.

6. Counterfeiting "Counterfeiting" means illegally imitating or forging.

7. Post Office In 1970 the United States Postal Service replaced the Post Office Department.

8. Copyrights and Patents Congress passes copyright and patent laws.

9. Courts Congress may establish a federal court system.

10. Piracy Congress protects American ships on the high seas.

11. Declare War Congress has the power to declare war.

12. Army This provision reveals the Framers' fears of a standing army.

13. Navy This clause allows Congress to establish a navy.

14. Rules for Armed Forces Congress may pass regulations that deal with military discipline.

15. Militia The "militia" is now called the National Guard. It is organized by the states.

16. National Guard Congress has the authority to pass rules for governing the National Guard's behavior.

17. Nation's Capital This clause grants Congress the right to make laws for Washington, D.C.

18. Elastic Clause This is the so-called "elastic clause" of the Constitution. The "necessary and proper" laws must be related to one of the 17 enumerated powers.

Section 9. Powers Denied to the Federal Government

1. Slave Trade Congress could not ban the slave trade before 1808.

2. Habeas Corpus A writ of habeas corpus requires a law official to bring a prisoner to court and show cause for holding the prisoner. The writ may be suspended only during wartime.

3. Bills of Attainder A "bill of attainder" is a bill that punishes a person without a jury trial. An "ex post facto" law is one that makes an act a crime after the act has been committed.

4. Direct Taxes The 16th Amendment allowed Congress to pass an income tax.

5. Tax on Exports Congress may not tax goods that move from one state to another.

13. To provide and maintain a Navy;

14. To make Rules for the Government and Regulation of the land and naval forces;

15. To provide for calling forth the Militia to execute the Laws of the Union, suppress Insurrections, and repel Invasions;

16. To provide for organizing, arming, and disciplining, the Militia, and for governing such Part of them as may be employed in the Service of the United States, reserving to the States respectively, the Appointment of the Officers, and the Authority of training the Militia according to the discipline prescribed by Congress;

17. To exercise exclusive Legislation in all Cases whatsoever, over such District (not exceeding ten Miles square) as may, by Cession of particular States, and the acceptance of Congress, become the Seat of Government of the United States, and to exercise like Authority over all Places purchased by the Consent of the Legislature of the State in which the Same shall be, for the Erection of Forts, Magazines, Arsenals, dock-Yards, and other needful Buildings;—And

18. To make all Laws which shall be necessary and proper for carrying into Execution the foregoing Powers, and all other Powers vested by this Constitution in the Government of the United States, or in any Department or Officer thereof.

Section 9

1. The Migration or Importation of such Persons as any of the States now existing shall think proper to admit, shall not be prohibited by the Congress prior to the Year one thousand eight hundred and eight, but a tax or duty may be imposed on such importation, not exceeding ten dollars for each Person.

2. The privilege of the Writ of Habeas Corpus shall not be suspended, unless when in Cases of Rebellion or Invasion the public Safety may require it.

3. No Bill of Attainder or ex post facto Law shall be passed.

4. No capitation, or other direct, Tax shall be laid unless in Proportion to the Census or Enumeration herein before directed to be taken.

5. No Tax or Duty shall be laid on Articles exported from any State.

6. No Preference shall be given by any Regulation of Commerce or Revenue to the Ports of one State over those of another: nor shall Vessels bound to, or from, one State, be obliged to enter, clear, or pay Duties in another.

7. No Money shall be drawn from the Treasury, but in Consequence of Appropriations made by Law; and a regular Statement and Account of the Receipts and Expenditures of all public Money shall be published from time to time.

8. No Title of Nobility shall be granted by the United States:—And no Person holding any Office of Profit or Trust under them, shall, without the Consent of the Congress, accept of any present, Emolument, Office, or Title, of any kind whatever, from any King, Prince, or foreign State.

Section 10

1. No State shall enter into any Treaty, Alliance, or Confederation; grant Letters of Marque and Reprisal; coin Money; emit Bills of Credit; make any Thing but gold and silver Coin a Tender in Payment of Debts; pass any Bill of Attainder; ex post facto Law, or Law impairing the Obligation of Contracts, or grant any Title of Nobility.

2. No State shall, without the Consent of the Congress, lay any Imposts or Duties on Imports or Exports, except what may be absolutely necessary for executing its inspection Laws: and the net Produce of all Duties and Imposts, laid by any State on Imports and Exports, shall be for the Use of the Treasury of the United States; and all such Laws shall be subject to the Revision and Controul of the Congress.

3. No State shall, without the Consent of Congress, lay any duty on Tonnage, keep Troops, or Ships of War in time of Peace, enter into any Agreement or Compact with another State, or with a foreign Power, or engage in War, unless actually invaded, or in such imminent Danger as will not admit of delay.

ARTICLE II

Section 1

1. The executive Power shall be vested in a President of the United States of America. He shall hold his Office during the Term of four years, and together with the Vice-President chosen for the same Term, be elected, as follows:

2. Each State shall appoint, in such Manner as the Legislature thereof may direct, a Number of Electors, equal to the whole Number of Senators and Representatives to which the State may be entitled in the Congress: but no Senator or Representative, or Person holding an Office of Trust or Profit under the United States, shall be appointed an Elector.

3. The Electors shall meet in their respective States, and vote by Ballot for two Persons, of whom one at least shall not be an Inhabitant of the same State with themselves. And they shall make a List of all the Persons voted for and of the Number of Votes for each; which List they shall sign and certify, and transmit sealed to the Seat of the Government of the United States, directed to the President of the Senate. The President of the Senate shall, in the Presence of the Senate and House of Representatives, open all the Certificates, and the Votes shall then be counted. The Person having the greatest Number of Votes shall be the President, if such Number be a Majority of the whole Number of Electors appointed; and if there be more than one who have such Majority, and have an equal Number of Votes,

6. Uniformity of Treatment Congress may not favor one state or region over another.

7. Appropriation Law All of the President's expenditures must be made with the permission of Congress.

8. Titles of Nobility This clause prevents the development of a nobility in the United States.

Section 10. Powers Denied to the States

1. Limitations on Power The states are prohibited from conducting foreign affairs, carrying on a war, or controlling interstate and foreign commerce. States are also not allowed to pass laws that the federal government is prohibited from passing.

2. Export and Import Taxes This clause prevents states from levying duties on exports and imports.

3. Duties, Armed Forces, War States cannot maintain an army or navy or go to war. States may not collect fees from foreign vessels or make treaties with other nations.

ARTICLE II. THE EXECUTIVE BRANCH

Section 1. President and Vice President

1. Term of Office The President enforces the laws passed by Congress. The President and the Vice President serve four-year terms.

2. Election The President and Vice President are not directly elected. Instead, the President and Vice President are elected by presidential electors from each state who form the Electoral College. Each state has the number of presidential electors equal to the total number of its senators and representatives.

3. Former Method of Election This clause describes the original method of electing the President and Vice President. The 12th Amendment changed this method.

4. Date of Elections Congress selects the date when the presidential electors are chosen and when they vote for President and Vice President. All electors must vote on the same day.

5. Qualifications The President must be a citizen of the United States by birth, at least 35 years old, and a resident of the United States for 14 years.

6. Vacancies If the President dies, resigns, is removed from office by impeachment, or is unable to carry out the duties of the office, the Vice President becomes President. (Amendment 25 deals with presidential disability.) If both the President and Vice President are unable to serve, Congress has the power to declare by law who acts as President.

7. Salary Originally, the President's salary was $25,000 per year. The President's current salary of $200,000 plus a $50,000 taxable expense account per year was enacted in 1969. The President also receives numerous fringe benefits including a $120,000 nontaxable allowance for travel and entertainment, and living accommodations in two residences—the White House and Camp David. However, the President cannot receive any other income from the United States Government or state governments while in office.

8. Oath of Office The oath of office is generally administered by the Chief Justice, but can be administered by any official authorized to administer oaths.

Section 2. Powers of the President

1. Military, Cabinet, Pardons Mention of "the principal officer in each of the executive departments" is the only suggestion of the President's cabinet to be found in the Constitution. This clause also makes the President, a civilian, the head of the armed services.

2. Treaties and Appointments The President is the chief architect of

then the House of Representatives shall immediately chuse by Ballot one of them for President; and if no Person have a Majority, then from the five highest on the List the said House shall in like Manner chuse the President. But in chusing the President, the Votes shall be taken by States, the Representation from each State having one Vote; a quorum for this Purpose shall consist of a Member or Members from two-thirds of the States, and a Majority of all the States shall be necessary to a Choice. In every Case, after the Choice of the President, the Person having the greatest Number of Votes of the Electors shall be the Vice-President. But if there should remain two or more who have equal votes, the Senate shall chuse from them by Ballot the Vice President.

4. The Congress may determine the Time of chusing the Electors, and the Day on which they shall give their Votes; which Day shall be the same throughout the United States.

5. No person except a natural born Citizen, or a Citizen of the United States, at the time of the Adoption of this Constitution, shall be eligible to the Office of President; neither shall any Person be eligible to that Office who shall not have attained to the Age of thirty-five years, and been fourteen Years a Resident within the United States.

6. In Case of the Removal of the President from Office, or of his Death, Resignation, or Inability to discharge the Powers and Duties of the said Office, the same shall devolve on the Vice-President, and the Congress may by Law provide for the Case of Removal, Death, Resignation or Inability, both of the President and Vice-President, declaring what Officer shall then act as President, and such Officer shall act accordingly, until the disability be removed, or a President shall be elected.

7. The President shall, at stated Times, receive for his Services a Compensation, which shall neither be encreased nor diminished during the Period for which he shall have been elected, and he shall not receive within that Period any other Emolument from the United States, or any of them.

8. Before he enter on the execution of his office, he shall take the following Oath or Affirmation "I do solemnly swear (or affirm) that I will faithfully execute the Office of President of the United States, and will to the best of my Ability, preserve, protect and defend the Constitution of the United States.

Section 2

1. The President shall be Commander in Chief of the Army and Navy of the United States, and of the Militia of the several States, when called into the actual Service of the United States; he may require the Opinion, in writing, of the principal Officer in each of the executive Departments, upon any subject relating to the Duties of their respective Offices, and he shall have Power to Grant Reprieves and Pardons for Offences against the United States, except in Cases of Impeachment.

2. He shall have Power, by and with the Advice and Consent of the Senate, to make Treaties, provided two-thirds of the Senators present concur; and he shall nominate, and by and with the Advice and Consent of the Senate, shall appoint Ambassadors, other public Ministers and Consuls, Judges of the supreme Court, and all other Officers of the United

States, whose Appointments are not herein otherwise provided for, and which shall be established by Law. But the Congress may by Law vest the Appointment of such inferior Officers, as they think proper, in the President alone, in the Courts of Law, or in the Heads of Departments.

3. The President shall have Power to fill up all Vacancies that may happen during the Recess of the Senate, by granting Commissions which shall expire at the End of their next Session.

Section 3

He shall from time to time give to Congress Information of the State of the Union, and recommend to their Consideration such Measures as he shall judge necessary and expedient; he may, on extraordinary occasions, convene both Houses, or either of them, and in Case of Disagreement between them, with respect to the Time of Adjournment, he may adjourn them to such Time as he shall think proper; he shall receive Ambassadors and other public Ministers; he shall take Care that the Laws be faithfully executed, and shall Commission all the Officers of the United States.

Section 4

The President, Vice-President and all civil Officers of the United States, shall be removed from Office on Impeachment for, and Conviction of, Treason, Bribery, or other high Crimes and Misdemeanors.

ARTICLE III

Section 1

The Judicial Power of the United States, shall be vested in one supreme Court, and in such inferior Courts as the Congress may from time to time ordain and establish. The judges, both of the supreme and inferior Courts, shall hold their Offices during good Behaviour, and shall, at stated Times, receive for their Services, a Compensation, which shall not be diminished during their Continuance in Office.

Section 2

1. The judicial Power shall extend to all Cases, in Law and Equity, arising under this Constitution, the Laws of the United States, and treaties made, or which shall be made, under their Authority; to all Cases affecting ambassadors, other public ministers and consuls; to all cases of admiralty and maritime Jurisdiction; to Controversies to which the United States shall be a party; to Controversies between two or more states; between a State and Citizens of another State; between Citizens of different States; between Citizens of the same State claiming Lands under Grants of different States, and between a State, or the Citizens thereof, and foreign States, Citizens or Subjects.

2. In all Cases affecting Ambassadors, other public Ministers and Consuls, and those in which a State shall be Party, the supreme Court shall have original Jurisdiction. In all the other Cases before mentioned, the

American foreign policy. He or she is responsible for the conduct of foreign relations, or dealings with other countries. All treaties, however, require approval of two-thirds of the senators present. Most presidential appointees serve at the pleasure of the President.

3. Vacancies in Offices The President can temporarily appoint officials to fill vacancies when the Senate is not in session.

Section 3. Duties of the President

Under this provision the President delivers annual State-of-the-Union messages and may call Congress into special session to consider particular problems. The President receives foreign diplomats and has the power of deciding whether or not to recognize foreign governments.

Section 4. Impeachment

This section states the reasons for which officials may be impeached and removed from office.

ARTICLE III. THE JUDICIAL BRANCH

Section 1. Federal Courts

The Constitution set up only the Supreme Court but provided for the establishment of other federal courts.

Section 2. Jurisdiction

1. General Jurisdiction American courts took over two kinds of traditional law from Great Britain. Common law was based on over five centuries of judicial decisions. Equity was a special branch of British law developed to handle cases where common law did not apply. Federal courts deal mostly with statute law, or laws passed by Congress, treaties, and cases involving the Constitution itself.

2. The Supreme Court Original jurisdiction means that the court has the authority to be the first court to hear a case. A court with appellate jurisdiction hears cases that have been appealed from lower courts.

3. Jury Trials Except in impeachment cases, anyone accused of a crime has the right to a trial by jury.

Section 3. Treason

1. Definition At least two witnesses must testify in court that someone has committed a treasonable act.

2. Punishment Congress determines the punishment for treason. The children of a person convicted of treason may not be punished.

ARTICLE IV. RELATIONS AMONG THE STATES

Section 1. Official Acts

This provision ensures that each state recognize the laws, court decisions, and records of all other states.

Section 2. Mutual Duties of States

1. Privileges Each state's citizens receive equal treatment in all states.

2. Extradition A person convicted of a crime must be returned to the state where the crime was committed.

3. Fugitive-Slave Clause Formerly enslaved persons could not become free persons by escaping to free states.

Section 3. New States and Territories

1. New States Congress has the power to admit new states. It also determines the basic guidelines for applying for statehood.

2. Territories Congress has power over federal land. Neither in this clause nor anywhere else in the Constitution is the federal government explicitly empowered to acquire new territory.

supreme Court shall have appellate Jurisdiction, both as to Law and Fact, with such Exceptions, and under such Regulations as the Congress shall make.

3. The trial of all Crimes, except in Cases of Impeachment, shall be by Jury; and such Trial shall be held in the State where the said Crimes shall have been committed; but when not committed within any State, the Trial shall be at such Place or Places as the Congress may by Law have directed.

Section 3

1. Treason against the United States, shall consist only in levying War against them, or in adhering to their Enemies, giving them Aid and Comfort. No Person shall be convicted of Treason unless on the Testimony of two Witnesses to the same overt Act, or on Confession in open Court.

2. The Congress shall have power to declare the Punishment of Treason, but no Attainder of Treason shall work Corruption of Blood, or Forfeiture except during the Life of the Person attainted.

ARTICLE IV

Section 1

Full Faith and Credit shall be given in each State to the public Acts, Records, and judicial Proceedings of every other State. And the Congress may by general Laws prescribe the Manner in which such Acts, Records, and Proceedings shall be proved, and the Effect thereof.

Section 2

1. The Citizens of each State shall be entitled to all Privileges and Immunities of Citizens in the several States.

2. A Person charged in any State with Treason, Felony, or other Crime, who shall flee from Justice, and be found in another State, shall on demand of the executive Authority of the State from which he fled, be delivered up, to be removed to the State having Jurisdiction of the crime.

3. No Person held to Service of Labour in one State, under the Laws thereof, escaping into another, shall, in Consequence of any Law or Regulation therein, be discharged from such Service or Labour, but shall be delivered up on Claim of the Party to whom such Service or Labour may be due.

Section 3

1. New States may be admitted by the Congress into this Union; but no new State shall be formed or erected within the Jurisdiction of any other State; nor any State be formed by the Junction of two or more States, or parts of States, without the Consent of the Legislatures of the States concerned as well as of the Congress.

2. The Congress shall have Power to dispose of and make all needful Rules and Regulations respecting the Territory of other Property belonging to the United States; and nothing in this Constitution shall be so construed as to Prejudice any Claims of the United States, or of any particular State.

Section 4

The United States shall guarantee to every State in this Union a Republican Form of Government, and shall protect each of them against Invasion; and on Application of the Legislature, or of the Executive (when the Legislature cannot be convened) against domestic Violence.

ARTICLE V

The Congress, whenever two-thirds of both Houses shall deem it necessary, shall propose Amendments to this Constitution, or, on the Application of the Legislatures of two-thirds of the several States, shall call a Convention for proposing Amendments, which, in either Case, shall be valid to all Intents and Purposes, as part of this Constitution, when ratified by the Legislatures of three-fourths of the several States, or by Conventions in three-fourths thereof, as the one or the other Mode of Ratification may be proposed by the Congress; Provided that no Amendment which may be made prior to the Year One thousand eight hundred and eight shall in any Manner affect the first and fourth clauses in the Ninth Section of the first Article; and that no State, without its Consent, shall be deprived of its equal Suffrage in the Senate.

ARTICLE VI

1. All Debts contracted and Engagements entered into, before the Adoption of this Constitution, shall be as valid against the United States under this Constitution as under the Confederation.

2. This Constitution, and the Laws of the United States which shall be made in Pursuance thereof; and all Treaties made, or which shall be made, under the Authority of the United States, shall be the supreme Law of the Land; and the Judges in every State shall be bound thereby, any Thing in the Constitution or Laws of any State to the Contrary notwithstanding.

3. The Senators and Representatives before mentioned, and the Members of the several State Legislatures, and all executive and judicial Officers, both of the United States and of the several States, shall be bound by Oath or Affirmation, to support this Constitution; but no religious Test shall ever be required as a Qualification to any Office or public Trust under the United States.

ARTICLE VII

The Ratification of the Conventions of nine States shall be sufficient for the Establishment of this Constitution between the States so ratifying the same.

Done in Convention, by the Unanimous Consent of the States present, the Seventeenth Day of September, in the Year of our Lord one thousand seven hundred and Eighty-seven, and of the Independence of the United States of America the Twelfth. In Witness whereof We have hereunto subscribed our Names.

Section 4. Federal Protection for States

This section allows the federal government to send troops into a state to guarantee law and order.

ARTICLE V. THE AMENDING PROCESS

Two methods of proposing and ratifying amendments are provided for. A two-thirds majority is needed in Congress to propose an amendment, and at least three-fourths of the states (38 states) must accept the amendment before it can become law. No amendment has yet been proposed by a national convention called by the states.

ARTICLE VI. NATIONAL SUPREMACY

1. Public Debts and Treaties This section promised that all debts the colonies had incurred during the Revolution and under the Articles of Confederation would be honored by the new United States government.

2. The Supreme Law The "supremacy clause" recognized the Constitution and federal laws as supreme when in conflict with those of the states.

3. Oaths of Office This clause also declares that no religious test shall be required as a qualification for holding public office.

ARTICLE VII. RATIFICATION OF THE CONSTITUTION

Unlike the Articles of Confederation, which required approval of all thirteen states for adoption, the Constitution required approval of only nine of thirteen states. Thirty-nine of the 55 delegates at the Constitutional Convention signed the Constitution. The Constitution went into effect in June 1788.

Signers
George Washington,
President and Deputy from Virginia

New Hampshire
John Langdon
Nicholas Gilman

Massachusetts
Nathaniel Gorham
Rufus King

Connecticut
William Samuel Johnson
Roger Sherman

New York
Alexander Hamilton

New Jersey
William Livingston
David Brearley
William Paterson
Jonathan Dayton

Pennsylvania
Benjamin Franklin
Thomas Mifflin
Robert Morris
George Clymer
Thomas FitzSimons
Jared Ingersoll
James Wilson
Gouverneur Morris

Delaware
George Read
Gunning Bedford, Jr.
John Dickinson
Richard Bassett
Jacob Broom

Maryland
James McHenry
Daniel of St. Thomas Jenifer
Daniel Carroll

Virginia
John Blair
James Madison, Jr.

North Carolina
William Blount
Richard Dobbs Spaight
Hugh Williamson

South Carolina
John Rutledge
Charles Cotesworth Pinckney
Charles Pinckney
Pierce Butler

Georgia
William Few
Abraham Baldwin

Attest: William Jackson,
Secretary

AMENDMENT 1 *Freedom of Religion, Speech, Press, and Assembly (1791)*

The 1st Amendment protects the civil liberties of individuals in the United States.

AMENDMENT 2 *Right to Bear Arms (1791)*

States have the right to keep a militia.

AMENDMENT 3 *Quartering Troops (1791)*

The government may not house soldiers in private homes.

AMENDMENT 4 *Searches and Seizures (1791)*

Americans wanted to make sure that such searches and seizures would be conducted only when a judge felt that there was "reasonable cause" to conduct them.

AMENDMENT I

Congress shall make no law respecting an establishment of religion, or prohibiting the free exercise thereof; or abridging the freedom of speech, or of the press; or the right of the people peaceably to assemble, and to petition the Government for a redress of grievances.

AMENDMENT II

A well-regulated Militia, being necessary to the security of a free State, the right of the people to keep and bear Arms, shall not be infringed.

AMENDMENT III

No soldier shall, in time of peace be quartered in any house, without the consent of the Owner, nor in time of war, but in a manner to be prescribed by law.

AMENDMENT IV

The right of the people to be secure in their persons, houses, papers, and effects, against unreasonable searches and seizures, shall not be violated, and no Warrants shall issue, but upon probable cause, supported by Oath or affirmation, and particularly describing the place to be searched, and the persons or things to be seized.

AMENDMENT V

No person shall be held to answer for a capital, or otherwise infamous crime, unless on a presentment or indictment of a Grand Jury, except in cases arising in the land or naval forces, or in the Militia, when in actual service in time of War or public danger; nor shall any person be subject for the same offence to be twice put in jeopardy of life or limb; nor shall be compelled in any criminal case to be a witness against himself, nor be deprived of life, liberty, or property, without due process of law; nor shall private property be taken for public use, without just compensation.

AMENDMENT VI

In all criminal prosecutions, the accused shall enjoy the right to a speedy and public trial, by an impartial jury of the State and district wherein the crime shall have been committed, which district shall have been previously ascertained by law, and to be informed of the nature and cause of the accusation; to be confronted with the witnesses against him; to have compulsory process for obtaining witnesses in his favor, and to have the Assistance of Counsel for his defence.

AMENDMENT VII

In suits at common law, where the value in controversy shall exceed twenty dollars, the right of trial by jury shall be preserved, and no fact tried by a jury, shall be otherwise reexamined in any Courts of the United States, than according to the rules of common law.

AMENDMENT VIII

Excessive bail shall not be required, nor excessive fines imposed, nor cruel and unusual punishments inflicted.

AMENDMENT IX

The enumeration in the Constitution, of certain rights, shall not be construed to deny or disparage others retained by the people.

AMENDMENT X

The powers not delegated to the United States by the Constitution, nor prohibited by it to the States, are reserved to the States respectively, or to the people.

AMENDMENT XI

The Judicial power of the United States shall not be construed to extend to any suit in law or equity, commenced or prosecuted against one of

AMENDMENT 5 *Rights of Accused Persons (1791)*

A grand jury determines whether there is enough evidence to bring the accused person to trial. A person may not be tried more than once for the same crime (double jeopardy). Members of the armed services are subject to military law. Persons may not be forced in any criminal case to be a witness against themselves.

AMENDMENT 6 *Right to Speedy, Fair Trial (1791)*

An accused person has the right to a speedy and public trial. This amendment also provides that legal counsel must be provided to a defendant.

AMENDMENT 7 *Civil Suits (1791)*

In civil cases where one person sues another for more than $20, a jury trial is provided for.

AMENDMENT 8 *Bail and Punishment (1791)*

Neither bail nor punishment for a crime shall be unreasonably severe.

AMENDMENT 9 *Powers Reserved to the People (1791)*

People's rights are not limited to those mentioned in the Constitution.

AMENDMENT 10 *Powers Reserved to the States (1791)*

The states or the people retain all powers except those denied them or those specifically granted to the federal government

AMENDMENT 11 *Suits Against States (1795)*

A lawsuit brought by a citizen of the United States or a foreign nation against a state must be tried in a state court.

AMENDMENT 12 *Election of President and Vice President (1804)*

This amendment changes the procedure for electing the President and Vice President as outlined in Article II, Section 1, Paragraph 3.

The electors are to cast separate ballots for each office. The votes for each office are counted and listed separately. The candidate who receives the most votes, providing it is a majority, is elected President. Other changes include: (1) a reduction from five to the three highest candidates receiving votes among whom the House is to choose if no candidate receives a majority of the electoral votes, and (2) provision for the Senate to choose the Vice President from the two highest candidates if neither has received a majority of the electoral votes.

The Twelfth Amendment does place one restriction on electors. It prohibits electors from voting for two candidates (President and Vice President) from their home state.

AMENDMENT 13 *Abolition of Slavery (1865)*

This amendment was the final act in ending slavery in the United States. It also prohibits the binding of a person to perform a personal service due to debt.

the United States by Citizens of another State, or by Citizens or Subjects of any Foreign State.

AMENDMENT XII

The Electors shall meet in their respective States and vote by ballot for President and Vice-President, one of whom, at least, shall not be an inhabitant of the same State with themselves; they shall name in their ballots the person voted for as President, and in distinct ballots the person voted for as Vice-President, and they shall make distinct lists of all persons voted for as President, and of all persons voted for as Vice-President, and of the number of votes for each, which lists they shall sign and certify, and transmit sealed to the seat of the government of the United States, directed to the President of the Senate;—The President of the Senate shall, in the presence of the Senate and House of Representatives, open all the certificates and the votes shall then be counted;—The person having the greatest number of votes for President, shall be the President, if such number be a majority of the whole number of Electors appointed; and if no person have such majority, then from the persons having the highest numbers not exceeding three on the list of those voted for as President, the House of Representatives shall choose immediately, by ballot, the President. But in choosing the President, the votes shall be taken by states, the representation from each state having one vote; a quorum for this purpose shall consist of a member or members from two-thirds of the states, and a majority of all the states shall be necessary to a choice. And if the House of Representatives shall not choose a President whenever the right of choice shall devolve upon them, before the fourth day of March next following, then the Vice-President shall act as President, as in the case of the death or other constitutional disability of the President.—The person having the greatest number of votes as Vice-President, shall be the Vice-President, if such number be a majority of the whole number of Electors appointed, and if no person have a majority, then from the two highest numbers on the list, the Senate shall choose the Vice-President; a quorum for the purpose shall consist of two-thirds of the whole number of Senators, and a majority of the whole number shall be necessary to a choice. But no person constitutionally ineligible to the office of President shall be eligible to that of Vice-President of the United States.

AMENDMENT XIII

Section 1

Neither slavery nor involuntary servitude, except as a punishment for crime whereof the party shall have been duly convicted, shall exist within the United States, or any place subject to their jurisdiction.

Section 2

Congress shall have power to enforce this article by appropriate legislation.

AMENDMENT XIV

Section 1

All persons born or naturalized in the United States, and subject to the jurisdiction thereof, are citizens of the United States and of the State wherein they reside. No State shall make or enforce any law which shall abridge the privileges or immunities of citizens of the United States; nor shall any State deprive any person of life, liberty, or property, without due process of law, nor deny to any person within its jurisdiction the equal protection of the laws.

Section 2

Representatives shall be apportioned among the several States according to their respective numbers, counting the whole number of persons in each State, excluding Indians not taxed. But when the right to vote at any election for the choice of electors for President and Vice-President of the United States, Representatives in Congress, the Executive and Judicial officers of a State, or the members of the Legislature thereof, is denied to any of the male inhabitants of such State, being twenty-one years of age, and citizens of the United States, or in any way abridged, except for participation in rebellion, or other crime, the basis of representation therein shall be reduced in the proportion which the number of such male citizens shall bear to the whole number of male citizens twenty-one years of age in such State.

Section 3

No person shall be a Senator or Representative in Congress, or elector of President and Vice-President, or hold any office, civil or military, under the United States, or under any State, who, having previously taken an oath, as a member of Congress, or as an officer of the United States, or as a member of any State legislature, or as an executive or judicial officer of any State, to support the Constitution of the United States, shall have engaged in insurrection or rebellion against the same, or given aid or comfort to the enemies thereof. But Congress may by a vote of two-thirds of each House, remove such disability.

Section 4

The validity of the public debt of the United States incurred for payment of pensions and bounties for service, authorized by law, including debts in suppressing insurrections or rebellion, shall not be questioned. But neither the United States nor any State shall assume or pay any debt or obligation incurred in aid of insurrection or rebellion against the United States, or any claim for the loss or emancipation of any slave; but all such debts, obligations and claims shall be held illegal and void.

Section 5

The Congress shall have power to enforce, by appropriate legislation, the provisions of this article.

AMENDMENT 14 *Rights of Citizens (1868)*

Section 1. Citizenship Defined By granting citizenship to all persons born in the United States, this amendment granted citizenship to former enslaved persons. The amendment also guaranteed "due process of law." By the 1950s, Supreme Court rulings used the due process clause to protect civil liberties. The last part of Section 1 establishes the doctrine that all citizens are entitled to equal protection of the laws. In 1954 the Supreme Court ruled, in *Brown* v. *Board of Education* of Topeka, that segregation in public schools was unconstitutional because it denied equal protection.

Section 2. Representation in Congress This section reduced the number of members a state had in the House of Representatives if it denied its citizens the right to vote. This section was not implemented, however. Later civil rights laws and the 24th Amendment guaranteed the vote to African Americans.

Section 3. Penalty for Engaging in Insurrection The leaders of the Confederacy were barred from state or federal offices unless Congress agreed to revoke this ban. By the end of Reconstruction all but a few Confederate leaders were allowed to return to public life.

Section 4. Public Debt The public debt incurred by the federal government during the Civil War was valid and could not be questioned by the South. However, the debts of the Confederacy were declared to be illegal. Former slave holders could not collect compensation for the loss of their enslaved persons.

Section 5. Enforcement Congress was empowered to pass civil rights bills to guarantee the provisions of the amendment.

AMENDMENT 15 *The Right to Vote (1870)*

Section 1. Suffrage for African Americans The right of African Americans to vote was not to be left to the states.

Section 2. Enforcement Congress was given the power to enforce this amendment.

AMENDMENT 16 *Income Tax (1913)*

This amendment authorized an income tax that was levied on a direct basis.

AMENDMENT 17 *Direct Election of Senators (1913)*

Section 1. Method of Election The right to elect senators was given directly to the people of each state. It replaced Article I, Section 2, Clause 1.

Section 2. Vacancies A state must order an election to fill a senate vacancy. A state may empower its governor to appoint a person to fill a Senate seat if a vacancy occurs until an election can be held.

Section 3. Time in Effect This amendment was not to affect any senate election or temporary appointment until it was in effect.

AMENDMENT 18 *Prohibition of Alcoholic Beverages (1919)*

This amendment prohibited the production, sale, or transportation of alcoholic beverages in the United States. Prohibition proved to be difficult to enforce, especially in states with large urban populations. This

AMENDMENT XV

Section 1

The right of citizens of the United States to vote shall not be denied or abridged by the United States or by any State on account of race, color, or previous condition of servitude.

Section 2

The Congress shall have power to enforce this article by appropriate legislation.

AMENDMENT XVI

The Congress shall have power to lay and collect taxes on incomes, from whatever source derived, without apportionment among several States, and without regard to any census or enumeration.

AMENDMENT XVII

Section 1

The Senate of the United States shall be composed of two Senators from each State, elected by the people thereof, for six years; and each Senator shall have one vote. The electors in each state shall have the qualifications requisite for electors of the most numerous branch of the state legislatures.

Section 2

When vacancies happen in the representation of any State in the Senate, the executive authority of such State shall issue writs of election to fill such vacancies: Provided, that the legislature of any State may empower the executive thereof to make temporary appointments until the people fill the vacancies by election as the legislature may direct.

Section 3

This amendment shall not be so construed as to affect the election or term of any Senator chosen before it becomes valid as part of the Constitution.

AMENDMENT XVIII

Section 1

After one year from ratification of this article the manufacture, sale, or transportation of intoxicating liquors within, the importation thereof into, or the exportation thereof from the United States and all territory subject to the jurisdiction thereof for beverage purposes is hereby prohibited.

Section 2

The Congress and the several states shall have concurrent power to enforce this article by appropriate legislation.

Section 3

This article shall be inoperative unless it shall have been ratified as an amendment to the Constitution by the legislatures of the several States, as provided in the Constitution, within seven years from the date of the submission hereof to the states of the Congress.

AMENDMENT XIX

Section 1

The right of citizens of the United States to vote shall not be denied or abridged by the United States or by any state on account of sex.

Section 2

Congress shall have power to enforce this article by appropriate legislation.

AMENDMENT XX

Section 1

The terms of the President and Vice President shall end at noon on the 20th day of January, and the terms of the Senators and Representatives at noon on the 3rd day of January, of the years in which such terms would have ended if this article had not been ratified; and the terms of their successors shall then begin.

Section 2

The Congress shall assemble at least once in every year, and such meeting shall begin at noon on the 3rd day of January, unless they shall by law appoint a different day.

Section 3

If, at the time fixed for the beginning of the term of the President, the President elect shall have died, the Vice President elect shall become President. If a President shall not have been chosen before the time fixed for the beginning of his term, or if the President elect shall have failed to qualify, then the Vice President elect shall act as President until a President shall have qualified; and the Congress may by law provide for the case wherein neither a President elect nor a Vice President elect shall have qualified, declaring who shall then act as President, or the manner in which one who is to act shall be selected, and such person shall act accordingly until a President or Vice President shall have qualified.

Section 4

The Congress may by law provide for the case of the death of any of the persons from whom the House of Representatives may choose a President whenever the right of choice shall have devolved upon them, and for

---

amendment was later repealed by the 21st Amendment.

AMENDMENT 19 *Woman Suffrage (1920)*

This amendment extended the vote to all qualified women in federal and state elections.

AMENDMENT 20 *"Lame-Duck" Amendment (1933)*

Section 1. New Dates of Terms This amendment fixed January 20 as Inauguration Day.

Section 2. Meeting Time of Congress "Lame-duck" sessions occurred every two years, after the November congressional election. That is, the Congress that held its session in December of an election year was not the newly elected Congress but the old Congress that had been elected two years earlier. This Congress continued to serve for several more months. The 20th Amendment abolished this lame-duck session, and provided that the new Congress hold its first session soon after the November election, on January 3.

Section 3. Succession of President and Vice President If the President-elect dies before taking office, the Vice President-elect becomes President. In the cases described, Congress will decide on a temporary President.

Section 4. Filling Presidential Vacancy If a presidential candidate dies while an election is being decided in the House, Congress may pass legislation to deal with the situation. Congress has similar power if this

---

occurs when the Senate is deciding a vice-presidential election.

Section 5. Beginning the New Dates Sections 1 and 2 affected the Congress elected in 1934 and President Roosevelt, elected in 1936.

Section 6. Time Limit on Ratification The period for ratification was limited to seven years.

AMENDMENT 21 *Repeal of Prohibition Amendment (1933)*

This amendment nullified the 18th Amendment. It is the only amendment ever passed to overturn an earlier amendment. It remained unlawful to transport alcoholic beverages into states that forbade their use. It is the only amendment ratified by special state conventions instead of state legislatures.

AMENDMENT 22 *Limit on Presidential Terms (1951)*

No President may serve more than two terms. Anyone who succeeds to the presidency and serves for more than two years of the term may not be elected more than one more time.

the case of the death of any of the persons from whom the Senate may choose a Vice President whenever the right of choice shall have devolved upon them.

Section 5

Sections 1 and 2 shall take effect on the 15th day of October following the ratification of this article.

Section 6

This article shall be inoperative unless it shall have been ratified as an amendment to the Constitution by the legislatures of three-fourths of the several States within seven years from the date of its submission.

AMENDMENT XXI

Section 1

The eighteenth article of amendment to the Constitution of the United States is hereby repealed.

Section 2

The transportation or importation into any State, Territory, or possession of the United States for delivery or use therein of intoxicating liquors, in violation of the laws thereof, is hereby prohibited.

Section 3

This article shall be inoperative unless it shall have been ratified as an amendment to the Constitution by conventions in the several States, as provided in the Constitution, within seven years from the date of the submission hereof to the States by the Congress.

AMENDMENT XXII

Section 1

No person shall be elected to the office of the President more than twice, and no person who had held the office of President, or acted as President, for more than two years of a term to which some other person was elected President shall be elected to the office of the President more than once.

But this Article shall not apply to any person holding the office of President when this Article was proposed by the Congress, and shall not prevent any person who may be holding the office of President, or acting as President, during the term within which this Article becomes operative from holding the office of President or acting as President during the remainder of such term.

Section 2

This article shall be inoperative unless it shall have been ratified as an amendment to the Constitution by the legislatures of three-fourths of the several States within seven years from the date of its submission to the States by the Congress.

AMENDMENT XXIII

Section 1

The District constituting the seat of Government of the United States shall appoint in such manner as the Congress may direct:

A number of electors of President and Vice President equal to the whole number of Senators and Representatives in Congress to which the District would be entitled if it were a State, but in no event more than the least populous State; they shall be in addition to those appointed by the States, but they shall be considered, for the purposes of the election of President and Vice President, to be electors appointed by a State; and they shall meet in the District and perform such duties as provided by the twelfth article of amendment.

Section 2

The Congress shall have power to enforce this article by appropriate legislation.

AMENDMENT XXIV

Section 1

The right of citizens of the United States to vote in any primary or other election for President or Vice President, for electors for President or Vice President, or for Senator or Representative in Congress, shall not be denied or abridged by the United States or any State by reason of failure to pay any poll tax or other tax.

Section 2

The Congress shall have power to enforce this article by appropriate legislation.

AMENDMENT XXV

Section 1

In case of the removal of the President from office or his death or resignation, the Vice President shall become President.

Section 2

Whenever there is a vacancy in the office of the Vice President, the President shall nominate a Vice President who shall take the office upon confirmation by a majority vote of both houses of Congress.

Section 3

Whenever the President transmits to the President pro tempore of the Senate and the Speaker of the House of Representatives his written decla-

AMENDMENT 23 *Presidential Electors for the District of Columbia (1961)*

This amendment granted people living in the District of Columbia the right to vote in presidential elections. The District casts three electoral votes. The people of Washington, D.C., still are without representation in Congress.

AMENDMENT 24 *Abolition of the Poll Tax (1964)*

This amendment ended poll taxes as a requirement to vote in any presidential or congressional election. In 1966 the Supreme Court voided poll taxes in state elections as well.

AMENDMENT 25 *Presidential Disability and Succession (1967)*

Section 1. Replacing the President The Vice President becomes President if the President dies, resigns, or is removed from office.

Section 2. Replacing the Vice President The President is to appoint a new Vice President in case of a vacancy in that office, with the approval of the Congress.

Section 3. Replacing the President With Consent If the President informs Congress, in writing, that he or she cannot carry out the duties of the office of President, the Vice President becomes Acting President.

Section 4. Replacing the President Without Consent If the President is unable to carry out the duties of the office but is unable or unwilling to so notify Congress, the cabinet and the Vice President are to inform Congress of this fact. The Vice President then becomes Acting President. The procedure by which the President may regain the office if he or she recovers is also spelled out in this amendment.

AMENDMENT 26 *Eighteen-Year-Old Vote (1971)*

This amendment made 18-year-olds eligible to vote in all federal, state, and local elections. Until then, the minimum age had been 21 in most states.

AMENDMENT 27 *Restraint on Congressional Salaries (1992)*

Any increase in the salaries of members of Congress will take effect in the subsequent session of Congress.

ration that he is unable to discharge the powers and duties of his office, and until he transmits to them a written declaration to the contrary, such powers and duties shall be discharged by the Vice President as Acting President.

Section 4

Whenever the Vice President and a majority of either the principal officers of the executive departments or of such other body as Congress may by law provide, transmit to the President pro tempore of the Senate and the Speaker of the House of Representatives their written declaration that the President is unable to discharge the powers and duties of his office, the Vice President shall immediately assume the power and duties of the office of Acting President.

Thereafter, when the President transmits to the President pro tempore of the Senate and the Speaker of the House of Representatives his written declaration that no inability exists, he shall resume the powers and duties of his office unless the Vice President and a majority of either the principal officers of the executive departments or of such other body as Congress may by law provide, transmit within four days to the President pro tempore of the Senate and the Speaker of the House of Representatives their written declaration that the President is unable to discharge the powers and duties of his office. Thereupon Congress shall decide the issue, assembling within forty-eight hours for that purpose if not in session. If the Congress within twenty-one days after receipt of the latter written declaration, or, if Congress is not in session, within twenty-one days after Congress is required to assemble, determines by two-thirds vote of both houses that the President is unable to discharge the powers and duties of his office, the Vice President shall continue to discharge the same as Acting President; otherwise, the President shall resume the power and duties of his office.

AMENDMENT XXVI

Section 1

The right of citizens of the United States, who are eighteen years of age or older, to vote shall not be denied or abridged by the United States or by any State on account of age.

Section 2

The Congress shall have power to enforce this article by appropriate legislation.

AMENDMENT XXVII

No law, varying the compensation for the services of Senators and Representatives, shall take effect, until an election of Representatives shall have intervened.

Underlying Principles

FOCUS

TERMS TO KNOW

popular sovereignty, enumerated powers, reserved powers, concurrent powers, supremacy clause

OBJECTIVES

- Define **popular sovereignty** and explain how it is reflected in the Constitution.

- Discuss the idea of **limited government.**

- Explain how **federalism** is related to popular sovereignty.

- Explain why and how the Framers of the Constitution provided for the **separation of powers.**

As you discovered in Chapter 2, many of our ideas about government began in England. By 1787, when the Constitution was written, Americans had experience governing themselves. This practical experience added to, and sometimes changed, the ideas that had come from England. The Constitution reflected these changing ideas and expressed a uniquely American way of thinking about government.

It is sometimes said that the Constitution is flawed because so many com- promises went into it. It is true that the delegates to the Constitutional Convention disagreed on details in the document, but they all strongly believed in and supported four of its basic principles: popular sovereignty, limited government, federalism, and separation of powers. These four ideas are the foundation on which our government is built.

Popular Sovereignty

Sovereignty is the right, or power, to rule. **Popular sovereignty** means that people should have the right to rule themselves.

In England, the idea of popular sovereignty led to the growth of a democratic government. The legislature, Parliament, was made up of representatives that the

Popular Sovereignty Elections are held at regular intervals in the United States. *How do you think voting in these elections is related to popular sovereignty?*

BALLOTS

State Governments The power to regulate trade within a state is reserved to state government. *How might federal regulation of all trade in the country cause problems?*

people elected. By choosing representatives who shared their ideas and points of view, the people ruled themselves.

This idea remained important to the English colonists who came to America. The Declaration of Independence is really a statement about popular sovereignty. It says that Americans, like English citizens, must be given the right to govern themselves. The same idea is echoed in the "We the People" phrase with which the Constitution begins.

For the writers of the Constitution, however, popular sovereignty was more than just an abstract idea. They designed a government whose actions would always reflect the will of the people.

Under the Constitution, the will of the people is expressed most strongly through elections. Voters elect representatives to Congress, and through the Electoral College, they elect a President and Vice President as well.

If elected officials fail to serve the people as they should, they can be removed from office. Under the Constitution, even the President can be dismissed if he or she commits a crime.

Limited Government

One danger of a democratic government is that the majority may try to limit or deny the rights of the minority. This is what happened to the American colonies when Parliament passed laws to punish the small group of citizens who lived in America.

The writers of the Constitution did not want to allow a similar situation to occur in the United States. They believed that a government must not be permitted to do certain things, even if the majority of citizens feels that the government should do them. They felt that the power of government should be limited.

Article I of the Constitution, which lists the powers denied to Congress, expresses the limits of our government most clearly. Among these are the powers to arrest people without charges or to punish people without a trial. The Bill of Rights, added to the Constitution in 1791, further limits the government.

Federalism

Federalism is another name for the federal system of government. In this system, the national government and the states share power. (In the United States, the national government is often called the federal government.)

Federal Assistance   After the floods of October 1994, the residents of Houston received disaster relief.   *What are some other events that might require such assistance?*

Federalism is related to the idea of popular sovereignty. Even in 1787, the United States was a large country, and people in different parts of the country had completely different ways of living. Many of the laws that made sense in a southern tobacco-growing state, for example, made little sense in a northern manufacturing state. By allowing each state to have its own government, the Constitution gave Americans the freedom to provide for their own needs.

Three Types of Power

In setting up a federal system, the writers of the Constitution divided the powers of government into three types:

1. **Enumerated powers** are those powers the Constitution specifically gives to the national government. These powers include controlling immigration, maintaining an army, and establishing a postal system.

2. **Reserved powers** are those that the Constitution gives to the states. Among these are the power to regulate trade within state borders, to set up schools, and to make rules for marriage and divorce.

3. **Concurrent powers** are those that the national and state government share. For example, both levels of government collect taxes, borrow money, and set up courts and prisons.

The Supremacy Clause

In a federal system, the laws of a state and the laws of the national government may conflict. To deal with this possibility, the writers of the Constitution included the supremacy clause. Found in Article VI, the **supremacy clause** states that the Constitution and the laws of the national government are the "supreme law of the land." In any conflict between national law and state law, the national law has the higher authority.

CHART STUDY

Federal and State Powers The Constitution is very clear about the powers of government. *What are three powers state and federal governments share?*

Enumerated Powers (Powers given to the federal government)	Concurrent Powers (Powers shared by state and federal governments)	Reserved Powers (Powers given to state governments)
■ Pass all laws necessary and proper to carry out its powers ■ Conduct foreign affairs ■ Raise and support an army ■ Regulate trade with other countries and among the states ■ Coin and print money ■ Establish a postal system ■ Govern United States territories, admit new states, and regulate immigration	■ Enforce the laws ■ Establish courts ■ Collect taxes ■ Borrow money ■ Provide for the general welfare	■ Regulate trade and commerce within the state ■ Establish local governments ■ Conduct elections, determine qualifications of voters ■ Establish a public school system ■ Provide for the public safety, health, and welfare within the state

Separation of Powers

English and European history is filled with stories of strong rulers who oppressed their people while gathering power and wealth for themselves. Having studied history, the Framers of the Constitution understood that too much power in the hands of one person—or one group—could be dangerous. The ideas of the French philosopher Baron de Montesquieu also influenced the Framers. Montesquieu believed that the best way to protect the liberty of the people was to clearly separate the legislative, executive, and judicial functions of government and assign each to a separate governmental branch.

The writers of the Constitution combined these ideas to create a new form of government. To protect against the abuse of power, they divided the government into legislative, executive, and judicial branches. They then created a system of checks and balances to ensure that no one branch would gain too much power.

★ SECTION 3 REVIEW ★

UNDERSTANDING VOCABULARY

Define popular sovereignty, enumerated powers, reserved powers, concurrent powers, supremacy clause.

REVIEWING OBJECTIVES

1 What is popular sovereignty, and how is it reflected in the Constitution?

2 Why does the Constitution provide for limited government?

3 How is federalism related to popular sovereignty?

4 Why and how did the Framers of the Constitution provide for the separation of powers?

How to Interpret a Political Cartoon

On the erection of the Eleventh PILLAR of the great National DOME, we beg leave most sincerely to felicitate "OUR DEAR COUNTRY,"

Rise it will.

D E L. | PEN. | N. JER. | GEOR. | CON. | MASSA. | MARY. | S° CARO. | N HAMP. | VIRG. | N.YORK. | N. CARO. | R. ISLAND

☞ The foundation good—it may yet be SAVED.

The FEDERAL EDIFICE.

ELEVEN STARS, in quick succession rise—
ELEVEN COLUMNS strike our wond'ring eyes,
Soon o'er the *whole*, shall swell the beauteous DOME,
COLUMBIA's boast—and FREEDOM's hallow'd home.
  Here shall the ARTS in glorious splendour shine !
And AGRICULTURE give her stores divine !
COMMERCE refin'd, dispense us more than gold,
And this new world, teach WISDOM to the old—
RELIGION here shall fix her blest abode,
Array'd in *mildness*, like its parent GOD !
JUSTICE and LAW, shall endless PEACE maintain,
And *the* " SATURNIAN AGE," *return again.*

Political cartoons are drawings that express a favorable or unfavorable opinion or point of view. They usually focus on public figures, political events, or economic or social conditions. Each cartoon contains useful clues to its meaning. These clues may come from labels or captions, the appearance and actions of figures, or the use of symbols— pictures that represent ideas or concepts.

How to Study a Cartoon

The first step in interpreting a political cartoon is to try to identify the clues. What is happening in the cartoon? What or who do the figures represent? To what do the symbols refer? Studying the clues helps you identify the subject and understand the cartoonist's point.

A Cartoon About Ratification

The cartoon above appeared in the Massachusetts *Centinel* in 1788, soon after New York ratified the Constitution. Study the cartoon in terms of its historical context, and answer the questions.

CITIZENSHIP IN ACTION

1 What do the pillars represent?

2 What purpose do the arches and the stars at the top of the pillars serve?

3 How do the last two pillars appear? What do you think they represent?

4 Do you think the artist has a favorable or unfavorable view of the last two states to ratify the Constitution? Explain.

A Living Constitution

FOCUS

TERMS TO KNOW
amendment, implied powers

OBJECTIVES

■ Describe the process for **amending the Constitution.**

■ Explain the considerations involved in **interpreting the Constitution.**

When the Constitution was signed in 1787, no one knew how well it would work. After all, the Articles of Confederation had been signed with high hopes, but they ended in near disaster.

For all anyone knew, government under the Constitution might also be a failure. Yet the Constitution has lasted more than 200 years, and it still has as much strength and vigor as it did when it was first written.

One key to the Constitution's success is its flexibility, or its ability to change with the times. The delegates to the Constitutional Convention could not have imagined a world in which automobiles, telephones, and computers were commonplace. Yet they wrote a document that has adapted to just such a world.

The Constitution's ability to adapt was built into the document from the very beginning. Its writers provided two ways for the Constitution to be changed: by amendment and by interpretation.

Amending the Constitution

Any change in the Constitution is called an **amendment.** Article V of the Constitution explains the two steps in the amendment process: An amendment must first be proposed, and then it must be ratified.

An amendment may be proposed in either of two ways: by a vote of two-thirds of the members of both houses of Congress or by a national convention. Two-thirds of the state legislatures must request a national convention. (Such a convention has never been called.)

Justice Sandra Day O'Connor
Members of the Supreme Court can change the Constitution through interpretation. *How else can the Constitution be changed?*

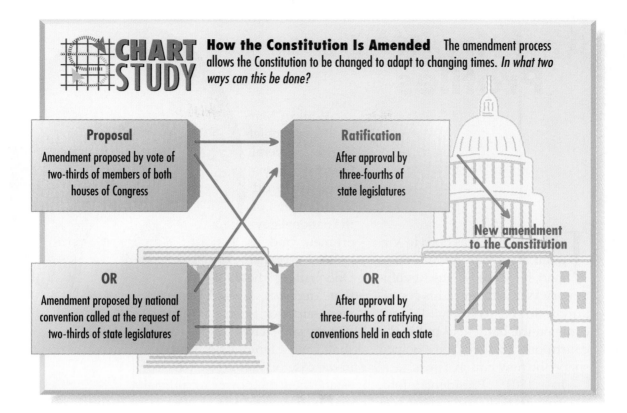

CHART STUDY

How the Constitution Is Amended The amendment process allows the Constitution to be changed to adapt to changing times. *In what two ways can this be done?*

Proposal
Amendment proposed by vote of two-thirds of members of both houses of Congress

Ratification
After approval by three-fourths of state legislatures

OR
Amendment proposed by national convention called at the request of two-thirds of state legislatures

OR
After approval by three-fourths of ratifying conventions held in each state

New amendment to the Constitution

Once an amendment has been proposed, three-fourths of the states must ratify it. The states have two ways to ratify an amendment: either by a vote in each state legislature or by calling special state conventions. Only one amendment, the Twenty-first Amendment, was ratified by means of state conventions. Congress proposed and the state legislatures ratified all others.

The writers of the Constitution deliberately made the amendment process difficult. After months of debate and compromise, they knew how delicate the structure of government can be. Making even one small change in the Constitution could have dramatic effects throughout the government. Therefore, the Constitution cannot be changed without the overwhelming support of the people.

At the same time, the ability to amend the Constitution is clearly neces-

sary. Constitutional amendments safeguard many freedoms we take for granted today, such as the abolition of slavery and the right of women to vote.

In the Declaration of Independence, Thomas Jefferson stated that people have the right to overthrow a government that does not protect their rights. If the Constitution could not have been amended to protect the rights of African Americans, women, and other oppressed groups, it—and our government—surely would not have survived.

Interpreting the Constitution

The writers of the Constitution knew that the world would change in ways they could not predict. For this reason, they attempted to keep the document as

American Profiles

John Marshall—Father of Constitutional Law

John Marshall was born in Virginia in 1755. As a young man, he served in the Revolutionary War. However, his contribution to his country did not come on the battlefield but in the courtroom, where he helped shape the new nation's laws.

In 1801 President John Adams named Marshall Chief Justice of the United States. During his 34 years on the Supreme Court, Marshall helped build the judicial branch into a powerful tool for protecting democracy.

While Marshall was chief justice, several Court decisions strengthened the power of the national government and its judicial branch. One ruling held that federal laws were superior to conflicting state laws. Marshall's most famous decision, in the case of *Marbury* v. *Madison*, established the power of judicial review (see page 292).

Marshall saw the Constitution as a living document destined "to endure for ages to come." He helped make this vision a reality.

PROFILE REVIEW

1 How did John Marshall help shape the role of the Supreme Court in the federal government?

2 How did the Court's ruling that federal laws are superior to state laws help strengthen the national government?

---

general as possible. Although they went into great detail about some matters, they left other matters open to interpretation.

The Necessary and Proper Clause

One phrase in the Constitution has probably been interpreted more often than any other. It is called the necessary and proper clause. In Article I where it lists the powers of Congress, the Constitution gives Congress the power "to make all Laws which shall be necessary and proper" to carry out its duties.

The necessary and proper clause allows Congress to exercise powers not specifically listed in the Constitution. These powers are known as **implied**

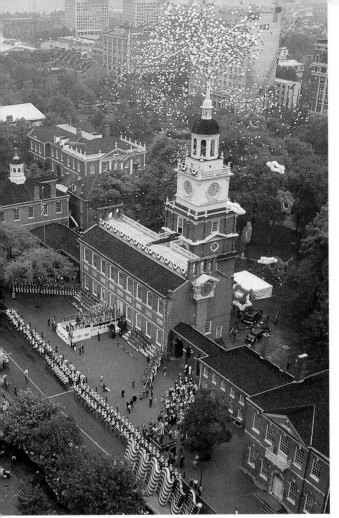

Constitutional Bicentennial In 1987 the two hundredth anniversary of the Constitution was celebrated in Philadelphia. *What is a strict interpretation of the Constitution?*

Other people believe in a strict interpretation of the Constitution. They feel Congress should only make the kinds of laws the Constitution mentions.

Another group of people say we should interpret the Constitution according to the intentions of its writers. These people feel that the writers of the Constitution, if they were alive today, would have approved of some implied powers but not others.

Role of the Supreme Court

The final responsibility for interpreting the Constitution rests with the Supreme Court. Over the years, the Court has interpreted the Constitution in different ways—sometimes strictly, sometimes loosely. Regardless of how it is interpreted, each new interpretation helps our government change and grow.

The Constitution of today is quite different from the document written in 1787. In the next 200 years, it will probably go through many more changes. However, the basic structure of our government—a finely tuned balance between the President, Congress, and the courts—will no doubt remain.

powers. Much of what the federal government does today—from regulating air pollution to licensing television stations—is based on the implied powers of Congress.

Of course, not everyone agrees which laws are "necessary and proper" and which are not. Some people feel Congress should be allowed to make any laws the Constitution does not specifically forbid. These people believe in a loose interpretation of the Constitution.

★ SECTION 4 REVIEW ★

UNDERSTANDING VOCABULARY
Define amendment, implied powers.

REVIEWING OBJECTIVES

1 What is the process for amending the Constitution?

2 What considerations are involved in interpreting the Constitution?

Identifying Key Terms

Choose the vocabulary term that best completes each of the sentences below. Write your answers on a separate sheet of paper.

Anti-Federalists   checks and balances
legislative   judicial   enumerated powers
concurrent powers   popular sovereignty

1. Congress, in making laws, is carrying out the _____ function of government.
2. In a democracy, the power of the people to rule themselves reflects the idea of _____.
3. The _____ were opposed to the power of the new central government.
4. The use of a presidential veto is an example of the system of _____.
5. _____ are specifically given to the federal government by the Constitution.
6. The Supreme Court and other federal courts are part of the _____ branch of government.
7. _____ are shared by both the federal government and the states.

Reviewing the Main Ideas

SECTION 1
1. What was the original purpose of the Constitutional Convention?
2. Why were small states unwilling to accept the Virginia Plan?

SECTION 2
3. Explain the importance of the system of checks and balances.
4. What is the purpose of the Preamble to the Constitution?

SECTION 3
5. In what ways does the Constitution express the idea of popular sovereignty?
6. How is the idea of limited government expressed in the Constitution?

SECTION 4
7. How did the writers of the Constitution allow for flexibility and change?
8. What is the difference between strict interpretation and loose interpretation of the Constitution?

Critical Thinking

SECTION 1
1. **Analyzing Information**   In what ways might the Constitution be viewed as not representative of the American people?

SECTION 2
2. **Using Reasoned Judgment**   What do you think are the major strengths and weaknesses of the Constitution?

SECTION 3
3. **Evaluating Information**   What are some of the advantages and disadvantages of our federal system of government?

SECTION 4
4. **Predicting Consequences**   What might happen if amendments were easier to propose and ratify?

Reinforcing Citizenship Skills

Look for political cartoons on the editorial pages of recent newspapers. Choose one. Decide what issue the cartoon addresses and what viewpoint it takes. You may need to scan the paper's headlines for additional information. Then list the details of the cartoon that helped you interpret it. Share your cartoon and interpretation with the class.

Cooperative Learning

In groups of three, interview fellow students and adults to find out what they know about the governmental powers specified in the Constitution. Prepare a list of questions to use in your interviews. To keep the interviews brief, you might use yes/no questions, such as "Does the Constitution give the government the power to regulate highways?" Compile the answers and present a report to your class.

Focusing on Your Community

Find out whether your community has a charter defining the structure of the government. If so, when was it adopted? What issues or information are included in it? Has the document ever been amended, and if so, how? In what ways is this document similar to or different from the United States Constitution? Prepare a short oral report on this charter.

Technology Activity

Using the Internet

Through the process of judicial review, the Supreme Court rules on the constitutionality of laws. Search the Internet to find information on a current case. You might use the following key words to focus your search: **Supreme Court decisions, Constitution.** Use the

information you find to write a brief report on the case and describe the constitutional issues that the case raises.

Analyzing Visuals

The United States Congress first met in New York City. In 1790 lawmakers decided to move the nation's capital to a site on the Potomac River between Maryland and Virginia. Until this capital was completed in 1800, Congress met in Philadelphia. Look at the map below, and answer the questions.

1. Geographically, do you think the site of the new capital was a wise choice? Why or why not?
2. Why do you think Congress chose to meet in Philadelphia while Washington was being built rather than staying in New York?
3. What do you think was the advantage of selecting a new site for the capital?

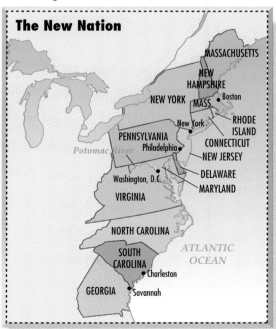

The New Nation

CHAPTER 4

The Bill of Rights

CIVIC PARTICIPATION

The Bill of Rights guarantees certain basic rights to all Americans. Among the most important is freedom of speech. This right allows Americans to speak out on issues and make their feelings known. It guarantees that people will not be punished for stating their beliefs. Contact a local organization concerned with civil liberties. Ask about incidents in your community that threatened the free speech of an individual or a group. Perhaps there were attempts to ban books from a library. How were these incidents resolved?

Working in Your Community

Interview your friends and neighbors. Should there be any limits to freedom of speech and, if so, what limits? Discuss ways you can speak out on community issues. ■

Your Civics Journal

As you learn about the Bill of Rights, think about how life in the United States might be different if we did not have these rights. Write your thoughts down in your civics journal. Include examples of things in your life that would be different without these freedoms.

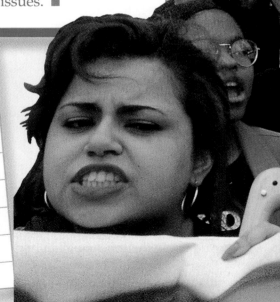

Free speech rally ➤

The Bill of Rights

FOCUS

TERMS TO KNOW
search warrant, indict, double jeopardy, due process of law, eminent domain, bail

OBJECTIVES

■ List the rights **the First Amendment** protects.

■ Explain how the Second, Third, and Fourth amendments are instrumental in **protecting against abuses of power** by the government.

■ Describe the role of the Fifth through Eighth amendments in **protecting the accused.**

■ Discuss the effectiveness of the Bill of Rights in **protecting other rights** that the Constitution does not specifically address.

The Constitution describes the powers and authority of the national government. The first 10 amendments to the Constitution, known as the Bill of Rights, describe the powers and rights of American citizens. These amendments, ratified in 1791, reflect the belief of the Framers of the Constitution in the principle of limited government. The amendments place strict limits on how the national government can use its power over the people.

The First Amendment

The First Amendment to the Constitution is probably the best known and most cherished part of the Bill of Rights. It protects five basic freedoms that are essential to the American way of life: freedom of religion, freedom of speech, freedom of the press, freedom of assembly, and freedom to petition the government. Because this amendment is so important and so far-reaching, we will look at it more closely later in this chapter.

Protecting Against Abuses of Power

The Second, Third, and Fourth amendments all help protect Americans against abuses of power by government officials or their representatives.

Muslims at Prayer   The First Amendment to the Constitution guarantees freedom of religion.   *What other freedoms does this amendment guarantee?*

The Second Amendment

The Second Amendment guarantees Americans the right to serve in a state militia and to bear arms.

If you look closely at the Second Amendment, you will see that it gives a specific reason for the right to bear arms: to maintain "a well-regulated militia." A militia, at the time this amendment was written, was a small, local army made up of volunteer soldiers. Such militias helped fight against Great Britain in the American Revolution. After independence, they helped defend the states and their communities. Because government money did not support militias, soldiers often had to supply their own weapons. The right of individuals to bear arms was therefore necessary for maintaining these militias.

Today we no longer have local volunteer armies in the United States. For this reason, some Americans question wheth-er the Second Amendment still gives individuals the right to have guns. Some federal court rulings reject the idea that this amendment gives individuals the right to own firearms for private use. Leaders in Congress and in the state legislatures continue to discuss what the "right to bear arms" really means in today's society. This question is the subject of Exploring Issues on page 313.

The Third Amendment

The Third Amendment limits the power of the national government to force Americans to quarter, or house, soldiers. In peacetime, soldiers may not move into private homes except with the owner's consent. In times of war, the practice is also prohibited unless people are requested to do so by law.

The British law requiring American colonists to house and feed British soldiers was one of the leading causes of the

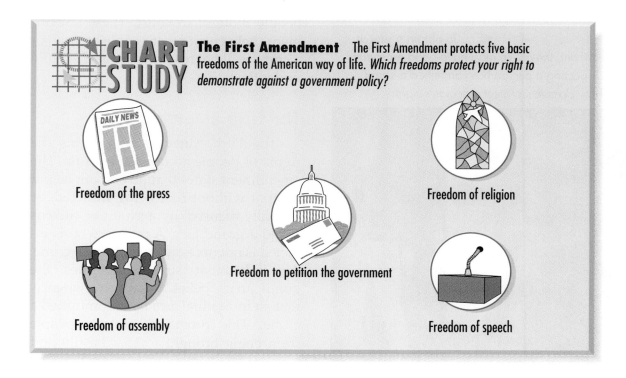

CHART STUDY

The First Amendment The First Amendment protects five basic freedoms of the American way of life. *Which freedoms protect your right to demonstrate against a government policy?*

Freedom of the press

Freedom of religion

Freedom to petition the government

Freedom of assembly

Freedom of speech

American Revolution. The Third Amendment has made it unlikely that Americans will ever be forced to open their homes to the military again. The amendment therefore protects us from an abuse of military authority.

The Fourth Amendment

The Fourth Amendment, sometimes known as the Privacy Amendment, protects Americans against unreasonable searches and seizures. No soldier, government official, or law enforcement official can search a person's home or take a person's property without a search warrant.

In some cases, however, searches and seizures may be "reasonable." If law enforcement officers believe an individual has committed a crime, they can ask a judge to issue a search warrant. A **search warrant** is a legal document that allows law enforcement officials to search a sus-

pect's home and take specific items they can use as evidence in court.

Judges do not give out search warrants easily, however. They must be convinced that the search will probably yield evidence. Without this safeguard the Fourth Amendment would have little meaning. Warrants could be issued readily and our privacy invaded. Without the Fourth Amendment, we would have little feeling of security in our homes. At any time of the day or night, a knock on the door could bring the police into our homes to invade our privacy and confiscate our possessions.

The Fourth Amendment is one of the most important safeguards we have for protecting the rights of individuals from the abuse of government power.

Protecting the Accused

Several of the first 10 amendments deal with the rights of people accused of committing a crime and the rights of people brought to court. These amendments help ensure that people accused of a crime will be treated fairly and equally under the law.

The Fifth Amendment

The Fifth Amendment protects the rights of people accused of a crime. The amendment states that no one can be put on trial without first being **indicted,** or formally accused, by a group of citizens called a grand jury. A person who is indicted is not necessarily guilty of a crime. An indictment simply indicates the grand jury's belief, based on evidence, that an individual *may* have committed a crime. This provision protects people from being brought to trial hastily and perhaps needlessly.

Search Warrants   To obtain a search warrant, the police must have good reason for suspecting a person has committed a crime. *How does this protect a person's rights?*

The Fifth Amendment also protects people from **double jeopardy.** This means that people who are accused of a crime and judged not guilty may not be put on trial again for the same crime.

In addition, the Fifth Amendment protects an accused person's right to remain silent. Throughout history, innocent people have been threatened, tortured, or bullied into confessing to crimes they did not commit. To prevent this, the Fifth Amendment guarantees that people cannot be forced to testify against themselves. This is called protection against self-incrimination.

The Fifth Amendment goes on to say that no one may be denied life, liberty, or property without **due process of law.** Due process means following procedures established by law and guaranteed by the Constitution. It also means that the laws themselves must be reasonable. Making it a crime to keep a diary would be unreasonable. Due process is an important protection for everyone.

Finally, the Fifth Amendment also protects a person's property rights. It limits the government's power of eminent domain. **Eminent domain** is the right of government to take private property—usually land—for public use. For example, if a home lies in the path of a proposed highway, the government may take the land and destroy the house. The Fifth Amendment limits this power and requires the government to pay a fair price for the property it takes.

The Sixth Amendment

The Sixth Amendment guarantees additional rights to people accused of crimes. It requires that they be told the exact nature of the charges against them. It also requires that the accused be al-

Trial by Jury The Sixth Amendment guarantees the right to trial by jury to anyone accused of a crime. *What other rights does this amendment guarantee?*

lowed a trial by jury. However, a person may ask to be tried only by a judge.

If an accused person asks for a jury trial, the trial must be speedy, public, and have an impartial jury. If possible, the trial should be held in the same area where the crime took place.

Accused individuals must have the right to hear and question all witnesses against them. They must also be permitted to call witnesses in their own defense. Finally, they are entitled to have a lawyer. Since the amendment was written, the Supreme Court has ruled that if an accused person cannot afford to hire a lawyer, the government must provide one. The government will pay the fees of this court-appointed lawyer.

The Seventh Amendment

The Fifth and Sixth amendments deal with people's rights in criminal cases—cases in which someone is accused of having committed a crime. Many court

CHART STUDY

The Bill of Rights The Bill of Rights describes the powers and rights of American citizens. *Which amendments deal with people accused of crimes?*

First Amendment	Protects five freedoms—of religion, speech, press, assembly, and petition
Second Amendment	Guarantees the right to serve in a state militia and to bear arms
Third Amendment	Limits the government's power to house soldiers in anyone's home
Fourth Amendment	Protects people from unreasonable searches and seizures
Fifth Amendment	Protects the rights of a person accused of a crime and guarantees that no one may be denied life, liberty, or property without due process of law
Sixth Amendment	Lists additional rights of a person accused of a crime, including the right to trial by jury and to be represented by a lawyer
Seventh Amendment	Guarantees the right to a jury trial in civil cases
Eighth Amendment	Prohibits excessive bail or fines; forbids cruel and unusual punishment
Ninth Amendment	Specifies that rights listed are not the only rights of the people
Tenth Amendment	States that powers not specifically assigned to the national government belong to the states or to the people

cases, however, result from disagreements between people or groups. For example, a person who is injured falling off a ladder with a defective rung may sue the ladder manufacturer. If the victim can prove the rung that broke was badly made, the court may require the manufacturer to pay the medical expenses. Cases like this one, in which no actual crime is involved, are called civil cases.

The Seventh Amendment guarantees the right to a jury trial in civil cases if the amount of money involved is more than $20. It does not, however, require a trial. Both sides may decide to have their dispute settled by a judge instead.

The Eighth Amendment

The Eighth Amendment deals with criminal cases. Although the Sixth Amendment guarantees a quick trial, sometimes weeks or months go by before a trial can be held. During that time, the accused has two choices: stay in jail or pay a sum of money called **bail.** The purpose of bail is to make sure that the accused person will appear in court for the trial. If the person appears at the proper time, the bail is returned. If the person fails to appear, the bail is forfeited.

The judge decides how much bail a person must pay. The Eighth Amendment forbids "excessive" bail—that is, an amount that is much too high. Excessive does not just refer to what a person can afford to pay. In determining bail, a judge considers various factors, including the type of crime committed, the record of the accused person, and the likelihood that the accused will appear in court. When a person is convicted of a crime, the Eighth Amendment protects him or her against having to pay excessive fines. Fines may vary, however, depending on the seriousness of the crime.

The Eighth Amendment also forbids "cruel and unusual punishments." For many years, Americans have debated what this really means. It is generally agreed that it means that punishment should be in proportion to the crime committed. For example, branding someone for stealing a loaf of bread would be considered cruel and unusual. People disagree strongly, however, about whether the death penalty for very serious crimes is cruel and unusual.

Protecting Other Rights

The people who wrote the Bill of Rights realized that they could not list every right that citizens have under the Constitution. At the same time, they wanted to guarantee that Americans would have every right possible. The last two amendments in the Bill of Rights help solve this problem.

The Ninth Amendment

The Ninth Amendment makes clear that the rights spelled out in the Constitution are not the only rights of the American people. Other, unwritten rights are just as valuable and may not be taken away. Therefore, although many basic freedoms we enjoy—such as the freedom to choose our friends, our spouses, and our careers—are not written down, they are still protected under the Constitution.

The Tenth Amendment

The Tenth Amendment is also a reminder of what the Constitution does *not* say. In this case, it concerns the principle of federalism. The Constitution talks about certain powers of national and state government. Many other powers of government—such as the power to set up schools or to license lawyers—are not mentioned at all.

Under the Tenth Amendment, any powers the Constitution does not specifically give to the national government are reserved for the states or for the people. (This amendment is the source of many of the reserved powers you learned about in Chapter 3.)

In this way, the Tenth Amendment prevents Congress and the President from becoming too strong. The government of the United States can only have powers the people give it.

★ SECTION 1 REVIEW ★

UNDERSTANDING VOCABULARY
Define search warrant, indict, double jeopardy, due process of law, eminent domain, bail.

REVIEWING OBJECTIVES

1 What rights does the First Amendment protect?

2 How are the Second, Third, and Fourth amendments instrumental in protecting Americans against abuses of power by the government?

3 What role do the Fifth through Eighth amendments play in protecting the accused?

4 In what way is the Bill of Rights effective in protecting other rights that the Constitution does not specifically address?

Exploring ISSUES

Congressional Term Limits

In recent years, Americans have become frustrated with government gridlock and politicians who seem out of touch and interested only in reelection. As a result, millions have signed petitions and gone to the polls to try to limit, by law, the number of terms a member of Congress can serve.

Arguments for Term Limits

Proponents argue that limiting terms would make Congress more responsive to the people. It would get rid of "career" politicians who are out of touch with the people and dependent on special-interest groups. Ordinary citizens should be elected to office, serve a few years, and then leave government to live under the laws they helped create. Term limits would bring in legislators with new ideas for dealing with the nation's domestic and foreign policy challenges.

Polls show a majority of Americans in favor of term limits, and 22 states already have established them for their own representatives. Republicans in Congress have promised a constitutional amendment that would limit terms.

Arguments Against Term Limits

One of the strongest arguments against term limits is that they run counter to democratic ideals. Opponents contend that voters already have the power to limit congressional terms by voting people out of office. Moreover, denying citizens the

Limiting the power of incumbents
(officeholders)

opportunity to reelect candidates takes away an important democratic right.

Opponents also argue that term limits are unconstitutional. The Constitution mentions age, citizenship, and residency requirements for members of Congress, and it stipulates the number of years for each term. It says nothing about the number of terms a member of Congress can serve. Opponents of term limits believe that the Constitution reflects the unwillingness of the nation's Founders to place further limits on elected representatives and their desire to give voters a greater voice in government.

DEVELOPING A POINT OF VIEW

1 What do you think are the strongest arguments for and against congressional term limits? Explain your answer.

2 What is your position on the issue?

SECTION 2

The First Amendment

FOCUS

TERMS TO KNOW
slander, treason, libel, petition

OBJECTIVES

■ Explain the principle of separation of church and state and how it relates to **freedom of religion.**

■ Describe two limits to **freedom of speech.**

■ Explain how **freedom of the press** has changed since the Bill of Rights was written.

■ Identify several types of activities protected by **freedom of assembly.**

■ Explain the meaning of the **right to petition.**

■ Explain why there must be **limits to these freedoms.**

For a democracy to work, its citizens must have access to information and ideas. They must be able to develop their own ideas and beliefs and to meet openly with others to discuss these ideas. They must also be able to express their ideas in public and to have their views on public matters heard by those who govern.

Such an open exchange of ideas is the hallmark of a free society. Access to new and different ideas allows a democracy to grow and change. It also ensures that the ideas of the people will be heard.

The First Amendment guarantees that Americans can do these things. The rights it discusses—freedom of religion, freedom of speech, freedom of the press, freedom of assembly, and freedom to petition—are the foundation on which American society rests. Without them, the rest of the Constitution would be meaningless.

Freedom of Religion

The First Amendment safeguards religious freedom in two ways. First, the amendment prohibits Congress from establishing an official religion in the United States. Many early colonists came to America because they wanted to be free to practice their religion in their own

Church and State   The First Amendment prohibits Congress from establishing an official religion in our country.   *Why has this been important to Americans?*

way. Some had come from England, where they were treated badly because they did not follow the official religion, the Church of England. To prevent the same thing from happening here, the Constitution follows the principle of "separation of church and state." Second, this amendment guarantees Americans the right to practice religion as they wish. The government may not favor one religion over another or treat people differently because of their religion.

Freedom of Speech

In some countries, people can be jailed for criticizing the government or for expressing their ideas, even if they do so in private conversations. The First Amendment, however, guarantees Amer-

Points of View   The government may not ban books, magazines, or newspapers that might offend or disturb some people.   *What is this principle called?*

icans the right to say what is on their minds, in public or in private, without fear of punishment.

Limiting Free Speech

Some limits to freedom of speech do exist, however. This freedom does not permit speech that harms other people. For example, if someone lies about another person to harm that person's reputation, the liar has committed a crime called **slander.** Yelling "Fire!" in a crowded theater is another example of speech that might harm others. Such acts may be punished under the law.

Freedom of speech does not include the right to endanger our government either. Giving military secrets to enemies of the United States, for example, is a very serious crime called **treason.**

Extending Free Speech

Over the years, freedom of speech has come to mean more than just spoken words. The word *speech,* as interpreted by the Supreme Court, can mean art, music, or even styles of clothing. The First Amendment thus allows us to decorate our houses as we like or to wear unusual clothing or hairstyles. As a result, the phrase "freedom of speech" is often replaced by a much broader idea, freedom of expression. The First Amendment protects almost all types of self-expression.

Freedom of the Press

The First Amendment allows Americans to express themselves in print as well as in speech. When the Bill of Rights was written, "the press" referred to printed publications such as books, newspapers, and magazines. Today the press includes many other means of com-

Groups and Organizations When people assemble to express their views, they are exercising a First Amendment right. *What else does freedom of assembly guarantee?*

municating information, such as radio, television, and computer networks.

Freedom of the press is limited in many of the same ways as freedom of speech. For example, no one is permitted to publish information that will harm other people's reputations or endanger the government. Printing lies about others is a serious crime called **libel.**

Freedom of the press not only protects our rights to publish information freely but also allows us to read what other people have published. The United States government cannot ban books, magazines, newspapers, or other printed materials that contain ideas most people find alarming or offensive. As a result, the American people are exposed to a wide variety of points of view.

Freedom of Assembly

The First Amendment protects our right to assemble in groups for any reason, so long as the assemblies are peaceful. We have the right to attend meetings, parades, political rallies, and public cele-

brations. Governments may make rules about when and where such activities can be held, but they cannot ban them.

The First Amendment also protects our right to form and join organizations such as social clubs, political parties, and labor unions. Freedom of assembly does not refer only to a gathering of people at a particular time or place. It also guarantees our right to belong to any group or organization, even if we never attend a meeting.

Right to Petition

Finally, the First Amendment guarantees all Americans the right to petition the government. A **petition** is simply a formal request. Often, we use the word *petition* to refer to a specific kind of document—a brief, written statement followed by the signatures of hundreds or thousands of people. Even a simple letter written by an individual, however, can be a petition.

The right to petition means the right to express our ideas to the government. If

A Formal Request A petition signed by a large number of citizens can greatly influence government policies. *Must a citizen join with others to file a petition?*

for example, does not permit practices, such as human sacrifice, that are against the law. Freedom of assembly does not permit groups to be so noisy or unruly that they break laws against disorderly conduct or disturbing the peace.

The First Amendment was never intended to allow Americans to do whatever they wanted. Unlimited freedom is not possible in a society of many people. The rights of one individual must be balanced against the rights of others and against the rights of the community. When the rights of the individual and the rights of the community conflict, the rights of the community must in most cases come first. Otherwise, the society will break apart.

we have a complaint or would like to see a particular law passed, we can write to our elected representatives and express our views. Our representatives are not obligated to act on our ideas. Sometimes, though, if enough people express their feelings about an issue, our leaders change their minds.

Limits to These Freedoms

You have already seen that freedom of speech and freedom of the press are limited. In addition, there are other limits to our First Amendment rights. These freedoms do not allow us to do things that break the law. Freedom of religion,

★ **SECTION 2 REVIEW** ★

UNDERSTANDING VOCABULARY
Define slander, treason, libel, petition.

REVIEWING OBJECTIVES

1 What is the principle of separation of church and state, and how is it related to freedom of religion?

2 What are two limits to freedom of speech?

3 How has freedom of the press changed since the Bill of Rights was written?

4 What types of activities are protected by freedom of assembly?

5 What is the meaning of the right to petition?

6 Why must there be limits to these freedoms?

SUPREME COURT CASE STUDIES
Brown v. Board of Education

In many states in the 1950s, African Americans went to separate schools, stayed at separate hotels, and even used separate restrooms. Segregation (separation) was not only a social custom, but it was also supported by state law. The United States Supreme Court had upheld these segregation laws in 1896 in the case of *Plessy* v. *Ferguson*. In that case, the Court ruled that separate facilities—railroad cars—for whites and African Americans were legal as long as they were equal.

Separate But Unequal

Separate, however, often was not equal, particularly in the case of public schools. All-white schools usually had better teachers and better equipment than schools for African Americans. In 1950 Oliver Brown tried to enroll his daughter Linda in a white school in Topeka, Kansas. When she was refused, Brown filed suit against the Topeka Board of Education.

The *Brown* Decision

The United States Supreme Court handed down its decision on May 17, 1954. Chief Justice Earl Warren read the Court's unanimous decision:

"Does segregation of children in public schools solely on the basis of race, even though the physical facilities . . . may be equal, deprive the children of the minority group of equal educational opportunities? We believe that it does. . . .

We conclude that in the field of public education the doctrine of "separate but equal" has no place. Separate educational facilities are inherently unequal."

The Court decided that segregated schools violated the Fourteenth Amendment's guarantee of equal protection of the laws and was unconstitutional.

Significance

In 1955, the Court ordered states with segregated schools to desegregate "with all deliberate speed." The federal courts in each state were assigned to oversee the process. Nevertheless, many states fought desegregation. Even today numerous schools remain segregated because whites and African Americans often live in different neighborhoods and belong to different school districts.

News of the *Brown* decision

REVIEWING THE CASE

1 Why did the Supreme Court decide that segregated schools violated the Fourteenth Amendment's guarantee of equal protection of the laws?

2 Why do you think the Court's decision in the *Brown* case met with so much resistance?

The Bill of Rights Extended

The Bill of Rights established rules for protecting the rights and liberties of citizens, but it did not apply to all Americans. In 1791 less than half of the American population enjoyed the full rights of United States citizens. Women, African Americans, and adults under age 21 were not granted the same rights as other Americans. None of these groups were permitted to vote. Most African Americans had no rights at all; as enslaved persons, they were considered property rather than people.

Even those who had the most power in American society—white, adult males—did not always have the full protection of the Bill of Rights. Because the Constitution left a great deal of power to the states, individual states were able to pass laws that violated certain rights.

Since 1791 the United States has experienced many changes, but the Constitution is flexible and has survived. It has been amended 27 times as conditions and attitudes have changed over the years. Some of these amendments changed the way government works. Others extended the rights of Americans, offering basic freedoms to those groups of people who were previously ignored. We will look closely here at eight amendments that extended the Bill of Rights. All the constitutional amendments are reprinted on pages 68–86.

Civil War Amendments

Three amendments were passed as a result of the Civil War. These amendments had a profound effect on Ameri-

Equal Treatment   In 1962 James Meredith became the first African American to attend the University of Mississippi.   *Which amendment deals with "equal protection of the laws"?*

can society because they extended the rights of the Constitution to African Americans.

The Thirteenth Amendment (1865)

The Thirteenth Amendment officially ended slavery in the United States and thus freed thousands of African Americans. It also outlawed any sort of forced labor, except as punishment for a crime.

The Fourteenth Amendment (1868)

Although African Americans gained their freedom in 1865, they did not receive full recognition as citizens until three years later. The Fourteenth Amendment defined a United States citizen as anyone "born or naturalized in the United States," a definition that included most African Americans.

To ensure the rights of African American citizens, the Fourteenth Amendment went even further. It required every state to grant its citizens "equal protection of the laws." State governments must treat all citizens equally. This part of the Fourteenth Amendment has been extremely important. In recent years it has been used to protect the rights of women, people with disabilities, and other groups whose rights have been abused.

Another part of the Fourteenth Amendment forbids state governments from interfering with the "privileges or immunities of citizens of the United States." State legislatures may not pass laws that interfere with rights granted by the national government. As a result of this provision, the protections in the Bill of Rights have been extended to state laws as well as national laws.

The Fifteenth Amendment (1870)

The Fifteenth Amendment extended the rights of African Americans even further by granting them **suffrage,** or the right to vote. This right was guaranteed

DID YOU KNOW?

Failed Amendments

For every amendment that is added to the Constitution, dozens, perhaps hundreds, never make it. Although some of these are absurd ideas, others are reasonable attempts to deal with government or social problems. Among the recently proposed amendments that have failed to become part of the Constitution is an amendment giving equal rights to women.

Here are a few other failed amendments:

The Senate shall be abolished (1876).

No United States citizen shall accept a foreign title of nobility (1910).

All acts of war shall be put to a national vote. All those affirming (voting yes) shall be registered as a volunteer for service in the United States Armed Forces (1916).

The nation shall hereafter be known as the United States of the Earth (1893).

The United States of the Earth

CHART STUDY

Amendments to the Constitution (Nos. 11–27)
Twenty-seven amendments have been added to the Constitution.
Which one deals specifically with woman's rights?

Eleventh Amendment (1795)
- Places limits on suits against states

Twelfth Amendment (1804)
- Revises procedure for electing the President and Vice President

Thirteenth Amendment (1865)
- Abolishes slavery

Fourteenth Amendment (1868)
- Defines United States citizenship; guarantees all citizens "equal protection of the laws"

Fifteenth Amendment (1870)
- Prohibits restrictions on the right to vote based on race and color

Sixteenth Amendment (1913)
- Gives Congress the power to levy an income tax

Seventeenth Amendment (1913)
- Enables voters to elect senators directly

Eighteenth Amendment (1917)
- Prohibits making, drinking, or selling alcoholic beverages (Prohibition)

Nineteenth Amendment (1920)
- Gives women the right to vote

Twentieth Amendment (1933)
- Changes the dates of congressional and presidential terms

Twenty-first Amendment (1933)
- Repeals Prohibition (Eighteenth Amendment)

Twenty-second Amendment (1951)
- Limits Presidents to two terms in office

Twenty-third Amendment (1961)
- Gives residents of the District of Columbia the right to vote

Twenty-fourth Amendment (1964)
- Abolishes poll taxes

Twenty-fifth Amendment (1967)
- Establishes procedures for succession to the presidency

Twenty-sixth Amendment (1971)
- Sets voting age at 18 years

Twenty-seventh Amendment (1992)
- Delays congressional pay raises until the term following their passage

only to men, however. Women, whether African American or white, were not guaranteed suffrage until 1920.

The Fifteenth Amendment was largely unsuccessful in guaranteeing African Americans the right to vote. Many states found legal ways to keep African American citizens from voting. Some states, for example, required voters to pay a **poll tax**—a sum of money paid in exchange for the right to cast a ballot. Because many African Americans were too poor to pay the poll tax, a large number remained unable to vote.

Voting Rights and Elections

A number of amendments passed in this century deal with voting rights. These amendments have helped guarantee universal suffrage.

The Seventeenth Amendment (1913)

According to Article I of the Constitution, the people were to elect members of the House of Representatives, but state legislatures were to choose members of the Senate. The Seventeenth Amendment allowed voters to elect their senators directly. This change in the electoral process gave Americans a greater voice in their government.

The Nineteenth Amendment (1920)

Although the Constitution did not grant suffrage to women, it did not explicitly deny them the right to vote. As a result, state legislatures used the powers granted under the Tenth Amendment to make their own laws about woman suffrage. The territory of Wyoming gave women the right to vote in 1869, and in the following years several other territories and states also gave women the vote.

Yet national recognition of women's right to vote was slow in coming. Suffragists such as Susan B. Anthony and Elizabeth Cady Stanton struggled courageously to win the right to vote. Many who believed that women should not have the same rights as men opposed them, however. The fight continued for almost 50 years, but gradually the suffrage movement overcame this opposition. Finally, in 1920 the Nineteenth Amendment gave women the right to vote in all national and state elections. As a result of the Nineteenth Amendment, women were brought into the political system and were granted full citizenship alongside men.

The Twenty-third Amendment (1961)

Our nation's capital, the city of Washington, is not part of any state. It occupies an area between Maryland and Virginia called the District of Columbia.

Because the District of Columbia is not a state, its residents originally were not allowed to vote in national elections. The Twenty-third Amendment granted residents of the District of Columbia the right to vote for President and Vice President, just as other Americans do.

Equal Rights for Women   In the 1980s Phyllis Schlafly (left) helped defeat ERA, an amendment to the Constitution calling for specific rights for women. Members of a woman's group (right) demonstrated for equal rights.   *What was the significance of the Nineteenth Amendment?*

Full Citizenship   Before 1971 18-year-old men could be sent to war, but they could not vote in most states.   *How did the Twenty-sixth Amendment change this situation?*

The Twenty-fourth Amendment (1964)

Nearly a century after the Fifteenth Amendment was adopted, many African Americans were still not able to vote. Many were among the poorer levels of society. As a result, they could not afford the poll taxes that several southern states required all voters to pay. These poll taxes affected not only African Americans but many poor whites as well.

In 1964 the Twenty-fourth Amendment made poll taxes illegal in national elections. Two years later the Supreme Court ruled that poll taxes were illegal in state elections as well. The elimination of the poll tax allowed many African American citizens to enjoy their full rights as voters for the first time.

The Twenty-sixth Amendment (1971)

Throughout our nation's history, people under the age of 21 have been sent into battle to fight for their country. By law, however, they were not old enough to vote for the leaders who sent them there. Although the Constitution did not specify a minimum age for voters, most states set that age at 21.

That situation was finally changed in 1971, a year when many young Americans were fighting in Vietnam. The Twenty-sixth Amendment lowered the minimum voting age to 18 for all national, state, and local elections. As a result, millions more Americans can now exercise their right to vote and enjoy the rights of full citizenship. (See Great American Documents on page 171.)

Since 1971 only one other amendment—the Twenty-seventh, dealing with congressional pay raises—has been added to the Constitution. In the future, however, more amendments will certainly be proposed and ratified. One of the strengths of our Constitution has been its ability to respond to changes in society. The amendment process has contributed to that flexibility.

★ SECTION 3 REVIEW ★

UNDERSTANDING VOCABULARY
Define suffrage, poll tax.

REVIEWING OBJECTIVES
1 What are the provisions of the three Civil War amendments?

2 What five other amendments concern voting rights and elections?

How to Run a Meeting

All organizations, clubs, and governing bodies hold meetings to take care of business and make important decisions. It is useful to know how effective meetings are run.

Student government

An Agenda

The first thing to do is to prepare an agenda, a list of matters to discuss and act on. Most agendas begin with the minutes (a record) of the last meeting and the treasurer's report. The organization's secretary prepares the minutes. The treasurer's report should include income and expenses since the last meeting and the current balance in the treasury. Next, the agenda should list old (unfinished) business, items held over from previous meetings, and new business.

When running a meeting, remember that you must control it. Go through the agenda item by item until all business is conducted. Give each person enough time to discuss an item before calling for a vote, but stop the discussion when it becomes repetitive or goes off the subject.

Rules of Order

After an item has been discussed, call for a motion on the matter. A motion is a statement describing what action the group may want to take on the matter. For example, someone may say, "I move that we approve the use of the school gym for our dance." Each mo-

tion requires a "second," or the backing of another person who says, "I second the motion." Then call for a vote, by a show of hands, a secret ballot, or a voice vote (saying aye or nay). If a majority agree with the motion, it is carried, or approved.

These rules are quite formal, but they do not have to be followed precisely. Just keep in mind that a meeting should be conducted with courtesy and common sense. Each member should respect the opinions of others.

CITIZENSHIP IN ACTION

1 Why is it important to prepare an agenda before each meeting?

2 How is being a class officer similar to being a member of a city council? How are the two jobs different?

Identifying Key Terms

Choose the vocabulary term that best completes each of the sentences below. Write your answers on a separate sheet of paper.

suffrage   search warrant
due process of law   indicted   bail
double jeopardy   slander

1. The person was charged with _____ as a result of damaging remarks she made at a public meeting.
2. Before a person can be put on trial, he or she must be _____ by a grand jury.
3. Many women fought long and hard to win the right of _____.
4. The principle of _____ protects a person from being tried for the same crime more than once.
5. The right to a fair trial is an important part of the principle of _____.
6. The police asked the judge to issue a(n) _____ so that they could look for evidence.
7. The lawyer for the accused claimed that the _____ set by the judge was excessive.

Reviewing the Main Ideas

SECTION 1

1. How does the Bill of Rights reflect the principle of limited government?
2. Explain the rights of accused persons that are protected by the Fifth and Sixth amendments.

SECTION 2

3. Explain why the First Amendment is essential to a democratic society.

4. In what way is freedom of assembly limited?

SECTION 3

5. Explain the significance of the Fourteenth Amendment.
6. How did the Seventeenth Amendment give Americans a greater say in their government?

Critical Thinking

SECTION 1

1. **Evaluating Information**   Which of the first 10 amendments do you think is the most important? Why?

SECTION 2

2. **Evaluating Information**   Should the government have the right to ban books that a majority of Americans find offensive? Why or why not?

SECTION 3

3. **Demonstrating Reasoned Judgment** Do you think our rights would be as well protected if they were not written down in the Constitution? Why or why not?

Focusing on Your Community

Investigate local rules about holding public meetings, political rallies, parades, and celebrations. Are permits required? What restrictions are there on when and where activities can be held? Has the community ever prevented a group from holding an activity? If so, why? On what grounds? Present your findings to the class.

Reinforcing Citizenship Skills

Think about topics that your class might discuss. Prepare an agenda, listing the items to be considered in order. Indicate which items you think will require a vote. Then write a description of how you would run the meeting. Share your agenda and report with the class.

Cooperative Learning

Work in groups of four to find information about a recent court case in which individuals sued others for infringing their rights (for example, slander or libel, illegal search and seizure, or wrongful arrest). Decide which amendments were involved in the case, and write a brief description of the case and its outcome. Then present your findings to the class. Discuss whether the results of the case showed a fair use of the amendments. Talk about how people's rights might sometimes be abused.

Technology Activity

Using a Word Processor

Find information on the Internet or your school or public library about any constitutional amendments that Congress or the states are considering proposing. (You might find information on the balanced budget that Congress has been debating during the past few sessions.) If you search the Internet, you might use the following key words to focus your search: **Constitution, amendments.** Use a word processor to write a letter to the editor of your local newspaper supporting or opposing the amendment and giving reasons for your opinions.

Analyzing Visuals

Photographs can be an important source of information about people and events. Like written documents, they can be used to analyze a particular moment in time. This photograph provides some insight into the struggle for equal rights. Study the photograph and then answer the questions below.

1. Is this a recent photograph? Why or why not?
2. To what does the sign in the photograph refer?
3. What rights are reflected in this photograph, and what right is this woman calling for?

CLOSEUP
THE NINETEENTH AMENDMENT

The Constitution gave states the right to determine who could vote. Most states permitted only white male property owners to vote. Gradually, the states dropped property ownership requirements. Women, however, were expected to leave politics to men.

In the 1830s many women became involved in reform movements. Those working to abolish slavery realized that they were fighting for rights for enslaved African Americans that they themselves did not enjoy.

In 1848 Lucretia Mott and Elizabeth Cady Stanton organized a Woman's Rights Convention in Seneca Falls, New York. In the "Declaration of Sentiments," the delegates declared that "all men and women are created equal."

After the Civil War, Congress adopted the Fifteenth Amendment, which extended suffrage to African American males. Women, however, still did not have this right.

Woman Suffrage Movement

In the early 1900s, a new generation of feminists, including Carrie Chapman Catt, Lucy Burns, and Alice Paul, took over the leadership of the woman's movement. They staged demonstrations, marches, and other forms of protest. Their actions helped increase support for the suffrage movement.

Starting in 1878, a woman suffrage amendment was introduced in Congress every two years. In 1918 the House of Representatives passed the amendment, and the Senate passed it the following year. By 1920 three-fourths of the states had ratified the amendment.

Early suffragists

CLOSEUP REVIEW

1 How did the movement to abolish slavery contribute to the woman's rights movement?

2 Why do you think that woman suffrage became the central issue of the woman's rights movement?

Multimedia Activities

Surfing the "Net"

The Twenty-seventh Amendment

In Chapter 3 you learned that any change in the Constitution is called an amendment. There are two steps in the amendment process. An amendment must be proposed, and then it must be ratified. Since 1971, only one amendment has been added—the Twenty-seventh. This amendment deals with congressional pay raises. To find out more details about the Twenty-seventh Amendment look on the Internet.

Getting There

Follow the steps below to gather information about the Twenty-seventh Amendment.

1. Go to your favorite search engine.
2. Type in the phrase *The United States Constitution*. Following this phrase, enter words like those below to focus your search:

   amendments
   27th amendment
   congressional pay
   Bill of Rights

The search engine should provide you with a number of links to follow. Links are pointers to different sites on the Internet and commonly appear as blue underlined words.

What to Do When You Are There

1. Click on the links to navigate through the pages of information.
2. Gather your findings.
3. Using a word processor, create a one-page report about your findings. Include whether or not, in your opinion, this is a good amendment. Discuss your findings.

Focus on Government

The Framework of Our Government

The United States Constitution has worked for more than 200 years largely because the Founders created a flexible Constitution that could change to meet the changing needs of the nation. The *Focus on Government* program referenced below explains how the Constitution has adapted to changes over the years.

Setting Up the Video

Using a bar code reader or an electronic keypad, work with a group of your classmates to view this video segment of the videodisc *Focus on Government:*

Side 1, Chapter 4
Lecture Launcher:
The Constitution—
A Living Document

Hands-On Activity

Use information from the video program and from your textbook to design an illustrated bulletin board display explaining which parts of the Constitution deal with the following situations. Illustrate the situations with photographs from magazines.

- A tax on luxury automobiles
- Construction of an interstate highway
- Controlling pollution from factories
- Launching the space shuttle

UNIT 3

Citizenship: Rights and Responsibilities

As American citizens, each of us has certain rights, such as the right to practice our religion as we wish and to freely express our opinions. To safeguard these rights for ourselves and future generations, we also have certain responsibilities. Each of us, for example, has the responsibility to obey the law.

In Unit 3 you will study your rights as a citizen and learn why it is important for all citizens to participate in the political process. ■

CHAPTERS IN THIS UNIT

New citizens with flag ➤

CHAPTER 5

The Citizen and the Community

CIVIC PARTICIPATION

As citizens, we are free to exercise our rights. In return we are expected to fulfill certain duties and responsibilities. By doing so, we help ensure that our government will be effective in serving our needs and protecting our rights. Contact your local government office or a volunteer organization in your community. Find out what you can do to help your community and the people living in it.

Working in Your Community

After you have obtained the information, volunteer some time every week to a service organization in your community. Let your friends, family, and neighbors know about the volunteer opportunities in the community and encourage them to volunteer their time as well. ■

Your Civics Journal

For one week, pay close attention to events in your community. Make a list of the specific challenges and problems facing your community during the week. Beside each entry in your journal, describe possible solutions to the challenge or problem.

Recycling newspapers ➤

The Rights of Citizens

FOCUS

TERMS TO KNOW
civil rights, discrimination, affirmative action, segregation

OBJECTIVES

■ Explain the three **categories of rights** contained in the Bill of Rights.

■ Discuss the need for **limits on rights** in our democratic society.

■ Describe how **the civil rights movement** of the 1960s resulted in broadening our rights as Americans.

The rights of Americans come from three sources—the Declaration of Independence and the Constitution, the laws Congress and state legislatures enact, and the interpretation of those laws by the courts.

In Chapter 2 you read Thomas Jefferson's inspiring words, contained in the Declaration of Independence:

>❞We hold these truths to be self-evident, that all men are created equal, that they are endowed by their Creator with certain unalienable rights, that among these are Life, Liberty, and the pursuit of Happiness.❞

The Declaration goes on to say that "to secure these Rights, Governments are instituted among Men, deriving their just powers from the Consent of the Governed."

Categories of Rights

Jefferson's words express the basic ideas of American democracy—that the government draws its power from the people and that it exists to preserve their rights. What exactly are those rights? As you learned in Chapter 4, the Bill of Rights guaranteed a number of very specific rights. In addition, in the 200 years since our government began, we have added more rights and safeguards through constitutional amendments and new laws. Most rights we now have as citizens fall into one of three broad categories: security, equality, and liberty.

Human Rights   Many countries do not accord their citizens basic human rights. *What are the three categories of rights Americans enjoy?*

Security

Security, in this case, means protection from unfair and unreasonable actions by the government. The government, for example, cannot arrest, imprison, or punish people or search or seize their property without good reason and without following certain rules. As you learned in Chapter 4, certain amendments in the Bill of Rights guarantee protection from such government actions. In addition, the principle of "due process of law" protects these rights for all Americans.

The due process clause, found in the Fifth and Fourteenth amendments, states that no person shall be deprived of "life, liberty, or property, without due process of law."

Due process means that the laws must be fair and reasonable, must be in accordance with the Constitution, and must apply to everyone equally. Most often, due process is applied to criminal laws, the laws dealing with people accused of crimes. People arrested or charged with a crime, for example, must be advised of their right to remain silent and to have an attorney if they wish to have one.

Due process also applies to property rights. If a state takes property to build a highway, it must pay the property owners a fair amount for their losses.

Equality

The right of equality means that everyone is entitled to the equal protection of all the laws in the United States. That is, all people have a right to be treated the same regardless of race, religion, or political beliefs. This right, along with that of due process, is found in the Fourteenth Amendment.

Free Expression This woman is protesting government policies. *How is free expression protected?*

Liberty

The rights with which we are most familiar—our fundamental freedoms—fall into this category. Most of these rights are spelled out expressly in the Bill of Rights. Our rights of freedom of expression—freedom of speech, press, religion, assembly, and petition—are found in the First Amendment. Our rights to own private property and to a trial by jury are contained in other amendments of the Bill of Rights.

The Bill of Rights was expanded after the Civil War by the so-called Reconstruction or Civil Rights amendments. These include the abolition of slavery and the extension of citizenship and voting rights to African American males. In addition, the rights guaranteed by the Bill of Rights were extended to the states. In this century other amendments have extended the right to vote to women, to citizens of the District of Columbia, and to 18- to 20-year-olds.

Limits on Rights

Our rights are not unlimited. The government can establish laws or rules to restrict certain rights to protect the health, safety, security, and moral standards of a community. Moreover, rights may be limited to prevent one person's rights from interfering with the rights of others. The restrictions of rights, however, must be reasonable and must apply to everyone equally.

Suppose you belonged to a group that wanted to hold a protest march down the main street of your city. Your right to do so is not completely unrestricted. Your organization may be required to obtain a permit from the city. The permit alerts the police department so it can reroute traffic and keep order. It also identifies the leaders of your group so they can be held responsible for any problems that might arise during the march.

The purpose of such a permit or other similar limitations is to prevent people from interfering with the rights of others when they exercise their own rights. Consider another example. Suppose you made a speech in a public place in which you urged your listeners to loot nearby stores. You would be interfering both with the right of the shop owners to protect their property and with the right of other people in the area to enjoy peace and order. If you made such a speech, you would probably be arrested for causing a riot.

Sometimes it is not easy for the government to establish laws that protect the rights of individuals on the one hand and the rights of the community on the other. In recent years, AIDS (Acquired Immune Deficiency Syndrome) has stricken many Americans. AIDS is a disease that destroys the body's immune system. Without an immune system, the body cannot fight back against infections and diseases.

DID YOU KNOW?

Uncle Sam

No one is really sure how Uncle Sam came to be a symbol of the United States. One story is that it came from the initials "U.S." stamped on government property during the War of 1812. A soldier supposedly asked what the "U.S." stood for, and another jokingly replied, "Uncle Sam." The nickname first appeared in print in 1813.

Cartoonists began to draw Uncle Sam with a goatee and striped trousers during the Civil War. He was used as a symbol of the United States during the Spanish-American War. The most familiar portrait, however, is the one on the "I Want You!" army recruiting posters of World Wars I and II.

Recruiting poster

Since the AIDS epidemic began in the early 1980s, public health officials and lawmakers at all levels of government have faced several dilemmas in trying to balance the rights of people with AIDS against the rights of the community. One such problem concerns the amount of funds and community resources that are to be used for AIDS research and for assistance to people with AIDS. In a democratic society, such problems frequently arise. That is why we need the lawmakers and the courts to try to find fair and reasonable compromises.

The Civil Rights Movement

In the 1950s and 1960s, many African Americans began an organized fight for their rights as citizens, or **civil rights.** The civil rights movement resulted in the passage of several new federal and state laws that have increased the rights not only of African Americans but also of all citizens.

Discrimination

Up to the 1960s, many state laws, particularly in the southern states, denied African Americans the same rights as other Americans. These laws allowed the states to practice **discrimination,** or unfair and less equal treatment toward a particular group. Some states, for example, forced African American students to attend separate schools and colleges. African Americans were required to ride in the back of buses and sit in separate sections in theaters and restaurants. They also had to use separate public rest rooms and water fountains and even stay at separate hotels.

Martin Luther King, Jr.   Martin Luther King, Jr., led many nonviolent protests against racial discrimination.   *What rights did the civil rights movement win for all Americans?*

The Civil Rights Act

The civil rights struggle resulted in the Civil Rights Act of 1964. This act gave African Americans equal protection under the law, as guaranteed in the Constitution. The act banned discrimination against African Americans in employment, voting, and public accommodations. This law, enacted to protect one group, also expanded the rights of everyone. It banned discrimination not only by race and color but also by sex, religion, or national origin.

The Voting Rights Act

The Voting Rights Act of 1965 empowered the federal government to intervene in places where African Americans were discriminated against in voter registration. Although the Fifteenth Amendment to the Constitution gave African American males the right to vote, that right was not well enforced. By the

1960s, several states had found ways, such as the poll tax, to discourage African Americans from registering and voting. Since the passage of the Voting Rights Act, African American voter registration has risen sharply. The law has also helped Hispanic Americans and other minorities register to vote.

Affirmative Action

New federal laws have also helped expand our rights through affirmative action. **Affirmative action** means taking special steps to help minorities and women gain access to jobs and opportunities that were denied them in the past because of discrimination. According to federal law, governments must apply affirmative action to give priority to hiring and promoting women and minorities in certain areas.

Affirmative action was meant to be only a temporary, short-term means of helping minorities and women reach the same economic levels as white males. Some affirmative action programs, however, have existed for more than 20 years. In recent years, the Supreme Court has begun to interpret affirmative action cases more strictly.

Equal Protection

The Fourteenth Amendment to the Constitution reaffirmed the principle of due process and established the idea of equal protection under the law. It did much more than that, however. It made the Constitution and the Bill of Rights apply not only to federal laws, but to state laws as well.

This meant that every citizen of the United States had the same rights as every other citizen. It also meant that if people felt their rights had been violated by a state or local law, they could take their complaint to a federal court, which could overturn the state or local law. This extension of federal laws to the state and local levels is called the nationalization of the Bill of Rights.

The most famous example of how the nationalization of the Bill of Rights helped expand American rights is the case of *Brown* v. *Board of Education of Topeka, Kansas* in 1954. In 1896 the Supreme Court had ruled that "separate but equal" public facilities for African Americans and whites were legal. The Court reversed that decision in the *Brown* case. It held that **segregation** in schools—that is, separating students because of race—was unconstitutional because it violated the Fourteenth Amendment's principle of equal protection under the law.

In the *Brown* case, the Court decided that separate schools could never be truly equal and therefore were illegal. As a result of this interpretation of the Constitution, no state or public school district can maintain separate schools for children of different races.

★ **SECTION 1 REVIEW** ★

UNDERSTANDING VOCABULARY

Define civil rights, discrimination, affirmative action, segregation.

REVIEWING OBJECTIVES

1 What are the three major categories of rights?

2 Why are our rights as Americans limited?

3 What gains did the civil rights movement of the 1960s win for all Americans?

The Duties and Responsibilities of Citizens

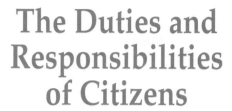

FOCUS

TERMS TO KNOW
duties, responsibilities, draft, toleration

OBJECTIVES

■ Explain the major **duties** of American citizens.

■ Discuss the **responsibilities** of American citizens.

As citizens of the United States, we are expected to carry out certain duties and responsibilities. **Duties** are things we are required to do; if we fail to perform them, we are subject to legal penalties, such as fines or imprisonment. **Responsibilities**, on the other hand, are things we should do; they are obligations that we fulfill voluntarily. Fulfilling both our duties and our responsibilities helps ensure that we have good government and that we continue to enjoy our rights.

Duties

Some countries require much from their citizens. In some countries, for example, citizens must serve in the armed forces for a period of time each year. In others, citizens are required to live in cities far away from their families and friends and to work at jobs assigned to them by the government.

The United States government asks much less of its citizens than many other countries. Nevertheless, the government does require its citizens to perform the following duties.

Obey the Laws

This is a citizen's most important duty. If citizens do not obey the law, the government cannot maintain order and protect the health, safety, and property of its citizens. The laws we must obey, including criminal laws, traffic laws, and local laws, all have a purpose. Criminal laws are designed to prevent citizens from harming one another; traffic laws prevent accidents; and local laws help people get along with one another.

Pay Taxes

Taxes pay for the government's activities. Without them, the federal government could not pay its employees, maintain an army and navy to defend its citizens, or help those in need. Your city could not hire police or firefighters, and your state could not pave roads or maintain prisons.

Citizens pay taxes in several ways. The federal government and some states and cities collect income taxes, a percentage of the wages people receive. Most states and some cities collect sales taxes. Your school district collects taxes on the residential and commercial property within the district.

Defend the Nation

In the United States, all men aged 18 and over are required to register with the government in case the country needs to **draft,** or call up, men for military service. Since the end of the Vietnam War, there has been no draft, and America's military has been volunteer. Nevertheless, the government has the authority to use the draft if the country should suddenly have to go to war.

Serve in Court

The Constitution guarantees every citizen the right to a trial by jury. To ensure this, every citizen must be prepared to serve on a jury. People can ask to be excused from jury duty if they have a good reason, but it is better to serve if possible. People on trial depend on their fellow citizens to render a fair and just verdict at their trials. Another duty of citizens is to serve as witnesses at a trial, if called to do so.

Attend School

In most states, people are required to attend school until age 16. This is important both to you and to the government because school is where you acquire much of the knowledge and skills you will need to be a good citizen.

In a free society, each person's opinion counts. You can voice your opinion in letters to the editor of a newspaper or to your congressional representatives, at government meetings, and in the voting booth. First, however, you need to learn how to arrive at an informed, well-reasoned opinion. This means examining all sides of an issue, separating facts from beliefs, and drawing your own conclusions.

Responsibilities

The responsibilities of citizenship are not as clear-cut as the duties. Because responsibilities are voluntary, people are not arrested or punished if they do not fulfill these obligations. The quality of our government and of our lives will diminish, however, if our responsibilities are not carried out.

Be Informed

Keep in mind that government exists to serve you. Therefore, one of your responsibilities as a citizen is to know what

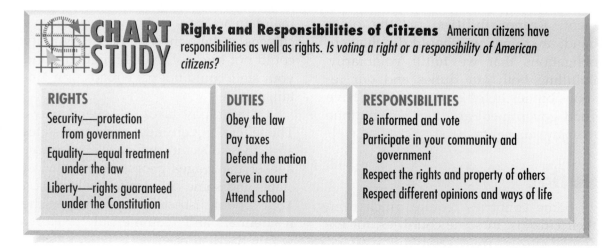

CHART STUDY **Rights and Responsibilities of Citizens** American citizens have responsibilities as well as rights. *Is voting a right or a responsibility of American citizens?*

RIGHTS	DUTIES	RESPONSIBILITIES
Security—protection from government	Obey the law	Be informed and vote
Equality—equal treatment under the law	Pay taxes	Participate in your community and government
Liberty—rights guaranteed under the Constitution	Defend the nation	Respect the rights and property of others
	Serve in court	Respect different opinions and ways of life
	Attend school	

the government is doing and to voice your opinion when you feel strongly about something the government has done or has failed to do. When the government learns that most people favor or oppose an action, it usually follows their wishes.

Government leaders make decisions every day that have an impact on your life. The state legislature, for example, may enact a law that raises or lowers the rates your parents pay for auto insurance. Your town council may vote to ban roller blading from all streets or to allow your next-door neighbor to operate a day-care center at home. Keeping informed about these issues and expressing your feelings about them ensure that government will act in the interests of all of its people.

Being informed also means knowing your rights and exercising them when you feel it is necessary. For example, people accused of crimes have the right to be represented by a lawyer. If people were unaware of those rights, they might not receive a fair trial.

Knowing your rights is the best way to preserve them. You will learn about many of your rights in this course. You can learn more about other rights, and also keep informed about the government and its laws, by reading books, newspapers, and magazines, listening to the news on radio and television, and discussing issues and events with teachers, family, and friends.

Vote

Voting is one of American citizens' most important responsibilities. By voting, people exercise their right of self-government. Voters choose the people who run the government, and in doing

so, they give their consent to that government. If people do not like the way an elected official is doing his or her job, it is their responsibility to choose someone else in the next election. Taking the responsibility to vote ensures that leadership is changed in a peaceful, orderly manner.

Participate in Government

Another responsibility of citizens is to participate in their community and in their government. Participating in your government and community is extremely important.

Think about what your community would be like if no one would serve as mayor, if no one would volunteer to fight fires or coach a baseball team, and if no one would ever speak out or do anything to help solve community problems. Communities and governments need people to participate. When people are

Working in Your Community   As Americans we have the responsibility to volunteer in our communities.   *What are some other responsibilities?*

Careers

Social Work

If you enjoy helping others, social work may be the career for you. Social workers help people deal with social and personal problems such as poverty, drug addiction, mental or physical illness, and criminal behavior.

Different Jobs

The kind of problems social workers deal with depends on where they are employed. Social workers in schools help troubled students. Those in child welfare agencies place children in foster or adoptive homes. Social workers employed by groups such as the Y.M.C.A. lead support groups for people with similar problems.

Hospitals hire social workers to help patients. Psychiatric social workers help people with mental or psychological problems. Social workers also work for the courts as probation or parole officers.

Requirements

Social workers usually need a master's degree in social work or psychiatric social work. Social work can be a very frustrating and

A social worker counseling a family

challenging career, but it can also be extremely rewarding for people who get satisfaction from helping others. To be a good social worker, you must really like people, and you must possess excellent problem-solving skills.

School TO WORK

Interview a social worker employed in your school district to learn what type of education and training the job requires. Also ask about the duties and responsibilities of the job. Share your interview results with your classmates.

involved in their communities, they are more likely to end up with well-run governments.

Respect Rights of Others

To enjoy your rights to the fullest, you must be prepared to respect other people's rights as well. For example, if you live in an apartment building, you have an obligation to keep the volume on your radio or television down so that it does not disturb your neighbors. You also expect them to do the same for you. Many of our laws have been enacted to encourage people to respect each other's rights. A person who continues to play a radio or television too loudly can be arrested for disturbing the peace.

Citizens have a responsibility to show the same respect for public property and for the property of others. Sometimes people who would not dream of breaking a neighbor's window will van-

A Multicultural Society   The United States is a multicultural society in which people, such as these Korean Americans, celebrate their ancestral land as well as their new country.   *What do we call respecting and accepting others?*

dalize their school or a city bus because "no one owns it." Yet, such public property belongs to us all, and we all pay if it is stolen or damaged.

Respect Diversity

Citizens have a responsibility to respect the rights of people with whom they disagree. Respecting and accepting others, regardless of their beliefs, practices, or other differences, is called **toleration**. It means giving people whose ideas you dislike a chance to express their opinions. Without toleration for the views of others, a real discussion or exchange of ideas is impossible. Under a democratic system of government, everyone should have a say. It is then up to the people to choose sensible ideas and discard offensive ones.

One of America's great strengths has always been the diversity of its people. Immigrants have brought a variety of religions, traditions, and lifestyles to this country, and they continue to do so. As citizens, we all have a responsibility to respect the practices and traditions of others when they are different from our own, just as we expect them to respect our differences. There are no degrees of citizenship in the United States. All citizens are equal and entitled to be treated the same.

★ SECTION 2 REVIEW ★

UNDERSTANDING VOCABULARY
Define duties, responsibilities, draft, toleration.

REVIEWING OBJECTIVES
1 What are the major duties of American citizens?

2 What are the responsibilities of American citizens?

How to Get the Facts

How will you decide which candidate to support? Responsible citizens use a variety of sources to find out about the candidates.

Newspapers

Most newspapers and many news magazines include both news and opinion. They usually indicate clearly what is news and what is opinion. Do not assume, however, that the news section is accurate and complete. The people who write the news have their own political preferences, which are likely to influence their reporting.

News Broadcasts

Commercial television and radio stations try to make stories dramatic, even if that means being less accurate. Therefore, commercial broadcasters present news that is short and exciting.

Talk Shows

In recent years political candidates have begun appearing on television and radio talk shows. The shows' hosts ask probing questions, and viewers can judge the candidate's answers and personalities accordingly.

Political Advertisements

Political advertising takes many forms: slick brochures, posters, newspaper ads, and TV commercials. These ads may be a good source of information, especially for finding out what a political party or candidate stands for or promises. Remember, however, that ads are designed to convince, not to inform.

League of Women Voters

The League of Women Voters is a nonpartisan organization that strives to present voters with clear, accurate information. One of the ways it does this is by sponsoring political debates.

Members of both parties respect the League for its thoroughness and fairness.

CITIZENSHIP IN ACTION

1 If political advertisements are so one-sided, why do you think people pay attention to them?

2 Choose an upcoming or recent election in your community and gather information on one of the candidates. Assess each source of information for its accuracy. Share your findings with the class.

The Citizen's Role in the Community

A **community** is a group of people who share the same interests and concerns. People usually think of their neighborhood or town when they are asked to identify their community. Most people, however, belong to several different communities. Your family, your school, and your town are communities. For some purposes, your state is a community, and so is the nation. You are even citizens of a global community.

Services Communities Provide

Each of the communities you belong to provides you with certain things. For example, your family and school teach you values, traditions, behavior, and co-operation. The government of your town or city provides laws, police and fire protection, schools, trash collection, and other services. These things are often called public services. **Public** means pertaining to the people in a community or for the use of all.

The services provided by a community vary according to the community's size and complexity. While a city provides police to protect its citizens from criminals, the federal government provides armed forces to protect the nation

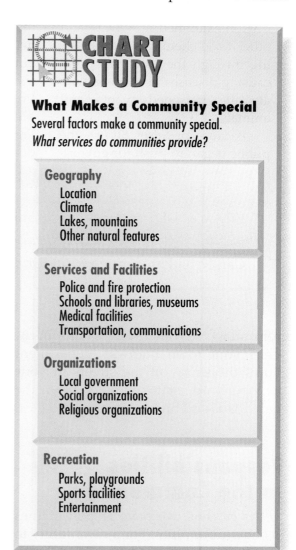

CHART STUDY

What Makes a Community Special

Several factors make a community special. *What services do communities provide?*

Geography
Location
Climate
Lakes, mountains
Other natural features

Services and Facilities
Police and fire protection
Schools and libraries, museums
Medical facilities
Transportation, communications

Organizations
Local government
Social organizations
Religious organizations

Recreation
Parks, playgrounds
Sports facilities
Entertainment

American Profiles

Rachel Carson

Rachel Carson (1907–1964) was a marine biologist and a gifted author. In 1958 she began writing a book about the effects of using the powerful insecticide DDT to control plant pests.

In her book *Silent Spring* Carson examined how DDT and other toxic chemicals were passing through the food chain and causing diseases in humans who ate the poisoned plants and animals.

Because of *Silent Spring*, the public began to push for government regulation. In 1972 the government finally banned all domestic use of DDT.

Rachel Carson died in 1964. She never saw the results of her work, but she was awarded the Presidential Medal of Freedom in 1980, years after her death.

PROFILE REVIEW

1 Why was DDT so dangerous to animals and humans?

2 What do you think America would be like today if Rachel Carson had not written *Silent Spring?*

---

from attack by other nations. Similarly, while your town highway department plows the snow off the streets in your neighborhood, state workers plow the main roads and highways.

Responsibilities to the Community

As citizens, we have responsibilities to our communities. For a community to be successful, its members must take an active role in it. One of the responsibilities of citizens is to help make their community a good place to work and live. Good citizens are concerned about the **welfare**—the health, prosperity, and happiness—of all members of the community. They are concerned about people who are poor as well as those who are rich.

Responsible citizens are also concerned about the welfare of the community as a whole. They may be concerned about the **environment,** or surround-

Civic Responsibility These students are fulfilling their responsibilities by helping clean up their community. *What are other responsibilities?*

to provide for the welfare of all its people or to solve all its problems. It counts on volunteers, who are unpaid workers, to help by doing some of the things that the government cannot afford to pay people to do.

People usually volunteer to do things they like. They may work in a hospital, fight fires, coach a little league baseball team, lead a scout troop, or help out in a classroom. In the summer of 1993, after floods in the Midwest, thousands of people from all over the nation volunteered to help with the cleanup.

Some volunteers raise money to help a good cause, such as buying uniforms for the high school band or providing food and shelter for the homeless. People of all ages and backgrounds perform volunteer work in the community. It is a very satisfying way of giving something back to the community for the help the community has given to them and to their families.

ings, of the community or about the quality of life. Safeguarding these things may require any number of government actions. It could mean cleaning up a toxic waste dump that is polluting the water supply, adding more police officers to combat drug trafficking, or building more parks and playgrounds.

Into Action

Concern for our communities is not enough, however. Our concern must be supported by action. No community or government has the money or resources

★ **SECTION 3 REVIEW** ★

UNDERSTANDING VOCABULARY
Define community, public, welfare, environment.

REVIEWING OBJECTIVES
1 What are some of the services that the many communities to which you belong provide?

2 What are your responsibilities to your community?

3 Why must citizens support their concern for their community with action?

Identifying Key Terms

Choose the word or phrase from the list below that best completes each sentence. Write the missing words on a separate sheet of paper.

segregation   civil rights   draft
welfare   duties   discrimination
toleration   affirmative action

1. By helping distribute food to the poor, the woman showed her concern for the _____ of the people in her community.
2. During the war, the thousands of men who fought in the armed services were fulfilling their _____ to their country.
3. The landlord was accused of _____ because he would not rent the apartment to the young Hispanic couple.
4. By hiring many African Americans and women, the company was following the policy of _____.
5. Before the 1960s, many schools in the South practiced _____, separating white and African American students.
6. Because the woman was not allowed to vote without paying a fee, her _____ were violated.
7. In the United States, all men aged 18 and over must register with the government in case the country needs to _____, or call up, men for military service.
8. Respecting and accepting others, regardless of their beliefs, policies, or other differences, is called _____.

Reviewing the Main Ideas

SECTION 1
1. What are the sources of our rights as citizens?
2. What two rights does the Fourteenth Amendment guarantee?
3. What rights were expanded by the Civil Rights amendments?

SECTION 2
4. Identify three ways in which citizens pay taxes.
5. Why do people have a responsibility to respect the rights of others?

SECTION 3
6. Explain how the services a community provides may vary.
7. Identify three actions a government might take to safeguard the welfare of the community.

Critical Thinking

SECTION 1
1. **Evaluating Information**   Do you think that affirmative action laws are a fair way to change past discrimination? Why or why not?

SECTION 2
2. **Analyzing Information**   Why is an educated population so crucial to maintaining the freedoms of a democratic society?

SECTION 3
3. **Evaluating Information**   Why are citizens' responsibilities to their communities such an important part of our democratic system?

Reinforcing Citizenship Skills

Choose an election in your community. Outline how you would become informed on the candidates and/or the issues. Then follow your outline and become an informed voter. Share your outline and your findings with the class.

Cooperative Learning

Working in groups of four, interview one of your community's officials to learn how you can begin taking an active role in the community. Members of your group may wish to volunteer for some sort of community service, perform the service, and report your experiences to your classmates.

Focusing on Your Community

The types of services communities provide vary according to different factors, such as the size of the community, the money available, and the community's needs. Find out what types of services your community offers. Research the different services that are available, who is eligible to receive these services, and how much money is available to provide these services. Find out also how interested citizens can become involved in helping to provide different community services. Present your findings to the class.

Technology Activity

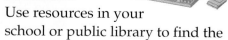

Using a Word Processor

Use resources in your school or public library to find the names and addresses of local not-for-profit agencies that need volunteers. Use a word processor to write one of these agencies to ask about volunteer needs. Share your findings with the class. You might also wish to follow-up with a visit to the agency and possibly volunteer to help.

Analyzing Visuals

While the democratic government of the United States guarantees a number of important rights, those rights also have limits. Study the cartoon, and then answer the questions.

1. Whom do you think the person in the cartoon represents? Why?
2. What is this person doing?
3. What do his thoughts suggest about the task faced by those involved in planning the new nation's government?

Parties and Politics

CIVIC PARTICIPATION

Political parties are an essential part of our democratic system of government. One of their functions is to select, or nominate, people from the party to run for elected office. Contact the local headquarters of the Democratic or Republican party. Find out how local and state candidates are nominated and who is involved in the process.

Working in Your Community

After you have obtained this information, interview people in your community who are active in a political party. If any of them have participated in the nominating process on the local or state level, ask them about their experiences. Prepare a brochure on the nominating process to distribute in your neighborhood. ■

Your Civics Journal

Find out how the Republican and Democratic parties stand on current issues. Record their positions in your civics journal. Note how your stand on an issue compares with that of each political party. Interview some classmates and add their views to your journal.

On the campaign trail ➤

SECTION 1

Kinds of Party Systems

FOCUS

TERMS TO KNOW
candidate, plurality, majority, coalition

OBJECTIVES

■ Describe the characteristics of **the two-party system** of the United States.

■ Explain the advantages and disadvantages of **multiparty systems.**

■ Identify the characteristics of **one-party systems.**

A political party is an organization made up of people who share similar ideas about the way the country should be governed. It offers people an opportunity to work with others to achieve certain political goals. Members of a party work to have their party's **candidates,** people seeking elected office, chosen as the government's leaders. Once elected, these candidates organize and run the government. They also work to get laws passed to carry out their party's programs.

Political parties are not unique to the United States. They exist in most countries. In the United States, we have a two-party system in which two major parties vie with each other to run the government. Some countries have a multiparty system in which several parties may compete. A third possibility is the one-party system in which only one party exists.

The Two-Party System

The United States has had a two-party system since its early days as a nation. Although the names of the parties have been different, one of two major parties has always been in power. Smaller political parties have also been formed, but these minor parties generally have had little impact on national elections.

For the most part, our two-party system has worked very well. If the voters are dissatisfied with the way one party is running the nation, they can elect candidates from the other party. The same process works on the state and local government levels.

Two-Party System The Republican and Democratic parties have different views on similar goals. *Which party believes the federal government should be more involved in education?*

CHART STUDY

1996 Party Platforms A platform describes a party's position on important public issues. *How did the Republican and Democratic positions on taxes differ?*

Democratic Party	Republican Party
Taxes	**Taxes**
▪ Favors tax cuts for some small businesses and the self-employed	▪ Favors an across-the-board tax cut
▪ Favors tax credits for research and development	▪ Promotes per-child tax credit for families
Rights	**Rights**
▪ Supports a woman's right to choose	▪ Supports a human life amendment to protect the rights of the unborn child
Education	**Education**
▪ Supports tax cuts for college tuition	▪ Promotes school choice at all levels of education
▪ Promotes expansion of work-study programs	▪ Supports increase in student loans and assistance for families preparing for college costs
Health	**Health**
▪ Favors portable medical coverage	▪ Advocates a health-care system in which providers respond to consumer choice
▪ Advocates shortening the approval process for new drugs	▪ Supports portable health insurance
The Economy	**The Economy**
▪ Advocates a balanced budget	▪ Advocates a balanced budget
▪ Advocates better training for wage earners	▪ Advocates reduction of tax burden on Americans

Republicans and Democrats

Sometimes it is difficult to tell the difference between the Republican and the Democratic parties. The parties are similar because the American people agree, to a large extent, about many political and social issues. Americans cherish their personal rights and freedoms. They believe that people should have an opportunity to get a good education and make a decent living. They also believe the government has a duty to protect the nation, preserve the environment, and help its citizens.

The essential difference between the two major parties is that they disagree on how to achieve these ends. For example, the Democrats tend to believe that the federal government should be more directly involved in providing housing, income, education, and jobs for the poor. The Republicans tend to believe that if they help the nation's economy grow, poor people will have a better chance of finding work and meeting their needs on their own.

Stability and Continuity

Our nation's Founders feared that political parties would divide the people and destroy the Republic. Our two-party system has been a stabilizing force, however. Both parties tend to stay near the center of a wide range of political opinions. Most Americans do not support extreme political ideas, such as government ownership of factories, and they do not want a completely different system of government. Because each party wants to gain the support of the largest possible number of votes, party policies are designed to appeal to many different groups of people. The parties usually avoid extreme positions that might cause voters to reject the party.

The two-party system has also provided continuity. Because each party is in power some of the time and out of power at other times, both parties have many members who are experienced not only in the art of politics but also in the busi-

ness of government. Thus, when a Democratic President takes over from a Republican, or vice versa, the transition is normally smooth.

Disadvantages

Two-party systems are not without disadvantages, however. The most important is that a two-party system can stifle the views of minority groups. In the United States, the news media give a great deal of coverage to the Democratic and Republican candidates for President. Candidates from other, minor parties usually receive very little attention, even though they may have important ideas to contribute.

For a minority viewpoint to be heard, it generally must be accepted and championed by one of the major parties. For example, the civil rights and woman's rights movements gained significant political power only when the Democratic party took up their ideas.

Multiparty Systems

In a multiparty system, three or more parties compete for control of the government. Multiparty systems are common in Europe and are also found in such countries as Israel and Japan.

One advantage of the multiparty system is that it provides voters with choices that represent a broader range of political ideas. Its major weakness, however, is that, with the vote divided among so many parties, it is sometimes difficult for one party to gain enough votes to form a government.

In countries where several major parties compete in each election, one party usually wins a **plurality,** that is, wins more votes or seats in the legislature than any other party. It may not, however, win a **majority** of votes, or more than half the votes cast. In most multiparty systems, a party must hold a majority before it can form a government. In that case, the top vote-getting party must form a **coalition,**

Multiparty System   In a multiparty system such as Italy's, one party may not win enough votes to form a government.   *How are governments often formed in multiparty systems?*

One-Party System   China is a one-party state; the government is made up of members of the Communist party.   *What is the main job of party members?*

or an alliance, with another party or parties so that together they command a majority of the votes.

The major problem with coalition governments is that the parties in the coalition often have very different ideas about how to run the government. These differences can become so great that the government is unable to accomplish anything and collapses. When that happens, the parties are forced to hold another election and, very likely, form another coalition. In Italy, for example, the repeated failure of coalition governments has resulted in more than 50 governments since the end of World War II, an average of about one a year.

One-Party Systems

A third type of party system is the one-party system. In such a system, the party and the government are nearly the same thing. In the People's Republic of China, for example, only one party—the Communist party—is allowed to exist. The party allows only candidates from its own party to run for office. As a result, positions in the government are filled only with Communist party members. The role of government officials is to carry out the decisions the party makes. There is no opposition. In many one-party systems, the head of the government is the head of the party as well.

In a one-party system, the main job of party members is to recruit new members, maintain party discipline, and carry out the party's orders. In exchange for their work for the party and government, upper-level party members are sometimes rewarded with special privileges and favors, such as vacation homes and the use of private stores and hospitals. Typically, only a small part of the population actually belongs to the party. In China, for example, only about 4 percent of the population belongs to the Chinese Communist party.

★ SECTION 1 REVIEW ★

UNDERSTANDING VOCABULARY
Define candidate, plurality, majority, coalition.

REVIEWING OBJECTIVES

1 What are some characteristics of the two-party system of the United States?

2 What are the advantages and disadvantages of multiparty systems?

3 What are the characteristics of one-party systems?

United States Political Parties

FOCUS

TERM TO KNOW
third party

OBJECTIVES

- Describe the **development of the two-party system** in the United States.

- Identify and discuss three **third parties** in the United States.

The first political parties in the United States began to form during the debate over the Constitution. Those who desired a strong national government, the Federalists, supported the Constitution and campaigned for its acceptance. The Federalist party became the first political party in the United States. Those who favored strong state governments formed the Anti-Federalist, or Democratic-Republican, party.

Development of the Two-Party System

The two parties represented not only different ideas about the government but also different groups of the population. The Federalist party drew much of its strength from New England merchants and bankers. The Democratic-Republicans relied on the support of the nation's small farmers, planters, shopkeepers, and laborers.

New Parties

After electing only two Presidents, George Washington and John Adams in the first years of the Republic, the Federalist party gradually disappeared. For several years, the Democratic-Republicans were unopposed. By the mid-1820s, however, the party began to break up into several groups. One group became the Democratic party, which continued to represent small farmers and working people. Another group became the Whigs, who arose to challenge the Democrats. The Whigs followed in the tradition of the Federalists and tended to represent northern bankers, merchants, manufacturers, and large plantation owners in the South.

The Republican Party

In the 1850s both parties split over the slavery issue. Proslavery voters stayed in the Democratic party, and Whigs and

George Washington The first President opposed the idea of political parties, but he supported Federalist principles. *What did the Federalist party stand for?*

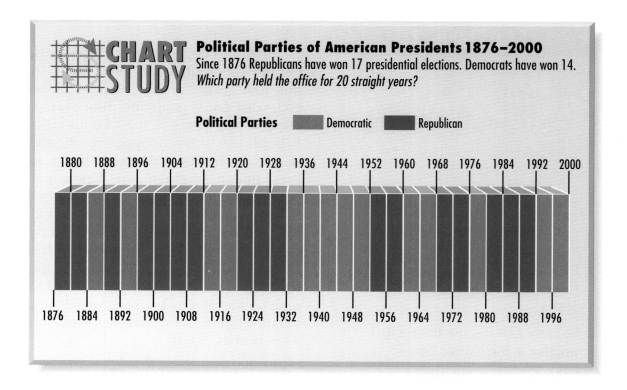

CHART STUDY

Political Parties of American Presidents 1876–2000
Since 1876 Republicans have won 17 presidential elections. Democrats have won 14.
Which party held the office for 20 straight years?

Political Parties ▮ Democratic ▮ Republican

1880 1888 1896 1904 1912 1920 1928 1936 1944 1952 1960 1968 1976 1984 1992 2000

1876 1884 1892 1900 1908 1916 1924 1932 1940 1948 1956 1964 1972 1980 1988 1996

antislavery Democrats formed a new party, the Republican party. In 1860 Abraham Lincoln became the first Republican to be elected President.

From the Civil War until today, the Democrats and the Republicans have remained the two major parties in the United States. After the Civil War, the Republicans emerged as the stronger of the two parties. Between 1865 and 1931, the Democrats were able to elect only two Presidents—Grover Cleveland and Woodrow Wilson.

Then, in 1932, it was the Democrats' turn. Franklin D. Roosevelt was elected President four times, and his successor, Harry S Truman, served nearly eight years. Since then, the presidency has switched back and forth between Democrats and Republicans, although the majority in Congress has usually been Democratic.

Third Parties

From time to time a minor party has arisen to challenge the Democrats and the Republicans. In the United States, we call these minor parties **third parties** because they challenge the two major parties rather than each other. No third party has ever won a presidential election. Third parties have, however, affected the outcome of some elections and influenced government and social policy.

The Populists and the Progressives

One of the most successful third parties was the Populist party of the 1890s. A coalition of farmers and working people, the Populists called for the direct election of United States senators and an eight-hour working day, as well as other

Third Parties   H. Ross Perot ran as an independent candidate in the 1992 and 1996 presidential elections.   *What percentage of the popular vote did he win in 1996?*

reforms. Although the Populists never won a presidential election, the two major parties eventually adopted many of their reform ideas.

Another important third party was the Progressive party, which split off from the Republicans in 1912 and ran former President Theodore Roosevelt as its candidate. Roosevelt took so many votes from the Republican candidate, William Howard Taft, that the Democratic nominee, Woodrow Wilson, won the election. In this case, the Progressive party played a "spoiler" role by taking votes away from the Republicans, the party closest to its own views.

Other Third Parties

Numerous third parties have sprung up throughout the nation's history. Normally, several third parties run candidates in every election year. In general, there are three kinds of third parties. Some are tied to a single issue, some to a particular political belief, and some to a single candidate.

The Prohibition party, formed in 1872, is a single-issue party. It opposes alcohol and would like to see it banned as it was in the 1920s. Parties such as the American Socialist party and the Libertarian party are third parties based on political beliefs. They run candidates in elections year after year, even though their political beliefs are too extreme for most Americans.

Third parties occasionally form around a single candidate when that person fails to receive support from one of the two major parties. George Wallace failed to receive the support of the Democratic party in 1968 and ran for President on the American Independent party ticket. In 1980 John Anderson lost the Republican nomination and ran as the candidate of the Independent party. In both 1992 and 1996 independent candidate H. Ross Perot challenged the ideas of both major party candidates. He won almost 19 percent of the votes in 1992 and 8 percent in 1996.

★ SECTION 2 REVIEW ★

UNDERSTANDING VOCABULARY
Define third party.

REVIEWING OBJECTIVES
1 How did the two-party system change and develop in the United States?

2 What are three American third parties?

Exploring ISSUES

The High Cost of Running for Office

Election campaigns have always cost money, but the amount of money required has increased dramatically in recent years. In 1976 the average cost of a United States Senate race was $610,000. By 1996 some candidates spent $15 million or more.

Although several developments explain this cost explosion, the most important is the use of television. Candidates have found that television commercials are the most effective way to win votes. Running these commercials in prime time can cost tens of thousands of dollars per minute.

Money from Special-Interest Groups

The Federal Election Campaign Act of 1971 placed campaign financing under government control. Among other things, the law limited individual contributions to a candidate to $1,000. This limit forced candidates to look for new sources of money.

Some funds come from political action committees (PACs). These are special-interest groups—such as labor unions, corporations, and medical associations—that provide funds to candidates who favor their position on issues. However, many people think candidates receiving PAC funds owe these groups favors.

Proposals for Reform

Some people say that the government should pay for election campaigns. In the case of presidential elections, a system is already in place. Taxpayers can contribute

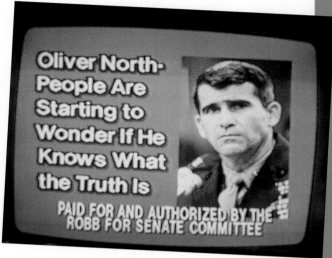

Television campaign

$3 of their income taxes to a campaign fund that is used to provide matching funds to candidates who raise money from outside sources.

Another proposal is to limit the amount of money each candidate can spend. However, in *Buckley* v. *Valeo,* the Supreme Court ruled that such a limit is unconstitutional because it restricts the candidate's right of free speech. Thus the free-speech guarantees of the First Amendment protect campaign commercials.

DEVELOPING A POINT OF VIEW

1 What is the possible effect of financing by a PAC?

2 Why has campaign fund-raising become more difficult and more controversial?

The Organization of United States Political Parties

FOCUS

TERMS TO KNOW

nominate, campaign, patronage, precinct, political machine, platform, plank

OBJECTIVES

- Describe **what party members do** for their party.

- Explain the basic **party organization** of the Democrats and the Republicans.

In the United States, anyone can become a member of a political party. It is not necessary to pay a fee, or take a test, or even vote. In most states, it is only necessary to declare yourself a member of a party when you register to vote. Which party you choose is entirely up to you.

In general, each of the two major parties has tended to attract certain kinds of people. Historically, the Democratic party has tended to appeal more to working people, Catholics, minorities, union members, and people in favor of government involvement in social policies. The Republican party has attracted more businesspeople, Protestants, and people against government involvement. These are only generalities, however. Each party includes members of all backgrounds, races, religions, and political beliefs. In Congress, for example, it is common to find Democrats whose political views are closer to those of some Republicans than to many of their fellow Democrats.

What Party Members Do

For most people, belonging to a political party involves little more than voting for the party's candidates on Election Day. Active party members do much more than just vote, however.

The major function of each party is to get its candidates elected to office. To achieve that goal, party members must first **nominate,** or name, the candidates they want to run for each office. Once the candidates have been chosen, each party embarks on an election **campaign,** an

Party Delegate A delegate to the national convention proclaims her support for Democratic candidates. *What is the major function of a political party?*

effort to gather support for its candidates and inform the voters of the party's stand on issues. Campaigns are a great deal of work, and many party workers and volunteers are needed to perform dozens of jobs. They may be asked to raise funds, poll voters, make telephone calls, stuff envelopes, arrange dinners and rallies, drive people to the polls, or register voters.

For some active party members, the work does not end when an election is over. Once a party's candidate is elected, the party helps the candidate organize and manage the government. For example, when a new President is elected, hundreds of job vacancies in the federal government must be filled. The President's party compiles lists of party members who contributed a great deal of time, energy, or money to the election campaign. The President consults these lists and often chooses people from them to fill positions in the government.

Giving jobs or special favors to party workers is called **patronage.** It is a way of rewarding people for their work and loyalty. Political patronage exists in both parties and at all levels of government and political organization. Many people work hard for their party in the hope of being rewarded with a patronage job. However, patronage has declined in importance with the rise of the civil service system, or merit appointment to government jobs.

Party Organization

The Democratic and Republican parties are organized at the local, state, and national levels, in very much the same way as the government. The local organization consists of a city, town, or county

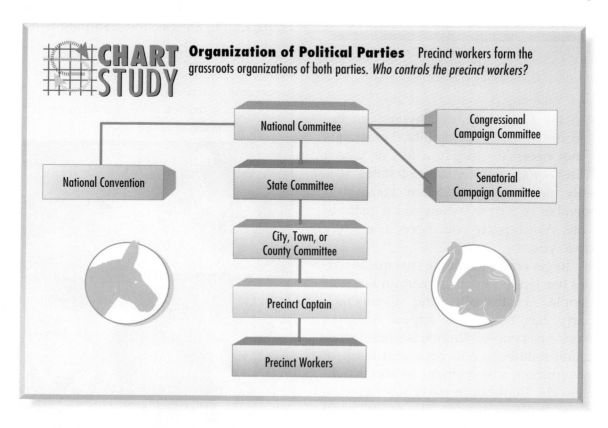

CHART STUDY **Organization of Political Parties** Precinct workers form the grassroots organizations of both parties. *Who controls the precinct workers?*

National Committee

Congressional Campaign Committee

National Convention

State Committee

Senatorial Campaign Committee

City, Town, or County Committee

Precinct Captain

Precinct Workers

Careers

Statistician

Statistician at work

Who will win the next election? How many consumers will buy a certain new product? People who try to answer such questions are statisticians.

curate picture by asking a sample of a few hundred people.

The Work

Statisticians work for the government gathering and interpreting data about the economy, health trends, and so on. They also work for industries and public opinion research organizations.

One way statisticians gather information is by taking samples. They cannot question all the adults in this country about their activities, but they can get a fairly ac-

Qualifications

To become a statistician, you should have an aptitude and an interest in mathematics and computers. Although some jobs are available for people with a bachelor's degree, many jobs require a graduate degree in

mathematics or statistics. If you think you want a career in statistics, you should take business, mathematics, and science courses in high school.

School TO WORK

To learn more about the work that statisticians do, design a sample opinion poll to conduct in your school. Choose some important community issues on which to poll your classmates. Conduct the poll and share your results with the class.

---

committee made up of people elected by their fellow party members. Each city or county is divided into election districts, or precincts. A **precinct** is a geographic area that contains a specific number of voters. A precinct may consist of one entire town or of several adjoining neighborhoods in a large city.

For each precinct, the local party committee appoints a precinct captain, whose job is to organize the party volunteers and get out the vote within the precinct. The precinct captain sends out

volunteers to hand out literature, register voters, and try to convince voters to support the party's candidates.

The local party organization is very important because it works to elect candidates at every level of government, from school board member to President of the United States. In a well-organized local party committee, the precinct captain is expected to know approximately how many votes are likely to be cast for the party's candidate, and he or she is expected to deliver them.

"Who Stole the People's Money? 'Twas Him" Thomas Nast attacked the Tammany Hall political machine in his cartoon. *How did Nast show the members of the Tammany ring answering the cartoon's title question?*

Sometimes a local party organization becomes so powerful that, year after year, only its candidates are elected to public office. Such a strong party organization is called a **political machine.** Political machines exist in a number of towns, cities, and counties throughout the United States.

Although political machines are not necessarily good or bad, most people think of them as harmful. If one party is in power for too long, it might become unresponsive to the needs of the community. Its politicians might forget that the party's main function is to serve the public. At its worst, a political machine might elect corrupt leaders who seek to enrich themselves and their associates at the expense of the people they are supposed to serve. One of the most famous—or infamous—political machines was New York City's Tammany Hall. Corrupt politicians controlled this organization, which ran New York in the late 1800s and early 1900s.

Above the local party committees are the state party committees. State committee workers concentrate on electing candidates to state offices—the governor, the attorney general, representatives to the state legislature, and so on. They also work within their state to elect their party's candidates for national office, such as their United States senators, representatives, and the President.

Each political party also has a national committee made up of representatives from each state. The committee is headed by a national chairperson who directs the committee's staff and speaks for the party on national issues. The national committee helps raise funds for the presidential election and organizes the party's national convention.

National Convention Party members nominate their candidates for President and Vice President at their party's national convention. *What other major decisions are made at the national conventions?*

The national convention is one of the most important responsibilities of the national committee. Held only once every four years, the national convention is where party members nominate their candidates for President and Vice President of the United States. During the convention, party members also formulate the party's **platform,** the statement of its goals and positions on various public issues. Each item in the platform is called a **plank.** A plank on the party's platform might, for example, call for new programs to improve education.

In addition to the national, state, and local committees, each political party has several congressional committees, including a Senatorial Campaign Committee and a Congressional Campaign Committee for the House. These committees seek to elect and reelect party members to the United States Senate and House of Representatives. Made up of members of Congress, the committees help out when a party member is in danger of losing a seat or when a vacant seat is up for grabs.

★ **SECTION 3 REVIEW** ★

UNDERSTANDING VOCABULARY
Define nominate, campaign, patronage, precinct, political machine, platform, plank.

REVIEWING OBJECTIVES
1 What are some of the things that party members do for their party?

2 What is the basic party organization of the Democrats and the Republicans?

How to Register to Vote

When you become 18 years old, you can begin to exercise one of your most important rights—the right to vote. Before you can do so, however, you must register.

Registration Procedures

The National Voter Registration Act took effect in January 1995. This law, known as the "motor voter" bill, allows citizens to get voter registration forms at motor vehicle offices when applying for a driver's license. After completing the forms, you mail or take them to a government office in your community.

You can also register in person at a county election bureau, or by mailing in special postcards obtained from any state or county office. Sometimes local citizens' groups hold voter registration drives at local malls, or they go door-to-door.

What the Forms Ask

Voter registration forms ask for your name, address, and age and often for your party preference. You can register as a Democrat, a Republican, an independent, or a member of some other party.

If you register as a Republican or a Democrat, you will be able to vote in primary elections, where you can choose your party's candidates for the general election. If you register as an independent voter, you may or may not be able to vote in primary elections.

Registering young voters

Requirements and Restrictions

When registering, first-time voters must show proof of citizenship, address, and age, such as a driver's license or a birth certificate. You can register to vote at any time, although most states have cutoff dates for specific elections.

Once registered, you are assigned to an election district according to your address. You do not need to reregister unless you change your address, name, or party. When you register, be sure to find out where your polling place will be.

CITIZENSHIP IN ACTION

1 What is the advantage of registering as a Republican or a Democrat?

2 Why do you think many citizens who are eligible to vote fail to register to vote?

The Role of Political Parties in the United States Today

FOCUS

TERMS TO KNOW

grassroots, accountable, nonpartisan

OBJECTIVES

- Discuss the five **basic functions of political parties.**

- Explain several factors that are causing a weakening of loyalty to **political parties today.**

Although the major purpose of American political parties is to elect candidates to public office, they also play an important role in helping the people of the United States practice self-government. The parties enable people to communicate with their government leaders and help ensure that government remains responsive to the people. The parties fulfill this role in a number of ways.

Basic Functions of Political Parties

Political parties have five basic functions that help them fulfill their role in government.

- They select and support candidates.
- They inform the public.
- They carry the message of the people to the government.
- They act as a watchdog over government activities.
- They serve as a link between different levels and branches of government.

Selecting and Supporting Candidates

Because candidates for public office have to compete in elections, each party tries to put up candidates who will win as many votes as possible. Each party wants to offer attractive, able candidates who have the experience needed to fill the offices they are seeking. This competition between the parties means that the voters are usually offered a choice of two or more qualified candidates.

After the parties select candidates, the election campaign begins. The parties support their candidates by helping

Republican Views   Haley Barbour, Republican National Committee Chairperson, answers reporters' questions.   *What function of a political party is he fulfilling?*

Speaker of the House Newt Gingrich became speaker after Republicans gained control of the House in 1995. *How do candidates get their views across to voters?*

Carrying the People's Message

In addition to presenting their views to the people, the parties listen to what the people have to say. Voters have ideas and concerns of their own and issues they want their leaders to address.

For example, perhaps voters across the country are concerned about crime. Each party develops a position on this issue and sets certain goals for how to solve the problem. In this way, the people's message can be carried to the highest levels of government in Washington.

Sometimes people in different areas feel very strongly about an issue. They may oppose a government policy or want stronger laws to protect the environment. A political movement that begins with the people is known as a **grassroots** movement. When a grassroots movement becomes strong enough, its ideas will probably be taken over by a political party.

Acting as Watchdogs

Between elections political parties act as "watchdogs" over government activities. Although it is not possible for an individual to keep a close watch on all government officials, political parties can do this very well.

Suppose, for example, that your town council has five Democrats and two Republicans. Although the Republicans lack enough votes to control the decision making on the council, they are still part of the government. They participate in all governmental meetings, inspect town records, talk to employees, and so on. The two Republicans are able to keep close track of the actions and behavior of the Democratic officials. Although they are out of power, the Republicans are serving the public interest by bringing

organize and raise money for election campaigns. They also help their candidates get their ideas and viewpoints across to as many voters as possible.

Informing the Public

In an election campaign, each party tries to tell the public what it has done and what it wants to do. It also points out what it believes the other party is doing wrong.

To get their views across, party candidates make speeches, publish and distribute pamphlets, and place ads in newspapers and magazines and on television and radio. As the parties present their views, the voters have an opportunity to learn about, compare, and make judgments about these views. In this way, the political campaign informs and educates the voters.

mistakes, wrongdoing, and problems to light. In this way, the Republican minority is holding the Democratic majority **accountable** to the people. Officials who want to keep their jobs must explain their actions to the voters.

Of course, the Republicans are acting as watchdogs out of self-interest. They would like to have more Republicans elected to the town council in the next election. The Democrats are also acting out of self-interest. If they know the public is watching, they will try to do a good job so they can be reelected.

Serving as a Link

Just as political parties carry the people's message to the government, they also help different levels and branches of government communicate and cooperate with one another. For example, suppose both the mayor of Cincinnati, Ohio, and the governor of the state are Democrats. As public officials in the same state and members of the same party, they may share similar goals and ideas. They may know each other well and perhaps have worked together on election campaigns or party business in the past. These connections may make it easier for them to work together on mutual problems.

Political Parties Today

Many people believe that the two major political parties are no longer as powerful as they once were. Over the last several years, they appear to have lost considerable strength and may continue to decline in the future.

Decline in Party Loyalty

Several factors have caused this decline. The primary factor is a weakening of party loyalty. People move from place to place more often, and party leaders can no longer count on stable neighborhoods and election districts where they can deliver the same number of votes each election. In addition, fewer people

Cooperation   Chicago Mayor Richard Daley (left), a Democrat, greets Illinois governor Jim Edgar, a Republican. *Why is it often difficult for officials of different parties to work together?*

vote in elections now than in the past. Although the reasons for this are unclear, it seems that many people believe their votes are no longer important.

Technological changes such as television have also weakened party loyalty. Years ago many voters would have voted for a particular candidate simply because he or she was their party's choice. Now many voters decide to vote for a candidate they have seen on television because they are attracted to the candidate, not the political party. In addition, because people are more sophisticated and better educated today than they were in the past, they are more likely to make up their own minds about candidates and issues. As a result, many voters prefer to register as independent voters. More people today are apt to split their votes between candidates of different parties. For many voters, the qualifications and personal characteristics of a candidate are as important as the political party.

Special-interest groups also have an increasing impact on voters' decisions. Dedicated to advancing a specific cause, special-interest groups support candidates who have good records for backing their causes. Some voters decide to vote

CHART STUDY

Who Votes, 1980–1996 Statisticians group voters by race, gender, age, and education to study voting trends. *In which two election years did the highest percentage of 18- to 20-year-olds vote?*

	Presidential Elections					Congressional Elections		
	1996	1992	1988	1984	1980	1994	1990	1986
Total, voting age (in millions)	193.5	185.7	178.1	170.0	157.1	190.3	182.1	173.9
Percent voting	48.8	61.3	57.4	59.9	59.2	44.6	45.0	46.0
White	51.0	63.6	59.1	61.4	60.9	46.9	46.7	47.0
African American	35.0	54.0	51.5	55.8	50.5	37.0	39.2	43.2
Hispanic American	38.0	28.9	28.8	32.6	29.9	19.1	21.0	24.2
Male	48.0	60.2	56.4	59.0	59.1	44.4	44.6	45.8
Female	49.0	62.3	58.3	60.8	59.4	44.9	45.4	46.1
18 to 20 years	31.0	38.5	33.2	36.7	35.7	16.5	18.4	18.6
21 to 24 years	33.0	45.7	38.3	43.5	43.1	22.3	22.0	24.2
25 to 34 years	35.0	53.2	48.0	54.5	54.6	32.2	33.8	35.1
35 to 44 years	49.0	63.6	61.3	63.5	64.4	46.0	48.4	49.3
45 to 64 years	58.0	70.0	67.9	69.8	69.3	56.0	55.8	58.7
65 years and over	54.0	70.1	68.8	67.7	65.1	60.7	60.3	60.9
School completed								
Elementary: 0 to 8 years	32.3	35.1	36.7	42.9	42.6	23.2	27.7	32.7
High School: 1 to 3 years	36.9	41.2	41.3	44.4	45.6	27.0	30.9	33.8
4 years	47.3	57.5	54.7	58.7	58.9	40.5	42.2	44.1
College: 1 to 3 years	62.1	68.7	64.5	67.5	67.2	49.1	50.0	49.9
4 years or more	75.4	81.0	77.6	79.1	79.9	63.1	62.5	62.5

Source: U.S. Dept. of Commerce, Bureau of the Census.

The 1996 Democratic National Convention Both political parties stage elaborate conventions to nominate their presidential candidates. *How has television affected political parties?*

for a candidate because their labor union, woman's rights group, environmental organization, or business association favors that candidate.

Nonpartisan Elections

Another trend that is weakening the parties is the increase in **nonpartisan,** or nonparty, elections. Some states require that certain elections, such as school board elections, be nonpartisan. Political parties are prohibited from participating, and candidates run on the strength of their own qualifications and personal appeal. The candidates organize and run their campaigns without help from any political party. After the election these officeholders owe nothing to a political party.

Despite all these factors, our two-party system is not about to disappear. Political parties are still the most effective means of raising the large sum of money necessary to campaign for national offices. In addition, state and federal election laws help preserve the two-party system by discouraging third parties and independent candidates. The two-party system is likely to remain an important part of our political system for many years to come as it has since the early years of the Republic.

★ SECTION 4 REVIEW ★

UNDERSTANDING VOCABULARY
Define grassroots, accountable, nonpartisan.

REVIEWING OBJECTIVES

1 What are the five basic functions of political parties?

2 What factors are causing a weakening of loyalty to political parties today?

Identifying Key Terms

Choose the vocabulary term that best completes each of the sentences below. Write your answers on a separate sheet of paper.

plurality   majority   coalition
platform   grassroots   nonpartisan

1. With 52 percent of the total vote, the candidate won by a _____.
2. During the convention, the party developed its _____, its list of all the programs it wanted to accomplish.
3. Although none of the candidates won more than 50 percent of the vote, one of them won by a _____.
4. With no political parties represented, the school board election was a _____ election.
5. The three largest parties formed a _____ government to govern the country.
6. The environmental movement was started as a _____ movement of people on the local level.

Reviewing the Main Ideas

SECTION 1
1. Explain how the two-party system works.
2. What are the major disadvantages of a two-party system and a one-party system?

SECTION 2
3. What role have third parties played in the United States political system?
4. What were the major successes of the Populist party?

SECTION 3
5. Identify different types of jobs that active party members are asked to perform.
6. What is the purpose of a party's national convention?

SECTION 4
7. Identify three ways in which parties and their candidates inform the public.
8. Explain how political parties carry the message of the people to the government.

Critical Thinking

SECTION 1
1. **Making Inferences**   The United States has many different groups of people. Why has our two-party system worked despite the differences among Americans?

SECTION 2
2. **Evaluating Information**   Why are third parties important in our democratic system of government?

SECTION 3
3. **Analyzing Information**   Explain why political machines do not usually result in good government. How do you think political machines could be controlled?

SECTION 4
4. **Predicting Consequences**   How do you think our political system would differ if all people were required to become members of a political party?

Reinforcing Citizenship Skills

Find out where you can obtain a voter registration card. Make a list of the information you will need for the card. Share your information with the class.

Cooperative Learning

Work with a partner to collect print ads that advertise a political candidate. Find out what office the candidate is running for, what political party is sponsoring the candidate, and what the candidate's views are. Share your findings with the class.

Focusing on Your Community

Investigate the political preferences of your community. Are most voters registered as Democrats or Republicans? Over the last three presidential elections, how did the majority of your community vote—Democratic or Republican? At the local level of government, which party does your community vote for most consistently? Report your findings to the class.

Technology Activity

Using E-Mail

Search the Internet for the e-mail addresses of the Democratic or Republican National Committees. You may use the following key words to focus your search: **Democratic Party; Republican Party; e-mail address, Congress.** Write and send electronic mail to the party of your choice asking the party's position on issues that concern you and your classmates.

Analyzing Visuals

The following circle graph shows the popular votes in the 1996 presidential election. Study the graph, then answer the questions below.

1. By what margin in both the number and percentage of votes did Democratic party candidate Bill Clinton defeat Republican candidate Bob Dole?
2. What percentage of the popular vote did the third-party candidate receive?
3. How might the results have been different if there had been only two candidates?

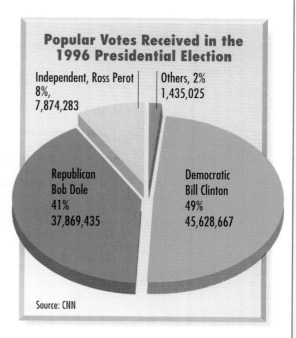

Popular Votes Received in the 1996 Presidential Election

Independent, Ross Perot 8%, 7,874,283

Others, 2% 1,435,025

Republican Bob Dole 41% 37,869,435

Democratic Bill Clinton 49% 45,628,667

Source: CNN

CHAPTER 7

Voting and Elections

CIVIC PARTICIPATION

The right to vote is one of the fundamental rights of citizens in a democratic society. Yet many Americans do not exercise this right. Contact the local chapter of the League of Women Voters or the county board of election commissioners to learn about the voting requirements in your state. Find out when and where a citizen can register to vote.

Find out also what forms a citizen needs to complete.

Working in Your Community

After you have obtained the information, conduct a poll in your neighborhood to learn who is registered to vote. If you have neighbors who are not registered, you might encourage them to do so and tell them the exact procedure they need to follow to register. ∎

Your Civics Journal

Every day for a week, read the local paper and listen to local TV news. Find out what major issues your community is facing, and keep a record of them in your civics journal. Next to each issue, indicate your position and tell what you would do if you were an elected official.

Registering to vote ➤

Voting

Voting is one of the major responsibilities of citizenship. It is the only time that citizens can directly bring about change in their government. Almost all Americans 18 years old or older have the right to vote. Like other rights, however, the right to vote is not absolute. It is subject to certain regulations and restrictions. The most significant regulation concerns who is actually eligible to vote on Election Day.

To be eligible to vote in most states, a person must be at least 18 years old, a resident of the state for a specified period of time, and a citizen of the United States. In most states, a person must be registered in order to vote. Registration usually takes place sometime before Election Day. (See Citizenship Skills, How to Register to Vote, on page 158.) The person's name is then added to a list of registered voters. On Election Day, election officials use this list to verify that the people who vote are eligible and to prevent people from voting more than once.

Preparing to Vote

Registering is only one part of getting ready to vote. It is equally important to learn about the candidates and the issues involved in the election. Voters can get this information from newspaper and magazine articles and from radio and television news programs or talk shows. Political parties also provide information about their candidates and their party's programs. Responsible voters use these different sources of information to prepare themselves for voting.

Most voters look for candidates whose opinions on particular issues are similar to their own. Voters who are concerned about protecting the environment, for example, would probably favor a candidate who advocates strong controls on pollution. Every election focuses on one or more issues. Responsible voters learn about those issues and about the candidates' stands on them.

Television News   Television is one good source of information about candidates and issues.   *From what other sources can voters get information?*

In a presidential election, a great deal of information about the candidates and the issues is usually available. On Election Day, however, voters also select candidates for local, state, and congressional offices. Although it is more difficult to learn about local candidates and issues than presidential ones, responsible voters try to get as much information as possible before casting their ballots.

Who Votes?

Collectively, the people who are eligible to vote in an election are called the **electorate.** Not everyone in the electorate votes, however. Between 1924 and 1992 turnout in presidential elections ranged from 48.9 to 63 percent. In the 1996 presidential election, only about 48.8 percent of the voting age population actually voted.

Factors That Limit Voting

Why don't more people vote? Some are not allowed to, for one reason or another. For example, inmates of mental hospitals are not allowed to vote in any state. In most cases people who have been convicted of serious crimes are denied the right to vote. In addition, thousands of people cannot vote in state and local elections because they moved recently and do not yet meet their new state's residency requirements. Others fail to vote because they are ill or away from home on Election Day.

Voter registration appears to be a major obstacle to voting. Some people find the registration requirements too complicated. Others say it is too difficult to get to a voter registration office during the working day. (Some states, however, now have mail-in registration.) Still others forget to reregister when they move.

Voter Registration   Citizens must register in order to vote.   *What is the purpose of registration?*

People without permanent addresses often cannot register because they do not meet state residency requirements. A new law now allows people to register to vote when they renew their driver's licenses. It is hoped that this will encourage more people to vote.

In the past, racial discrimination often prevented African Americans from registering to vote. Several southern states discriminated against their African American citizens by imposing poll taxes or by requiring people to pass a literacy test in order to register. The **literacy test** was a test given to prove that the voter could read and write and understand public issues. In some cases, whites were not required to take the test. In others, whites and African Americans were

SECTION 2

Election Campaigns

FOCUS

TERMS TO KNOW

caucus, primary election, propaganda, canvassing, PAC

OBJECTIVES

- Describe the three procedures for **nominating candidates** for public office.

- Identify three important campaign tools used in **running for office.**

- Discuss sources of private and public funds for **financing election campaigns.**

In the United States political system, every election is a two-part process. First, each party nominates its candidates for public office, and then the candidates run against each other for election. The first part of this process, the nomination of candidates, varies widely from state to state.

Nominating Candidates

In state, local, and congressional elections, a candidate can be nominated to run for a public office in one of three ways—in a caucus, a nominating convention, or a primary election. Each state decides which method it will use.

In presidential elections, the candidates are chosen by a combination of these methods.

Caucuses

A **caucus** is a meeting of political party members to conduct party business. Originally, the caucus was a private meeting of important people in the community. Sometime in the mid-1700s, it was used to nominate people for public office. Later, as political parties developed, they used caucuses as well. Today caucuses are used primarily for nominating candidates for local office. Some states also hold caucuses for nominating presidential candidates.

Nominating Conventions

By the 1830s, caucuses were considered undemocratic and became very unpopular. People criticized them because only party leaders were involved in nominating candidates. Nominating conventions, which were considered more democratic, replaced caucuses. The party members in a particular area elected

---

Caucuses   The voters in Iowa select their candidates in party caucuses.   *How does a caucus differ from a primary election?*

---

delegates to attend the nominating convention. These delegates would then choose the party's candidates. Nominating conventions are used today in only a few places to choose candidates for state and local offices. Presidential nominating conventions are discussed later in this section.

Primary Elections

A **primary election** is held among party members to nominate candidates to run for office. Primaries may be either closed or open. Closed primaries are more common. In a closed primary, only declared party members may vote. Voters can add their names to the list of one party or the other either when they register to vote or when they go to the polling place. Then, in the primary election, registered Democrats and Republicans are directed to voting machines or are given ballots that list only their party's candidates.

In an open primary, voters do not have to register with one of the parties. They choose the party to vote for after entering the voting booth. The major advantage of an open primary is that the privacy of voters is preserved. Critics of open primaries, however, say that they undermine party loyalty because a voter can switch from party to party. They also point out that open primaries enable the voters of one party to cross over and vote in the opposing party's primary. In this way, party members can choose weak opponents to run against their own party's candidates.

Getting on the Primary Ballot

How do candidates get their names on a primary ballot to begin with? In most primary elections, party members

Candidate Selection Congressional candidate J.C. Watts addressed the Republican convention in 1996. *What happens at national conventions?*

meet and select a candidate for each office. This list of candidates, called a slate, is then placed on the party's ballot. Usually, each candidate also circulates a nominating petition that a certain number of party members must sign. If no one challenges these candidates, they run unopposed in the primary election. Party members who wish to challenge the party's nominees, however, may also circulate nominating petitions for other candidates. If these petitions receive enough signatures, these candidates are also placed on the primary ballot.

Nominating Presidential Candidates

The Democratic and Republican parties each choose their presidential and vice-presidential nominees at a national convention held during the summer of election year. Party delegates from all the states meet at this convention to vote for the candidate of their choice.

Campaign Techniques   Film star Bruce Willis appeared at a rally with President George Bush during the 1992 election campaign. *What is the technique of using celebrities called?*

The nominating process actually begins in February of that year, when candidates seeking the parties' nomination run in the New Hampshire primary. From then until June, potential candidates run in other primaries or state caucuses throughout the country.

In some states with primary elections, voters vote directly for the candidates they prefer. In others, they vote for delegates to the national convention who support a particular candidate.

Although most states hold primaries, several, including Iowa, Minnesota, Maine, and Michigan, hold caucuses where party delegates meet and vote on presidential candidates.

Each state sends a certain number of delegates to attend each party's national convention. The state's population determines the number of delegates. At the convention the candidate who receives a majority of the delegates' votes wins the presidential nomination. This candidate then chooses a vice-presidential running mate. Together these candidates are called "the ticket."

Running for Office

Nominating candidates is only the first part of the election process. Once candidates are chosen, they spend several weeks or months in an election campaign, trying to convince the public to vote for them. Each candidate has a campaign organization to help run the campaign. In some races, such as for the city council or the school board, a candidate's campaign organization may have only a few workers. A presidential campaign, on the other hand, can involve thousands of people.

A campaign organization is responsible for acquainting voters with the candidate's name, face, and position on the issues. It must also convince voters to like and trust the candidate. Each party uses several different techniques, or campaign tools, to accomplish this.

Endorsements

One common campaign tool is the endorsement. When a famous and popular person supports or campaigns for a candidate, it is an endorsement. The endorser may be a movie star, a famous athlete, a popular politician, or some other well-known individual. In 1996, for example, the well-known singer and actress Barbra Streisand often campaigned for the Democratic candidate, Bill Clinton. The idea behind endorsements is that if voters like the person making the endorsement, they may decide to vote for the candidate.

Endorsements are a kind of propaganda technique. **Propaganda** is an attempt to promote a particular person or idea. Propaganda techniques are a means of trying to persuade or influence voters to choose one candidate over another.

Endorsements are only one type of propaganda technique used in political campaigns. You will read about others in Chapter 8.

Advertising and Image Molding

How the voters perceive a candidate is often more important than whether a candidate is qualified. Political campaigns therefore try to create an image of the candidate that will appeal to voters.

Political campaigns spend much time and money in an effort to create the right image for a candidate. Much of that money goes for advertising. Political advertisements are a very effective campaign tool that allow a party to present only its candidate's position or point of view. They also enable a candidate to attack an opponent without offering an opportunity to respond.

For local campaigns, a party may do little more than buy newspaper advertisements and hang up posters. In state and national campaigns, however, a great deal of campaign advertising is done on television. Television ads can present quick and dramatic images of a candidate and his or her ideas. For example, the image of a candidate talking with unemployed steelworkers conveys a concern for industry and employment as well as a concern for people and their problems. Such television images tend to stay in the viewer's mind.

Congresswoman Maxine Waters of California Politicians use symbols such as the American flag to suggest that they represent the nation's best interests. *What other tools are used to build a candidate's image?*

Using Television

Television advertising has come under increasing criticism. Because most ads are only 30 seconds long, they do not allow candidates to discuss issues and ideas in detail. In addition, some candidates use TV ads to create negative images of their opponents. Although this "negative campaigning" is often viewed as unfair, it can also be very effective.

In addition to campaign advertisements, television is useful to candidates in other ways. In presidential or statewide campaigns, candidates often appear in TV news broadcasts or on talk shows answering reporters' questions, making speeches, or talking to voters. Such appearances help them keep their names and faces in front of the voters.

Campaign Funds   Actor Danny DeVito joined President Clinton at a fund-raising dinner.   *Where else do politicians get funds?*

Canvassing

Another important campaign tool is **canvassing,** or going through neighborhoods asking for votes or taking public opinion polls. At the local level, candidates and campaign workers often "knock on doors" to solicit votes and hand out campaign literature.

At the national level, campaign organizations conduct frequent polls to find out how their candidates are doing. News organizations and public opinion research companies also take polls to see which candidate is leading in a particular election.

Financing Election Campaigns

It takes money to buy the television ads, buttons, bumper stickers, posters, and literature that a candidate needs to run an effective campaign. How much is needed depends on the race.

A small-town mayoral race may require only a few hundred or few thousand dollars. A state legislative or congressional race can cost several hundred thousand dollars. A presidential race can cost hundreds of millions. The 1996 presidential race, for example, is estimated to have cost $390 million.

Private Funding

Where does all of this money come from? A small portion, probably less than 10 percent, comes from individual donors who feel strongly enough about a candidate to contribute money to his or her campaign. The political parties also work hard all year to raise money for the party's campaign treasury. They hold $1,000-a-plate dinners or other fund-raising events such as concerts, rallies, and parties. Often, they also write to party members and ask them for donations.

In addition to money from individuals and fund-raising events, about

Public Money   When taxpayers fill out their income tax forms, they can check off a box to contribute $3 to the Presidential Election Campaign Fund.   *Why was this fund created?*

one-fourth of each party's funds come from political action committees, better known as PACs. (See Exploring Issues, The High Cost of Running for Office, on page 152.) **PACs** are political fund-raising organizations established by corporations, labor unions, and other special-interest groups. PAC funds come from voluntary contributions of company employees, stockholders, and union members. A PAC uses its funds to support presidential, congressional, and state and local candidates who favor the PAC's position on issues.

Public Funding

The largest share of the money spent in presidential campaigns comes from the public. Public funding of presidential elections began in the 1970s. At that time, Congress created the Presidential Election Campaign Fund to prevent wealthy candidates from buying their way into office by outspending their opponents. Taxpayers can contribute $3 to the fund each year by checking off a box on their federal income tax form.

The Presidential Election Campaign Fund allots money for both the primary and general elections. In general, major party candidates can qualify for funds to campaign in the primary elections if they can raise $100,000 on their own. After the national convention, the two major party candidates receive equal shares of money

from the fund, so long as they agree not to accept any other direct contributions. In 1996 Bill Clinton and Bob Dole each received $61.8 million. Because Ross Perot captured more than 5 percent of the vote in the 1992 election, he received $29 million in 1996.

Congress also passed the Federal Election Campaign Act in 1971, which limits individual and PAC contributions to presidential candidates to $1,000 and $5,000, respectively. This law was intended to prevent large contributors from buying special favors—such as appointment to public office or changes in the laws—from winning candidates.

★ SECTION 2 REVIEW ★

UNDERSTANDING VOCABULARY
Define caucus, primary election, propaganda, canvassing, PAC.

REVIEWING OBJECTIVES
1 What are the three procedures for nominating candidates for public office?

2 What are three important campaign tools used in running for office?

3 What are some sources of private and public funds for financing election campaigns?

How to Read an Election Map

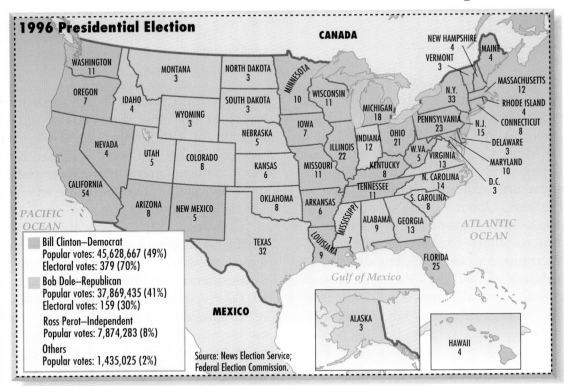

1996 Presidential Election

CANADA

NEW HAMPSHIRE 4
VERMONT 3
MAINE 4

WASHINGTON 11
MONTANA 3
NORTH DAKOTA 3
MINNESOTA 10
WISCONSIN 11
N.Y. 33
MASSACHUSETTS 12

OREGON 7
IDAHO 4
SOUTH DAKOTA 3
MICHIGAN 18
RHODE ISLAND 4

WYOMING 3
IOWA 7
PENNSYLVANIA 23
N.J. 15
CONNECTICUT 8

NEBRASKA 5
ILLINOIS 22
INDIANA 12
OHIO 21
DELAWARE 3

NEVADA 4
UTAH 5
COLORADO 8
KANSAS 6
MISSOURI 11
KENTUCKY 8
W.VA. 5
VIRGINIA 13
MARYLAND 10

CALIFORNIA 54
TENNESSEE 11
N. CAROLINA 14
D.C. 3

ARIZONA 8
NEW MEXICO 5
OKLAHOMA 8
ARKANSAS 6
S. CAROLINA 8

PACIFIC OCEAN

TEXAS 32
MISSISSIPPI 7
ALABAMA 9
GEORGIA 13
ATLANTIC OCEAN

LOUISIANA 9

FLORIDA 25

MEXICO

Gulf of Mexico

Bill Clinton—Democrat
Popular votes: 45,628,667 (49%)
Electoral votes: 379 (70%)

Bob Dole—Republican
Popular votes: 37,869,435 (41%)
Electoral votes: 159 (30%)

Ross Perot—Independent
Popular votes: 7,874,283 (8%)

Others
Popular votes: 1,435,025 (2%)

Source: News Election Service;
Federal Election Commission.

ALASKA 3

HAWAII 4

Some special-purpose maps relate political information to geography. The information includes political boundaries and place-names. Boundaries show the location and size of regions, populations, nations, states, districts, counties, or any other political divisions. Place-names identify the divisions and other features, such as cities and ports.

What This Map Shows

The election map above is an example of a special-purpose map. It shows the results of the presidential election of 1996. The map identifies each state and the number of its electoral votes. The map key explains the meaning of the colors and includes the totals of each candidate's electoral and popular votes.

Use the map and key to answer these questions.

CITIZENSHIP IN ACTION

1 Which state has the most electoral votes? Which candidate won this state?

2 In which geographic region did Clinton get the most electoral votes?

3 Which vote was closer—the electoral or the popular vote?

4 A candidate needs a majority of electoral votes to win. If Dole had won California, Illinois, and Ohio, would he have been elected?

Elections

Once the campaign hoopla is over and Election Day arrives, it is up to the voters to decide who will win or lose. These important decisions are made at the nation's **polling places,** or polls—the locations where votes are cast. Polling places are usually set up in town halls, schools, firehouses, and other public buildings. Each voter must vote at an assigned polling place, determined by his or her place of residence.

At the Polls

Exact hours vary, but polling places are generally open from early morning until 7 or 8 P.M. to give people time to vote before or after work. Election board workers who make sure that voters are properly registered and do not vote more than once staff each polling place. Typically, each party also stations a poll watcher at each polling place. The poll watchers make sure that the election is conducted fairly and that only qualified voters are allowed to vote.

Casting Votes

Upon entering the polling place, voters give their names to an election worker, who checks the names against a master list. The voters are then given a ballot and directed to a voting booth.

Voters cast their ballots in one of three ways—by computerized machine, by mechanical machine, or by paper ballot. In all three, the candidates are usually listed according to their party and the office they are seeking. With a computerized voting machine, votes are cast by

Casting Ballots   These voters are casting their votes by paper ballot.   *Why must each voter check in with an election board worker?*

Election Returns   At election time, television networks monitor voting results and pass them on to viewers.   *How are election predictions made?*

touching certain spots on the screen, by pushing certain buttons, or by marking a ballot. The machine then "reads" the ballot electronically and records the votes. With a mechanical voting machine, votes are cast by pulling small levers next to the names of the candidates chosen. With a paper ballot, a square is marked or a hole punched next to the names of the candidates chosen. All three systems enable voters to vote a **straight ticket,** for all the candidates of a single party. In some states, people who want to vote a straight ticket must vote for each of the party's candidates individually. In other states, voters can indicate their preference by voting for the party rather than the individual candidates. Voting for candidates of different parties is called voting a **split ticket.** It is also possible to vote for someone not on the ballot. This is called a write-in vote.

Absentee Ballots

Voters who cannot get to the polls on Election Day can use an absentee ballot to vote. People who know they will be away on Election Day and people who are too sick to get to the polls commonly use absentee ballots. A voter must request an absentee ballot from the local election board sometime before Election Day. On Election Day, these ballots are opened and counted either at the polling place or at the election board.

Counting the Votes

In a major election, the news media and the party workers attempt to predict the winners as soon as possible. To do this, they ask voters leaving polling places how they voted. This is known as an **exit poll.** By taking a sample of voters at key polling places, specialists can often predict the winners.

When the polls close, the election workers count the votes at the polling place and take the ballots and the results—called returns—to the election board. The election board then counts the returns for the entire city or county. Gathering all the returns and tallying the results can take several hours.

In national and state elections, the news media often use early returns, as well as the results of their own exit polls, to make a projection of the winners. That is why the television networks can project winners while people are still voting.

General Elections

In a general election, the voters cast ballots for candidates for various national, state, and local offices. The general election is always held on the first Tuesday after the first Monday in November. The ballot may include the names of candidates for governor, the state legislature, the county government, and local offices. In certain years, the ballot will also list presidential and congressional candidates.

For all races except the presidential race, the candidate who wins a majority of the **popular vote**—votes cast directly by the people—is elected to office. In a presidential race, the voters are actually electing people called electors, who hold **electoral votes** and are part of the Electoral College system. You read about the creation of the Electoral College in Chapter 3.

Presidential Elections in the Electoral College

When a person votes for a Republican or Democratic presidential candidate, he or she is really voting for a Republican or Democratic elector. About a month after the November general election, these electors assemble in each state to cast their votes for President. If the Republican presidential candidate has won the popular vote in the state, then the Republican electors get to cast all the state's electoral votes. The Democratic electors do not cast any votes. This procedure is known as the "winner-take-all" system.

The number of electoral votes for each state is determined by its representation in Congress. For example, Michigan, which has 16 United States representatives and 2 United States senators, has 18 electors. There is a total of 538 electoral votes, and the presidential

candidate who receives 270 or more of these votes wins the electoral vote and the election.

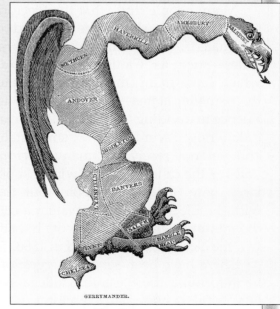

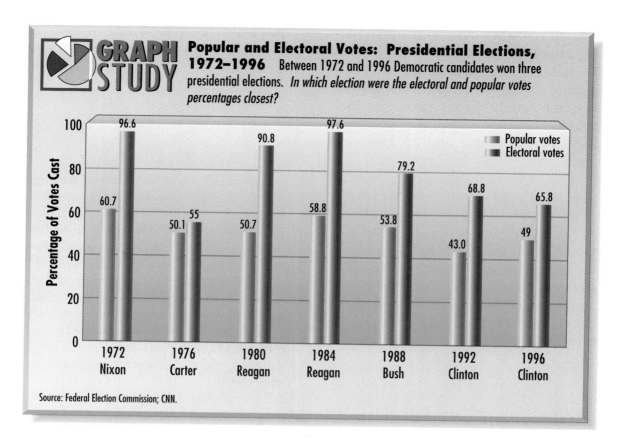

GRAPH STUDY

Popular and Electoral Votes: Presidential Elections, 1972–1996 Between 1972 and 1996 Democratic candidates won three presidential elections. *In which election were the electoral and popular votes percentages closest?*

Percentage of Votes Cast

Legend: Popular votes, Electoral votes

Year	Candidate	Popular	Electoral
1972	Nixon	60.7	96.6
1976	Carter	50.1	55
1980	Reagan	50.7	90.8
1984	Reagan	58.8	97.6
1988	Bush	53.8	79.2
1992	Clinton	43.0	68.8
1996	Clinton	49	65.8

Source: Federal Election Commission; CNN.

Critics of the Electoral College

Many people think that the Electoral College system should be changed or eliminated. They charge that large states—such as California and Texas, which have many more electoral votes than smaller states—have too much influence in deciding the election. One candidate might win five or six small states and yet not receive as many electoral votes as the candidate who wins just one large state. Critics also point out that with the Electoral College system a candidate can lose the popular vote but still win the election, as happened in 1888.

There have been several suggestions for reforming the Electoral College system. Under one plan, electoral votes would be based on the percentage of the popular vote. If a candidate won 55 percent of a state's popular vote, for example, he or she would also get 55 percent of the electoral votes. Any change in the Electoral College system would take time because it would require a constitutional amendment.

Voting on Issues

In some elections at the state or local level, voters may be asked to vote on issues as well as on candidates. This allows voters to participate more directly in the lawmaking process. Twenty-four states provide for lawmaking through the initiative. An **initiative** is a method by which citizens propose laws or state constitutional amendments. They do this by circulating a petition asking for the proposed new law, or **proposition.** If the petition receives a certain number of signatures, the proposition is put on the ballot. For example, California voters

Fair Elections   No campaigning is allowed beyond a certain point at a polling place. *What is a recall election?*

petitioned to put a proposition on the ballot in 1994 that dealt with rights of illegal immigrants.

A **referendum** is a method by which voters can approve or reject a measure passed by the state legislature or by the local government. All the states except Delaware use the referendum to vote on state constitutional amendments.

Special Elections

From time to time, state or local governments also hold certain kinds of special elections. Runoff elections may be held when none of the candidates for a particular office wins a majority of votes in the general election. The runoff is held to determine the winner.

Another kind of special election is the recall election. In a **recall,** voters can vote to remove a public official from office. Like the initiative, the recall begins with a petition. Voters may recall an official because of wrongdoing or because they do not like his or her position on issues. In many states voters can recall only local officials, but in 16 states they can recall state officials as well.

Sometimes, if an election is very close, the loser may contest, or challenge, the results. The loser then has the right to demand a recount of the votes. In very close races, a small mistake such as failing to include the votes from a single voting machine can change the election results. Occasionally, a disputed election cannot be resolved by a recount and requires another election. In the case of a national election, a dispute may be referred to Congress for settlement. In presidential elections, if neither candidate wins a majority of the electoral votes, the House of Representatives elects the President. This happened in the elections of 1800 and 1824.

★ SECTION 3 REVIEW ★

UNDERSTANDING VOCABULARY
Define polling place, straight ticket, split ticket, exit poll, popular vote, electoral vote, initiative, proposition, referendum, recall.

REVIEWING OBJECTIVES

1 What are three methods of casting votes at the polls?

2 In general elections, how does the election of presidential candidates differ from the election of all other public officials?

3 What are two types of special elections?

Identifying Key Terms

Choose the vocabulary term that best completes each of the sentences below. Write your answers on a separate sheet of paper.

primary election   canvassing   recall
electoral vote   initiative   referendum

1. In most states, each party's candidate for governor is chosen in a(n) _____.
2. The new law proposed by the state legislature was submitted to the voters for their approval in a(n) _____.
3. The voters proposed a new tax law through a(n) _____.
4. The _____ election was held to remove a corrupt official from public office.
5. The Republican presidential candidate won the election by winning both the popular vote and the _____.
6. The party workers spent many hours _____ the neighborhood to get support for their candidate.

Reviewing the Main Ideas

SECTION 1
1. Name three groups of people who are not allowed to vote.
2. What methods did southern states once use to prevent African Americans from voting?

SECTION 2
3. Identify three methods that have been used to nominate candidates for public office.
4. What is the purpose of endorsements?

5. What is the purpose of political action committees, or PACS?

SECTION 3
6. How are television news programs able to predict the winners of elections before all the polls are closed?
7. What is the "winner-take-all" system?

Critical Thinking

SECTION 1
1. **Analyzing Information**   What do you think political parties could do about the problem of voter apathy?

SECTION 2
2. **Identifying Alternatives**   Do you think it is better to have the government pay for election campaigns or to let each candidate raise funds privately?

SECTION 3
3. **Assessing Information**   Do you think the Electoral College system should be abolished? Explain why or why not.

Cooperative Learning

In groups of four, research the results of the last major election in your state. (You might look in back issues of newspapers or contact groups such as local or state election boards or the League of Women Voters.) Try to find out how many people in your state voted in the election and the percentages of different groups who voted (for example, people of different ages, ethnic or racial groups, gender, and educational background.) Write a brief report summarizing the voting trends you discover. Discuss your findings with the class.

Reinforcing Citizenship Skills

Find out about the last national election for President and/or Congress and state governors. Look for an election map that shows national results in a newspaper or newsmagazine from that time. Determine from the map how many states the two major political parties dominated, depending on who was elected. Look for information on which states, if any, may have switched. Report your findings to the class.

Technology Activity

Using a Spreadsheet

The United States has one of the lowest voter participation rates of any democratic nation. Some experts believe other nations have more participation because they assess penalties on citizens who do not vote. Find information about voter participation rates in other nations and create a spreadsheet with the following headings: Country, Voting Age, Voter Participation Rate, Penalties for Not Voting.

Focusing on Your Community

Laws about voter registration vary from place to place. Contact the local election board to find out what the requirements for registration are in your community. Then design a brochure encouraging people to register. It should include the following information: local residency requirements, when and where people can register for an election, the procedure for registering, and the types of identification needed.

Analyzing Visuals

The graph below shows the percentage of eligible voters of different age groups that voted in recent elections. Study the graph and answer the questions.

1. Which age group remained the most stable in voting participation during this period?
2. Which age group showed the smallest decrease in participation between 1980 and 1996? What factors might explain this decrease?
3. Describe the general trend in voter participation since 1980.

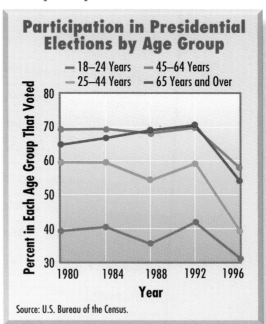

Participation in Presidential Elections by Age Group

— 18–24 Years   — 45–64 Years
— 25–44 Years   — 65 Years and Over

Percent in Each Age Group That Voted

Year

Source: U.S. Bureau of the Census.

Public Opinion and Interest Groups

CIVIC PARTICIPATION

America is a diverse nation in which many different groups of people hold many different viewpoints. The members of some groups form organizations to try to persuade government officials to support their views. Contact an organization involved in local issues in your area, such as the Sierra Club or the local parent-teacher organization. Find out what issues are most important to this group and how it tries to influence government officials.

Working in Your Community

Interview people in your neighborhood to find out their opinions on the issues that were raised. If their opinions are similar to those of the group you contacted, encourage them to learn more about the group and perhaps become active in it. ■

Your Civics Journal

During the next week, think about issues important to you that some organized group in your community or state has raised. Perhaps they concern the environment, school safety, or job opportunities. Note these issues in your civics journal, and jot down ideas for dealing with them.

Voicing special concerns ➤

Public Opinion

FOCUS

TERMS TO KNOW
public opinion, mass media, interest group, pollster

OBJECTIVES

- Identify and discuss several **factors affecting public opinion.**

- Explain different methods of **measuring public opinion.**

What is public opinion? **Public opinion** is a term that refers to the attitudes or opinions of a large group of people about a particular issue or person. Our elected representatives, at all levels of government, care a great deal about public opinion. It is the way these leaders learn what the people want.

The term *public opinion* is misleading, however. It suggests a uniformity of opinion that does not exist. In fact, most Americans agree on very few issues. On any given issue, different groups of the "public" often hold different viewpoints. For example, some may favor greatly increasing the nation's military forces; others may urge the government to do everything possible to halt the arms race. Between these two positions, however, are many shades of opinion. On almost any public issue, there are two or more public opinions.

Factors Affecting Public Opinion

Many factors affect a person's opinion on any public issue. Age, gender, income, hobbies, race, religion, occupation, and so on may play a role. The family of a government employee, for example, probably feels differently about the proposed government pay raise than the family of a factory worker. An African American woman may favor affirmative action employment laws, whereas a white man may not.

Other factors affect public opinion as well. The economic situation usually has an enormous impact on public opinion. If United States steel mills are booming and the nation's steelworkers are fully employed, most people would probably not object to allowing some foreign steel to be imported into the country. In hard times, when the steel mills are laying off workers, public opinion would probably oppose importing steel.

Public Opinion   The news media influence how people view candidates and issues. *How can photographs affect a candidate's image?*

✳ Mass Media

The **mass media,** news information sources that include television, radio, newspapers, and magazines, heavily influence public opinion. Every day, newspapers sell about 60 million copies nationwide, and more than one person may read each of these copies. Television news may reach another 60 million Americans each day, and some 10 million people subscribe to weekly newsmagazines.

The media influence public opinion not only by the numbers of people they reach but also by how they cover issues and events. The media can emphasize certain issues and events and downplay others in ways that can influence people's opinions.

Public Officials

Political leaders and public officials can also exert a strong influence on public opinion. When the voters elect people to office, they put their trust in those officials and rely on their opinions. Public officials get opportunities to state their views in speeches, press conferences, television interviews, and in newspaper and magazine articles. In doing so, they hope to persuade people to support their positions on issues.

People who share a similar point of view about an issue sometimes work together to promote that point of view. Such a group is called an **interest group** or a special-interest group. Interest groups try to influence public opinion by making people aware of issues and changing their attitudes. A recent example involves the animal rights movement. Animal rights groups have worked to make people aware of the treatment of animals used for laboratory

Special-Interest Groups   Special-interest groups use various tactics to make the public aware of their concerns.   *How do you think interest groups influence public opinion?*

testing and for making fur coats. These groups hope to change people's attitudes about buying products that have been tested on animals. They also hope to persuade people not to buy fur coats.

Measuring Public Opinion

It is possible to get some idea of what the public's opinion is on any given issue. One way is to look at election results. If voters elect a particular candidate, presumably many of them agree with that candidate's ideas and programs. Elections are not a very reliable guide to public opinion, however. People vote for candidates for various reasons. Perhaps they liked a particular candidate's appearance or felt he or she was capable. Perhaps they voted a straight party ticket. Election results can provide only a broad idea of public opinion, not an accurate assessment of opinions on specific issues. The election of a Republican President, for example, may reflect a desire for reduced government spending. It does not, however, indicate which specific programs the public would like to see cut.

Public Opinion Polls

The most accurate way to measure public opinion is through a public opinion poll. In Chapter 7, you learned that people who take polls collect information by questioning certain groups. Hundreds of organizations conduct public opinion polls. Two of the best known are the Gallup Poll and the Harris Survey. Although most organizations take polls about consumer products, some concentrate on public issues and political campaigns.

Polling organizations have made a science out of taking polls. **Pollsters,** the people who take polls, follow specific techniques to make sure their polls are accurate. By asking about 1,500 people their opinions on an issue, pollsters can get an accurate idea of how most Americans feel about that issue.

Random Samples

Pollsters usually question a group of people selected at random all over the United States. They have found that such a random sample will probably include people of nearly all races, incomes, genders, ages, and viewpoints. Because the sample reflects the characteristics of the entire population, it presents a reasonably accurate picture of public opinion.

To find out what people really think, pollsters must be careful how they word the questions in a poll. For example, the question, "Do you favor cutting taxes?" might get a different answer from the same person as the question, "Do you favor cutting taxes if it means letting poor people go hungry?" The second question is called a loaded question be-

Opinion Polls Political cartoons may focus on political leaders, government policies, or public opinion. *What does this cartoon say about the relevance of opinion polls?*

cause it is biased, or written in a way that will get a certain, in this case negative, response.

The Effect of Polls

Political parties and news organizations frequently hire polling organizations to take political polls. The results are then released to the public. Some critics feel that these polls not only measure public opinion but also affect it. They argue that the polls may influence many voters to support a candidate who is leading in the polls.

Public opinion polls may also have the opposite effect, that is, influencing people not to vote at all. For instance, in the 1994 gubernatorial race in Ohio, polls declared Republican George

Voinovich the winner weeks before the election. As a result, some voters did not bother to vote on Election Day because they thought the race had already been decided.

★ **SECTION 1 REVIEW** ★

UNDERSTANDING VOCABULARY
Define public opinion, mass media, interest group, pollster.

REVIEWING OBJECTIVES

1 What factors are important in affecting public opinion?

2 What are two methods of measuring public opinion?

SUPREME COURT CASE STUDIES
Muller v. Oregon

The National Consumers' League was one of the first public-interest groups to use federal courts to help change working conditions. The league was established in the 1800s to deal with social problems and political corruption in cities.

Unregulated working conditions

The Issue

In the 1800s, working conditions in factories and mines were disgraceful. At the turn of the century, groups such as the league began demanding laws that would regulate working conditions for women and children.

In 1906 Oregon passed a law limiting the number of hours women could work in factories and laundries. One laundry owner, Curt Muller, ignored the law. He claimed that it interfered with his right of contract—his right to arrange working conditions with his employees.

The Case

Oregon prosecuted Muller, and the case—*Muller v. Oregon*—went to the United States Supreme Court. The National Consumers' League hired Louis Brandeis to defend the Oregon law before the Court. In his argument to the Court, Brandeis took an unusual tack. Instead of arguing about the law, he presented research showing that long working hours affected the health and capabilities of women, causing them to make mistakes and be less productive.

The Court unanimously upheld the Oregon law. It ruled that states could pro-

tect women workers if they could provide a reasonable justification for doing so. In this case, it ruled that women's "unique physical structure and maternal functions" were sufficient justification.

The Impact

The *Muller* case opened the door for similar social reforms. It was also the first time an interest group had convinced the Supreme Court to protect the interest of the general public instead of the interests of business tycoons and rich property owners.

REVIEWING THE CASE

1 Why did Muller believe the Oregon law was unconstitutional?

2 What role did the National Consumers' League play in the case?

Interest Groups

FOCUS

TERMS TO KNOW
bias, impartial

OBJECTIVES

- Identify three **types of interest groups.**

- Describe various **techniques interest groups use** to try to influence public opinion.

People form or join interest groups because there is strength in numbers. Although one person might not have much luck convincing the town board to start a waste recycling program, a homeowners' association of 300 members would be able to exert much more influence. The town board members would find it more difficult to oppose 300 voters than to oppose only one. Interest or special-interest groups are also called pressure groups because they try to influence or pressure the government into adopting certain policies or taking specific actions.

Interest groups are an important part of our democratic process. Different interest groups constantly bombard public officials with opinions and demands. These groups often hold conflicting views on an issue. For example, while labor unions might demand a higher minimum wage, business groups might urge that it be kept at the current level. Because an interest group usually holds one particular viewpoint, we say it has a **bias,** or one-sided point of view. To be biased is the opposite of being **impartial**—or considering all viewpoints equally.

Types of Interest Groups

Interest groups vary greatly in size and influence. Some have only a handful of members and a few hundred dollars to spend a year. Others have several million members and multimillion-dollar budgets. Some large interest groups have a national headquarters and hundreds of regional chapters, and others have a small local organization that meets in a member's living room.

Interest Groups The Gray Panthers work for legislation to protect the interests of older Americans. *What is such legislation likely to involve?*

Trade Associations   Trade associations often use billboard campaigns to convince people they need a product or service.   *What is the message about milk in this ad?*

An individual can belong to a number of different interest groups. Perhaps a person is a member of a labor union, the National Association for the Advancement of Colored People (NAACP), and the local parent-teacher organization and also contributes to the National Wildlife Federation. The First Amendment, which guarantees "the right of the people peaceably to assemble, and to petition the Government for a redress of grievances" protects the right to belong to interest groups. Individuals are free to decide whether to belong to any interest groups and to choose which ones to join.

Economic Interest Groups

Some of the largest and most powerful interest groups in the United States are based on economic interests. These include business organizations, professional associations, labor unions, and industrial or trade associations.

The national Chamber of Commerce, with more than 200,000 members, and

the National Association of Manufacturers (NAM), which represents more than 13,000 manufacturing companies, are two of the largest business organization interest groups. Many business organizations represent specific kinds of businesses. These are called industry or trade associations. One of the largest is the Tobacco Institute, which represents cigarette manufacturers. This association is frequently involved in fighting proposed laws to restrict or ban smoking around the country. Other trade associations include the National Association of Printing Ink Manufacturers and the California Redwood Association. Trade associations exist for nearly every kind of business in the United States.

Business organizations are interested in shaping the government's policy on such economic issues as free enterprise, imports and tariffs, the minimum wage, new construction, and government contracts for construction and manufacturing. The Aerospace Industries Association of America, for instance, encourages the federal government to build rocket ships, space stations, and satellites.

While business groups represent the owners and operators of businesses, labor unions focus on wages, working conditions, and benefits such as pensions and medical care for workers. Unions pressure the government to pass laws that will benefit and protect their workers. The largest labor organization in the United States is the American Federation of Labor–Congress of Industrial Organizations (AFL-CIO), an association of unions whose members do all kinds of work. The International Airline Employees Association and the National Football League Players Association, for example, are both AFL-CIO unions. Many other unions, such as the National Education Association for teachers, are independent and also represent workers in specific industries.

Professional associations are made up of members of specific professions. Many doctors belong to the American Medical Association (AMA), and many lawyers belong to the American Bar Association (ABA). Accountants, journalists, real estate agents, and many other kinds of professional people also have their own organizations.

Other Types of Interest Groups

Many people belong to interest groups that work to promote their particular ethnic group, age group, or gender. These organizations include the NAACP and Congress of Racial Equality (CORE) for African Americans, the National Organization for Women (NOW) and National Women's Political Caucus for women, and the American Association of Retired Persons (AARP) and National

Environmental Issues   The Sierra Club works to protect wilderness areas and parks for future generations.   *What other environmental concerns draw interest groups?*

Council of Senior Citizens for older Americans.

Another category of interest groups covers those working for specific causes. For example, the Sierra Club, the National Wildlife Federation, and Greenpeace are concerned with environmental issues.

All the interest groups discussed so far are considered private groups, each pursuing issues of interest to its own members. Some groups, however, work to benefit all or most of society. These groups are called public interest groups. One example is Common Cause, an organization of 250,000 members that

 **CHART STUDY**

Types of Propaganda Techniques Political parties use various techniques to promote their candidates. *How does name-calling differ from the other techniques?*

NAME-CALLING

"Candidate A is the candidate of liberals and Communists."

ENDORSEMENT

Popular movie star says, "I'm voting for Candidate A, and so should you."

GLITTERING GENERALITY

"Candidate A is the one who will bring us peace and prosperity."

THE BANDWAGON

"As the polls show, Candidate A is going to win the election. Vote for A, and be part of this great victory."

JUST PLAIN FOLKS

"My parents were immigrants. I understand the problems of ordinary Americans."

STACKED CARDS

"Candidate A has the best record on the environment."

SYMBOLS

"I pledge allegiance…"

works to expose corruption and favoritism in government. The League of Women Voters is a nonpartisan group that promotes voting and educates voters about candidates and issues.

Techniques Interest Groups Use

All interest groups want to influence public opinion both to increase their memberships and to convince people of the rightness of their causes. They attempt to do this in a number of ways. Many use direct-mail campaigns to recruit members. They target potential new members by using subscriber or membership mailing lists from magazines or groups with a similar viewpoint.

Interest groups also advertise on television or in newspapers and magazines. Perhaps you have seen ads urging you to drink milk or to buy cotton clothing. Trade associations sponsor these types of ads. Interest groups also stage protests or organize public events to get free coverage in the news media. For example, a peace group might demonstrate at a local defense plant, or a business group might ask for coverage of its annual "Businessperson of the Year" dinner.

In Chapter 7, you learned that political parties use propaganda to promote a particular idea or viewpoint. Interest groups also use propaganda techniques to advance their causes. Here are some common propaganda techniques that political parties and their candidates and interest groups use.

Endorsements

Political candidates and interest groups often get famous people such as movie stars, rock stars, or sports figures to endorse, or support, them. In the 1996 presidential race, for example, movie actor and singer Barbra Streisand made appearances in support of Bill Clinton. The idea behind endorsements is that if people admire the person endorsing a candidate or product, they will endorse the candidate or product, too.

Stacked Cards

Card stacking is a technique that presents only one side of an issue by distorting the facts. For example, a group advocating nuclear power might present only facts that would make nuclear power seem safe, omitting any that might indicate safety problems.

The Bandwagon

Getting on the bandwagon means convincing people that everyone else agrees with the interest group's viewpoint or that everyone is going to vote for a certain candidate. This technique tries to appeal to many people's desire to be on the winning team.

Glittering Generality

A glittering generality is a statement that sounds good but is essentially meaningless. For example, in the 1994 congressional campaigns, candidates from both parties called for a "return to family values." The statement is a glittering generality.

Symbols

Political candidates and interest groups use and misuse symbols when appealing to the public. For example, one candidate for public office might salute the flag at every public event to appear more patriotic than his or her opponent.

Techniques   President Clinton and Vice President Gore help to build a house during the 1996 presidential campaign.   *Which propaganda technique does this demonstrate?*

Just Plain Folks

Political campaigns often use countless photographs of candidates wearing hard hats, talking to factory workers, eating pizza or tacos, or even milking cows. The idea of this plain-folks appeal is to make people think that the candidate is just like them, with the same desires and concerns.

Name-calling

Name-calling is an attempt to turn people against an opponent or an idea by using an unpleasant label or description for that person or idea. In the 1990s, for example, Republicans often referred to their opponents as "tax-and-spend Democrats," and some people called candidates who opposed welfare and affirmative-action programs "racists." Name-calling is meant to harm the image of a person, group, or idea. One should therefore always consider the accuracy of the label.

★ SECTION 2 REVIEW ★

UNDERSTANDING VOCABULARY
Define bias, impartial.

REVIEWING OBJECTIVES

1 What are three general types of interest groups?

2 What are some of the techniques interest groups use to try to influence public opinion?

How to Distinguish Fact From Opinion

Facts are statements that can be proved. Opinions are statements that express feelings, attitudes, or beliefs. Although opinions may be stated very persuasively, they are not always based on facts. For this reason, you should check the accuracy of information before using it to make a decision.

Questions to Ask

Is the information factual? Decide whether the information seems believable, and then look for evidence to verify that the facts are correct.

Do I have all the facts? Try to learn all the facts that relate to an issue. The more facts you have, the more confidence you can have in the information.

From where did the information come? Eyewitness accounts and physical evidence are good sources of information. Information based on rumor or unreliable sources may be suspect.

How up-to-date is the information? Information should be current and timely.

Is the information accurately stated? Information presented in an emotional manner may be an expression of an opinion, bias, or point of view rather than of fact. Look for information presented in an impartial manner.

Testing Your Ability

The following is an excerpt from President Theodore Roosevelt's 1907 message to Congress. Read the excerpt and answer the questions.

President Theodore Roosevelt

"The land law system which was designed to meet the needs of fertile and well-watered regions of the Middle West has largely broken down when applied to the drier regions of the great plains, the mountains, and much of the Pacific slope. . . . Three years ago a public-lands commission was appointed. . . . Their examination . . . showed the existence of a great fraud upon the public domain.. . . The recommendations [of the commission] are . . . so just and . . . so essential to our national welfare, that I feel confident . . . that they will ultimately be adopted."

CITIZENSHIP IN ACTION

1 What facts did Roosevelt offer to support his claims about the land law system?

2 What words indicate that Roosevelt is expressing an opinion?

Interest Groups and Public Policy

FOCUS

TERMS TO KNOW
lobby, lobbyist

OBJECTIVES

■ Identify three **functions of interest groups.**

■ Explain what **lobbies** are and how lobbyists try to accomplish their goals.

Many people think special-interest groups are harmful to American democracy because they exert too much influence over political decisions. In reality, interest groups serve a number of useful functions.

Functions of Interest Groups

The major contribution of interest groups is to bring issues and concerns to the attention of the public, lawmakers, and policymakers. They do this by presenting facts and opinions to support their positions and to counter the arguments of their opponents. For example, much of the current concern about air and water pollution can be traced to information and arguments from interest groups.

Another important function of interest groups is to represent the interests and concerns of specific groups. For example, the United Auto Workers Union represents automobile assembly line workers. Although politicians may not listen to the concerns of one autoworker, they are likely to listen to a group representing hundreds of thousands of voters. As a member of an interest group, an individual can thus have a greater influence on the political system.

A third contribution of interest groups is their support of political candidates who favor their interests and goals. Many large groups, such as the American Association of Retired Persons (AARP), have PACs that contribute funds

Political Influence Members of large interest groups can have considerable influence on political life. *To which interest group does this woman belong?*

to the campaigns of selected candidates. Some interest groups also rate lawmakers according to how they voted on certain issues. Such ratings help voters decide which candidates to support.

Lobbies

One of the primary goals of interest groups is to influence public policy. An anti-abortion group wants the government to pass laws outlawing abortion. Railway commuters want the government to run more trains at lower fares. The NAACP wants the courts to enforce laws against discrimination. Interest groups affect public policy and bring about changes by lobbying.

To **lobby** is to try to get government officials to support a group's goals. The word dates from the 1830s, when it described how people would wait in the lobbies of statehouses to ask politicians for favors. The people who lobby politicians are called **lobbyists.** They are either paid employees or volunteers who work for interest groups. Their job is to persuade government officials to support their group's policies.

Lobbying Government

Lobbying takes place at the local, state, and federal levels of government. It occurs in all branches of government, but most lobbying focuses on Congress and the state legislatures. Lobbyists spend much of their time trying to persuade lawmakers to reject or enact laws that will affect their interest groups.

Lobbyists must have a good understanding of how the government functions. They must know where to go and whom to see. The federal government and each state government have hun-

Lobbying An effective lobbyist knows where to go and whom to contact about the concerns of an interest group. *What do you think would be some concerns of autoworkers?*

dreds of departments, offices, and agencies, but a good lobbyist knows which department to contact about a particular concern. Lobbyists must also be skilled at making contacts with lawmakers, legislative aides, and other government officials. Some lobbyists are former legislators with many contacts in government. Others are lawyers or public relations consultants who specialize in lobbying.

What Lobbyists Do

How do lobbyists go about their jobs? Suppose Congress is considering a bill to allow oil exploration on national park lands in Alaska. Lobbyists for business and oil industry groups would promote the bill, and lobbyists for environmental groups would probably oppose it. Each side would research the issue and submit reports, news articles, and statistics supporting its views. The

Consumer Advocate Ralph Nader frequently speaks out against government agencies and public policies. *How does this help consumers?*

lobbyists might also testify at a House or Senate committee hearing on the bill.

These activities provide lawmakers with a tremendous amount of information. Because Congress deals with thousands of bills each year, lobbyists play an important role in making legislators aware of the merits and drawbacks of many bills. Lobbyists sometimes even submit their own drafts of bills for lawmakers' consideration.

Using Public Opinion

Another way that lobbyists try to persuade lawmakers is by arousing public opinion. They often encourage their interest group's members to write or telephone key legislators. If these lawmakers receive enough mail supporting a proposed bill, they may be persuaded to vote for the bill. Yet lawmakers usually know when a small but active interest group rather than a majority of the public is pressuring them.

The job of lobbyists does not end once a law is enacted. Their interest groups are also concerned with making sure that laws are carried out, enforced, and stand up in court. For example, if an oil exploration bill is approved, environmental groups are likely to watch the whole operation carefully. They want to make sure that the oil companies observe any provisions aimed at protecting the environment. If not, lobbyists for the environmental groups will lobby various government departments or agencies to see that the law is enforced.

Sometimes lobbyists initiate court actions on behalf of their interest groups. The American Civil Liberties Union has gone to court to defend all kinds of interest groups, including students, police officers, and even Communists. Public Citizen, Inc., a consumer group Ralph Nader leads, has brought suits against various companies for violating consumer protection laws.

Regulation of Lobbies

In the past, lobbying was criticized severely because some lobbyists tried to win legislators' votes by providing them with fancy meals and free trips. Some lobbyists also provided large campaign contributions and even used bribery.

Today most lobbyists are ethical and professional. Instead of trying to buy votes, they rely on their ability to present the facts and make persuasive arguments to influence public officials. Nevertheless, many people still criticize lobbyists and their special-interest groups. They feel that some interest groups, because of their power and influence, have an unfair advantage over their opponents. These groups can afford to spend a great deal of money trying to promote or defeat legislation. Groups

PAC Spending These PACs spent the most in 1995–1996. *What are PACs trying to do when they contribute to political campaigns?*

PAC	Amount Spent
Emily's List (group supporting women for political office)	$9,190,660
Democratic Republican Independent Voter Education Committee	6,214,520
Association of Trial Lawyers of America Political Action Committee	3,322,980
National Rifle Association Political Victory Fund	2,950,770
Campaign America	2,921,813
National Education Association Political Action Committee	2,562,574
American Federation of State, County and Municipal Employees	2,418,440
AT&T Corp. Political Action Committee	2,207,903
American Medical Association Political Action Committee	2,027,521
Machinists Non-Partisan Political League	1,962,259

Source: Federal Election Commission, 1996.

such as the National Rifle Association and the Tobacco Institute can amass enormous PAC funds to spend on the campaigns of legislators who support their causes.

To prevent abuses among lobbyists, Congress passed the Federal Regulation of Lobbying Act in 1946. This law requires lobbyists at the federal level to register themselves and their interest groups and to report all lobbying expenditures. The law has not been very effective, however, because it applies only to people whose primary job is lobbying. People who claim that only a small portion of their time is spent lobbying are not required to register. As a result, only about one-fifth to one-quarter of all lobbyists are registered. The law does not provide for any means of enforcement. Most states have lobbying laws. Some state laws are more effective than the federal law.

Federal and state laws that require a waiting period before former officials can become lobbyists also restrict lobbying. The terms of these laws vary from state to state. A typical law might bar a former state legislator from lobbying the legislature or its committees for one or two years after leaving office. The purpose of these laws is to prevent ex-public officials from taking unfair advantage of their inside knowledge and close friendships with former associates on behalf of special-interest groups. Unfortunately, these laws have proved inadequate, especially at the federal level. In recent years, for example, the Department of Defense has come under increasing criticism because many military officers retire and seek jobs with defense industries.

★ SECTION 3 REVIEW ★

UNDERSTANDING VOCABULARY
Define lobby, lobbyist.

REVIEWING OBJECTIVES

1 What are three functions of interest groups?

2 What are lobbies and how do lobbyists try to accomplish their goals?

Identifying Key Terms

Choose the vocabulary term that best completes each of the sentences below. Write your answers on a separate sheet of paper.

interest group   bias   mass media
pollster   lobby   impartial

1. The interest group had a(n) _____ toward one particular candidate because they agreed with his views.
2. The homeowners' association could be considered a(n) _____ because members were all concerned with similar issues.
3. In considering all sides of the issue, the legislator tried to remain _____.
4. Most people look to the _____ as their source of news and information.
5. The group planned to _____ congressional leaders to get them to change their views on the issue.
6. According to the _____, the results of the survey indicated that public opinion was divided on the issue.

Reviewing the Main Ideas

SECTION 1
1. What factors can influence a person's opinion on public issues?
2. Why do some people criticize public opinion polls?

SECTION 2
3. Why do people form interest groups?
4. Why are interest groups an important part of our democratic system?
5. Identify and explain three propaganda techniques interest groups use.

SECTION 3
6. What are the main tasks of lobbyists?
7. What are the provisions of the Federal Regulation of Lobbying Act of 1946?

Critical Thinking

SECTION 1
1. **Analyzing Information**   What role do you think public opinion polls should play in the political process? Explain.

SECTION 2
2. **Demonstrating Reasoned Judgment** Do you think interest groups are a positive or a negative force in politics? Explain your answer.

SECTION 3
3. **Determining Cause and Effect**   How effective is lobbying as a means of influencing public officials to support a particular cause? Explain.

Reinforcing Citizenship Skills

In a newspaper or newsmagazine, find a report on or an actual transcript of a political speech of a candidate for office or a government official. Many newspapers publish the complete text of the President's annual State of the Union Address. Look through the report or the transcript and mark in some way the facts this person gave about one issue. Analyze these facts and decide if they are believable and complete. Then look for a stated opinion about this same issue. Share your findings with the class.

Cooperative Learning

In groups of four, research a current issue in the news. As an interest group, decide what your position is on this issue. Then write four paragraphs or prepare an oral presentation to illustrate your position, using four different propaganda techniques. Share your results with the class.

Focusing on Your Community

Investigate some of the special-interest groups in your community. You may be able to locate the names of some of these groups through a local newspaper or television station. Once you have a list, ask the following questions. How many of them have local offices with full-time staffs? How many are local branches of national organizations? How many employ full-time lobbyists? Choose one of the interest groups to investigate further. Find out the group's major issues and concerns. What methods does the group use to try to inform the public and to influence public opinion? What activities is it involved in at the local, state, or national level? How effective has it been in changing policy or influencing the public? Share your findings with the class.

Technology Activity

Using a Spreadsheet

Review the issues you noted in your civics journal that you began keeping when you began studying this chapter. Imagine that you belong to an interest group concerned with one of these issues. You have been asked to survey public opinion on this issue. Use a word processor to write a 20-question public opinion survey. Distribute the questionnaires to 30 people in the community. When you have the results, use a spreadsheet to tabulate the responses.

Analyzing Visuals

The political cartoon below expresses an opinion on the influence of lobbyists. Study the cartoon, then answer the questions.

1. What do the oxen's words suggest about politicians?
2. What is about to happen in the picture?
3. What does the choice of the wagon and oxen suggest about the cartoonist's viewpoint?

CLOSEUP
POLITICAL LABELS

What does it mean to be a liberal, a conservative, a moderate, a radical, or a reactionary? Political labels can be very confusing. It is helpful to think of these labels as describing a spectrum, or line, of political ideas.

The Political Spectrum

At one end of the political spectrum are reactionaries, who favor a return to more traditional policies. At the other end are radicals, who favor sweeping changes in government policies. In between are conservatives, moderates, and liberals.

Conservatives generally believe that the role of government should be limited, and that individuals should be responsible for their own well-being. They oppose government regulation and favor traditional values. Conservatives often seek to reinstate prayer in school, curb affirmative action programs, and ban abortions. Conservatives tend to be Republican.

Liberals believe that government should help meet the needs of individual citizens and protect and extend their rights. They often support affirmative action, public housing, and programs for the poor. Most liberals are Democrats or independents.

Moderates follow a course between conservatism and liberalism. They may support government action in some areas and reject it in others.

Other Labels

The terms *the left* or *left wing* and *the right* or *right wing* may be used to refer to liberals and conservatives, respectively. These terms are based on a custom in the French National Assembly of seating liberals on the left, conservatives on the right, and moderates in the middle.

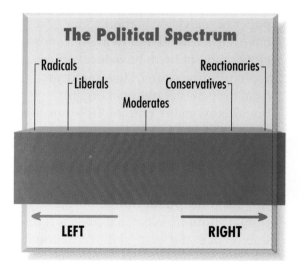

The Political Spectrum

Radicals — Liberals — Moderates — Conservatives — Reactionaries

LEFT — RIGHT

CLOSEUP REVIEW

1 What is the basic difference between conservatives and liberals?

2 How did the terms *left wing* and *right wing* originate?

Multimedia Activities

Surfing the "Net"

The Electoral College

When you studied general elections in Chapter 7, you read about the Electoral College. You learned that when a person votes for a Republican or Democratic presidential candidate, he or she is really voting for a Republican or Democratic elector. The following Internet activity will help you learn about your state's electoral votes.

Getting There

Follow the steps below to find information about your state's electoral votes.

1. Go to your favorite search engine.
2. Type in the phrase *Electoral College*. Following this phrase, enter words like those below to focus your search:

    votes   electors

The search engine should provide you with a number of links to follow. Links are pointers to different sites on the Internet and commonly appear as blue underlined words.

What to Do When You Are There

1. Click on the links to navigate through the pages of information.
2. Using a word processor, create a fact sheet that answers the following questions:
   - How many electors does your state have?
   - How many electoral votes did the winning candidate receive in the last presidential election?
   - How many electoral votes did the losing candidate receive?

Focus on Government

A Nation of Immigrants

The United States is often called a "nation of immigrants." Many Americans today can look at their own personal heritage and trace their roots outside of the United States. The **Focus on Government** programs referenced below show Ellis Island in New York harbor as the entry point for millions of immigrants when they arrived in the United States. Also, the program explains the naturalization process by which immigrants can become citizens.

Side 1, Chapter 8
Electronic Field Trip, Ellis Island

Setting Up the Video

Using a bar code reader or an electronic keypad, work with a group of your classmates to view these video segments of the videodisc **Focus on Government:**

Side 1, Chapter 9
Lecture Launcher:
Citizenship in the United States

Hands-On Activity

Work with a group of your classmates to determine the national origin of students in your group. Have each group member do a short report on one of these countries. Present the reports to the class.

UNIT 4

The National Government

YOUR ROLE AS A CITIZEN

Under our federal system, the executive, legislative, and judicial branches share the responsibility of governing the nation. They derive their power from the American people. As citizens, we have a responsibility to learn about the officials who represent us and to express our views through voting.

In Unit 4 you will study the branches of government and learn how government works. ∎

CHAPTERS IN THIS UNIT

The campaign trail ➤

CHAPTER 9

Congress

CIVIC PARTICIPATION

Congress is the most direct expression of American democracy. When citizens express their views to their representatives in Congress, they actually become part of the lawmaking process. Contact the offices of your representative in Congress and of one of your senators. Find out what legislation they currently support and if they plan to introduce any new bills in Congress.

Working in Your Community

Make an outline of the positions of your senator and representative. Share the information with your neighbors. Find out what your neighbors think about legislation pending in Congress. Encourage them to express their views to their members of Congress. ■

Your Civics Journal

As you study about Congress, pay attention to the important national issues discussed in newspapers and on television. Consider how you would deal with these issues if you were a member of Congress. Write your ideas in your civics journal.

Our nation's Capitol ➤

How Congress Is Organized

FOCUS

TERMS TO KNOW

bicameral, gerrymandering, constituent, franking privilege, immunity, expulsion, censure, session

OBJECTIVES

- List the qualifications and terms of office for members of **the House of Representatives.**

- List the qualifications and terms of office for members of **the Senate.**

- Describe the **salary, benefits, and privileges** members of Congress receive.

- Identify the three types of **congressional sessions.**

As you learned in Chapter 3, one of the major conflicts at the Constitutional Convention in 1787 concerned state representation in the new Congress. Delegates from the smaller states wanted each state to have equal representation. Delegates from larger states wanted representation to be based on population, which would give them a greater voice in government.

The Great Compromise, which established a **bicameral,** or two-house, Congress, settled the dispute. In the upper house, the Senate, each state would have an equal number of representatives—two. In the lower house, the House of Representatives, each state's population would determine its representation.

Although Article I of the Constitution makes some distinctions between the powers of the two houses, the houses are more alike than different. Each house is made up of elected members who carry out similar duties and enjoy similar privileges.

The House of Representatives

According to the Constitution, members of the House of Representatives, known as representatives, must meet only three qualifications: they must be at least 25 years old, they must have been United States citizens for at least 7 years, and they must live in the states they represent. In practice, however, representatives usually meet several other

Congressional Representation
Congressman John Conyers of Michigan meets with constituents in his Washington office.
How are the number of representatives for each state determined?

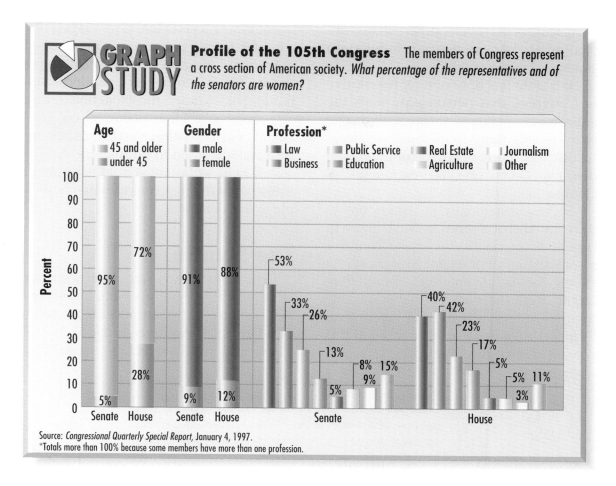

GRAPH STUDY

Profile of the 105th Congress The members of Congress represent a cross section of American society. *What percentage of the representatives and of the senators are women?*

Age
- 45 and older
- under 45

Gender
- male
- female

Profession*
- Law
- Business
- Public Service
- Education
- Real Estate
- Agriculture
- Journalism
- Other

Age: Senate — 95%, 5%; House — 72%, 28%

Gender: Senate — 91%, 9%; House — 88%, 12%

Profession — Senate: 53%, 33%, 26%, 13%, 5%, 8%, 9%, 15%

Profession — House: 40%, 42%, 23%, 17%, 5%, 5%, 3%, 11%

Source: *Congressional Quarterly Special Report,* January 4, 1997.
*Totals more than 100% because some members have more than one profession.

qualifications as well. Most representatives have had successful careers in law or business. Many have also had experience in state and local government or in other forms of public service.

Representatives are elected for two-year terms. Because these terms all begin and end at the same time, it is possible for the House to have an entirely new membership every two years. In reality, however, this never happens. In recent elections, 70 to 80 percent of the current House members have been reelected.

The Constitution does not limit the number of terms a representative may serve. In recent years, however, public opinion has increasingly favored term limitations. A number of states have already passed laws limiting the terms of

representatives. Congress is considering a constitutional amendment that would set term limits.

The number of representatives is fixed at 435. The Constitution guarantees each state at least one representative, but the number of additional representatives depends on the state's population. Some small states, such as Wyoming and Vermont, have only one representative. California, the state with the largest population, has 52.

When the Census Bureau counts the population every 10 years, it studies population changes to see whether each state's number of representatives needs to be adjusted. After the 1990 census, for example, some states such as Florida, Texas, and California gained some representatives, while other states, including several eastern and midwestern states, lost representatives.

If a state has only one representative in Congress, that person represents the entire state. States with more than one representative are divided into sections, or districts. Each of these congressional districts elects one representative to Congress.

State legislators, who often try to draw the districts' lines in ways that will benefit them politically, create congressional districts. For example, if most of a state's legislators are Republican, they might draw the lines so that some districts have more Republican voters than Democratic ones. Districts created in this way are often oddly shaped.

Dividing a state into odd-shaped districts for strictly political reasons is called **gerrymandering.** Despite many attempts to stop this practice, gerrymandering remains legal under most circumstances. The major restriction is that all congressional districts within a state must be approximately equal in population. All the state's representatives should have about the same number of **constituents,** or people in their districts.

The Senate

The Constitution sets slightly stricter requirements for membership in the Senate. Senators must be at least 30 years old, United States citizens for at least 9 years, and residents of the states they

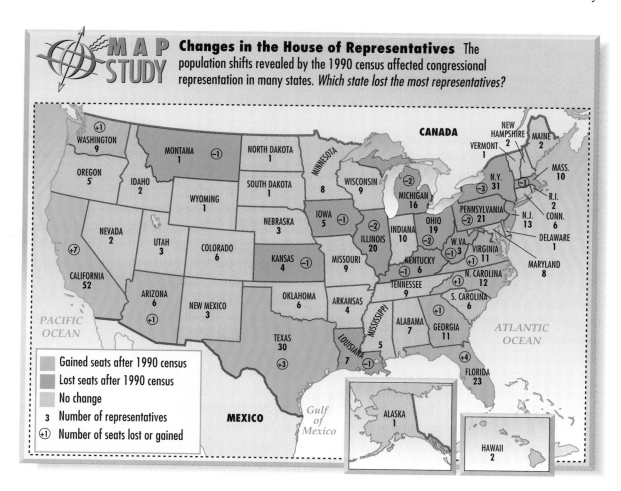

MAP STUDY **Changes in the House of Representatives** The population shifts revealed by the 1990 census affected congressional representation in many states. *Which state lost the most representatives?*

Gained seats after 1990 census
Lost seats after 1990 census
No change
3 Number of representatives
+1 Number of seats lost or gained

Senate Leaders Tom Daschle and Trent Lott One-third of the senators run for reelection every two years. *How many years is the term of office for senators?*

represent. Most senators also have a great deal of government experience; many are former members of the House of Representatives.

Senators serve six-year terms, but not every senator's term begins at the same time. Every two years, one-third of the senators must run for reelection. As a result, at least two-thirds of the Senate always consists of experienced members. There is currently no limit to the number of terms a senator may serve, but a constitutional amendment being considered would set a two-term limit.

Two senators represent each state. The Senate therefore has 100 members. Unlike representatives, senators do not represent specific districts. The entire state elects each senator.

Salary, Benefits, and Privileges

Although members of Congress get to set their own salary, they rarely give themselves a raise. They are afraid of the public's response to such an action. Early in 1989, for example, Congress was considering a salary increase of 51 percent. Protests from angry voters caused the

DID YOU KNOW?

Congressional Mail

Each year, members of Congress receive tons of mail from their constituents. That does not include the approximately 5,000 mailings they receive daily from lobbying groups. In 1993 Senator Barbara Boxer of California received more mail than any other member of Congress—more than 10,000 letters each day from her constituents.

Congressional aides have the daunting task of opening, sorting, and responding to this mail. They also must respond to letters sent electronically by computer. Letter-opening machines help open envelopes. Aides must then remove the letters from the envelopes, sort them according to subject, read them (sometimes while deciphering handwriting), and write replies. Despite the challenge, aides try to respond to every letter—electronic or otherwise. After all, letters to Congress are an important way for the citizens of the country to be heard.

Congressional aide with mail

House and the Senate to vote down the raise, but a compromise was reached later that year. The yearly salary of both senators and representatives is currently $133,600 a year.

In addition to their salary, members of Congress receive other benefits. They are given free office space, parking, and trips to their home state. They have budgets to pay for assistants, office staff, and supplies. They receive discounts on many services such as medical care, video production, and even haircuts. They are also given a **franking privilege,** the right to send job-related mail without paying postage. Recent criticism of many congressional privileges has led to calls for reform. When Republicans took control of Congress in January 1995, they cut staff and reduced other privileges of members.

The Constitution grants senators and representatives **immunity,** or legal protection, in certain situations. For example, members of Congress may not be arrested while doing their job, or while traveling between home and work, unless they have committed a very serious crime. They also may not be sued for anything they say or write while carrying out their duties. This immunity allows members of Congress to say and do what they believe is right, without fear of interference from outsiders.

Of course, the guarantee of immunity does not mean that members of Congress are free to break the law. Senators and representatives are expected to set an example of good, honest behavior for the rest of the country. A member of Congress who acts dishonestly or irresponsibly may face **expulsion** and be forced to

Congressional Benefits   Representative Susan Molinari of New York meets with members of her staff.   *Who pays the salaries of congressional aides?*

Oath of Office   Members of the 104th Congress take their oath of office at the opening of the new session.   *How many sessions does each Congress have in which to do its work?*

sions begin on January 3 and continue until November or December, although recesses, or vacations, interrupt them.

In addition to regular sessions, Congress may also meet in special sessions. In times of crisis, the President has the power to call Congress into session to deal with pressing problems. Special sessions have been rare in recent times because Congress is already in session during most of the year.

On some occasions, the House and the Senate may meet together in a joint session of Congress. Little real work can be accomplished at a joint session, so its value is mostly ceremonial. A joint session is held each year when senators and representatives gather to hear the President's State of the Union address.

leave Congress. Expulsion requires a two-thirds vote of either house and is reserved for only the most serious crimes. **Censure,** or formal disapproval, punishes less serious offenses. Members who are censured must endure the embarrassment of having their misbehavior made public.

Congressional Sessions

The entire House of Representatives is elected every other year, and each "new" Congress is given a number to identify its two-year term. For example, the first Congress met in 1789, and the 105th Congress began meeting in 1997.

Congress carries out its work in two regular time periods, or **sessions.** One session is held each year of the two-year term. In the early years of the Republic, each session of Congress lasted only a few months. Today, however, Congress meets regularly for most of the year. Ses-

★ SECTION 1 REVIEW ★

UNDERSTANDING VOCABULARY
Define bicameral, gerrymandering, constituent, franking privilege, immunity, expulsion, censure, session.

REVIEWING OBJECTIVES
1 What are the qualifications and terms of office for members of the House of Representatives?

2 What are the qualifications and terms of office for members of the Senate?

3 What salary, benefits, and other privileges do members of Congress receive?

4 What are three types of congressional sessions?

How Congress Works

FOCUS

TERMS TO KNOW

majority leader, minority leader, party whip, speaker of the house, president *pro tempore*, standing committee, sub-committee, select committee, joint committee, conference committee, seniority system

OBJECTIVES

- Describe the roles of the **congressional leaders.**

- Identify three types of **congressional committees.**

- Explain the rules and traditions that determine **committee membership** in the House and the Senate.

Over the years, Congress has found it increasingly difficult to accomplish its work. This difficulty is due partly to the growing complexity of modern life and partly to the size of the two houses. The Senate, which began with 26 members in 1789, has 100 members today. The increase in the House has been even greater—from 65 to 435 members.

Such large groups are not always able to work together smoothly. As a result, the House has developed strict rules to help it conduct its business. These rules specify when bills can be introduced, how long they can be debated, and most other parts of the lawmaking process.

The Senate also has rules to help it work efficiently. Because it is much smaller, however, it can operate on a more informal basis. Few of the rules by which the House and Senate operate are in the Constitution. These regulations, however, have become a permanent part of how our government works.

Congressional Leaders

The Democratic and Republican leaders in each house decide much of what happens in Congress. Within the Senate and the House of Representatives, the party to which more than half the members belong is called the majority party. The other party is called the minority party.

At the beginning of each congressional term, the members of each party meet to choose new leaders. Among the leaders they choose are floor leaders and party whips.

Newt Gingrich A member of the majority party, Republican Newt Gingrich became speaker of the house in 1995. *What does the speaker of the house do?*

Floor Leaders and Party Whips

Floor leaders try to make sure that the laws Congress passes are in the best interests of their own political party. Each house of Congress has two floor leaders—a Democrat and a Republican. The majority party's floor leader is called the **majority leader;** the minority party's floor leader is called the **minority leader.**

A **party whip** assists each floor leader. The whip's job is to keep track of how party members vote and to persuade all members of his or her party to vote together on issues.

Speaker

In addition to these party leaders, each house of Congress also has one overall leader. In the House of Representatives, this leader is the **speaker of the house.** A member of the majority party, the speaker is usually an experienced, respected member of the House. The speaker is in charge of nearly everything that occurs while the House is in session.

President *Pro Tempore*

According to the Constitution, the official leader and president of the Senate is the Vice President of the United States. The Vice President, however, takes no part in the legislative process of the Senate. Moreover, the Vice President may only vote when there is a tie.

Because of other duties, the Vice President is rarely present while the Senate is in session. The **president** *pro tempore,* or president "for the time being," handles day-to-day leadership of the Senate. By tradition, this largely honorary position goes to the most senior member of the majority party.

President *Pro Tempore*   Following the 1994 elections, Strom Thurmond of South Carolina assumed this position in the Senate. *What is the role of the president pro tempore?*

Congressional Committees

Each house of Congress must consider thousands of bills, or proposed laws, in the course of a session. To make it possible to handle so many bills at one time, each house has developed a system of committees. Every new bill goes to a committee, where it is researched, discussed, and often revised. The committee then decides whether the full House or Senate should vote on the bill.

Congress has three types of committees: standing committees, select committees, and joint committees. A **standing committee** is a permanent committee that specializes in a particular topic. For example, both the Senate and the House have standing committees to deal with agriculture, commerce, and veterans' affairs. When a bill dealing with any of these topics is introduced, it is sent immediately to the appropriate committee.

Standing committees are divided into **subcommittees,** smaller groups that handle more specialized problems. In the Senate, for example, the Banking, Housing, and Urban Affairs Committee has subcommittees to deal with each area.

Both the Senate and the House sometimes form temporary committees to deal with issues that need special attention. These **select committees** meet for a few months or perhaps a few years, until they complete their assigned task.

Occasionally, the Senate and the House form **joint committees,** which include members of both houses. Like select committees, joint committees usually meet for a limited period of time to consider specific issues. A special type of joint committee, called the **conference committee,** helps the House and the Senate agree on the details of a proposed law. You will learn more about conference committees later in the chapter.

Committee Membership

Most members of Congress have strong preferences about which committees they would like to serve on. In general, certain committees are considered more desirable than others.

A senator who belongs to the Foreign Relations Committee, for example, is

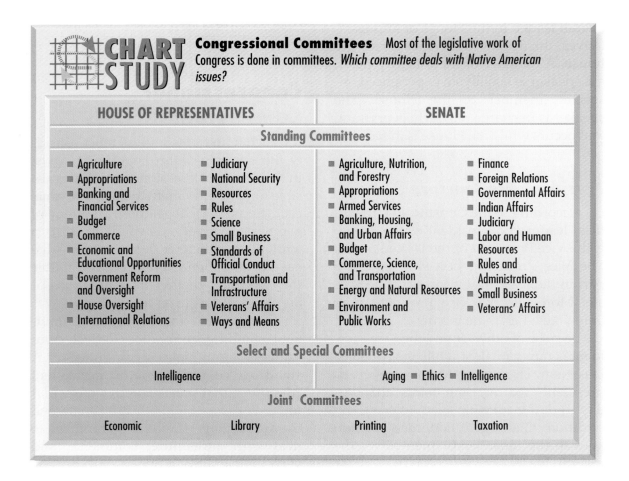

CHART STUDY **Congressional Committees** Most of the legislative work of Congress is done in committees. *Which committee deals with Native American issues?*

HOUSE OF REPRESENTATIVES		SENATE	
Standing Committees			
■ Agriculture ■ Appropriations ■ Banking and Financial Services ■ Budget ■ Commerce ■ Economic and Educational Opportunities ■ Government Reform and Oversight ■ House Oversight ■ International Relations	■ Judiciary ■ National Security ■ Resources ■ Rules ■ Science ■ Small Business ■ Standards of Official Conduct ■ Transportation and Infrastructure ■ Veterans' Affairs ■ Ways and Means	■ Agriculture, Nutrition, and Forestry ■ Appropriations ■ Armed Services ■ Banking, Housing, and Urban Affairs ■ Budget ■ Commerce, Science, and Transportation ■ Energy and Natural Resources ■ Environment and Public Works	■ Finance ■ Foreign Relations ■ Governmental Affairs ■ Indian Affairs ■ Judiciary ■ Labor and Human Resources ■ Rules and Administration ■ Small Business ■ Veterans' Affairs
Select and Special Committees			
Intelligence		Aging ■ Ethics ■ Intelligence	
Joint Committees			
Economic	Library	Printing	Taxation

Labor and Human Resources
Nancy Landon Kassebaum of Kansas served as chair of the Senate Committee on Labor and Human Resources in the 104th Congress. *Who chooses committee members?*

likely to influence international affairs. In contrast, a senator who serves on the Labor and Human Resources Committee —which selects and oversees government employees—is not likely to accumulate a significant amount of fame or power.

Role of Party Leaders

The leaders of the political parties control committee membership. By tradition, the chairperson of each committee is almost always a member of the majority party. Each chairperson is a powerful leader who controls the committee's activities.

The majority party is also allowed to select more than half of the committee members. For example, if 60 percent of House members are Democrats, 60 percent of each House committee will be Democratic as well. As a result, the majority party has a great deal of control over what takes place in each committee as well as in each house of Congress.

Seniority System

Party leaders traditionally make committee assignments according to the **seniority system.** In this system the most desirable committee assignments are given to the senators and representatives who have served the longest in Congress. Moreover, within each committee, the member with the longest record of service is almost always made chairperson. Many people—especially younger members of Congress—feel that the seniority system is unfair. The most influential representatives and senators, who earned their status through seniority, are unwilling to reduce their own authority by changing the system. However, in 1995 the House voted to limit a committee chairperson to three consecutive terms.

★ **SECTION 2 REVIEW** ★

UNDERSTANDING VOCABULARY
Define majority leader, minority leader, party whip, speaker of the house, president *pro tempore,* standing committee, subcommittee, select committee, joint committee, conference committee, seniority system.

REVIEWING OBJECTIVES
1 What are the roles of the congressional leaders?

2 What are three types of congressional committees?

3 What rules and traditions determine committee membership in the House and the Senate?

How to Write Your Representative

If you need help dealing with a federal agency or getting information about the government or if you want to voice your opinion about an issue, you can write your House representative or your senators. Members of Congress depend heavily on mail to find out how we, their constituents, feel about issues.

The Congressional Directory

If you do not know the name of your senators or representative, you can find out from your local library or county election bureau. You can also refer to the *Congressional Directory,* a book containing detailed information about Congress. This book is found in most libraries throughout the United States.

Suggestions to Follow

- Address the member of Congress as "The Honorable" (Name) on the envelope and the letter, and use the title *Representative* or *Senator* in the salutation.

- Address a letter to your representative to the Longworth House Office Building, Washington, D.C. 20515. Address letters to senators to the Dirksen Senate Office Building, Washington, D.C. 20510.

- If you are writing to express an opinion on an issue, be courteous and stick to the subject.

- If you are writing for help with a problem, explain the problem clearly and enclose photocopies of documents that help prove your case.

- Be sure to include your return address.

104 Michigan Avenue
Poplar Bluff, IA 50010
January 15, 1995

The Honorable Luis Rodriguez
Longworth House Office Building
Washington, D.C. 20515

Dear Representative Rodriguez:

As you know, there is a bill pending in Congress to fund the building of a new veterans' hospital in our city. I am writing to urge you to support this bill.

The disabled veterans in our area have to travel a great distance to go to the nearest veterans' hospital. It is very inconvenient and time-consuming for veterans and their families to travel so far for medical care. A new hospital in our city would also create new jobs to help our economy.

Please let me know your position on this issue.

Sincerely,

Julia Imhoff
Julia Imhoff

Letter to a representative

CITIZENSHIP IN ACTION

1 What are three reasons why people write to their representatives in Congress?

2 Name an issue about which you would like to write your congressional representatives.

Congressional Powers

FOCUS

TERMS TO KNOW
expressed powers, impeach, appropriations

OBJECTIVES

■ Explain both the **expressed and implied powers** of Congress.

■ Name and describe two **non-legislative powers** of Congress.

■ List four **special powers of Congress.**

■ Summarize the three basic **limits to congressional power** in the Constitution.

The writers of the Constitution believed strongly in the principle of limited government. As a result, they placed clear limits on the powers of Congress. These restrictions determine what Congress and each of its houses may or may not do. You have already learned about congressional powers and their limits in Chapter 3.

Expressed and Implied Powers

Expressed powers, also known as delegated powers, are one type of congressional power. Expressed powers are those listed specifically in Article I of the Constitution. Among them are the power to collect taxes, to borrow money, to regulate foreign and interstate commerce, to set up a postal system, to maintain armed services, to declare war, and to regulate immigration and naturalization.

As you learned in Chapter 3, implied powers are those not stated explicitly in the Constitution. The implied powers of Congress come from the necessary and proper clause, often called the elastic clause. The clause is called elastic because it allows Congress to stretch its authority to carry out its expressed powers.

For example, one expressed power of Congress is to maintain an army and a navy. Using its implied powers, Congress has expanded this expressed power and has built a huge military network, including service academies and intelligence-gathering organizations in addition to the United States Army, Navy, Air Force, and Marines.

Implied Powers   United States troops landed in Port-au-Prince, Haiti, on September 14, 1994.   *On which power is the extensive military network based?*

Presidential Appointments   Steven Breyer testified at the hearing on his nomination to the Supreme Court.   *Why does the Senate hold hearings on presidential nominees?*

Nonlegislative Powers

The Constitution also grants Congress a number of nonlegislative powers. These enable the government to operate more effectively and help Congress serve as a check on the other branches of government. One such power, the power to propose amendments to the Constitution, was discussed in Chapter 4.

Congress also has the power to investigate. Most congressional hearings and fact-finding commissions are part of the lawmaking process. Congress needs to gather information to use in drafting and evaluating legislation, but it can also use its investigative powers in another way. It can review the activities of the executive branch to find out whether the government is administering the laws efficiently and as intended by Congress.

One of Congress's most important nonlegislative powers is the power to

impeach—to accuse government officials of wrongdoing, put them on trial, and if necessary remove them from office. Any federal official—including the President, the Vice President, or a judge—can be impeached if suspected of committing a serious crime.

The impeachment process begins in the House of Representatives, where a list of charges against the accused official is drawn up. If a majority of members vote to accept these charges, the Senate then has the power to act as a jury and decide the official's guilt or innocence. A two-thirds vote in the Senate is necessary to convict and to remove a person from office.

Special Powers of Congress

The Constitution has reserved special powers for each house of Congress. One of the House of Representatives' special powers, the power to begin impeachment proceedings, has just been discussed. The House also has the power to choose the President if no candidate wins a majority in the Electoral College. This has happened only twice—after the elections of 1800 and 1824.

One of the House's most important special powers is to introduce tax bills and **appropriations** bills, bills that involve money. The Senate votes on money bills, but all such bills must start in the House. For this reason, the political party that controls the House also has a great deal of control over the nation's purse strings.

The special powers of the Senate include acting as the jury in an impeachment trial and ratifying treaties with other nations. Although the President

American Profiles

Patsy Mink

Early in her youth, Patsy Takemoto Mink decided to devote her life to public service. In 1964 she was elected a United States representative from her home state of Hawaii. She lost a bid for the Senate in 1976, but she returned to the House in 1990.

Mink has been a tireless champion of such issues as equal rights for women and for people with disabilities, educational funding for young people, and fairness in the private and public sectors.

Throughout her years in public service, Mink has found strength in our nation's diversity. She once declared that America's "strength lies in all our diversities converging in one common belief, that of the importance of freedom as the essence of our country."

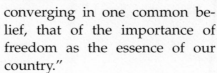

PROFILE REVIEW

1 What groups have received most of Patsy Mink's attention?

2 Does Patsy Mink think our nation's diversity is a strength or a weakness?

---

may sign a treaty, it is not binding unless a two-thirds vote in the Senate ratifies it.

The Senate also has the power to approve or reject the President's appointments of certain high government officials. The Senate usually accepts the President's choice, but there are exceptions. In 1989, for example, the Senate refused to approve President Bush's appointment of John Tower as secretary of defense. The Senate expressed doubts about Tower's character and his ability to handle the job. In 1993 the nomination of Zoë Baird, President Clinton's appointee for attorney general, was withdrawn before the Senate had a chance to vote. At issue was her hiring of illegal aliens and failure to pay social security taxes on their wages.

Limits to Congressional Power

As you may remember, the Constitution includes some clear statements about things Congress may *not* do.

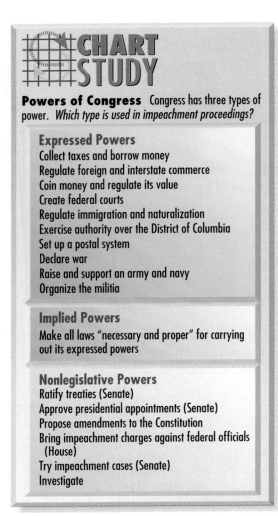

CHART STUDY

Powers of Congress Congress has three types of power. *Which type is used in impeachment proceedings?*

Expressed Powers
Collect taxes and borrow money
Regulate foreign and interstate commerce
Coin money and regulate its value
Create federal courts
Regulate immigration and naturalization
Exercise authority over the District of Columbia
Set up a postal system
Declare war
Raise and support an army and navy
Organize the militia

Implied Powers
Make all laws "necessary and proper" for carrying out its expressed powers

Nonlegislative Powers
Ratify treaties (Senate)
Approve presidential appointments (Senate)
Propose amendments to the Constitution
Bring impeachment charges against federal officials (House)
Try impeachment cases (Senate)
Investigate

According to Article I, Congress may not favor one state over another, tax interstate commerce, or tax exports.

Article I also forbids Congress from enacting laws that would interfere with the legal rights of individuals. Congress may not pass bills of attainder and ex post facto laws or suspend the writ of habeas corpus. These important legal rights will be discussed in Chapter 16.

The Constitution also reserves many powers for the states. Congress cannot interfere with these powers, which include the right to make marriage and divorce laws. The Bill of Rights and other amendments also deny Congress certain powers. (See Chapter 4.)

Additional restrictions on congressional power come from the Constitution's system of checks and balances. As you will see later in this chapter, the President has the power to veto a bill passed by Congress. The Supreme Court can also declare a law unconstitutional. This process will be discussed in Chapter 12.

A final restriction on the power of Congress is a result of economics. Nearly every law requires the government to spend a certain amount of money. Some government programs, such as social security, cost billions of dollars. While the government's budget is huge, it is still limited. Therefore, Congress cannot pass every law it might like to pass, simply because the money is not available. The need to set priorities and to consider what laws and programs the government can best afford limits the power of Congress.

★ SECTION 3 REVIEW ★

UNDERSTANDING VOCABULARY
Define expressed powers, impeach, appropriations.

REVIEWING OBJECTIVES
1 What are Congress's expressed and implied powers?

2 What are two nonlegislative powers of Congress?

3 What are four special powers of Congress?

4 What are the three basic limits to congressional power in the Constitution?

How a Bill Becomes a Law

FOCUS

TERMS TO KNOW

pigeonhole, filibuster, cloture, voice vote, standing vote, roll-call vote, pocket veto

OBJECTIVES

- Explain the procedure for **introducing a bill** in Congress.

- Describe **the work of committees,** including three actions a committee can take when it receives a bill.

- Discuss the rules for **debating a bill** in the House and in the Senate.

- Identify three methods of **voting on a bill.**

- Outline a President's options for **signing or vetoing a bill.**

Each year, Congress considers thousands of bills. Of these, only a few hundred become laws. Congressional committees, negative votes in one or both houses of Congress, or presidential vetoes kill the rest. The process by which a bill becomes a law is complicated and may require a great deal of time and effort.

Every bill starts with an idea. Some of these ideas come from members of Congress. Citizens who write to their representatives suggest some. Many ideas come from lobbyists representing various interest groups. Others come from the President or from officials in the executive branch. A senator or representative must sponsor a bill before Congress will consider it.

Introducing a Bill

A member of Congress who wants to sponsor a bill has to draft it, or put the idea in written form. The representative's or senator's staff usually drafts the bill.

A senator introduces a bill by making a formal announcement in the Senate. In the House, a representative introduces a bill by dropping it into the "hopper," a box used specifically for this purpose. The bill then receives a number. A House bill might be called HR 1266.

After a bill is introduced, it is sent to the standing committee that is concerned with the subject of the bill. For example,

Consumer Lobbyist   Many ideas for bills come from lobbyists representing interest groups. *How are these bills introduced in Congress?*

Senator Robert Byrd—A Filibuster Expert Senators can prevent discussion of a bill by talking endlessly until the bill's sponsor withdraws it. *How else can a bill be killed?*

a bill dealing with airline safety would probably be sent to the Commerce, Science, and Transportation Committee in the Senate or the Transportation and Infrastructure Committee in the House.

The Work of Committees

A committee has several options when it receives a bill. If the committee members dislike the bill, they can "kill," or reject, it immediately, or they can **pigeonhole** it—set it aside without even considering it. This is what happens to most bills in committee.

Suppose, however, that most committee members favor the bill. The committee might decide to keep the bill as it is, or it might decide to make some changes. It might even decide to throw out the bill and write a new one dealing with the same subject.

At this point, the bill would be passed to a subcommittee for further work and study. By law, the subcommittee must hold public hearings at which people affected by the bill can express their opinions. These people have an opportunity to present arguments in support of or against the bill.

Based on information from hearings and from other research, the subcommittee might make other changes in the bill. When the subcommittee has finished its work, the bill is returned to the full committee. The full committee may make additional changes before voting on the bill. If a majority of the committee votes to approve the bill, it is sent to the full Senate or House for consideration.

Debating a Bill

Because the House of Representatives has many members and a great deal of work to do, it can devote only a small amount of time to any one bill. The Rules Committee of the House helps to schedule the consideration of bills. This committee can decide when a bill will be debated and for how long. It can even kill a bill by refusing to give it time for debate.

The rules for debate in the House are fairly complicated. In some cases, the House speeds up the debate process by meeting as a "Committee of the Whole," a special gathering of all House members. The rules for debate within a committee are more informal, so debates can proceed more quickly and easily.

In the Senate, the debates are freer. For one thing, senators are allowed to speak for an unlimited amount of time.

This freedom means that one or more senators may kill a bill by talking until the bill's sponsor withdraws it. This tactic is known as a **filibuster.**

A vote for cloture, which requires the support of 60 members of the Senate, can end a filibuster. **Cloture** limits a senator to one hour of debate. Cloture votes are rare, however, and a filibuster is often an effective way to kill a bill.

Voting on a Bill

After a bill has been debated, it is brought to a vote. Voting is done in one of three ways. The simplest is a **voice vote,** in which those who support a bill say yea, and those opposed say nay. A voice vote is usually used for bills that are clearly popular or unpopular.

A more exact method of voting is the **standing vote** in which members who support a bill are asked to stand and be counted. Then members who oppose the bill are asked to stand and be counted.

Roll-call Votes

A third method is the roll-call vote. In a **roll-call vote,** each member's name is called individually, and he or she is asked to vote yea, nay, or present. (A vote of "present" means "no opinion.") In a roll-call every person's vote is a matter of public record, so constituents can find out how their representatives in Congress have voted on an issue. This knowledge may have an effect on the way a senator or representative votes.

Conference Committees

Often, the House and Senate pass different versions of the same bill. For example, the House version of a bill on airline safety might require aircraft to be

Roll-call Vote   This type of vote provides a public record of each member's vote. *Why should roll-call votes affect the way members of Congress vote?*

replaced after 20 years. The Senate version, on the other hand, might specify 25 years. When two versions of the same bill are passed, the conflicting bills are sent to a conference committee made up of members from both houses. The conference committee works to reach a compromise and write a revised bill that will satisfy both houses. When its work is done, the conference committee sends the revised bill to the House and Senate for another vote. Unless both houses pass the same version of a bill, it cannot become a law.

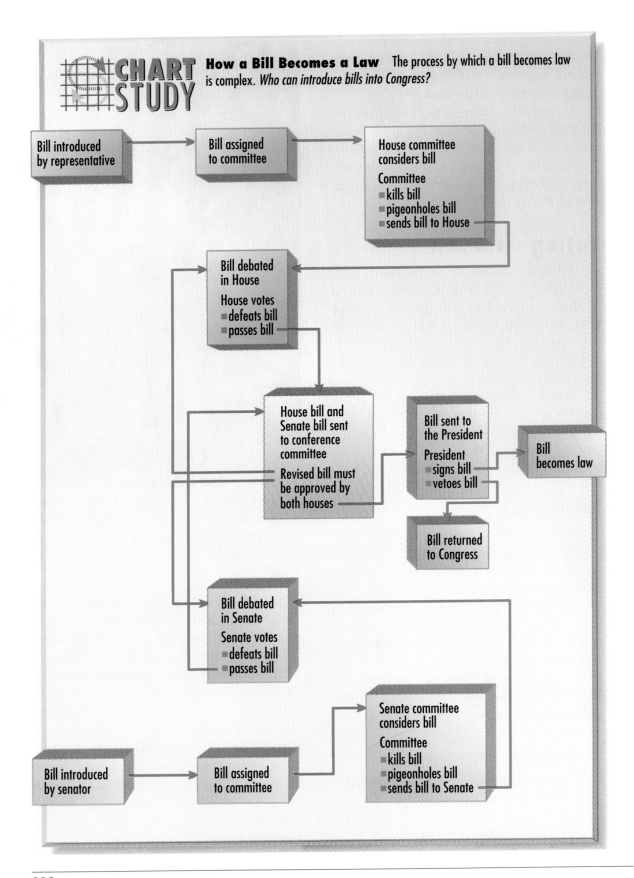

CHART STUDY

How a Bill Becomes a Law The process by which a bill becomes law is complex. *Who can introduce bills into Congress?*

Bill introduced by representative

Bill assigned to committee

House committee considers bill

Committee
- kills bill
- pigeonholes bill
- sends bill to House

Bill debated in House

House votes
- defeats bill
- passes bill

House bill and Senate bill sent to conference committee

Revised bill must be approved by both houses

Bill sent to the President

President
- signs bill
- vetoes bill

Bill becomes law

Bill returned to Congress

Bill debated in Senate

Senate votes
- defeats bill
- passes bill

Senate committee considers bill

Committee
- kills bill
- pigeonholes bill
- sends bill to Senate

Bill introduced by senator

Bill assigned to committee

Signing a Bill Into Law   President Clinton signed the Crime Bill on September 13, 1994.   *How can the President prevent a bill from becoming law?*

Signing or Vetoing a Bill

After both houses of Congress pass a bill, it is sent to the President. If the President approves of the bill and signs it, the bill becomes a law. The President, however, may also decide to veto the bill. Many bills survive months of work and debate in Congress only to be killed by a presidential veto.

A President may also choose to do nothing about a bill. If the President lets 10 days pass without signing a bill, and Congress is in session, the bill becomes a law without the President's signature. If Congress is not in session, the bill is considered dead after the 10 days. Killing a bill in this way is called a **pocket veto.**

Presidents sometimes use the pocket veto for political reasons. The President may want to veto a particular bill but knows that the veto would be unpopular with the public. In that case, the President might prefer to let the bill die quietly.

If the President vetoes a bill, Congress has one last chance to save it. Congress can override the President's veto by a two-thirds vote in each house. Only the most popular bills can be rescued in this way, however. To keep a good relationship with the President, many members of Congress prefer not to challenge a veto—especially if the President is a member of their own party.

★ SECTION 4 REVIEW ★

UNDERSTANDING VOCABULARY
Define pigeonhole, filibuster, cloture, voice vote, standing vote, roll-call vote, pocket veto.

REVIEWING OBJECTIVES
1 What is the procedure for introducing a bill in Congress?

2 What are three actions a congressional committee can take when it receives a bill?

3 What are the rules for debating a bill in the House and in the Senate?

4 What are three methods of voting on a bill?

5 What are a President's options for signing or vetoing a bill?

Identifying Key Terms

Choose the vocabulary term that best completes each of the sentences below. Write your answers on a separate sheet of paper.

censure   impeach   appropriations
pigeonhole   filibuster   pocket veto

1. By not acting on the bill for 10 days, the President was using his _____.
2. The congressional committee members decided to _____ the bill when they set it aside without consideration.
3. Only rarely have the House and Senate used their power to _____ government officials and remove them from office.
4. Without a three-fifths vote, the Senate was unable to stop the senator's _____.
5. The senators voted to _____ their colleague for conduct unbecoming a senator.
6. All _____ bills, those involving the spending of money, must start in the House.

Reviewing the Main Ideas

SECTION 1
1. What qualifications does the Constitution require for United States representatives and senators?
2. What happens in the House of Representatives after the Census Bureau has counted the population?

SECTION 2
3. Describe the responsibilities of floor leaders and party whips.
4. Explain the difference between standing committees and select committees.

SECTION 3
5. Describe three special powers the Constitution grants to Congress.
6. Explain the difference between expressed and implied powers.

SECTION 4
7. How are bills introduced in the Senate and in the House of Representatives?
8. Identify three methods of voting on bills in Congress.

Critical Thinking

SECTION 1
1. **Analyzing Information** Why do you think the Constitution did not include other qualifications for members of Congress?

SECTION 2
2. **Evaluating Information** Do you think that government by committee makes the role of individual members of Congress less important? Why or why not?

SECTION 3
3. **Developing a Point of View** Do you think Congress has enough power to assume its responsibilities and accomplish its work? Explain.

SECTION 4
4. **Evaluating Information** Do you think the people should play a greater role in making the laws that govern them? Why or why not?

Reinforcing Citizenship Skills

Identify a state or national issue that is important to you. Find out the names of your United States representative and senators. Then compose a letter to one of them about the issue. Explain your opinion clearly and courteously. Be sure to use correct letter format.

Cooperative Learning

With a group of five, select one of the congressional committees listed on page 220. Find out more about this committee and what bills it is currently studying. Choose one of these bills and make recommendations on whether the bill should be rejected, pigeonholed, or sent to Congress for consideration. Present your report to the class. Ask the class to role-play the part of Congress and vote on the issue.

Technology Activity

Using a Word Processor

Review your journal on your ideas about how you would deal with issues if you were a member of Congress. Then use a word processor to write a persuasive essay that describes your goals, explains your reasons, and encourages readers to vote for you when you run for election. Remember as you write your essay that a major responsibility of a member of Congress is to reflect the opinions of the voters.

Focusing on Your Community

Find out about an issue Congress debated during the last year that has had an impact on your community. Find out what your representative's and senators' stands were on this issue and how they voted on any related bills.

Analyzing Visuals

Until recently, most members of Congress were white males. Now things are beginning to change. Study the table below. Then answer the questions.

1. Which group has shown the largest increase in Congress?
2. In which year were the greatest increases seen?
3. Based on the information in this table, what do you think might happen in future elections?

Minority Representation in Congress

	1991	1993	1995	1997
Women	31	54	57	60
African Americans	26	40	40	38
Hispanic Americans	12	19	18	18
Native Americans	1	1	1	1
Asian Americans	7	9	8	5

Source: *Congressional Quarterly.*

CHAPTER 10

The Presidency

CIVIC PARTICIPATION

The presidency is the nation's highest elected office. To carry out their responsibilities, Presidents rely on the offices and departments of the executive branch. Contact a federal information center to find out about the responsibilities of various divisions of the Executive Office of the President. Be sure to obtain addresses and phone numbers. Find out what these offices can do to help citizens.

Working in Your Community

Use the information you obtain to prepare a brochure that lists the executive offices, outlines their roles, and provides addresses and phone numbers. Distribute this brochure in your neighborhood. ■

Your Civics Journal

During the next week, pay attention to the news to find what actions the President has taken on different issues. Write down your findings in your civics journal. Next to each entry, indicate your stand on the issue and whether or not you agree with the President's actions.

Visiting the White House ➤

The President and Vice President

The presidency is the most important office in the United States and one of the most important in the world. As head of the executive branch of government, the President must make decisions that affect the lives of all Americans. The President receives advice and assistance in carrying out the responsibilities of the office from the **cabinet,** a group made up of the heads of the executive departments, the Vice President, and other important officials.

The President

The Constitution lists only three requirements to become President of the United States. The President must be a native-born (not naturalized) citizen of this country. He or she must be at least 35 years old and must have lived in the United States for at least 14 years. In theory, anyone who meets these qualifications can become President.

In practice, however, the requirements for becoming President are more complex. Almost all our Presidents have shared similar characteristics. Every President in American history has been a white male. All but one have been Protestant, and many have been of British ancestry. Most, but not all, attended college, and many began their careers as lawyers.

Only in the past few decades has the presidency become a possibility for a wider range of Americans. John F. Kennedy, a Catholic, was elected President in 1960. In 1984 the Democratic party nominated Geraldine Ferraro as its first female vice-presidential candidate. Four years later Jesse Jackson, an African American male, ran a close second in the race to become the Democratic candidate for President.

Presidency   President Clinton confers with Secretary of the Treasury Robert Rubin. *What are the constitutional requirements for the presidency?*

Salary and Benefits

The President receives a salary of $200,000 per year, plus another $50,000 per year for expenses and up to $100,000 per year for travel. Congress sets the President's salary and cannot change it during the President's term.

In addition, the President and his or her family enjoy free lodging in the White House and the use of Camp David, a mountain estate in Maryland. They receive the finest possible medical care and personal protection. They also have hundreds of assistants to help them with their public and personal activities. The President also enjoys the power, prestige, and respect that come with the office.

Vice Presidency   President Clinton and Vice President Gore meet regularly for political discussions.   *What are the qualifications for the vice presidency?*

Election and Terms of Office

Presidential elections are held every four years. You have already learned much about the presidential election process—how presidential candidates are nominated and about the role of the Electoral College.

The presidential election process—like the presidency itself—depends heavily on tradition. The law does not require political parties to nominate presidential candidates. Nor are members of the Electoral College required by law to select either party's candidate. These traditions have been with us for so long, however, that they have almost taken on the force of law.

Sometimes long-established traditions are turned into law. For example, the Constitution originally placed no limit on the number of terms a President could serve. George Washington, who felt that eight years was enough for any President, stepped down after two four-

year terms. Following Washington's example, no President served more than two terms until 1940, when President Franklin D. Roosevelt was elected to a third term. In 1944 Roosevelt was elected to a fourth term.

After Roosevelt's death, Congress proposed a constitutional amendment that would prevent any President from breaking the two-term tradition again. The Twenty-second Amendment, ratified in 1951, limits each President to two terms in office.

The Vice President

The Vice President is the only other member of the executive branch mentioned in the Constitution. Article II says that if the President dies or leaves office, the Vice President automatically takes on all the powers of the President. For this reason, the qualifications for the vice presidency are the same as those for the presidency.

Nixon's Successor   Gerald Ford became President in August 1974 when Richard Nixon resigned from the presidency.   *Which amendment deals with presidential succession?*

As you may remember from Chapter 9, the Vice President serves as president of the Senate. Although the Constitution assigns the Vice President no other official duties, many Presidents have given their Vice Presidents major responsibilities. Most recent Vice Presidents have taken part in cabinet meetings and have helped make important government decisions.

Salary and Benefits

The Vice President earns a salary of $171,500 per year, plus $10,000 per year for expenses. The Vice President also receives many of the same benefits as the President, including a free residence, a large staff, and a variety of personal services.

Election and Terms of Office

The procedure for electing the Vice President has changed since the Constitution was written. Originally, members of the Electoral College voted for two candidates for President. The candidate who received a majority of electoral votes became President, and the candidate who came in second became Vice President.

This procedure caused problems. With more than one person from each political party competing for the presidency, it was difficult for any candidate to win a majority of the electors' votes. The adoption of the Twelfth Amendment in 1804 solved the problem. This amendment allowed the Electoral College to vote separately for President and Vice President.

Although the number of four-year terms a Vice President can serve is not limited, no Vice President has ever served more than two terms.

Presidential Succession

In 1841 William Henry Harrison became the first President to die in office. His death raised many questions. While the Constitution says that the Vice President should assume the "powers and duties" of the presidency, no one was sure what that meant. Should the Vice President remain Vice President while doing the President's job? Should the Vice President become President? Should a special election be called to elect a new President?

Vice President John Tyler settled the matter. He declared himself President and served out the remainder of Harrison's term. Since Tyler's time, eight other Vice Presidents have taken over the presidency following the death or resignation of a President.

Congress eventually decided that the selection of a President was too important to be left to tradition. In 1947 Congress passed the Presidential Succession

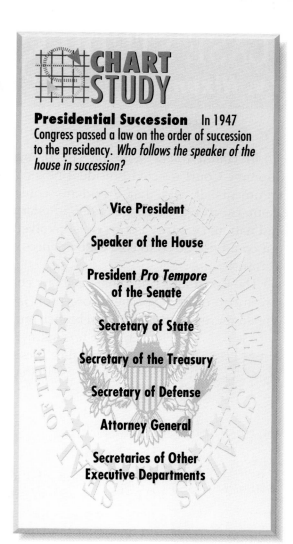

Presidential Succession In 1947 Congress passed a law on the order of succession to the presidency. *Who follows the speaker of the house in succession?*

Vice President

Speaker of the House

President *Pro Tempore* of the Senate

Secretary of State

Secretary of the Treasury

Secretary of Defense

Attorney General

Secretaries of Other Executive Departments

The new President then chooses another Vice President, whose selection both houses of Congress must approve. The amendment also allows the Vice President to become "Acting President" if the President is temporarily unable to carry out the duties of office.

The Twenty-fifth Amendment has already been used three times. The first was in 1973, when Vice President Spiro Agnew resigned. President Richard Nixon replaced him with Gerald R. Ford, a representative from Michigan. In 1974, when Nixon resigned from the presidency, the amendment was used a second time. Gerald Ford became the new President and chose Nelson A. Rockefeller, former governor of New York, to be his Vice President.

In 1985 the Twenty-fifth Amendment was used again. President Ronald Reagan, who was about to undergo surgery, informed Congress that he would be unable to carry out his presidential duties during the operation. As a result, Vice President George Bush served as Acting President for about eight hours.

Act, which indicates the line of succession after the Vice President. According to this law, if both the President and Vice President die or leave office, the speaker of the house becomes President. Others in line include the president *pro tempore* of the Senate and the members of the cabinet.

Twenty years later, Congress ended all remaining questions about presidential succession by passing a constitutional amendment. The Twenty-fifth Amendment, ratified in 1967, says that if the President dies or leaves office, the Vice President legally becomes President.

★ **SECTION 1 REVIEW** ★

UNDERSTANDING VOCABULARY
Define cabinet.

REVIEWING OBJECTIVES

1 What are the qualifications and terms of office for the President?

2 What are the qualifications and terms of office for the Vice President?

3 What are the constitutional provisions for presidential succession?

SUPREME COURT CASE STUDIES
United States v. Nixon

While the doctrine of "separation of powers" works fairly well, sometimes one branch finds itself in conflict with another. A dramatic conflict occurred during the Watergate affair.

The Watergate Affair

The affair began when people linked to President Richard Nixon's reelection committee were caught breaking into the offices of the Democratic National Committee in the Watergate building in Washington. Special Prosecutor Leon Jaworski led an investigation into the President's possible involvement in the case.

The Tapes

Jaworski asked Nixon to turn over 64 tapes of conversations with White House aides on the Watergate affair. The President refused. He claimed that executive privilege—the right to have confidential discussions to conduct the nation's business—protected the tapes. He also argued that the courts—the judicial branch—had no right to interfere in a dispute between the President and Jaworski, who was a member of the Justice Department, part of the executive branch.

Special Prosecutor Leon Jaworski

The Case

In *United States* v. *Nixon* (1974), the Supreme Court rejected President Nixon's arguments. It said that Presidents could claim executive privilege when military and national security issues were involved but could not do so to conceal evidence of a crime.

The Court also ruled that, as a law enforcement officer, Special Prosecutor Jaworski represented the judicial branch and had a right to seek evidence from the President in a criminal proceeding.

The Results

As a result of the Court's ruling, President Nixon was forced to turn over the tapes. These conversations revealed his involvement in a cover-up, and this led to his resignation.

REVIEWING THE CASE

1 What arguments did President Nixon use to try to withhold the 64 tapes?

2 What did the Supreme Court rule in *United States* v. *Nixon?*

The President's Major Roles

The Constitution holds one person—the President—responsible for carrying out the duties of the executive branch. As the nation has grown, the duties and responsibilities of the executive branch have also grown. In carrying out these tasks, the President takes on several different roles. These include Chief Executive, chief diplomat, and commander in chief.

Chief Executive

The most important job of the President is to carry out the nation's laws. Article II of the Constitution gives the President the responsibility to "take care that the laws be faithfully executed."

When Congress passes a law, a number of issues must be resolved before the law can take effect and be enforced. Suppose, for example, that Congress passes a law requiring all cosmetics to have labels listing their ingredients. Although the law seems relatively simple, many questions must be answered. How big should the labels be? In what order should the ingredients be listed? Which products should be considered "cosmetics"? (For example, is hair spray a cosmetic or simply a grooming aid?) What action should be taken if manufacturers break the law?

Congress cannot possibly deal with all these details when it writes a bill. Instead, the executive branch of the government determines the specific provisions of each new law. The President, of course, does not attend to such details personally. Overseeing the execution of national laws is the responsibility of the hundreds of agencies and millions

Chief Executive President Clinton speaks to reporters at a press conference. *Why do you think a President's words are newsworthy?*

CHART STUDY

Powers and Duties of the President These illustrations show the many roles of the President of the United States. *Which is the President's most important role?*

Chief Executive

Carries out the nation's laws
Issues executive orders
Appoints cabinet members
and other officials

Commander in Chief
Has final authority over all military matters

Chief Diplomat

Deals with foreign countries
Appoints ambassadors
Makes treaties

Chief of State
Represents the whole nation

Party Leader

Supports party members
in election campaigns
Helps unify party
and give it direction

Judicial Leader
Appoints judges to Supreme Court and other federal courts
Can issue pardons and reprieves

Legislative Leader

Proposes legislation
Prepares federal budget
Approves or vetoes
legislation

---

of executive branch employees. This large network of individuals and agencies is called the federal **bureaucracy.** The President heads this bureaucracy in his role as the Chief Executive.

Issuing Executive Orders

One of the President's most important tools for executing laws is the power to issue executive orders. An **executive order** is a rule or command the President issues that has the force of law. Executive orders are often, though not always, is-

sued during times of crisis. During World War II, for example, President Franklin Roosevelt issued executive orders that put certain important industries under the direct control of the government.

According to the Constitution, only Congress has the power to make laws. Issuing executive orders, however, is generally considered part of the President's duty to "take care that the laws be faithfully executed."

Decisions any agency of the executive branch makes are also considered executive orders and have the force of law. For example, if the Federal Trade Commission—part of the executive branch—decides that cosmetics' labels must use lettering one-eighth of an inch high, cosmetics manufacturers must obey this rule as they would a law Congress passes.

Appointing Officials

Because the President shares power with others in the government, it is important that these people be reliable and competent. It is also important that these people share the President's values and ideas so that they will support the President's policies and see that they are carried out.

The Constitution gives the President the power to appoint many government officials. Among these officials are ambassadors, judges, heads of government agencies, and members of the cabinet. Except for judges, the President can also remove most officials from office after they have been appointed. The Senate must approve almost all the President's appointments.

Chief Diplomat

Another role of the President is that of chief diplomat. The President and the executive branch have primary responsibility for dealing with other countries. The Constitution gives the President two important powers: the first is the power to appoint ambassadors; the second is the power to make treaties.

Appointing Ambassadors

An **ambassador** is an official representative of a country's government. The President appoints about 150 ambassadors, each of whom is sent to a different country as a representative of the United

Peace Accord   Prime Minister Rabin of Israel (left) and Palestine Liberation Organization Chairman Arafat (right) signed an accord in Washington in 1993.   *Which presidential role did President Clinton play in this meeting?*

States. As you may remember, the President needs the approval of the Senate in order to appoint ambassadors.

Ambassadors are sent only to those countries where the United States recognizes, or accepts, the legal existence of the government. If the government of a certain country is thought to hold power illegally, the President can refuse to recognize that government. In that case, no American ambassador will be sent, and that country will not be allowed to send an ambassador to the United States.

Making Treaties

The second important power of the President as chief diplomat is the power to make treaties. A **treaty** is a formal agreement between two or more countries. The Constitution gives the President the power to make treaties with

The Power to Make Treaties   In January 1993, President George Bush and Russian President Boris Yeltsin signed the START II treaty.   *What is a treaty?*

"the advice and consent of the Senate." The Senate must approve the treaty by a two-thirds vote. Only then can it be signed into law.

Often Presidents bypass the Senate by making executive agreements instead of treaties. An **executive agreement** is an agreement between the President and the leader of another country. It has the force of law but does not require Senate approval. Most executive agreements deal with fairly routine matters.

Commander in Chief

The Constitution gives Congress the power to maintain an army and the power to declare war. In keeping with the system of checks and balances, however, it makes the President the commander in chief, or leader, of the armed forces. Only the President can order American soldiers into battle.

Military power can sometimes threaten a nation's government. Many times in history, the military leaders of a country have used force to take over their government. The writers of the Constitution hoped to avoid this danger by making the President, a nonmilitary person, the commander of the armed forces. For the same reason, they divided responsibility for the military between the executive and legislative branches.

The War Powers Act

Occasionally, however, the President has used the power as commander in chief in ways that have threatened the system of checks and balances. For example, Congress never declared war in Korea and Vietnam. Yet the United States became involved in an armed conflict in Korea after President Truman sent troops to fight there, and in Vietnam under Presidents Eisenhower, Kennedy, Johnson, and Nixon.

In 1973, following the Vietnam War, Congress passed the War Powers Act,

Commander in Chief President Lyndon Johnson visited American troops in Vietnam. *Why does the Constitution give the President leadership of the armed forces?*

which limits the President's authority to wage war. This law requires the President to notify Congress immediately when troops are sent into battle. These troops must be brought home after 60 days unless Congress gives its approval for them to remain longer or unless it declares war.

Peacetime Role

During an actual war—one that Congress declares—the President may be given special powers. For example, the President can order the United States Army to take over the government of another country.

During peacetime, the President can use the armed services for a variety of purposes. In 1995, for example, President Clinton sent United States troops to Bosnia to take part in the NATO peacekeeping force. Presidents can also call out government troops to keep order within the United States. President Eisenhower did this in 1957, in Little Rock, Arkansas, when attempts to integrate public schools led to clashes between groups of angry citizens and the local police.

★ SECTION 2 REVIEW ★

UNDERSTANDING VOCABULARY
Define bureaucracy, executive order, ambassador, treaty, executive agreement.

REVIEWING OBJECTIVES

1 What are the President's responsibilities as Chief Executive?

2 What two powers does the President have as chief diplomat?

3 Which military responsibilities are given to the President as commander in chief and which to Congress?

SECTION 3

The President's Other Roles

FOCUS

TERMS TO KNOW

pardon, reprieve, amnesty

OBJECTIVES

- Identify five ways in which the President in the role of **legislative leader** can influence congressional legislation.

- Explain how the President in the role of **party leader** can help the party and its members.

- Identify two powers the Constitution gives the President as **judicial leader.**

- Describe the President's role as **chief of state.**

I n addition to acting as Chief Executive, chief diplomat, and commander in chief, the President plays several other important roles in the nation. These include legislative leader, party leader, judicial leader, and chief of state. Not all these roles come directly from the Constitution, but all are vital parts of the President's job.

Legislative Leader

Every President comes into office with ideas about what kind of place the United States should be. No President, however, can make major changes in American life without the cooperation of Congress. Any attempts to change the nation require new laws, and only Congress can pass new laws.

The President can, however, play a large part in the legislative process. By developing a close relationship with the members of Congress—especially those who belong to the President's party—the President can often get Congress to pass laws that will advance his or her program.

Introducing Legislation

Suppose, for example, that the President wants a bill introduced in Congress. A member of the President's staff will first draft the bill according to the President's instructions. The President will then ask a senator or representative to introduce the bill in Congress. Once a bill has moved into congressional committee, the President may speak individually to the committee members and encourage them to approve it.

Legislation   President George Bush signed the Americans with Disabilities Act in 1990.   *What tactics can a President use to persuade Congress to pass a particular bill?*

When it is time for the full House or Senate to vote on a bill the President supports, the President may use a variety of tactics to encourage passage of the bill. Those tactics might include telephoning members of Congress, inviting them to the White House to discuss the bill, or even promising not to veto another bill that a member of Congress supports. Another tactic the President might use is to appeal to the American people by making a speech on television. If the speech is convincing enough, the voters may pressure their senators or representatives to pass the legislation. President Ronald Reagan, known as "the Great Communicator," used this technique successfully a number of times.

Influencing Legislation

The President also has more formal ways to influence legislation. Once a year, as required by the Constitution, the President makes a State of the Union address to Congress. In this speech the President presents the administration's goals for the coming year. Shortly afterward the President submits a budget to Congress, which recommends how the government should raise and spend money to reach those goals. Congress is not required to accept the President's budget, but it often does.

The President may also call a special session of Congress to consider urgent matters. This is rarely necessary today because Congress now meets for most of the year.

Party Leader

When a political party's candidate is elected President, that person becomes the leader of the party. This role carries no special powers or privileges. Like all political party members, however, the President does try to help the party. One way a President can do this is by appointing party members to government jobs through patronage, the system of rewarding party workers with jobs or special favors. Another way is by making speeches and personal appearances in support of party members who are running for election.

DID YOU KNOW?

America's First Ladies

First Ladies—the wives of our Presidents—have distinguished themselves in unique and interesting ways. Eleanor Roosevelt worked tirelessly for the young, the disadvantaged, and minorities. "Lady Bird" Johnson waged a campaign to beautify the nation's highways. Barbara Bush crusaded against illiteracy. Hillary Clinton worked to improve health care for all Americans.

First Ladies also have delighted Americans with their ingenuity and style. Dolley Madison saved documents from a burning White House during the War of 1812. Helen Taft let a cow graze on the White House lawn to provide milk for the kitchen. Jacqueline Kennedy redecorated the White House and made it a living museum for the nation.

Hillary Rodham Clinton

Although it is not always obvious, the President's role as party leader influences much of what happens in the national government. When making treaties, appointing officials, suggesting legislation, or executing laws, the President tries to consider the goals and interests of the party—as well as the country. In return, members of the President's party—in all levels and branches of government—try to act in ways that will help the President.

Judicial Leader

The Constitution gives the President the power to appoint judges to the Supreme Court and other federal courts. This power is one of the most important that the President holds.

As you will discover in Chapter 12, the Supreme Court has a great deal of in-

---

Appointments   President Clinton nominated and the Senate confirmed the appointment of Ruth Bader Ginsburg to the Supreme Court.   *What is the role of Supreme Court justices?*

fluence. It has final authority to determine whether a law is acceptable under the Constitution. Through this power to interpret the law and the Constitution, it can greatly affect life in America. Most Presidents try to appoint Supreme Court justices whose point of view is similar to their own. President Ronald Reagan, for example, appointed two Supreme Court justices—Antonin Scalia and Anthony Kennedy—who shared his views on civil rights, religion, and family values.

Once appointed, a Supreme Court justice usually holds that position for life. Therefore, by appointing new justices to the Supreme Court, Presidents can continue to influence the country long after they have left office.

The President also plays another, somewhat smaller, role in the judicial system. The Constitution gives the President the power to help an individual convicted of breaking federal laws. The President may grant a **pardon** to someone—that is, issue a declaration of forgiveness and freedom from punishment. The President may issue a **reprieve,** an order to delay a person's punishment until a higher court can rule on the case. If a large number of people have violated a federal law, the President also has the power to grant amnesty. **Amnesty** is similar to a pardon, except that it applies to a group rather than an individual.

Chief of State

Americans, like citizens all over the world, want their government to have a human face. Congress and the Supreme Court are groups with no distinct personality. The President, however, is an individual with familiar ways of speaking and acting. Unlike members of Congress,

Chief of State   President Clinton and all the living former Presidents of the United States attended the funeral of Richard Nixon in 1994.   *What does the President represent as chief of state?*

the President represents people from all 50 states. For most Americans, therefore, the President is a symbol of the United States government.

People want to admire the President and the First Family. They like to feel that the President is special. When the President greets a hero or throws the first pitch at a baseball game, many Americans feel good about their country.

The President's role as chief of state is mostly symbolic. The President may demonstrate America's support of the arts by inviting musicians to perform at the White House. The President may express United States respect for another nation by attending the funeral of its leader.

The role of chief of state is often difficult to distinguish from the President's other roles. For example, when the President meets with leaders of other nations to discuss important matters, these occasions usually involve speeches and ceremonies in which the President acts as chief of state. When the discussions turn to the business at hand, however, the President once again assumes the role of chief diplomat or Chief Executive.

How to Use Primary Sources

Much of what we know as history is really historians' interpretations of past events. How accurately these events are portrayed depends upon how much information historians have and on the quality of that information.

Types of Sources

Accounts of events or descriptions of conditions made by participants and on-the-scene observers are called primary sources. They include people's diaries, journals, public records, and other personal and public documents.

Library research

Sources of information such as newspaper editorials and biographies are called secondary sources. They are not the accounts of eyewitnesses, but they are based on those primary sources. Historians use both primary and secondary sources to reconstruct the past.

A Secondary Source

The following is a brief account of a historical event.

In 1928 the Republican national convention chose Herbert Hoover as its candidate for President. The convention chairman told Hoover that the nation was indebted to him for the services he had performed. After World War I, Hoover administered relief programs that helped Europe recover from the war. He also served as secretary of commerce under Presidents Harding and Coolidge. Hoover won the election of 1928 and became the thirty-first President.

A Primary Source

The following is an excerpt from Hoover's letter of reply to the chairman.

"You convey too great a compliment when you say that I have earned the right to the presidential nomination. No man can establish such an obligation. . . . My country owes me no debt. It gave me schooling, independence of action, opportunity for service and honor.

My whole life has taught me what America means. I am indebted to my country beyond any human power to repay. . . . It has called me into the cabinets of two Presidents. By these experiences I have observed the burdens and responsibilities of the greatest office in the world."

CITIZENSHIP IN ACTION

1 What reasons did Hoover give for not accepting the chairman's compliment?

2 Why are primary sources so important to historians?

The Executive Office

FOCUS

TERMS TO KNOW
administration, domestic

OBJECTIVES

■ Identify and describe the basic functions of the three most important offices within **the Executive Office of the President.**

■ Explain the difference between the EOP and **the executive departments.**

The executive branch is organized like a pyramid. The President, as Chief Executive, is at the very top of the pyramid. Directly below the President are a number of powerful officials, usually hand-picked by the President. Below these are many levels of lesser officials and managers. At the bottom of the pyramid are hundreds of thousands of people, from messengers to security guards to lawyers, who carry out the day-to-day work of the executive branch.

In general, the people at the top of the pyramid are the ones who set goals and make important decisions. Because the President or the President's closest advisers appoint them, they tend to be replaced every time a new President is elected. This group is usually referred to as the President's **administration.**

The Executive Office of the President

President Franklin D. Roosevelt created the Executive Office of the President (the EOP) in 1939. The people in the EOP are responsible for providing advice and helping Presidents do their job. Over the years, Presidents have changed the organization of the EOP according to their needs. The most important of the EOP offices are the White House Office, the Office of Management and Budget, and the National Security Council.

The White House Office

The core of the Executive Office of the President is the White House Office, which consists of the President's closest advisers and personal staff. Only the highest government officials get to meet with the President personally. Others must deal with the President's assistants in the White House Office.

The most powerful official in the White House Office is the chief of staff.

Executive Office   Top administration officials and advisers meet to discuss current issues.   *Who is the most powerful official in the White House Office?*

Budget Director Alice Rivlin heads the Office of Management and Budget. *What is the function of this office?*

The chief of staff decides who gets to see the President and which matters are important enough to be brought to the President's attention. It is often said that the chief of staff, rather than the President, really runs the White House.

Another member of the White House Office, the President's press secretary, is often in the public eye. The press secretary provides reporters with news about, and statements from, the President. Most of the President's other assistants do their work behind the scenes. Among them are speechwriters, clerical staff, and experts in many fields who advise the President.

Office of Management and Budget

Earlier in this chapter, you learned that the President submits a proposed budget to Congress each year. Preparing this budget is the responsibility of the Office of Management and Budget, or OMB. To prepare a realistic budget, the OMB must gather many statistics about the country's economy.

The budget director, the head of the OMB, meets often with the President. Together, they decide how much money should be allotted to each government program and where that money should come from. The result of their work is presented in the proposed budget that is given to Congress. This budget is the clearest statement of the administration's plans and goals for the coming year.

The National Security Council

Matters affecting the safety and security of the United States are among the most urgent a President must deal with. Faced with a possible threat from a hostile country, the President must make life-and-death decisions in a matter of hours or even minutes. The National Security Council helps the President make such decisions. Its members include the Vice President, the secretary of state, and the secretary of defense.

The National Security Council also supervises the Central Intelligence Agency (CIA). The CIA is responsible for gathering information about other governments. To do so, it uses undercover agents, informants, spy satellites, and other techniques.

Other Offices Within the EOP

The Council of Economic Advisers helps the President make important decisions about domestic policy. **Domestic** refers to matters affecting only the United States. The council advises the President about the nation's economy and helps the President make decisions about taxes, inflation, and foreign trade.

The other offices within the EOP are the Council on Environmental Quality, the Office of Science and Technology Policy, the Office of Administration, the

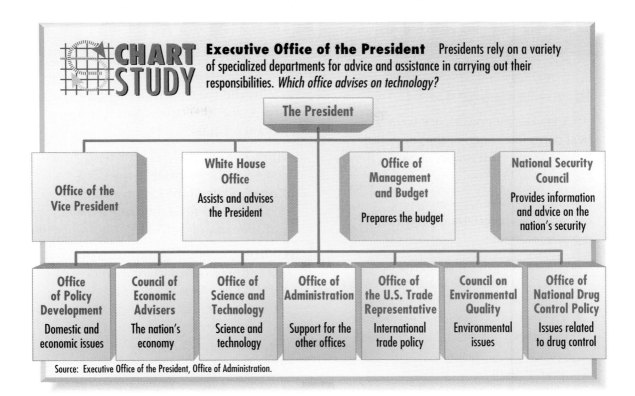

CHART STUDY **Executive Office of the President** Presidents rely on a variety of specialized departments for advice and assistance in carrying out their responsibilities. *Which office advises on technology?*

The President

Office of the Vice President

White House Office
Assists and advises the President

Office of Management and Budget
Prepares the budget

National Security Council
Provides information and advice on the nation's security

Office of Policy Development
Domestic and economic issues

Council of Economic Advisers
The nation's economy

Office of Science and Technology
Science and technology

Office of Administration
Support for the other offices

Office of the U.S. Trade Representative
International trade policy

Council on Environmental Quality
Environmental issues

Office of National Drug Control Policy
Issues related to drug control

Source: Executive Office of the President, Office of Administration.

Office of the United States Trade Representative, and the Office of National Drug Control Policy. Together, the offices of the EOP allow the President to make careful and informed decisions about our country's future.

The Executive Departments

The EOP is only a small part of the President's administration. Many more people work in the 14 executive departments. These departments can be distinguished from the EOP by the kind of work they do. The EOP exists to serve and advise the President. The executive departments, on the other hand, play a direct role in governing the country. The officials in these departments use the power the President gives them to make and enforce regulations. The heads of the executive departments make up the President's cabinet. The executive departments and the cabinet will be discussed at length in the next chapter.

★ **SECTION 4 REVIEW** ★

UNDERSTANDING VOCABULARY
Define administration, domestic.

REVIEWING OBJECTIVES
1 What are the three most important offices within the Executive Office of the President, and what are their functions?

2 What is the difference between the EOP and the executive departments?

Identifying Key Terms

Choose the vocabulary term that best completes each of the sentences below. Write your answers on a separate sheet of paper.

bureaucracy   executive order
ambassador   executive agreement
reprieve   amnesty

1. After her appointment, the new _____ to Italy was congratulated by the press.
2. The executive branch of government includes a large _____ that deals with the day-to-day work of government.
3. During wartime, a President may need to issue an _____ to see that a policy is carried out quickly.
4. President Reagan granted the illegal aliens _____ so they would not be prosecuted for their illegal status.
5. The convicted man's punishment was delayed when he was granted a(n) _____.
6. Senate approval was not required for the _____ made between the President and the leader of the People's Republic of China.

Reviewing the Main Ideas

SECTION 1
1. Why were Presidents not elected for more than two terms before 1940?
2. What was the Presidential Succession Act of 1947?

SECTION 2
3. What is the role of the federal bureaucracy?

4. Why did the Constitution place limits on the President's power to appoint officials?

SECTION 3
5. What is the purpose of the President's State of the Union address?
6. Why is the President's role as chief of state important?

SECTION 4
7. Identify two important members of the White House Office and describe their responsibilities.
8. What is the responsibility of the Central Intelligence Agency?

Critical Thinking

SECTION 1
1. **Evaluating Information** Should a President be allowed to serve more than two terms? Why or why not?

SECTION 2
2. **Developing a Point of View** Do you think there should be more limits on the President's power? Explain why or why not.

SECTION 3
3. **Putting Ideas Together** In Great Britain the roles of chief executive and chief of state are played by two different people. Do you think this system would work in the United States? Why or why not?

SECTION 4
4. **Analyzing Information** Why do you think an EOP was not needed before 1939? How did previous Presidents manage without this office?

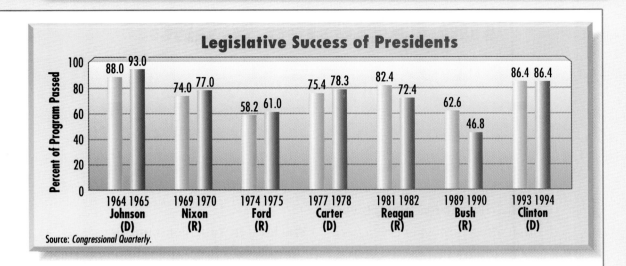

Legislative Success of Presidents

Percent of Program Passed

Year	President	Party	Value
1964	Johnson	(D)	88.0
1965	Johnson	(D)	93.0
1969	Nixon	(R)	74.0
1970	Nixon	(R)	77.0
1974	Ford	(R)	58.2
1975	Ford	(R)	61.0
1977	Carter	(D)	75.4
1978	Carter	(D)	78.3
1981	Reagan	(R)	82.4
1982	Reagan	(R)	72.4
1989	Bush	(R)	62.6
1990	Bush	(R)	46.8
1993	Clinton	(D)	86.4
1994	Clinton	(D)	86.4

Source: *Congressional Quarterly.*

Reinforcing Citizenship Skills

Choose a recent or historical event for which you will be able to locate primary and secondary sources of information. Compare the primary source with one secondary source. Prepare a report for the class in which you describe the event and compare the information in the primary and secondary sources.

Technology Activity

Using E-Mail

Search the Internet for the President's e-mail address. You might want to use the following key words to focus your search: **White House, president, e-mail address.** Then review your civics journal on presidential actions or policies. Decide how one of these policies might affect you as a citizen. Then consider what you would have done. Write and send electronic mail to the President. Clearly explain your feelings about any recent actions and suggest what you would have done.

Analyzing Visuals

Successful passage of bills requires Congress and the President to work together. Study the graph above. Then answer the questions.

1. What President had the worst record?
2. Overall, to what political party did most successful Presidents belong?

Cooperative Learning

With a partner, select a President you admire. Prepare a short biography. Then one partner will present your biography to the class; the other will read an excerpt from the President's speeches.

Focusing on Your Community

Ask various people in your community how they feel about the current President's performance. Limit your questions to one issue, such as foreign policy. Report your findings to the class.

CHAPTER 11

The Executive Branch

CIVIC PARTICIPATION

The executive branch of the federal government has far-reaching powers that affect almost every aspect of our lives. Its departments and agencies set standards for our food, monitor the quality of our air, and print the money we use. Find out which federal departments or agencies have offices in your area. Visit or call some of these offices to learn what services they provide for your community.

Working in Your Community

Ask your neighbors about their experiences with federal agencies. Find out whether they were successful in obtaining the information or assistance requested or were frustrated by bureaucracy and red tape. ■

Your Civics Journal

As you study this chapter, record the major issues in the news in your civics journal. Next to each entry, indicate what departments, agencies, or commissions in the federal government would most likely be involved in each issue.

The Executive Departments

The executive departments are among the most important parts of the executive branch. With huge staffs and multibillion dollar budgets, they carry out much of the work of the executive branch.

Each of these departments is responsible for a certain area of government. The head, or "secretary," of each executive department is a member of the President's cabinet. As cabinet members, the secretaries advise the President on issues related to their particular department. As department heads, the secretaries often make policy decisions of far-reaching effect.

Development of the Cabinet

Although the Constitution mentions neither a cabinet nor executive departments, it was clear from the start that the President would need assistance to carry out the presidential duties. Right after President Washington took office, he asked Congress to provide funding for three executive departments. These were the Department of State, the Department of the Treasury, and the Department of War. Over the years, Presidents have continued to add departments to the executive branch. The most recent addition is the Department of Veterans Affairs, which was formed in 1989. Today there are 14 executive departments. (See the chart on page 259.)

As the number of departments has grown, the size of the President's cabinet has increased as well. In addition to the department heads, most cabinets now in-

President's Cabinet President Clinton meets regularly with the members of his cabinet. *What powers do members of the President's cabinet possess?*

CHART STUDY

Executive Departments The heads of the 14 executive departments are members of the cabinet. *Which department manages public lands?*

Department of State (1789)
Plans and carries out the nation's foreign policy

Department of the Treasury (1789)
Collects, borrows, spends, and prints money

Department of Defense (1949)
Manages the armed forces

Department of Justice (1870)
Has responsibility for all aspects of law enforcement

Department of the Interior (1849)
Manages and protects the nation's public lands and natural resources

Department of Agriculture (1889)
Assists farmers and consumers of farm products

Department of Commerce (1903)
Supervises trade, promotes United States tourism and business

Department of Labor (1913)
Is concerned with the working conditions and wages of United States workers

Department of Health and Human Services (1953)
Works for the health and well-being of all Americans

Department of Housing and Urban Development (1965)
Deals with the special needs and problems of cities

Department of Transportation (1966)
Manages the nation's highways, railroads, airlines, and sea traffic

Department of Energy (1977)
Directs an overall energy plan for the nation

Department of Education (1979)
Provides advice and funding for schools

Department of Veterans Affairs (1989)
Directs services for veterans

clude the Vice President and other important government officials. For example, President Clinton included the United States representative to the United Nations, the heads of several executive agencies, his chief of staff and press secretary, and various members of the Executive Office of the President in cabinet meetings.

The President chooses the heads of the 14 executive departments, but the Senate must approve them. Since the time of Washington, these cabinet members have been called secretaries. The head of the Labor Department, for example, is the secretary of labor. The only exception is the head of the Justice Department, who is the attorney general.

Although the secretaries have great power as leaders of their departments, they have virtually no power as members of the cabinet. The President is not required to accept the cabinet's advice on issues. Some Presidents, such as Franklin Roosevelt, relied heavily on advisers outside the cabinet, but the cabinet has played an influential role in the administration of many Presidents.

Secretary of State Warren Christopher and Hosni Mubarak of Egypt
The secretary of state helps the President plan foreign policy. *What is the purpose of American consulates?*

Three of the most important cabinet departments are the original three executive departments: the departments of State, Treasury, and Defense. (The Department of War became part of the Department of Defense in 1949.)

Department of State

One of the responsibilities of the President is to create a **foreign policy,** a plan for dealing with other nations. The Department of State, or State Department, is the executive department that helps the President with this responsibility.

As a member of the cabinet, the secretary of state helps the President plan foreign policy. The Department of State is then responsible for carrying out this foreign policy and for managing United States relationships with other countries. To help in this task, the State Department employs many experts in foreign affairs. These experts gather information and

help the President understand events and issues in different parts of the world.

The State Department also sets up American government offices, known as **embassies,** in foreign nations. An ambassador, an official representative of the United States government, runs each embassy. These ambassadors and their staffs handle the details of foreign relations with a particular country. From time to time, the secretary of state also meets with foreign leaders to discuss matters of common interest.

Another function of the State Department is to protect the rights of Americans working or traveling abroad. In about 170 different locations around the world, the State Department has set up offices called **consulates** to help Americans in various countries. An official called a **consul** heads each of the consulates. The consulates also work to improve American business opportunities and business interests in foreign countries.

The State Department is also responsible for issuing passports to American travelers. A **passport** is an official document that identifies a traveler as an American citizen. When a citizen of a foreign country visits the United States, the State Department issues a **visa**—a permit allowing the person to remain here for a certain amount of time.

Department of the Treasury

In 1996 the budget of the United States government was about $1.6 trillion. The task of handling the nation's money belongs to the Department of the Treasury. It is responsible for collecting, borrowing, and spending the money that the nation requires. The head of the de-

Careers

Government Office Worker

The government is the largest employer in the United States. Most government employees work in offices and do the same kind of work as people in other businesses.

Responsibilities

Employees who keep records up-to-date and in the right place are called file clerks. File clerks classify, store, update, and get information for other workers. They also review files from time to time and remove information that is no longer needed. File clerks handle paper files in folders, mechanized files that rotate, micro- film files, and computer disk files.

Government clerk

Opportunities

File clerks work at all levels of government, from the White House to a mayor's office. Because the job of file clerk does not require much work experience, some people become file clerks to get into government service.

Training

Government file clerks must have a high school diploma and pass a civil service test. If you want to advance to other office jobs, however, you should learn as many office skills as possible.

School TO WORK

Obtain a sample local, state, or federal civil service exam from the appropriate government agency. Use the test and information from the agency to prepare a written report on how to qualify for a specific civil service position.

---

partment, the secretary of the treasury, is an important financial adviser to the President.

The Treasury Department has several divisions that carry out specific jobs. For example, the Internal Revenue Service (IRS) collects income taxes from individuals and businesses. The United States Customs Service collects taxes on items that are brought into the United States from other countries. The Bureau of the Mint designs and produces United States coins, and the Bureau of Engraving and Printing prints paper money.

Some divisions of the Treasury Department perform tasks that are not directly related to money. The Secret Service, for example, was originally set up to find counterfeiters—people who print imitation money and try to pass it off as real. Although the Secret Service still does this job, it now has a more important one—to protect the President and the Vice President and their families.

Armed Forces in Haiti   The Department of Defense is responsible for carrying out the orders of the commander in chief.   *Who are the Joint Chiefs of Staff?*

Department of Defense

Originally, two executive departments, the Department of War and the Department of the Navy, managed the armed forces of the United States. These were combined into the National Military Establishment, which became the Department of Defense in 1949. The Department of Defense now oversees the army, the navy (including the marine corps), and the air force. It is the largest department in the executive branch, with about 825,000 civilian employees and an annual budget of about $270 billion.

Each armed service has its own division within the Department of Defense. A secretary of the army, a secretary of the navy, and a secretary of the air force head these subdepartments, but none is a member of the cabinet.

The Department of Defense carries out most of the President's duties as commander in chief. Civilians, however, hold most of the department's power. By law, the secretaries of the army, navy, and air force, as well as the secretary of defense, may not be military officers.

Military officers may, however, serve as advisers. The President and the secretary of defense consult the Joint Chiefs of Staff on all important military decisions. The Joint Chiefs are made up of the highest-ranking officers from each of the armed services.

★ SECTION 1 REVIEW ★

UNDERSTANDING VOCABULARY
Define foreign policy, embassy, consulate, consul, passport, visa.

REVIEWING OBJECTIVES

1 How did the cabinet develop?

2 What are the responsibilities of the Department of State?

3 What are five divisions within the Department of the Treasury, and what are their responsibilities?

4 What is the basic organization of the Department of Defense?

Exploring ISSUES

The Right to Privacy

A 14-year-old student was seen smoking in the girls' lounge of a New Jersey high school. One of the school's assistant principals searched her purse and found cigarettes—and also marijuana. The student was suspended from school and charged in juvenile court.

The Issue

Did the assistant principal have a right to search the student's purse? Should the student have been protected by the Fourth Amendment prohibition against unreasonable searches and seizures?

The Case

In 1985 the United States Supreme Court ruled in favor of the school. It found that the assistant principal had reasonable grounds to suspect that the student was violating school rules or the law. This case—*New Jersey* v. *T.L.O.*—is one of the many cases involving the right to privacy that come before the courts each year.

Impact

Finding a balance between the right of privacy and the protection of society can be difficult. Several questions about privacy have arisen in recent years. These include:

▼ Can job applicants be required to take lie detector tests?

▼ Can a company sell the confidential information in its computerized personnel files to another company?

Students at their lockers

▼ Can a company fire a person for dating an employee of a rival company?

Most of these questions have not yet been resolved. Congress, however, has already taken steps to limit the use of lie detector tests. Labor unions are also bringing suits and seeking contract clauses to protect workers from unjustified invasions of their privacy in the workplace. The courts have also ruled that testing workers for drug use is lawful in some circumstances.

DEVELOPING A POINT OF VIEW

1 What was the Supreme Court's ruling in *New Jersey* v. *T.L.O.?*

2 Is it fair for the government to force train crews to submit to drug tests after an accident? Why or why not?

Other Executive Departments

The original three executive departments were established in 1789. Over the next 200 years, as the nation grew, additional executive departments were added to help carry out the work of the government. Today there are a total of 14 executive departments. We will look briefly at each of these additional departments, in the order in which they were established.

Departments Created in the Nineteenth Century

During the nineteenth century, three executive departments were established to meet the needs of a growing nation.

Department of Justice

The Department of Justice was not established until 1870, after the Department of the Interior. Nevertheless, it is usually considered the fourth-oldest department because the attorney general, who heads the department, was the fourth member of George Washington's original cabinet.

The attorney general was originally the nation's lawyer and represented the United States government in court. The Justice Department still fulfills this function, but the attorney general almost never appears in court personally.

Over the years, the duties of the Justice Department have expanded to in-

Law Enforcement   Attorney General Janet Reno answers reporters' questions at a press conference.   *Which part of the Department of Justice investigates most federal crimes?*

Conservation   Park rangers at Mammoth Cave National Park in Kentucky help manage and conserve public lands.   *What is the role of the Fish and Wildlife Service?*

clude a wide range of law enforcement activities. Whenever a federal law is broken, the Justice Department is responsible for investigating the crime, tracking down the lawbreakers, putting them on trial, and punishing them if they are found guilty.

The Federal Bureau of Investigation, or the FBI, one of the best-known divisions in the Justice Department, conducts investigations and arrests suspects. Those convicted of breaking federal laws are usually sent to federal prisons, which the Bureau of Prisons operates.

Another part of the Justice Department is the Immigration and Naturalization Service, or INS. The INS is responsible for enforcing the nation's immigration laws.

The Department of the Interior

As pioneers moved westward in the mid-1800s, vast areas of land were added to the United States. The Department of the Interior was established in 1849 to manage that land. Today the Interior Department is primarily responsible for the management and **conservation,** or protection, of the nation's public lands and natural resources.

The best-known part of the Interior Department is the National Park Service, which oversees nearly 80 million acres of land in national parks across the country. The Interior Department also includes the Fish and Wildlife Service, which maintains wildlife refuges and protects endangered animals.

The Bureau of Indian Affairs, another division of the Interior Department, manages land set aside for the use of Native Americans. These areas, called reservations, are home to more than 800,000 people.

Department of Agriculture

The Department of Agriculture, or USDA, became an executive department in 1889. Its job is to help both farmers and the consumers of farm products.

Food Safety and Inspection Service
USDA inspectors help maintain the quality and safety of meat and poultry. *What is the purpose of the Agricultural Research Service?*

Divisions of the USDA that benefit farmers include the Agricultural Research Service, which develops new crops and better ways to grow them, and the Farmers' Home Administration, which lends money to farmers who want to expand their farms.

One agency within the USDA that benefits consumers is the Food Safety and Inspection Service, which helps maintain the quality and safety of meat and poultry. Another is the Food and Nutrition Service, which distributes food stamps to millions of needy families.

Like the Interior Department, the Agriculture Department is also concerned with conservation. The USDA's Soil Conservation Service protects the rich soil of American farms, and its Forest Service maintains nearly 200 million acres of national forests.

Departments Created in the Early 1900s

The early 1900s were a time of great economic and social change. Two important issues were the growth of business and the rights of workers. Two new executive departments were established to help deal with these issues.

Department of Commerce

The Department of Commerce was established in 1903 to encourage the growth of American business. It supervises international trade, promotes tourism and business, and collects information about the country's economic well-being.

The Commerce Department also offers a number of services that are less directly related to commerce. The Bureau of the Census, which you learned about in Chapter 1, is part of the Commerce Department. So is the National Patent and Trademark Office, which keeps official records of inventions and product names. The National Institute of Standards and Technology, another part of the Commerce Department, sets standards for units of measurement such as inches, pounds, and quarts. These are the official measures against which all others are compared.

The Commerce Department also oversees the National Oceanic and Atmospheric Administration (NOAA), which conducts ocean research and keeps track of atmospheric conditions. Our daily weather forecasts usually come from the National Weather Service, part of the NOAA. Warnings about hurricanes, floods, and other potentially destructive natural events come from this organization.

Department of Labor

In the late 1800s, labor unions pressured the federal government to pass laws against unfair labor practices. The Department of Labor was established in 1913 to enforce those laws.

One of the most important parts of the Department of Labor is the Occupational Safety and Health Administration (OSHA). OSHA sets health and safety standards that employers must meet to protect their workers from physical harm. The Department of Labor also includes the Unemployment Insurance Service, which provides financial aid to workers who have been forced to leave their jobs.

The Bureau of Labor Statistics (BLS), another division of the Department of Labor, collects information about the job market and working conditions. This information is available to the public and is particularly useful to people planning their careers.

Departments Created Since 1950

Since 1950, six executive departments have been created, almost doubling the size of the President's cabinet. These departments deal with issues that are increasingly important to many Americans.

Department of Health and Human Services

In 1953 President Dwight D. Eisenhower established the Department of Health, Education, and Welfare to work for the health and well-being of Americans. It was renamed the Department of Health and Human Services in 1979,

when the Department of Education was made a separate department.

The Department of Health and Human Services (HHS) is concerned with the welfare of Americans. Several of its divisions, including the Social Security Administration and the Family Support Administration, provide financial support for people who might otherwise live in poverty.

Most HHS programs, however, benefit all Americans. The Public Health Service, for example, works to keep Americans free from illness. It includes the Centers for Disease Control and Prevention, which conducts research into prevention and cures for diseases, and the National Institutes of Health, which supports other health-related research.

Department of Health and Human Services The Centers for Disease Control and Prevention protects the nation's health. *Which group oversees the safety of all foods, drugs, and cosmetics?*

Department of Transportation

The Department of Transportation (DOT) was formed in 1966 to manage the country's highways, railroads, airlines, and sea traffic. It also promotes transportation safety. Among its different agencies, the National Highway Traffic Safety Administration sets standards for the safety of automobiles, and the Federal Aviation Administration oversees the airline industry. One of the best-known parts of the DOT is the United States Coast Guard, which undertakes search and rescue operations at sea and also serves as an ocean-based police force.

Department of Energy

In 1973 America was hit by its first "energy crisis." The price of gasoline and home heating oil skyrocketed, and these widely used fuels were often in short supply. Americans wondered whether they would have to live with permanent shortages of energy. In 1977 President Jimmy Carter created the Department of Energy to work out and direct an overall energy policy for the nation. The department regulates the development and use of United States oil and gas resources. It also conducts research into ways to use these fuels more efficiently and to develop other sources of energy, such as nuclear energy and solar energy. The Department of Energy also regulates the nation's nuclear power industry.

Department of Education

In the mid-1970s critics charged that the United States was falling behind in education. Although the nation's goal was to provide free education for everyone, the number of people who could not read was increasing. Moreover, students

Improving Neighborhoods   The Department of Housing and Urban Development provides federal grants to state and local governments.   *What kinds of projects are eligible?*

The Food and Drug Administration (FDA), which oversees the safety of all foods, drugs, and cosmetics sold in the United States, is also part of HHS.

Department of Housing and Urban Development

In 1965 President Lyndon Johnson established the Department of Housing and Urban Development, or HUD, to deal with the special problems of cities. HUD operates programs that distribute federal grants to state and local governments. These grants help pay for such projects as rebuilding slums, improving neighborhoods, and building low-income housing. HUD also works with cities and towns to plan for growth.

Special Needs The Department of Veterans Affairs is concerned with the special interests and needs of veterans. *When was this executive department created?*

helps schools meet the special needs of students who are disadvantaged or have disabilities.

Department of Veterans Affairs

About 27 million living Americans have served in the armed forces. Many of these people receive special services from the government, such as inexpensive life insurance and financial aid for education. Some also have special needs, such as medical care for injuries or disabilities received during military service.

For many years, a government agency called the Veterans Administration met these needs. In 1989, however, the Veterans Administration became an executive department. It received a new name, the Department of Veterans Affairs, and the head of the department became a member of the cabinet.

in Europe and Asia were performing better than American students in science and mathematics.

Many people felt that the system of education in the United States had to be improved. To help meet this goal, President Carter set up the Department of Education in 1979. (Until that time, education had been part of the Department of Health, Education, and Welfare.)

Although responsibility for education lies primarily with the states and with local communities, the Department of Education offers advice and assistance whenever possible. It distributes federal money to states and school districts to help fund such programs as bilingual education, health and drug education, and vocational training. The department also

★ SECTION 2 REVIEW ★

UNDERSTANDING VOCABULARY
Define conservation.

REVIEWING OBJECTIVES

1 What three executive departments were created in the nineteenth century, and what are their responsibilities?

2 What are the two executive departments created in the early twentieth century, and what are their responsibilities?

3 What are the responsibilities of the six executive departments created since 1950?

How to Read an Organization Chart

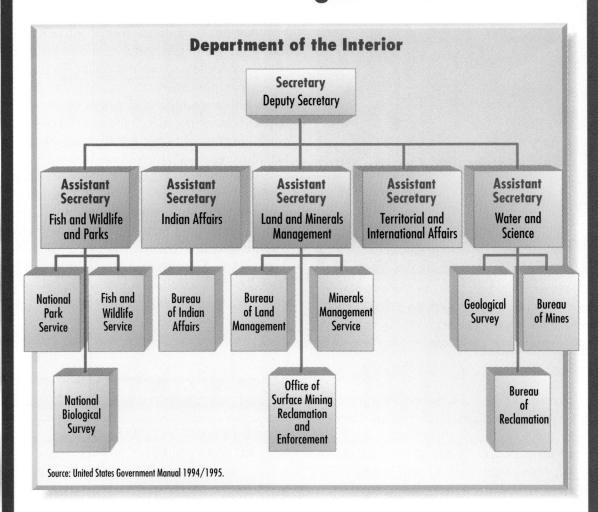

Department of the Interior

Secretary
Deputy Secretary

Assistant Secretary — Fish and Wildlife and Parks
Assistant Secretary — Indian Affairs
Assistant Secretary — Land and Minerals Management
Assistant Secretary — Territorial and International Affairs
Assistant Secretary — Water and Science

National Park Service
Fish and Wildlife Service
Bureau of Indian Affairs
Bureau of Land Management
Minerals Management Service
Geological Survey
Bureau of Mines

National Biological Survey
Office of Surface Mining Reclamation and Enforcement
Bureau of Reclamation

Source: United States Government Manual 1994/1995.

An organization chart is a diagram that shows the relationship of different offices or divisions within an organization. It shows the lines of command and communication. It helps you understand the structure of the whole organization as well as the relationship of its various parts.

The organization chart above shows the basic structure of the Department of the Interior. Use the information on the chart to answer the questions that follow.

CITIZENSHIP IN ACTION

1 What role does the deputy secretary of the interior play in the organization of the department?

2 Who is responsible for the National Park Service?

Independent Agencies

FOCUS

TERMS TO KNOW

executive agency, regulatory commission, government corporation

OBJECTIVES

- Identify the basic responsibility of **executive agencies.**

- Explain the purpose of **regulatory commissions.**

- Compare **government corporations** with private corporations.

L arge as they are, the executive departments can handle only a small part of the executive branch's responsibilities. Other organizations within the executive branch, known as independent agencies, take care of the rest. Such agencies may be created by the President, and funded by Congress, whenever a need for a certain type of work arises.

As a result, today's government includes hundreds of independent federal agencies. Their responsibilities are not always clearly defined, and their work may sometimes overlap. In general, however, they can be divided into three types: executive agencies, regulatory commissions, and government corporations.

Executive Agencies

An **executive agency** is an independent agency responsible for dealing with certain specialized areas of government. The President chooses and the Senate approves the heads, or administrators, of the executive agencies.

The National Aeronautics and Space Administration (NASA) is an executive agency that we hear about every time a space shuttle is launched. NASA has

CHART STUDY

Executive Agencies These agencies handle specialized areas of government. *What is the role of the Commission on Civil Rights?*

Farm Credit Administration (FCA)—1933
Supervises loans to farmers by federal banks

Central Intelligence Agency (CIA)—1947
Gathers political and military information on foreign nations

General Services Administration (GSA)—1949
Maintains federal office buildings and property

National Science Foundation (NSF)—1950
Promotes scientific research

Small Business Administration (SBA)—1953
Protects the interests of small businesses

Commission on Civil Rights—1957
Gathers and evaluates information on discrimination

National Aeronautics and Space Administration (NASA)—1958
Develops and administers the space program

National Foundation on the Arts and the Humanities—1965
Provides grants for the promotion of the arts

Environmental Protection Agency (EPA)—1970
Protects and enhances the environment

Action—1971
Administers programs of voluntary service including the Peace Corps

Regulatory Commissions These agencies control certain types of businesses and industries. *Which are concerned with workers' rights?*

Federal Reserve System
Establishes general monetary policies

Federal Trade Commission (FTC)
Prevents monopolies and unfair business practices

Securities and Exchange Commission (SEC)
Regulates the stock market

Federal Communications Commission (FCC)
Regulates radio and television

National Labor Relations Board (NLRB)
Protects the rights of employees

Equal Employment Opportunity Commission (EEOC)
Works to eliminate job discrimination

Consumer Product Safety Commission (CPSC)
Develops standards of safety for consumer goods

The FCC

For example, the Federal Communications Commission, or FCC, regulates the television, cable TV, radio, and telephone industries. It exercises its executive power whenever Congress passes a law involving one of those industries. In 1970, for instance, when Congress banned cigarette commercials from television broadcasts, the FCC was responsible for enforcing the law.

More often, however, the FCC exercises its legislative power. Congress has given the FCC the power to regulate radio and television transmissions. Using this power, the FCC has set aside certain frequencies for special uses. FCC decisions have the force of law. Anyone who transmits music over the police band, for example, can be charged with a crime.

The FCC also has a judicial function. For example, anyone who wants to own a television station must obtain a license. In exchange for this license, the owner must demonstrate that the TV station will be run in a way that will benefit the general public. If there are two or more applicants for a license to run a station, the competing sides must present evidence in support of their qualifications. The FCC then awards the license to one of the applicants.

Impartiality

To keep regulatory commissions impartial, Congress has been careful to protect them from political pressure. A board runs each commission and the President appoints and the Senate approves board members. The terms of office of these board members are long—in some cases, as long as 14 years—and the starting dates of the terms are staggered. Furthermore, Democrats and Republicans must

responsibility for the nation's space flights and research program. About 21,600 people work for NASA.

Regulatory Commissions

Regulatory commissions are independent agencies that protect the public by controlling certain types of businesses and industries. (See the chart on this page.) Each commission has executive, legislative, and judicial powers.

Delivering the Mail The U.S. Postal Service became a government corporation in 1970. *How do government corporations differ from executive departments and agencies?*

receive nearly equal representation on each commission's board.

Because of these safeguards, regulatory commissions tend to be impartial. Their decisions are made to benefit the public rather than to please the members of political parties or interest groups. Nevertheless, many Americans feel that regulatory commissions are a bad idea. They feel that Congress has placed too much power in the hands of too few people. Some people also feel that regulatory commissions make unnecessary rules.

Government Corporations

Many government agencies, especially those that provide services to the public, are set up as government corporations. A **government corporation** is similar to a private corporation, except that the government rather than individuals owns and operates it. The President,

with Senate approval, chooses a board of directors and a general manager to run each corporation.

Government corporations are supposed to be more flexible than regular government agencies. They are more likely to take risks and to find innovative solutions. However, all government corporations operate under instructions from Congress, and their flexibility varies considerably. Today the executive branch includes more than 50 government corporations. The best known of these is the U.S. Postal Service.

Originally an executive department called the Post Office Department, the Postal Service became a government corporation in 1970. As an executive department, the Post Office consistently lost money. Since becoming a corporation, the U.S. Postal Service (USPS) has done a better job of balancing its budget. In part this is because Congress passed legislation giving the USPS "the exclusive right, with certain limited exceptions, to carry letters for others." Only the Postal Service may deliver first-class mail.

★ **SECTION 3 REVIEW** ★

UNDERSTANDING VOCABULARY
Define executive agency, regulatory commission, government corporation.

REVIEWING OBJECTIVES

1 What is the basic responsibility of executive agencies?

2 What is the purpose of regulatory commissions?

3 How do government corporations differ from private corporations?

The Federal Bureaucracy

FOCUS

TERMS TO KNOW

red tape, spoils system, merit system, civil servant

OBJECTIVES

- Explain the **structure of the federal bureaucracy.**

- Describe the **development of the civil service system.**

- Identify and describe the two agencies responsible for employment in **the civil service today.**

For more than 200 years, Americans have watched the executive branch grow and expand. Today almost 3 million government employees assist the President.

The government has grown for several reasons. The most obvious is that the United States itself has grown. The nation's population is now nearly 60 times larger than it was in George Washington's time. More important, however, the federal government has involved itself in the lives of Americans in ways that the writers of the Constitution never imagined. In 1787 there were no telephones, radios, cars, planes, or satellites. There were also no food safety inspections, no programs to provide low-cost housing, no unemployment insurance policies, and no social security benefits, which we cannot imagine living without today. Each of these benefits requires regulation or administration by the federal government.

Structure of the Federal Bureaucracy

The federal bureaucracy is well known for its red tape. **Red tape** is a term that refers to inefficiency caused by too many rules and regulations. For example, even a simple task—such as making a correction on an income tax return—can involve speaking with several different federal employees and filling out dozens of forms.

Red Tape   The paperwork involved in dealing with the federal government can be overwhelming.   *What is the advantage of requiring strict procedures?*

Some of this red tape results from poor planning or bad management. Most of it, however, is a necessary part of the way a bureaucracy works. Each person in a bureaucracy has a specialized function and operates within a strict chain of command. Only certain people have decision-making power; most people are responsible only for carrying out specific duties. A great deal of paperwork is required to get the proper authorization at different stages of any task. This system may be time-consuming and annoying. It does, however, help ensure that cases are handled consistently. This way the bureaucracy treats everyone equally.

Very specific procedures are also necessary to keep decision making to a minimum. If each person in the bureaucracy made individual decisions, the result would be chaos.

Bureaucracies function best when the people who work in them are well trained and well qualified. Managers should be good at giving clear instructions, and those who carry out the instructions should be skilled at their work.

Development of the Civil Service System

Originally, the executive branch was small enough for Presidents to be able to choose most of their employees personally. Early Presidents tried to appoint the most qualified people to federal jobs. They also, however, tended to appoint members of their own party, who shared similar views.

Spoils System

When Andrew Jackson became President in 1829, party loyalty became even more important. Jackson openly gave out

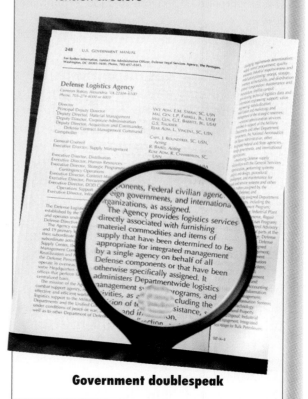

Civil Service   President James A. Garfield was assassinated by a disappointed office seeker who had hoped to find a job through the spoils system.   *What was the spoils system?*

federal jobs as rewards to people who had helped his campaign or done him favors in the past. It didn't matter whether these people were qualified for the jobs they were given. This practice of giving jobs as a reward for party loyalty is called the **spoils system.** The term comes from the saying "to the victor belong the spoils."

The spoils system continued for more than 50 years. During that time, the executive branch grew larger, and the number of incompetent federal workers increased as well. In addition to being unqualified, many government employees were also dishonest and took advantage of their power. As a result, Americans began to demand that something be done about changing the spoils system.

Merit System

After several unsuccessful attempts to end the spoils system, Congress passed the Pendleton Act (also called the Civil Service Act) in 1883. The Pendleton Act replaced the spoils system with a **merit system,** by which government jobs would be given to those most qualified.

The Pendleton Act divided government jobs into two categories, unclassified and classified. Jobs in the unclassified category could still be filled by appointment. Jobs in the classified category, however, would be given to the people who scored highest on tests relating to job skills. The Pendleton Act created an agency called the Civil Service Commission to give the tests and to award jobs to the highest scorers. The

Office of Personnel Management
This federal agency administers civil service tests and hires workers for government jobs. *Which agency deals with civil service promotions?*

name of the agency reflected the idea that government employees are **civil servants**—workers whose primary duty is to serve the government and its citizens.

The Hatch Act

Workers who got jobs through the civil service system were supposed to be promoted on the basis of their job performance. Many believed, however, that managers would tend to promote people who shared their political beliefs rather than people who were good workers. They also feared that government employees would be asked to help one party or another in an election. To meet these concerns, Congress passed the

Hatch Act in 1939. The act forbids any civil servant to work in a political campaign or to get involved in party politics.

The Civil Service Today

In 1978 two federal agencies replaced the Civil Service Commission. The first, the Office of Personnel Management, administers civil service tests and hires workers for government jobs. It also trains new workers and decides on the salary and benefits for each job.

The second agency, the Merit System Protection Board, deals with promotions within the civil service system. It makes sure that promotions are based entirely on merit. It also makes sure that no government worker is discriminated against for personal or political reasons.

The rise of the civil service system has not eliminated the red tape from the federal bureaucracy. It has, however, guaranteed that the executive branch, despite its large size, will work as efficiently as possible.

★ **SECTION 4 REVIEW** ★

UNDERSTANDING VOCABULARY
Define red tape, spoils system, merit system, civil servant.

REVIEWING OBJECTIVES
1 What is the basic structure of the federal bureaucracy?

2 How did the civil service system develop?

3 What two agencies are responsible for employment in the civil service today?

Identifying Key Terms

Choose the vocabulary term that best completes each of the sentences below. Write your answers on a separate sheet of paper.

embassy   regulatory commission
consulate   government corporation
spoils system   merit system

1. Under the _____, people were given government jobs without regard to their qualifications.
2. Government employees are promoted according to the _____.
3. The employees at the United States _____ in Taipei, Taiwan, worked to improve United States business interests in that city.
4. The U.S. Postal Service is an example of a(n) _____.
5. The _____ was responsible for controlling use of radio frequencies throughout the nation.
6. The _____ was run by the newly appointed ambassador.

Reviewing the Main Ideas

SECTION 1
1. Name three important divisions of the Department of the Treasury.
2. What positions make up the Joint Chiefs of Staff?

SECTION 2
3. Identify two important agencies within the Department of Health and Human Services.
4. Why was the Department of Energy created in 1977?

SECTION 3
5. What is an executive agency?
6. Why are regulatory commissions protected against political pressures?

SECTION 4
7. Why is red tape a necessary part of a bureaucracy?
8. How did the spoils system change the federal bureaucracy?

Critical Thinking

SECTION 1
1. **Determining a Point of View**   Do you think the Department of Defense should be under civilian control? Why or why not?

SECTION 2
2. **Evaluating Information**   Which of the executive departments do you think has the greatest effect on you and your family? Why?

SECTION 3
3. **Evaluating Information**   Government corporations, such as the U.S. Postal Service, are protected from certain types of competition. Do you think this is fair? Why or why not?

SECTION 4
4. **Determining Cause and Effect**   What effect does the civil service system have on the work of the federal bureaucracy?

Reinforcing Citizenship Skills

Find an almanac or other resource that gives information on the divisions of the Department of Health and Human Services. Then create an organization chart that shows the department and the relationship of its various parts. Share your chart with the class.

Cooperative Learning

With three other students, interview a local government official about the government bureaucracy in your community. Ask what he or she considers well-managed programs and why. Ask what methods he or she would recommend to improve the operation of government at the local level. Report your findings to the class.

Focusing on Your Community

Jobs within the government bureaucracy are found at every level of government. Research the different types of government jobs in your community. Find out how many people work for the local government. Find out how people apply for these jobs, what qualifications are necessary, and what the salaries are. Prepare a report to present to the class.

Technology Activity

Using the Internet

Search the Internet for information on one of the executive departments, agencies, or commissions of the federal government. You may want to use the name of the organization as the key words to focus your search. Use the information you find on the Internet to write a paragraph explaining current policies and responsibilities of the organization.

Analyzing Visuals

The second half of the twentieth century has seen many changes in the federal government. The following pictograph shows the number of federal civilian employees from 1935 to 1995. Study the graph and then answer the questions.

1. How many people were employed by the federal government in 1935? In 1995?
2. Why do you think there were so many federal employees in 1945?
3. Explain the increase in the number of people employed by the federal government between 1935 and 1995.
4. What do you think has happened to the numbers of civilian employees at the state and local levels?

Civilian Employees of the Federal Government, 1935–1995

| 1935 |
| 1945 |
| 1955 |
| 1965 |
| 1975 |
| 1985 |
| 1995 |

= 500,000 people

Source: U.S. Bureau of the Census.

CHAPTER 12

The Judicial Branch

CIVIC PARTICIPATION

The judicial system of the United States is one of the nation's most important institutions. Its function is to interpret the laws and to preserve and protect the rights the Constitution guarantees. As such, it plays a vital role in the system of checks and balances that protects our democracy. Look in your local library for information on the federal court system. Find out the location of the nearest federal district court and court of appeals and the names of the judges on these courts.

Working in Your Community

Using this information, prepare a file for your school library. Include the locations of the nearest federal courts, the names of their judges, and a summary of how the federal court system works. ■

Your Civics Journal

During the next week, look in newspapers or listen to news programs for stories about criminal arrests, lawsuits, or court cases. How do these stories illustrate the strengths and weaknesses of the judicial system? Write your ideas in your civics journal, including specific examples.

A federal courthouse ➤

The Federal Court System

FOCUS

TERMS TO KNOW

inferior court, criminal case, civil case, suit, jurisdiction, exclusive jurisdiction, concurrent jurisdiction

OBJECTIVES

■ Explain the difference between **criminal and civil cases.**

■ Identify five areas of **federal court jurisdiction.**

From 1781 to 1789, when the United States was governed by the Articles of Confederation, there was no national court system. Each state had its own laws and its own courts. There was no way to guarantee that people would receive equal justice in all the states.

To deal with this problem the writers of the Constitution provided for a federal judiciary. Article III of the Constitution established a national Supreme Court. It also gave Congress the power to establish other **inferior courts,** or courts of lower authority. This power was given to Congress as a way of checking the power of the judicial branch.

Over the years, Congress has added two types of lower courts to the federal judiciary system. In 1789 it passed the Judiciary Act, which created the federal district courts. Much later, in 1891, Congress created the appeals courts. The federal court system now has three levels—the district courts at the bottom, the appeals courts in the middle, and the Supreme Court at the top. You will learn what each of these courts does later in this chapter.

Criminal and Civil Cases

The United States really has two separate court systems—the state courts and the federal courts. The state courts hear the vast majority of legal disputes. Most **criminal cases**—cases in which juries decide whether people have committed crimes—are tried in state courts. The state courts also hear most **civil cases**—cases in which two sides disagree over some issue. In a civil case, one party, or person, involved sues or takes legal action against another party. The complaint

Civil Cases   Attorneys consult with the judge during a trial.   *In which type of court are most criminal cases tried?*

the first person makes to the court is called a **suit,** or lawsuit. A party in a lawsuit can be a person, a company or business, or a level of government. You will learn more about the state court system in Chapter 13.

Federal Court Jurisdiction

Article III of the Constitution gives the federal courts **jurisdiction**—the authority to hear and decide a case—only in certain specific areas. These are cases that involve one of the following:

1. *The Constitution.* For example, if a person feels that a constitutional right such as freedom of speech has been violated, that person has a right to be heard in a federal court.

2. *Federal laws.* The federal courts try people accused of federal crimes such as tax evasion, kidnapping, and bank robbery. Federal courts also hear civil cases that involve federal laws.

3. *Admiralty and maritime laws.* These concern crimes and accidents that happen on the high seas or are related to the seas. One recent case involved a dispute over rights to the riches recovered from a sunken ship 160 miles off the coast of South Carolina.

4. *Disputes in which the United States government is involved.* The government, for example, could take a company to court for failing to live up to a contract to deliver supplies to a government department. Individuals or companies can also take the government to court. For example, if a United States Army van struck your car or the Department of the Interior

Haitian Refugees   A Coast Guard patrol rescues people fleeing Haiti.   *In which type of court do maritime law cases come to trial?*

Jurisdiction The Constitution gives the federal courts authority to hear cases in certain specific areas. *What are two of these areas of federal court jurisdiction?*

failed to pay your company for equipment, you could sue the government.

5. *Controversies between states.* In any disagreement between states, the states can ask the federal courts to settle the matter.

6. *Controversies between citizens of different states.* For example, if a person in Maine cheats a person in Iowa, the case can be brought before a federal court. Federal law limits the jurisdiction of federal courts in these cases to suits involving $50,000 or more.

7. *Disputes involving foreign governments.* In any dispute between a foreign country and the United States government, an American company, or an American citizen, the case will be heard in a federal court.

8. *United States ambassadors, ministers, and consuls serving in foreign countries.* For example, if a diplomat assigned to the United States Embassy in Moscow is accused of breaking an American law, the case may be heard in the federal courts.

In most of these areas, the federal courts have **exclusive jurisdiction,** which means that only the federal courts may hear and decide cases. By giving the federal courts jurisdiction in these instances, the writers of the Constitution left all other matters to the state courts. In some circumstances, however, a case can be heard in either the state or federal courts. In these instances, the state and federal courts are said to share jurisdiction, or to have **concurrent jurisdiction.** For example, crimes that violate both state and federal laws may be tried in either the federal or state courts. Concurrent jurisdiction also occurs when an individual appeals a conviction on constitutional grounds. The conviction can be appealed through the state and federal courts up to the United States Supreme Court.

★ SECTION 1 REVIEW ★

UNDERSTANDING VOCABULARY
Define inferior court, criminal case, civil case, suit, jurisdiction, exclusive jurisdiction, concurrent jurisdiction.

REVIEWING OBJECTIVES

1 What is the difference between criminal and civil cases?

2 What are five areas in which the federal courts have jurisdiction?

The Lower Federal Courts

At the top of the federal court system is the Supreme Court. Then come the lower courts—the district courts and appeals courts.

District Courts

United States district courts make up the lowest level of the federal court system. **District courts** are the federal courts where trials are held and lawsuits are begun. Before a federal case can be filed and heard in an appeals court or the Supreme Court, it must be heard in a district court. For this reason, district courts are said to have **original jurisdiction,** or the authority to hear cases for the first time. In addition, district courts are the only federal courts in which jury trials are held.

The district courts are so named because each has jurisdiction or authority over a specific geographical area or district. Each state has at least one district court, and more populous states may have as many as three or four. There is also a district court in the District of Columbia and in some of the territories of the United States.

About 90 percent of the work of the federal courts takes place in district courts. They handle about 300,000 criminal and civil cases each year. Criminal cases can include mail fraud, income tax evasion, bank robbery, and treason. Civil cases include disputes involving labor relations, public lands, copyright and patent laws, and civil rights.

The Constitution clearly states where federal cases shall be tried. Article III says that "such Trial shall be held in the State where the said Crimes shall have been committed." This provision helps

Jury Trials   District courts are the only federal courts that hold jury trials.   *What kinds of criminal cases are tried in district courts?*

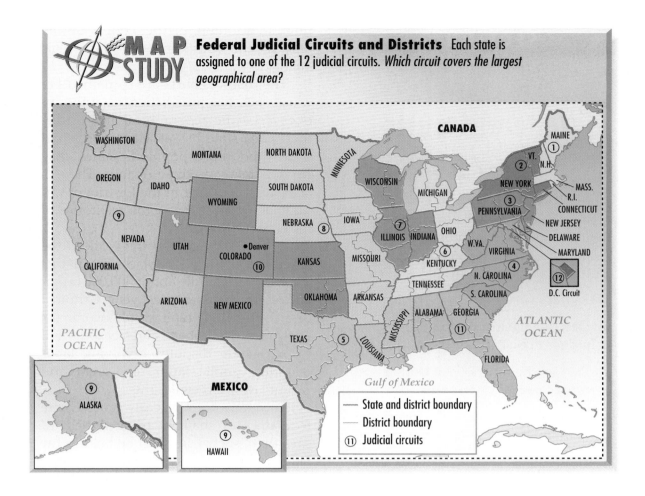

MAP STUDY

Federal Judicial Circuits and Districts Each state is assigned to one of the 12 judicial circuits. *Which circuit covers the largest geographical area?*

State and district boundary
District boundary
⑪ Judicial circuits

ensure that people accused of federal crimes can get a fair trial. The accused will be tried by people familiar with the area where the crime was committed. In addition, witnesses for the defense will be available to testify without having to travel great distances.

District Court Judges

Each district court has at least two judges. Some courts in more populous districts have many more judges because of a higher volume of work. It is the responsibility of each district court judge to decide on the procedures to be followed in court and to explain the law involved in a case to the jury. Judges also decide

on the punishment or fine when the jury finds the defendant guilty. The President of the United States appoints and the Senate approves district court judges. District court judges currently receive a salary of $133,600 per year.

The Constitution provides that federal judges be appointed "during good behavior." In effect, they are appointed for life unless guilty of some serious crime. The Constitution also provides that the government cannot reduce the salaries of federal judges during their term in office. The writers of the Constitution included these two provisions to help ensure an independent judiciary. Because federal judges cannot be removed from office without cause or punished with a reduction in salary, they can remain free from political influence and cannot be forced to make rulings favorable to anyone in power. They are free to decide each case strictly in terms of the legal issues, no matter how unpopular their decisions may be politically.

Other District Court Officials

In addition to judges, district courts have several other officials. Each district court has a **magistrate,** who issues court orders and hears the preliminary evidence in a case to determine whether the case should be brought to trial. By doing this, the magistrate helps protect criminal suspects from being unfairly charged and tried. Magistrates may also hear minor cases.

Every district court also has a United States attorney. The United States attorney is the government's lawyer. It is his or her job to prove that a suspect has committed a crime. It is also the attorney's job to represent the government in civil cases in which the government is involved. Usually, a United States attorney runs a large office with dozens of assistant United States attorneys who perform most of the trial work.

Serving Subpoenas

Another district court official is the United States marshal. The **marshal** arrests suspects, delivers defendants to court, and serves people with subpoenas. A **subpoena** is a court order requiring someone to appear in court. The President, with Senate approval, appoints United States attorneys and marshals.

In addition to these officials, each district court also has many clerks, deputy clerks, secretaries, and other workers who keep track of court cases, file legal papers, help the public, and perform other jobs that help the court operate efficiently.

Facing the Music

Although the Supreme Court tries to choose cases that raise important legal or constitutional questions, sometimes the circumstances of a case may take the Court into unusual areas.

In the case of *Ward* v. *Rock Against Racism,* which the Court heard in 1989, the issue was whether a New York City law violated the freedom of expression of rock and roll bands.

The law required musicians performing at a city-owned bandshell in Central Park to use a city-supplied sound system and a sound technician so that it could regulate the volume of the music. Rock Against Racism, a group of rock bands, argued that this interfered with artistic expression.

The Court upheld the New York law. It ruled that the city could place certain restrictions on the "time, place and manner" of expression without violating the First Amendment. The city had the right to turn down the volume.

Central Park concert

United States Courts of Appeals

Above the district courts in the federal court system are the United States **courts of appeals.** These courts are also called federal appeals courts, circuit courts of appeals, or appellate courts.

Jurisdiction

Federal courts of appeals have only **appellate jurisdiction.** They hear only cases that have come to them on appeal from the lower district courts or from federal regulatory agencies. For example, the lawyer for the losing side in a civil case may decide to appeal a district court's verdict. The lawyer may feel that the district court judge followed the wrong procedure or did not apply the law correctly. Some new evidence may have turned up that could change the verdict.

Rulings by a federal regulatory agency may also be appealed if the people or groups involved feel the agency applied a rule or made a decision unfairly. Suppose, for example, that the Food and Drug Administration (FDA) refuses to approve the use of a new drug. The company that manufactures the drug can ask the appeals court to review the FDA's decision.

Congress established the present appeals-court system in 1891 to ease the burden of the Supreme Court, which was receiving more appeals each year than it could handle. Today each of the 12 United States courts of appeals has jurisdiction over a **circuit,** or a particular geographical area. Each court receives cases from the district courts within its own circuit. If a person appeals a case that originated in the federal district court in Denver, Colorado, for example, the case would go to the United States Court of Appeals for the Tenth Circuit. (See the map on page 286.)

Appeals Court Judges

Each appeals court has from 6 to 27 judges. Like other federal judges, they are appointed for life. Their salaries are currently $141,700 a year. Appeals court judges do not preside over trials. There are no juries in appeals courts. Instead, a panel of at least three judges hears arguments from the attorneys for each side and reviews lower court trial records.

The judges do not decide on the guilt or innocence of a defendant. They rule only on whether the defendant's rights have been protected and on whether he or she received a fair trial. The panel may make one of three rulings: to uphold the lower court's verdict, to overturn the lower court's decision, or to **remand** (return) the case to the lower court for a new trial. The decision of the appeals court is usually final. In some cases, however, the decision may be appealed to the United States Supreme Court, which can decide whether or not to hear the case.

Appeals People who disagree with the verdict received in a district court can appeal it in one of the federal appeals, or circuit, courts. *How many circuits are there?*

UNITED STATES
COURT OF APPEALS
FOR THE
FEDERAL CIRCUIT

Special Courts Members of the military who are convicted in a court-martial may appeal the decision to the Court of Military Appeals. *What other special courts were created by Congress?*

Special Federal Courts

In addition to the district and appeals courts, Congress has also created several special courts. These include:

- *United States Tax Court.* This court hears appeals dealing with federal tax laws. Taxpayers who have a dispute with the Internal Revenue Service may take their case to this court.

- *United States Court of Federal Claims.* This court hears cases of citizens who sue the government for money claims. If the court feels that the claim has merit, it will uphold the suit and award a sum of money. Congress must then appropriate the money to pay the claim.

- *United States Court of Military Appeals.* This is the appeals court for the armed forces. When people in the service are accused of breaking a federal or military law, they are tried at a **court-martial,** a trial before a panel of military officers. Military personnel who have been court-martialed may appeal their verdicts to the United States Court of Military Appeals.

- *United States Court of International Trade.* This court hears disputes arising from tariff and trade laws. For example, if the government prevents an importer from bringing certain goods into the country, the importer may take the case to the court of trade.

★ SECTION 2 REVIEW ★

UNDERSTANDING VOCABULARY
Define district court, original jurisdiction, magistrate, marshal, subpoena, court of appeals, appellate jurisdiction, circuit, remand, court-martial.

REVIEWING OBJECTIVES

1 What are the responsibilities of judges in district courts?

2 What are the functions of United States courts of appeals?

3 What are three special federal courts, and what are their functions?

Great American Documents

Democracy in America

Alexis de Tocqueville was a French judge who came to America in 1831 to study prison reform and American democracy. He spent two years traveling around the country interviewing political leaders and ordinary citizens about how the American political system worked. At that time American democracy was still unfamiliar to most of the world.

Think About It

As you read the following excerpt, think about the importance of the federal court system in our society.

Tocqueville's Work

Tocqueville returned to France and published a book called *Democracy in America*. It was an instant success.

What Tocqueville tried to do was analyze American society and its political system. He was very interested in learning how Americans were able to keep control of their government and prevent it from being taken over by dictators or kings.

Tocqueville's View of the Supreme Court

In the following excerpt from *Democracy in America*, Tocqueville discusses the role the Supreme Court plays in protecting democracy.

The peace, the prosperity, and the very existence of the Union are vested in [entrusted to] the hands of the . . . Federal judges. Without them the Constitution would be a dead letter: the executive branch appeals to them for assistance against the encroachments [extension] of the legislative power; the legislature demands their protection against the assaults [attempts to gain power] of the executive; they defend the Union from disobedience of the states, the states from the exaggerated claims of the Union, the public against private interests, and the conservative spirit of stability against the fickleness [changing nature] of the democracy. Their power is enormous, but it is the power of public opinion. They are all powerful as long as the people respect the law.

The Impact of Tocqueville's Work

Democracy in America had a great impact abroad. This blueprint of how to create a democratic government was widely read and debated in European countries as they struggled to establish democracies.

INTERPRETING SOURCES

1 Why do you think Tocqueville was so interested in how American democracy worked?

2 What did he mean when he said that without the Supreme Court, the Constitution would be a "dead letter"?

3 Why was *Democracy in America* so important in Europe?

The United States Supreme Court

FOCUS

TERMS TO KNOW
judicial review, unconstitutional

OBJECTIVES

■ Explain how the case of *Marbury* v. *Madison* affected **the power of the Supreme Court.**

■ Explain how a President may try to influence the Court through the appointment of **Supreme Court justices.**

The United States Supreme Court is the highest court in the land. It is the final court to which anyone can appeal a legal decision. According to the Constitution, the Supreme Court has original jurisdiction in only two instances. It can preside over trials in cases that involve diplomats from foreign countries and in cases in which a state is involved. For example, if one state sues another state, the Supreme Court can try the suit. In fact, the Court very rarely hears these two kinds of cases. They are usually tried in the federal district courts.

In all other instances, the Supreme Court has appellate jurisdiction. Its main responsibility is to hear appeals in cases originating in lower courts. Although about 6,000 or more cases are appealed to the Supreme Court each year, the Court selects fewer than 150 for a full hearing and review. In general, the Court hears appeals only in cases that pose significant legal or constitutional questions or are of great public interest and concern. The Supreme Court decides not to hear many cases and remands others to the lower courts with a short opinion stating its reasons for ordering a retrial. Whether the Court hears a case or not, its decision cannot be appealed.

The Power of the Supreme Court

The Supreme Court enjoys a great deal of power and prestige. The legislative and executive branches must follow the Supreme Court's rulings. The fact that the Court is removed from politics

Justice Ruth Bader Ginsburg   The main responsibility of Supreme Court justices is to hear appeals in cases originating in lower courts. *How do the justices select the cases they hear?*

Judicial Review

One of the most important powers of the Supreme Court is the power of judicial review. **Judicial review** means that the Court can review any federal or state law to see if it is in agreement with the Constitution. If the Court decides that a law or action is **unconstitutional**—in conflict with the Constitution—it has the power to nullify, or cancel, that law or action. The power of judicial review thus makes the Supreme Court the final authority on the Constitution and laws of the United States.

Marbury v. Madison

The power of judicial review is not mentioned in the Constitution. This power was established officially in 1803 in the case of *Marbury* v. *Madison*. On his last night in office, President John Adams signed an order making William Marbury a justice of the peace (a kind of judge) for the District of Columbia. When Thomas Jefferson took office as President the next day, he told Secretary of State James Madison not to carry out Adams's order.

William Marbury took his case directly to the Supreme Court, which he claimed had jurisdiction as a result of a provision in the Judiciary Act of 1789. John Marshall, the chief justice, wrote an opinion turning down Marbury's claim. He noted that the Constitution did not give the Court jurisdiction to decide Marbury's case. In his opinion, Marshall set out three basic principles of judicial review.

- The Constitution is the supreme law of the land.
- When there is a conflict between the Constitution and any other law, the Constitution must be followed.

Supreme Court   The Supreme Court is the highest court of appeals in the United States.   *Which justice wrote the opinion that established the power of judicial review?*

Landmark Decisions of the Supreme Court These decisions help determine the rights of citizens. *What early decision did* Brown *v.* Board of Education *overturn?*

Marbury v. Madison (1803)
Established the Supreme Court's power of judicial review

Dred Scott v. Sandford (1857)
Ruled that Congress could not prohibit slavery in United States territories and that enslaved African Americans and their descendants were not United States citizens

Plessy v. Ferguson (1896)
Established the "separate but equal" doctrine that permitted segregation

Muller v. Oregon (1908)
Ruled that states could protect women workers if the states had a reasonable justification

Schenck v. United States (1919)
Held that free speech could be limited if there was a "clear and present danger" that illegal action might result from the speech

Brown v. Board of Education (1954)
Established that the "separate but equal" doctrine was unconstitutional

Gideon v. Wainwright (1963)
Declared that a person accused of a major crime had the right to legal counsel during a trial

Reynolds v. Sims (1964)
Held that unequal representation violated the Fourteenth Amendment and established the principle of "one person, one vote"

Miranda v. Arizona (1966)
Ruled that police officers must inform suspects of their rights at the time of arrest

New York Times v. United States (1971)
Held that prior restraint or censorship was unconstitutional unless the government could prove serious and immediate harm to the nation

Roe v. Wade (1973)
Legalized a woman's right to an abortion under certain circumstances

United States v. Nixon (1974)
Established that Presidents could claim executive privilege in cases where military and national security issues were involved but could not use it to conceal evidence of a crime

Webster v. Reproductive Health Services (1989)
Ruled against the use of public funds and buildings for counseling about and performing abortions

■ The judicial branch has a duty to uphold the Constitution. It must be able to determine when a law conflicts with the Constitution and to nullify, or cancel, unconstitutional laws.

The power of judicial review serves as an important check on the legislative and executive branches of government. It prevents them from straying too far from the Constitution when they make and carry out new laws.

Controversial Decisions   Local police and United States marshals stood guard as protesters demonstrated outside an abortion clinic. *What Supreme Court decision do the protesters probably oppose?*

Checking the Court's Power

Judicial review gives the Court a position of great influence, but it does not make the Court all powerful. Congress can get around a Supreme Court ruling by changing a law in such a way that it no longer conflicts with the Constitution. Congress can also adopt an amendment to the Constitution, which then changes the Constitution.

In addition, the Supreme Court must rely on the executive branch to carry out its decisions. The executive branch almost always enforces Supreme Court rulings, but in the case of *Worcester* v. *Georgia,* it did not. When Chief Justice John Marshall ordered the state of Georgia to stop violating federal land treaties with the Cherokee nation in 1832, President Andrew Jackson refused to enforce the order. The President is reported to have said: "John Marshall has made his decision; now let him enforce it."

Controversy and the Court

Despite its power and prestige, the Supreme Court sometimes becomes involved in controversy. Some of its decisions anger certain groups of people. These people might pressure Congress to pass a new law or constitutional amendment that will get around the Court's ruling. One of the Court's most controversial decisions was in the 1857 case of *Dred Scott* v. *Sandford,* in which the Court ruled that the Constitution did not prohibit slavery in the territories (in this instance, the Minnesota Territory, where Scott had been taken). The Court's decision went on to say that African Americans were not citizens and therefore could not sue in the federal courts. That ruling was overturned in 1868 by the Fourteenth Amendment, which stated that all "persons born or naturalized in the United States and subject to the jurisdiction thereof are citizens of the United States."

Controversial decisions of recent years have included *Brown* v. *Board of Education* (1954), which outlawed school segregation, and *Roe* v. *Wade* (1973), which legalized abortion.

Supreme Court Justices

The Supreme Court is made up of eight associate justices and one chief justice. Until recently, all the justices who had served on the Supreme Court were men. In 1981, however, President Ronald Reagan appointed Sandra Day O'Connor to the Court, and President Bill Clinton appointed Ruth Bader Ginsburg to the

Thurgood Marshall Justice Marshall served on the Supreme Court from 1967 to 1991. *Why was Justice Marshall's appointment significant?*

Court in 1993. Thurgood Marshall, who was appointed in 1967, was the first African American justice to serve on the Court. After Marshall retired in 1991, Clarence Thomas—also an African American—was appointed to the Court. Supreme Court justices serve for life. Associate justices currently receive a salary of $164,100 and the chief justice receives $171,500.

Although the Constitution does not set any qualifications for serving on the Supreme Court, all justices have been lawyers and most have been judges or law professors. Some have also been public officials. William Howard Taft was the only person to become chief justice after serving as President of the United States.

The Constitution gives the President the power to appoint Supreme Court jus-

tices, with the consent of the Senate. The Senate usually approves the President's choices. Occasionally, however, the Senate will turn down a President's nominee because of doubts about the qualifications or legal philosophy of that person. This happened in 1987, for example, when the Senate rejected Robert Bork because of his legal philosophy. The appointment of Clarence Thomas in 1991 was almost derailed when a former employee, Anita Hill, accused him of misconduct. After hearings were held, however, his appointment was confirmed.

Presidents usually try to appoint justices who share their political beliefs or view of the law. Once appointed to the Court, however, a justice is under no obligation to follow the President's line of thinking. Nevertheless, if a President has the opportunity to name several justices to the Court, it is likely that many of the President's views will be reflected in the Court's decisions. In this way, a President may affect the way cases are decided far into the future.

★ SECTION 3 REVIEW ★

UNDERSTANDING VOCABULARY
Define judicial review, unconstitutional.

REVIEWING OBJECTIVES
1 How did the case of *Marbury* v. *Madison* affect the power of the Supreme Court?

2 How may a President try to influence the Court through the appointment of Supreme Court justices?

How to Read a Flow Chart

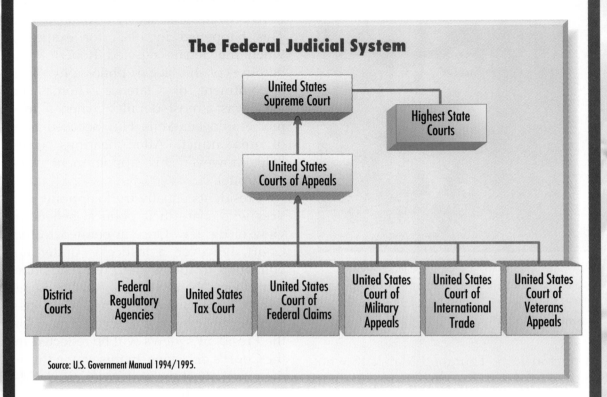

The Federal Judicial System

United States Supreme Court

Highest State Courts

United States Courts of Appeals

District Courts | Federal Regulatory Agencies | United States Tax Court | United States Court of Federal Claims | United States Court of Military Appeals | United States Court of International Trade | United States Court of Veterans Appeals

Source: U.S. Government Manual 1994/1995.

A flow chart is a diagram that shows movement in a system or illustrates how a system works. The flow chart on this page shows how the various parts of the federal judicial system are related. The arrows indicate the flow of authority (appeals) from the lowest courts (shown at the bottom of the chart) up to the Supreme Court. You can trace the route of an appeal from any of the lower courts or agencies. The higher courts have the power to review the decisions of the lower courts under their jurisdiction.

Use the information on this flow chart of the judiciary system to answer the following questions.

CITIZENSHIP IN ACTION

1 Which court has the power to review the decisions of the highest state courts?

2 To what court can decisions of district courts be appealed?

3 What courts review the decisions of federal regulatory agencies?

4 The Constitution established the Supreme Court and gave Congress the power to create lower courts. Why do you think the Framers of the Constitution placed the Supreme Court above all other courts?

The Court at Work

FOCUS

TERMS TO KNOW
brief, docket, adversary, writ of certiorari, majority opinion, concurring opinion, dissenting opinion

OBJECTIVES

■ Explain what the Supreme Court does in **deciding which cases to hear.**

■ Explain **how cases reach the Court** from lower courts.

■ Describe how Supreme Court justices arrive at **Court decisions and opinions.**

The Supreme Court conducts its business each year from October until the following June or July. For the first two weeks of each of these months, the Court is said to be "sitting," or in session. This is the time when justices hear arguments—usually 30 minutes for each side in a case. The justices also announce what cases they have decided to hear, discuss and vote on current cases, and announce their decisions.

A two-week recess, during which the justices do most of their work, follows each two-week session. When the Court is in recess, justices decide which cases to hear, research the cases that will come before them, and write their opinions on cases heard during the previous session. They also use this time to read the written arguments, or **briefs,** that the attorneys have prepared.

Deciding Which Cases to Hear

An important task of Supreme Court justices is to decide whether to hear a case. The justices review a list of possible cases and consider their merits. For a case to be heard, at least four justices must vote for it. After a case has been accepted, it is placed on the Court **docket,** or calendar. It is assigned a number as well as a date when it will be brought before the Court.

The justices of the Supreme Court decide to hear only certain kinds of cases. They usually decide to hear a case if it involves a significant constitutional question. In most instances, such questions center around the Bill of Rights and other amendments and deal with issues such as freedom of speech, equal protection of the laws, and fair trial.

Court in Session Justices Ruth Bader Ginsburg and Sandra Day O'Connor are the first women to serve on the Supreme Court. *What do the justices do while the Court is in session?*

Careers

Court Reporter

Court reporters are stenographers, or shorthand reporters. They are responsible for recording everything that is said in a legal proceeding.

What Court Reporters Do

Court reporters use special stenotype machines to take notes. After the proceedings, they dictate their notes into a machine for transcription at a later time. Every word said in the trial or hearing must be included in the official transcript.

Qualifications

To become a court reporter, you must be able to take at least 160 words of dictation per minute. You need at least a high school diploma and preferably an associate degree or certification from a fully qualified preprofessional training program.

In addition to being quick and accurate, court reporters must be able to concentrate on the task in a busy setting with many distractions. Most jobs involve

Court reporter operating stenotype machine

repetitive work with little independent decision making. However, by keeping accurate records, court reporters play a vital role in the American judicial system.

School to WORK

Arrange to visit a courtroom in session and note the role the court reporter plays in the proceedings. If possible, interview the reporter about his or her job and report your findings to the class.

The justices always choose cases that involve a real dispute between two **adversaries,** or opposing sides. In other words, the cases must deal with real people and events.

The justices also select cases that involve legal issues rather than political questions. By choosing these kinds of cases, the justices cannot be accused of interfering in matters that the legislative or executive branch should decide.

Finally, the justices tend to select cases that are of importance to the entire country rather than just to the individuals or groups involved. Such cases will have a broader application to the nation's laws.

How Cases Reach the Court

You have already learned that nearly all cases come to the Supreme Court on appeal from a lower court. Most of the appeals reach the Court by a request for a **writ of certiorari** (Latin for "to make

Hugo Black During his 34 years of service, Supreme Court Justice Black wrote many dissenting opinions. *How do dissenting and concurring opinions differ?*

more certain"). A writ of certiorari directs a lower court to send its records on a case to the Supreme Court for review. This happens if one of the parties involved in a case claims that the lower court made an error in the case. Sometimes a lower court will ask the Supreme Court to make a ruling in a case because it is not sure how to apply the law to the case.

Court Decisions and Opinions

While the Court is in session, the justices meet privately on Wednesdays and Fridays to discuss and vote on each case. At these meetings, the chief justice asks each associate justice to give his or her opinion of the case. Opinions are given in order of the justices' time on the Court, with the longest-serving justice first and the newest justice last. Then a vote is taken, starting with the newest justice and ending with the chief justice.

A majority vote of the Court determines the outcome of a case. If all nine justices are present, the vote must be at least 5 to 4. Sometimes, because of illness or other reasons, all nine justices do not vote. A minimum of six justices is required, however, to hear and decide a case. In the event of a tie vote, the lower court's decision is upheld.

Most Supreme Court decisions are accompanied by an opinion explaining why the justices made that decision. Usually the chief justice asks an associate justice who voted with the majority to write the **majority opinion.** A justice who agrees with the majority decision but has different reasons writes a **concurring opinion.** Justices who oppose the majority decision issue **dissenting opinions.**

Dissenting opinions sometimes become majority opinions in later cases. This happened when Justice Hugo Black argued in a dissenting opinion in 1942 that poor people suspected of crimes are entitled to an attorney. Black's dissenting opinion became the basis for a majority opinion he wrote 21 years later in *Gideon v. Wainwright.* (See page 416.)

★ SECTION 4 REVIEW ★

UNDERSTANDING VOCABULARY
Define brief, docket, adversary, writ of certiorari, majority opinion, concurring opinion, dissenting opinion.

REVIEWING OBJECTIVES
1 How does the Supreme Court decide which cases to hear?

2 How do cases reach the Court from lower courts?

3 How are the Supreme Court's decisions and opinions reached?

Identifying Key Terms

Choose the vocabulary term that best completes each of the sentences below. Write your answers on a separate sheet of paper.

criminal case   civil case
concurrent jurisdiction   appellate jurisdiction
court of appeals   judicial review

1. In instances where either state or federal courts can hear a case, the courts are said to have _____.
2. The case against the man accused of robbing the store was a(n) _____.
3. Convinced that the presiding judge had applied the law incorrectly, the defense lawyer decided to take the case to the _____.
4. Courts that hear only cases sent to them from the lower courts are said to have _____.
5. The Supreme Court used its power of _____ in deciding that the law was unconstitutional.
6. The case involving a boundary dispute between two neighbors was a(n) _____.

Reviewing the Main Ideas

SECTION 1
1. Identify three types of cases in which the federal courts have exclusive jurisdiction.
2. In what instances do state and federal courts usually share concurrent jurisdiction?

SECTION 2
3. What is the function of district courts?

4. Describe the work of judges of the appeals courts.

SECTION 3
5. What three principles of judicial review were established in *Marbury* v. *Madison*?
6. What are the two ways that Congress can get around a Supreme Court decision?

SECTION 4
7. Identify three activities of Supreme Court justices while the Court is sitting, or in session.
8. What happens to a case before the Supreme Court in the event of a tie vote by the justices?

Critical Thinking

SECTION 1
1. **Analyzing Information**   Why do you think the federal courts were given exclusive jurisdiction over certain types of cases?

SECTION 2
2. **Developing a Point of View**   How important do you think appeals courts are in providing fair and equal treatment under the law? Explain.

SECTION 3
3. **Evaluating Information**   What influence do you think the power of judicial review has on the legislative and executive branches of government? Explain.

SECTION 4
4. **Making Inferences**   Which do you think is probably more important in Supreme Court cases, oral arguments or written briefs? Explain.

Reinforcing Citizenship Skills

In the library, find out more about the process by which a case moves into and through a district court. Then create a flow chart that shows this movement. You may wish to use a particular kind of case, such as tax evasion or a public land dispute. Share your chart with the class.

Cooperative Learning

With a group of two other students, play the roles of federal judges. One judge is appointed for life, a second judge is required to run for election every four years, and the third judge is dependent on the renewal of his or her appointment by political leaders every four years. Stage a conversation with the class in which you discuss the advantages and disadvantages of your situations and the possible consequences to providing "equal protection of the laws" to all.

Technology Activity

Using a Word Processor

The American judicial process is often slow. Review your civics journal about the judicial system. Then use a word processor to write an essay in support of the present system, despite its problems. Suggest what might happen if the system were changed to provide speedy trials at the expense of due process of law.

Focusing on Your Community

Find out where the nearest federal district courts are located. How many cases does your district court handle each year? What types of cases does it handle? Where is the nearest appeals court? Present your findings in a written report.

Analyzing Visuals

The United States courts are supposed to protect the rights of citizens and to judge everyone equally and fairly. Study the depiction of justice in the picture below. Then answer the questions.

1. What does the blindfold symbolize?
2. What ideal of justice is symbolized by what the figure is holding in her left hand?
3. What does the sword symbolize?

CLOSEUP
WATERGATE

In June 1972, during President Richard Nixon's reelection campaign, police arrested five men at the Watergate building in Washington, D.C. The men were charged with breaking into the Democratic party headquarters. The burglary marked the beginning of the so-called Watergate affair.

In the months that followed, evidence was found linking the burglary and other illegal acts to members of the President's staff. The White House denied any connection.

The burglary suspects were tried and found guilty. One burglar testified before a Senate committee that several White House officials were involved. Then presidential counsel John Dean testified that the President himself had been involved.

President Nixon resigns

Congressional Hearings

During its hearings, the Watergate Committee learned that President Nixon had made tape recordings of conversations in his office. The committee believed it could discover the truth of the President's involvement by listening to these tapes. Nixon, however, claimed "executive privilege" and refused to hand them over.

The affair came to a head in July 1974, when the Supreme Court ruled that Nixon had to turn over the tapes. On one, the President was heard discussing how to cover up White House involvement in the burglary. This tape was a "smoking gun"—concrete evidence of Nixon's role.

Impeachment or Resignation?

Meanwhile, the House Judiciary Committee recommended impeaching the President. It charged Nixon with obstruction of justice, abuse of power, and contempt of Congress. The next steps would have been a full House vote on the charges and an impeachment trial. The process never went that far. On August 9, 1974, Nixon resigned—the first President ever to do so.

CLOSEUP REVIEW

1 What was the "smoking gun"?

2 Why do you think Nixon resigned from office rather than go through an impeachment trial?

Multimedia Activities

Surfing the "Net"

The Census Bureau

The Bureau of the Census keeps track of our country's population. Use the Internet to find out the latest projections of the United States and world populations.

Getting There

Follow the steps below to find information about population projections.

1. Go to your favorite search engine.
2. Type in the phrase *Census Bureau*. Following this phrase, enter words like those below to focus your search:

> population
> current U.S. population
> world statistics

The search engine should provide you with a number of links to follow. Links are pointers to different sites on the Internet and commonly appear as blue underlined words.

What to Do When You Are There

1. Click on the links to navigate through the pages of information.
2. Search until you find the population projection for the United States. Write this number down and the time you recorded it.
3. Search until you find the world's population projection. Write this number and the time you recorded it down.
4. Present your statistics to the class and explain their meaning. Explain whether, in your opinion, these numbers will be larger or smaller by tomorrow.

Focus on Government

The Presidency

The presidency is the nation's highest elected office. The presidency comes with many responsibilities and challenges. The ***Focus on Government*** programs referenced below explain the different roles of the President and student opinions of personal characteristics of a good President.

Side 2, Chapter 29
Lecture Launcher:
The Presidency

Setting Up the Video

Using a bar code reader or an electronic keypad, work with a group of your classmates to view these video segments of the videodisc ***Focus on Government:***

Side 2, Chapter 30
Lecture Launcher:
Presidential Leadership

Side 2, Chapter 33
Speaking Out:
The Character of the Presidency

Hands-On Activity

Use ideas from the video programs to design a bulletin board display of magazine clippings demonstrating the different roles of the President.

Be certain to include examples of the following roles:

- lawmaker
- diplomat
- policymaker

UNIT 5

State and Local Government

YOUR ROLE AS A CITIZEN

The relationship between the American people and government is closest at the state and local levels. As citizens one of our most important roles is to work with local leaders to improve our communities and solve problems affecting their well-being.

In Unit 5 you will learn about state and local governments. You will study how they are organized and how they affect our lives. ■

CHAPTERS IN THIS UNIT

13 State Government

14 Local Government

15 Community Issues

A town meeting ➤

State Government

CIVIC PARTICIPATION

State governments rather than the federal government have the most impact on your daily life. When you make a purchase, you probably pay a state sales tax. Your state maintains many of the roads you ride on. State funds help pay for your school and textbooks. Contact the information office of your state government. Find out the names of the top state officials, both elected and appointed, and their areas of responsibility.

Working in Your Community

Prepare an organizational chart of your state government that shows major state officials and their responsibilities. Share this chart with your neighbors. Encourage them to contact these state officials to express their opinions on specific state policies. ■

Your Civics Journal

Read the newspaper to find out what problems your state faces. Perhaps the state has a large budget deficit, or the crime rate has increased sharply. List the problems in your civics journal. Describe what the state is doing to solve the problems and what you would do if you were governor.

Governor talks at school ➤

SECTION 1

The Federal System

FOCUS

TERMS TO KNOW
federalism, extradition

OBJECTIVES

- Explain the **constitutional basis for federalism.**

- Describe the basic features of **state constitutions.**

- Identify and describe three examples of **federal-state cooperation.**

- Give an example of **cooperation between states.**

As you learned in Chapter 2, the first American states behaved like 13 separate countries when the Articles of Confederation were in force. Each state wrote its own constitution, set up its own government, and made its own laws. When the states banded together under the United States Constitution, they gave up some of their independence. States could no longer print their own money, for example, or tax items imported from other states. Nevertheless, each state continued to govern itself much as it had in the past.

This system, in which the power to govern is shared between the national government and the states, is called the federal system, or **federalism.** Our federal system allows the people of each state to deal with their needs in their own way. At the same time, it lets the states act together to deal with matters that affect all Americans.

Constitutional Basis for Federalism

The Constitution does not list the powers of state governments, as it does for the national government. Instead, it specifies what the state governments may *not* do. Article I of the Constitution forbids the states to make treaties, coin money, tax imports or exports, keep an army in peacetime, or declare war. In addition, several amendments to the Constitution prevent state governments from taking away rights granted by the federal government. The most important of these amendments is the Fourteenth, which guarantees all Americans "equal protection of the laws."

Law Enforcement   State police officers play an important role in enforcing the state's laws.   *What happens if state and federal laws conflict?*

While some powers are denied to the states, many others are given to both Congress *and* the states. These concurrent powers include the powers to tax and to borrow money.

Reserved Powers

As you learned in Chapter 4, the Tenth Amendment gives the states additional authority. According to this amendment, state governments may exercise all powers not given to the federal government or denied to the states. These powers, you may recall, are called reserved powers. Among them are the powers to make marriage and divorce laws, to regulate education, and to conduct elections.

In general, each state is responsible for the safety and welfare of its own citizens. State governments often use their reserved powers to meet this responsibility. They set up police forces and other law enforcement operations. They build roads and bridges. They regulate business and trade within their borders. They set educational requirements and provide funding for schools. They organize local governments for counties, cities, and towns. State government touches almost every activity in Americans' lives. (See the chart on page 90.)

Supremacy Clause

The Framers of the United States Constitution recognized that the powers of the states may sometimes conflict with those of the federal government. For this reason they declared in Article VI that the Constitution and the laws Congress makes shall be the "supreme law of the land." If state and federal law conflict, the federal law has the greater authority and power. One famous use of this "su-premacy clause" occurred after the Eighteenth Amendment was ratified in 1919. The amendment made it illegal to sell alcoholic beverages anywhere in the United States. Each state had had its own laws about the use of alcohol, but the Eighteenth Amendment became the supreme law of the land and the state laws lost their power.

State Constitutions

Each state has its own constitution. Like the United States Constitution, a state constitution is a plan of government. It is also the highest law in the state, just as the United States Constitution is the highest law in the nation.

Article IV of the United States Constitution requires each state to have a "republican form of government." (A *republic* is a word meaning representative

Sovereign States   The Arkansas legislature meets in a building modeled after the United States Capitol in Washington, D.C.   *What do all 50 state governments have in common?*

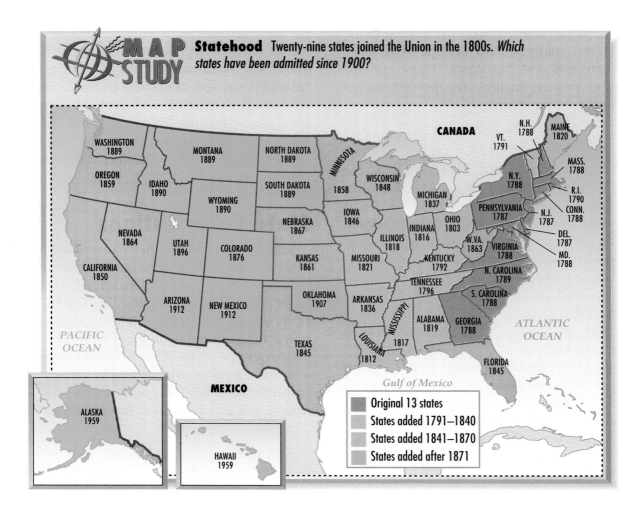

MAP STUDY

Statehood Twenty-nine states joined the Union in the 1800s. *Which states have been admitted since 1900?*

CANADA

N.H. 1788
MAINE 1820
VT. 1791
MASS. 1788
N.Y. 1788
R.I. 1790
CONN. 1788
PENNSYLVANIA 1787
N.J. 1787
DEL. 1787
MD. 1788

WASHINGTON 1889
MONTANA 1889
NORTH DAKOTA 1889
MINNESOTA 1858
WISCONSIN 1848
MICHIGAN 1837
OREGON 1859
IDAHO 1890
SOUTH DAKOTA 1889
OHIO 1803
WYOMING 1890
IOWA 1846
INDIANA 1816
W.VA. 1863
VIRGINIA 1788
NEBRASKA 1867
ILLINOIS 1818
NEVADA 1864
UTAH 1896
COLORADO 1876
KANSAS 1861
MISSOURI 1821
KENTUCKY 1792
N. CAROLINA 1789
CALIFORNIA 1850
TENNESSEE 1796
S. CAROLINA 1788
ARIZONA 1912
NEW MEXICO 1912
OKLAHOMA 1907
ARKANSAS 1836
MISSISSIPPI
ALABAMA 1819
GEORGIA 1788
LOUISIANA 1812
1817
TEXAS 1845
FLORIDA 1845

PACIFIC OCEAN
ATLANTIC OCEAN
Gulf of Mexico
MEXICO

ALASKA 1959
HAWAII 1959

Original 13 states
States added 1791–1840
States added 1841–1870
States added after 1871

democracy.) Other than that, however, the Constitution does not say anything about how a state's government should be set up. It would be possible, therefore, for the 50 states to create 50 completely different systems of government.

Not surprisingly, however, nearly every state government closely resembles the federal government. The reason for this is simple: The early state constitutions served as models for the writers of the United States Constitution. Since then, most states have used the United States Constitution as a model for their own constitutions.

A typical state constitution begins with a preamble, which cites the goals and ideals of the state's citizens. All state constitutions provide for three branches of government—legislative, executive, and judicial—and assign certain powers and duties to each branch. Every state constitution also includes a bill of rights, which in most cases is similar to the United States Bill of Rights.

The amendment process is an important part of every state constitution. While the procedure for changing the constitution varies from state to state, it is usually a two-step process similar to amending the United States Constitution. An amendment must first be proposed, generally by the legislature; then it must be ratified by the voters. As the role of state governments has changed, some state constitutions have been amended hundreds of times.

Despite their basic similarities, the constitutions of different states vary significantly. Every state has its own ideas about what makes a good government. Nebraska, for example, is the only state with a one-house legislature. (The other states have bicameral legislatures similar to that of the United States Congress.) In Delaware the legislature rather than the voters ratifies amendments.

Federal-State Cooperation

The states and the federal government do not always agree. They do, however, tend to work together most of the time.

The United States Constitution ensures a certain amount of federal-state cooperation. Article IV, which requires every state to have a "republican form of government," includes the idea that the United States will defend that form of government if it is threatened. The Constitution says that the federal government will protect each state against invasion and domestic violence. When local or state police cannot control violent incidents within a state, the governor may call for the assistance of federal troops.

In return, the states provide certain services to the federal government. For example, the states hold elections for federal offices—such as President and Vice President—as well as for state and local offices. This is considered part of the reserved powers of the states.

The states and the federal government also cooperate in ways not called for in the Constitution. For example, state and federal agencies often share

Federal Relief   Vice President Gore visited flooded areas along the Mississippi in July 1993 as part of federal relief efforts.   *What does the Constitution say about federal assistance to states?*

Partnership The Port Authority of New York and New Jersey runs transportation facilities serving both states. *In what other ways do states cooperate?*

information. A state police force may help the FBI catch a criminal, or the Federal Bureau of Prisons may share prison management techniques with a state's justice department.

Although not required to do so by the Constitution, the federal government provides funding for many state services. For example, federal agencies help pay for student lunches in public schools and for the construction of state highways. By helping states pay for services that they could not otherwise afford, the federal government also helps the country as a whole.

Cooperation Between States

The Constitution helps ensure that states cooperate with each other as well as with the federal government. According to Article IV, each state must give "full faith and credit" to the laws and court decisions of other states. This

means that each state must accept and uphold these laws and decisions. For example, if a couple is married according to the laws of one state, every other state must accept that marriage as legal.

Article IV also ensures another type of cooperation. Often, someone who breaks the law in one state will flee to another state to avoid punishment. A state cannot legally punish a person for breaking the laws of another state. If requested to do so, however, a governor usually orders that a person charged with a major crime be returned to the state where the crime was committed. Returning a suspected criminal in this way is called **extradition.**

States cooperate in other ways as well, especially when they share a border. The neighboring states of New York and New Jersey, for example, are partners in an agency called the Port Authority. The Port Authority controls three airports, a seaport, a bus terminal, and other transportation facilities that serve both states.

★ SECTION 1 REVIEW ★

UNDERSTANDING VOCABULARY
Define federalism, extradition.

REVIEWING OBJECTIVES

1 What is the constitutional basis for federalism?

2 What are the basic features of all state constitutions?

3 What are three examples of federal-state cooperation?

4 What is an example of cooperation between states?

Exploring ISSUES

The Second Amendment and Gun Control Laws

The Second Amendment of the Constitution deals with the right to bear arms. The United States has changed a great deal since this amendment was adopted in 1791. At that time, settlers needed guns to shoot animals for food and to defend themselves in a hostile world.

Confiscated handguns

Guns in the United States

Today there are more than 100 million guns in the United States. Most of these are rifles and handguns that law-abiding people keep for hunting or for protection. Still, guns cause many injuries and deaths, and Americans remain divided over the issue of gun control.

Arguments For and Against Gun Control

Some people support gun control laws that ban all handguns. They feel that these small, easily hidden guns make it too easy to kill people. Opponents of gun control argue that gun ownership is as important a right as freedom of speech. Moreover, opponents say, gun control laws do not keep guns out of the hands of criminals, and such laws deprive citizens of the means to protect themselves against armed criminals.

The National Rifle Association (NRA) has long opposed any kind of restraints on gun ownership. Over the years the NRA has built a powerful lobby of gun owners and their supporters. It has been quite suc-

cessful in blocking gun control laws and defeating pro-gun control candidates at the national and state levels.

Recent Actions

In recent years the spread of semiautomatic assault rifles has caused a change in public opinion about gun control. Many states have introduced or enacted laws to ban them. The federal government has enacted legislation imposing a partial ban on assault rifles. It also passed a law, the Brady Bill, requiring a waiting period for the purchase of handguns. Such legislation has not ended the debate. Americans remain deeply divided over the issue of gun control.

DEVELOPING A POINT OF VIEW

1 Why do you think the authors of the Bill of Rights wanted to make gun ownership a constitutional right?

2 List the main arguments for and against gun control laws.

The State Executive Branch

FOCUS

TERMS TO KNOW
commute, parole

OBJECTIVES

■ List and describe several characteristics of **the office of governor.**

■ Describe the **powers and duties of the governor.**

■ Identify **executive officials and agencies** found in most states.

The executive branch of a state government is similar to the executive branch of the federal government. A chief executive, the governor, leads the state executive branch. The governor plays a number of other roles in addition to chief executive, including those of party leader and chief of state. As the President does in the federal government, the governor delegates powers to a number of state executive departments and agencies.

The Office of Governor

Each state constitution includes a set of qualifications for the office of governor. In most states a governor must be an American citizen, at least 30 years old, and a resident of the state for at least 5 years. As for most other elected offices, however, there are also unofficial qualifications for the office of governor. Most governors have previously held public office or been active in state politics. Many have had successful careers in law or business. In the past most governors have been men, and this has not changed very much. In 1997, only 2 of the nation's 50 governors were women.

The voters of each state elect their governor directly. There is no Electoral College in state elections. Other than that, governors are nominated and elected in much the same way that a President is.

Once elected, the governor in most states serves a four-year term. In nearly every state, a governor can be impeached if he or she commits a crime while in office. In several states, the voters themselves can take steps to remove a governor from office by demanding a special "recall" election.

Governor of Hawaii   The citizens of Hawaii elected Ben Cayetano in 1994.   *How long is the term of office for governor in most states?*

Governor's Powers In cases of emergency, the governor may call up the National Guard to protect the state or provide relief and shelter for its citizens. *What are the governor's responsibilities as chief executive?*

Each state constitution sets up a line of succession in case the governor dies, resigns, or is removed from office. In most states the first person in line is the lieutenant governor. The role of the lieutenant governor is similar to that of the Vice President in two respects. The lieutenant governor takes over the governorship if the governor dies or leaves office. The lieutenant governor usually presides over the state senate.

Powers and Duties of the Governor

Like the President, a governor plays several important roles. A governor's most important role is as the state's chief executive. As chief executive, the governor is responsible for executing laws the state legislature passes. To help with this responsibility, the governor issues executive orders to a large state bureaucracy. The governor has the power to appoint some of the officials in this bureaucracy, usually with the approval of the state senate. The governor also has the power to veto bills the legislature passes. In most states it is the governor's responsibility to prepare a budget for the state and submit it to the legislature.

The governor is also the state's chief legislator. Although only the state legislature can pass laws, the governor can play a part in proposing laws. For example, the governor may suggest laws that he or she thinks should be passed. Governors also try to convince the legislature to pass certain bills. They may do this formally, by making speeches to the legislature, or informally, by speaking privately to lawmakers.

In addition to executive and legislative responsibilities, all governors have certain judicial responsibilities. Like the President, governors have the power to offer pardons and reprieves to convicted criminals. They can also **commute,** or reduce, a criminal's sentence. For example, if a criminal has been sentenced to death, a governor may decide to commute the sentence to life in prison. Governors also have the power to grant a prisoner a **parole,** an early release from prison, with certain restrictions. Usually committees or boards under the governor's supervision—rather than the governor personally—make decisions regarding pardons, sentences, and paroles.

Governors play a number of other roles as well. Every governor is commander in chief of the National Guard, a state militia that may be called up to protect the state and its citizens during emergencies. Every governor is a party leader who tries to help out his or her

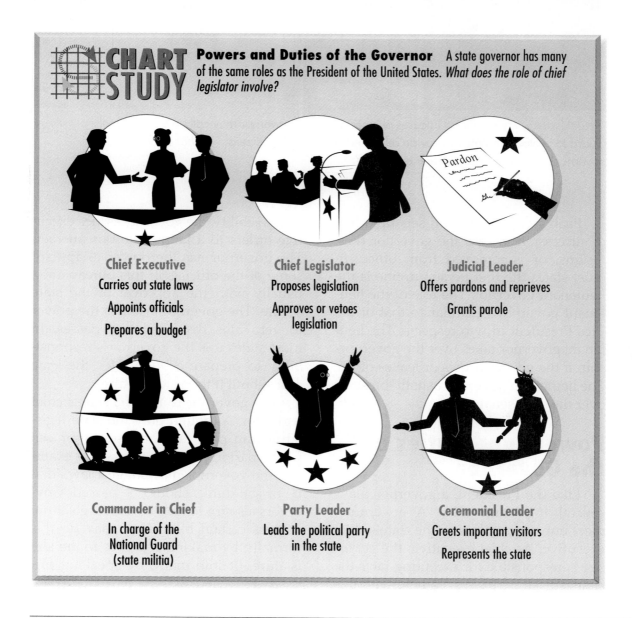

CHART STUDY **Powers and Duties of the Governor** A state governor has many of the same roles as the President of the United States. *What does the role of chief legislator involve?*

Chief Executive
Carries out state laws
Appoints officials
Prepares a budget

Chief Legislator
Proposes legislation
Approves or vetoes legislation

Judicial Leader
Offers pardons and reprieves
Grants parole

Commander in Chief
In charge of the National Guard (state militia)

Party Leader
Leads the political party in the state

Ceremonial Leader
Greets important visitors
Represents the state

Highway Repairs A paving crew works on a stretch of highway in North Carolina. *Which department of state government oversees highway construction and maintenance?*

standards and oversees the state's public schools. A treasurer supervises the state's funds, pays money from the treasury, and sometimes acts as chief tax collector. An auditor or comptroller, who makes sure that no government money is spent without approval from the governor and the legislature, supervises the treasurer's work.

In addition, every state has a number of executive departments, agencies, boards, and commissions. Some of these, such as departments of justice, of agriculture, and of labor, are similar to departments in the federal government. Other departments exist only in state governments. For example, nearly all states have a department (or board) of health, which administers programs in health education and disease prevention. Most states have a department of public works and a department of highways to supervise construction of public buildings, dams, bridges, and roads. Most states also have a state welfare board, which helps people who are disadvantaged or unemployed.

political party while governing the state. Finally, every governor is a chief of state, or ceremonial leader, who greets important visitors or represents the state on ceremonial occasions.

Executive Officials and Agencies

Although not every governor has a cabinet, each state has a number of high officials who advise the governor on important issues. The governor sometimes selects these officials. More often, however, voters elect executive officials.

While the top government officials vary from state to state, most states have a few important officials in common. Usually a secretary of state is responsible for keeping the state's records. An attorney general acts as the state's lawyer and legal adviser. A superintendent of public instruction (sometimes called a commissioner of education) sets educational

★ **SECTION 2 REVIEW** ★

UNDERSTANDING VOCABULARY
Define commute, parole.

REVIEWING OBJECTIVES

1 What are several characteristics of the office of governor?

2 What are some of the powers and duties of the governor?

3 What executive officials and agencies are found in most states?

SUPREME COURT CASE STUDIES
Reynolds v. Sims

When the nation was young, each county or town had a representative in the state legislature. By the early 1900s, more and more people were moving to cities and suburbs. The old formula for assigning legislative seats was no longer fair. A county with 2,000 residents and a city with 100,000 people might each have 1 representative. The legislators from rural areas controlled the state legislatures and paid little attention to the needs of city dwellers.

The Significance of the Case

The ruling required every state to draw up new voting districts, each with an approximately equal number of voters. This ruling has become known as the "one person, one vote" rule, meaning that each vote counts equally no matter where a voter lives. States also had to draw up new congressional districts for members of the United States House of Representatives. Today the "one person, one vote" rule applies to every election in the country.

The Case

Many people realized that apportioning seats by area instead of population was very unfair. In 1964 the United States Supreme Court heard the case of *Reynolds* v. *Sims*, which involved the apportioning of legislative seats in Alabama. At that time the Alabama legislature had 43 rural state representatives for every urban one and 16 rural senators for every senator from a city or suburb.

Overrepresented rural areas

The Court ruled that voters in the most populous districts were underrepresented and that this unequal representation violated the Fourteenth Amendment's guarantee of citizens' equal protection under the laws. As a result both houses of the state legislature had to be reapportioned according to the population, not area.

REVIEWING THE CASE

1 Why was apportioning legislative seats by area unfair to cities and suburbs?

2 How do you think the "one person, one vote" rule affected city residents?

The State Legislative Branch

State legislatures vary in name and size. In some states the legislature is called the general assembly; in others, it is called the legislative assembly. Most states, however, simply call it the legislature. New Hampshire has the largest legislature, with more than 400 members, and Nebraska has the smallest, with only 49 members.

The similarities, however, outweigh the differences. With one exception, every state legislature has two houses. The upper house is always called the senate, and the lower house is usually called the house of representatives. The one exception is Nebraska, which has a **unicameral,** or one-house, legislature. Its single house is called the senate.

Legislative Districts

Each state legislature divides its state into many election districts. The people in these districts elect their own representatives to the state legislature. Generally, there is one set of districts to elect state senators and another to elect state representatives. For many years senate districts were based on land area, and house districts were based on population. This system resulted in unequal representation in many state senates. For example, a city district and a county district would each be represented by 1 senator, even though the city district might have 10 times more people.

The United States Supreme Court's "one person, one vote" decision (see *Reynolds* v. *Sims* on page 318) ended this

State Legislatures   Nebraska's legislature has only 49 members, making it the smallest in the country.   *In what other way does Nebraska's legislature differ from that of other states?*

Election Districts The Texas House of Representatives has 150 members elected from 150 districts. *What is apportionment?*

situation in 1964. The Court ruled that all election districts must be equal, or nearly equal, in population. As a result many states had to change the apportionment of their legislatures. **Apportionment** is the distribution of legislative seats according to population.

Legislators

Each state constitution lists the qualifications for membership in its legislature. Generally, legislators must be American citizens and must live in the district they represent. They must also have reached a certain age—usually 25, 21, or 18. A legislator's term may be 2 or 4 years, depending on the state.

Originally, membership in the state legislature was not intended to be a full-time job. Many state legislatures met for only a few months every two years, and legislators took time off from their jobs to serve. For this reason the pay for legislators is still fairly low.

As the duties of state governments have grown, however, the responsibilities of state legislators have increased. Many legislatures meet for at least six months a year, and some meet year-round. As a result many state legislators have become full-time public servants, and their salaries are now increasing.

The Legislative Process

State legislatures operate much like the United States Congress. Ideas for bills come from many sources, including the executive branch, interest groups, individuals, and legislators themselves. After a state senator or representative introduces a bill in the legislature, the bill is sent to an appropriate committee. State legislatures, like Congress, have various committees that study bills, hold hearings, and revise the bills if necessary. A committee may recommend that a bill be passed or that it be killed. If the two houses pass different versions of a bill, the bill is sent to a conference committee.

As in the United States Congress, each house of a state legislature has a leader. A speaker usually presides over the state house of representatives, and a president (often the lieutenant governor) usually presides over the state senate. These leaders have a great deal of control over legislation.

After the legislature passes a bill, it is sent to the governor, who may sign the bill, veto it, or pocket-veto it. In many states, the governor has another option as well—a **line-item veto**—which means that the governor can approve certain parts of the bill and veto others.

If the governor vetoes all or part of a bill, the legislature may vote to override

Education California has one of the nation's largest university systems. *Why are many state universities facing financial problems?*

the veto. As in the United States Congress, however, few vetoes are successfully overridden.

Problems Facing States

In recent years Americans have begun to expect more and more from their state governments. They demand better public transportation, better schools, and better services for people who are disabled or disadvantaged. They expect their state governments to protect the environment, regulate business, and reduce crime and drug abuse.

Budget Squeeze

Unfortunately, most states have found it difficult or impossible to pay for these services. Most legislators will not vote to raise taxes because they know that such a vote may cost them reelection. In the past, federal grants helped pay for programs that state taxes could not sup-

port. However, many of those grants have been eliminated as the federal government has faced its own budget squeeze.

Borrow or Cut Services?

As a result many state governments have been faced with a difficult choice: to borrow increasing amounts of money or to cut essential services. Neither solution is satisfactory. Paying interest on borrowed money is expensive and adds to the drain on a state's treasury. On the other hand, cutting services—at a time when crime, homelessness, and pollution are rising—may be considered unwise and irresponsible.

The Supreme Court's "one person, one vote" ruling increased the representation of city dwellers in state legislatures. Because cities are where crime, drug abuse, and unemployment are highest, legislators are under great pressure to deal with these issues.

★ **SECTION 3 REVIEW** ★

UNDERSTANDING VOCABULARY
Define unicameral, apportionment, line-item veto.

REVIEWING OBJECTIVES
1 How are legislative districts organized at the state level?

2 What are the basic qualifications of state legislators?

3 In what ways is the legislative process in the states similar to that of the federal government?

4 What are some of the problems facing states and state legislatures?

Developing a Multimedia Presentation

With a multimedia presentation, you can easily capture the attention of your audience by presenting information in an interesting way. Multimedia is the mixture of text, video, audio, and animation in an interactive computer program. To create a multimedia presentation, you will combine computer and video images, along with television, sound, and video.

Learning the Skill

To develop a multimedia production, you will need traditional computer graphic tools and draw programs, animation programs that make still images move, and authoring systems to tie everything together. Before you start, assess your computer to determine what its capabilities are. Your production can be modified to the tools you have.

Practicing the Skill

Before you begin creating a multimedia presentation, answer the following questions:

■ Which forms of media would be most effective for a presentation like this? Do you want sound, video, animation, photographs, and graphics?

■ Which of these elements does your computer support?

■ What kind of software program, software system, or authoring system do you need?

■ Is there a "do-it-all-program" that would enable you to develop the type of presentation you want?

■ Of all the available media forms, which is most appropriate for each segment of your presentation?

APPLYING THE SKILL

Use these guidelines to plan a multimedia presentation about your state's constitution. Be sure to include a complete outline of the text, as well as the multimedia applications.

A Completed Multimedia Presentation

The State Judicial Branch

The federal court system, which you read about in Chapter 12, handles only a small portion of the nation's judicial workload. Most of the legal matters that arise within a state—robberies, assaults, sale and use of illegal drugs, broken contracts, child custody battles, and so on—are the responsibility of the state court system.

Lower State Courts

Each year, state and local courts decide millions of cases. To handle the enormous number of cases as efficiently as possible, most states have set up several different kinds of courts. At the lowest level are justice courts, which handle minor matters in local communities.

Small local courts almost always handle less serious crimes, known as **misdemeanors.** These courts do not have juries. Instead, a single judge hears and decides each case. The voters of the community usually elect lower court judges.

In many rural areas and small towns, the local court is called a justice court and the judge is called a **justice of the peace.** In larger towns and small cities, local courts may be called police courts or **magistrate courts.** These courts handle minor cases such as traffic violations or disturbing the peace. They may also handle civil cases involving small sums of money, usually less than $1,000. If someone is found guilty, the punishment may be a small fine or, occasionally, a short jail term.

Most larger cities have municipal courts that serve the same purpose. These are often divided into specialized courts—traffic courts, juvenile courts, and small-claims courts. Small-claims courts hear civil cases involving small amounts of money.

A Civil Wedding   A judge marries a young couple in a civil ceremony.   *What kinds of cases do lower court judges usually hear?*

Higher State Courts

Courts called general trial courts handle more serious crimes, known as **felonies.** These courts deal with criminal cases involving major crimes such as robbery, murder, and arson. They also hear civil cases involving large amounts of money.

General Trial Courts

Depending on the state and on the way the court system is organized, a general trial court may be called a district court, a county court, a common pleas court, a circuit court, or a superior court. No matter what they are called, however, general trial courts have the same responsibility: to determine whether someone is guilty or not guilty of a serious crime.

Unlike lower courts, general trial courts may use a jury to determine a defendant's guilt or innocence. The job of the judge in a general trial court is to guide the jury and, in some cases, to decide on a sentence.

Appellate Courts

Sometimes the decision of a general trial court may be appealed to an appellate court. The basis for appeal is usually that the general trial court violated one of the defendant's constitutional rights to a fair trial.

An appellate court has no jury. Instead, a panel of judges reviews the records of the trial court's proceedings. If the judges feel that the defendant did not have a fair trial, they can decide—by a majority vote—to overturn the lower court's decision.

The highest state court is the supreme court, in some states called the court of appeals. The supreme court consists of a panel of judges, usually elected by the voters.

Like the United States Supreme Court, the state supreme court hears arguments from lawyers representing both sides of a case, reviews the evidence, and makes a decision by majority vote. Except for cases involving federal law or the United States Constitution, the decisions of the state supreme court are final.

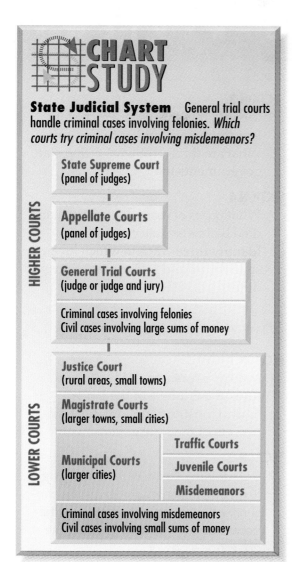

CHART STUDY

State Judicial System   General trial courts handle criminal cases involving felonies. *Which courts try criminal cases involving misdemeanors?*

HIGHER COURTS

State Supreme Court
(panel of judges)

Appellate Courts
(panel of judges)

General Trial Courts
(judge or judge and jury)

Criminal cases involving felonies
Civil cases involving large sums of money

LOWER COURTS

Justice Court
(rural areas, small towns)

Magistrate Courts
(larger towns, small cities)

Municipal Courts
(larger cities)

| Traffic Courts |
| Juvenile Courts |
| Misdemeanors |

Criminal cases involving misdemeanors
Civil cases involving small sums of money

However, the United States Constitution guarantees a fair trial to every individual, no matter how much that trial costs. For this reason state courts cannot cut their services.

Most state court systems have too few judges and too little space to handle the huge number of cases that come before them each year. Because of this, months may pass before a person who is accused of a crime finally receives a trial. A defendant who cannot afford bail may remain in jail during those months—even if he or she is innocent.

One way the courts have tried to speed the legal process and cut costs is by plea-bargaining with defendants. In a **plea bargain,** a defendant agrees to plead guilty to a crime in exchange for a reduced sentence or some other form of leniency. A guilty plea makes a court trial unnecessary. Few people believe that plea-bargaining is a good solution to the problem of overcrowded courts. No one, however, has found a better solution that does not involve spending money.

Cases that do involve federal law or the Constitution may be appealed to the United States Supreme Court.

Problems Facing the State Courts

Running a state court system is costly. It involves paying the salaries of court officials and clerical staff and maintaining court buildings. Most state court systems face a severe shortage of funds.

★ **SECTION 4 REVIEW** ★

UNDERSTANDING VOCABULARY
Define misdemeanor, justice of the peace, magistrate court, felony, plea bargain.

REVIEWING OBJECTIVES
1 What are three types of lower state courts?

2 What are three types of higher state courts?

3 What are some of the problems facing the state courts?

Identifying Key Terms

Choose the vocabulary term that best completes each of the sentences below. Write your answers on a separate sheet of paper.

unicameral   apportionment
misdemeanor   felony   justice of the peace
plea bargain   commute

1. Some people felt that the new _____ of election districts was unequal.
2. After reviewing the case, the governor decided to _____ the criminal's sentence to life imprisonment.
3. The traffic violation was a(n) _____ and was therefore handled by the local justice of the peace.
4. The defendant decided to plead guilty in a(n) _____ in exchange for a reduced charge.
5. The murder case, a(n) _____, was handled by the general trial court.
6. Only one state, Nebraska, has a(n) _____ legislature.
7. The marriage was performed by a(n) _____ in a small rural town.

Reviewing the Main Ideas

SECTION 1

1. Identify three features of state constitutions that are similar to those of the United States Constitution.
2. What is the significance of the supremacy clause?

SECTION 2

3. Identify three roles that a governor has in common with the President.
4. What judicial powers do governors have?

SECTION 3

5. Identify three ways in which state legislatures are similar to Congress.
6. What are three problems facing state governments today?

SECTION 4

7. What types of cases are usually handled by lower state courts?
8. Identify three ways in which lower state courts and higher state courts differ.

Critical Thinking

SECTION 1

1. **Making Inferences** Why do you think the Framers of the United States Constitution did not list the powers of the state governments?

SECTION 2

2. **Determining Cause and Effect** High-level officials in many states are chosen by the voters rather than by the governor. How does this affect the governor's power?

SECTION 3

3. **Identifying Alternatives** What do you think is the best way for states to solve their money problems? Why?

SECTION 4

4. **Evaluating Information** Do you think judges in state courts should be appointed or elected? Explain.

Reinforcing Citizenship Skills

In a current almanac, select a table that shows some type of information about the states such as agricultural production or crime rates. Study the table until you are familiar with the information. Then copy a part of the table, or bring the book to class to share with your classmates. Report on your findings.

Cooperative Learning

With a group of 3 other students, develop 10 survey questions about your state government. Then interview several family members, adults, and students to find out what they know about state government. Also survey their impressions of your state government. Share your results with the class.

Focusing on Your Community

Find out about your local court system. What types of lower courts does your community have? Is there a general trial court or appeals court in your community? Prepare a short oral report of your findings.

Technology Activity

Using the Internet

Search the Internet to find issues and challenges currently facing your state's policymakers. You might use the name of your state or the following as key words to help focus your search: **issues, legislation, state laws.** Study the information you find and determine how you feel about a particular issue or challenge. Then search the Internet to find your state representative's e-mail address. Write

and send electronic mail to the legislator describing your position on the issue and asking how the legislator views the issue.

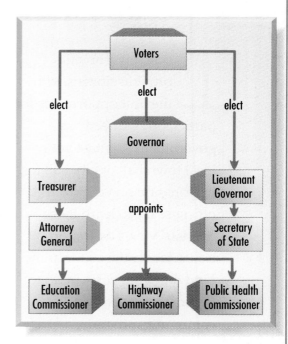

Analyzing Visuals

The diagram above shows the organization of the executive branch of a typical state. Study the diagram and answer the questions.

1. Which state officials are usually chosen by the voters?
2. How can the voters show their approval or disapproval of the way the state attorney general and state treasurer perform their duties?
3. What avenue of complaint might there be for people dissatisfied with a commissioner?

CHAPTER 14

Local Government

CIVIC PARTICIPATION

Local governments provide citizens with the best opportunity for participating directly in government. Contact your local town hall or city hall for information on your local officials. Try to learn these officials' views on important issues facing the community. Find out what you can do to become involved in community affairs.

Working in Your Community

When you have this information, choose an issue facing the community. Organize a meeting of friends and neighbors to discuss the issue. Draft a petition stating the group's ideas and recommendations for dealing with the issue. Circulate the petition in the community to gather signatures, and then present it to local government officials. ■

Your Civics Journal

As you study this chapter, think about some of the problems facing your local government. If your community has a local newspaper, look through it for ideas. Write the problems in your civics journal. Note which level of government deals with the problem and what is being done.

San Francisco skyline ➤

County Government

FOCUS

TERMS TO KNOW
charter, ordinance

OBJECTIVES

- Describe the basic **organization of county government.**

- Identify and describe the roles of various **county officials.**

- Explain reasons for the **growth of county government.**

U nder our federal system, each city, town, and county has its own local government. Unlike the federal and state governments, which are basically similar, these local governments vary greatly in size and structure. The United States Constitution grants no power to local governments. In fact, it does not even mention their existence. Instead, the states establish all local governments. Usually, state constitutions describe the duties and powers of local governments. The only powers a local government has are those that the state gives it. Most often, a state grants these powers in a **charter,** or plan of government. This charter describes the local government and gives it authority over its affairs.

Because each state's history and geography are different, each has set up different kinds of local governments.

One type, county government, is found in every state except Connecticut and Rhode Island.

The United States has more than 3,000 counties. These counties vary greatly in size and in population. In some states counties are known by other names. In Alaska they are known as boroughs; in Louisiana they are called parishes. No matter what their size is or what they are called, however, these counties have one thing in common— they provide services for their citizens.

Organization of County Government

A group of officials called a county board governs most counties. In some places this group is known as the board

County Government   A county board may have both legislative and executive powers. *How do county governments raise money for county facilities and services?*

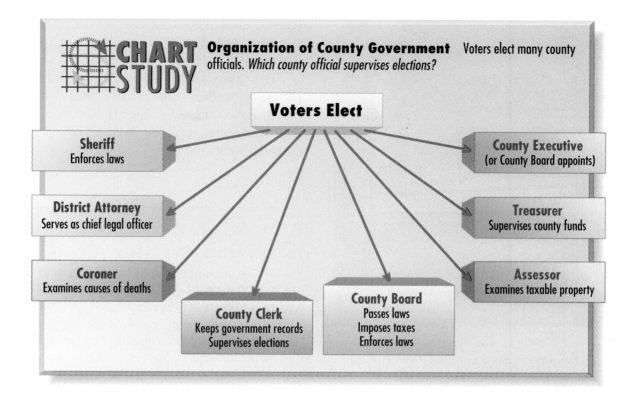

CHART STUDY

Organization of County Government Voters elect many county officials. *Which county official supervises elections?*

Voters Elect

Sheriff
Enforces laws

District Attorney
Serves as chief legal officer

Coroner
Examines causes of deaths

County Clerk
Keeps government records
Supervises elections

County Board
Passes laws
Imposes taxes
Enforces laws

County Executive
(or County Board appoints)

Treasurer
Supervises county funds

Assessor
Examines taxable property

---

of supervisors, board of commissioners, or county court. The voters elect the county board members, who are sometimes called supervisors, commissioners, or freeholders. Usually, each board member represents a particular district within the county. While board members' terms of office vary, the most common term is four years.

The county board has legislative powers and can pass laws for the county. A law passed by a county board or other local government is often known as an **ordinance.** Ordinances may deal with such matters as regulating business, improving regional transportation, and protecting the health and safety of county residents.

A county board can also raise money by imposing property taxes or sales taxes. This money is used to pay county employees, to maintain county roads and buildings, and to provide services such as law enforcement. In addition, many counties also provide recreation facilities, hospitals, and public libraries for their residents.

Because it is also the county government's responsibility to administer and enforce laws, a county board may have executive powers as well as legislative powers. For example, many county boards employ inspectors to check buildings for safety violations. Many also set up special departments to enforce liquor and food service laws.

County Officials

The executive powers of a county board are often shared with a number of other elected or appointed officials. The

Sheriff's Duties The sheriff's department patrols the water in the Saint Clair River in Michigan. *What is the main role of a sheriff?*

roles of these officials are similar to those of executive officials in the state government.

The sheriff is the county's chief law enforcement officer. The sheriff's department, which usually includes deputies and uniformed officers, enforces court orders and manages the county jail. In some counties the sheriff's department shares law enforcement duties with a separate police department.

The district attorney (DA) is the county's chief legal officer. The DA investigates crimes, brings charges against suspected lawbreakers, and prosecutes the cases in court.

The coroner is an official who tries to establish the cause of unusual or suspicious deaths. The coroner usually works closely with the sheriff's department or the police department.

The county clerk is similar to the state government's secretary of state. The county clerk keeps official government records and often supervises county elections.

The assessor examines all taxable property within the county and estimates how much it is worth. The county's property tax is based on the assessor's estimate.

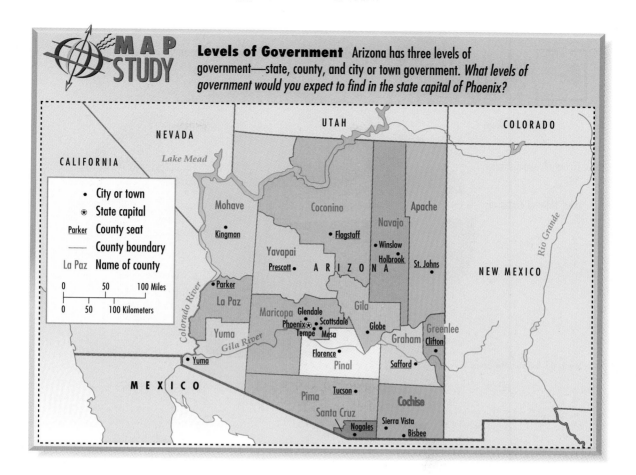

MAP STUDY

Levels of Government Arizona has three levels of government—state, county, and city or town government. *What levels of government would you expect to find in the state capital of Phoenix?*

The county treasurer, like the state treasurer, supervises the county's funds and makes payments from the treasury. He or she may also be the chief tax collector. An auditor, who makes sure that none of the county's money is spent without approval from the county board, supervises the treasurer's work.

Growth of County Government

County governments were first set up to provide a few basic services that residents could not provide for themselves, such as law enforcement and road construction. Over the past century, the role of county government has grown enormously throughout the United States. As large cities became increasingly crowded, many of their residents moved into the surrounding counties. Many rural areas have turned into densely packed suburbs, filled with shopping centers, highways, and housing developments.

Because of this growth, county governments have been forced to provide more and more services. Most counties provide water, sewer, and sanitation services. Many also operate large, modern police departments and hospitals. To manage these increased services, county governments have begun to maintain large bureaucracies similar to those of

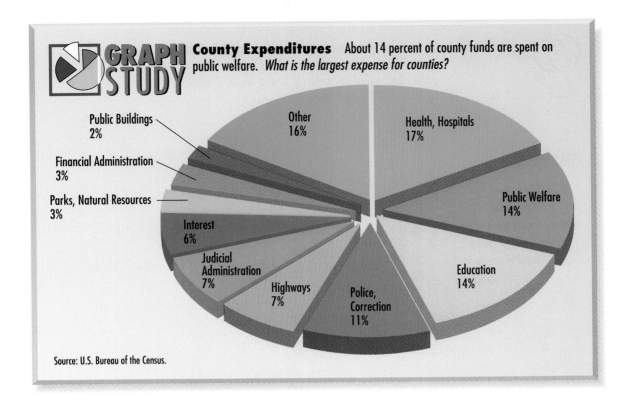

GRAPH STUDY

County Expenditures About 14 percent of county funds are spent on public welfare. *What is the largest expense for counties?*

- Public Buildings 2%
- Financial Administration 3%
- Parks, Natural Resources 3%
- Interest 6%
- Judicial Administration 7%
- Highways 7%
- Police, Correction 11%
- Other 16%
- Health, Hospitals 17%
- Public Welfare 14%
- Education 14%

Source: U.S. Bureau of the Census.

state governments. Among the government agencies found in many counties are the board of health, the welfare board, the hospital board, and the planning commission.

The increased demand for services has put a strain on many counties. The old form of county government, in which executive duties are divided equally among many officials, is often slow and inefficient. As a result, many county governments have been reorganized to operate more like state governments.

Under a new form of government that many counties have adopted, the county board operates only as a legislature. A powerful official called a county executive, or county manager, handles all executive responsibilities. Sometimes the county board hires the county executive. More often, however, the voters elect the executive. The county executive appoints top officials, manages the bureaucracy, and submits proposed bills to the legislature.

★ **SECTION 1 REVIEW** ★

UNDERSTANDING VOCABULARY
Define charter, ordinance.

REVIEWING OBJECTIVES

1 What is the basic organization of county government?

2 What are the titles of various county officials, and what are their duties?

3 What are some of the reasons for the growth of county government?

Great American Documents

The Shame of the Cities

In the early years of this century, penniless immigrants poured into cities and lived in cold, dark firetraps. Whole families worked six or seven days a week to scratch out a living.

Political Machines

Think About It

As you read the following excerpt, think about the importance of the media in exposing corruption.

In many large cities, powerful political machines arose that took advantage of the poor. Political leaders continued in office year after year, growing rich from taxpayers' dollars. Voters could have broken the machine's power but did nothing. Often this was because they were bribed with jobs or money.

The Muckrakers

Into this world stepped the muckrakers, a group of publishers, writers, and artists. They were called muckrakers because they raked the "muck," or filth, to expose political corruption and social ills.

One of the most famous muckrakers was Lincoln Steffens. Traveling from city to city, he exposed the corruption of politicians who were stealing millions from city treasuries while failing to provide basic services. Steffens's articles were collected in a book, *The Shame of the Cities* (1904), the source of the following quotation.

New York City tenement

T*he great truth I tried to make plain was that bribery is no ordinary felony, but treason . . . [and that] corruption . . . is not an occasional offense, but a common practice . . . the effect is literally to change the form of our government from one that is representative of the people to an oligarchy [government by the few], representative of special interests.*

Steffens and other muckrakers tried to educate the public and set a reform movement in motion. Soon people began demanding and winning changes.

INTERPRETING SOURCES

1 Why was the work of the muckrakers so important to the American public?

2 What do you think Steffens meant when he said that bribery was treason?

Town, Township, and Village Governments

FOCUS

TERMS TO KNOW

township, special district, user fee

OBJECTIVES

■ Describe the history of **town government.**

■ Explain the organization of **township government.**

■ Identify the basic responsibilities of **village government.**

■ Identify three kinds of **special districts.**

Just as states are divided into counties, many counties are divided into smaller units. In New England, these units are called towns. In many other eastern and midwestern states, they are called **townships.** Each town or township also has its own government. Like county governments, local governments get their power directly from the state.

The relationship between county governments and local governments varies from state to state. In New England, town governments meet the needs of most communities, and counties are basically judicial districts. In some parts of the country, county and township governments share power, but in the South and West, county governments tend to be more important than township governments. The two forms of government usually have a cooperative relationship, dividing responsibilities between them.

Town Government

Town government is one of the oldest forms of government in the United States. It began in the New England colonies, where colonists generally settled in small villages and towns. In most cases, farmers living in outlying areas were also considered town members. From the very beginning, these New England colonists met regularly with their neighbors to discuss problems that involved everyone. A majority vote settled any disagreements.

Eventually, "town meetings" became the colonists' form of local government. Citizens rather than elected representa-

Town Clerk   In some towns the clerk takes care of the day-to-day details of local government.   *How are decisions made in town governments?*

Careers

Firefighter

Fighting a fire

Putting out fires is hard, dangerous, dirty work. The hours are long and the working conditions are miserable. Nevertheless, many men and women become firefighters because saving lives and property is a vital and rewarding job.

Working as a Firefighter

When a fire breaks out, seconds count in saving lives and property. Therefore, each firefighter must perform a specific job as part of a highly trained team. Some firefighters drive the fire trucks, others operate hoses, and still others search burning buildings for fire victims.

Some fire-fighters become fire inspectors or fire science specialists. These specialists inspect buildings to spot fire hazards and make sure the buildings have adequate fire-detection and fire-fighting equipment.

Training

Most firefighters usually work for towns, cities, or private companies. In many small towns, firefighters are unpaid volunteers who fight fires in their spare time. To become a professional firefighter, you should be a high school graduate. You must pass a civil service test and a rigorous physical exam. If accepted, you will undergo several months of apprenticeship training.

School TO WORK

Find out from your local fire department the exact requirements for becoming a firefighter. Present your findings to the class in the form of an oral report. Conclude the report by asking a firefighter to speak with your class about the job.

tives made all important decisions. Because each citizen had a direct say in the government, the town meeting was a form of direct democracy. You read about direct democracy in Chapter 1.

A number of small New England towns still hold town meetings today. These meetings are usually held once a year. The time and place and the topics to be discussed are announced in advance. All town residents who are registered to vote are encouraged to attend the town

meeting. One by one, the topics on the agenda are discussed and then voted upon.

Because town meetings are held so rarely, they are useful only for making broad policy decisions. They cannot handle the day-to-day details of government. For this reason each New England town elects a number of officials, called selectmen, to run the local government between meetings. (Despite the name, selectmen may be women.) The town may also elect executive officers similar to those in a county government, such as a clerk, a treasurer, and an assessor.

Some New England towns have replaced the traditional town meetings with representative town meetings. In these towns the citizens elect people to represent them at the town meeting. Other towns have eliminated town meetings entirely. These towns are run much like counties, with a board of selectmen or a town council doing the job of a county board.

Township Government

New York, New Jersey, and Pennsylvania were organized somewhat differently than New England. The counties in these states were divided into smaller units called townships, a term borrowed from Great Britain. These townships set up local governments similar to those of New England towns.

Midwestern Townships

Midwestern townships have a different history. As the United States expanded westward, it acquired new land that was not yet settled. As this land was obtained, Congress divided it into square blocks, which were called townships. Townships were sections of land, not units of government. As settlers moved into these areas, however, they set up local governments similar to those in the eastern states. These governments, called civil townships, generally kept the same borders that Congress had originally established. For this reason many midwestern townships appear perfectly square on a map.

Today some township governments are like town governments, holding township meetings similar to town meetings in New England. Most townships, however, have governments similar to those of counties. In most cases a small group of elected officials called a town-

Township Government   Some midwestern states have local governments known as civil townships.   *What is the origin of midwestern townships?*

ship committee, board of supervisors, or board of trustees has legislative responsibilities. A township supervisor usually heads this committee or board.

Township and County Responsibilities

Over the years county governments have taken over a number of responsibilities originally held by township governments. In some cases county and township governments work together to provide local services. Law enforcement duties, for example, may be divided between county and township police forces. Township officials may supervise county elections, and county officials may oversee the maintenance of township roads.

Village Services Village governments can collect taxes to spend on libraries and other projects for the community. *What is the main disadvantage of becoming a village?*

Village Government

A village is the smallest unit of local government. Villages almost always lie within the boundaries of other governments, such as townships or counties. In some areas villages are known as boroughs. (These should not be confused with Alaskan boroughs, which are similar to counties rather than to villages.)

The population of some rural communities may be quite small—a few hundred people, or even fewer. Communities this small often have no need for their own government. County or township governments provide for most of their needs. Occasionally, however, community members find some reason to band together. They may be dissatisfied with the services the county provides, or they may want to set up their own school system. In that case they may organize the community as a village and

request permission from the state to set up a village government.

As in a township, the government of a village usually consists of a small board of trustees the voters elect. Most villages also elect an executive, similar to a town manager. This official is usually known as the chief burgess, or president of the board, or sometimes as the mayor.

The village board has the power to collect taxes and spend money on projects that benefit the community. Those projects may include building and maintaining roads, establishing schools and public libraries, or setting up recreation facilities. The board may hire officials to supervise these projects and provide other services.

Becoming a village has both advantages and disadvantages. The main disadvantage is that residents must often pay higher taxes to support the village government. In return, however, they

Special Districts Small communities often band together to create a school district. *What are some other types of special districts in local government?*

often get better services. Becoming a village also improves the community's status. As a result, visitors, new residents, and businesses may be attracted to the village, bringing money and other resources with them.

Special Districts

Local governments sometimes have special problems or needs. To deal with these matters, they may request permission from the state to create units of government called special districts. A **special district** is set up to deal with a single issue or provide a single service.

Special districts are sometimes set up for financial reasons. For example, one small village may not be able to afford a fully equipped fire department. By pooling their resources, however, several villages may be able to set up a fire department to serve the entire area.

In other instances a special district may be established to deal with a regional issue. For example, several communities may use the water in a reservoir. Managing this water is beyond the authority of any of the individual communities.

A board or commission, which may be elected or appointed, runs a special district. The board sometimes has the power to collect taxes from district residents to pay for the service it provides. Some boards levy **user fees** to raise money. For example, a water district charges residents a fixed price for every gallon of water they use.

One of the most common types of special district is the school district. Small communities often band together to build schools and hire faculty and staff. An elected school board or board of education usually runs a school district. The United States has about 15,000 school districts.

★ SECTION 2 REVIEW ★

UNDERSTANDING VOCABULARY
Define township, special district, user fee.

REVIEWING OBJECTIVES

1 How did town government begin in the United States?

2 What is the basic organization of township government?

3 What are the basic responsibilities of village government?

4 What are three kinds of special districts?

How to Deal With Government Bureaucracy

Dealing with government bureaucracy can be frustrating and difficult. Sometimes you must explain your problem over and over again before reaching the right department or official. You may also have to stand in line for hours or come back another day because you failed to bring the right form or document.

Planning and Preparation

You can take much of the frustration out of dealing with the government by doing as much planning and information gathering as possible beforehand.

- If you need to contact a government department, look up its number in a local telephone directory. Government numbers may be grouped together in a special section or listed alphabetically in the white pages. If no number is listed for a specific department, call the main number and ask for the department or briefly explain your business. With large government bureaucracies, you may be transferred two or three times before reaching the right person.

- After reaching the proper department, explain your problem and listen carefully for instructions. Have pencil and paper handy to take notes. You may be told to write to a certain official, to send photocopies of documents, or to send in an application fee. Be sure to get the correct names and addresses, and follow all instructions carefully.

Dealing with paperwork

- In some cases you will have to appear in person. Get the address of the office and find out when it is open. Make a list of the documents you need to take.

The key to dealing with government bureaucracy is to expect delays and rerouting. Sometimes you may be surprised to find your problem quickly and efficiently resolved.

CITIZENSHIP IN ACTION

1 What can you do to make it easier to deal with a government bureaucracy?

2 Why do you think it is difficult for a large government bureaucracy to serve the public efficiently?

SECTION 3

City Government

FOCUS

TERMS TO KNOW
home rule, mayor, ward, member-at-large, metropolitan area

OBJECTIVES

- Describe the organization of a **mayor-council government.**

- Compare a **council-manager government** with the mayor-council plan of city government.

- Describe the organization of a **commission government.**

- Describe the organization and responsibilities of a **metropolitan government.**

- Identify and discuss several **challenges facing local governments.**

C ity government is the most common form of local government. When people think of the word *city*, they often think of skyscrapers, neon lights, and hundreds of thousands, or perhaps millions, of people. A city, however, can be as small as 2,500 people. Whether a community is called a city really depends on whether or not its residents consider it to be one.

Most of the features that characterize a city cannot be measured or counted. Cities are usually important centers of business, art, and education. Their residents often live more closely together than the residents of towns or suburbs. Cities frequently depend heavily on particular industries, such as manufacturing, high technology, or trade. They usually have special problems as well, such as high rates of crime or drug abuse, homelessness, and large numbers of people with AIDS.

For whatever reason, the people who live in a particular community sometimes begin to think of that community as a city. When that happens, they may apply to the state legislature for a city charter. As you know, a charter is a document that grants power to a local government.

A city charter is much like a constitution, describing the type of city government, its structure, and its powers. The state legislature still maintains control, however. It may change the powers granted to the city government at any

Bustling Cities   Many cities are regional centers of business, education, and art.   *What are some of the special challenges of cities?*

time. In recent years many state legislatures have begun to grant home rule to cities. **Home rule** allows cities to write their own charters, choose their own type of government, and manage their own affairs. Cities must still follow state law.

A city charter usually sets up one of four types of government: the mayor-council form, the council-manager form, the commission form, or the metropolitan form.

Mayor-Council Government

The oldest and most widely used type of city government is the mayor-council form. Under this form of city government, responsibility for governing the city is divided between separate legislative and executive branches. The legislative branch consists of a group of officials called the city council. A chief executive called the **mayor** heads the executive branch. It also includes officials such as a clerk, a treasurer, a comptroller, and a city attorney. Separate departments handle police and fire protection, recreation, roads and buildings, health and welfare, and other matters.

Some cities are divided into voting districts called **wards**. Each ward elects a representative to the city council. In other cities, however, some or all of the members of a city council are known as members-at-large. A **member-at-large** is elected by the entire city.

The voters elect the mayor, most often for a four-year term. The powers of the mayor vary from city to city. Some cities follow a strong-mayor plan, which

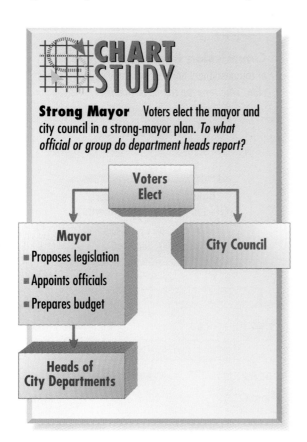

CHART STUDY

Strong Mayor   Voters elect the mayor and city council in a strong-mayor plan. *To what official or group do department heads report?*

Voters Elect

Mayor
- Proposes legislation
- Appoints officials
- Prepares budget

City Council

Heads of City Departments

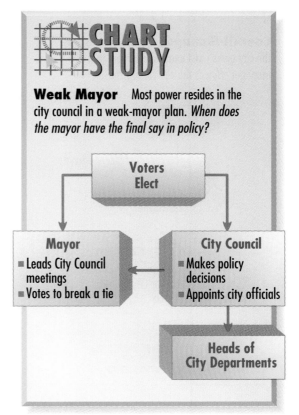

CHART STUDY

Weak Mayor   Most power resides in the city council in a weak-mayor plan. *When does the mayor have the final say in policy?*

Voters Elect

Mayor
- Leads City Council meetings
- Votes to break a tie

City Council
- Makes policy decisions
- Appoints city officials

Heads of City Departments

gives the mayor a great deal of power over city affairs. Under this plan the mayor has many of the same powers as a governor or the President. He or she can veto bills the city council passes and also appoint and dismiss different city officials. A strong mayor also submits an annual budget to the city council and takes the lead in proposing legislation.

Many cities, however, still follow a weak-mayor plan. Under this plan the mayor has only limited executive power. The city council makes most policy decisions, and the mayor's veto power is restricted. In addition, the city council rather than the mayor chooses the heads of most city departments. The mayor usually leads city council meetings and votes only to break a tie.

The weak-mayor plan dates from the nation's early days, when memories of unfair British officials were still vivid. Even today many Americans want to prevent any one official from having too much power. The weak-mayor plan achieves that goal, but it also makes a city government much less efficient.

Council-Manager Government

Today a growing number of cities have adopted another type of city government—the council-manager form. In

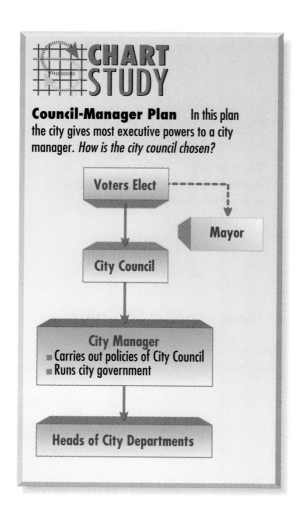

CHART STUDY

Council-Manager Plan In this plan the city gives most executive powers to a city manager. *How is the city council chosen?*

Voters Elect

Mayor

City Council

City Manager
- Carries out policies of City Council
- Runs city government

Heads of City Departments

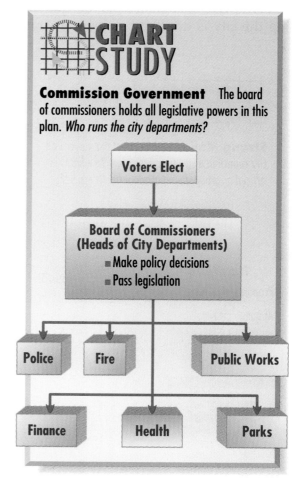

CHART STUDY

Commission Government The board of commissioners holds all legislative powers in this plan. *Who runs the city departments?*

Voters Elect

Board of Commissioners
(Heads of City Departments)
- Make policy decisions
- Pass legislation

Police Fire Public Works

Finance Health Parks

this type of city government, the voters also elect a city council. They may even elect a mayor, but he or she has almost no power. Instead, most of the executive powers are held by an official called a city manager. This manager is responsible for carrying out the council's policies and running the city government.

City Manager

A city manager is selected by the city council rather than the voters. City managers are almost always professional executives who know how to get things done. Because they are not elected, they are free from political pressures that might interfere with getting a job done.

A council-manager government operates like a large corporation. In the business world, a company's directors would probably fire an ineffective manager. In a city, the city council is likely to dismiss a city manager who does not run the city efficiently. Unlike the situation in a large corporation, however, money may limit the effectiveness of council-manager government. The top managers of successful corporations often receive millions of dollars in salaries and benefits. Most cities cannot afford to reward their executives this generously. As a result they often have trouble attracting the best managers away from the business world.

Disadvantages

Although the council-manager form of government is usually very efficient, many Americans do not approve of it. They feel that any official as powerful as a city manager should be elected, not appointed. Otherwise, the needs and wishes of voters—especially minority voters—may not be taken into account.

Commission Government   In this form of government, the voters elect commissioners, who run the city departments.   *How are the executive and legislative functions handled?*

Commission Government

A third type of city government is the commission form. A commission government has no separation of legislative and executive powers. Instead, separate departments, each of which handles a different set of responsibilities, govern the city. Some of the most common departments are police, fire, finance, health, and public works. The elected heads of these departments, called commissioners, perform executive duties for their particular department. They also meet together as a commission, with legislative power to pass city ordinances and make policy decisions.

In some cities either the commission or the voters choose one commissioner to be mayor. The mayor has no special powers and usually has only a ceremonial role. Still, he or she remains

Transportation Needs   The Bay Area Rapid Transit (BART) system serves the San Francisco metropolitan area.   *How does a metropolitan government differ from a special district?*

an equal member of the commission and continues to manage a government department.

The commission form of government was developed in Galveston, Texas, in 1901. Nearly destroyed by a tidal wave, the city decided that a commission government was the best way to handle the emergency. Since that time, however, other cities have found that a commission government is not always efficient in running a city. Without clear leadership, a commission is often unable to set and meet goals. Each commissioner is likely to concentrate primarily on his or her own department, without considering the problems of the city as a whole.

Metropolitan Government

The influence of a city does not stop at the city borders. Suburbs surround nearly every major city. Together, the city and its suburbs form a unit called a **metropolitan area.**

The different local governments in a metropolitan area often have many needs in common. For example, because many people live in the suburbs and work in the city, a good transportation system is essential to people in both places.

Some metropolitan areas have begun to deal with these regional issues by forming metropolitan governments. A metropolitan government is similar to a special district in that it involves several local governments. However, a metropolitan government usually has more than one area of responsibility. It may, for example, handle the transportation, water, and energy needs of people in the area. An elected board usually runs a metropolitan government.

City and suburban residents may also form metropolitan councils to help them solve common problems. A metropolitan council is a regional organization made up of local elected officials, such as mayors and county supervisors. A metropolitan council does not have any special powers. It is simply an organization that discusses metropolitan issues, shares information, helps coordinate the policies of different local governments, and seeks solutions to regional problems.

Challenges Facing Local Governments

The same financial problems that confront state governments also affect local governments. Community residents demand an increasing number of services but are unwilling or unable to support those services through increased taxes.

This problem is especially serious in cities. Crime, homelessness, drug abuse,

Maintenance Keeping bridges in good repair requires regular maintenance. *How do local governments handle the costs involved?*

AIDS, and pollution have been rising steadily in urban areas. At the same time, many of the industries and businesses that help provide cities with jobs and revenue have closed or moved elsewhere. In addition, as conditions in cities get worse, many people who can afford to leave move to the suburbs. Many of those who remain are poor and cannot afford higher taxes. As a result, cities are finding it increasingly difficult to raise enough money to solve their problems.

Because of their financial difficulties, many local governments cannot afford to pay for services and the maintenance of buildings, parks, and roads. When a problem arises, they look to another unit of government to solve it. This happens because of the overlapping jurisdiction of local governments. For example, most villages are located in townships, which in turn are located in counties. Under these circumstances, it is often difficult to

know which government is responsible for what. If a town bridge needs repair, for example, the town may ask the county to pay for the work. The county, in turn, may insist that the town should pay for the work. As the dispute goes back and forth, the bridge goes unrepaired.

Part of the solution to problems facing local governments lies in greater cooperation between the different levels of government. In some cases this cooperation may be purely financial. Cooperation between governments may also take other forms. Increasingly, local governments are getting together to discuss their regional problems and to work out solutions. The idea of a metropolitan government, which was described earlier, is an important step in this direction.

★ SECTION 3 REVIEW ★

UNDERSTANDING VOCABULARY
Define home rule, mayor, ward, member-at-large, metropolitan area.

REVIEWING OBJECTIVES
1 What is the basic organization of a mayor-council government?

2 How does a council-manager government compare with a mayor-council form of government?

3 How is a commission government organized?

4 What is the basic organization of a metropolitan government, and what are its major responsibilities?

5 What are some of the challenges facing local governments?

Identifying Key Terms

Choose the vocabulary term that best completes each of the sentences below. Write your answers on a separate sheet of paper.

ordinance   special district
home rule   metropolitan area
ward   member-at-large

1. The city council included one _____, elected by all the voting districts.
2. The three neighboring towns applied for permission to create a(n) _____ to handle their water resources.
3. The city was granted _____, which allowed it to write its own charter.
4. The influence of the city had spread to its surrounding suburbs, creating a(n) _____.
5. Voters in the city's twenty-third _____ voted for the Republican candidate for mayor.
6. The town board passed a(n) _____ requiring all new house lots to be at least one acre in size.

Reviewing the Main Ideas

SECTION 1

1. Give two examples of a county board's legislative power and two of its executive power.
2. Why has county government become more important in recent years?

SECTION 2

3. What are some advantages and disadvantages of establishing a village government?
4. Identify two reasons for a special district.

SECTION 3

5. What is one disadvantage of the city commission form of government?
6. Identify and describe the two types of mayor-council plans of city government.
7. Why are many cities having financial problems?

Critical Thinking

SECTION 1

1. **Evaluating Information**   What are the advantages and disadvantages of the county executive type of county government?

SECTION 2

2. **Demonstrating Reasoned Judgment** Which do you think is more effective, state or local government? Give reasons for your answer.

SECTION 3

3. **Identifying Alternatives**   What do you think could be done to encourage cooperation among the local governments in a region?

Focusing on Your Community

Find out about your local government and its leaders. If you live in a town, village, or city, find out who the chief executive is. Is the position a full- or part-time job? What are some of the main issues facing your community? How are local officials trying to deal with these problems? Prepare a short oral report.

Cooperative Learning

Working with three other students, find a map of your county and locate the

LEVY DESCRIPTION	ASSESSED VALUE	TAXABLE VALUE	TAX RATE	TAX AMOUNT
COUNTY GENERAL TAX	28,500	28,500	10.99118	313.25
TOWN GENERAL TAX	28,500	28,500	10.19789	290.64
TOWN HIGHWAY TAX	28,500	28,500	5.37885	153.30
FIRE	28,500	28,500	4.21016	119.99
LIGHT	28,500	28,500	.62177	17.72
WATER	28,500	28,500	11.02086	314.09
SEWER	28,500	28,500	5.80978	165.58
TOTAL **				1,374.57

TAXPAYER'S RECEIPT

STATEMENT OF COUNTY, TOWN TAXES FOR 1995

COLLECTOR'S ADDRESS

BANK   BILL NO.

JAN. INTEREST FREE	1ST HALF PAYMENT	2ND HALF PAYMENT	TOTAL TAX
	687.29	687.28	1,374.57
INTEREST % PENALTY			
FEB. 1 %	694.16	694.15	1,388.31
MAR. 2 %	701.04	701.03	1,402.07
APR. 3 %	707.91	707.90	1,415.81
MAY 4 %	714.78	714.77	1,429.55

boundaries for your town, township, or city. Then write five questions about jurisdiction for various regional services. For example, who maintains the roads in the middle of town? Contact your local government offices to find the answers. Share your results with the class.

Technology Activity

Using E-Mail

Search the Internet to find the e-mail address of a local television station or newspaper. You may want to use the following key words to focus your search: **television station call letters, city or town name, e-mail address.** Then review the entries in your civics journal on local government problems. Choose an issue that involves the question of jurisdiction. Write and send electronic mail to at least one local news outlet about the importance of cooperation among local governments. Share your e-mail letter with the class.

Analyzing Visuals

A large part of a county's and town's revenue comes from property taxes. Above is an example of an annual property tax bill. Study the bill, then answer the questions.

1. What are the special districts for which taxes are collected?
2. To which special district is the greatest amount of tax paid? The lowest?
3. How much in penalties does this resident pay if taxes are paid in May?

Reinforcing Citizenship Skills

Think of a reason for which you would need to contact a government office, such as applying for a driver's license or a building permit. Outline the steps you would take and the information you would collect before calling the office. Include a few questions you would ask. Share your plan with the class.

CHAPTER 15

Community Issues

CIVIC PARTICIPATION

In recent years the responsibilities of state and local governments have increased dramatically because of such issues as rising crime rates, homelessness, and environmental pollution. Contact the offices of your local government to find out what is being done to solve local problems and how volunteers can help. Find out when the town board or city council meets.

Working in Your Community

After you have obtained the information, interview people in the neighborhood to find out what they think should be done about various problems the community faces. Tell them about the town board or city council meetings, and encourage them to attend or to become involved in community activities. ■

Your Civics Journal

As you study this chapter, keep a list of issues you consider to be very important to your community. Perhaps your school is overcrowded, or the air is becoming more polluted. Next to your list of issues, write ideas of what you think should be done about each issue.

Community volunteers ➤

Dealing With Community Issues

FOCUS

TERMS TO KNOW

public policy, infrastructure, priorities, resources, master plan, zoning board, bond

OBJECTIVES

■ Discuss factors involved in **making public policy.**

■ Identify several issues communities must consider when **planning for the future.**

■ Identify some of the **difficult questions** communities face as they plan for the future.

■ Identify five ways of **financing public policy.**

S chools, businesses, and other organizations usually have policies, or rules, that guide their actions. These policies allow decisions to be made consistently. Most businesses, for example, have policies about hiring, promoting, and firing employees.

Federal, state, and local governments also make policies. A policy a government makes is called a **public policy** because it affects all members of the public. A public policy is not a law. In many cases it is not even written down. In-stead, a public policy is a general agreement among government leaders about how they intend to deal with certain issues or problems.

Making Public Policy

The ideas for policies, like those for laws, come from many different sources. They may originate with members of the legislative, executive, or judicial branches. Party leaders or interest groups may propose them. Members of the media, such as newspaper journalists and television commentators, may even suggest them.

One other important source of policy ideas, especially at the local level, is private citizens. Often, just one person can have a great effect on the policies of local government. In Oakland, California, for example, a man named Robert Patten believed that the beauty of a scenic road near his home should be preserved. When a storage company began building a large, unattractive warehouse near the road, Patten acted immediately. He gath-

Citizen Action Citizens may take part in a demonstration on public issues. *Where do ideas for public policy originate?*

Careers

EPA Inspector

EPA inspector

The Environmental Protection Agency, or EPA, is the federal agency responsible for protecting the environment. It employs thousands of inspectors to oversee the enforcement of pollution control laws and regulations.

Activities and Responsibilities

EPA inspectors work throughout the United States, inspecting air, water, and soil for evidence of pollution. Their work may involve travel and hazardous conditions. Investigating the cause and extent of pollution requires EPA inspectors to visit places where pollution might occur and test for pollutants and collect samples for analysis. Inspectors might visit industrial plants and test nearby water supplies to make sure the water quality meets government standards. They monitor the air quality of major cities and in the vicinity of large factories. They also inspect dump sites and surrounding areas for toxic wastes or other hazardous materials. After completing their investigation, EPA inspectors compile reports of their findings and initiate action to stop further pollution.

Education and Training

EPA inspectors learn about pollution and its causes, environmental regulations, and proper inspection procedures through a combination of education and on-the-job training. EPA inspectors generally have a college education with a specialization in environmental or biological science, plus several years of experience in the field. As with most government jobs, EPA applicants must pass a civil service examination.

School TO WORK

Use library resources or Internet sources to find information on current job opportunities with the EPA. Use the information to create a help-wanted brochure for the agency.

---

ered his neighbors' signatures on a petition and complained to the city government. As a result the city convinced the storage company to make some changes in the building's design. The city also changed its policy about what kinds of buildings would be allowed near the road.

Changing a public policy is not always easy, however. It may take months or even years. During that time disagreements about what the public policy should be or how a policy should be changed may arise. Like congressional committees, local governments often do research and hold public hearings before

Improving the Infrastructure   Governments build roads and bridges to make transportation easier.   *What is an infrastructure?*

making policy decisions. The policy that results is often a compromise that reflects many points of view.

Planning for the Future

Making policies to solve current problems is not always effective. The most useful public policies are usually those that try to prevent problems before they occur. This requires looking at what is likely to happen in the future and planning for it now. A growing number of local governments are setting up planning commissions to do this kind of work. A planning commission is an advisory board whose members may include government leaders, businesspeople, local residents, and architects.

Short-term Plans

Local governments and their planning commissions make both short-term and long-term plans. A short-term plan is a policy designed to be carried out over the next few years. For example, Oakland's decision to protect the scenic road near Robert Patten's home is a short-term plan. In the future the Oakland planning commission may change its mind.

Long-term Plans

A long-term plan is a broader, less detailed policy than a short-term plan. It is designed to be followed over 10, 20, or even 50 years. To make long-term plans, a planning commission must make educated guesses about a community's future needs. For example, it might try to determine future transportation, education, and recreation needs by looking at recent population and economic patterns.

Difficult Questions

Planning for a community always involves searching for answers to a number of difficult questions. Take, for example, a small town whose local computer software company suddenly becomes successful. As the company expands, it builds several new buildings. Attracted by the growing economy, other businesses move into the town. People flock to the town to work for these companies.

A situation like this raises a number of questions for a local government. For example, will increased traffic cause problems on local roads and highways? Should the town build new roads to accommodate more vehicles, or should it encourage the development of public transportation? What other demands will the growing population place on the town's **infrastructure**—its system of roads, bridges, water, and sewers? If the infrastructure needs to be expanded, how will the town pay for the work?

Evaluating Priorities and Resources

Hundreds of local governments and planning commissions around the country face questions like these every year. The answers to such questions usually depend on two things—priorities and resources. **Priorities** are the goals a community considers most important or most urgent. In setting priorities, a community must first decide what it values most. For example, is it more important to have commercial success or a peaceful place to live? While assessing its values, a community must also determine its more specific goals and rank them in order of importance. For example, a community may decide that its most important goal is to attract business. Following that may be goals of improving community services, preserving open spaces, upgrading the school system, and so on.

Once a community has set its priorities, it must look closely at its **resources.** These are the materials, people, and money available to carry out the community's goals. Suppose, for example, that a community has decided to improve its public transportation system. Is there enough money to build and maintain a new trolley system, or would an expanded bus system be more affordable? Which system will attract the most riders and earn the most revenue? To plan effectively, a community must consider how much money and what other resources are available.

Creating a Master Plan

After setting priorities and evaluating resources, a planning commission makes practical decisions about the community's future. It usually expresses these decisions in a document called a **master plan,** which states a set of goals and explains how the local government will respond to the changing needs of its citizens over time.

Priorities and Resources   Local governments may set aside land and funds to create parks.   *Why do you think communities want parks?*

A planning commission normally submits its master plan to the local government, which then decides whether to accept and enforce it. If the master plan is accepted, the local government is responsible for carrying it out. The legislative branch must approve funds for any projects outlined in the plan. The executive branch makes rules and regulations to enforce the plan. In many communities an important commission called a **zoning board** decides where houses, stores, factories, and offices may be built. For example, the zoning board may set up a residential zone in which no businesses are allowed.

Communities often have a housing board, which makes sure that the community has safe, affordable housing. Often, a recreation department will set aside land for parks and athletic fields. If a public transportation system is part of the master plan, a special commission is usually set up to build or improve it.

Financing Public Policy

No local government can carry out any of its plans without first deciding how it is going to pay for them. Taxes are the most common source of revenue for local governments.

Different Kinds of Taxes

Nearly every local government imposes a tax on property—the land and buildings—within its borders. Some places also impose a property tax on items such as boats or cars. The advantage of a property tax is that it is a steady source of revenue. The main disadvantage is that a property tax is difficult to apply fairly. No mathematical formula can determine how much a piece of property is worth. Tax assessors can only make estimates.

An increasingly popular source of local revenue is the sales tax. With a sales tax, people pay a fixed percentage of the

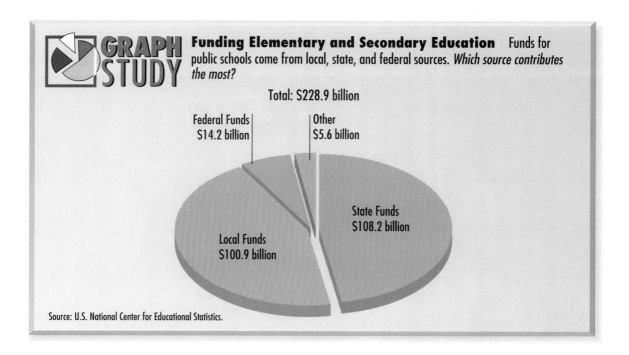

GRAPH STUDY

Funding Elementary and Secondary Education Funds for public schools come from local, state, and federal sources. *Which source contributes the most?*

Total: $228.9 billion

Federal Funds $14.2 billion

Other $5.6 billion

State Funds $108.2 billion

Local Funds $100.9 billion

Source: U.S. National Center for Educational Statistics.

Public Transit Washington's subway system is one of the newest in the country. *Are subway fares considered taxes or user fees?*

purchase price—usually 5 to 8 percent—in addition to the purchase price. The advantage of a sales tax is that it is easy to collect. The major disadvantage of a sales tax is that it puts an unfair burden on low-income families.

An income tax, the chief source of revenue for the federal government and for many states, also appears at the local level. Many large cities have income taxes. The primary advantage of an income tax is that the burden falls most heavily on those who can most afford to pay. The main disadvantage is that it is more difficult and costly to enforce.

Businesses pay most of these kinds of taxes and a variety of other taxes. For example, many communities require certain businesses to have a license to operate. To receive its license, a business must pay a fee to the government.

Other Sources of Income

One common source of revenue is user fees. These include tolls charged on roads and bridges and fares for public transportation. User fees are often considered a fair way to raise money because they require only those who use government services to pay for them. Like sales taxes, however, user fees fall hardest on low-income people.

Many local governments find that they must borrow money to pay for the services they provide. They may borrow money from banks, but more often they borrow money from the public by issuing bonds. A **bond** is an IOU or promissory note from the government. For example, if you pay $100 for a bond, the government promises to pay the $100 back—with interest—by a certain date. Issuing bonds is an easy way for a local government to raise money quickly. The drawback, however, is that the government must eventually pay back not only the amount of the bond but also interest.

★ SECTION 1 REVIEW ★

UNDERSTANDING VOCABULARY
Define public policy, infrastructure, priorities, resources, master plan, zoning board, bond.

REVIEWING OBJECTIVES

1 What are some of the factors involved in making public policy?

2 What are several issues communities must consider when planning for the future?

3 What are some of the difficult questions communities face as they plan for the future?

4 What are five ways of financing public policy?

Social Issues

C ities are often portrayed as dirty, noisy, crowded, and dangerous places. The areas outside cities are portrayed as quiet, orderly, and clean. Such distinctions are becoming a thing of the past. As the populations of cities have spilled over into surrounding areas, urban troubles have followed. Changes in family structure, movement between different regions, and changes in the makeup of American society have also brought new challenges to many areas in the nation. People everywhere must now deal with issues such as crime, inadequate housing, and declining standards of education.

Education

In 1991 more than $228 billion was spent on public education in United States elementary and secondary schools. Local governments supplied about 45 percent; the rest came from federal and state funds. Of all the services local governments provide, education is the most expensive.

Despite the money being spent, many Americans have become increasingly unhappy with the public education system. Students often feel that the subjects they study in school have little to do with their lives. Teachers, faced with students who seem uninterested in learning, are frustrated with their jobs and work for a salary that is low compared to salaries for many other jobs. Parents complain that their children are not learning basic skills and are not being taught values and ideas from their own cultural traditions. In addition, problems

Magnet School By focusing on special subjects in magnet schools, educators hope to improve public education. *Which level of government has the primary responsibility for education?*

American Profiles

Christine Todd Whitman

In 1994 Christine Todd Whitman became the fiftieth governor of New Jersey. Christie Whitman, as she is known, is the first woman ever elected to that office.

Political Background

Whitman's family was influential in the Republican party. After college she became active in Republican politics, and she later held a number of Republican staff jobs. In 1990 she ran for the United States Senate in New Jersey and almost upset Senator Bill Bradley.

In her campaign for governor, Whitman pledged to reduce taxes, cut government spending, and make New Jersey's government smaller and more responsive to the people. As governor, she is working hard to keep her promises. She is already well on her way to cutting state income taxes. Conservative on financial issues, she is more moderate on social issues.

The Future

Whitman's victory and success so far have made her a rising star in the Republican party—perhaps even a future vice-presidential candidate. For Whitman, her priority now is New Jersey and the welfare of its citizens.

PROFILE REVIEW

1 What are some of her positions on political issues?

2 Why is Whitman a rising star in the Republican party?

---

such as high dropout rates, drug abuse, and crime plague many schools.

Some problems have worsened as families move from the cities to the suburbs. Rapidly expanding suburban communities are unable to build schools or hire teachers fast enough to handle the growing number of students. Back in the cities, lower-income families cannot afford to maintain their school buildings or pay their teachers adequately.

Local governments have begun to tackle these problems in a variety of ways. To improve the quality of education, for example, some areas have begun experimenting with "magnet schools," which allow students to focus on particular fields, such as science or the arts.

Urban Renewal   Community volunteers help fix up houses in need of repair. *What other steps are being taken to help homeless people?*

Magnet schools bring together students from rich and poor communities, and they are supported by everyone in the area. By allowing students to concentrate on what they do best, magnet schools encourage students to work harder.

Another idea for improving education is to give parents publicly financed vouchers to help pay the cost of sending children to private schools. This "school choice" plan is being tried in a number of places around the nation. (See page 473.) Still another idea is to let private companies run public school districts. Supporters of this idea argue that it would improve education by making schools more competitive.

Housing

A critical issue in many communities is adequate, affordable housing. In many communities and city neighborhoods, rising real estate values have forced out lower-income families. Many move to less desirable areas, but some cannot find

any affordable housing at all. These people may join the growing number of homeless individuals and families who roam the nation's streets.

Another aspect of the housing problem involves the decline of certain neighborhoods into slums. Many buildings in these areas are run-down and dangerous, and they often lack hot water and heat.

Urban Renewal

Cities have approached the housing problem in different ways. Some cities have tried to eliminate slums through urban renewal projects. **Urban renewal** means rebuilding old neighborhoods, often by tearing down old buildings and replacing them with new ones. In recent years the trend in urban renewal has been to convert old buildings into fashionable shops and living spaces. In many cities young, well-to-do professional people are buying slum buildings and turning them into attractive residences. While urban renewal may improve the appearance of cities, it does not always solve the underlying problems. If poor neighborhoods become middle-class neighborhoods, poor families will have an even harder time finding housing.

Low-Income Housing

Many communities have tried to solve the housing problem by building low-income housing—blocks of houses and apartments set aside for low-income families. Unfortunately, most governments cannot afford to build enough housing units to satisfy the demand. Even after low-income housing has been built, it can be very expensive to maintain. Many communities, faced with shortages of funds, have had to cut back on repairs and upkeep of their low-income housing. The result is often a government-owned slum.

Crime

Crime is a serious problem in many communities. Crime rates are usually highest in cities, where poverty and crime often go hand-in-hand. For people who have struggled in poverty with dead-end, minimum-wage jobs, robbery or drug dealing may seem like a practical way to make a better living. For other people, employment may not even be an option. Many of the poorest inner-city residents—sometimes called the underclass—drop out of school early and spend much of their time on the streets. Crime is often the only way of life these people know.

Many cities have set up programs to try to help poor people improve their lives. These programs may include after-school tutoring and government-funded summer jobs for young people and job training and counseling for adults. Such programs give people the skills they need to work their way out of poverty.

In recent years, with the increased use of illegal drugs, crime has become a major problem in suburbs and small towns as well as cities. Drug addicts often steal to get the money they need to buy drugs. Drug dealers often engage in violent crimes as they fight over territory.

Many communities are fighting drug-related crime through education. By teaching young people how to "say no" to drugs, they hope to put the drug dealers out of business.

When possible, communities have tried to expand their police forces. Often, however, there are simply no funds available for more law enforcement officers. In that case many communities have formed neighborhood watch programs, in which ordinary citizens are trained to spot and report any suspicious activity in their neighborhoods.

Job Training   Some communities offer high school students and adults job-training classes.   *What is the purpose of these classes?*

Cleanup Campaign Volunteers work in the "Adopt a Highway" program to keep a section of roadway free of litter. *Why do communities benefit from volunteer work?*

Outlook for the Future

Given enough money, local governments could go a long way toward solving their social problems. They could raise teachers' salaries, build low-income housing, fix up decaying neighborhoods, hire additional police, and do much more. Unfortunately, as has been mentioned many times, money is in short supply. The challenge facing communities, therefore, is to find solutions to their problems without relying on higher taxes or federal funds.

Many communities are beginning to meet that challenge by taking advantage of their greatest resource—their citizens. If given enough encouragement, citizens are often willing to devote time and energy to helping their communities. **Voluntarism,** the tradition of unpaid community service, has always been an important part of American life.

Community volunteers help their neighborhood schools by getting involved with parent-teacher organizations and by tutoring students. They help homeless people by opening shelters, running soup kitchens, and organizing clothing drives. They help fight crime by participating in neighborhood watch programs. They help poor families by giving money, clothing, and food to community service organizations.

Recent court decisions extending the "one person, one vote" rule have given some citizens—those from minority groups in particular—a greater voice in their local government. This increased participation has led to increased voluntarism as well. When people feel appreciated and valued as members of a community, they become more willing to devote themselves to that community.

★ **SECTION 2 REVIEW** ★

UNDERSTANDING VOCABULARY
Define urban renewal, voluntarism.

REVIEWING OBJECTIVES

1 What are two problems associated with the public education system?

2 What are two ways in which communities have tried to solve housing problems?

3 What are two ways in which communities are trying to solve the problem of crime?

4 What is the outlook for the future regarding the efforts of communities to solve their problems?

How to Use a Library

When you need information about a particular topic, the best place to look is in your local library.

Card Catalogs

Most libraries still have card catalogs that organize references to books according to subject, title, and author. Many libraries are now replacing these with computerized catalogs that allow you to get the same information faster.

Articles and Reference Sources

You can find references to magazine articles on a topic in the *Reader's Guide to Periodical Literature.* Some libraries also have a computer InfoTrak system that lists articles by subject or author.

The reference section of your library also has encyclopedias, almanacs, atlases, dictionaries, and other research aids in book form. Some libraries carry reference materials on CD-ROM, a computer disk that can hold an entire encyclopedia or other reference work. Libraries may also offer computer databases from which material can be printed.

Most libraries also have a news index or digest, such as *Facts on File.* This allows you to find references to newspaper articles on a topic.

The Librarian as a Resource

The librarian will help you locate the information you need. The librarian knows the library's resources and can direct you to useful collections.

Electronic card catalog

CITIZENSHIP IN ACTION

Practice your library skills by researching a community issue in which you are interested. Then complete the following tasks.

1 List the main topic and subtopics you will use to find information.

2 Write the author, title, and call number of a book about your topic.

3 Write the title of two newspaper articles and two magazine articles about your topic, and include the name and date of the newspaper(s) and magazine(s).

4 Locate these four articles and read them. Write short summaries of the main points.

Environmental Issues

FOCUS

TERMS TO KNOW
landfill, recycling

OBJECTIVES

■ Discuss the problem of **resource shortages,** and identify possible solutions to such shortages.

■ Identify some of the sources of **air and water pollution.**

■ Explain how some communities are dealing with the problem of **waste disposal.**

■ Describe what communities are doing to resolve the issue of **land use.**

■ Discuss the **outlook for the future** in regard to the solution of environmental problems.

When the oil tanker *Exxon Valdez* ran aground off the coast of Alaska in March 1989, it spilled 10 million gallons of oil in Prince William Sound. The oil killed countless fish, birds, otters, and other wild creatures and blackened hundreds of miles of coastline.

The *Valdez* oil spill reminded Americans of the high price we pay for living in an industrialized society. Every time we turn on a light, drive a car, or throw away trash, we harm our environment.

Often, that damage is small and easy to ignore. Sometimes, as in Prince William Sound, the damage is much greater.

Protecting the environment is a national, and worldwide, concern. Most often, however, the battles to protect the environment are fought at the local level. Nearly every town and city has its own environmental problems and is searching for ways to solve them.

Resource Shortages

As their populations grow, communities place greater demands on their energy and water resources. Many local areas are having trouble meeting this demand. Existing power plants often cannot produce enough electricity to meet people's needs, especially on hot summer days when air conditioners are running.

In many western states, where rainfall is limited, the demand for water is an even greater problem than the demand for electricity. As the populations of these

Oil Spill   Workers try to clean oil off the shore after the *Exxon Valdez* spill.   *Where and when did the* Exxon Valdez *run aground?*

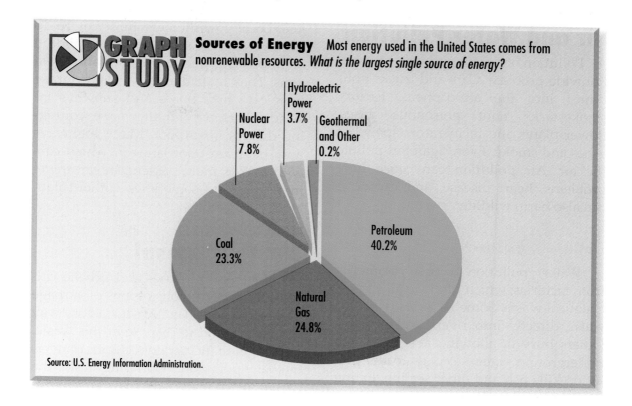

Sources of Energy   Most energy used in the United States comes from nonrenewable resources. *What is the largest single source of energy?*

Hydroelectric
Power
3.7%

Geothermal
and Other
0.2%

Nuclear
Power
7.8%

Petroleum
40.2%

Coal
23.3%

Natural
Gas
24.8%

Source: U.S. Energy Information Administration.

states grow, housing developments are built in desert areas and the demand for water is greatly increased.

New Power Plants

Americans disagree about solutions to these problems. Some believe that the best answer is new power plants and reservoirs. This solution has many drawbacks, however. Coal- and oil-burning power plants pollute the air. Nuclear power plants can be dangerous. Reservoirs alter the landscape and destroy the habitats of many wild creatures. Moreover, building power plants and digging reservoirs are very expensive.

Conservation

Other people believe the best answer is conservation. People can conserve electricity by buying energy-efficient ap-pliances and turning off unnecessary lights. They can conserve oil and natural gas by adjusting thermostats, installing more efficient furnaces, and insulating their homes. They can conserve water by putting weights in toilet tanks, taking shorter showers, and reducing or eliminating lawn watering. This solution has drawbacks as well, however. Conservation is very difficult to enforce. Except in times of emergency, most Americans resent actions that interfere in their personal lives. They do not want to be told how much water or power to use.

Scientists are working on a third solution—energy sources that do not harm the environment. In the future we may get much more of our electricity from sunlight, wind, water, or less harmful forms of nuclear energy. So far, however, none of these technologies is ready for large-scale use.

Air and Water Pollution

Pollution of our air and water is a nationwide problem. Cars and trucks pour fumes into the atmosphere. Factory smokestacks emit poisonous gases. Power plants and incinerators spew out ashes and smoke. Even cigarettes pollute the air. Air pollution can cause lung problems, heart disease, and cancer. It can also harm wildlife.

Polluted Water

Water pollution comes primarily from factories, which produce all sorts of chemical waste. Some factories pour this waste directly into rivers and streams. Others bury it, allowing it to seep into underground water supplies. Water pollution kills fish and other sea life. Eating fish from polluted waters can also cause severe illness in people. Drinking polluted water can be dangerous or even deadly.

Controlling Pollution

The federal government, through the Environmental Protection Agency, has done much to stop industrial pollution of air and water. Federal regulations strictly limit the amounts and kinds of waste that factories can discharge. Unfortunately, budget cutbacks in recent years have kept many of these regulations from being enforced. As a result state and local governments have had to take more responsibility for protecting the air and water.

Pollution factories produce can be regulated much more easily than pollution individuals produce. In many cities, cars and trucks are the primary source of air pollution. The only way to ease this problem is to persuade people to drive less. Local governments are trying to do this in two ways. First, they are building or improving public transportation systems. They hope that this will encourage people to take buses and subways instead of cars. Second, they are encouraging drivers to carpool. Many highways now have car-pool lanes in which cars with two or more passengers can travel more quickly—sometimes without paying the usual tolls.

Waste Disposal

Together, industries and private citizens produce millions of tons of garbage and trash each year. No satisfactory way has been found to dispose of this waste. Burning it in incinerators creates dangerous air pollution. Dumping it in the ocean does not work, as New Jersey residents discovered when hospital debris washed up on their beaches in 1988. Much waste in recent years has been

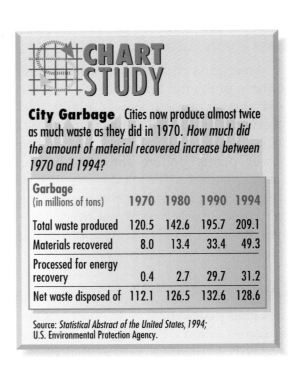

CHART STUDY

City Garbage Cities now produce almost twice as much waste as they did in 1970. *How much did the amount of material recovered increase between 1970 and 1994?*

Garbage (in millions of tons)	1970	1980	1990	1994
Total waste produced	120.5	142.6	195.7	209.1
Materials recovered	8.0	13.4	33.4	49.3
Processed for energy recovery	0.4	2.7	29.7	31.2
Net waste disposed of	112.1	126.5	132.6	128.6

Source: *Statistical Abstract of the United States, 1994;* U.S. Environmental Protection Agency.

buried at huge sites called **landfills.** Existing landfills are nearly full, however, and few Americans are willing to have new ones opened.

Recycling

Recycling has become an increasingly popular way to dispose of some waste. In **recycling,** old materials are reused to make new ones. For example, used paper and paper products can be shredded, bleached, and processed to make new paper. One new, innovative recycled paper product is mulch, which landscapers use on newly seeded lawns. Many towns and cities now have voluntary recycling programs, and some have passed laws requiring recycling. The federal government is doing the same by requiring federal agencies to use more recycled paper. It hopes that this will stimulate investment in more recycling plants. Unfortunately, only a few kinds of waste are suitable for recycling. Glass, aluminum, paper, and certain kinds of plastic can be recycled successfully. Other common kinds of waste—such as plastic foam—cannot be recycled.

Precycling

Once again, the best solution seems to be conservation. Many communities with active recycling programs are now encouraging *pre*cycling—using only products that can be recycled. Consumers may be asked to buy peanut butter in glass jars instead of plastic ones. Some stores encourage consumers to return bags by offering a rebate. Businesses are encouraged—and sometimes required by law—to eliminate unnecessary packaging. In Berkeley, California, for example, businesses are not allowed to sell products in plastic foam. Many record-

ing companies have reduced the amount of packaging on compact discs. In some communities, high school students have taken the initiative in the conservation

Historic District   The Beacon Hill section of Boston is now an historic district, part of the city's efforts to preserve its past.   *Why are land-use policies controversial?*

Many communities now set aside land for parks or wildlife refuges and restrict the use of certain types of land. For example, a hotel built on beachfront property may be required to allow public access to the beach.

Preservation

Many communities try to hold on to their history as well as their land. To protect important historical sites, some communities set up historic districts in which no changes can be made without special approval. Individual buildings can be protected in a similar way by being declared landmarks.

The planning process described earlier in this chapter also helps preserve land and buildings. Planning commissions and zoning boards can help keep expansion under control. They can prevent developers from building houses or shopping centers in places where they would do more harm than good.

Conflicting Interests

Not everyone agrees that limiting growth is a good idea, however. Many people object to restrictions that prevent businesses from bringing money into the community. There is always controversy when a piece of land is set aside as a park or a historic district. The controversy becomes especially strong when that land is known to contain an important resource, such as oil or minerals. In this time of energy shortages, many people feel that access to resources is more important than history or beauty.

Nevertheless, communities now tend to be more cautious in deciding land use issues. Too many farms, forests, marshes, and beaches have already been lost.

effort. They have, for example, led campaigns to ban the use of plastic foam in school cafeterias.

Land Use

Land is a scarce resource; we have only a fixed amount of it. Every time farmland is paved over for a shopping center or a housing development replaces a forest, we lose a valuable part of the environment. Many communities have learned this lesson too late, after productive farmland and scenic areas have been destroyed.

Communities have begun to protect their land in several different ways.

Auto-Emissions Testing Many communities require testing of auto emissions to control pollution. *In what other ways are states trying to reduce auto emissions?*

Outlook for the Future

Solving environmental problems is difficult and expensive. Especially in these days of limited funds, state and local governments cannot do the job by themselves. Communities have had to find new ways to think about these issues and work on solutions.

One positive development is the increase in cooperation between governments. In Chapter 14, you read about special districts and metropolitan governments. Environmental issues have recently led to cooperation on an even larger scale. For example, the governors of 12 northeastern states joined together to ask the Environmental Protection Agency to impose a strict program to reduce auto emissions in their region. The plan would require all new cars to run on alternative fuels or electricity or to be fitted with emissions-control equipment.

Similarly, the states of Pennsylvania, Maryland, and Virginia have joined forces with the city of Washington, D.C., to fight water pollution in the Chesapeake Bay.

Communities are also beginning to depend more on private businesses and citizens. In many towns and cities, privately owned companies provide free recycling services to local residents. These companies make money by selling the bottles, cans, and stacks of paper to other companies that can recycle them.

Similarly, energy and water use in many communities is being reduced significantly through the efforts of individuals. As conservation becomes a way of life for more Americans, the nation may come closer to solving its environmental problems.

★ **SECTION 3 REVIEW** ★

UNDERSTANDING VOCABULARY
Define landfill, recycling.

REVIEWING OBJECTIVES
1 Why are resource shortages a problem, and what are two possible solutions to such shortages?

2 What are some of the sources of air and water pollution?

3 How are some communities dealing with the problem of waste disposal?

4 What are communities doing to resolve the issue of land use?

5 Why has the outlook for the future improved in regard to the solution of environmental problems?

Identifying Key Terms

Choose the vocabulary term that best completes each of the sentences below. Write your answers on a separate sheet of paper.

priorities   urban renewal
resources   bonds   infrastructure
zoning board

1. The goal of the city's _____ project was to rebuild old neighborhoods.
2. In setting its _____, a community must balance its goals and its resources.
3. The planning board turned down a proposal to build a recreation center because the town lacked the _____ required.
4. The _____ ruled that only residential buildings could be built in that particular part of the town.
5. To pay for the new school, the community issued _____.
6. Much of the city's _____ was badly in need of repair.

Reviewing the Main Ideas

SECTION 1
1. What is the role of a planning commission?
2. Identify and explain two nontax sources of local revenue.

SECTION 2
3. What have local governments done to try to improve their systems of public education?
4. What is the effect of rising real estate values on the housing problem?
5. Identify three voluntary activities that can help solve a community's social problems.

SECTION 3
6. Identify four environmental issues communities face.
7. What are some ways in which communities have attempted to solve their waste problems?

Critical Thinking

SECTION 1
1. **Identifying Alternatives**   Which do you think is more important, long-term or short-term planning? Why?

SECTION 2
2. **Analyzing Information**   How do you think communities should try to deal with the problem of crime?

SECTION 3
3. **Evaluating Information**   Which of the environmental issues discussed do you think is most critical today? Explain.

Reinforcing Citizenship Skills

Select a community issue you might want to research, such as landfills or recycling. Visit your local library and find at least three resources for your topic, such as a magazine article, a book, and a computer database. Write down the titles and authors of these resources and note other information needed to locate them in the library. Share your findings with the class.

Cooperative Learning

With a group of two other students, decide what your position is on this statement: The country's need for re-

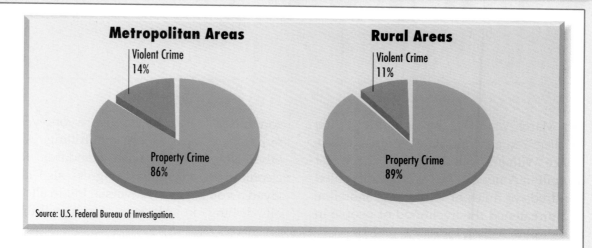

Metropolitan Areas

Violent Crime
14%

Property Crime
86%

Rural Areas

Violent Crime
11%

Property Crime
89%

Source: U.S. Federal Bureau of Investigation.

sources is more important than environmental concerns. Research information that will help you support your position. Prepare an argument for a debate with other groups in your class. Then discuss the results with your class.

Focusing on Your Community

What are the most important environmental problems in your community? Research their causes, and find out what local government, businesses, and individuals are doing to solve the problems. How successful have these efforts been? What can you, as an individual, do? Prepare a short oral report for the class.

Technology Activity

Using a Word Processor
Review the community issues you listed in your civics journal. Choose the issue you

consider most important in your community. Gather information about the issue, including various proposals or programs for dealing with the issue. Then use a word processor to prepare a report for the class.

Analyzing Visuals

Many people are concerned about violent crime—murder, rape, robbery, and assault—in their communities. However, property crime, including burglary and motor vehicle theft, are also a problem. Look at the two circle graphs above. Then answer the questions.

1. What do the two areas have in common?
2. In which area is property crime a greater percentage of all crimes committed?
3. In which area are more violent crimes committed?
4. In what ways are these percentages different from what you thought they might be?

CLOSEUP
THE VALDEZ OIL SPILL

On March 24, 1989, the oil tanker *Exxon Valdez* ran aground on a reef in Alaska's Prince William Sound, causing the worst oil spill in American history. The oil fouled hundreds of miles of wilderness shoreline and threatened the livelihood of people in the Alaskan fishing industry.

Responsibility for the Spill

The spill focused attention on the question of responsibility—for preventing such catastrophes, punishing violators, and supervising cleanup. Under federal law, whoever causes an oil spill—in this case, the Exxon Oil Company—must clean it up. The United States Coast Guard, however, is responsible for supervising any cleanup in ocean waters.

The state was responsible for regulating the Alaskan oil industry, both to prevent spills and to plan for cleanup operations. The state failed in these duties by allowing the oil industry to reduce its emergency response measures.

After the Spill

After the accident both the state and federal governments asserted their authority. Alaska charged the tanker's captain with several violations of state law. The state legislature cancelled a long-standing tax break for two large oil fields.

At the federal level, congressional committees held hearings on the spill. One committee voted to impose a one-year moratorium on offshore oil drilling. Another voted to establish standards for cleaning up oil spills. Congress also delayed a vote on a controversial bill to allow oil drilling in Alaska's Arctic wildlife preserve.

Victim of the oil spill

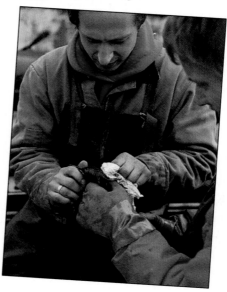

CLOSEUP REVIEW

1 What were the responsibilities of the federal and state governments in the *Valdez* oil spill and cleanup?

2 Why do you think Congress postponed a vote on oil drilling in the Arctic wildlife preserve?

Multimedia Activities

Surfing the "Net"

E-Mail Your Government Official

The most important role the representatives we send to Congress have is carrying the message of the people back to the government. With the Internet, constituents can communicate with their representatives very rapidly, and can usually expect an immediate response. To find out how you can e-mail your state's representatives follow the instructions below.

Getting There

Find out the name of your representative in Congress. Think of any issues, concerns or questions that you might like to discuss with them.

1. Go to your favorite search engine.
2. Type in the word *Congress*. Following the word *Congress*, enter words like those below to focus your search:

   e-mail address

   your representative's name

The search engine should provide you with a number of links to follow. Links are pointers to different sites on the Internet and commonly appear as blue underlined words.

What to Do When You Are There

1. Click on the links to navigate through the pages until you find your representative's e-mail address.
2. Using your e-mail service, write a letter about your concerns or interests to your representative.
3. When you receive your response, share your news with your class.

Focus on Government

The Federal System

Our federal system of government reserves many powers for the states. The states, in turn, give power to towns and cities within their boundaries. The *Focus on Government* programs referenced below help explain this sharing of power.

Setting Up the Video

Using a bar code reader or an electronic keypad, work with a group of your classmates to view these video segments of the videodisc *Focus on Government:*

Side 3, Chapter 46
Lecture Launcher:
Organization of State Government

Side 3, Chapter 47
Lecture Launcher:
State Government in Action

Hands-On Activity

Use ideas from the video segments and resources in your community to learn about the organization of your state government or of your local government. Use this information to create a flow chart showing how governmental power is distributed among the three branches of government. Use the charts on pages 327, 331, 343, and 344 as guides.

UNIT 6

Law and the Individual

YOUR ROLE AS A CITIZEN

The United States is a nation of laws. These laws are very important to the nation and its citizens. Our system of laws brings order into our lives and allows people to live together peacefully. It also protects our individual rights. Laws are only effective, however, if people respect and obey them.

In Unit 6 you will study the nation's legal system and learn about its importance in our lives. ■

CHAPTERS IN THIS UNIT

CHAPTER 16

Legal Rights and Responsibilities

CIVIC PARTICIPATION

The Constitution and Bill of Rights contain important provisions safeguarding the legal rights of Americans. In return, our system of laws gives American citizens a number of responsibilities, including the duty to serve on a jury. Contact your local county court to find out how it selects the names of people for jury duty. Ask when it sends out jury notices, how frequently a person may be called for jury duty, and under what circumstances a person may be excused.

Working in Your Community

After you have obtained the information, interview neighbors and family friends who have been called for jury duty. Find out whether they actually served on a jury and how they feel about jury duty. ■

Your Civics Journal

As you study this chapter, think about the legal rights and responsibilities we have as American citizens. Keep a list of these in your civics journal. Next to each entry, explain why the right or responsibility is important and how it affects our lives.

Swearing in a witness ➤

The Source of Our Laws

FOCUS

TERMS TO KNOW

jurisprudence, *stare decisis*

OBJECTIVES

■ Identify and describe two **early systems of law.**

■ Identify three systems of law based on **Roman law.**

■ Explain how **English law** has influenced American law.

■ Explain the role of the executive, legislative, and judicial branches in **the American legal system.**

Laws are rules that are binding on all the people living in a particular community, state, or nation. Laws help bring order into our lives. They provide penalties to discourage people from committing crimes. They enable people to settle disagreements peacefully through a fair system of justice. They protect our rights as citizens against abuses by other people, organizations, and the government. They also promote the welfare of society as a whole by protecting it against certain dangers.

Although not all laws are good, good laws share certain characteristics. Good laws are fair. People in similar circumstances will be treated equally under the law. Good laws are also reasonable. In England in the 1700s, a person who stole a loaf of bread might have been hanged. Today such harsh punishment for a similar crime would be considered unreasonable. Good laws must be understandable. If laws are too complicated, people may break them without meaning to or realizing it. Finally, good laws are enforceable. The government's ability to enforce a law often depends on the people's willingness to obey it.

When the writers of the Constitution created a new government, they based the nation's system of laws on ideas, traditions, customs, and laws passed down from generation to generation. Some of these ideas date back thousands of years.

Early Systems of Law

The earliest laws were probably passed from one generation to the next by word of mouth. Then, after people learned to write, they began to write down their laws.

Code of Hammurabi An ancient tablet depicts King Hammurabi handing down his code of laws. *How long ago was the Code of Hammurabi written?*

About 4,000 years ago, King Hammurabi of ancient Babylon had a series of laws compiled into a list, or code of laws. This Code of Hammurabi is one of the earliest written codes of law. The code not only listed Babylon's laws but also included the punishments for breaking them. Although some of the punishments were very harsh, the code was a great benefit to the people. It ensured that the law would be followed and everyone would be treated in the same way.

Another early set of written laws was the Ten Commandments found in the Bible. The Ten Commandments are a set of moral rules about how people should behave toward one another. Many of these rules still govern our behavior today. The commandments "thou shalt not steal" and "thou shalt not kill" are reflected in our laws prohibiting theft and murder.

Religion was an important source for many of these early laws. Leaders believed that their authority and their laws came from God or from gods. One reason people obeyed the laws was because they feared the anger of their gods.

Roman Law

The ancient Romans developed an elaborate legal system that they took to all the lands they conquered in Europe, Africa, and Asia. The Romans made a science of the law, which they called **jurisprudence,** a word we still use to mean the study of the law. Over the centuries, Roman law became very complex. In the sixth century, the Emperor Justinian I produced a simplified system of laws called the Justinian Code.

More than 1,000 years after the Justinian Code was written, its ideas were taken over by the French Emperor Napoleon. Napoleon updated the Justinian

English Law By tradition these English lawyers, called barristers, wear wigs for court appearances. *What two principles of American law came from English law?*

Code and called it the Napoleonic Code. Like the ancient Romans, Napoleon carried his laws to all the lands he controlled. One of those lands was Louisiana, which France sold to the United States in 1803. The laws of the state of Louisiana are still based on the Napoleonic Code.

English Law

The most important source of American laws is English law. Perhaps the greatest contribution is the English system of common law, or law based on court decisions rather than on a legal code. Beginning in the 1100s, English monarchs sent judges throughout the English countryside to hold trials and administer the law. The decisions of these judges set precedents that became part of the common law. A second significant contribution is the idea of citizens' rights. As the power of English monarchs decreased and the power of Parliament increased, the English people began to acquire certain rights of citizenship (see Chapter 2).

Stare Decisis Judges' rulings have the force of law. *What two factors do judges use in making their rulings?*

When English settlers came to the American colonies in the 1600s and 1700s, they brought their traditions of common law and rights of citizenship with them. Today these ideas are an important part of our legal system. This is true on the federal level and in all states except Louisiana.

The American Legal System

While ideas and traditions from the past have influenced our legal system, today's laws come from the authority of the Constitution. As you know, the Constitution is the basic law of the land. It is the most important source of our nation's laws. The Constitution gives each branch of government a role in making, enforcing, and interpreting the law.

The legislative branches of government—Congress, state legislatures, and city and town councils—make most laws. While the main role of the execu-tive branch is to carry out these laws, in doing so it sometimes makes laws as well. For example, the President has the power to issue executive orders, which have the force of law. Executive departments and agencies also make rules and regulations to carry out the law. These, too, have the force of law.

Many laws come from the judicial branch as well. Although the courts do not pass laws or regulations, they do interpret them. They base their rulings on written laws and on the precedents of previous cases. These rulings are then used to build decisions about similar cases in the future. This process is called ***stare decisis,*** which is Latin for "let the decision stand." Such judicial rulings have the force of law unless a higher court overturns them. As you learned in Chapter 12, the Supreme Court has a special duty to make sure local, state, and federal laws agree with the Constitution and to strike down conflicting laws.

★ SECTION 1 REVIEW ★

UNDERSTANDING VOCABULARY
Define jurisprudence, *stare decisis.*

REVIEWING OBJECTIVES

1 What were two early systems of law, and what did they contain?

2 What three systems of law were based on Roman law?

3 In what two ways has English law influenced American law?

4 What roles do the executive, legislative, and judicial branches have in the American legal system?

Great American Documents

The Emancipation Proclamation

When the Civil War began in 1861, many Northerners believed that the purpose of the war was to reunite the nation. By the summer of 1862, however, many people were pressuring President Lincoln to take a stand against slavery. In September Lincoln acted, warning the Confederate states to abandon their rebellion by the first day of 1863. After that, he would declare the enslaved people in all rebellious states free. True to his word, Lincoln signed the Emancipation Proclamation on January 1, 1863.

Think About It

As you read the following excerpt, think about the role of the President in making the nation's laws.

Presidential Authority

The proclamation was an executive order that freed enslaved African Americans in the Confederate states. Some questioned whether the President had the authority to issue an order overruling state laws. Lincoln based his order on military necessity. As commander in chief, he felt he had authority to take any action to reunite the nation.

Excerpt From the Proclamation

Whereas on the 22d day of September, A.D. 1862, a proclamation was issued by the President of the United States, containing among other things, the following, to wit:

That on the 1st day of January, in the year of our Lord 1863, all persons held as slaves within any state or designated part of a state, the people whereof shall then be in rebellion against the United States, shall be then, thenceforward, and forever free; and the executive government of the United States, including the military and naval authority thereof, will recognize and maintain the freedom of such persons and will do no act or acts to repress such persons, or any of them, in any efforts they may make for their actual freedom. . . .

And upon this act, sincerely believed to be an act of justice, warranted [authorized] by the Constitution upon military necessity, I invoke [ask for] the considerate [thoughtful] judgement of mankind and the gracious favor of Almighty God.

The rest of the enslaved persons in the United States were officially freed after the war. On December 18, 1865, the Northern states ratified the Thirteenth Amendment, which abolished slavery.

INTERPRETING SOURCES

1 Why do you think Lincoln asked for "the considerate judgement of mankind" in the proclamation?

2 The proclamation had little effect on the lives of most enslaved African Americans in 1863. Why, then, do you think it is considered such an important document?

Legal Rights and Responsibilities

In some countries people can be jailed for very little reason. They may be accused of actions—such as demonstrating or criticizing the government—that would not even be considered crimes in the United States. These people may never be told the charges against them or be given the opportunity to defend themselves. Instead, they may be kept in prison for years or even executed without ever having a trial. Their families and friends may not be told where they are or even if they are alive.

In the United States, we have legal rights that protect us from these kinds of abuses. The Constitution outlines these rights, stating how we are to be treated if we are accused of a crime. These rights are an important safeguard of the freedom we cherish in our system of democracy.

Basic Legal Rights

The Constitution guarantees our basic legal rights. One of these rights concerns what is called a writ of habeas corpus. A **writ of habeas corpus** is a court order that guarantees a person who is arrested the right to appear before a judge in a court of law. The officials holding the person must show good reasons why the prisoner should not be released. If they cannot give good reasons, the person must be set free. A writ of habeas corpus is an important legal right because it prevents people from being arrested and put in prison without cause. Article I,

Legal Rights   A person accused of a crime has the right to a trial in a court of law. *What is a writ of habeas corpus?*

Careers

Paralegal Aide

Paralegal aide

Paralegal aides perform much of the routine work involved in preparing lawsuits, contracts, wills, and other legal documents. They do research in law books and public records, interview clients, trace the ownership of properties, fill out tax returns, write reports, and do many other jobs.

Employment

Most paralegals work for private law firms. Some are employed by the government or by large corporations. Paralegals who work for corporations are called corporate legal assistants. They are often involved in labor negotiations, contracts, and financial matters.

Education

Paralegals need a high school diploma plus two to four years of instruction in a paralegal training program. Many private schools, as well as some colleges and law schools, offer paralegal training.

Paralegals can become very knowledgeable about legal procedures and cases. They work primarily in the law office or in public record offices. Sometimes they assist an attorney in court during a criminal or civil trial. Paralegals must have a keen eye for detail and the ability to analyze data. They must also be discreet and mature because they are involved in handling many confidential matters.

School to Work

Contact the local office of the American Bar Association or an attorney's office to find information on the training that paralegals in your community must have. If possible, interview a paralegal to learn more about this career and share your findings with the class.

Section 9, of the Constitution guarantees this right by stating that "the privilege of the writ of habeas corpus shall not be suspended, unless when in cases of rebellion or invasion the public safety may require it." Habeas corpus has been suspended only twice in the nation's history—during the Civil War and in Hawaii after the Japanese attack on Pearl Harbor in 1941. In both instances the Supreme Court later held that the suspensions were unconstitutional.

Article I of the Constitution states that "no bill of attainder or ex post facto law shall be passed." A **bill of attainder** is a law that punishes a person accused of a crime without a trial or a fair hearing in court. An **ex post facto law** is a law that would allow a person to be punished for an action that was not against the law when it was committed. For example, an ex post facto law making it a crime to buy lottery tickets could be applied to someone who bought tickets

Right to Counsel An attorney confers with an accused person. *What Supreme Court decision requires states to provide an attorney to people too poor to hire their own?*

One special legal safeguard included in the Constitution concerns the crime of treason, which is the only crime the Constitution defines. Article III states that people can be convicted of treason only if they wage war against the United States, join its enemies, or give aid and comfort to the enemy. Moreover, no one can be convicted of treason without proof. Treason is defined so that the government cannot misuse the law to punish people for political activities. In some countries, criticizing the government is considered treason. The Constitution prevents this from happening in the United States.

Rights of Persons Accused of a Crime

The Constitution includes several specific rights that protect citizens accused of crimes. These rights ensure that accused persons are treated fairly and receive every chance to defend themselves. Each of these rights is based on a time-honored principle of English and American law—a person is presumed innocent unless and until proven guilty in a court of law.

before the law was passed. By banning ex post facto laws, the Constitution guarantees that people cannot be punished unfairly if the laws are changed later.

Two other important legal rights the Constitution guarantees are the rights of due process and equal protection of the laws. In Chapter 4 you learned that due process requires the government to follow certain procedures in enforcing the law. The right of due process helps guarantee that an accused person will receive a fair trial and will be granted all of his or her constitutional rights before being convicted of a crime. Equal protection of the laws helps guarantee that a person accused of a crime will not be treated differently from others because of race, religion, sex, or other factors. For example, judges will not let lawyers ask any questions or make comments during a trial that appear to be prejudiced or unfairly biased.

Under the principle of "innocent until proven guilty," the prosecutor, the government's lawyer, must prove that an accused person is guilty. The accused does not have to prove his or her own innocence. Furthermore, only a judge or jury can decide that a person is in fact guilty of a crime. Until convicted, or found guilty, of a crime, a person can only be considered a suspect.

The following are specific legal rights the Constitution guarantees. Each one protects people accused of a crime and ensures that they will be treated fairly.

Grand Jury

The Fifth Amendment provides that no person can be held for a serious crime unless evidence of it is presented to a grand jury. A **grand jury** is a group of from 16 to 23 citizens that hears evidence a prosecutor presents. The grand jury decides whether there is enough evidence to indicate that a crime has been committed. If there is sufficient evidence, the grand jury issues an indictment, or formal charge, that names the suspect and states the charge(s) against the suspect.

Self-Incrimination

The Fifth Amendment also states that "no person . . . shall be compelled in any criminal case to be a witness against himself." This means that a person does not have to answer questions that may incriminate that person, or show his or her involvement in a crime. Sometimes when being questioned by a prosecutor, a person may say, "I decline to answer on the grounds that it may tend to incriminate me." This is known as "taking the Fifth," or exercising the right to remain silent. If this right against self-incrimination is misused—to protect others, for example—the judge may hold the person in contempt of court. **Contempt of court** means that the judge believes the person is obstructing or interfering with the judicial process. A person charged with contempt of court may be jailed.

Adequate Defense

Every person accused of a crime has the right to an adequate defense during a trial. The Sixth Amendment lists several specific rights to help ensure this. First, people accused of crimes have the right to be informed of the nature and cause of the accusations against them. They also have the right to hear and question the witnesses who testify against them and to subpoena witnesses who can testify on their behalf. A subpoena is a court order requiring a person to appear in court.

Finally, they have the right to counsel, which means they have a right to be represented by an attorney, or lawyer. This right to an attorney applies to every step in the legal process, from the moment a person is formally charged with a crime to the end of the appeals process.

Before 1963 people charged with crimes in some state courts had to face trial without an attorney if they were too poor to hire one. In that year, however, the Court in *Gideon* v. *Wainwright* ruled that states had to provide attorneys to people who were too poor to afford their own. (See page 416.)

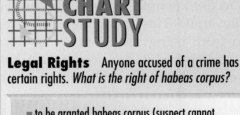

CHART STUDY

Legal Rights Anyone accused of a crime has certain rights. *What is the right of habeas corpus?*

- to be granted habeas corpus (suspect cannot be held without a hearing)
- to be told what the accusation is
- to be represented by a lawyer
- to refuse to answer any questions that may be incriminating
- to have a grand jury hearing
- to have a speedy and public trial
- to have a trial by an impartial jury
- to hear and question opposing witnesses during trial
- to subpoena their own witnesses
- to be protected from double jeopardy
- to appeal a verdict or sentence to a higher court
- to have equal protection of the laws

Bench Trial   A person accused of a crime can choose to be tried by a judge rather than by a jury.   *How many people usually are on a jury?*

Speedy and Public Trial

The Sixth Amendment also guarantees accused people the right to a speedy, public trial. This guarantee prevents them from being forced to spend long periods in jail while awaiting trial. A federal criminal trial must begin within 100 days of a person's arrest, unless there are good reasons to delay it. Some states have also set specific time limits for the prosecution to bring a case to court. The suspect can ask for delays for certain reasons, but if the prosecutor delays for too long, the state must dismiss the charges.

Trial by Jury

A person accused of a crime also has the right to a trial by an impartial jury. Impartial means that the jury members will be people who do not know anyone involved in the case and have not already made up their minds about the case. Jury members must be drawn from the area where the crime was committed.

The juries that hear trials are called trial juries or **petit juries** to distinguish them from grand juries. A trial jury is usually composed of 12 citizens, although some states permit juries of as few as 6 people. The jury is usually required to reach a unanimous verdict.

An accused person can waive, or give up, the right to a jury trial and be tried by a judge instead. This kind of trial is called a **bench trial.** A person might request a bench trial to avoid the long drawn-out process and expense of a jury trial.

Double Jeopardy

The Fifth Amendment protects an accused person from double jeopardy. You should remember from Chapter 4 that double jeopardy means a person cannot be tried twice for the same crime. Suppose, however, that a person breaks both federal and state law while committing a crime. In that case the person can be tried for the federal crime in a federal court and for the state crime in a state court. A person can also be retried for the same crime if the first trial ends in a hung jury, a jury that cannot reach a verdict. In addition, people may be tried again for the same crime if a higher court finds that the first trial was in any way unfair.

Appeals

Anyone convicted of a crime always has the right to appeal an unfavorable verdict or sentence. The person may feel that the judge or prosecutor made errors in conducting the trial, that there was not enough evidence for the jury to reach its verdict, or that new evidence would result in a different verdict.

Punishments and Fines

The Constitution also has provisions concerning punishments. The Eighth Amendment bars the government from imposing excessive bail or fines or from using cruel and unusual punishment. These provisions ensure that courts must follow reasonable standards in setting bail and for determining fines or other punishments for people convicted of crimes.

Setting Bail

When a person is arrested and brought before a judge, the judge determines the amount of bail. This amount must be reasonable in relation to the crime. A judge could not reasonably set bail at $100,000 for a motorist accused of running a red light, for example.

The main purpose of bail is to ensure that the accused person will appear in court for trial. After the trial, the person gets back the money. If a judge is convinced that the person will show up for trial and is unlikely to harm anyone, the judge may set a low bail or release the person without bail.

The prohibition against cruel and unusual punishment was originally meant to prevent such things as branding or burning a person at the stake. It has come to mean that the punishment should be in proportion to the crime. For example, it would be considered cruel and unusual punishment to sentence a person to life in prison for writing a bad check.

Capital Punishment

In recent years the Supreme Court has considered whether capital punishment (the death penalty) is cruel and unusual punishment. In 1972 the Court struck down all state capital punishment laws, although not because it found the death penalty cruel and unusual. Instead, it found that the death penalty was being applied unfairly and was used primarily on poor or African American people.

Since 1972 many states have passed new capital punishment laws, which have also been brought before the Supreme Court. State laws that made the death penalty mandatory for certain crimes, such as killing someone while committing another crime, were ruled unconstitutional. The Court ruled that these laws were too harsh because they did not allow judges to consider the individual circumstances of each case. Other state laws have established a two-stage process in capital punishment cases. First, a jury trial determines guilt or innocence. Then a separate hearing determines the degree of punishment. The Court has upheld these laws.

House Arrest In some cases people convicted of a crime are placed under house arrest rather than sent to prison. *Is house arrest a punishment or a fine?*

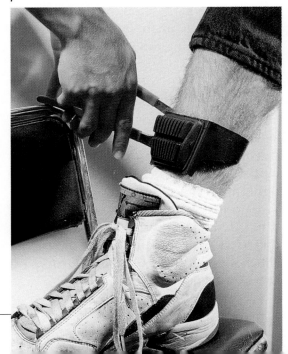

Responsibilities An important civic responsibility is to assist police in their investigations. *Why should citizens help the police?*

Two other actions have had a further impact on capital punishment laws. In 1991 the Supreme Court ruled that the number of appeals by death-row prisoners could be limited. In the past such appeals restricted the actual use of the death penalty by postponing executions for many years. Also, a crime bill Congress passed in 1994 expanded the death penalty to include about 60 offenses, including terrorism and drive-by shootings. These actions, along with the spread of capital punishment laws, have come in response to rising rates of violent crime.

Legal Responsibilities

American citizens have a number of legal responsibilities. By fulfilling them, citizens ensure that the legal system works as it should and that their legal rights are protected.

Serving on a jury and testifying in court are both important responsibilities. The legal right to a jury trial can only be effective if people are willing to serve on juries and appear in court.

Other responsibilities include obeying the laws and cooperating with police and other law enforcement officials. Earlier you learned that the government's ability to enforce a law depends to a great extent on people's willingness to obey it. Similarly, the ability of law enforcement officials to arrest and prosecute criminals depends on people's willingness to become involved and tell what they know about a crime.

Another responsibility of citizens is to work peacefully to change unfair, outdated laws. This might involve gathering voters' signatures on petitions to place an issue on the ballot for a vote or contacting legislators and asking them to change the law. For our legal system to be effective, people must care enough to participate in it.

★ SECTION 2 REVIEW ★

UNDERSTANDING VOCABULARY
Define writ of habeas corpus, bill of attainder, ex post facto law, grand jury, contempt of court, petit jury, bench trial.

REVIEWING OBJECTIVES

1 What are three basic legal rights of all citizens, and what do these rights mean?

2 What are five specific rights of persons accused of a crime, and how do these rights work?

3 What are people's legal rights concerning punishments and fines?

4 What are the basic legal responsibilities of all citizens?

SUPREME COURT CASE STUDIES
Miranda v. Arizona

Under federal law, anyone arrested for a crime must be informed of certain rights:

- The right to remain silent; any statements made can be used against you in court.
- The right to have an attorney present during any questioning.
- The right to have a court-appointed attorney if you cannot afford one.
- The right to stop answering questions at any time.

The Case

Informing suspects of their rights is now routine. It was only in 1966, however, in the case of *Miranda* v. *Arizona,* that the Supreme Court ruled that this procedure must be followed. These rights are known as the "Miranda rights."

Ernesto Miranda was tried and convicted of kidnapping and raping an 18-year-old woman in Arizona. After his arrest Miranda was questioned by the police and made an oral and written confession. At his trial the police testified they had warned him that a written statement could be used against him, but they had not warned him about oral statements. Nor had they told him he had the right to have an attorney present during the questioning.

The Ruling

The Supreme Court overturned Miranda's conviction, stating that it violated his Fifth Amendment right to remain silent and his Sixth Amendment right to counsel.

Since 1966 the Court has continued to uphold the basic principles of the case. In 1984 it stated that the "Miranda rules" apply to any case in which a person is taken into custody. Yet the Court has also ruled that the right to have an attorney present applies only after formal charges are made, not from the time of arrest.

Ernesto Miranda (right)

REVIEWING THE CASE

1 What are the four Miranda rights?

2 Why is it important for a suspect to have his or her attorney present when being questioned by the police?

Types of Laws

FOCUS

TERMS TO KNOW

civil law, lawsuit, plaintiff, defendant, contract

OBJECTIVES

■ Explain the difference between **criminal law and civil law.**

■ Identify and describe three **other types of law.**

O ur legal rights and responsibilities are important because we are a nation of laws. The United States has many laws. There are laws against drunk driving, robbing a store, selling drugs, harming another person, and so on. These laws can be divided into several categories—criminal law, civil law, constitutional law, administrative law, and international law.

Criminal Law and Civil Law

Two types of law affect Americans most directly—criminal law and civil law. These laws help maintain a peaceful and orderly society. People who break these laws generally find themselves in the courtroom.

Criminal Law

Whenever people commit a crime, such as murder, they are not only harming their victims, they are also harming the victims' families, friends, coworkers, employees, and neighbors. Criminal laws are laws that seek to prevent people from deliberately or recklessly harming each other or each other's property.

Law enforcement officers enforce criminal laws, and the courts impose penalties for breaking these laws. The safety and well-being of the entire community is affected whenever someone breaks a criminal law.

Civil Law

Civil law is concerned with disputes between people (or groups of people) or between the government and its citizens. Suppose, for example, that you slip on ice on your neighbor's sidewalk and break a leg. According to your local law, property owners are responsible for keeping their

---

Personal Injury   Someone who falls and is injured on an icy sidewalk may sue the property owner or business responsible for cleaning the walks.   *Is this a civil or a criminal matter?*

sidewalks clear of ice. If your neighbor does not do this and you are injured as a result, you have a right to sue your neighbor to recover the costs of your medical treatment and other damages.

When one person wrongs or injures another in any way, the injured person may decide to bring a lawsuit. A **lawsuit** is a legal action in which a person or group sues to collect damages for some harm that is done. The party (person, group, or organization) who files the lawsuit is the **plaintiff.** The party being sued, in this case the neighbor, is the **defendant.**

Many civil cases involve breach of contract. A **contract** is an agreement between two or more parties. It may be a written agreement or an oral one. Breach of contract means the failure to fulfill the terms of a contract. The terms of any contract are enforceable by law. Suppose, for example, that you order something from a mail-order catalog and charge it to your credit card. The mail-order company has, in effect, made a contract with you. If you do not receive the merchandise, the mail-order company has broken the contract. If the company fails to return your money, you can take it to court.

Another type of civil law involves family issues and problems. Family law deals with such things as divorce, child custody, adoption, alimony, child support, and spouse and child abuse.

Other Types of Law

Although Americans are most familiar with criminal law and civil law, some other types of law also exist. These laws affect our daily lives less directly than criminal and civil law, but they are still very important.

Constitutional Law

The Eighth Amendment prohibits excessive fines and cruel and unusual punishment. This constitutional law serves as the guiding light for our courts and legislatures whenever they deal with punishments and fines. Constitutional laws are those laws found in the United

DID YOU KNOW?

It's the Law

Did you know that it is illegal to fish for whales on Sunday in Ohio or to put pennies in your ear in Hawaii? Over the course of the nation's history, thousands of odd laws like these have been passed. Some have been repealed. Many are still in effect. The following are some unusual laws from around the nation.

- Farmers in North Carolina may not use elephants to plow their fields.
- It is illegal to lasso fish in Knoxville, Tennessee.
- In Florida a person may not sleep under a hair dryer.
- Residents of Amarillo, Texas, cannot take a bath on the main street during business hours.
- A person may not tie an alligator to a fire hydrant in Detroit, Michigan.

Enforcing the law

Types of Law   The Coast Guard patrols the territorial waters of the United States to ensure that no vessels from other countries are fishing illegally.   *Under what type of law does this action fall?*

States Constitution. As the highest laws in the land and the laws that dictate how the government works, constitutional laws have enormous influence on our lives.

Administrative Law

If the Federal Aviation Agency issued an order requiring commercial airlines to install a new type of safety device, that would be an example of administrative law. Administrative law refers to all of the rules and regulations that the executive branch of government must make to carry out its job.

International Law

If Canada and the United States had a dispute over fishing in the territorial waters of either nation, that would be a matter of international law. International law refers to any laws that affect the United States and other nations. These laws might involve military and diplomatic treaties, trade regulations, international agreements concerning fishing rights, and so on.

★ SECTION 3 REVIEW ★

UNDERSTANDING VOCABULARY
Define civil law, lawsuit, plaintiff, defendant, contract.

REVIEWING OBJECTIVES
1 What is the difference between criminal law and civil law?

2 What are three other types of law, and how would you describe them?

How to Serve on a Jury

When you reach 18 years of age, you will be eligible to serve on a jury. Jury duty is one of the primary responsibilities of United States citizenship. Procedures for jury selection vary from state to state, but jurors are always chosen at random. Prospective jurors receive a notice to appear in court at a specific date and time. Failure to obey the notice is a punishable offense.

Receiving a jury notice does not mean you will automatically serve on a jury. More people are called than are needed. You may be on standby or not needed at all. You may be selected for a case and then dismissed because the case is settled before going to trial.

Selecting a Jury

The lawyers in a case select jurors and alternates. Prospective jurors are questioned to determine whether they can be fair and impartial. Lawyers can reject a certain number of jurors who they believe will not be favorable to their clients. After jury selection is complete, the judge administers an oath to the jurors and instructs them on court procedures and rules of evidence.

Reaching a Verdict

After lawyers present all their arguments and evidence, the judge instructs the jury on the laws that apply to the case. The jury goes to a private room to discuss the evidence and decide on a verdict. In a criminal trial, the verdict is "guilty" or "not guilty" and must be unanimous. In civil cases the verdict is

Jurors taking their oath

"for the plaintiff" or "for the defendant." After reaching its verdict, the jury returns to the courtroom to announce its decision.

In reaching a verdict, jurors must determine the truth by considering only the evidence presented. They must not be influenced by a person's personality or appearance, by speculation, by information in the media, or by public opinion. They must set aside personal emotions and prejudices and never discuss the case outside the courtroom. They must also uphold the principles of the Constitution.

CITIZENSHIP IN ACTION

1 On what basis are jurors selected?

2 What are a juror's responsibilities?

3 Why is jury duty an important obligation of citizens?

Identifying Key Terms

Choose the vocabulary term that best completes each of the sentences below. Write your answers on a separate sheet of paper.

contempt of court   writ of habeas corpus
bench trial   grand jury   plaintiff
contract   double jeopardy   *stare decisis*

1. The two partners signed a _____ specifying the terms of their agreement.
2. The _____ guaranteed the man's right to appear before a judge to determine whether he was being held legally.
3. The _____ had been injured in an accident and was bringing suit against the bus company.
4. By basing its ruling on the precedents of other cases, the Supreme Court was following _____.
5. The constitutional provision against _____ protected the man from being tried for the crime a second time.
6. The accused waived her right to a jury trial in favor of a _____.
7. The _____ handed down the indictment after hearing the arguments of attorneys for both sides in the case.
8. The judge felt that the witness was obstructing the trial and held him in _____.

Reviewing the Main Ideas

SECTION 1
1. Identify four characteristics of good laws.
2. How did English law influence the development of American law?
3. Describe the role of the judicial branch in making laws.

SECTION 2
4. Why is the crime of treason defined in the Constitution?
5. What does "taking the Fifth" mean?
6. Identify three rights that guarantee individuals will have an adequate defense during a trial.

SECTION 3
7. Name three types of law.
8. Give at least two reasons why a person might file a lawsuit.

Critical Thinking

SECTION 1
1. **Evaluating Information**   Why do you think laws are important to our society?

SECTION 2
2. **Identifying Alternatives**   Are there any other legal rights you think people should have? Explain.

SECTION 3
3. **Analyzing Information**   Which types of law do you think might be most difficult to enforce? Why?

Focusing on Your Community

Lawyers often specialize in a particular type of law. Find out about specialties of the lawyers in your community. How many lawyers deal with criminal law, with international law, and so on? What is the most common type of law practiced? With what types of law are most of the legal cases in the community involved? Prepare a short report for the class.

Reinforcing Citizenship Skills

Imagine that you have received a jury notice in the mail. Write a description of what you would do next and what you would expect to happen. Then note what you plan to tell the judge about your understanding of a juror's responsibilities. Share your writing with the class.

Cooperative Learning

With a group of three other students, develop five questions about the American legal system—such as, do you believe that people accused of crimes have too many rights? Do you think juries are a fair way to try someone for a crime? Survey several adults and other students. Share your results with the members of your class, and discuss their opinions of our legal system.

Technology Activity

Using a Computerized Card Catalog

Search a computerized card catalog to find your local library's holdings on the history of legal systems and the evolution of law in the United States. (You may need to review the technology skill on using a computerized card catalog on page 16.) Find the sources on the library shelves, then use the information you find to write a two-page description of the history and foundations of the American legal system.

Analyzing Visuals

Copyright laws protect a person's work and creative ideas from others who might claim those ideas as their own or use them without the permission of the artist or author. The copyright notice reproduced above is typical of what you will see in most books. Study the notice, then answer the questions that follow.

1. On what date does this copyright become effective? Who holds the copyright?
2. What does this copyright protect?
3. What exception to the law does the notice cite?
4. Who is given permission to reproduce material from the book? Why?
5. How might someone else legally use material from the book?

CHAPTER 17

Civil and Criminal Law

CIVIC PARTICIPATION

Americans are very concerned about the issue of law and order. Each year millions of people are charged with crimes. Millions more go to court to try to resolve legal disputes. As citizens, we can help maintain law and order by obeying laws, respecting the rights of others, and being aware of current laws. Contact your local police department or town court to find cut about any new or altered laws, such as a change in the local speed limit. Do some background research on your local laws.

Working in Your Community

After you have obtained the information, prepare a pamphlet describing a number of local laws and the punishments or fines for breaking them. Distribute this pamphlet in your neighborhood. ■

Your Civics Journal

As you study this chapter, think about how juveniles and adults are treated differently by our justice system. Record your ideas in your civics journal. Try to provide specific examples of different treatment based on cases discussed in the media.

Civil Cases

FOCUS

TERMS TO KNOW

suit of equity, injunction, complaint

OBJECTIVES

■ Identify four types of **lawsuits.**

■ Explain the difference between lawsuits and **suits of equity.**

■ Summarize the basic **court procedure in civil cases.**

As you have learned, a civil case, or civil suit, is a legal action one person or party brings against another. Civil cases usually involve disputes over rights, property, or agreements. For example, if an employer refuses to hire someone because the person is African American or female, that person could bring a civil suit against the employer for discrimination. Civil cases are classified as lawsuits or suits of equity.

Lawsuits

In a lawsuit a person or group brings legal action to collect damages for some harm that has been done. Lawsuits involving damages of a few thousand dollars or less are often handled in a small-claims court, and the people involved can act as their own attorneys. Lawsuits involving more money, however, often require lawyers and juries in larger civil courts.

Our judicial system allows many different kinds of lawsuits. They may involve property disputes, or breach of contract, or family matters, such as divorce. Many lawsuits deal with negligence, or personal injury. A negligence suit is filed when a person has been injured or killed or when property has been destroyed because someone else has been careless or negligent. Most cases involving auto accidents are negligence suits.

Suits of Equity

Suits of equity are a special kind of lawsuit. They seek fair treatment in a situation where there is no existing law to help decide the matter. Suits of equity are often brought to prevent a damaging action from taking place. For example, a

Injury Claims Someone who has been injured or suffered property damage in an auto accident may sue the person who caused the accident for carelessness. *What is the legal term used for this kind of suit?*

Civil Suits   Lawsuits involving major sums of money often go to civil court where they are heard by a jury.   *What is the first step in filing a lawsuit?*

group of citizens could file a suit of equity to try to prevent the state from building a highway through a local park.

While a jury may decide lawsuits, a judge usually decides suits of equity. In deciding a suit of equity case, a judge may issue an injunction. An **injunction** is a court order commanding a person or group to stop a certain action. In the case above, for example, the judge might issue an injunction to stop construction of the highway.

Court Procedure in Civil Cases

Each year an enormous number of civil suits are filed in American courts. Some courts are faced with so many civil cases that it can take several years for a

case to go to trial. Many civil suits, perhaps the majority, never make it to trial at all. They are usually settled out of court, when the parties involved agree on a settlement.

Let's look at how a lawsuit proceeds through the court system. Suppose John Maloney is riding in a city bus one day and suffers head injuries and a broken arm when the bus is in an accident. Mr. Maloney decides to file a lawsuit against the city to recover the costs of hospital and doctor bills, lost income from days missed at work, and other expenses. Mr. Maloney becomes the plaintiff, or person filing the lawsuit and making the complaint. The party he is suing, in this case the city, is the defendant.

Mr. Maloney hires an attorney who prepares and files a **complaint,** a formal notice that a lawsuit is being brought. It

Settlement Out of Court Most lawsuits never come to trial. *What document notifies someone that he or she is being sued?*

names the plaintiff and defendant and describes the nature of the complaint. The court then sends the defendant (the city) a summons, which announces that the defendant is being sued and sets a date and time for appearance in court.

After receiving the summons, the defendant's attorneys get a copy of the complaint and file a written answer with the court in which they deny or admit each of Mr. Maloney's claims. Next, the attorneys for each side exchange documents known as pleadings, which narrow down the issues and legal points raised by both sides in the case. For example, Mr. Maloney originally may have sued the bus manufacturer as well as the city. In the pleadings he may agree to drop that part of the suit because it is clear to both sides that the manufacturer was not at fault in the accident.

When the case finally goes to court, the attorneys for the plaintiff and defendant each present their side of the case. Then they await a verdict.

Exploring ISSUES

Fighting Crime

Although most people agree that crime is a serious problem in the United States, they do not agree on what should be done. The solutions offered fall into two distinct approaches to fighting crime: prevention and punishment.

Preventing Crime by Attacking Its Cause

Many Americans think the best way to fight crime is to identify and deal with its causes. They believe a number of factors—such as a lack of education and good employment, a low standard of living, an unstable home environment, and poor self-esteem—contribute to crime.

Advocates of the prevention approach believe crime can be reduced by helping people improve their lives. To this end, they endorse government-run or privately sponsored social programs as well as education and job training. They also view programs such as Big Brother and Big Sister and antidrug programs as ways to help individuals deal with social and emotional problems that may lead to crime.

Punishment as a Deterrent

Other Americans point out that millions of people face social, economic, and personal problems without resorting to crime. Instead, they believe that the best way to fight crime is through punishment.

Supporters of this approach argue that the criminal justice system is too easy on criminals and offers no real deterrent to crime. They believe that punishing crimes

Arresting a suspect

swiftly and severely is such a deterrent. They advocate expanding police forces, imposing harsher sentences, and making sure that convicts serve their full terms.

Finding a Solution

There does not appear to be an easy way to fight crime. Perhaps the solution will be found in a combination of approaches—prevention and punishment. While addressing the social problems that lead to crime, stricter punishment for those who break the law might also act as a deterrent.

DEVELOPING A POINT OF VIEW

1 What do you think is the strongest argument for fighting crime through prevention?

2 Defend the punishment approach against the claim that it ignores the causes of crime.

3 Which approach to crime fighting do you support? Explain your answer.

SECTION 2

Criminal Cases

FOCUS

TERMS TO KNOW
penal code, larceny, vandalism, fraud, mandatory sentence

OBJECTIVES

- Identify two general **types of crime** and several specific kinds of crime in each category.

- Identify four functions of **penalties for crimes.**

When people break the law, they are committing a crime and are subject to a certain punishment. In the United States, each state determines what actions are considered crimes within the state. These crimes are defined in the state's criminal laws, called the **penal code.** The federal government also has a penal code that defines federal crimes such as income tax evasion, kidnapping, and drug smuggling.

Types of Crime

Crime is very costly to American society. Each year thousands of people are killed, millions are injured, and billions of dollars in goods and services are lost as a result of crime. In addition, it costs the federal and state government billions of dollars annually to combat crime. Crime also takes a toll in the fear and anxiety it arouses in people throughout the nation.

Crime can be divided into two general categories—crimes against people and crimes against property. Most crimes against people are violent crimes in which the victim is either injured or killed. These crimes include murder, manslaughter (the accidental killing of a person), rape, assault (physical injury or threat of injury), and kidnapping.

Crimes Against Property

Crimes against property are the most common type of crime. Burglary, robbery, and theft are all forms of **larceny,** the taking of property unlawfully. Other common crimes against property are **vandalism** (the deliberate destruction of property) and fraud. **Fraud** means taking property by dishonest means or misrepresentation. For example, convincing someone to invest in a nonexistent gold mine would be fraud.

Victimless Crimes

Certain crimes, such as unauthorized gambling or the use of illegal drugs, are considered victimless crimes or crimes against morality. Laws against victimless crimes are very difficult to enforce because there is no victim to bring a complaint. Some people argue that these activities should not be crimes because they do not hurt anyone except the person involved.

In fact victimless crimes often do harm others. People frequently steal to get money to purchase illegal drugs. Gamblers sometimes bet more than they can afford and borrow money from illegal money lenders called loan sharks. Moreover, victimless crimes are often under the control of criminal gangs that commit many violent crimes against society.

Penal Codes

The penal code in most states establishes different degrees of seriousness to many of these crimes. For example, a first-degree murder is one in which a person plans and carries out a killing deliberately or hires someone else to do it. A second-degree murder is one in which there is an intent to kill, but it is not planned beforehand. Instead, it is carried out on the spur of the moment, often in a fit of anger. Manslaughter occurs when one person kills another by accident, or without meaning to.

The reason for establishing different classifications, or degrees of seriousness, for certain crimes is to set appropriate penalties. In general, the more serious the crime, the harsher the punishment. The courts tend to treat crimes against people more seriously than crimes against property because of the great harm these crimes can do to the victims and to society as a whole.

Penalties for Crimes

People convicted of crimes are usually punished by fines and/or imprisonment, depending on the nature and severity of the crime. For many minor crimes and misdemeanors, punishment may be only a small fine or a few days or weeks in jail. Long-term imprisonment is the most common kind of punishment for felonies or serious crimes.

Criminal penalties serve several functions. First, they provide punishment in which a criminal pays for an offense against a victim and against society. Criminal penalties also help protect society by keeping dangerous criminals "off the streets." Lawbreakers who are in prison cannot continue to commit

Rehabilitation Prisoners may receive job training so that they can return to society after release from prison. *What two other functions does punishment serve?*

crimes against others. Another function of criminal penalties is to keep others from committing the same crime. They serve as a warning or an example; others tempted to commit the same crime can see what their punishment would be if they were caught. Finally, criminal penalties can play a role in preparing lawbreakers to reenter society. Through counseling, education, and vocational training, some prisons help inmates learn skills that will help them lead productive lives after prison.

Determining the sentence, or punishment, of a person convicted of a crime is one of the most complicated and difficult aspects of the criminal justice system. Because the circumstances in each case are different, judges may hand down very different sentences for similar crimes.

In the past, most states used a system of indeterminate sentences and parole in

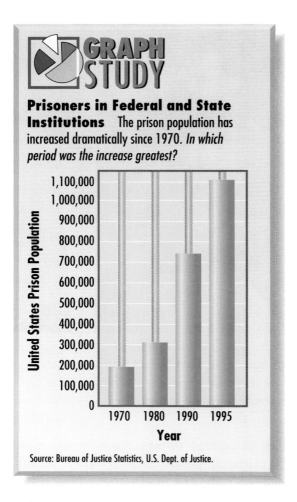

GRAPH STUDY

Prisoners in Federal and State Institutions The prison population has increased dramatically since 1970. *In which period was the increase greatest?*

United States Prison Population (y-axis): 0, 100,000, 200,000, 300,000, 400,000, 500,000, 600,000, 700,000, 800,000, 900,000, 1,000,000, 1,100,000

Year (x-axis): 1970, 1980, 1990, 1995

Source: Bureau of Justice Statistics, U.S. Dept. of Justice.

penalizing criminals. An indeterminate sentence is one in which a judge gives a minimum and maximum sentence, and a prisoner may be released for good behavior after completing the minimum sentence. However, the rising crime rate has prompted more and more states to switch to determinate sentencing, which involves sentences for a specific period of time and no time off for good behavior.

A prisoner may also be eligible for parole, or early release, after serving a certain part of the sentence. A parole board reviews each request for parole and decides whether or not to grant it. If parole is granted, the person is set free but must report to a parole officer periodically until the maximum sentence has expired.

Some people criticize indeterminate sentences and parole. They feel that many sentences turn out to be much shorter than originally intended. Some states have tried to deal with this issue by establishing mandatory sentences. With a **mandatory sentence,** a judge must impose whatever sentence the law directs. Mandatory sentences, however, present another problem. They sometimes force judges to impose much harsher sentences than the circumstances of the crime justify.

At the federal level, the courts are trying a third method to find a fairer system of sentencing criminals. Starting in 1987, the federal government abolished parole. Instead, it established a range of sentences that judges may apply to each of 43 "offense levels," or categories of crimes. Under this system, similar crimes receive similar punishments, although judges have some leeway in considering the individual circumstances in each case. If the new system proves to be workable and more just, individual states may model their sentencing procedures on the federal system.

★ **SECTION 2 REVIEW** ★

UNDERSTANDING VOCABULARY
Define penal code, larceny, vandalism, fraud, mandatory sentence.

REVIEWING OBJECTIVES

1 What are two general types of crime, and what are several specific kinds of crime in each category?

2 What are four functions of penalties for crimes?

Court Proceedings in Criminal Cases

FOCUS

TERMS TO KNOW

summons, arraignment, prosecution, testimony, cross-examination, acquittal, hung jury

OBJECTIVES

■ Describe the procedure when **arresting a suspect** of a crime.

■ Explain the **hearing, indictment, and arraignment** phases of a criminal case.

■ Define **plea bargaining** and explain its importance.

■ Outline the basic procedure of **the trial.**

■ Explain what happens during **the verdict and sentencing** parts of a criminal case.

The justice system treats misdemeanor cases and felony cases quite differently. Misdemeanor cases are usually handled in a minor court, such as traffic court or municipal court. Most felony cases are tried in county courts. The police do not usually arrest misdemeanor suspects. Instead, they issue a ticket, requiring payment of a fine, or a **summons,** directing someone to appear in court for a hearing on the charge. For felony cases, the procedure is much more formal and involved.

Arresting a Suspect

Suppose an undercover police officer observes Hannah Jones exchanging packets of white powder for money on a downtown street. The officer immediately arrests her, searches her, and finds a large amount of cash and 30 small packets of what seems to be cocaine. The officer also informs Ms. Jones of her rights as soon as she is arrested.

Whenever the police arrest anyone, they are required to read the suspect his or her rights. These include the right to remain silent and the right to have an attorney present when being questioned by police. (For a detailed discussion of the "Miranda rights," see page 389.)

After her arrest, Ms. Jones is taken to the local police station, where she is booked, or charged with a crime. As part

Miranda Rights Police officers are required to read a suspect his or her rights. *What rights are included?*

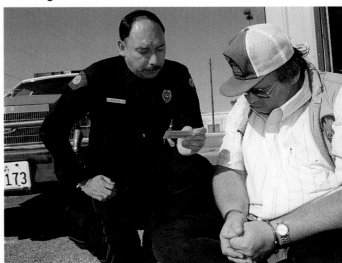

of the booking procedure, Ms. Jones is photographed and fingerprinted. During this time she is also allowed to call an attorney, or lawyer. If she cannot afford a lawyer, the state will provide one.

Hearing, Indictment, and Arraignment

A few hours later, Ms. Jones and her attorney appear before a municipal judge for a preliminary hearing. The judge hears the charges against the suspect and sets bail. For minor offenses, the judge has the option of releasing suspects on their own recognizance. This means they are released without having to pay bail. Instead, they promise to appear in court when they are called.

After the preliminary hearing, the judge sends Ms. Jones's case to a grand jury, which hears the evidence against the suspect. The grand jury decides whether to indict the suspect—to issue a formal charge—or to dismiss the case if it feels there is not enough evidence for a trial.

The Supreme Court has not required the states to use grand juries. In many cases the prosecutor will present a formal accusation, and the judge will decide whether to indict the suspect.

After it is decided to charge a person with a crime, an arraignment is held. An **arraignment** is a hearing where the suspect pleads guilty or innocent to the charges. The judge at the arraignment will then set a court date for the trial.

Plea Bargaining

Sometimes after reviewing the charges and evidence against a suspect, a lawyer may urge the defendant to accept a plea bargain. A plea bargain is an agreement in which the accused person agrees to plead guilty, but to a lesser charge. Plea bargaining helps avoid a lengthy and expensive trial. It also ensures that a person will be punished for committing a crime.

The majority of criminal cases never go to trial but are handled through plea

DID YOU KNOW?

Community Cops

Years ago, police officers used to be part of the community. They knew everyone on the beats they walked. They could take the time to solve problems and catch criminals. Then police were put in squad cars, trained to be more objective, and required to answer many more calls each day.

Now police departments across the country are retraining law enforcement personnel to again become part of their communities. Police officers are being told to try to solve individual crimes rather than just take down information for a report and leave.

One officer might work with a storekeeper on ways to reduce shoplifting. Others may try to find rehabilitation programs for drug abusers who want to kick the habit. This kind of police work takes more time, but it builds bridges between the police and the community. It may also reduce crime much more successfully than other methods.

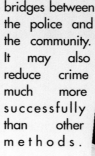

Community policing

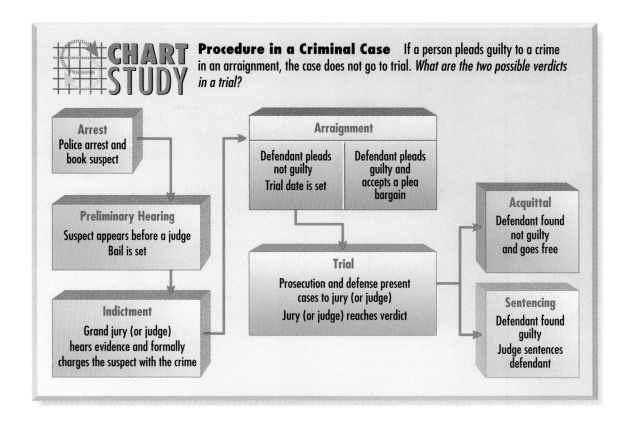

CHART STUDY

Procedure in a Criminal Case If a person pleads guilty to a crime in an arraignment, the case does not go to trial. *What are the two possible verdicts in a trial?*

Arrest
Police arrest and book suspect

Preliminary Hearing
Suspect appears before a judge
Bail is set

Indictment
Grand jury (or judge) hears evidence and formally charges the suspect with the crime

Arraignment

| Defendant pleads not guilty Trial date is set | Defendant pleads guilty and accepts a plea bargain |

Trial
Prosecution and defense present cases to jury (or judge)
Jury (or judge) reaches verdict

Acquittal
Defendant found not guilty and goes free

Sentencing
Defendant found guilty
Judge sentences defendant

bargaining. While plea bargaining saves the government a great deal of time and money, many people object to it. They criticize it because it often results in light sentences for serious crimes. Without plea bargaining, however, the criminal justice system would be even more backed up, and people accused of crimes would have very long waits before their cases came to trial.

The Trial

In preparing for her trial, Ms. Jones's lawyers interview witnesses, research the state's drug laws, and gather as much information about the case as possible. When the trial begins, the first step is selecting the jurors.

After the jury has been selected, the attorneys for each side make an opening statement in which they outline the case they will present. In criminal trials the state's side of the proceedings is called the **prosecution,** and the lawyer for the state is called the prosecutor. The accused person's, or defendant's, side is the defense, and his or her lawyer is the defense attorney.

After the opening statements, the prosecution presents its case first, followed by the defense. Each side calls witnesses, who take an oath to tell the truth about what they know. The statements a witness makes under oath are called **testimony.**

After a witness testifies for one side, the other side is allowed to cross-examine, or question, the witness. The questions asked in **cross-examination** are often designed to cast doubt on the truth or reliability of the witness's testimony. Finally, each side makes a closing

The Verdict   The foreman of the jury delivers the jury's decision on whether the defendant is guilty or not guilty.   *Who chooses the foreman?*

statement summarizing the testimony and evidence. The judge then "instructs" the jury, or explains the law that pertains to the case.

The Verdict and Sentencing

The last part of a trial begins when the jury withdraws to deliberate, or think over and discuss the case and reach a verdict. After choosing a foreman (who may be a man or a woman) to lead the discussion, the jurors review the evidence and legal arguments they have heard. Finally, they take a vote. In most states juries are required to reach a unanimous vote in finding a defendant guilty or not guilty.

If the jury feels that the prosecution has not proven its case, it can decide on **acquittal**—a vote of not guilty. To find a defendant guilty, a jury must believe that the evidence and testimony prove a suspect's guilt beyond a reasonable doubt. In the case of Hannah Jones, the jury finds her guilty of selling cocaine.

Sometimes a jury cannot agree on a verdict. When that happens, the judge declares a **hung jury** and rules the trial a mistrial. With a mistrial the prosecution must decide whether to drop the charges or ask for a retrial.

When a defendant is found guilty, the judge sets a court date for sentencing. In some cases a jury recommends a sentence. Most often, however, the judge determines the sentence after considering the defendant's family situation, previous criminal record, employment status, and other relevant information.

★ SECTION 3 REVIEW ★

UNDERSTANDING VOCABULARY
Define summons, arraignment, prosecution, testimony, cross-examination, acquittal, hung jury.

REVIEWING OBJECTIVES

1 What is the procedure when arresting a suspect of a crime?

2 What happens during the hearing, indictment, and arraignment phases of a criminal case?

3 What is plea bargaining, and how is it an important part of the legal process in criminal cases?

4 What is the basic procedure of a trial?

5 What happens during the verdict and sentencing parts of a criminal case?

Using a CD-ROM

CD-ROM stands for Compact Disc, Read-Only Memory. A CD-ROM can hold huge amounts of information, making it a perfect storage place for games, simulations, and reference books.

Learning the Skill

Because a CD-ROM is a special type of disk, you must have a CD-ROM drive on your computer to use it. Some CD-ROMs need to be loaded onto the computer's hard drive before they can be used. Once this has been done, you are ready to get started in your search for information.

Suppose you want to learn more about American law in the 1600s. One good source for this information is *Facts On File: Landmark Documents in American History.*

Accessing the Documents As you access the document, the first screen to appear will be the main menu. You can choose. **DOCUMENT TITLE, SUBJECT, HISTORICAL TIME PERIOD, YEAR, PEOPLE,** or **ADVANCED SEARCH.** You might enjoy looking at each category to learn all the ways to find information on this disk. For now, choose SUBJECTS.

Using the Subject Screens This screen reveals many topics. Scroll down the list until you come to **Habeus Corpus Act of 1679.** Highlight this selection and then click on **VIEW DOCUMENT.**

To find out more about your topic, select **ABOUT THIS DOCUMENT.**

Using Other Types of CD-ROMs

Remember that CD-ROMs differ in design, so be sure to read all instructions on each computer screen as you move from one to another. If you need assistance, access HELP on the screen, or consult someone who is experienced in using the CD-ROM.

Learning About CD-ROMs

APPLYING THE SKILL

Use what you know about CD-ROMs to locate and learn about an important court case in the United States. Note who was involved, the year it happened, and what the outcome was.

Juveniles and the Court System

FOCUS

TERMS TO KNOW

juvenile, juvenile delinquent, offender

OBJECTIVES

■ Identify two factors that contribute to **juvenile delinquency.**

■ Explain the primary role of **juvenile courts.**

■ Describe the basic procedure in **dealing with juvenile offenders.**

■ Identify several options judges have for **punishing juvenile offenders.**

Children and teenagers commit many crimes each year. Some of these crimes are misdemeanors such as shoplifting or driving without a license. Others, however, are serious crimes and felonies such as burglary, rape, and murder. Moreover, the number of serious crimes children and teenagers commit has increased dramatically.

Each state establishes a certain age when people are considered adults for the purposes of applying criminal laws. In some states the age is 16, in others 18. Anyone under that age limit is considered a **juvenile,** a person not yet legally an adult. Our justice system treats juveniles who commit crimes somewhat differently than it treats adults.

Juvenile Delinquency

A child or teenager who commits a serious crime or repeatedly breaks the law is often called a **juvenile delinquent.** Some researchers who have studied the problem of juvenile crime have explored ways of preventing juvenile delinquency and of preventing juvenile **offenders,** or lawbreakers, from becoming adult criminals. Their studies have shown that children who are abused or neglected or who suffer emotional or mental problems are more likely than others to get into trouble with the law. They have also shown that children who grow up in poverty, in overcrowded slums where drug and alcohol abuse are widespread, are more likely to become delinquents.

Although these factors may contribute to juvenile delinquency, they do not explain why some children commit crimes. Many children who grow up in poverty or are abused do not become criminals. Moreover, children from all backgrounds and levels of society can and do become juvenile delinquents.

Gangs Crimes committed by members of gangs are a growing problem. *At what age are people no longer considered juveniles?*

American Profiles

Marion Wright Edelman

Although children cannot vote or pay taxes, they have a powerful voice speaking for them—Marion Wright Edelman. She is the founder and president of the Children's Defense Fund, a group that works to get federal funding for children.

Edelman grew up in South Carolina, attended Yale Law School, and became the first African American woman to practice law in Mississippi. In the 1960s she worked with the NAACP Legal Defense Fund.

In 1973 she started the Children's Defense Fund (CDF). The CDF uses statistics to show how malnutrition, poverty, and poor education affect the nation's children. Through its reports, the CDF has helped convince Congress to increase funding for children's programs, even in years when other social programs were cut.

PROFILE REVIEW

1 How does the CDF seek to influence Congress to provide money for children's programs?

2 If Congress reduced or eliminated funds for these programs, how might that affect the nation's children?

Juvenile Courts

When juveniles are charged with committing crimes, their cases are handled in separate courts called juvenile courts. The primary goal of juvenile courts is to try to rehabilitate juvenile offenders and correct their behavior rather than to punish them.

The juvenile court system was set up in the late 1800s as a result of reforms in the judicial system. Before that time, juvenile offenders over age 14 were treated like adults. They received the same sentences for crimes and were sent to the same prisons as adult criminals.

The guiding principle of juvenile courts is to do whatever is in the best interest of the children. The courts handle two kinds of cases: neglect and delinquency. Cases of neglect involve children who are neglected or abused by their

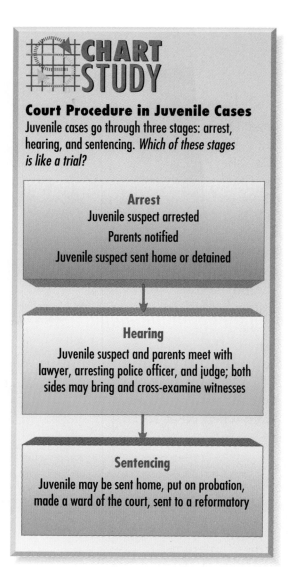

CHART STUDY

Court Procedure in Juvenile Cases
Juvenile cases go through three stages: arrest, hearing, and sentencing. *Which of these stages is like a trial?*

Arrest
Juvenile suspect arrested

Parents notified

Juvenile suspect sent home or detained

Hearing
Juvenile suspect and parents meet with lawyer, arresting police officer, and judge; both sides may bring and cross-examine witnesses

Sentencing
Juvenile may be sent home, put on probation, made a ward of the court, sent to a reformatory

Dealing With Juvenile Offenders

When a child is arrested, the police notify his or her parents. Depending on the crime, the child may be sent home or kept in a juvenile detention center until it is time to appear in court.

Juvenile Court System

At the court appearance, the juvenile and his or her parents meet with their lawyer, the judge, the police officer who made the arrest, and the probation officer who investigated the case. This meeting, or hearing, is similar to a trial, but it is less formal. Only the parties involved are allowed to attend the hearing. As in a trial, both sides are allowed to call and cross-examine witnesses. There is no jury, however. Juveniles do not have the right to a jury trial. In most cases, a judge decides whether the juvenile is delinquent (guilty) or nondelinquent.

The juvenile court system provides several special protections for juveniles. First, the identity of juveniles is kept secret. Juveniles' criminal records are also kept from the public, and in some cases they may be erased when the offender becomes an adult. In addition, when juveniles are arrested, they are not fingerprinted or photographed.

Supreme Court Rules

In 1967 the Supreme Court established certain rules for juvenile cases.
- The parents or guardians of the juveniles must be notified of their arrest as soon as possible.
- Juveniles and their parents must be notified in writing of all the charges against them.
- Juveniles have the right to remain silent and have an attorney.

parents. A juvenile court has the power to place these children with other families in foster homes, where they will be protected and cared for.

Delinquency cases involve children who commit crimes. Juvenile courts also handle offenses that are considered illegal for juveniles but not for adults. These offenses include such things as running away from home, playing hooky from school, and violating local curfew ordinances.

Sentencing   If a juvenile is found guilty of committing a crime, the judge determines the punishment.   *What does it mean to become a ward of the court?*

■ Juveniles have the right to confront witnesses against them.

These rights were established by the Supreme Court in *In re Gault* (*in re* means in the matter of). In this case 15-year-old Gerald Gault of Phoenix, Arizona, was charged with making indecent telephone calls to a neighbor. His parents were not informed of his arrest. When his case came up for a hearing, Gerald Gault did not have an attorney, and the neighbor was not questioned. The judge sent Gault to a reformatory until age 21—a period of 6 years. If he had been an adult, the most he could have received was a $50 fine and a few months in jail. In overturning the decision, the Supreme Court ensured that juveniles would enjoy most of the legal rights of adults.

Punishing Juvenile Offenders

Juvenile court judges can sentence juvenile offenders in different ways. They may simply send young children or first offenders home with a stern lecture. Offenders with a previous history of delinquency may be placed in a special training school or in a reformatory.

Juveniles who have been neglected or have a poor home life may become wards of the court. The court becomes their guardian and can supervise their lives until adulthood. Judges may place juveniles with serious mental or emotional problems in a hospital or institution. Judges may also put juveniles on probation, which means that they can live at home and go to school as long as they obey the court's rules.

One criticism of the juvenile court system is that juveniles who commit major crimes sometimes receive very light sentences and are soon released. In many states juvenile court judges may now refer serious cases to the criminal courts, or prosecutors may ask the state courts to order a suspect to be tried as an adult.

★ SECTION 4 REVIEW ★

UNDERSTANDING VOCABULARY
Define juvenile, juvenile delinquent, offender.

REVIEWING OBJECTIVES

1 What are two factors that contribute to juvenile delinquency?

2 What is the primary role of juvenile courts?

3 What procedure do the police and the court system follow in dealing with juvenile offenders?

4 What options do judges have for punishing juvenile offenders?

Identifying Key Terms

Choose the vocabulary term that best completes each of the sentences below. Write your answers on a separate sheet of paper.

complaint   prosecution   plea bargain
acquittal   injunction   arraignment

1. The injured woman's lawyer filed a(n) _____ against the city bus company.
2. After hours of deliberation, the jury felt the evidence was not convincing and voted for _____.
3. The _____ asked the jury to find the defendant guilty on all counts.
4. The defense attorney recommended that his client accept a(n) _____ in exchange for a lighter sentence.
5. At the _____ the defendant pleaded not guilty to the charge.
6. The judge issued a(n) _____ to stop construction of a new highway.

Reviewing the Main Ideas

SECTION 1

1. Identify and describe two types of lawsuits.
2. What is the purpose of a suit of equity?

SECTION 2

3. In what ways are victimless crimes harmful to others?
4. Describe the parole system.

SECTION 3

5. What are the main steps people accused of a crime go through in the legal process before a trial?

6. What is the main purpose of plea bargaining?

SECTION 4

7. Identify four rules the Supreme Court established for juvenile cases.
8. What special protections do the juvenile courts provide for juveniles?

Critical Thinking

SECTION 1

1. **Evaluating Information**   Do you think that civil cases should be tried before a jury? Why or why not?

SECTION 2

2. **Determining a Point of View**   Do you think that imposing longer prison sentences on people convicted of violent crimes would prevent others from committing similar crimes? Why or why not?

SECTION 3

3. **Analyzing Information**   How does the idea of "guilty beyond a reasonable doubt" protect the rights of defendants?

SECTION 4

4. **Determining Cause and Effect**   What are some factors that contribute to juvenile delinquency? What do you think could be done to help prevent juveniles from committing crimes?

Reinforcing Citizenship Skills

Describe a decision that a young person might face today, such as the choice to go to college or to get a job after high school. List the six steps of the decision-making process. Write the questions and information you would consider at each step and what your answers might be. Write what you think would be a wise decision. Share your results with the class.

Cooperative Learning

In groups of four, prepare arguments, pro or con, for debating the following statement: The Miranda rule should be suspended so criminals can be prosecuted more easily. Support your arguments with your own opinions, information from the chapter, and other research. Debate this issue with the rest of the class.

Focusing on Your Community

Find out what types of civil cases are filed most frequently in your community. What percentage of these cases is won by the plaintiff? What types of crime are committed most often? What percentage of these cases results in a guilty verdict? What types of crime do juveniles commit most frequently? What types of punishment do juveniles usually receive from the court? Prepare a short written report.

Technology Activity

Using the Internet

Search the Internet to find information on juvenile law in your state. You may use the name of your state or any of the following as key words to focus your search: **juvenile law, juvenile court, law, state law**. Use the information you find to create a flow chart showing the process that juveniles accused of crimes must follow in your state.

Analyzing Visuals

The criminal justice system has three parts—police work, judicial and legal proceedings, and corrections (prisons, jails, probation, and parole). Study the graph below on federal, state, and local government expenditures. Then answer the following questions.

1. Which level of government spent the most money on police work?
2. Which level spent the largest portion of its budget on corrections?
3. Why do you think the federal government spent less on all areas of the criminal justice system than did state and local governments?

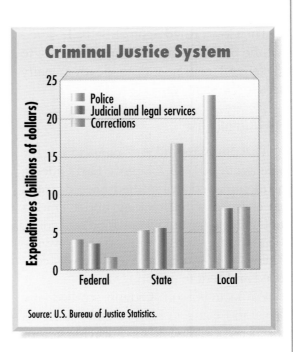

Criminal Justice System

Expenditures (billions of dollars)

- Police
- Judicial and legal services
- Corrections

Federal   State   Local

Source: U.S. Bureau of Justice Statistics.

CLOSEUP
THE RIGHT TO COUNSEL

The Sixth Amendment to the Constitution states that a person accused of a crime shall "have the assistance of counsel for his defense." This amendment was adopted in 1791, but it was not applied to state courts until 1963.

The Betts Case

In 1942 the Supreme Court considered the issue in *Betts* v. *Brady.* Smith Betts had been accused of robbing a store in Maryland. Unable to afford an attorney, he was convicted and sentenced to eight years in prison. In an appeal to the Supreme Court, Betts argued that his Sixth Amendment right to counsel and Fourteenth Amendment right to due process had been violated.

The Court ruled against Betts. It stated that the Sixth Amendment applied only to the federal courts and to death penalty cases in the state courts.

The Gideon Case

The Supreme Court considered the issue again in 1963. Clarence Earl Gideon, an unemployed drifter, had been arrested and charged with breaking into a Florida pool hall and stealing some food and coins. The Florida courts refused to provide Gideon with an attorney, and he was convicted and sent to prison.

While in prison, Gideon studied law books and came to believe that his rights had been violated. The Supreme Court

Clarence Earl Gideon

agreed to hear the case and assigned a lawyer to represent Gideon.

In 1963 the Court ruled in Gideon's favor, overturning the *Betts* decision. Justice Hugo Black wrote the opinion, declaring, "any person . . . who is too poor to hire a lawyer, cannot be provided a fair trial unless counsel is provided."

CLOSEUP REVIEW

1 What reason did the Supreme Court give for ruling against Betts?

2 Why did Betts and Gideon argue that failing to provide them with attorneys violated due process?

Multimedia Activities

Surfing the "Net"

Supreme Court Justices

The Constitution gives each branch of government a role in making, enforcing, and interpreting the law. In particular, the Supreme Court of the United States has a specific duty of making sure local, state, and federal laws are constitutional. To find out more information about the Supreme Court, go to the Internet.

Getting There

Follow the steps below to find information about current Supreme Court justices.

1. Go to your favorite search engine.
2. Type in the phrase *The United States Supreme Court.* Following this phrase, enter words like those below to focus your search:

judicial branch	decisions
justices	White House

The search engine should provide you with a number of links to follow. Links are pointers to different sites on the Internet and commonly appear as blue underlined words.

What to Do When You Are There

1. Click on the links to navigate through the pages of information.
2. Using a word processor, create a biographical sketch on each justice. Include in your information their educational background and their most recent decision.
3. Design a bulletin board with pictures of our current justices and their individual biographical information.

Focus on Government

The FBI

The Federal Bureau of Investigation is a division of the Department of Justice. This division conducts investigations and arrests suspects for violating federal laws. The ***Focus on Government*** program referenced below shows the training given to FBI agents and police officials.

Setting Up the Video

Using a bar code reader or an electronic keypad, work with a group of your classmates to view this video segment of the videodisc ***Focus on Government:***

Side 2, Chapter 39
Electronic Field Trip:
The FBI Training Academy

Hands-On Activity

Interview a local police officer and ask questions about training and how the local police department interacts with law enforcement from a federal level. Compare this account of training with the training you learned about on the video program. Using a word processor, write a report of your findings.

UNIT 7

The Free Enterprise System

As American citizens, we live in a land of economic opportunity. Our economy provides us with a great variety of jobs, goods, and services that enable us to live better lives. We can contribute to the nation's economic success by taking advantage of these opportunities.

In Unit 7 you will study the American free enterprise system and learn how it works and how it affects our lives. ■

CHAPTERS IN THIS UNIT

★ CHAPTER 18 ★

The American Economic System

In our economic system, the people who make goods or provide services are extremely important to the well-being of the nation. These businesses give job opportunities to millions of Americans. Contact your local chamber of commerce to learn about some of the major businesses or industries in your area. Find out what goods or services these businesses provide, how many people they employ, and how long they have been in the area.

Working in Your Community

Next conduct a business survey in your neighborhood. Find out where people work, what type of work they do, and how long they have worked. Encourage the people you survey to learn more about local businesses. ■

Your Civics Journal

As you study this chapter, think about how our economic system works and how it affects your daily life. Write your ideas in your civics journal. Consider the advantages or disadvantages of our system, and note these in your journal too.

Having a snack in town ➤

Making Economic Decisions

conomics is the study of how things are made, bought, sold, and used. It helps answer such questions as where do these products come from? Who makes them? How are they made? How do they get to the stores? Who buys them? Every country has its own economic system, or way of producing the things its people want and need. A country's economic system helps determine how basic economic decisions will be made.

Goods and services help satisfy people's needs and wants. Goods include food, clothing, cars, tools, jewelry, television sets, and anything else that can be grown or manufactured. Services are things people do for others in exchange for money or something else of value. Barbers, doctors, waiters, and entertainers all provide services.

The goods and services a country can produce depend upon its resources. **Resources** are the things used in making goods and providing services. They include tools; natural resources such as wood, soil, and water; and human resources, the people who provide the necessary labor, skills, and knowledge.

A country with many resources is capable of satisfying its people's wants and needs better than a country with few resources. The United States is fortunate to be rich in resources such as fertile soil,

Goods and Services   This waitress provides a service by bringing food (a good) to restaurant clients.   *What three kinds of resources determine the goods and services produced in a country?*

trained workers, forests, and water. No country, however, has all the resources it needs. Even the United States has a scarcity, or limited supply, of some resources, such as nickel, zinc, and certain other minerals. Scarcity is a problem all countries must face.

A scarcity of resources affects the economic decisions a country and its people will make. For example, a country with a scarcity of good farmland may need to buy most of its food from other countries rather than grow its own. Scarcity affects individual decisions as well. For most people, money is a limited resource. They must make decisions about how to spend the money.

Scarcity affects decisions concerning what and how much to produce, how goods and services will be produced, and who will get what is produced.

Deciding What and How Much to Produce

The people who buy and use products are called **consumers.** Much of a country's economy is geared to providing consumers with goods and services.

The amount of each good or service available to consumers is the **supply.** The amount of a good or service that consumers are willing to buy is the **demand.** The demand for a product is influenced by its supply, its price, and the number of people who want to buy it.

In most economic systems, supply and demand are important factors in determining what kind of goods and services are made available and in what quantity. The following is an example of how these factors work.

With the invention of the compact disc (CD) player came a need for com-

Supply and Demand   Companies base how much they produce on consumers' demand. *How do supply and demand affect the price of goods and services?*

pact discs to play on the new machines. To fill this need, record companies began to produce compact discs. Their decisions about what music to put on disc were based on demand. If more people want to listen to rock than to classical music, recording companies will produce more rock CDs than classical ones. Decisions about how many CDs to produce are also based on demand.

The forces of supply and demand also affect the price of goods and services. When the supply of a product is low and the demand for it is high, the price will be high. When supply is high and demand is low, however, the price will usually drop. For example, suppose there is a gasoline shortage during the summer, when families are taking their vacations. This will probably cause the price of gasoline to increase because people will be willing to pay more to make sure they have gasoline. If the supply of gasoline increases, or the demand decreases, gasoline merchants will probably lower their prices.

Most often a balance exists between supply and demand and price. This balance is based on what consumers are willing to pay for a product and on what producers are able to charge for it.

Under the system of supply and demand, the consumer plays the most important role in determining what goods and services will be offered and how much will be produced. The producer's or manufacturer's role is to adjust production and price according to the consumer's decisions.

Deciding How Goods and Services Will Be Produced

What determines how goods and services are produced? Who makes them? How are they made? What resources are needed to produce them? The production of any good or service requires four elements—capital, land and natural resources, labor, and management. Let's look at how these four elements are involved in making a product.

Capital

Money used to produce goods and services is called financial capital. Businesses need capital to get started and to

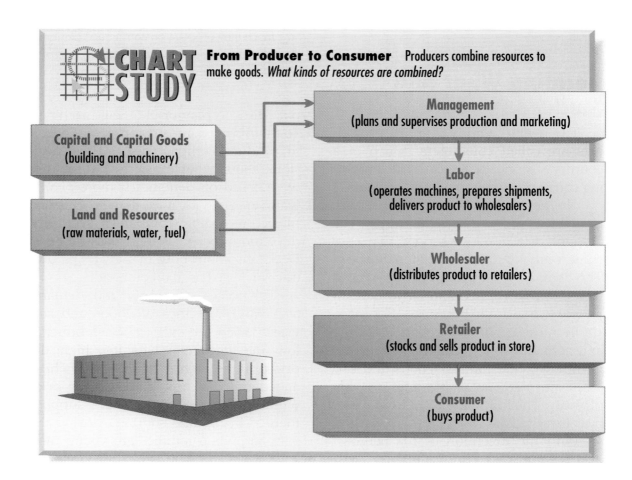

CHART STUDY **From Producer to Consumer** Producers combine resources to make goods. *What kinds of resources are combined?*

Capital and Capital Goods (building and machinery)

Land and Resources (raw materials, water, fuel)

Management (plans and supervises production and marketing)

Labor (operates machines, prepares shipments, delivers product to wholesalers)

Wholesaler (distributes product to retailers)

Retailer (stocks and sells product in store)

Consumer (buys product)

continue operating. For example, several years ago, Robert and Marion Keller decided to start a business producing potato chips. The Kellers used some of their savings and also borrowed money from the bank to start their business. They used this capital to buy a small building and also to purchase several machines that would make the potato chips. The building and the machines are called **capital goods**—the tools, buildings, and machines used to make goods and provide services. Capital goods are different from consumer goods, which are the goods produced for people to buy. The potato chips are a consumer good.

Land and Natural Resources

Earlier you read about resources. All businesses use land and natural resources—materials that come from the earth. A business might need some type of crop or a mineral such as iron or a supply of water to make its product. A business will also need a supply of energy, perhaps from electricity, coal, or gas.

Once the Kellers' business was ready to go into operation, they needed several resources to produce their potato chips. First, they needed potatoes, which they arranged to buy from several farmers in the area. They also needed vegetable oil in which to cook the chips and a good supply of water to clean the potatoes and machines. Finally, they needed electricity to provide light and to run the machines.

Labor

Workers are important in the production of all goods and services. Because the Kellers could not do all the work themselves, they hired people to help them. Some people move the potatoes from a storage area to the machines. Oth-

ers operate the machines that wash and slice the potatoes and that cook and package the chips. Still others prepare boxes for shipment and deliver the potato chips to stores. Each person does just

Division of Labor   By learning specialized tasks, workers can produce more goods at lower unit costs.   *How does this benefit consumers?*

one kind of job. This is called **division of labor.** A division of labor helps manufacturers produce large quantities of goods more quickly and cheaply.

Labor is an important element of production not only because workers make goods or provide services but also because they earn money that they use to buy other goods and services. This produces jobs and money for other workers.

Management

Managers are the people who plan and supervise the production of goods and services. They make important decisions about what kind and how many goods will be produced, how and where they will be sold, and so on. The deci-

sions managers make can have an important impact on a business and the people who work in it. For example, the managers of the Kellers' business may decide to make a new type of potato chip. If consumers do not like the new chip, the result could be decreased sales and the layoff of some workers.

Taking Risks

Making management decisions involves taking risks. So does starting and owning a business. The people who start new businesses are called **entrepreneurs.** Entrepreneurs risk their money and devote their time and energy to building a profitable business. If they are successful, one of their rewards will be making more money from their business than they put into it.

The total amount of money a business makes is its **gross income.** Much of this income is used to pay salaries, to pay bills for supplies and other expenses, and to pay off bank loans. Some money is also used to pay taxes and fees for licenses. If possible, money is reinvested to meet the future needs of the business. The money that remains is the **profit.** Business owners receive this profit as a reward for taking the risk of starting the business.

One well-known and very successful entrepreneur is Steven Jobs. In 1975, when Jobs was only 20 years old, he started the Apple Computer Company with Stephen Wozniak in Jobs's garage. They had only $1,300 in financial capital. Jobs and Wozniak believed that they could produce an affordable, easy-to-use computer that people would want to use in their homes. Within 5 years the Apple company was worth $1.2 billion and Jobs was a multimillionaire.

Advertising Businesses use commercials and ads to help persuade consumers to buy their goods and services. *Suggest three places where advertising appears.*

Deciding How Goods and Services Will Be Distributed

Another important part of making economic decisions is deciding who will receive the goods and services that have been produced. The Kellers could make all the potato chips in the world, but they would not make any money unless they got the chips to people who wanted them. Getting goods to consumers is called **marketing.**

Marketing involves several factors, including advertising, distribution, storing, and selling. To encourage people to buy their product, the Kellers call their potato chips "Keller's Best." They put this name on the packages so people can recognize their brand of chips. The Kellers also advertise their chips on television to tell people about their product and to create a demand. When a company advertises its product, it tries to reach as many people in as wide an area as possible. The extent of the advertising budget depends, in large part, on how much money a company can afford to spend.

The Kellers have their own fleet of trucks to ship, or deliver, their potato chips. The trucks take the chips to **wholesalers,** businesses that buy large quantities of products and store them in warehouses. Wholesalers buy products from manufacturers at a wholesale price—a lower price than a consumer pays in a store. When the retail stores sell the product to consumers, they charge a higher price, called the retail price, to make a profit.

★ SECTION 1 REVIEW ★

UNDERSTANDING VOCABULARY
Define resources, consumer, supply, demand, capital goods, division of labor, entrepreneur, gross income, profit, marketing, wholesaler.

REVIEWING OBJECTIVES

1 What two important factors are involved in deciding what and how much to produce?

2 What four elements are involved in deciding how goods and services will be produced?

3 What is the role of marketing in deciding how goods and services will be distributed?

SUPREME COURT CASE STUDIES
Punitive Damages

In civil suits, plaintiffs can ask for two kinds of damages—compensatory and punitive. *Compensatory damages* means the amount needed to pay for medical costs, lost income, damaged property, and other expenses. *Punitive damages* means an amount the jury may set to "punish" a defendant for negligence or wrongdoing.

The Case and Decision

In the case of *Browning-Ferris Industries v. Kelco Disposal,* the Supreme Court was asked to overturn a punitive damage award to Kelco Disposal as being "wildly excessive." A jury had decided that Browning-Ferris had illegally tried to force Kelco Disposal out of business. It awarded Kelco $51,000 in compensatory damages and $6 million in punitive damages. Browning-Ferris argued that such a large award was illegal under the Eighth Amendment to the Constitution, which bars "excessive fines."

In 1989 the Court did not overturn the award. The Eighth Amendment, it said, was intended to prevent the government from imposing excessive punishments on citizens, not to restrict decisions in private lawsuits.

Seeking damages

A Continuing Concern

Punitive damages remain a concern for businesses. Large awards used to be very rare, but in recent years many companies have been hit with multimillion-dollar awards.

Plaintiffs also have cause for concern. In cases where many people are suing a company, the first few plaintiffs whose suits are brought to trial may receive large awards. Those who file suit later may find that little money remains. Multiple claims have forced some companies into bankruptcy.

Unless and until the Supreme Court reconsiders the issue, some remedies do exist. Several states have rules that limit the amount of punitive damages that may be awarded. In others, judges often reduce punitive damage awards they think are excessive.

REVIEWING THE CASE

1 Why did the Supreme Court rule against Browning-Ferris?

2 How can large punitive damage awards work against plaintiffs?

Economic Systems

FOCUS

TERMS TO KNOW
traditional economy, command economy, market economy, capitalism, free enterprise, mixed economy

OBJECTIVES

■ Describe the main features of **traditional economies.**

■ Describe the main features of **command economies.**

■ Describe the main features of **market economies.**

■ Explain how **mixed economies** are a combination of other economic systems.

The way the American people make economic decisions is not the only way to make these decisions. Economists have identified three basic kinds of economic systems—the traditional economy, the command economy, and the market economy. In each of these systems, economic decisions are made differently. For example, in a command economy, the government makes economic decisions; in a market economy, the consumers make these choices. Rarely, however, does a country have only one kind of system. Most nations have a combination of economic systems.

Traditional Economies

In a **traditional economy,** economic decisions are made according to customs handed down from one generation to another. People supply the goods they need by hunting, farming, gathering, and making things by hand. Traditional economies are largely untouched by technology. Farmers use the same methods their parents and grandparents did. People make their clothing and tools and build their homes the same way their ancestors did. In a traditional economy, economic activities generally center around the family and the ethnic group or other social unit. In addition, men and women often have different economic roles and perform different tasks. Traditional economies exist primarily in rural, nonindustrial areas of the world. Some traditional economies can be found in parts of Africa, South America, Asia, and the Middle East.

Following the Past Traditional economies use the methods of past generations to produce goods. *What group is the major focus of economic activity in a traditional economy?*

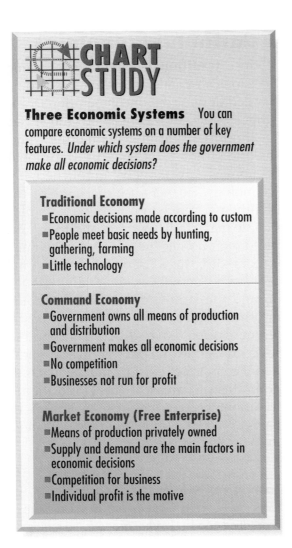

Command Economies

In a **command economy,** the government makes all economic decisions. It decides what products to make, how many to make, how to make them, and who gets them. The leaders of the government direct the economy as they see fit. The government also controls the means of production—the factories, farms, natural resources, transportation systems, and stores. In a command economy, the individual has little, if any, influence on basic economic decisions.

Until the collapse of the Soviet Union in 1991, the economy of that nation was primarily a command economy controlled by the government. The Soviet people had little or no say in economic matters. The government told the manager of each farm and factory what to produce and provided the necessary money and raw materials. The government also determined how much to produce by setting weekly, monthly, and yearly production quotas, or goals, for each factory and farm. A shoe factory, for example, would be expected to produce a certain number of shoes each month.

Disadvantages of Command Economies

One of the major characteristics of a command economy is that there is no competition. The government does not have its factories, for example, compete with one another. As a result, consumers have little or no choice about what type of refrigerator or what style of shoes to buy. In addition, consumer goods may be poorly made or in short supply. Factories are more concerned with meeting quotas than with producing well-made goods. Farms and factories tend to be poorly run, and shortages of goods are common.

In addition, although the government in a command economy often provides low-cost housing, free medical care, and free education, the citizens have no individual freedoms. Nor do the people have basic human rights. They must even work at the jobs the government dictates.

Advantages of Command Economies

On the other hand, because the government in a command economy owns the factories and farms, it is able to set the prices of goods. Factories and farms

Fixed Prices   The government sets the prices for all the goods sold in this store in Cuba.   *What kind of economic system does Cuba have?*

are in business to provide the goods that the government wants to produce. Therefore, the government can set low prices for consumer goods, and it can provide financial support for factories that lose money. Consumers can thus be assured of buying goods at reasonable prices when they are available.

Since the collapse of the Soviet Union, only a few nations have primarily command economies. The best known are the People's Republic of China, North Korea, and Cuba.

Market Economies

The word *market* refers to buying and selling. A market can be a physical place—such as a supermarket or a shopping mall—where buyers and sellers come together to exchange goods and services. It can also mean a demand by consumers for certain goods and services.

In a **market economy,** individual consumers make basic economic decisions according to the principles of supply and demand. People are free to buy, sell, and produce whatever they want, whenever they want, and any way they want. They can also work wherever they want. In addition, individuals own the means of production in a market economy. Many nations in the world today, including the United States, have some form of market economy.

Market economies are often called capitalist economies. In **capitalism,** individuals put their capital, or money, into a business in hopes of making a profit. This profit motive is what influences

Careers

Bank Teller

Bank teller

When you go to a bank, a bank teller often handles your money. The bank teller's job is to process a customer's transactions.

Tasks

The work of a bank teller is very exacting. Tellers are responsible for every cent they handle. Their job includes helping customers deposit or withdraw money and referring customers to other bankers.

Training

Tellers need an aptitude for using computers, and they must be quick, accurate, and honest. They should have a pleasant personality and enjoy working with people. Tellers must also understand peoples' financial needs and how they can be satisfied with bank products. Applicants should have taken mathematics and business courses in high school.

A bank teller's job is an entry-level position. After a few years, a teller can be promoted to a personal banker, or to a management position such as branch manager.

School TO WORK

Visit a local bank to interview someone in their human resources department to learn what qualities and training they look for in bank tellers. Conclude your interview by asking how current technological changes are affecting the jobs of tellers.

people to take the risk of starting a business enterprise.

An important characteristic of capitalism is free enterprise. In a system of **free enterprise,** people enjoy many economic freedoms. These include the freedom of individuals to own their own property, to go into business for themselves, and to buy and sell things to make a profit. Business owners are free to compete with others. Competition helps determine prices. Because consumers have freedom of choice, they are likely to choose the product that offers the best quality at the lowest price.

Mixed Economies

Pure forms of command or market economies are rare. In most cases a country's economic system combines these principles in what is known as a mixed economy. In a **mixed economy,** individuals and the government share the decision-making process. In mixed economies most of the means of production are privately owned, but the government also plays an important role in guiding and regulating the economy. Mixed economies are the most efficient way of providing consumers with goods

Mixed Economy Our economy is a mixed economy. The federal government provides some services, such as passenger train service, directly to consumers. *What other government actions make this a mixed economy?*

and services. At the same time, government regulation prevents business owners from cheating or abusing workers and consumers.

The economy of the United States can be considered a mixed economy. Although it is primarily a market economy, it also combines features of other economic systems. For example, the federal, state, and local governments play a large role in regulating and promoting the American economy. Various agencies regulate businesses to ensure that they sell safe products, that they do not pollute the environment, and that they do not cheat consumers. (You will learn more about the role of government in the American economy in Chapter 19.)

The United States government also promotes the economy by providing services to businesses and consumers. For example, the federal and state governments have built extensive highway systems that have helped promote travel and the transportation of goods. The government also owns and operates

some businesses itself, such as the U.S. Postal Service and Amtrak, the federally owned passenger rail system.

★ **SECTION 2 REVIEW** ★

UNDERSTANDING VOCABULARY
Define traditional economy, command economy, market economy, capitalism, free enterprise, mixed economy.

REVIEWING OBJECTIVES

1 What are the main features of a traditional economy?

2 What are the main features of a command economy?

3 What are the main features of a market economy?

4 In what ways can mixed economies be considered a combination of other economic systems?

How to Locate Government Figures

Statistics are facts expressed as numbers. You can find statistics on almost any topic, from the life expectancy of Americans to federal government spending on national defense.

Using Statistical Abstracts

The *Statistical Abstract of the United States*, published annually by the Department of Commerce and the Bureau of the Census, is an extremely useful resource. The book's table of contents shows the categories into which information is divided, and the index explains where to locate statistics on specific topics. The government also publishes the *United States Government Manual*, with information about all departments of the federal government, and the *State and Metropolitan Area Data Book.*

Information Through the GPO

The Government Printing Office (GPO) in Washington, D.C., publishes thousands of books and pamphlets on the nation's government, economy, and people. You can locate these government reference materials by using a brochure called the *Subject Bibliography Index.*

Library Resources

Many government reference materials can be found in the reference section of your library. Your library will also have general almanacs that include both statistics and other information. The *World Almanac,* for example, includes profiles on the world's nations, facts

Government publications

about American states and cities, and data on many other topics.

References on government figures are also available on microfilm and microfiche and in computer files in many libraries. A computer system called Info-Trac will help you locate articles on specific subjects in government publications. Some libraries may provide on-line applications, such as TELNET, which connects users to information databases.

CITIZENSHIP IN ACTION

1 What is one of the best sources of statistics about the United States?

2 What new types of resources might be found in libraries today?

3 Why is statistical information important?

Organization and Management

FOCUS

TERMS TO KNOW
sole proprietorship, partnership, corporation, incorporate, stocks, stockholder, common stock, dividend, preferred stock, limited liability, cooperative, nonprofit organization

OBJECTIVES

- Discuss the advantages and disadvantages of **sole proprietorships.**

- Discuss the advantages and disadvantages of **partnerships.**

- Explain how **corporations** raise money.

- Describe **cooperatives and nonprofit organizations.**

A new business must be organized and managed in a way that will help it produce goods or services as effectively and efficiently as possible. For example, as sole owners of a potato chip company, the Kellers make major decisions about the company. However, they also have managers who make decisions about specific aspects of the company, such as production, advertising, and shipping. The decisions these managers make have an important effect on the whole company. If a manager does not order enough potatoes, for example, the company will fall behind in production and lose sales and money as a result.

Businesses are organized and managed in three basic ways—as sole proprietorships, partnerships, and corporations. How a particular business is organized depends on its size, its purpose, and the number of owners.

Sole Proprietorships

A **sole proprietorship** is a business that one person or a married couple who choose to share the business, income, assets, and risk owns. Almost three-quarters of the businesses in the United States—about 17 million businesses—are sole proprietorships. Sole proprietorships are almost always small businesses because very few individuals can afford to start a large business. Typical sole proprietorships include

Sole Proprietorship This baker is a sole proprietor. *How many sole proprietorships are there in the United States?*

such businesses as gas stations, barbershops, restaurants, grocery stores, and newsstands.

Sole proprietorships have both advantages and disadvantages. The proprietors are their own bosses. They decide what to make or sell, how much to charge customers, and what hours to work. They also receive all the profits when their businesses are successful. Sole proprietors must, however, take all the risks of starting and operating a business. They provide all the capital to start and run the business. They pay all the bills, hire all the employees, and usually must work long hours. If their business fails, they lose all the money they put into it. When a proprietor dies or retires, the business often comes to an end as well.

Partnerships

A **partnership** is a business two or more people own. Doctors and lawyers often form partnerships. Construction companies, auto dealerships, and advertising firms are also frequently partnerships. While partnerships tend to be larger than sole proprietorships, they still are usually relatively small businesses.

People set up partnerships for various reasons. Sometimes it is to pool their capital because individually they do not have enough money to start a business. People may also form partnerships to combine different skills. For example, one partner in a clothing business may be a talented designer while the other is a good manager with a head for business. People often form partnerships to share the workload and the duties and decision making a business requires.

In a partnership, the partners also share the profits and financial risks. However, if the business should fail, each partner is still responsible for the whole amount of the loss. When people form a partnership, they usually sign a written partnership agreement that spells out the responsibilities and rights of each partner.

One of the greatest disadvantages of partnerships involves disagreements among partners. If partners have a serious falling out and want to end the partnership, it can be very complicated to do so. Disagreements over who will get what may have to be resolved in court. Another disadvantage is that if one partner dies, a new partnership must be legally formed.

Partnership When two or more people pool their resources to start a business, they may form a partnership. *Who assumes the risk in a partnership?*

Corporations

A **corporation** is a large business that has many owners. Starting and operating a large business requires more money than most individuals or even groups of partners can afford. A business of this

American Profiles

Linda Alvarado

Women and minorities often face difficult challenges on the road to business success. Linda Alvarado, the head of a highly successful contracting firm in Colorado, has faced that challenge head on. She started in the construction business in the 1970s, when women rarely worked in the field. In 1976 Alvarado established her own company, which she has built into a multimillion-dollar business.

In 1993 Alvarado broke another barrier as co-owner of the Colorado Rockies. She became the first—and only —Hispanic American to own one of the major league baseball teams.

Alvarado meets regularly with many other women in business to share advice and discuss concerns. "There are still too many doors that need opening for women and minorities," she says. Alvarado has worked hard to help open those doors.

PROFILE REVIEW

1 Why did Alvarado face special difficulties building her business?

2 How has Alvarado used her success to help others?

---

sort, however, can be set up and maintained by forming a corporation.

Suppose several entrepreneurs wanted to start a computer software company. Their first step would be to **incorporate.** To do this, they apply for a charter from the state, which gives them permission to form a corporation. Incorporation gives a company some of the legal rights and obligations of individuals. For example, a corporation can enter into contracts and buy and sell property, but it must also pay taxes and it can be sued.

The entrepreneurs who formed the new corporation decide they need $5 million to build a factory, purchase equipment, and hire workers. As a corporation, the company can raise this money by selling shares of ownership— shares in the business—to hundreds or thousands of people. The shares of ownership are called **stocks,** and the people who buy them are called **stockholders.** When a person buys shares in a company, he or she is investing money in the company. Like entrepreneurs, investors

Corporation   The largest businesses in the country take the form of corporations. *Who owns a corporation?*

are gambling that the company will make a profit for them.

An investor who buys stock in a corporation can share in its profits and its risks. Most people who invest in a corporation buy **common stock.** If the company makes a profit for the year, the owner of common stock receives a share of the profit called a **dividend** for each share of stock owned. The size of the dividend on common stock usually depends on how large a profit the company makes. Some people buy **preferred stock.** These people receive a fixed dividend each year regardless of whether the company makes a profit, and they are paid before common stockholders. Some investors buy corporate bonds. In effect, these people lend the company money. In return, the company pays them interest each year for the use of their money whether or not the company makes a profit.

Corporations offer several advantages. One advantage is that a great

many people share the risk. For example, if the company should fail, a stockholder who has invested $500 in the company can only lose that $500 and no more. This is called **limited liability.** Another advantage is that the death of an owner—a stockholder—does not interrupt the operation of the company. Even after an owner dies, his or her shares of stock continue to exist. These shares can be inherited by the stockholder's heirs or sold to other people.

A business with hundreds or thousands of owners must have a system for making important decisions. Corporations are run by boards of directors. This board makes important policy decisions and hires managers to oversee the day-to-day operations of the company. One way stockholders can take part in a corporation is to attend its annual stockholders' meeting. Any stockholder can come to these meetings and question the company's directors. The stockholders

Nonprofit The American Red Cross helps people and communities that have suffered in natural disasters. *Who runs a nonprofit organization?*

example, can sell food to members more cheaply than retail stores can because it is not in business to make a profit. Cooperatives are often small enough so that all members can vote on business decisions. Sometimes, like a corporation, a cooperative may elect a board of directors to make decisions.

Nonprofit organizations are similar to cooperatives. They are in business to provide goods or services, not to make a profit. As a result they can also charge lower fees for their goods or services. Many nonprofit organizations are charities, such as the American Red Cross and the American Cancer Society, whose purposes are to collect money to help the victims of disasters, to pay for research, or to educate the public about their causes. Nonprofit corporations are usually run by boards of directors.

can also elect the directors by voting their shares of stock. This means that stockholders may cast one vote for each share of common stock they own. Thus stockholders can elect new directors if they do not like the way the company is run.

Cooperatives and Nonprofit Organizations

In addition to the three major types of business organizations, people may organize to conduct business in two other ways.

A **cooperative** is an organization in which a number of people share the costs of a business or buy and sell goods or services at the lowest possible prices. Many farmers form cooperatives so they can share in the costs of storing and shipping their products.

Groups of consumers also form cooperatives. The most common kinds are food stores, preschools, and apartment buildings. A cooperative food store, for

★ **SECTION 3 REVIEW** ★

UNDERSTANDING VOCABULARY
Define sole proprietorship, partnership, corporation, incorporate, stocks, stockholder, common stock, dividend, preferred stock, limited liability, cooperative, nonprofit organization.

REVIEWING OBJECTIVES

1 What are the advantages and disadvantages of sole proprietorships?

2 What are the advantages and disadvantages of partnerships?

3 How do corporations raise money?

4 What are cooperatives and nonprofit organizations?

Identifying Key Terms

Choose the vocabulary term that best completes each of the sentences below. Write your answers on a separate sheet of paper.

supply and demand   market economy
corporation   entrepreneur
dividend   limited liability   profit

1. In a _____, individuals own the means of production.
2. After forming a _____, the owners sold stock to raise capital.
3. In a capitalist system, the forces of _____ determine most prices.
4. The owner's _____ was a result of owning a corporation.
5. The company had a good year and paid a _____ to all its stockholders.
6. After investing her time and money to start the business, the _____ was happy to see that the business was prospering.
7. After the partners paid their bills and taxes they found they had made a nice _____ for the year.

Reviewing the Main Ideas

SECTION 1
1. How do supply and demand affect each other?
2. How does a division of labor affect production?
3. What is the function of marketing, and what does it involve?

SECTION 2
4. Identify and describe three basic types of economic systems.

5. What type of economic system is a "mixed economy"?

SECTION 3
6. What are the disadvantages and advantages of the sole proprietorship type of business organization?
7. What are some of the reasons people form partnerships?
8. What are some of the advantages of a corporation?

Critical Thinking

SECTION 1
1. **Demonstrating Reasoned Judgment** How can the supply of resources affect a country's economy?

SECTION 2
2. **Evaluating Information** Which type of economic system do you think provides the most stable economy? Explain why.

SECTION 3
3. **Expressing a Point of View** Do you think cooperatives and nonprofit organizations serve a useful purpose? Explain.

Reinforcing Citizenship Skills

Locate a source of statistics on the United States in your library. One good source would be the *Statistical Abstract of the United States*. Select a topic that has a statistical table, such as the unemployment rate for different age groups. Study the table. Then write a summary of what the statistics show. Share your findings with the class.

Cooperative Learning

Meet in groups of four to discuss how to get capital to start a business. To begin with, you need to prepare a business plan. Your plan should describe your product or service and explain why the product or service is needed, how you plan to make or provide it, how your business will be run, what resources you need, and how you plan to use the capital. Write your plan, then present it to the class. Ask the class if it would finance the business outlined in your plan.

Focusing on Your Community

What are the major businesses in your community? What goods or services do they provide? Which businesses employ the most people? What types of goods or services do the sole proprietorship businesses in your community provide? Which corporations have offices, plants, or warehouses in the area? Prepare an oral report for the class.

Technology Activity

Using a Word Processor

Imagine that you are writing to a young person who lives in a nation in eastern Europe, such as Poland, that is trying to develop a market economy. Use a word processor to write a letter in which you explain what it is like to live in a "mixed" economy with its system of free enterprise. Keep in mind that the person has lived his or her entire life under a command economy and knows very little about a market economy. Discuss the system's advantages and disadvantages.

Analyzing Visuals

The table below shows the net income during the 1980s and early 1990s of proprietorships, partnerships, and corporations. Use the table to answer the following questions.

1. Which type of business showed a loss during the mid-1980s?
2. Which type of business has shown steady growth with no losses?
3. Which type of business showed a decline between 1988 and 1991?
4. Which type of business showed the largest jump in income in a two-year period? When did this increase occur?

Net Income for Different Types of Ownership (In billions of dollars)

Year	Proprietorships	Partnerships	Corporations
1980	55	8	239
1985	79	-9	240
1987	106	-5	328
1988	126	15	413
1989	133	14	389
1990	141	17	371
1991	142	21	345
1992	154	43	402
1993	156	67	498

Source: U.S. Internal Revenue Service.

★ CHAPTER 19 ★

Government and the Economy

CIVIC PARTICIPATION

The government's economic policies are aimed at strengthening the economy, solving economic problems, and protecting the economic interests of citizens. Ask a local librarian for help in finding information on recent government economic policies. Focus on such topics as tax policies, banking regulations, and efforts to balance the budget and curb inflation.

Working in Your Community

After you have obtained the information, prepare a fact sheet outlining these policies. Share this sheet with neighbors, and ask how the policies have affected their lives. Encourage them to write their elected representatives to express their views on government economic policies. ■

Your Civics Journal

For the next week, think about the advantages and disadvantages of labor unions and how they affect your life and the nation's economy. Write these ideas in your civics journal.

18mo
24mo
TRANS TEXAS.
(210)
182
BRADSTREET.
(232)
FORD BACON
156
187
BECHTOL
267
(200)
AIRPORT ACQ
(194)
148
248
(191)
APPLICATION for EMPLOYMENT

Measuring the Economy

FOCUS

TERMS TO KNOW

business cycle, recession, depression, fiscal policy, monetary policy, gross domestic product (GDP), standard of living, inflation

OBJECTIVES

■ Describe the four phases of **the business cycle.**

■ Identify two factors experts look at in **measuring economic performance.**

■ Explain how **inflation** affects people's standard of living.

In the United States, the government makes many decisions that affect the nation's economy. These decisions are aimed at improving the economy and solving economic problems, as well as protecting the interests of the nation's citizens.

The American economy continually changes as the government, as well as consumers and entrepreneurs, make economic decisions. To help the economy operate efficiently, the government must know what the economy is doing. For this reason the government regularly measures the economy and compares its performance to that in other years.

The Business Cycle

The ups and downs of the economy are known as the **business cycle.** This cycle has several phases, or parts. During the first phase, the economy is improving and business activity is increasing. Throughout this period of expansion, businesses produce more goods and hire more employees, and consumers buy more goods and services. This phase is often called a period of prosperity.

The second phase takes place when economic activity has peaked. Businesses are working at full capacity and stores are selling in record amounts. Eventually, this boom period slows and the economy enters its third phase. During this period of decline, people buy fewer goods and services than before. Companies do not sell as many goods, so they cut back on production and lay off workers. Some companies may be forced out of business.

During the fourth phase of the business cycle, production is at its lowest point and unemployment is very high.

The Period of Prosperity During the first phase of the business cycle, companies hire more employees. *What else happens during this period?*

HELP WANTED
COUNTER & GRILL
NO EXPERIENCE
NEEDED
WILL TRAIN

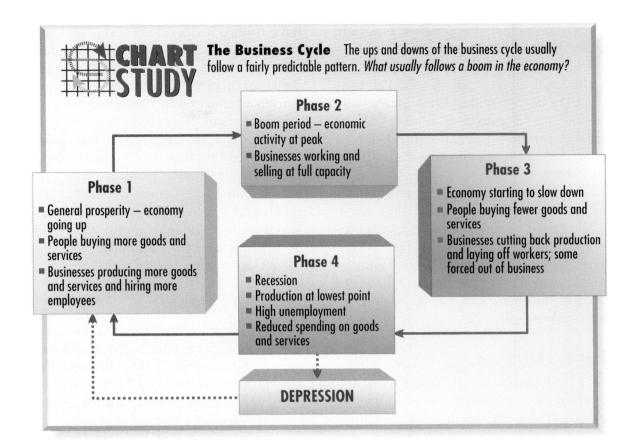

The Business Cycle The ups and downs of the business cycle usually follow a fairly predictable pattern. *What usually follows a boom in the economy?*

Phase 2
- Boom period — economic activity at peak
- Businesses working and selling at full capacity

Phase 1
- General prosperity — economy going up
- People buying more goods and services
- Businesses producing more goods and services and hiring more employees

Phase 3
- Economy starting to slow down
- People buying fewer goods and services
- Businesses cutting back production and laying off workers; some forced out of business

Phase 4
- Recession
- Production at lowest point
- High unemployment
- Reduced spending on goods and services

DEPRESSION

Most people have less money to spend on goods and services. Such a decline in economic activity is often called a **recession.** Eventually, however, the economy will enter a new expansion phase, and the business cycle will continue its ups and downs.

The model of the business cycle can help experts predict what will happen to the economy. Unfortunately, no one can predict how long a particular phase will last or how good or bad the economy will get. Sometimes, for example, a recession lasts for a long period of time and the economy becomes very bad. A severe recession is called a **depression.** The worst depression in the United States was the Great Depression, which began in 1929 and lasted until the start of World War II in 1939.

The Great Depression and Government Involvement

During the Great Depression, thousands of businesses were forced to close and millions of people were unemployed. Families lost their homes and farms because they had no money to pay their mortgages. Banks failed and people lost their life savings. Millions of people were hungry and homeless.

Until the Great Depression, the government was not very involved in the economy. Many people felt that the economy could take care of itself. In the early 1930s, however, the economy was so terrible that the government had to act.

When Franklin Roosevelt took office as President in 1933, his administration took a number of steps to get the country back on its feet. Roosevelt's program, called the New Deal, put millions of people to work on government projects such as building parks and schools. The government also provided low-cost loans so people could purchase homes, and it started the social security fund, which provided people with income during their retirement.

Many of the government agencies set up during the Depression still exist. While these agencies cannot prevent economic slowdowns, they do help soften the effects of recessions. The government also uses two other methods—fiscal policy and monetary policy—to help regulate the business cycle.

Fiscal Policy

Fiscal policy refers to the way the government taxes citizens and spends money. The government can use different fiscal policies to affect the business cycle. For example, in a recession, the government may spend more money on highway and public housing construction to help keep companies in business and workers employed. People with jobs have money to spend on goods and services, which increases demand. With factories producing more goods to meet the demand of both government and consumers, the economy begins to expand and comes out of its recession. The government might accomplish the same thing by cutting taxes. A tax cut is a fiscal policy that stimulates production by giving people more money to spend on goods and services. The government can also use fiscal policy to control the peaks of the business cycle, by raising taxes or cutting spending.

Monetary Policy

Monetary policy refers to the way the government regulates the amount of money in circulation. The Federal Reserve System, or the "Fed," acts as a bank for banks. It has an important role in the government's monetary policy.

One way that the Fed can regulate the nation's monetary policy is by raising or lowering the interest rates on its loans to commercial banks. When the rate is higher, commercial banks will borrow less money. They, in turn, will have less

Depression Breadline   During the Great Depression, millions of Americans lost their jobs and had to rely on handouts for survival.   *What did the government do to end the Depression?*

Fiscal Policy   By ordering military aircraft during a recession, the government helps keep people employed.   *What are some other measures the government might take to stimulate the economy?*

money to lend to individuals and businesses. As a result, spending will gradually decrease and the economy will slow down.

By using its powers, the Fed can increase the money supply during a recession and thus help the economy expand. In doing so, it can offset the fluctuations of the business cycle.

Measuring Economic Performance

The government conducts studies of different parts of the economy on a regular basis to find out how the economy is doing. Economists seek answers to such questions as how many people are working this month? How much did consumers spend last year? How much money did the steel industry make last year? The answers to these questions are called economic indicators because they indicate how the economy is performing.

Gross Domestic Product

One of the important indicators economists use is the **gross domestic product,** or **GDP.** The GDP is the total value, in dollars, of all the final goods and services produced within the nation each year. That is, it is the total value of all the cars, planes, television sets, running shoes, toothbrushes, and so on produced in this country. The GDP also includes all the money spent on doctors, restaurant meals, car repairs, and other services performed during the year. The GDP does not include goods or services produced by American citizens or American-owned companies outside the United States. It does, however, include goods

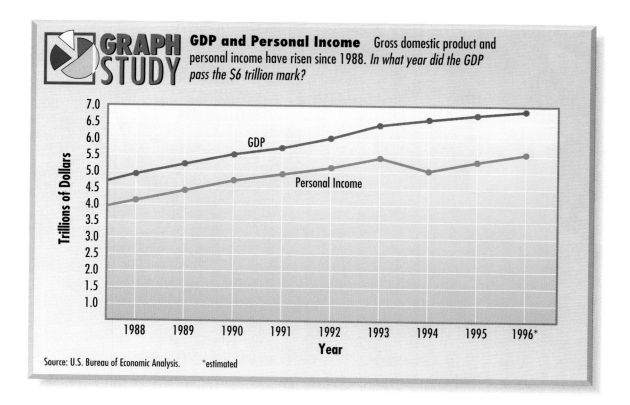

GRAPH STUDY

GDP and Personal Income Gross domestic product and personal income have risen since 1988. *In what year did the GDP pass the $6 trillion mark?*

Source: U.S. Bureau of Economic Analysis.   *estimated

and services produced by foreign-owned companies within this country.

The GDP tells economists how many goods and services are being produced and available for purchase, how much consumers are spending, and how these factors compare to those of other years. If the GDP is higher this year than last year, then the economy is expanding. If it is lower, the economy is declining. Economists study GDP figures over a period of years to analyze business cycle patterns. They also use the GDP to compare the economic performance of the United States with that of other countries.

Other Economic Indicators

Economists look at other economic indicators, such as personal income and disposable income, as well. Personal income is the total amount of income individuals receive before paying income

taxes. Disposable income refers to the money consumers have to spend on goods and services after their taxes are paid. These indicators help tell economists about people's **standard of living,** their quality of life based on the amount of goods and services they can purchase and leisure time they have.

Inflation

During the business cycle, inflation sometimes threatens people's standard of living. **Inflation** is a general rise in the prices of goods and services. Remember that when the economy is expanding, people have more money to purchase goods and services. As a result, the demand for those goods and services increases. As the demand increases, prices rise because people are competing to buy things.

Effects of Inflation

During a period of inflation, the prices of almost all goods and services will rise, and people have to keep paying more for the things they buy. Because their money buys less than it did before, their standard of living declines.

Sometimes companies are able to pay their workers more to help them keep up with inflation. Inflation is especially hard on retirees and other people with fixed incomes, however, because their incomes do not increase along with prices. Inflation also hurts people who save money. Their savings will probably buy less when they go to spend it.

Attempts to Control Inflation

The government tries to control inflation to prevent a decline in the standard of living. As you read earlier, government may try to slow the economy by raising the interest rate. Higher interest rates make it more expensive to borrow money and put a damper on economic activity. The government may also reduce the amount of money in circulation by raising taxes and cutting its own spending. Businesses, workers, and consumers can help control inflation as well. When businesses and workers increase their productivity (produce more goods and services) so that supply is greater than demand, prices drop. When consumers save more money and spend less, they, too, reduce demand and cause a decrease in prices.

Controlling the economy is a complicated balancing act. Sometimes an action the government takes to control one aspect of the economy has other, unavoidable consequences. For example, actions that help reduce inflation can also increase unemployment. The economy is

Effects of Inflation Inflation makes it especially hard for retirees on a fixed income to make ends meet. *What measures can the government take to control inflation?*

very complex and changes constantly. Economic experts often have different views on the course of action the government should take to keep the economy in good shape.

★ SECTION 1 REVIEW ★

UNDERSTANDING VOCABULARY
Define business cycle, recession, depression, fiscal policy, monetary policy, gross domestic product (GDP), standard of living, inflation.

REVIEWING OBJECTIVES
1 What are the four phases of the business cycle?

2 What are two factors experts look at in measuring economic performance?

3 How does inflation affect people's standard of living?

Government and Business

At the beginning of the 1800s, most American businesses were small, family-run concerns that made and sold a few goods. By the end of the 1800s, however, many businesses had developed into enormous, multimillion-dollar enterprises. During this time, the government took a **laissez-faire** approach to businesses. (*Laissez-faire* is a French phrase that means to "allow to do.") In a laissez-faire economy, the government lets businesses do what they want and does not interfere.

The power of the large corporations led to many abuses, and many Americans wanted the government to do something to control unfair business practices. In this century, the government has generally become more involved in regulating businesses.

The Growth of Monopolies

As businesses grew larger, many became monopolies. A **monopoly** exists when one company or small group of people control the supply of all, or most of, a particular good or service. With a monopoly, there is little or no competition. Consumers therefore have no choice if they want to buy a product provided by a monopoly. Because a monopoly has no competitors, it can produce goods of poorer quality or charge higher prices than it would if it had to compete with other companies.

Monopolies are formed in one of two ways—through mergers or through trusts. In a **merger** two or more companies agree to join together and form one large company. In a **trust** several companies remain separate but have only one board of directors to make decisions for all the companies. Instead of competing,

Monopoly Monster   In the 1880s Standard Oil controlled every aspect of the oil business.   *Why did monopolies need government regulation?*

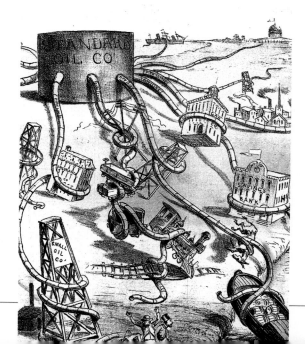

the companies cooperate in making decisions about their products. One of the best-known trusts was the Standard Oil Trust, organized by John D. Rockefeller in the 1880s. Standard Oil controlled every aspect of the oil business—drilling, shipping, refining, and selling.

As monopolies grew stronger and competition decreased, the federal government began to take steps to regulate them. In 1890 Congress passed the Sherman Antitrust Act, which outlawed monopolies and trusts. Unfortunately, the law was very vague and therefore difficult to enforce. In 1914 Congress enacted a new law, the Clayton Antitrust Act, that was easier to enforce because it listed specific business activities that were illegal. To help enforce the Clayton Act, Congress created the Federal Trade Commission (FTC). The FTC was given the power to investigate businesses to determine whether they were monopolies. It could also order them to stop breaking the law.

Monopolies Today

Some monopolies still exist today. For example, the people of a community can only buy their electricity, water, or cable television service from one company. These companies are called public utilities because they provide services to everyone in a community. Public utilities are legal monopolies. They are allowed to exist because it is cheaper and more efficient to let only one company provide such services to a community. The government, however, closely regulates public utilities.

Sometimes even legal monopolies are broken up. In 1982 the American Telephone and Telegraph Company (AT&T) was forced to break up its virtual monopoly on local telephone services in the

Monopoly Breakup   The breakup of AT&T in 1982 enabled other telephone companies to compete for customers.   *Why did the government break up the AT&T monopoly?*

United States. The government felt that competition would bring consumers lower prices and improved services.

Conglomerates

The government also keeps a close eye on conglomerates. A **conglomerate** is formed by the merger of companies that supply a variety of different goods and services. For example, a communications conglomerate may own several newspapers, printing plants, paper mills, and television stations. The danger with a conglomerate is that it might gain too large a share of a part of the economy and be able to control prices and competition. When that happens, the government can step in and break up the conglomerate.

Deregulation

For many years the government closely regulated a number of important industries that were not monopolies or

Assistance for Farmers The Soil Conservation Service teaches farmers about soil conditions. *What other government departments provide services for businesses?*

conglomerates. It did this to protect the interests of consumers. For example, trucking companies, airlines, and banks were regulated and had to provide services and set prices according to government rules. In the late 1970s and 1980s, some national leaders felt the government was interfering too much in these industries. They felt that **deregulation,** removing government restrictions, would better serve the public by increasing competition. In the case of the airlines, deregulation did stimulate competition, which led to lower prices. However, deregulation also resulted in the merger or disappearance of some airlines, the elimination of flights, and in some cases the raising of air fares again.

Government Assistance

The government's relationship with business is not limited to regulating and restricting. Various government depart-ments and agencies also provide services to businesses. For example, farmers can learn about soil conditions from the Soil Conservation Service, fishers can find out about ocean weather conditions from the National Weather Service, and a business owner can get help selling goods to Italy from the Department of Commerce.

The Department of Commerce also includes the Bureau of the Census, which compiles records on the nation's population. This information is very useful to businesses. Census records tell a great deal about consumers, such as where people live, how much they earn, and how many children they have. Business can use this information to help decide where to locate a factory, shopping mall, or movie theater.

Another federal agency, the Small Business Administration, helps people start new businesses. It advises them on how to go about setting up and operating a business, and it makes low-cost loans to help them get their businesses underway.

Exploring ISSUES

The Health-Care Debate

Each year, the United States spends billions of dollars on health care. Yet millions of Americans go without health care because they cannot afford health insurance. Moreover, rising medical costs create a great financial burden. These problems have led to a public debate about the nation's health-care system.

Health-Care Reform

In 1994 President Bill Clinton called for a sweeping reform of the health-care system. He proposed universal health care for all Americans, achieved through government funding and regulation of the health-care and health-insurance industries. The plan was abandoned because of fears that it would be too expensive and too complicated.

Most Americans are wary of giving the government control of the health-care system and fear that the quality of care would suffer. Another idea is to reform the health-insurance industry to ensure that more people are covered by insurance. Congress moved in this direction in 1996 when it passed a law ensuring that people who change jobs would be eligible for medical insurance even if they had a history of medical problems.

Managed Care

An important development in health care today is the movement toward "managed care." The term refers to a system in

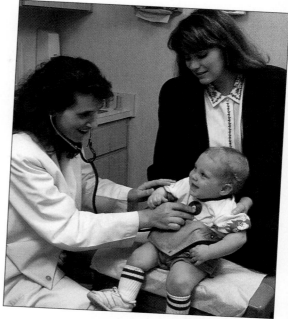

The health-care system

which costs are contained by limiting a patient's choice of doctors and treatments.

Managed care usually involves groups known as health maintenance organizations, or HMOs. HMOs stress prevention and seek to cut costs by limiting tests, referrals to specialists, and lengthy hospital stays. HMOs do help lower costs, but critics charge that they often lower the quality of care as well. Nevertheless, the number of people who belong to HMOs and other managed-care systems continues to grow.

DEVELOPING A POINT OF VIEW

1 What are two basic problems with the health-care system?

2 What role should the government have in providing health care?

Government and Labor

FOCUS

TERMS TO KNOW
labor union, collective bargaining, strike, closed shop, open shop, mediation, arbitration

OBJECTIVES

■ Describe **the formation of labor unions** in the United States.

■ Identify and describe two basic features of **labor-management relations** between union workers and employers.

■ Describe three **government actions** in labor-management relations.

■ Discuss the status of **labor unions today.**

The nation's workforce is an important part of the economy. Workers not only produce goods and services but also use their wages to buy the goods and services that are available. Because workers are so important, government takes a special interest in them and in their relation to businesses.

The Formation of Labor Unions

In the 1800s the nation's workers were treated very badly. Wages were low, and working conditions were poor and often dangerous. Workers who complained were fired and quickly replaced. Many workers began to band together to try to get better working conditions, shorter hours, and higher pay. They formed organizations of workers called **labor unions** to achieve their goals.

The first groups of workers to form unions were craftspeople—skilled workers, such as plumbers and carpenters, who worked at specific trades. In 1886 many different craft, or trade, unions formed a large association of unions called the American Federation of Labor (AFL). Within 15 years the AFL had grown to nearly half a million members.

In the meantime factory and mine workers began to form unions called industrial unions. These unions were organized not by craft but by factory or industry. For example, people who worked in a textile factory could join that factory's union regardless of what type of work they did. These industrial

Union Power   Union members in New York attended a rally in the early 1900s.   *What was the association of industrial unions called?*

unions also formed an association of unions, which was called the Congress of Industrial Organizations (CIO). In 1955 the AFL and CIO joined together to become the AFL-CIO, which represents more than 80 unions and 13 million workers. Many other unions that are independent of the AFL-CIO also exist.

Labor-Management Relations

Once workers had formed unions, they had to find ways to convince employers to raise wages and improve working conditions. Business owners often resisted the unions' demands, however, because paying higher wages or buying safer equipment would force them to raise their prices or reduce their own profits. In addition, business owners could no longer arrange terms with individual workers. Instead, they had to negotiate conditions and terms of employment with representatives of the union. This kind of negotiation is called **collective bargaining.**

Union Tactics

If a business owner rejected a union's demands, union members might **strike,** or refuse to work. Striking workers usually formed a picket line, or a kind of human fence, at the entrance to the business. The purpose of picketing was to prevent nonunion workers from entering and taking the strikers' jobs. Striking and picketing are still the major methods unions use to force companies to negotiate with them. In addition, unions may call for a work slowdown, in which workers perform their jobs so slowly that production decreases.

Management Tactics

Business owners quickly developed ways of getting back at striking workers. In some cases, they went to court and obtained injunctions. With these court orders, they could use the police, and sometimes even federal troops, to break up a strike. Companies would also keep blacklists of the names of union leaders

DID YOU KNOW?

An Owl Saves the Trees

The rare spotted owl lives in the national forests of Washington and Oregon, where some of the nation's oldest and largest evergreen trees grow. In the early 1980s, environmental groups went to court to prevent logging in these forests. Environmentalists claim that the spotted owl is an endangered species. They say that cutting down the forests destroys the owl's home and reduces the chance of the bird's survival.

Under the federal plan approved in 1994, access to national forests in the Northwest is now restricted. The timber industry can cut a limited amount of lumber, while many areas of forest are protected. Neither the timber industry nor environmentalists are happy with the plan. It is hoped, however, that the plan will help save both the spotted owls and millions of acres of ancient forest.

Protected species

On Strike Union members whose demands are rejected often resort to striking. *What benefits do union members seek?*

and strikers. These blacklists would be sent to other companies. When union workers went looking for new jobs, these other companies would often refuse to hire them. Sometimes a company might simply lock its doors and wait until the workers ran out of money and had to return to work.

Today companies and unions still use collective bargaining to settle their disputes. In addition to higher wages, unions often seek other benefits, such as medical, dental, and life insurance, longer paid vacations, more sick days, and safer working conditions. Unions are also very concerned about job security. They want to ensure that members can only be fired or laid off under certain conditions.

Government Actions

During the early years of the labor movement, many strikes and lockouts were very violent. By the 1930s the government had moved into the role of ref-

eree between labor and management. In 1935 Congress enacted the National Labor Relations Act. This law guaranteed the right of all workers to join a union. It also created a government agency, the National Labor Relations Board (NLRB), which would judge the fairness of actions by employers and unions.

In 1947 Congress passed the Taft-Hartley Act, which imposed some limits on unions. The Taft-Hartley Act banned closed shops and featherbedding. A **closed shop** is a factory or business in which workers cannot be hired unless they are union members. Featherbedding refers to a union practice that forces a company to employ more workers than needed. However, the law did allow union shops. In a union shop, workers do not have to be union members to be hired, but they must join the union within 30 days to keep their jobs.

Many states now have right-to-work laws, which guarantee that no one may be forced to join a union. These states only allow **open shops,** in which workers are free to choose whether or not to join a union. Unions do not like open shops because nonunion workers receive the benefits the unions have negotiated for their own members, without having to pay union dues or support the union.

Labor Unions Today

Labor unions are not as strong as they once were. In some cases unions have lost power because industries in which unions were prominent—such as steel and automaking—have become less important to the American economy. In other cases businesses have moved to areas of the country where there are no unions or unions are weak.

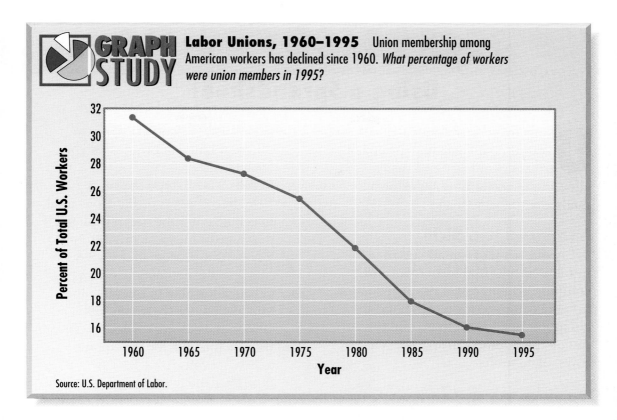

GRAPH STUDY

Labor Unions, 1960–1995 Union membership among American workers has declined since 1960. *What percentage of workers were union members in 1995?*

Percent of Total U.S. Workers

Year

Source: U.S. Department of Labor.

Nonetheless, labor unions are still a significant factor in the economy. In the 1960s César Chavez formed the United Farm Workers union and organized the migrant farmworkers who harvest the nation's food crops. In recent years unions have successfully organized many public and service employees, such as hospital workers and firefighters.

Strikes are far less common today than they were in the past. In most cases employers and unions prefer to settle disputes peacefully, through mediation and arbitration. In **mediation** a third party listens to both sides and then suggests a solution, which is not binding on either side. If both sides accept the mediator's recommendation, the dispute is settled. **Arbitration** is similar to mediation except that both sides agree beforehand to accept the arbitrator's decision no matter what it may be.

★ **SECTION 3 REVIEW** ★

UNDERSTANDING VOCABULARY
Define labor union, collective bargaining, strike, closed shop, open shop, mediation, arbitration.

REVIEWING OBJECTIVES
1 What factors led to the formation of American labor unions?

2 What are two basic features of labor-management relations between union workers and employers?

3 What have been three government actions in labor-management relations?

4 What is the status of labor unions today?

TECHNOLOGY SKILLS

Using a Spreadsheet

Using an electronic spreadsheet, you can manage large groups of numbers quickly and easily, allowing the computer to perform mathematical functions.

Learning the Skill

A spreadsheet is made up of numbered cells that form rows and columns. By entering a simple equation into the computer, you command the computer to add, subtract, multiply, or divide the numbers in specific cells, rows, or columns.

Changing the Spreadsheet Use a mouse or the cursor keys on the computer to move to the cell you choose. That cell will be highlighted or have a border around it. If you change a number in any cell, the computer will automatically change the totals to reflect the new number. The computer will even copy a formula from one cell to another.

Practicing the Skill

Suppose you want to know the net income of sole proprietorships, partnerships, and corporations in the United States since 1990. Use these steps to create a spreadsheet that will provide this information. Use the sample below that shows you the lettered cells.

A1	A2	A3	A4	A5	A6	A7	A8	A9
B1	B2	B3	B4	B5	B6	B7	B8	B9
C1	C2	C3	C4	C5	C6	C7	C8	C9
D1	D2	D3	D4	D5	D6	D7	D8	D9

1. In cells B1, C1, and D1, type the different kinds of businesses you wish to track.
2. In cells A2-A8, type the years 1990-1996. In cell A9, type the word total.
3. In cell B2 enter the net income for that type of business in 1990. Repeat this process in rows 3-8, filling in the net income each year.
4. Create a formula to calculate the total net income between 1990 and 1996 in the category listed in cell B1. The formula for the equation tells what cells (B2 + B3 + B4 + B5 + B6 + B7 + B8) to add together. Each spreadsheet program is slightly different, so check your program documentation to get the correct formula.
5. Copy the formula down in the cells for the other two types of business organization.
6. Use the process in steps 4 and 5 to create and copy a formula to calculate the net income of businesses each year from 1990 to 1996.

APPLYING THE SKILL

Create a spreadsheet you can use to track weekly price changes in two grocery items over a three-week period and determine which item has shown the greatest price changes.

Government and Banking

B anking is a business that deals in money. It is a very large and important part of the American economy. As with business and labor, the federal government regulates the banking industry.

Financial Needs

To function in our economy, consumers must satisfy a range of financial needs. For example, people need to have a place where they can save and store their money safely. They also need ways that allow them to make their purchases conveniently. Consumers also have the need for credit—to be able to borrow money that they will repay in the future.

Financial Institutions

Various financial institutions satisfy consumers' financial needs. The most common institutions are banks, savings banks, and credit unions.

Banks and Savings Banks

Banks and savings banks are businesses that are privately owned and operated. They can be chartered—allowed to do business—by either a state government or the federal government. The federal government, however, supervises most banks because they are members of the Federal Reserve System.

Credit Unions

Credit unions are institutions that are owned by their members. To join a credit union, an individual must share the same

Credit Consumers often need credit to purchase a car. *What is credit?*

MAP STUDY

Federal Reserve Districts There are 12 districts in the Federal Reserve System of the United States. *Which district consists of only one state?*

(11) Federal Reserve districts
• Federal Reserve Bank locations

characteristic that links the other members of the credit union. In the past, most credit unions were composed of people who worked for the same employer or in the same job, such as a teachers' credit union. Today many people with a common characteristic form credit unions, such as religious groups or even residents of a single town. Credit unions with state charters are supervised by their state. The National Credit Union Administration (NCUA) supervises federally chartered credit unions.

Meeting Financial Needs

Banks and credit unions provide a variety of products and services to satisfy consumers' needs. Deposit accounts provide people with an opportunity to keep their money in a safe place. As an additional benefit, people usually earn money—**interest**—on the money that they keep in deposit accounts.

Financial institutions are able to pay interest to depositors because they satisfy another important consumer need— the need to borrow money. Banks make mortgage loans to people who want to purchase homes and consumer loans to people who want to purchase cars, to finance their education, or to satisfy other needs. Banks make loans based upon an individual's ability and willingness to repay the money. To further protect themselves, banks often require borrowers to pledge property they own to secure the loan. On a home loan, the home and property secure the loan. On auto loans, the car being purchased is used as security and is called **collateral**.

Financial institutions satisfy a full range of other financial needs. Checking accounts and credit cards allow people to make purchases conveniently without using cash. Travelers checks allow people to travel anywhere in the world without worrying about the risk of carrying cash. Banks also offer investment services that allow consumers to place their funds in products that might allow them to earn a higher rate of interest, or, in some cases, to take advantage of tax benefits.

The Government's Role in the Banking Industry

During the 1800s many American banks lent too much money and did not keep enough cash on hand. As a result depositors sometimes lost faith in a bank and demanded their money back. This was called "a run on the bank." If the bank did not have enough money to pay its depositors, it might fail, and depositors who did not withdraw their money in time would lose their savings.

Federal Reserve System

In 1913 Congress created the Federal Reserve System to put a stop to such bank failures. The new system set up 1 Federal Reserve Bank in each of 12 districts around the nation. All national banks were required to maintain a legal reserve—the amount of money that the government requires a bank to keep on hand to pay depositors who want to withdraw their money. Member banks had to keep part of their cash reserves on deposit at a Federal Reserve Bank. Then in the event of a run on the bank, the

bank could use this cash reserve to meet its depositors' demands.

The Federal Reserve is the bank for other banks. Individuals and companies cannot do business with a Federal Reserve Bank. Commercial banks, however, may borrow money from the Federal Reserve to lend to their customers.

Despite the establishment of the Federal Reserve System, many banks failed in the 1930s during the Great Depression. Thousands of people lost their money.

Federal Deposit Insurance Corporation

To protect individual depositors from losing their life savings in cases like these, the federal government created the Federal Deposit Insurance Corporation (FDIC) for bank depositors and the National Credit Union Share Insurance Fund for credit union depositors. These two programs ensure that depositors will be repaid if a financial institution fails.

★ **SECTION 4 REVIEW** ★

UNDERSTANDING VOCABULARY
Define interest, collateral.

REVIEWING OBJECTIVES

1 What are some financial needs of consumers?

2 What are two types of financial institutions?

3 How do financial institutions help meet financial needs?

4 What is the government's role in the banking industry?

Identifying Key Terms

Choose the vocabulary term that best completes each of the sentences below. Write your answers on a separate sheet of paper.

recession   inflation   strike
deregulation   mediation
monopoly   collateral

1. Since it had no competition, the _____ could charge whatever price it wanted for its product.
2. To get the loan from the bank, the couple had to use their car as _____.
3. With business very slow and unemployment increasing, the nation seemed headed for a _____.
4. Prices kept going up and up because of the high rate of _____.
5. Recent _____ removed many government controls from the industry.
6. After _____, the third party recommended that the company meet the union's demands.
7. Unable to reach agreement with the company, the union called for a _____.

Reviewing the Main Ideas

SECTION 1
1. How does the business cycle affect the economy?
2. What is the difference between fiscal policy and monetary policy?

SECTION 2
3. Why was the Sherman Antitrust Act difficult to enforce?
4. Why does the government allow public utility companies to operate as monopolies?

SECTION 3
5. What methods can unions use to try to improve wages and working conditions?
6. What government actions have reduced the power of the unions?
7. What methods can employers and unions use to try to settle disputes peacefully?

SECTION 4
8. What are some of the services banks provide?
9. How does the government protect depositors' savings in banks?

Critical Thinking

SECTION 1
1. **Synthesizing Information** What are the advantages and disadvantages of using fiscal and monetary policies to regulate the nation's economy?

SECTION 2
2. **Expressing a Point of View** Do you think a laissez-faire approach to business is good for individuals and small companies? Explain.

SECTION 3
3. **Determining Cause and Effect** What factors do you think have helped lead to the decline of labor unions in the United States?

SECTION 4
4. **Analyzing Information** Why do you think some customers use bank investment services rather than simple savings accounts?

Reinforcing Citizenship Skills

The government publishes the President's plan for federal expenditures for the coming year. In the library try to find a source that has a circle graph of this information. Study the graph and note the percentages of the two largest and two smallest categories. Share your information with the class.

Cooperative Learning

With two other students, develop several questions you might ask local business people about their experiences with the business cycle, inflation, and government regulation. Report your findings to the class.

Focusing on Your Community

Some local governments adopt policies, such as tax breaks and highway improvement, to stimulate business activity in the community. Find out what types of assistance your local government provides to businesses and what policies it has to encourage or discourage the location of businesses in your community.

Technology Activity

Using a Spreadsheet

Search the Internet or find information in your local library about economic indicators. Economic indicators are certain statistics that economists study to chart economic growth. For example, economists study the unemployment rate. A rise in the rate suggests that the nation is entering a recession. A fall in the rate suggests an economic recovery. Use the information you find to create a spreadsheet with the following headings: Economic Indicator, 1990, 1997, Today. Use the completed spreadsheet to evaluate the health of the American economy.

Analyzing Visuals

The head of the Federal Reserve System is often in the news. In the political cartoon below, Alan Greenspan is the head of the "Fed." Study the cartoon, and then answer the following questions.

1. What is the general outlook for the American economy according to Uncle Sam?
2. How does Uncle Sam's mood contrast with that of Greenspan?
3. What does Greenspan suggest will happen?
4. How might this affect the American economy?

CHAPTER 20

Financing Our Governments

CIVIC PARTICIPATION

As taxpayers, American citizens share most of the burden of financing local, state, and federal governments. In return, we receive a host of services that make our lives better and more secure. Contact your local town hall or city hall for information about the current budget, including sources of revenue and expenses. How much state or federal money does the community receive for local programs?

Working in Your Community

After you have this information, ask neighbors about their views on local expenditures and taxes. Share your community's budget with them. What changes, if any, would they make in local taxes and spending and in state and federal funding for local programs? ■

Your Civics Journal

As you study this chapter, think about the various services your local, state, and federal governments provide. Write these in your civics journal, along with your feelings about the importance of these services. What changes, if any, would you make in these services?

West Point cadets ➤

★ SECTION 1 ★

The Power to Tax

E very government has expenses. It must pay the salaries of elected officials and public employees. It must also pay for the services it provides to citizens. Government spending is one of the most controversial aspects of government policy. Some people feel that governments should spend less. Others feel governments should spend more. Almost everyone has different ideas about what the money should be spent on. People's feelings about public spending generally reflect their deepest beliefs about the purpose of government.

Governments, like individuals, must receive money before they can spend it. Money governments receive is generally called **revenue.** While governments get revenue from a variety of sources, the most important source is taxes. State and local governments usually get 60 to 80 percent of their revenue through taxes. The federal government gets nearly all of its revenue from taxes.

Taxation

The power to tax is an important source of a government's strength. Laws and regulations are worthless unless a government can raise the money necessary to carry them out. For this reason governments have almost always required their citizens to pay some form of taxes. Ancient Mesopotamian farmers had to give a portion of their crops to the government. Ancient Romans paid sales taxes, just as we do today.

Sometimes governments abuse their power to tax. Many times throughout history, citizens have turned against their government because they believed their taxes were unfair. One such revolt led to the American colonists' decision to declare independence from Britain in 1776.

Tea and Taxes   British taxes on a shipload of tea angered American colonists, and they threw the tea into Boston Harbor.   *Why is a government's power to tax important?*

When the American Revolution was over, citizens denied their new government the power to tax in order to avoid similar revolts. Under the Articles of Confederation, the government could request—but not demand—contributions from the states. The inability to raise money was a major weakness of the Confederation government.

The United States Constitution, on the other hand, included provisions on the power of taxation. The writers of the Constitution realized that the federal government needed a reliable source of revenue to operate effectively. At the same time, they wanted to prevent Congress from abusing its power to tax, as the British Parliament had done. For this reason they gave Congress a *limited* power to tax.

Limits on Taxation

The writers of the Constitution gave Congress "the power to lay and collect taxes." However, they placed certain restrictions on this power to prevent abuses. They wanted to make sure that the people being taxed would have a voice in the tax law. For this reason all tax bills must be introduced in the House of Representatives, where representation is based on population. They also wanted to be sure that the taxes would fall fairly on all citizens. Thus the Constitution requires that any tax the federal government imposes must apply uniformly throughout the country.

In addition, the Constitution restricts the power of state governments to collect taxes. Unlike the federal government, states are not permitted to tax interstate or foreign commerce. Also, as the result of an 1819 Supreme Court decision, states may not tax the federal government.

Limits on Taxation   Angry citizens protest increased property taxes.   *Which amendment to the Constitution ensures that tax laws apply equally to all?*

One of the most important limits on the taxation power of state governments is the Fourteenth Amendment. The amendment's guarantee of "equal protection of the laws" to all citizens prevents states from taxing one group of citizens more heavily than another—without good reason. For example, a state government may not require Republicans to pay heavier taxes than Democrats. It may, however, require wealthy people to pay more taxes than poor people.

Many state constitutions further limit taxation. The limits may include the kinds of taxes the state legislature can pass and how high those taxes can be. As you discovered in Chapter 14, local governments get their powers directly from state governments. Therefore, all restrictions on state taxation—whether found in the United States Constitution or in state constitutions—apply to local governments as well.

Local Taxes   A property owner pays local taxes.   *What is an example of a tax collected in the most convenient way possible?*

Principles of Taxation

No one enjoys paying taxes. Taxpayers complain less, however, when they feel that their government is collecting taxes fairly and using the money wisely. In 1776 the English economist Adam Smith developed four guidelines for taxation.

The first guideline is that taxes should be *based on a person's ability to pay.* In other words wealthy people should be taxed at a higher rate than poor people. Such a tax, in which people who earn more money pay more taxes, is known as a **progressive tax.** A **regressive tax,** on the other hand, is one in which people pay the same amount no matter how wealthy or poor they are. A regressive tax places a heavier burden on the poor.

Smith's second guideline is that a tax should be *clear and straightforward.* People should be able to figure out exactly how much they must pay in taxes. When this guideline is followed, people can plan their finances wisely.

The third guideline is that a tax should be *collected in the most convenient way possible.* A sales tax, for example, should be paid when the sale is made.

Smith's final guideline is that each tax should be *collected efficiently.* Whenever a government collects a tax, a small portion of the revenue goes to pay for the cost of tax collection. According to this guideline, collection costs should be kept as low as possible so that more tax money can be spent for the public good.

Most economists add a fifth guideline that Adam Smith did not include. This guideline is that taxes should be *reasonable.* When taxes are high, people and businesses have less money to save and invest. Moreover, people may not work as hard because they know they will have to pay the government a large portion of the money they earn.

★ SECTION 1 REVIEW ★

UNDERSTANDING VOCABULARY
Define revenue, progressive tax, regressive tax.

REVIEWING OBJECTIVES

1 What is the importance of taxation?

2 What are three limits on taxation found in the United States Constitution?

3 What are four basic principles of taxation?

SECTION 2

Types of Revenue

FOCUS

TERMS TO KNOW
income tax, tax return, exemption, deduction, taxable income, property tax, sales tax, excise tax, tariff

OBJECTIVES

- Explain why **income taxes** are considered progressive taxes.

- Explain how **property taxes** are determined.

- Identify and compare two kinds of **sales taxes.**

- Identify and describe three **other types of taxes** the federal government imposes.

- Identify three sources of **nontax revenue.**

There is no such thing as a perfect tax. No single form of taxation can satisfy all the guidelines you read about in the preceding section. For this reason most governments use several different kinds of taxes to raise revenue. The advantages of one tax can help make up for the disadvantages of another.

Income Taxes

An **income tax** is a tax on income—the money an individual or business earns. The Sixteenth Amendment, passed in 1913, gave the government the power to levy, or collect, such a tax. Today the federal government gets about half its total revenue from income taxes. Most states and many cities have income taxes as well and rely on these as an important source of revenue.

The United States levies two types of income taxes—personal and corporate. Individuals pay personal income taxes based on the money they earn each year. Corporations pay corporate income taxes based on their annual profits.

Filing Tax Returns

The deadline for paying personal income tax is generally April 15 of each year. By that date, each taxpayer must submit a form called a **tax return** to the Internal Revenue Service, the government's tax collector. To fill out the tax return, taxpayers must first figure out exactly how much income they received during the past year. Each taxpayer then subtracts a certain amount of money called an **exemption.** In 1996 the exemption the federal government allowed was $2,550 plus $2,550 for each dependent, or person the taxpayer supported.

Income Taxes   Most people must file their personal income tax returns by April 15. *What is a corporate income tax?*

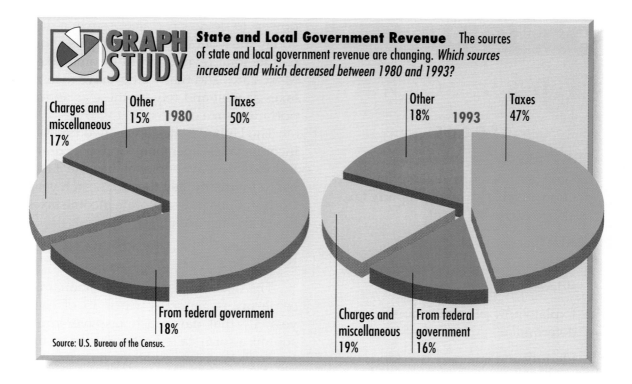

GRAPH STUDY

State and Local Government Revenue The sources of state and local government revenue are changing. *Which sources increased and which decreased between 1980 and 1993?*

1980
- Charges and miscellaneous 17%
- Other 15%
- Taxes 50%
- From federal government 18%

1993
- Other 18%
- Taxes 47%
- Charges and miscellaneous 19%
- From federal government 16%

Source: U.S. Bureau of the Census.

For example, a taxpayer with an unemployed spouse would claim an exemption of $5,100.

A taxpayer may sometimes subtract additional amounts of money, called **deductions,** for such things as medical expenses and charitable contributions. The amount that remains after the taxpayer has subtracted all possible exemptions and deductions is called **taxable income.** The taxpayer must pay the government an income tax based on a certain portion of this taxable income.

Withholding Taxes

To make the payment and collection of personal income taxes more convenient, the federal and state governments have set up a system of tax withholding. Under this system employers regularly subtract a certain portion of money from each employee's paycheck. This money is sent directly to the federal and state

governments. As a result most taxpayers owe only a small amount of income tax when they submit their tax returns. Some taxpayers may have too much money withheld from their paychecks. These taxpayers are entitled to a tax refund after submitting their tax returns.

The federal income tax and most state income taxes are progressive. People with higher incomes must pay a greater percentage in taxes. For example, in 1994 an unmarried taxpayer whose taxable income was less than $22,750 had to pay 15 percent (or no more than $3,412.50) to the federal government. An unmarried taxpayer whose taxable income was between $22,751 and $55,100 had to pay 15 percent on the first $22,750 and 28 percent on the rest. People with higher incomes paid rates of 31, 36, and 39.6 percent. The reason for this system is that people with lower incomes must spend a larger percentage of their earnings on necessities such as food and housing. People with higher incomes generally have more money to spend on non-necessities. As a result they can afford to take on a bigger share of the tax burden.

Property Taxes

A **property tax** is a tax based on the value of property. Governments usually define *property* to mean real estate, but personal items such as cars and jewelry may also be taxable. Property taxes are the primary source of revenue for local governments. Some state governments impose property taxes as well, as do many of the nation's school districts.

Before a government can collect property tax, it must send an assessor to examine a taxpayer's property. Using written reference material and past experience, the assessor decides what each piece of property is worth. Property tax is usually worked out as a percentage of the assessed value. The local government sets this tax rate according to the needs of the community. In one community it might be 4.5 percent ($4,500 on a house assessed at $100,000). In another it might be only 2 percent ($2,000 on a house assessed at $100,000).

As the costs of government have increased, property owners have had to pay higher property taxes. Many property owners have objected to paying these high taxes. In 1978 California taxpayers voted to lower property taxes throughout the state. Since then, voters in a number of other states have followed with similar "taxpayer revolts." As a result of this pressure to lower property taxes or limit increases, many state and local governments have been forced to cut their spending drastically.

Sales Taxes

A **sales tax** is a tax placed on the sale of various products. The purchaser pays this tax at the time of purchase. The seller collects the sales tax and sends the money to the government. Sales taxes are a popular way to raise revenue because they are so easy to collect. Almost every state government has some form of sales tax, as do many county and city governments.

Property Taxes   Many communities depend on property taxes to finance schools. *How are property taxes determined?*

Tolls   Motorists must pay tolls for the use of some highways, bridges, and tunnels.   *What kind of revenue are tolls?*

traffic regulations or for failing to meet clean air and water standards.

In recent years an increasing number of states have begun to raise revenue through government-run lotteries. These games of chance, in which people buy numbered tickets, offer large amounts of cash as prizes for those whose numbers are drawn. Lotteries have proven to be very successful at raising revenue, and more than half the states now have them. Many people disapprove of lotteries, however, because they feel that states should not be encouraging gambling.

Many state and local governments get from 9 to 47 percent of their revenue from nontax sources such as rents, tolls, and fees. The federal government, however, gets less than 2 percent of its revenue from nontax sources.

federal government often leases the rights to dig mines or drill for oil on federal land. Renting or leasing is preferable to selling because it provides a steady source of income.

Tolls are another regular source of income. State and local governments often charge tolls for the use of highways and bridges. The federal government charges tolls for the use of canals the United States owns.

All governments also collect fees and fines. State governments, for example, require licenses for driving, getting married, hunting, and fishing. People who want to obtain such licenses must pay a fee to the government. The federal government charges fees for such services as registering copyrights, preparing passports, and providing copies of documents. In addition, governments collect fines from individuals and organizations. The fines might be for violating

★ SECTION 2 REVIEW ★

UNDERSTANDING VOCABULARY
Define income tax, tax return, exemption, deduction, taxable income, property tax, sales tax, excise tax, tariff.

REVIEWING OBJECTIVES
1 Why are income taxes considered progressive taxes?

2 How are property taxes determined?

3 What are two kinds of sales taxes, and how are they different?

4 What are three other types of taxes the federal government imposes?

5 What are three sources of nontax revenue?

Using the Internet

To learn more about almost anything, learn to use the Internet. The Internet is a global "network" that offers opportunities to explore exciting features such as electronic mail, games, on-line discussion groups, and even shopping. To enjoy the Internet and its services, you must have three things:
1) a computer,
2) a modem, to enable your computer to send and receive data over a telephone line, and
3) an Internet service provider, such as America Online or a local Internet service provider, that will grant you entry to the Internet.

Learning the Skill

The easiest way to access sites and information on the Internet is to use a Web browser. This will allow you to view and explore information on the World Wide Web. The World Wide Web is made up of documents called Web pages. Each Web page has its own address, or URL, many URLs begin with http://. As you become familiar with the Internet and its various features, you will see how easy it is to locate information by using the proper Web site.

Practicing the Skill

This chapter focuses on financing our governments. Follow these steps to learn more about government finances.
1. Log on to the Internet and access a World Wide Web search tool, such as Yahoo at
   http://www.yahoo.com

Lycos at
   http://www.lycos.com
WebCrawler at
   http://www.webcrawler.com

2. Search by selecting one of the listed categories or by typing in the category you want to find.
3. Continue your search by scrolling down the list that appears on your screen. When you select an entry, click on it to access the information. Sometimes, the information you first access will not be exactly what you need. If so, continue searching until you find the information that you want.

Checking Out the Internet

APPLYING THE SKILL

Follow this procedure to locate information about the budget of the federal government. Use the information you gather to create a chart or graph depicting how the government allocates it funds.

How Governments Spend Their Money

FOCUS

TERMS TO KNOW
budget, expenditures, deficit, national debt, balanced budget, grant-in-aid

OBJECTIVES

- Describe the steps in **the budget process** of the federal government.

- Identify the largest **expenditures** of the federal, state, and local governments.

- Explain some of the problems caused by **budget deficits.**

- Identify and describe the most common form of **intergovernmental revenue.**

B ecause governments have limited revenues, they must make choices. If more money is spent on one item, less money must be spent on another. Spending an extra $1 billion on space exploration, for example, may result in less money for programs to feed the hungry. Making decisions like these is one of the most difficult duties of government.

To decide how best to spend its money, a government must set priorities. It must determine the importance of its various goals and spend its money accordingly. The greatest amount of money will be spent on the most important items. Lesser amounts of money will be spent on less important items.

The Budget Process

A government's spending priorities are presented in the form of a **budget,** a plan for managing and spending money. A budget always has two parts. The first part lists the government's revenues, or receipts, and indicates how much money is expected from each source. The second part lists the government's outlays, or **expenditures**—the items on which the government plans to spend money and the amount it plans to spend on each.

Budgets are almost always annual; they list revenues and expenditures for a one-year period. This one-year period is usually a fiscal year rather than a calen-

NASA The federal government has spent billions of dollars on the space program of the National Aeronautics and Space Administration. *How do governments decide how to spend their funds?*

dar year. While a calendar year always runs from January 1 to December 31, a fiscal year can begin at any time. For example, the federal government's fiscal year runs from October 1 of one calendar year to September 30 of the next. Most state and local governments also use those dates for their fiscal years.

Preparing the Budget

Because the federal government spends such an immense amount of money—more than $1 trillion—the federal budget is a huge document. Preparing the budget requires the work of hundreds of people over several months.

The budget process begins each year in the Office of Management and Budget (OMB), a division of the Executive Office of the President. The head of the OMB, the budget director, asks every federal department and agency to estimate the amount of money it will need for the coming fiscal year. At the same time, members of the OMB staff estimate the amount of money the government can expect to take in during the same period.

With this information, the budget director meets with the President to discuss priorities. Based on recommendations of the President and the President's advisers, the budget director works out the first draft of the budget with the help of the OMB staff, who fill in the details. The completed budget is often more than 1,000 pages long.

Passing the Budget

Once the President has approved the OMB's work, the budget is sent to Congress for approval. The President usually marks the occasion with a nationally televised speech, explaining and defending the spending priorities that have

Budgets Laura D'Andrea Tyson, head of the National Economic Council, is one of the officials involved in planning the budget. *Who else participates in preparing the budget?*

been established. Congress, however, almost never accepts the President's budget as it is. Many members of Congress have different priorities from those of the President. So, after weeks or months of congressional debate, the budget usually emerges with major changes.

By the time both houses of Congress pass the budget, it includes a great many compromises. Many federal agencies must accept less funding than they requested. The President may have to abandon some goals that were considered important. Members of Congress may have to give up programs that would benefit their constituents. As a result of these compromises, however, the federal budget is better able to meet the needs of the country as a whole.

State Budgets

Most state and local governments follow a similar process in preparing their own budgets. Usually the leader of the executive branch, with the advice of

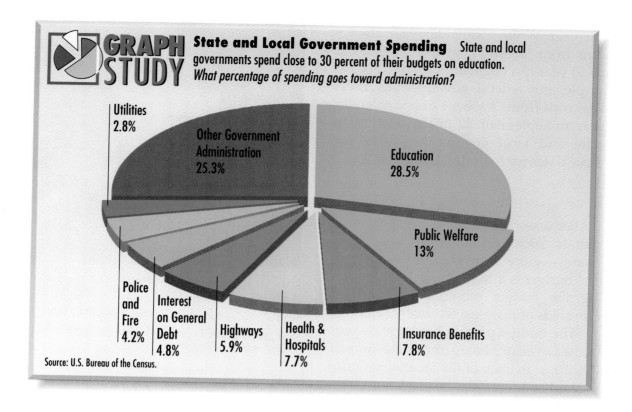

GRAPH STUDY

State and Local Government Spending State and local governments spend close to 30 percent of their budgets on education. What percentage of spending goes toward administration?

Utilities 2.8%

Other Government Administration 25.3%

Education 28.5%

Public Welfare 13%

Police and Fire 4.2%

Interest on General Debt 4.8%

Highways 5.9%

Health & Hospitals 7.7%

Insurance Benefits 7.8%

Source: U.S. Bureau of the Census.

experts and political leaders, submits a budget to the legislature. The legislature then makes some changes and passes the revised version. Of course, no state or local budget requires as much work as the federal budget. In a small town, the budget process may take days rather than months. Nevertheless, the task of making choices and compromises is a difficult and often painful process at all levels of government.

Expenditures

Each year's budget tends to be somewhat different from the one before. Some budgetary changes are due to outside events, such as world crises or natural disasters. More often, however, the changes are due to political developments, such as the election of new leaders who have new ideas and priorities.

During the early 1990s, the spending priorities of the federal government began to shift somewhat because of political changes in the country. However, the government did not radically change its pattern of spending. Each year the government spends the largest part of its budget on social security, medicare, national defense, and interest payments on loans.

The expenses in state and local budgets are much different from those of the federal budget. State governments do not have to pay for national defense, social security, or medicare. They also borrow much less money than the federal government does, so interest payments are not as great an expenditure.

The largest expense for nearly every state and local community is education. Educational spending accounts for more than one-third of the average state budget. Among the other major expenses are social services (aid to needy people), transportation, and public safety.

Budget Deficits

Governments often choose to spend more money than they take in. An excess of government expenses over government revenues is called a **deficit**. The federal government has had a deficit every year since 1970. In 1992 the deficit was at its peak—$290 billion. Since then, the deficit has gone down significantly.

Borrowing Money

To make up for a deficit, governments must borrow money to meet their expenses. Although some of the money is borrowed from banks, most of it comes from issuing bonds. A bond is a way for a government to borrow money from individuals. If you have ever bought a United States savings bond, you have lent money to the federal government. The government has promised to pay back what you paid for the bond plus interest.

Government deficits have occurred because American citizens ask more of their governments but are unwilling to pay higher taxes. Candidates who pledge to raise taxes almost always lose elections. As a result government leaders have been left with a difficult choice. They can either cut back on government programs or borrow more money. They have almost always decided to borrow more money.

The National Debt

The huge federal deficit has caused a number of problems for the country. The most severe problem is the effect it has on the national debt. The **national debt** is the total amount the government owes

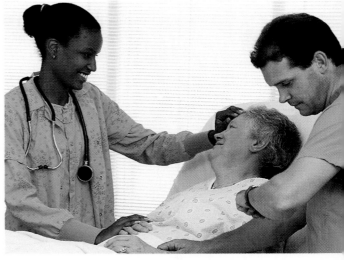

Medicare   Social security and medicare are the two largest items in the federal budget. *What is the largest item in a state budget?*

on money it has borrowed. Each year's deficit adds to this debt and increases the interest that must be paid on it. In 1996 that interest payment was more than $345 billion. To pay this interest without cutting other expenses, the federal government has to continue borrowing money, which adds to the national debt.

Another problem is the deficit's effect on the economy. Only a limited amount of money is available for borrowing. If the federal government borrows much of that money, very little is left for individuals and businesses to borrow. This may result in higher interest rates—the "price" for borrowing money—which in turn discourages investment and slows economic growth.

Balancing the Budget

To overcome these problems, the federal government has been making great efforts to cut the federal deficit and "balance the budget." A **balanced budget** is a budget in which expenditures do not

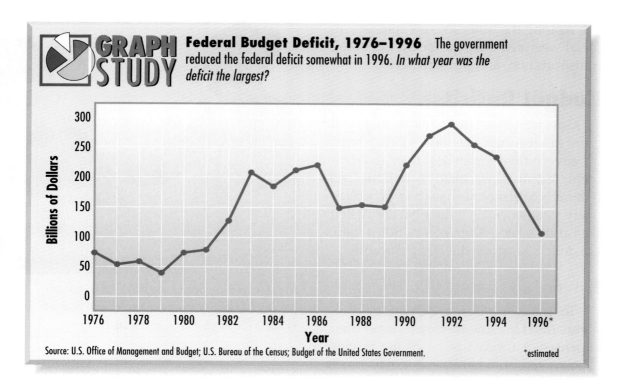

GRAPH STUDY

Federal Budget Deficit, 1976–1996 The government reduced the federal deficit somewhat in 1996. *In what year was the deficit the largest?*

Source: U.S. Office of Management and Budget; U.S. Bureau of the Census; Budget of the United States Government.

*estimated

exceed revenues—in other words, a budget with no deficit. An important step toward reducing the deficit came in 1985, when Congress passed the Gramm-Rudman-Hollings Act. This law required federal spending to be reduced by a certain amount each year. The Clinton administration made some progress toward reducing the deficit by cutting federal spending. In 1995, the Republican-controlled Congress tried to pass an amendment to the Constitution requiring a balanced budget by 2002. The amendment did not get the necessary votes in the Senate.

Most state constitutions require balanced budgets. When these governments cannot raise enough revenue to meet their expenses, they are not allowed, by law, to borrow money. Instead, they must cut services. In many communities, library hours have been cut and school activities have been limited in order to meet the restrictions of a balanced budget.

Intergovernmental Revenue

When state and local governments are short of funds, they often turn to the federal government for help. Financial aid from the federal government may take several different forms.

Federal Grants

By far the most common form of federal assistance is the grant-in-aid. A **grant-in-aid** is a sum of money given for a specific purpose, such as building highways or low-income housing. To receive a grant-in-aid, a state or local government must meet certain conditions. For example, it might have to agree to let minority-owned companies do a certain part of the work on the project.

A block grant is a combination of specific grants-in-aid. The federal government usually gives block grants for

Special Education   Some federal funds go to special education programs.   *What educational items do state grants pay for?*

general categories, such as transportation. A grant may be used for any purpose within that particular category.

State Grants

States also provide grants to local governments. For education, a city or town may depend on assistance from both the state government and the federal government. In many schools, for example, state grants help pay for textbooks, while federal funds help pay for school lunch programs. Money for special programs, such as education for students with learning disabilities, may also come from federal grants.

Debate Over Federal Grants

Many Americans criticize federal grants. They feel that the huge bureaucracy needed to manage these grants is too expensive. They also argue that state and local governments often waste money by requesting grants for projects they do not really need. Other people argue that federal grants enable communities to pro-

vide services they could not afford otherwise. In their view, while the federal government may not be completely efficient, it is the best way we have of providing help to people who need it.

In recent years, intergovernmental financing has moved in several directions. First, in its efforts to reduce the budget deficit, the federal government has made fewer and smaller grants to states than it did in the past. Second, there has been a trend to give states more freedom in deciding how to spend federal grants.

In 1995 Congress passed legislation in response to state complaints about the financial burdens of federal regulations. This legislation makes it harder for the federal government to impose new regulations, such as environmental laws, on states without putting up the money to pay for them. Such laws are known as unfunded mandates.

★ SECTION 3 REVIEW ★

UNDERSTANDING VOCABULARY
Define budget, expenditures, deficit, national debt, balanced budget, grant-in-aid.

REVIEWING OBJECTIVES
1 What are the main steps in the budget process of the federal government?

2 What are the largest expenditures of the federal, state, and local governments?

3 What are some of the problems caused by budget deficits?

4 What is the most common form of intergovernmental revenue?

Identifying Key Terms

Choose the vocabulary term that best completes each of the sentences below. Write your answers on a separate sheet of paper.

revenue   progressive tax   deductions
deficit   regressive tax   sales tax

1. For the last several years, the government had a _____ because its expenses exceeded its receipts.
2. More than half of the federal government's _____ comes from income taxes.
3. The tax was a _____ because the wealthy paid more than the middle class.
4. The state placed a 4 percent _____ on all products except food.
5. The _____ placed a heavier tax burden on the poor.
6. The family was able to claim several _____ on their income tax return.

Reviewing the Main Ideas

SECTION 1
1. Why is taxation such an important government power?
2. How does the Constitution limit the federal government's power to tax?

SECTION 2
3. What is tax withholding, and what is its purpose?
4. How are property taxes determined?

SECTION 3
5. In what ways is the federal budget a compromise document?
6. What choices do government leaders have when faced with a deficit?

7. What factors may contribute to annual changes in the federal budget?

Critical Thinking

SECTION 1
1. **Developing a Point of View**   Do you think Americans would be willing to pay higher taxes in return for more services? Why or why not?

SECTION 2
2. **Evaluating Information**   What type of government revenue do you think is the most fair? Explain.

SECTION 3
3. **Identifying Alternatives**   What do you think the government's spending priorities should be? Give reasons for your answer.

Reinforcing Citizenship Skills

In an almanac, find a table that shows some budget information, such as the interest paid on the national debt, over a period of time. Explain how you could show this information on a line graph or bar graph. Indicate which type of graph would be better.

Cooperative Learning

In groups of four, survey family members, local businesspeople, and other adults on the subject of taxes. Ask for their ideas on how the taxation system might be changed. Also look for news reports in newspapers and magazines on tax increases or cuts at the local, state, and national levels.

Changing Tax Rates

Income	Tax Bracket	Percent Decrease	Tax Decrease
$25,000	15%	4%	$150
$50,000	28%	3%	$420
$75,000	31%	2%	$465
more than $100,000	36%	1%	$360

Focusing on Your Community

The revenues and expenditures of every community are somewhat different, depending on the resources and needs of the community. Find out what your community's major expenditures and major sources of revenue are. What are local property tax rates and sales tax rates? What grants, if any, does the community receive from the state or federal government? Has the community had to cut services in recent years because of budget problems? If so, what services have been cut? Prepare a brief oral report for the class.

Technology Activity

Using the Internet

Search the Internet to find information on this year's individual income tax forms. You might use the following key words to focus your search: **treasury, Internal Revenue Service, income tax.** Once you have located the information, calculate your income tax if you were single, had no other dependents, claimed the standard deduction, and earned $23,000 for the year.

Analyzing Visuals

The federal government is constantly revising tax rules and rates in an effort to raise revenues without overtaxing its citizens. The table above shows how one proposed change would affect different levels of taxpayers. Study the table, then answer the following questions.

1. At which income level would people see the greatest percentage decrease in taxes?
2. At which income level would people see the smallest percentage decrease in taxes?
3. At which income level would people see the largest reduction in their tax bill?
4. Do you think this proposed tax plan would be fair? Explain why or why not.

CHAPTER 21

The Economy and the Individual

CIVIC PARTICIPATION

As a consumer, your economic decisions can have a far-reaching effect on other individuals and on your community and the country, as well as on yourself. Contact a local consumer league to learn about your rights as a consumer. What protections and what economic responsibilities do consumers have? Try to find out how the economic decisions of people in your area have affected local businesses.

Working in Your Community

After you have obtained the information, prepare a pamphlet on consumer rights. List the various rights consumers have, and provide the names, addresses, and phone numbers of consumer groups to contact with problems. Distribute this pamphlet to people in your neighborhood. ■

Your Civics Journal

As you study this chapter, keep a list in your civics journal of the economic decisions you make each day. The list might include budgeting, purchasing items, and saving or borrowing money. Next to each entry, note the factors involved in your decision.

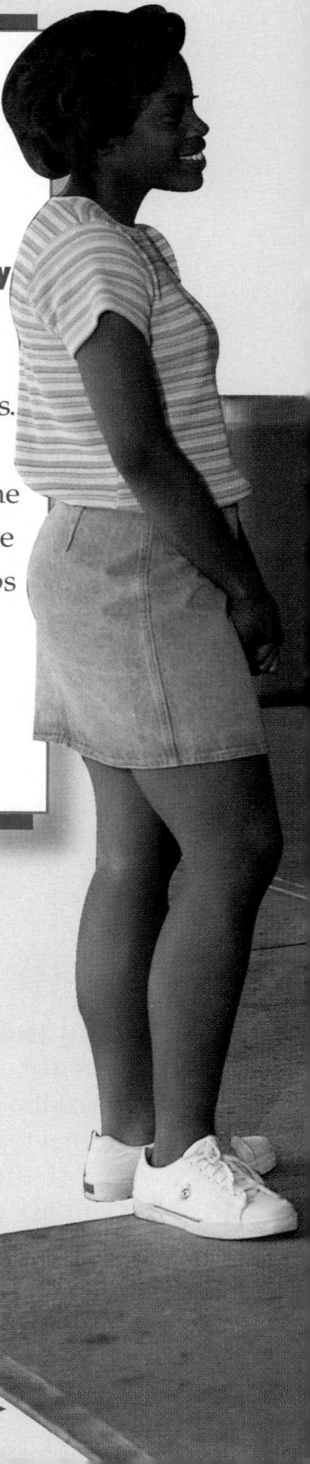

Buying movie tickets ➤

Buying Goods and Services

FOCUS

TERMS TO KNOW
fixed expenses, flexible expenses, unit price

OBJECTIVES

- Identify the two major budget categories people should consider when **planning a budget.**

- Describe strategies consumers should use when **shopping for quality.**

- Describe strategies consumers should use when **shopping for value.**

- Explain how consumers can achieve success in **avoiding impulse buying.**

E very time you buy a product, you expect to receive quality merchandise and to be treated with respect in exchange for your money. If some stores and businesses fail to satisfy you, you can look for others that will work harder to please you. This is one of your rights as a consumer.

In earlier chapters you discovered that with every right come certain responsibilities. With the right to vote, for example, comes the responsibility of staying informed about issues and candidates. In the same way, our rights as consumers require some responsibility on our part. We should find out as much as we can about the products we buy so that we can recognize good quality. We should also find out where we can get the best value for our money. We cannot rely on stores and businesses to protect us; we must protect ourselves.

Planning a Budget

In Chapter 20 you read about how governments use budgets to manage their finances. Individuals and families

Rights and Responsibilities When you buy something, you have a right to expect quality and a responsibility to recognize it. *What are other consumer rights and responsibilities?*

also use budgets to plan their spending. Although governments usually plan budgets for an entire year, most individuals plan their budgets month by month.

As you have learned, a budget has two parts: income and expenditures. The first step in planning a monthly budget is to determine monthly income. Common sources of income include a job, an allowance, or interest from money in the bank.

Determining Expenses

Once an individual or a family has determined its income, it must decide how that money will be spent. A large portion of the money in most people's budgets goes toward **fixed expenses**—expenses that are the same from month to month. Common fixed expenses include rent, loan payments, and insurance premiums. Other expenses vary from month to month. Some of these **flexible expenses,** such as heating bills and clothing purchases, vary according to the time of year. Others, such as entertainment expenses, depend on the spender's changing needs and wants.

Not all money in a budget goes toward expenses. Many people try to set some money aside for saving or investing. We will look more closely at saving later in the chapter.

Balancing Your Budget

Very few people have enough income to cover all their needs and wants. As a result people must set priorities and make decisions that will allow them to balance their budgets—to make sure that expenditures do not exceed income. Several possibilities exist. One possibility is to increase income by getting a better-

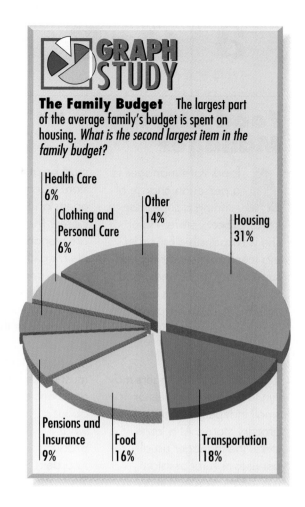

GRAPH STUDY

The Family Budget The largest part of the average family's budget is spent on housing. *What is the second largest item in the family budget?*

- Health Care 6%
- Clothing and Personal Care 6%
- Other 14%
- Housing 31%
- Pensions and Insurance 9%
- Food 16%
- Transportation 18%

paying job or by working more hours each week. Another is to decrease fixed expenses, by moving to a less expensive apartment, for example. Most people, however, find that the most practical decision is to decrease their flexible expenses. They may try to spend less on food, clothing, or entertainment. They may also decide to avoid buying things they do not really need, such as jewelry or compact discs.

Shopping for Quality

Because income is limited, it makes sense to try to "get the most for your money." This does not necessarily mean

Careers

Food Store Manager

Hundreds of decisions every day

A food store manager is a person in charge of running a supermarket or grocery store. He or she is responsible for ordering merchandise, hiring and supervising employees, and making all decisions concerning the store's operation and maintenance.

Responsibilities

Food store managers may run large supermarkets or small independently owned grocery stores. At a large store, the manager usually supervises several assistant managers, who run separate departments of the store.

Food store managers work long hours and usually must be at the store when it opens and closes. They are responsible for all the money the store makes, and they must keep accurate records. They also oversee the advertising and promotion of the store and its products.

Food store managers must make hundreds of decisions each day about what products to order. They also must work well with people.

Training

Most food store managers are high school graduates. They usually work their way up to the position of manager, perhaps starting as a checkout clerk and then becoming an assistant manager and finally a manager.

School to WORK

Food stores often hire students to work part-time as checkers or baggers. You might explore the possibility of applying for such a job to learn more about the career opportunities food stores provide.

---

buying a large number of products; it means buying good-quality items that will last longer than poorly made goods.

You can use several methods to find out about the quality of a product before buying it. One way is to talk to trusted people, such as parents and friends, who may be familiar with the product. Another is to visit the library and check recent issues of magazines such as *Consumer Re-* *ports* and *Consumers' Research.* These and similar magazines test thousands of products each year for safety, effectiveness, convenience, and reliability. They then publish the results for the benefit of consumers, those who buy goods or services. Specialized magazines, such as *PC Magazine, High Fidelity,* or *Car and Driver,* evaluate certain kinds of products, such as computers, stereos, or cars.

Another important way to determine the quality of a product is to look at it carefully and, if possible, try it. It is always a good idea to try on clothing, test electronic equipment, or examine furniture before buying it. The more consumers know about a product, the easier it is to judge its quality.

Consumers can find much of what they need to know about a product on its label. A number of federal and state labeling laws require manufacturers to attach certain information to the product itself or to the package the product comes in. The ingredients in packaged foods, for example, must be listed on the outside of the package. Many foods and medicines must be stamped with a date that indicates how long they will be safe to use. Tags on clothing must describe what the clothing is made from and how it can be cleaned. Labels on many kinds of products must identify any safety or health risks associated with using the product. Even if two products seem to be alike, the labels may reveal that one is better than the other. For example, one brand of lemonade may contain real juice, while another contains only lemon flavoring.

Shopping for Value

Once a consumer decides that a product is worth buying, the next step is finding out where to buy it at the best possible price. To do this, it is useful to check advertisements in newspapers, call stores and ask about prices, or visit stores in person.

CHART STUDY

Consumer Ratings Price and quality vary for different brands of any consumer product. *Which compact disc player received the highest basic rating?*

Brand and type	Price	Basic rating	Error correction	Dynamic range	Convenience	Remote control	Type of player
Corvac ZX-600	$175	4	4	4	3	–	MC
Vonex CD-NL80	$220	2	4	3	2	✓	CC
Vonex Mini CD-2B	$195	3	2	4	4	✓	SP
Top-Tech DCP-R2L	$280	5	5	5	4	✓	CC
TKU DL-9990	$250	4	4	4	4	✓	CC
Automain C16-3000	$175	4	3	4	2	✓	MC
Centura 8PLX	$98	2	1	3	1	–	SP

Scale: 1 ———— 5
Poor   Excellent

*single player = SP
*carousel changer = CC
*magazine changer = MC

Comparing Prices Unit pricing allows consumers to compare prices of competing brands and of different quantities of the same brand. *What are some other ways to check prices?*

Shopping by Mail Mail-order companies have lower overhead expenses than stores and can often charge lower prices for their goods. *What is a disadvantage of buying by mail?*

Comparing Prices

In some areas, grocery stores help shoppers compare prices by displaying unit prices for many of the products. A **unit price** is the price for a standard unit of measurement. For example, a 4-ounce bar of soap for 52 cents may seem like a better buy than a 6-ounce bar for 72 cents. Their unit prices, however, would show that the 4-ounce bar costs 13 cents per ounce, while the 6-ounce bar costs only 12 cents per ounce. An increasing number of local governments are requiring their stores to use unit pricing.

Another good place to check prices is in mail-order catalogs. Many products available from mail-order companies are less expensive than items sold in stores because mail-order companies do not have to rent and decorate stores or pay salaries to salespeople. A disadvantage of buying by mail is that the consumer does not see a product before buying it. Many mail-order companies, however, allow people to return items if they are not satisfied with them.

Looking for Bargains

A good way to get products at lower prices is to wait for a sale. Many stores sell items at a discount, or lower price, at particular times of the year. For example, outdoor barbecue grills may go on sale in September, as the summer is ending.

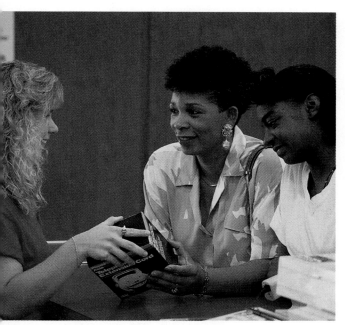

Return Policy If you do buy on impulse, make sure you know the store's policy on returns. *Why should you save your receipts?*

Avoiding Impulse Buying

While buying wisely requires a good deal of work and thought, many businesses try to get consumers to buy without thinking. For example, supermarkets may place certain items near checkout lines, hoping that shoppers will toss them into their carts while waiting to pay for purchases. Many stores hold special "one-day sales" as a way to encourage people to buy products without taking time to compare prices at other stores. Salespeople may try to pressure shoppers to buy products they do not need.

These sales techniques can be very effective. Many people do not realize their mistake until after they have spent their money. Wise shoppers often make it a rule never to buy anything without planning in advance. Even if a salesperson of-fers a deal that seems too good to resist, a wise shopper will insist on thinking about it and will then do some research and comparison shopping. If the salesperson persists and says that the deal is "now or never," it is best to hold off. Consumers should never yield to pressure to make a purchase they may regret later.

The best protection is to buy from businesses that allow customers to change their minds after they have made a purchase. Before handing over money, smart shoppers first find out a store's return policy. This policy may be posted on a wall or printed in small type on a store's "sales contract." An acceptable policy will allow customers to return merchandise within a few days in exchange for a full refund. It is always important to save sales receipts because stores usually require them as proof of the price and date of purchase.

★ SECTION 1 REVIEW ★

UNDERSTANDING VOCABULARY
Define fixed expenses, flexible expenses, unit price.

REVIEWING OBJECTIVES

1 What two major budget categories should people consider when planning a budget?

2 What strategies should consumers use when shopping for quality?

3 What strategies should consumers use when shopping for value?

4 How can consumers become successful in avoiding impulse buying?

Contracts

A contract is a legally binding agreement between two or more people. The terms of a contract spell out the rights and obligations of each of the parties under the terms of the agreement. Contracts can be oral. For instance, if you agree to cut your neighbor's grass for $5 an hour, you have made an oral contract. Most contracts, however, are written.

Think About It

As you read the following material, think about the importance of contracts in preventing and settling disputes.

The Elements and Language of Contracts

A contract has three elements: an offer, an acceptance, and a "consideration"—an exchange of something of value. Your neighbor *offered* you a job cutting the grass, which you *accepted* in return for a *consideration* of $5 an hour.

The language in contracts may seem difficult to understand. When writing a contract, lawyers use terms that have very specific legal meanings. In an apartment lease, for example, the contract will refer to the Landlord, the Tenant, and the Premises. The *Landlord* is the person who owns the apartment (the *Premises*), and the *Tenant* is the person who rents it.

A Sample Lease

Here are a few of the terms and conditions that are often included in an apartment lease.

1. Tenant shall pay Landlord as rent for the Premises the sum of $500 monthly in advance, until termination of this lease.
2. Tenant shall not permit anything to be thrown out of the windows; nothing shall be placed on outside windowsills; no parrot, dog, or any other animals shall be kept within or about the Premises.
3. Landlord will supply hot and cold water to the Premises at all faucets and fixtures. Landlord will also supply heat, by means of the heating system and fixtures provided by the Landlord.

Each paragraph or clause of a lease contract spells out one or more specific rights or obligations of each party. A typical lease may have 10 to 20 such paragraphs.

The Purpose of Contracts

The main purpose of any contract is to protect the parties involved. Because the terms of a written contract are spelled out in detail, it provides a clear understanding of what is expected of each party. If one party fails to comply with a contract, the other party may sue in court.

INTERPRETING SOURCES

1 What is the purpose of a contract?

2 What are the three elements of a contract?

Saving, Borrowing, Buying on Credit

People's incomes and expenses vary widely. Some people take in much more money than they need to cover their basic expenses. These people usually save or invest the money they have left over. Other people take in much less money than they need. These people must make up the difference by borrowing money or buying on credit.

Saving

Saving money can be a difficult habit to establish. Some people feel they should enjoy every penny they earn. As a result they spend their money as quickly as it comes in, often buying goods or services they may not really need.

There are, however, many good reasons for saving money. Most people cannot make certain major purchases, such as a car or a house, without putting aside money to help pay for them. Savings also come in handy in emergencies. In addition, of course, people can use savings for luxuries, such as a new stereo system or a trip to Hawaii.

Saving Regularly

To make it easier for people to save, some employers will withhold a fixed amount from employees' paychecks. This money is automatically deposited into participating employees' savings accounts. Many people, however, handle the responsibility themselves. Each week or month, they budget a small amount of money to put aside for savings.

At one time people saved money by stuffing it into a mattress. Today, however, most people put their savings in a

Saving for the Future Using today's technology, you can deposit money in your savings account at any time. *What are some of the main reasons for saving money?*

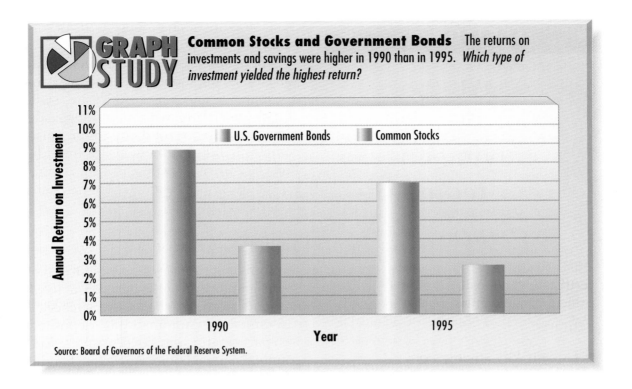

GRAPH STUDY

Common Stocks and Government Bonds The returns on investments and savings were higher in 1990 than in 1995. *Which type of investment yielded the highest return?*

Annual Return on Investment

■ U.S. Government Bonds   ■ Common Stocks

Year: 1990, 1995

Source: Board of Governors of the Federal Reserve System.

bank, a savings and loan association, or a credit union. Depositing money in any one of these organizations is a way of increasing your savings because the money in a savings account earns interest.

Banks and Credit Unions

Banks and credit unions offer several kinds of savings accounts. A regular savings account pays a relatively small amount of interest. A savings certificate, or **certificate of deposit** (CD), pays higher interest but requires the saver to keep the money in the CD account for a specific length of time. Although keeping money in a bank generally does not earn depositors the highest available interest rates, it is a relatively safe way of saving. As you learned in Chapter 19, the federal government insures each depositor's account in member banks up to $100,000.

Another way to save money is to buy government bonds. After a certain number of years, the owner of a savings bond can sell it for a higher price than he or she paid for it.

Investments

A third way of saving money is to invest it. **Investment** is the buying of something the purchaser expects to increase in value. Investment carries a risk, but it can also pay off handsomely. Imagine, for example, that you buy shares in a small recording company. If the company is successful, your investment might earn you a good deal of money. If it is unsuccessful, however, you might lose all the money you invested. A share of stock may increase—or decrease—in value.

People who are looking for a safer investment may put money in mutual funds. The experts who manage these funds use the money to buy stocks and bonds in many different areas. Because the investments are varied and carefully selected, these funds usually make money for their investors over time.

Investment benefits not only individuals but also the economy. It helps individuals increase their savings. It also helps businesses by giving them the money they need to grow and expand. Banks invest their depositors' money in stocks, in bonds, and in loans to people and businesses, which keeps the economy running and expanding.

Borrowing

Often people have to spend more money than they have in their savings accounts. Very few people, for example, have saved the thousands of dollars needed to pay for a college education, to start a business, or to buy a home. In situations like these, most people must borrow money.

Places to Borrow

The usual places to borrow money are banks, savings and loan associations, and credit unions. To borrow money, people must prove they are good risks. They must show they can repay the loans, with interest, in a reasonable amount of time.

Some people who cannot get loans from banks borrow money from finance companies instead. Finance companies are private businesses that lend money. They often lend to high-risk borrowers, but they charge very high rates of interest in return.

If a bank or finance company feels there is some chance a person will not be able to repay a loan, it will ask for collateral. If you borrow money to buy a car, for example, the bank may require that you offer the car as collateral. In this case, although you have full use of the car, the

A Loan for Learning   Many parents need to borrow money for their children's college educations.   *Where might they borrow this money?*

bank remains the car's legal owner until you have repaid the loan.

Most loans must be paid back in installments, usually a certain amount of money each month. At first these monthly payments cover only the interest on the loan. Little by little, however, they also begin to pay back the **principal**—the amount of money borrowed.

Risks of Borrowing

Borrowing money can be dangerous. If a borrower is unable to keep up with loan payments, the bank may seize the collateral. For example, even if the borrower has repaid 80 percent of a car loan, the bank may take the car along with the money already paid on the loan.

Sometimes people borrow money from a finance company to pay back other loans. Eventually they may borrow more money than they can possibly

Paying with "Plastic" Using a credit card is convenient—provided that you can pay the bills. *What is the main disadvantage of easy credit?*

issue credit cards. A person may use a credit card in any business that accepts the card. The business collects the purchase price from the credit card issuer, which sends a monthly bill to the cardholder. The cardholder may pay the bill all at once or in installments. Late payment may result in additional charges.

Problems With Credit

Buying on credit can be a convenient way to make purchases. Unfortunately, the availability of easy credit encourages people to spend money they do not have. When customers are unable to pay their bills, a store has the right to **repossess,** or take back, the items they bought on credit, as well as keep any money they have already been paid. In addition, the high interest rates on credit cards cause people's debts to mount rapidly.

In the past the federal government encouraged the use of credit cards by allowing taxpayers to deduct interest payments on their income taxes. These interest payments on credit card debts are no longer deductible.

repay. People in this situation may be forced to declare **bankruptcy,** a legal statement that one cannot pay one's debts. The courts take over their financial assets and distribute them to creditors.

Buying on Credit

Buying on credit is another way to borrow money. In this case the money is borrowed from a store or business.

Charge Accounts and Credit Cards

The simplest way to buy on credit is to use a charge account. A charge account is a line of credit that a particular store extends to its regular customers. At the end of the month, the store sends the customer a bill for that month's purchases.

Another way to buy on credit is with a credit card. Banks and some businesses

★ **SECTION 2 REVIEW** ★

UNDERSTANDING VOCABULARY
Define certificate of deposit, investment, principal, bankruptcy, repossess.

REVIEWING OBJECTIVES
1 Why is saving money important?

2 What are the dangers of borrowing money?

3 What are the dangers of buying on credit?

Insuring Against Risk

FOCUS

TERMS TO KNOW
insurance, premium, liability insurance, beneficiary, social security, medicare, medicaid

OBJECTIVES

■ Identify and describe five kinds of **private insurance.**

■ Identify and describe four kinds of **social insurance.**

L ife is full of dangers and surprises. A breadwinner may die suddenly, leaving his or her family with no source of income. A flood may wash away a farmer's crop. A fire may destroy an apartment building, leaving dozens of residents injured and hundreds of others homeless. Few people are prepared to deal with such events. Even if they have money in the bank, it is rarely enough to rebuild their lives.

For these reasons many Americans rely on insurance to help them through a crisis. **Insurance** is a type of investment that protects the investor against unpredictable events. It can help pay for hospital bills and for repairs to homes or cars. It can also supply financial support to people who have lost their primary source of income.

Insurance can be classified into two basic categories, depending upon who provides it. Private companies provide one kind of insurance, and the federal government provides the other.

Private Insurance

Most Americans have some type of insurance on their car, their home, their health, and perhaps even their life. Private insurance companies provide this insurance, and individuals and businesses pay for it. Insurance companies sell policies, which protect policyholders against certain risks. A car insurance policy, for example, will protect against the risks of car accident or theft.

How an Insurance Policy Works

To get an insurance policy, a person must make payments, called **premiums,** to an insurance company. These premiums must be paid regularly, usually a certain amount each month or every few months. If a policyholder does not pay the premiums, the insurance company

Insuring Against Disaster Fortunately for this homeowner, her insurance policy covered the flood damage that destroyed her home. *How does someone get an insurance policy?*

Retirement Funds Most people start collecting full social security benefits when they reach age 65. *Who pays for the social security program?*

cancels the policy. An insurance company keeps some of the money it receives from premiums in a reserve fund it uses to pay policyholders' claims.

An insurance policy guarantees that a policyholder will collect money for any expenses the policy covers. If the holder of a car insurance policy has an accident while driving, the insurance company will pay the driver's medical expenses. It will also pay the medical expenses of other people hurt in the crash, and it may pay to repair damage to the car.

Types of Insurance

Automobile insurance is only one of many kinds of insurance. Other common types include health insurance, liability insurance, property insurance, and life insurance.

Most property owners have liability insurance. If someone is injured on another person's property, the property

owner may be legally liable, or responsible, for the injured person's medical expenses. **Liability insurance** pays these expenses for the property owner and helps protect against financial liability.

Property insurance helps people repair or replace property that is damaged, stolen, or destroyed. It is possible to get insurance policies that cover specific events such as fire or flood. More often people get "umbrella policies," which protect against a variety of dangers.

Life insurance provides money to help support a policyholder's family after the policyholder dies. When purchasing a life insurance policy, the policyholder must provide the name of a **beneficiary**—the person who will receive the amount of money stated in the policy from the insurance company.

Social Insurance

Much of the federal government's social insurance program began in the Great Depression of the 1930s, when millions of Americans lost their jobs and savings. To help them, President Roosevelt proposed an assortment of government programs called the New Deal.

Social Security

The cornerstone of the New Deal was the Social Security Act, which Congress passed in 1935. The **social security** program set up two different kinds of insurance: old-age and survivors insurance and unemployment insurance.

Every employer and employee must pay a social security tax on wages and salaries. This tax goes into a special fund. When a person reaches age 62, he or she can begin to receive payments from that fund. If the person waits until age 65, however, the payments will be larger. If a

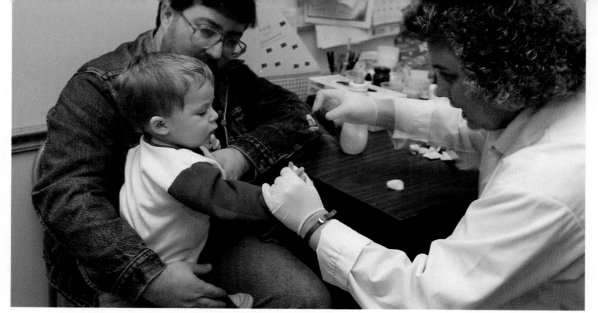

Medical Relief   The medicaid program helps pay the medical bills of low-income families.   *For what does medicare provide?*

worker is forced to retire early due to illness or disability, benefits may begin before age 62.

Some people die before they are old enough to collect old-age benefits. When this happens surviving family members receive social security payments instead.

Unemployment Insurance

Social security taxes do not pay for unemployment insurance. Instead, every employer must pay a payroll tax to the federal government. This money helps support people who are out of work.

Workers who have lost their jobs must register with a state employment office. If they meet certain conditions, they can receive weekly payments for a certain number of months.

Medicare and Medicaid

Two of the government's most important programs—medicare and medicaid—went into effect in 1965. **Medicare** provides health and hospitalization in-

surance to people age 65 and older. **Medicaid** helps pay the health care costs of low-income people, no matter what their age. Because health-care costs have risen rapidly in recent years, the cost of medicare and medicaid programs has risen as well. Social security, medicare, and medicaid account for more than $500 billion of annual federal spending.

★   **SECTION 3**   ★

UNDERSTANDING VOCABULARY

Define insurance, premium, liability insurance, beneficiary, social security, medicare, medicaid.

REVIEWING OBJECTIVES

1 What are five kinds of private insurance?

2 What are four kinds of social insurance?

How to Protect Your Rights as a Consumer

While many federal and state laws protect consumers, you can help protect yourself by reading and understanding product labels, which you have already learned about. You should also know how to read and use a warranty.

Warranties

A warranty is a guarantee of a product's performance. All products come with an "implied" warranty, which is that you have a right to expect a product to do what it is supposed to do. Some products have a written warranty, which specifies the purchaser's rights and responsibilities. Before buying a product, read its warranty and look for answers to the following questions.

How to Read a Warranty

- *What kind of warranty is it?* A "full" warranty covers an entire product. A "limited" warranty covers only certain parts of the product.
- *What is the length of the warranty?* Warranties are valid for a specified time after the date of purchase.
- *Whom does it protect?* Most warranties protect only the original purchaser.
- *What does it cover?* Most warranties cover defective parts and workmanship and specify what

Many products come with warranties

the manufacturer will pay for. Most warranties do not cover products purchased outside the United States or from unauthorized dealers; products damaged by accident, misuse, or neglect; unauthorized repairs; or improper installation.

- *What are your obligations?* You must sometimes register a warranty by mailing a card enclosed with the product to the manufacturer. When returning defective goods, you must usually supply the sales receipt.

Answer the questions below.

CITIZENSHIP IN ACTION

1 What is a limited warranty?

2 Do you think warranties provide adequate protection for consumers? Why or why not?

Protecting Consumer Rights

FOCUS

TERM TO KNOW
fraudulent

OBJECTIVES

■ Explain **the role of government** in protecting consumer rights.

■ Explain the **role of private organizations** in protecting consumer rights.

Throughout much of history, consumer rights could be summed up in one Latin phrase: *caveat emptor,* or "let the buyer beware." Sellers routinely lied and cheated, and any buyers who fell for the sellers' tricks were thought to deserve what they got.

Today government regulations protect consumers and help ensure they will be treated fairly and honestly. In addition, consumers can turn to a number of private organizations if they feel they have been treated unfairly.

The Role of Government

Over the years, Congress has passed a number of laws that protect consumer rights. Many of these laws involve labeling. For example, the Fair Packaging and Labeling Act requires that every package have a label identifying its contents and how much it weighs. In addition, the Food, Drug, and Cosmetic Act requires packages to list their ingredients according to the amount of each. Other laws protect consumers' health and safety. An early example is the Pure Food and Drug Act, passed in 1906. It requires manufacturers of foods, cosmetics, and drugs to prove their products are safe.

Executive agencies of the federal government handle much of the work of enforcing the laws that protect consumer rights. As you learned in Chapter 11, hundreds of such agencies exist, and their responsibilities often overlap. One important federal agency is the Food and Drug Administration, or FDA, which oversees the safety of food, drugs, and cosmetics. Other agencies include the Federal Trade Commission (FTC), which guards against false advertising; the Consumer Product Safety Commission, which prevents companies from selling

Consumer Protection FDA officials inspect food-preparation plants regularly to ensure that safety and hygiene standards are met. *What are some other executive agencies that protect consumer rights?*

hazardous products; and the U.S. Postal Service, which cracks down on individuals and companies that sell products that are **fraudulent,** or make false claims, through the mail.

State governments also play a role in protecting consumers. Many states, for example, regulate car repair services and used car sales. Some states have their own restrictions on advertising or labeling. In California any product suspected of causing cancer—even gasoline—must be labeled with a health warning.

On the local level, nearly every city or county has commissions to deal with consumers' complaints about public utilities, such as electricity, water, and cable television. Most cities also have health inspectors who check restaurants and food-processing plants for unsanitary conditions.

The Role of Private Organizations

The federal and state governments have been quite successful in regulating manufacturing, advertising, and sales practices. Government bureaucracies, however, do not usually have the time or money to deal with the problems of individuals.

As a result private groups and organizations have largely taken on the task of protecting individual consumers. Sometimes these organizations are able to resolve consumers' problems by themselves. At other times they pressure the appropriate government agencies to come up with solutions.

Better Business Bureaus

One of the oldest consumer groups in the United States is the Better Business Bureau, founded in 1912. There are more than 200 local better business bureaus in communities around the country, in addition to the national bureau that sets standards for the local groups. Surpris-

ingly, business owners rather than consumers run better business bureaus. These businesspeople recognize that the key to success lies in earning the trust of their customers. Better business bureaus provide information about local businesses and warn consumers about dishonest business practices. They also investigate consumer complaints and try to resolve them in a way that will satisfy everyone concerned.

Many communities also have local consumer leagues. These groups serve much the same purpose as better business bureaus, but consumers rather than businesspeople run them. In addition to handling customer complaints, they may help educate consumers about their rights. They may also issue "seals of approval" to businesses or products they recommend.

Consumer Interest Groups

Over the past 30 years, another type of group—the consumer interest group—has become quite common. The primary purpose of consumer interest groups is to bring consumer problems to the government's attention. These groups pressure the government to pass new laws and regulations that will protect consumers. Through education, publicity, and organizing efforts at the national and local levels, consumer interest groups have attracted broad public support for their causes.

The growth of these groups is due largely to the leadership of Ralph Nader, who has worked tirelessly on behalf of consumer rights. Early in his career, Nader worked for the passage of stricter automobile safety laws. He also helped convince Congress to ban dangerous chemicals from foods. In 1971 he founded a consumer interest group called

Help in the Community   Better business bureaus give consumers information about local businesses.   *What else do better business bureaus do?*

Public Citizen, Inc. Other national groups such as the National Consumer League have since joined Nader's group. Many states and communities now have consumer interest groups as well.

★ SECTION 4 REVIEW ★

UNDERSTANDING VOCABULARY
Define fraudulent.

REVIEWING OBJECTIVES
1 What role does the government play in protecting consumer rights?

2 What are three private consumer groups, and what is their role in protecting consumer rights?

Identifying Key Terms

Choose the vocabulary term that best completes each of the sentences below. Write your answers on a separate sheet of paper.

investment   bankruptcy   repossess
unit price   premium   beneficiary

1. Peter was worried that the company might _____ his car because he had fallen behind in his payments.
2. The man felt that his stocks were a good _____.
3. The shopper checked the _____ to see which product was really cheaper.
4. The policyholder always paid each _____ on her policy on time.
5. The store owner was so far in debt that he had to declare _____.
6. The woman named her son as _____ of her life insurance policy.

Reviewing the Main Ideas

SECTION 1
1. What is one advantage and one disadvantage of buying from mail-order catalogs?
2. What are some of the methods stores use to encourage impulse buying?

SECTION 2
3. Describe two ways to buy on credit.
4. What are the general requirements for getting a loan?

SECTION 3
5. What is the purpose of insurance?
6. Why did the federal government set up the social security system?

SECTION 4
7. Why is the task of protecting individual consumers primarily the concern of private groups and organizations?
8. What actions do better business bureaus take in protecting consumers?

Critical Thinking

SECTION 1
1. **Demonstrating Reasoned Judgment** What do you think are the most important factors to consider when shopping for a product? Explain.

SECTION 2
2. **Determining Cause and Effect** The savings rate of Americans is very low compared to that of citizens of other industrialized nations. Why do you think this is so?

SECTION 3
3. **Evaluating Information** Most states require drivers to have car insurance. Do you think people should be required to have other kinds of insurance as well? Explain why or why not.

SECTION 4
4. **Expressing a Point of View** Do you think there are sufficient government regulations to protect consumers? Why or why not?

Reinforcing Citizenship Skills

Choose a product, such as a compact disc player, that would come with a warranty. List the information you would like to know about the warranty. If possible, obtain an example of a

Ratings of Fast-food Chains

Chain	Freshness of Food	Variety of Food	Speed of Service	Employee Courtesy	Cleanliness	Convenient Location	Good Place for Kids
Mickey O's	3	2	2	2	2	1	1
Happy Days	3	2	3	3	4	3	3
Barby's Best	2	3	2	3	3	5	5
Burgers n' BBQ	3	2	2	5	3	2	1
Chicken Licken	5	5	4	4	5	5	5

1 Top rating ———— 5 Lowest rating

warranty. Check what the warranty includes against your list.

Cooperative Learning

In groups of three, ask family members and other adults about prices paid for common products in years past. Ask about grocery items, haircuts, cars, and so on. Compare these prices with current prices and determine how much more or less expensive these goods or services are today. Share your group's findings with the class.

Technology Activity

Using a Spreadsheet

Select several financial institutions in your community and contact them to learn the interest rate they are currently charging for automobile loans. Then construct a spreadsheet showing the various interest rates and the monthly payments on a $10,000 loan for 3, 4, and 5 years. Construct the spreadsheet to show the total cost of the loan over each repayment period.

Focusing on Your Community

Find out how your local government or private groups protect consumer rights in your community. What ordinances protect consumers? How are complaints handled? What private organizations help consumers? Prepare a report for the class.

Analyzing Visuals

Consumers are often asked to give their opinions about goods and services. The chart above shows consumers' ratings of fast-food chains. Study the chart and then answer the questions.

1. Which fast-food chain did consumers like the most? Which did they like the least?
2. What did consumers think was the best feature of the chains?
3. Which two features received the lowest overall ratings?

CLOSEUP
RECYCLING

Today many states, counties, and municipalities are wrestling with the problem of what to do with the millions of tons of trash and solid waste that Americans generate each year. These materials are filling up the nation's landfills. Many of them also release harmful air pollutants when burned.

Bans on Products

Some places are responding to this problem by banning the use of certain products so they do not present disposal problems later on. Minneapolis, Minnesota, for example, has banned the use of most throwaway plastic food packaging in grocery stores and fast-food outlets.

Incineration

Plastic goods are not the only materials contributing to the waste disposal problem. Newspapers, aluminum cans, old tires, glass, and even leaves and grass clippings are rapidly piling up in the nation's landfills. As these landfills reach capacity, communities are searching for other, more acceptable solutions to the waste problem. One alternative is to burn waste products in incinerators. This method, however, can also be harmful to the environment. Even the most modern incinerators release some

toxic fumes that can pollute the air and endanger the environment.

Recycling

More and more local governments are turning to recycling as a solution to the waste problem. In many communities, residents are required to sort their cans, glass, plastics, and newspapers and place them in special receptacles.

Technology takes on old tires

An increasing number of private companies have discovered that there are profits to be made in recycling. For example, one plant in California burns old tires to produce electricity. The process, which creates very little air pollution, also recovers the minerals zinc and gypsum for resale.

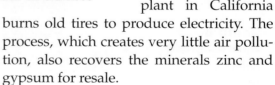

CLOSEUP REVIEW

1 Why has disposing of solid waste become such a problem for American communities?

2 What measures does your community take to recycle waste?

Multimedia Activities

Surfing the "Net"

The Lemon Law

Many products have warranties that guarantee a product's performance. Sometimes consumers experience problems where manufacturers might not honor a warranty. In those cases consumers can turn to their state's lemon laws for protection. The lemon law is a law that protects consumers who have warranties for their goods. There is also a federal lemon law that applies to all 50 states. To find out about your state lemon law, look on the Internet.

Getting There

Follow the steps below to find out more information about lemon laws in your state.

1. Go to your favorite search engine.
2. Type in the phrase *lemon laws*. Following this phrase, enter words like those below to focus your search:

> your state's name   warranties
> consumer   federal

The search engine should provide you with a number of links to follow. Links are pointers to different sites on the Internet and commonly appear as blue underlined words.

What to Do When You Are There

1. Click on the links to navigate through the pages of information.
2. Using a word processor, write an article about your state's lemon laws and the steps consumers can take legally to solve their problems. Share your findings with the class.

Focus on Government

Financing Our Government

The Constitution allows the government to collect taxes to finance its operations. The **Focus on Government** program referenced below examines some of the ways that local governments tax and spend.

Setting Up the Video

Using a bar code reader or an electronic keypad, work with a group of your classmates to view this video segment of the videodisc **Focus on Government:**

Side 3, Chapter 40
Lecture Launcher:
Taxing and Spending

Hands-On Activity

Use ideas from the video program and from the chapters in this unit to design a multimedia display featuring images of services that your community provides to its residents. You might be able to find illustrations of these services from the local newspaper or a member of your group might be able to photograph these services being used. Make transparencies or slides of some of the images and write a script to narrate your presentation as you show your classmates the images.

YOUR ROLE AS A CITIZEN

The world seems smaller than it did only 50 years ago. Modern transportation and communication have brought people around the globe closer together. As a result, countries today are more dependent on one another. As citizens of the United States and members of the global community, we have a responsibility to keep informed about developments in other nations and the world. ■

CHAPTERS IN THIS UNIT

Comparative Government

CIVIC PARTICIPATION

Each nation of the world has a unique history, as well as its own cultural values, political interests, and economic needs. These factors influence how a nation governs itself. Contact the embassy or consulate of a country you are interested in. Ask for information about the country's history, government, people, culture, and economy. Try to find out about the country's relations with the United States.

Working in Your Community

After you have obtained the information, prepare a fact sheet on the country. Then ask some neighbors and friends what they know about the country and its relations with the United States. Share the information on your fact sheet with them. ■

Your Civics Journal

As you study this chapter, scan newspapers, magazines, and TV broadcasts for stories about other countries. In your civics journal, list the countries mentioned and the main points of the stories. Next to each entry note what you think these stories reflect about life in that country.

British Parliament ➤

Great Britain

Great Britain is officially known as the United Kingdom of Great Britain and Northern Ireland. It includes England, Scotland, Wales, and Northern Ireland. The United States owes many traditions to Great Britain, including our representative system of government and the belief that citizens have certain basic rights.

Despite shared ideals, the British and American governments are quite different. Britain is a **constitutional monarchy** with a king or a queen who serves as the symbolic head of state but does not run the government. Centuries ago Britain's monarchs had a great deal of power, but they no longer do.

Great Britain has a **parliamentary government** ruled by elected representatives. In a parliamentary system, the executive and legislative branches are not separated, and their functions overlap. This is unlike the American system, in which there is a separation of powers.

Great Britain also has what is called an unwritten constitution. Instead of a single document like the United States Constitution, it has a collection of documents, parliamentary acts, and court decisions that serve as a guide to government. Many of these date back hundreds of years, and they serve as a record of British political traditions.

The Parliamentary System

Great Britain's parliamentary system developed over many centuries. At one time, powerful monarchs who governed as they saw fit ruled the nation. Yet many early rulers also consulted with important nobles and religious leaders. In the late 1200s, the monarchs began to include representatives of towns and counties in

Queen Elizabeth II The British monarch performs many ceremonial duties but has little real power. *What is the monarch's role in a constitutional monarchy?*

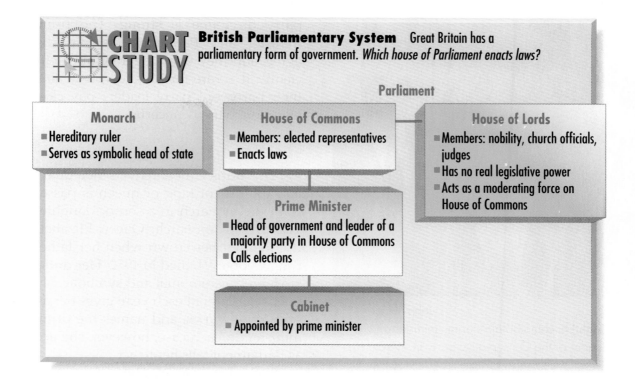

CHART STUDY

British Parliamentary System Great Britain has a parliamentary form of government. *Which house of Parliament enacts laws?*

Parliament

Monarch
- Hereditary ruler
- Serves as symbolic head of state

House of Commons
- Members: elected representatives
- Enacts laws

House of Lords
- Members: nobility, church officials, judges
- Has no real legislative power
- Acts as a moderating force on House of Commons

Prime Minister
- Head of government and leader of a majority party in House of Commons
- Calls elections

Cabinet
- Appointed by prime minister

their meetings. Gradually, these meetings, or parliaments, began to take on more and more of the duties and powers of government. At the same time, the monarchs became less and less powerful.

House of Commons

Today the British Parliament makes all of the nation's laws. The Parliament has two houses—the House of Commons and the House of Lords. The lower house, the House of Commons, is the main legislative body. It includes 650 members of Parliament, or MPs. Each MP represents a **constituency,** or the people in a particular election district.

MPs are elected in a general election. These elections have no set dates, but they must be held at least once every five years. The head of the government, the prime minister, can call for an election any time he or she thinks that members of the ruling party have a good chance of

being reelected. If an MP dies or resigns between general elections, a new MP is chosen in special local elections, called **by-elections.**

House of Lords

Parliament's upper house, the House of Lords, is not an elected body. It is made up of about 800 nobles with inherited titles, 26 bishops and archbishops of the Church of England, 15 judges, and more than 200 life peers. Life peers are people who have been given titles in reward for their achievements. Members of the House of Lords serve for life.

The House of Lords has no real legislative power beyond delaying and debating proposals. If it rejects a bill, the House of Commons can still pass it and make it law. The main function of the House of Lords is to act as a moderating force by watching closely and criticizing the work of the House of Commons.

State Visit to Japan John Major (right) became Britain's prime minister and leader of the Conservative party in 1990. *What are the main differences between the Conservative and the Labour parties?*

The Prime Minister

The head of Britain's government (or administration, as it would be called in the United States) is the prime minister. The people do not elect the prime minister. He or she is the leader of the majority party in the House of Commons and is chosen by the MPs of that party. A new prime minister is chosen when a different party gains the majority in the House of Commons after a general election.

The prime minister chooses ministers, or officials, to run various executive departments. Most of these ministers are MPs of the majority party. The ministers of the most important departments make up the cabinet.

Because the same party controls the executive and legislative functions, Britain's parliamentary system has fewer checks and balances than the United States government. At the same time,

party discipline is strong. The prime minister and Parliament seldom disagree, and they work together quite efficiently. It is rare for MPs to vote against their party, but party leaders pay close attention to their concerns.

The Monarchy

The British monarchy is hereditary, and the title of king or queen is passed from the monarch to a son or daughter. The present monarch, Queen Elizabeth II, inherited her crown when her father, King George VI, died in 1952. Her duties are largely ceremonial and symbolic. She opens Parliament each year, gives her assent to new laws, and names the prime minister. In each case, however, she acts as Parliament tells her to act.

Some people today question the need for the monarchy because the monarch has no real power. Others, however, argue that abolishing the monarchy would destroy Britain's unwritten constitution. Abolishing the monarchy would also deprive Britain of a cherished symbol of the nation and its people.

Political Parties

Two major political parties, the Conservative party and Labour party, dominate Great Britain's political system. The Conservative party is similar to the Republican party in the United States. It stresses private enterprise, less government regulation, and tradition. The Labour party, like the Democratic party in the United States, favors a more active government role.

Britain's political parties are based more on social and economic class than are American parties. In general, the upper class supports the Conservative party, while the Labour party attracts

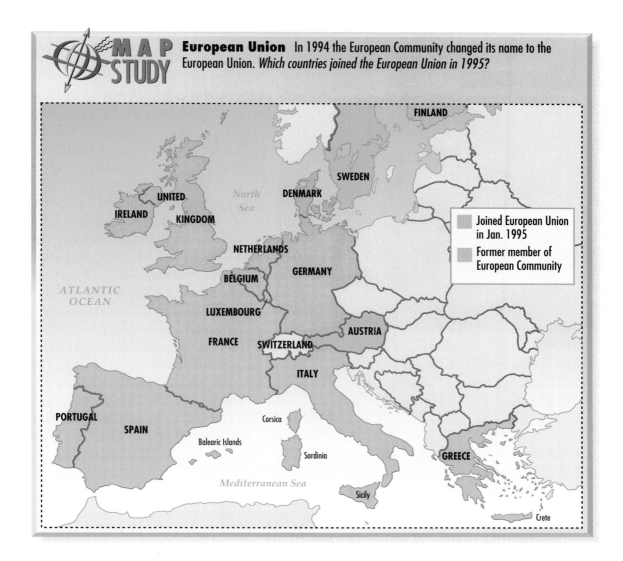

European Union In 1994 the European Community changed its name to the European Union. *Which countries joined the European Union in 1995?*

Joined European Union in Jan. 1995

Former member of European Community

FINLAND

SWEDEN

DENMARK

UNITED KINGDOM

IRELAND

North Sea

NETHERLANDS

GERMANY

BELGIUM

LUXEMBOURG

ATLANTIC OCEAN

AUSTRIA

FRANCE

SWITZERLAND

ITALY

PORTUGAL

SPAIN

Corsica

Balearic Islands

Sardinia

GREECE

Mediterranean Sea

Sicily

Crete

working-class voters. A large, shifting block of voters comes from the middle class. A few minor parties, such as the Social Democrats and the Liberals, draw most of their support from middle-class voters who distrust the two major parties.

The Conservative party has controlled the British government since 1979. For most of that time, Prime Minister Margaret Thatcher headed the government. After her resignation in 1990, John Major became prime minister.

The primary role of the opposition party in Great Britain is to question and criticize the government and its policies. The opposition forms a **shadow cabinet** made up of members of its own party who would govern if the party took control. Each shadow cabinet member follows the activities of a government cabinet member and is ready to take over should the governmental fall.

Great Britain Today

Until the middle of this century, Great Britain ruled many colonies in different parts of the world. Today those colonies

European Link Britain's physical isolation from Europe ended with the opening of the Channel Tunnel in 1994. *What advantages does membership in the European Union offer?*

are independent nations. Most are members of the Commonwealth of Nations, a loose association of former British colonies, including Canada, Australia, India, and 47 other independent nations. The heads of these nations meet periodically to discuss military, economic, and political matters. While Great Britain often plays a leadership role at Commonwealth meetings, it has no real authority over other members.

United Nations

Great Britain belongs to the United Nations (UN), where it is a permanent member of the Security Council, the UN's chief policy-making body. It is also a member of the North Atlantic Treaty Organization (NATO), a military alliance made up of the United States, Canada, and various European countries.

European Union

For centuries, Britain saw itself as separate from Europe. Now, however, its role in the world is tied firmly to the rest of Europe as a member of the European Union (EU). The European Union, formed in 1994 from the earlier European Community (EC), is an organization of 15 European nations. Its goal is to integrate the economies of member nations, coordinate social developments, and work toward establishing common defense and foreign policies. Although national borders remain, member nations trade freely with one another, and citizens can travel and live in any EU country. Such movement toward a unified Europe has met resistance from some Europeans who fear the loss of national identity and independence. Most observers believe that the European Union will strengthen the economies of Great Britain and the other EU members and give members collective strength in world politics.

★ SECTION 1 REVIEW ★

UNDERSTANDING VOCABULARY
Define constitutional monarchy, parliamentary government, constituency, by-elections, shadow cabinet.

REVIEWING OBJECTIVES

1 How does Great Britain's parliamentary system work?

2 What are Great Britain's two major political parties, and what is their role in government?

3 What is the world role of Great Britain today?

Russia

FOCUS

TERMS TO KNOW
totalitarian, cold war, glasnost, perestroika, coup

OBJECTIVES

- Describe how **the Soviet Union** developed, and discuss the policies of some of its leaders.

- Explain the factors and events that led to **the Soviet collapse.**

- Describe the main features of **Russia's emerging political system.**

- Identify and describe some of the problems facing **Russia today.**

Russia is an enormous country. It spans two continents—Europe and Asia—and has a population made up of many different groups and nationalities.

Throughout much of its history, powerful monarchs called czars ruled Russia. In 1917 a group of communist revolutionaries known as Bolsheviks overthrew the czar and created a new state.

The Soviet Union

Led by Vladimir Lenin, these revolutionaries ruled the country through a dictatorship in which a few Communist party leaders made all the decisions. They abolished private property, redistributed land, and took control of all industry and agriculture. Under communist rule, Russia became a **totalitarian** state, one in which the government controlled most aspects of life.

In 1922 the nation became the Union of Soviet Socialist Republics (USSR), or the Soviet Union. The Soviet Union included not only Russia but several other neighboring republics that were absorbed into the new nation. Eventually, the Soviet Union consisted of 15 different republics.

Joseph Stalin

After Lenin died in 1924, Joseph Stalin became leader of the Soviet Union. He ruled the nation ruthlessly for almost 30 years. During that time, he murdered and imprisoned millions of people who tried to oppose him. He forced farmers to

Communism   Lenin and his Bolshevik revolutionaries seized power in 1917 and established the world's first communist government. *What kinds of decisions did the communist leaders make?*

End of the Cold War   Soviet leader Mikhail Gorbachev met with President Reagan and other Western leaders as he introduced political and economic reforms.   *What did Gorbachev's glasnost policy involve?*

The Soviet Collapse

In 1985 Mikhail Gorbachev rose to power in the Soviet Union. Younger and more open to new ideas than previous Soviet leaders, Gorbachev understood that years of communist policies had weakened the Soviet economic system. To save the country, he attempted to make radical changes in the Soviet economy and government.

Glasnost and Perestroika

Gorbachev introduced several reforms aimed at making Soviet society more democratic. These changes were called **glasnost,** which means openness. Gorbachev's regime encouraged new ideas and permitted people to criticize the government openly. It also relaxed censorship rules on books, films, and newspaper and magazine articles. In 1991 free elections were held for the first time since 1917.

Glasnost was part of a broader policy called **perestroika,** or restructuring. Gorbachev hoped to revitalize the nation's economy by allowing people to own private property and start small businesses. He also permitted farmers to hold leases on land.

A Referendum and Coup

As Soviet society became more open, the other Soviet republics began to challenge the power and authority of the Russian republic. In March 1991 Soviet voters approved a national referendum that granted all the republics greater independence. Some hardline Communists, however, feared that this policy would destroy the country. In August 1991 they staged a **coup,** an attempt to overthrow the government. They

give up their land and work on large state-owned farms. He also tried to industrialize rapidly and make the nation a world power. In 1953 Stalin died, and a succession of communist leaders who continued many of Stalin's harsh policies followed.

The Cold War

After World War II, the Soviet Union dominated Eastern Europe, forcing countries there to become Soviet dependencies with communist governments. Soviet actions during these years convinced the United States and its allies that the Soviet goal was to expand its power and influence. Much of the world soon divided into two hostile camps—the free nations of the West and the communist nations. The bitter struggle between the two sides came to be known as the **cold war** because it more often involved a clash of ideas than a clash of arms.

arrested Gorbachev and imposed a state of emergency.

As the hardliners tried to consolidate their power, Soviet citizens responded. People in Moscow, the nation's capital, built barricades in streets, held demonstrations, and ignored government curfews. A popular politician named Boris Yeltsin rallied public support for democracy and urged soldiers and bureaucrats not to support the coup. Resistance soon spread beyond Moscow to other cities.

Faced with such opposition, the coup collapsed in two days. Gorbachev returned to Moscow, but Yeltsin had become a national hero. On December 25, 1991, Gorbachev resigned as Soviet president, and the Union of Soviet Socialist Republics ceased to exist.

Russia's Emerging Political System

A loose alliance of former Soviet republics, called the Commonwealth of Independent States (CIS), replaced the Soviet Union. Boris Yeltsin became president of the largest of these republics, the Russian Federation.

Under this arrangement, each republic is independent, but economic and

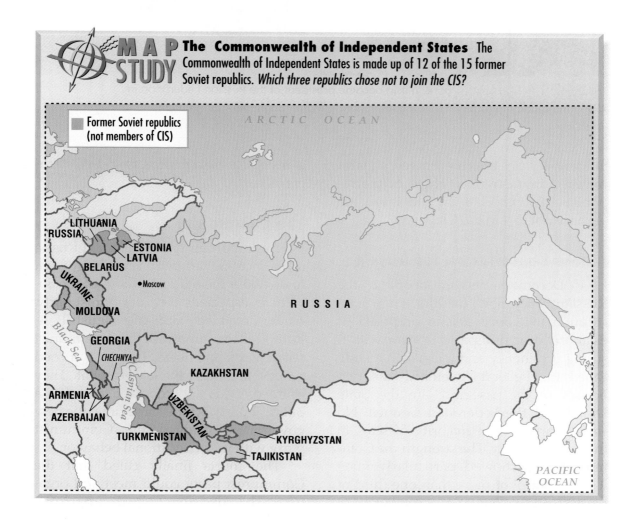

MAP STUDY **The Commonwealth of Independent States** The Commonwealth of Independent States is made up of 12 of the 15 former Soviet republics. *Which three republics chose not to join the CIS?*

Russian President   Boris Yeltsin became president of the Russian Federation in 1991 and quickly introduced a new constitution. *What did the new constitution establish?*

military policies are coordinated under a central administration. Three of the republics—Estonia, Latvia, and Lithuania—chose not to join the CIS.

A New Constitution for Russia

In December 1993 the people of the Russian Federation voted for a new constitution that Boris Yeltsin proposed. It established a multiparty system with a strong presidency and a legislative body called the Federal Assembly. The two houses of the assembly are the State Duma and the Federation Council. No single party won a majority of seats in the new assembly. The strength the Communist party showed, particularly when it won control of more than one-third of the seats in the Duma in December 1995,

alarmed Russian reformers and Westerners alike.

The Communist Party

An important question facing Russia in the post-Soviet period has been what to do about the old institutions of the Soviet era, especially the Communist party. After the failed coup of August 1991, Boris Yeltsin outlawed the Communist party. Party members, however, turned around and sued the government. They claimed it was undemocratic to outlaw a political party. At the same time, the new government charged the Communist party with unconstitutional behavior.

The courts finally ruled that the Communist party could meet and organize. This decision helped propel the

Communists to their 1995 victory in the parliamentary elections.

For a time it looked as though the Communist candidate for president, Gennady Zyuganov, might defeat Boris Yeltsin in the hotly contested 1996 presidential race. In the end, however, Yeltsin won the election to another term.

Russia Today

The old Soviet system created an illusion of economic security, social order, and world power. Today Russia faces economic uncertainty, increasing social chaos, and the loss of national prestige and power.

Economic Problems

Since the collapse of the Soviet state, Russia has experienced staggering inflation. Under communism, inflation was hidden through price controls. This policy led to serious shortages of many consumer products, forcing people to wait hours in line to buy a loaf of bread or a bottle of milk. Today more items are available in the shops but at prices beyond the reach of many Russians.

Although inflation moderated somewhat in 1996, it remained a serious problem for the fledgling democracy. In addition, many Russians resented the growing gap between the rich and the poor. Under Communist rule, the gap had existed, but it had been much less obvious.

Under the Soviet system, people were guaranteed jobs even when there was no work. Today, however, many Russians are losing their jobs and unemployment is soaring. The new Russian government is struggling to solve these problems by finding a way to balance private enterprise with economic security.

At times the upheaval has been so great that workers have not been paid for months at a time. Such hardships only

DID YOU KNOW?

Young Russian Entrepreneurs

Since the collapse of the Soviet Union in 1991, Russian citizens are learning firsthand how to be capitalist entrepreneurs. New privately owned shops have sprung up throughout the country. Sidewalk entrepreneurs peddle their wares along city streets. The All-Russia Exhibition Center in Moscow, formerly a shrine to communist economic triumph, is now a huge shopper's paradise filled with items from around the world. Such a place was unthinkable under the old communist system, and many Russians are awed and overwhelmed by the change.

The people at the forefront of this amazing transition are, perhaps not surprisingly, the young people of Russia. Most new capitalist entrepreneurs are only in their 20s. Thousands are only teenagers. In tune with the world around them and aware of the possibilities before them, this young generation is creating a new economy to take the place of the old one.

Russian entrepreneurs

made the transition to full-scale democracy more difficult.

Social Problems

The social order in Russia is also in great upheaval. During the Soviet era, the Communist party and secret police ensured social stability by crushing or silencing opponents of the system. Harsh punishment and full employment deterred crime.

Today Russia is a more open society. This openness, however, has increased tensions and released angry feelings that were hidden under communist rule. Organized crime and corruption are on the rise, and the number of ordinary crimes has skyrocketed.

These social problems threaten Russia's political and economic progress. They also play into the hands of certain extremists who promise that they will return the country to the peace and prosperity of the Soviet era.

Russia and the World

Another issue facing Russia today is its place in the world. The Commonwealth of Independent States is a fragile alliance, and Russia's role in it is greatly diminished. Some politicians have called for measures that will force some or all former Soviet republics back under Russian control.

No longer a superpower, Russia has lost strength and prestige in international affairs and is searching for a new role. In the last few years, Russia has tried to establish better relations with the United States and the nations of Western Europe. It has cooperated in the reduction of nuclear arsenals, supported actions against old Soviet allies, and asked Western nations for financial aid. The nation has also sought a role in Western economic and military partnerships, such as the European Union and NATO.

Uncertain Future

Despite efforts to reform its society and define its role in the world, Russia's future is still uncertain. Although the power of the Communist party is broken and the old Soviet system has been rejected, a return to communism and dictatorship is possible. In the elections of 1993, 1995, and 1996, many Russians voted for antidemocratic parties. Nevertheless, the pro-democracy faction retained control and forged onward with reforms.

The 1996 news that President Yeltsin would need heart surgery clouded the prospects for futher reform, however. Despite the news, reform-minded Russians tried to remain optimistic about the future.

★ SECTION 2 REVIEW ★

UNDERSTANDING VOCABULARY
Define totalitarian, cold war, glasnost, perestroika, coup.

REVIEWING OBJECTIVES

1 How did the Soviet Union develop, and what were the policies of some of its leaders?

2 What factors and events led to the Soviet collapse?

3 What are the main features of Russia's emerging political system?

4 What are some of the problems facing Russia today?

Exploring ISSUES

Getting In

Refugees to the United States

	Africa	Asia	Latin America	Middle East/ South Asia	Other*	Total
1980	955	163,799	6,662	2,231	33,469	207,116
1985	1,953	49,970	138	5,994	9,990	68,045
1990	3,494	51,611	2,309	4,991	56,912	119,317
1994	5,856	43,581	6,437	5,861	50,944	112,679

Source: U.S. Department of State, Bureau for Refugee Programs.   * "Other" includes Eastern Europe and the former Soviet Union

Who may come to the United States and who may not? That question has long been a subject of controversy. So many foreigners want to come to the United States that the government has had to impose limits. The question of who should be admitted as a refugee is equally controversial.

The Refugee Question

The United States government claims that its refugee policy is "nation-neutral" and that it accepts refugees from any country as long as they can prove "a well-established fear of persecution" in their own countries. Yet refugees from unfriendly nations gain asylum more easily than those from nations with which the United States has friendly relations. American refugee policy changes with world events. If violence and oppression erupt in a country, the United States may issue more visas to refugees from that country.

DEVELOPING A POINT OF VIEW

1 According to the table, in what year did the United States receive the largest number of refugees? From which region did the largest number of refugees come?

2 Why do you think the government makes gaining asylum in the United States harder for refugees from friendly nations than from unfriendly nations?

Japan

FOCUS

TERMS TO KNOW

oligarchy, sovereignty, consensus, faction, trade deficit

OBJECTIVES

- Identify the main features of **the Japanese constitution.**

- Describe the structure of **the Japanese government.**

- Identify and describe Japan's main **political parties.**

- Discuss some of the challenges facing **Japan today.**

Japan is an island nation on the western edge of the Pacific Ocean. For centuries it was one of the most isolated countries in the world. Its seaports were closed to all foreign trade and travel in order to protect Japanese culture from outside influence. In the 1850s Japan opened its ports to foreign trade. It quickly modernized and soon became an important world power.

Before World War II, Japan had a parliamentary form of government with political parties. Many Japanese, however, still believed Emperor Hirohito to be divine, or descended from the gods. By 1940 Japan was an **oligarchy,** a system of government in which a small group of people hold power. A small group of business and military leaders controlled the country and abolished all political parties. After Japan's defeat in the war, the United States occupied the country for seven years and helped Japan restructure its government and rebuild its economy.

The Japanese Constitution

The Japanese constitution was enacted in 1947, during the American occupation. It set up a parliamentary government that recognizes the **sovereignty,** or supreme power, of the people. It also guarantees many of the same civil rights as those in the United States Constitution. Under the Japanese constitution, the emperor and his descendants continue to reign but have no power. Like the British monarchs, they serve only as symbols of their country. The Japanese constitution also includes a unique

Emperor of Japan   Akihito, shown here in ceremonial dress, became emperor in 1989. *In what way is the emperor's role similar to that of the British monarch?*

statement in which the Japanese people forever reject war as a part of national policy and declare that they will never maintain offensive military forces.

The Japanese Government

Japan has a bicameral legislature called the Diet. Its upper house, the House of Councillors, has 252 members who each serve six-year terms. The people elect the members of the House of Councillors, but this house has very little power. Its main role is to advise the government.

The lower house, the House of Representatives, has 511 members elected from 123 election districts. Each of these districts elects three to five representatives to serve four-year terms. The representatives may stand for election sooner, however, if—as happens in a parliamentary system—the government is dissolved and new elections are held. Like the British House of Commons, the Japanese House of Representatives is Japan's most powerful legislative body. Its duties are to make laws and treaties, approve budgets, determine taxes, and spend public funds.

The Japanese people have a long tradition of group cooperation, political unity, and social harmony. They like to conduct business in a low-key, quiet manner and avoid confrontation. Members of the Diet, therefore, try to reach decisions through compromise and **consensus**—by broad, general agreement—and avoid argument and dissent.

The Prime Minister

The Diet elects Japan's head of state, the prime minister. The person who holds this office is usually the leader of

House of Representatives Members of Japan's most powerful legislative body try to avoid confrontation when reaching decisions. *What are the main duties of the House of Representatives?*

the majority party in the House of Representatives. The prime minister selects the members of the cabinet and the ministers of government departments. Together, the prime minister and these leaders form the executive branch of the government. The prime minister and at least one-half of the cabinet ministers must be members of the Diet. As a result, the executive and legislative functions are combined.

Japanese Bureaucracy

Japan has a large bureaucracy to carry out many of the administrative and technical duties of the government. This bureaucracy plays an especially important role in coordinating the actions of government and business. Japanese companies compete fiercely for business, but they also cooperate on general policies. The bureaucracy helps oversee this cooperation and guide the nation's economic growth.

Political Parties

Japan is a multiparty democracy. Yet for almost 40 years one party, the Liberal Democratic party (LDP), dominated Japanese government and politics. Despite its name, the LDP is a conservative party that represents Japan's powerful business interests and middle class. The LDP is really a coalition of parties made up of several smaller **factions,** or groups. These factions differ from one another in certain respects, but all favor private enterprise and ties with the United States.

In July 1993, the LDP lost control of the Diet for the first time since 1955 because of major corruption scandals. Since then, a coalition of parties has run the country. The Japanese Socialist party (JSP), one of the parties in this coalition, was for years the major opposition party.

Party Politics   Until 1993 the Liberal Democratic party (LDP) dominated Japanese government and politics.   *What brought down the LDP?*

It had favored placing more controls on capitalism and breaking with the United States. After the JSP became part of the government, however, it moved closer to LDP policies.

Japan Today

After its devastation in World War II, Japan rebuilt its economy so successfully that it became one of the richest nations in the world. Its spectacular economic success provided a model for many other Asian regions, such as South Korea, Singapore, Taiwan, and Hong Kong.

The Japanese Economy

Toward the end of the 1980s, the pace of Japanese economic growth slowed, and the country experienced a recession that extended well into the 1990s. In 1995 a severe earthquake devastated the city of Kobe, causing more economic disruption. Many thought that the country would not have an economic downturn because the powerful Japanese bureaucracy would be able to maintain uninterrupted economic growth. The recession showed that, although the Japanese economy is still very strong, it is not invincible.

Japan's economic development has made it a major world power. Yet the nation has been reluctant to take on a role of international leadership. Slowly, however, this reluctance is disappearing. In recent years Japan has begun to provide foreign assistance to other nations. In 1991, for example, the nation pledged billions of dollars to support the Persian Gulf War against Iraq. This was the first time that Japan had become involved in any war effort since its defeat in World War II.

Trade Tensions   President Clinton met with Japan's minister of foreign trade in an effort to ease tensions between the two countries.   *What is a major cause of the tensions?*

Japan and the United States

Japan's relationship with the United States is also changing. Its economic strength has led to increased tensions with the United States. A major cause of these tensions is the trade imbalance between the two nations. Japan sells more goods to the United States than it buys, which leaves the United States with a large trade deficit. A **trade deficit** is the amount by which a country's spending on imports exceeds the amount received from exports.

Many Americans believe that Japan's economic success hurts the United States economy. They have demanded that Japan adopt more open trade policies. The two countries have agreed on several changes in trade policy that they hope will ease tensions and create a fairer trade balance.

Finally, despite Japan's constitutional ban on maintaining offensive military forces, the United States has pressured Japan in recent years to take over more of its own defense. Since World War II, the United States has provided this defense. Many Americans feel that our country should no longer continue this policy.

★ SECTION 3 REVIEW ★

UNDERSTANDING VOCABULARY
Define oligarchy, sovereignty, consensus, faction, trade deficit.

REVIEWING OBJECTIVES

1 What are the main features of the Japanese constitution?

2 How is the Japanese government organized?

3 What are Japan's main political parties, and what ideas do they support?

4 What are some of the challenges facing Japan today?

How to Use an Atlas

Atlases are reference books containing maps. They usually have different types of maps that present various kinds of geographic and social information. Maps can focus on areas of any size—from a city block to a whole continent or the world.

Using an atlas

General-Purpose Maps

Most atlases have general-purpose maps, such as physical and political maps. *Physical maps* show natural features such as mountains, deserts, and rivers. *Political maps* show the boundaries between countries and often smaller divisions such as states or counties.

Special-Purpose Maps

Atlases may also contain special-purpose maps. *Geologic maps* might show the location of the earth's volcanoes and earthquake zones. *Climate maps* present information about rainfall, air temperature, and winds. Other maps might show the distribution of natural resources.

Some special-purpose maps present information about people, such as the distribution and movement of people in a region or where different languages are spoken. *Economic activity maps* might show how people use the land—what crops are grown and what products are manufactured. Other special-purpose maps show forms of government, how people voted in elections, and transportation systems.

Changes in political, economic, social, and cultural conditions are the special concern of *historical atlases*. A historical atlas presents maps on specific places, events, and conditions in the past.

Other Information Atlases

Atlases often contain useful information that is not presented in maps. Some atlases have chronologies, glossaries, geographical dictionaries, and statistics. Many include photographs, tables, diagrams, charts, and graphs.

CITIZENSHIP IN ACTION

1 What types of information can be shown in maps?

2 What other kinds of information, besides maps, are often found in atlases?

Mexico

Mexico is the southern neighbor of the United States, and the two countries share a long, common border. Officially called the United Mexican States, Mexico is the most populous Spanish-speaking country in the world.

The present government of Mexico was established in 1917 after a long and bitter revolution and civil war. Since then, Mexico's leaders have struggled to build a modern nation from a unique heritage that combines Spanish and Native American cultures.

The Government

Mexico, like the United States, is a federal republic. It has 31 states and a federal district surrounding the capital of Mexico City. Each state has its own constitution and is governed by a governor and state legislature.

The structure of Mexico's government is also similar to that of the United States. There are three separate branches of government. A president, elected for a single six-year term, heads the executive branch. The president has the power to appoint cabinet ministers, supreme court justices, and high military officers. The president also has the power to recommend legislation to the legislative branch.

Mexico's bicameral legislature consists of the Senate and Chamber of Deputies. The 64 senators—2 from each state and 2 from the Federal District—are elected to 6-year terms. The 500 members of the Chamber of Deputies are elected to 3-year terms. Of these, 300 are chosen directly by the people in local electoral districts. The other 200 deputies are chosen from party candidates according to the proportion of the popular vote each party receives in the general election.

Mexico's Government Mexico's legislature consists of the Senate and the Chamber of Deputies. *How many members sit in each house?*

The federal judicial system consists of circuit courts, district courts, and a supreme court. The president appoints the 26 supreme court justices.

The Political System

Mexico has a multiparty system with many different parties. In reality, however, one party has dominated Mexican politics and government. This ruling party, the Partido Revolucionario Institucional (PRI), or the Institutional Revolutionary party, has dominated the government for more than 65 years. The PRI controls the presidency, the legislature, and the judiciary. The PRI also controls most state governorships and town **mayoralties,** or mayors' offices.

The major opposition parties in Mexico are the National Action party (PAN), a conservative group formed in 1939, and the left-leaning Democratic Revolutionary party (PRD).

During the national election of August 1994, these opposition parties made a great effort to take control from the PRI. Unusual bitterness marked the election, and the first PRI candidate for the presidency was assassinated. In the end, Ernesto Zedillo Ponce de León of the PRI did win the presidential election, but he received only 50 percent of the vote—the lowest ever for a PRI candidate.

Mexico Today

Mexico is a deeply divided country. Millions of Mexicans live in extreme poverty, while a small number of wealthy landowners and entrepreneurs control the political and economic life of the country.

The huge gap between the rich and poor was highlighted in January 1994, when a peasant rebellion erupted in the rural, southern state of Chiapas. This revolt shocked many Mexicans and con-

Mexico's Ruling Party   Voters attended a rally for PRI candidate Ernesto Zedillo Ponce de León during the 1994 election campaign.   *What was the result of the election?*

A Divided Country The 1994 peasant revolt in Chiapas highlighted the huge gap between rich and poor in Mexico. *What happened in late 1994 to make matters worse?*

vinced them of the urgent need for both economic and political reforms to deal with the country's poverty.

Economic Reforms

Some of Mexico's recent leaders have initiated reforms. During his presidency from 1988 to 1994, Carlos Salinas de Gortari reduced Mexico's debt, lowered inflation, and attracted foreign investment. He also changed industry through **privatization,** the selling of state-owned companies to private entrepreneurs. In 1993 President Salinas ushered in a new era by signing the North American Free Trade Agreement (NAFTA) with Canada and the United States. This treaty reduces tariffs and other trade barriers.

Economic Challenges

Despite these success stories, Mexico is still struggling. Economic reforms have primarily benefited the wealthy. Many other Mexicans continue to face unemployment and **underemployment,**

work that does not use their skills to the fullest. As a result thousands of Mexicans cross the United States border in search of work. This tide of illegal immigrants has created tensions between the two countries.

The situation in Mexico grew worse in 1994 when an economic slowdown led the government to devalue the peso. This **devaluation,** which lowered the value of the nation's currency in relation to other currencies, raised doubts about Mexico's ability to pay its debts.

Turning Point

In response to pressing demands for political reform, President Zedillo has promised to take steps to end the PRI's monopoly of power. He has also vowed to reform the electoral system.

Mexico appears to be at a turning point. If it can improve the lives of its citizens and achieve political reform, it can move forward. If not, Mexico risks sliding into a period of instability.

★ SECTION 4 REVIEW ★

UNDERSTANDING VOCABULARY
Define mayoralty, privatization, underemployment, devaluation.

REVIEWING OBJECTIVES
1 What is the basic structure of the government of Mexico?

2 How does the political system of Mexico differ from that of the United States?

3 What is the major problem facing Mexico today?

Identifying Key Terms

Choose the vocabulary term that best completes each of the sentences below. Write your answers on a separate sheet of paper.

privatization   parliamentary government
consensus   sovereignty   glasnost
devaluation

1. Under the policy of _____, Soviet society became more democratic and open.
2. The members of Japan's parliament, or Diet, try to make decisions based on _____ rather than confrontation.
3. In Great Britain's _____, executive, legislative, and judicial functions overlap.
4. The _____ of the people is the basic principle of democratic government.
5. During _____ of Mexico's industry, state-owned companies were sold to individual entrepreneurs.
6. The people had to pay more for imported goods after the _____ of their currency.

Reviewing the Main Ideas

SECTION 1
1. Describe the main features of the British Parliament.
2. Compare the political parties of Great Britain with those of the United States.

SECTION 2
3. What happened when the Soviet Union became a communist country?
4. What are some of the advantages and disadvantages of a more democratic society for the Russian people?

SECTION 3
5. How did Japan's government change after World War II?
6. How has Japan's economic success affected its role in the world?

SECTION 4
7. Describe the relationship between Mexico and the United States.
8. How might Mexico's economic problems affect its government?

Critical Thinking

SECTION 1
1. **Analyzing Information**   Why do you think Great Britain continues to have a monarchy, even though the monarch has no real power?

SECTION 2
2. **Predicting Outcomes**   Do you think that democracy has a chance to work in Russia? Explain your answer.

SECTION 3
3. **Analyzing Information**   What do you think might be the advantages and disadvantages of Japan's consensus-type decision making?

SECTION 4
4. **Evaluating Information**   Why is Mexico at a turning point? How might the results of change affect the United States?

Reinforcing Citizenship Skills

In an atlas, locate climate maps for at least two of these countries: Great Britain, Russia, Japan, and Mexico. List the average rainfall and summer and winter temperatures for each country.

Comparing National Statistics

Country	Population Density (per sq. mile)	Life Expectancy		Economic Rates		
		Male	Female	Growth	Unemployment	Inflation
United Kingdom	622	74	80	2.1%	10.3%	2.6%
Russia	22	64	74	-12%	1.4%	21%
Japan	857	77	82	0.4%	2.9%	0.7%
Mexico	123	70	77	0.4%	10.7%	8%

Source: *1996 Information Please Almanac; World Almanac and Book of Facts 1996.*

Which country has the highest average rainfall and temperatures? Share your findings with the class.

Cooperative Learning

In a group of three, select a country of the world. Do research on the country's political system. Compare this system to that of the United States. Then prepare a report in which you compare government structures and analyze the advantages and disadvantages of different features of the political systems. Present your report to the class.

Technology Activity

Using E-Mail

Choose a nation not discussed in this chapter. Then search the Internet for the e-mail address of the United Nations delegation or embassy of your chosen nation. Send electronic mail asking for the population density, life expectancy, and economic rates of the nation. Share what you learn with the rest of the class.

Analyzing Visuals

A table is a useful way to compare information about different countries. Study the table above. Then answer the following questions.

1. Which of the countries has the lowest population density per square mile?
2. In which country do people live the longest on average?
3. Which country has the greatest growth rate?
4. Which country shows the best overall economic health? Why?

Focusing on Your Community

Find out if any people in your community have come from Great Britain, Russia, Japan, Mexico, or other countries. Try to interview these people and ask them questions about the political system of the country they came from. Ask what it was like to live under that system of government and what role citizens had in their government. Prepare an oral report for the class.

CHAPTER 23

International Relations

CIVIC PARTICIPATION

Both cooperation and conflict characterize international relations. In its international relations, the United States pursues its own interests as a sovereign nation. These interests sometimes bring the nation into conflict with others. At the same time, as a member of the United Nations, our country works with others in trying to resolve conflicts around the world. Contact the Public Affairs Office of the Department of State in Washington, D.C., for information on United States relations with two foreign countries.

Working in Your Community

After you have this information, interview neighbors and friends to find out what they know about our relations with these countries. Share your information with them. ■

Your Civics Journal

During the next week, be on the lookout for stories in the media about United States relations with foreign countries. In your civics journal, list the countries that are mentioned and next to each country note its relationship with the United States.

United Nations tour ➤

United States Foreign Policy

FOCUS

TERMS TO KNOW
foreign policy, national security, diplomacy, foreign aid, alliance, trade sanction, embargo, isolationism, collective security, disarmament

OBJECTIVES

- Identify and describe four basic **goals of American foreign policy.**

- Describe **who conducts foreign policy.**

- Explain **how foreign policy is conducted.**

- Describe the basic elements of the **postwar foreign policy** of the United States.

- Describe some foreign policy challenges facing the United States **after the cold war.**

One of the basic tasks of government is to develop strategies and principles to guide the nation's relations with other countries. These strategies and principles are known as **foreign policy.** A nation's foreign policy outlines its position on important issues and determines how the nation will deal with other nations on those issues. Because the United States is a world leader, foreign policy plays a central role in our government.

Goals of American Foreign Policy

In developing foreign policy, a nation has a series of goals it hopes to achieve. The United States has four basic foreign policy goals. The most important is **national security,** the ability to keep the country safe from attack or harm.

Another important goal is international trade. In today's global economy, trade with other nations is vital to economic prosperity. Trade creates markets for American products and jobs for American workers. It also brings foreign products to American consumers.

A third goal of American foreign policy is promoting world peace. Even a war far from United States shores can disrupt trade and endanger our national security. The United States thus works hard to get countries to cooperate and solve their conflicts peacefully.

International Cooperation When Iraqi soldiers invaded Kuwait in 1990, the United States called on other nations to help fight the invaders. *Why is the United States concerned about promoting world peace?*

This country's fourth foreign policy goal concerns democracy and human rights. Americans believe strongly in democracy and in basic human rights. Through its foreign policy, the nation encourages other countries to guarantee rights for their people by adopting and maintaining democratic ideals. When people are denied rights, they are more likely to rebel against their government. Promoting democracy thus encourages peace and helps protect the national security of the United States.

Who Conducts Foreign Policy?

As the nation's chief diplomat, one of the President's major roles is formulating foreign policy. Among the President's powers are the power to negotiate treaties and to appoint ambassadors and other diplomats.

Several government officials and agencies help the President plan and carry out foreign policy. The Department of State has the primary responsibility for carrying out American foreign policy. It supervises United States diplomats and gathers information to help the President make foreign policy decisions.

The Department of Defense helps with foreign policy by carrying out the President's military decisions. It maintains United States troops at military bases around the world and ensures that the nation will react quickly to any military crisis.

The National Security Council (NSC) informs and advises the President on foreign policy issues. It analyzes information and coordinates the nation's military and foreign policy goals. The NSC also supervises the Central Intelligence

Foreign Affairs   The President plays a major role in formulating foreign policy. *Which government department has primary responsibility for helping the President in this role?*

Agency (CIA). Known as the nation's spy agency, the CIA gathers information about governments and political movements around the world.

Congress and the American people also play important roles in making foreign policy. Only Congress has the power to declare war or appropriate money to carry out foreign policy goals. In addition, the Senate must ratify all treaties the President negotiates and approve the President's nominees for ambassadors.

The American people affect foreign policy through the leaders they elect. They can also participate in special-interest groups, such as environmental, peace, and human rights organizations that are concerned with various foreign policy issues.

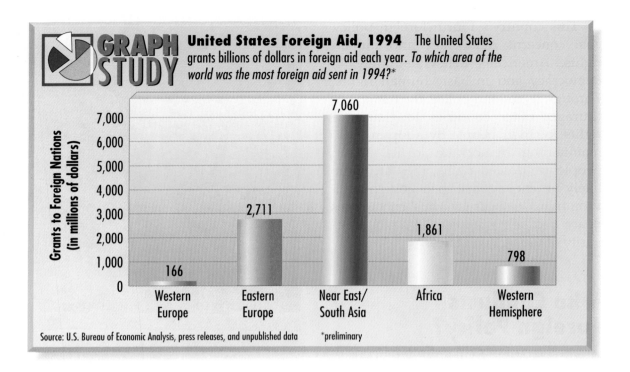

GRAPH STUDY

United States Foreign Aid, 1994 The United States grants billions of dollars in foreign aid each year. *To which area of the world was the most foreign aid sent in 1994?**

Grants to Foreign Nations (in millions of dollars)

Western Europe	166
Eastern Europe	2,711
Near East/South Asia	7,060
Africa	1,861
Western Hemisphere	798

Source: U.S. Bureau of Economic Analysis, press releases, and unpublished data   *preliminary

How Foreign Policy Is Conducted

Governments carry out foreign policy in a variety of ways. One way is through **diplomacy,** the process of conducting relations with foreign governments. Diplomacy is used to settle disagreements as well as to cooperate in such tasks as uniting against a common enemy or establishing trade relations. The President often meets with foreign leaders to discuss foreign policy issues or to negotiate treaties and agreements. The secretary of state, ambassadors, and other diplomats are engaged in most of the nation's day-to-day diplomacy.

Foreign Aid

Another way of carrying out foreign policy is through **foreign aid**—money, military assistance, food, or other supplies given to help other countries. One of this nation's greatest foreign aid tri-umphs was the Marshall Plan, a program established after World War II to help Western Europe rebuild factories and businesses destroyed in the war.

Alliances

A third way of carrying out foreign policy is through alliances. **Alliances** are formal agreements or unions among nations. Some alliances are based on defense. One of the most important defense alliances of the United States is the North Atlantic Treaty Organization (NATO). You will learn more about NATO later in the chapter.

Alliances may also be formed for economic or other reasons. The European Union, which you read about in Chapter 22, promotes the political and economic strength of Europe. The Organization of Petroleum Exporting Countries (OPEC) is an alliance of oil-rich nations that works to control the quantities and price of oil around the world.

International Trade

Foreign policy may also be carried out through trade measures. These generally involve agreements about the terms of international trade—what products may be traded, the tariffs involved, and the rules by which products may be traded back and forth. Sometimes trade measures include **trade sanctions,** or efforts to punish a nation by imposing certain trade barriers. Trade sanctions may include boycotts, tariffs, or **embargoes,** which prohibit ships, planes, trains, or trucks from entering or exiting a nation's ports or crossing its borders.

Postwar Foreign Policy

In the years between World War I and World War II, American foreign policy was characterized by **isolationism.** This means that the nation did not form alliances with other countries, and it remained neutral in international disputes and wars. One exception to this policy occurred in Latin America, where the United States sometimes stepped in to protect its interests in this hemisphere.

The Cold War

Two events at the end of World War II changed American foreign policy forever. The first was the use of the atomic bomb, the most fearsome weapon the world had ever seen. The other event was the Soviet occupation of Eastern Europe and the formation of communist governments there. This action convinced the United States and its allies that the goal of communism was to take over the world. These events led to fierce competition between the forces of democracy and communism, which became known as the cold war.

Foreign Policy Changes The use of the atomic bomb to end World War II marked a significant change in American foreign policy. *What other events contributed to the cold war?*

The cold war dominated American foreign policy from the late 1940s to the end of the 1980s. (See page 518.) At first, the United States tried to deal with the communist threat through a policy of containment, using money and military power to prevent Soviet expansion. To promote containment, the United States and other nations signed defense treaties and agreed to protect each other in the event of communist attack. The policy of containment prevented communist advances in Greece and Turkey. In the 1950s the policy led to the Korean War, and in the 1960s it led to United States involvement in the Vietnam War.

Another cold war foreign policy was the idea of **collective security,** the formation of political and military alliances to protect member nations from communist aggression. One of the most important alliances was the North Atlantic Treaty Organization. Formed in 1949 by the United

American Profiles

Jesse Jackson

A Baptist minister, the Reverend Jesse Jackson came of age during the civil rights movement of the 1960s. He has become a national political figure and a prominent spokesman for equal rights. In 1988 he ran for the Democratic party's presidential nomination.

Jackson has also spoken on behalf of minorities and oppressed people around the world. In his numerous trips abroad, he has worked for human rights causes ranging from the release of prisoners in Cuba to an end to racial inequality in South Africa. Jackson has also lobbied Japanese leaders on the rights of minority workers.

Always outspoken, Jackson is often at odds with official United States policy. Nonetheless, he has become a respected citizen diplomat.

PROFILE REVIEW

1 What are some of Jackson's major accomplishments?

2 How has Jackson demonstrated the qualities of responsible citizenship?

States, Canada, and several European nations, NATO's main purpose was to protect members from Soviet aggression and maintain a balance of power in Europe.

The Arms Race

In the years following World War II, the United States and the Soviet Union were engaged in an escalating arms race. Each side tried to gain military advantage by increasing the numbers and kinds of nuclear and conventional (nonnuclear) weapons. Relations between the two countries began to improve in the 1970s. One sign of better relations was arms control and **disarmament,** or arms reduction. In the 1980s the United States signed several arms control treaties with the Soviet Union that limited the growth of nuclear arms and slowed the arms race.

In 1989 events in the Soviet Union and Eastern Europe ended the cold war. The Soviet Union began moving toward a democratic form of government, and one by one the nations of Eastern Europe ousted their communist governments.

Since the collapse of the Soviet Union in 1991, relations between Russia and the United States have improved dramatically.

After the Cold War

The end of the cold war forced the United States to reconsider its foreign policy. The nation must now decide how to respond to the new challenges of the emerging world order.

Nuclear Threat

One challenge for American foreign policy is the continued existence of nuclear weapons and the possibility of their development by hostile nations. In 1994 tensions erupted between the United States and North Korea over suspicions that the Koreans were developing nuclear weapons. The issue was resolved, at least temporarily, through negotiations. There is also the problem of thousands of nuclear weapons from the former Soviet Union, some of which may be slipping into the hands of other nations. The United States has tried to address this problem by providing Russia with money to dismantle and dispose of its weapons.

Relying on International Cooperation

In the cold war era, crises in different parts of the world had a global impact because of the involvement of the world's two superpowers. Now crises are more localized and restricted to smaller regions. As the world's only superpower, the United States could act as a "supercop" to deal with these problems. Instead, American leaders have favored a policy of international cooper-

ation. When Iraq invaded its neighbor Kuwait in 1990, the United States enlisted the support of other nations to fight in the Persian Gulf War against Iraq. In 1992 the United States obtained United Nations support for a humanitarian intervention in Somalia, which was torn apart by civil war. In 1994 the United States sought international cooperation before landing in Haiti to oversee the return to power of the country's democratically elected president.

Increasingly, the United States is trying to deal with international problems by bringing countries or groups together to negotiate. In the mid-1990s, for example, the United States helped Israel and the Palestine Liberation Organization (PLO) reach an agreement designed to end hostility and violence.

★ SECTION 1 REVIEW ★

UNDERSTANDING VOCABULARY
Define foreign policy, national security, diplomacy, foreign aid, alliance, trade sanction, embargo, isolationism, collective security, disarmament.

REVIEWING OBJECTIVES
1 What are four basic goals of American foreign policy?

2 Who conducts foreign policy?

3 Explain how foreign policy is conducted.

4 How did the foreign policy of the United States change after World War II?

5 What are some foreign policy challenges facing the United States after the cold war?

SUPREME COURT CASE STUDIES
The Pentagon Papers

One of the basic principles of freedom of the press is the idea of "no prior restraint." This means that the government cannot decide beforehand what the press cannot discuss or write about. To do so would amount to censorship and would violate the First Amendment.

Background of the Case

In 1971 the federal government tried to prevent *The New York Times* from publishing a series of articles based on a secret report prepared for the Department of Defense. The newspaper had received the secret documents from Daniel Ellsberg, one of the authors of the report. The documents, which became known as the Pentagon Papers, detailed United States involvement in the Vietnam War. They also showed that the government had misled the public about its early involvement in Vietnam.

The first articles appeared in *The New York Times* on June 13 and June 14, 1971. The Nixon administration sought, and won, a federal injunction halting publication of further articles. The *Times* immediately appealed to the Supreme Court. Meanwhile, the *Washington Post* began printing articles based on the papers. It became apparent that other newspapers would do the same, forcing the government to seek injunctions against each one.

The Case and the Court's Decision

The Supreme Court took the case, *New York Times Co. v. United States.* The *Times* argued that the injunction was unconstitutional and amounted to censorship. The government claimed that the articles were damaging to national security because the war was still going on.

In its decision, the Supreme Court ruled 6 to 3 against the injunction, finding that the government had not shown sufficient "justification for the imposition of such a restraint." The court thus upheld the principle that censorship or prior restraint is a violation of the First Amendment.

Daniel Ellsberg

REVIEWING THE CASE

1 Why would allowing the government to decide beforehand what can be printed or broadcast destroy freedom of the press?

2 Do you agree with the decision in the Pentagon Papers case? Explain why or why not.

The United Nations

Internationalism is the idea that individual nations promote common aims through membership in an organization made up of many nations. One such organization, the League of Nations, was formed after World War I. The United States, however, refused to join the League. Without United States participation, the League was a weak, ineffectual organization that was unable to prevent World War II. When World War II ended, the United States realized it could not make the same mistake again. It therefore became a leader in forming a new international organization—the United Nations.

The Structure of the United Nations

The United Nations is a large international organization with nearly 200 member nations. Its main headquarters is in New York City. The organization's main purposes are to maintain international peace, develop friendly relations among nations, promote justice and cooperation, and seek peaceful solutions to international problems.

The General Assembly

The General Assembly is the legislative body of the United Nations. Each member nation is represented in the General Assembly and has a single vote. The assembly holds regular and special sessions to debate international issues and make recommendations to member nations. The General Assembly also elects a secretary-general.

The Security Council

The Security Council is the peacekeeping arm of the United Nations. It has 15 members, including 5 permanent members—the United States, Great Britain, Russia, France, and China. The General Assembly elects the 10 nonpermanent members for 2-year terms.

The United Nations Representatives of member nations meet regularly at the United Nations headquarters in New York. *What are the main purposes of the organization?*

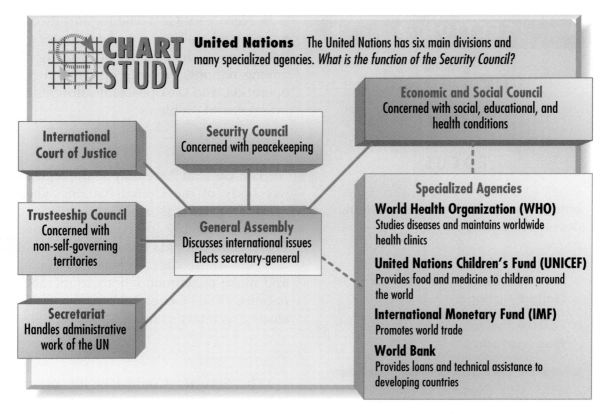

CHART STUDY

United Nations The United Nations has six main divisions and many specialized agencies. *What is the function of the Security Council?*

International Court of Justice

Security Council
Concerned with peacekeeping

Economic and Social Council
Concerned with social, educational, and health conditions

Trusteeship Council
Concerned with non-self-governing territories

General Assembly
Discusses international issues
Elects secretary-general

Specialized Agencies

World Health Organization (WHO)
Studies diseases and maintains worldwide health clinics

United Nations Children's Fund (UNICEF)
Provides food and medicine to children around the world

International Monetary Fund (IMF)
Promotes world trade

World Bank
Provides loans and technical assistance to developing countries

Secretariat
Handles administrative work of the UN

Each country on the Security Council has one vote, but any permanent member can veto a motion. This veto gives the permanent members a great deal of power to block actions.

The Security Council meets throughout the year and holds emergency sessions to consider new crises. It often asks quarreling nations to solve differences peacefully. It can also send UN troops, drawn from various nations, to try to prevent or stop a war.

International Court of Justice

The International Court of Justice, also known as the World Court, is the judicial arm of the United Nations. Its headquarters is in The Hague, Netherlands. The court has 15 judges appointed by the General Assembly. They hear disputes between nations and issue decisions based on international law.

UN Agencies

Specialized, semi-independent agencies do much of the most important and least appreciated work of the UN. These agencies include the World Health Organization (WHO), the United Nations Children's Fund (UNICEF), the International Monetary Fund (IMF), and the World Bank.

These agencies oversee a wide range of international issues. They help nations combat hunger, disease, poverty, ignorance, and other problems. The WHO, for example, helps fight disease and promote health.

UN agencies play an important role by providing money and expert assistance in health, agriculture, and other fields to poor nations. Countries that are still struggling to build industrial economies and meet the basic needs of their people are called **developing nations.**

Nations such as Japan and the United States that have already built strong industrial economies are often called **developed nations.**

The Role of the United Nations Today

Throughout the cold war, critics of the UN complained that small nations whose voting strength was equal to that of large nations like the United States dominated the organization. Such criticism, and a lack of cooperation among more powerful members, made the UN less effective in settling disputes and preventing wars than many had hoped.

New Efforts to Promote Peace

Since the late 1980s, the UN has taken a more visible and effective role in peacekeeping efforts. For example, when Iraq invaded Kuwait in 1990, the UN Security Council voted to condemn Iraq and place trade sanctions on the country. It also set a deadline for Iraq to withdraw its troops from Kuwait. When the deadline passed, a coalition of nations led by the United States and sanctioned by the UN attacked and defeated Iraq in the Persian Gulf War.

Since the Persian Gulf War, the UN has sent peacekeeping troops to oversee elections in Cambodia, to provide humanitarian aid to starving people in Somalia, and to monitor the peace settlement in Bosnia.

Problems Facing the United Nations

Many problems face the United Nations today. Its troops are not well-enough armed to stand up against strong

Ongoing Efforts United Nations troops in Bosnia helped monitor the peace settlement that ended Bosnia's bloody civil war. *Where do United Nations funds come from?*

local armies, and the organization lacks adequate funds. Money for running the UN and its activities comes from dues paid by member nations. Many countries, including the United States, however, have not paid all the money they owe. Still, the greatest problem facing the UN is the inability or unwillingness of members to cooperate.

★ **SECTION 2 REVIEW** ★

UNDERSTANDING VOCABULARY
Define internationalism, developing nation, developed nation.

REVIEWING OBJECTIVES
1 What is the structure of the United Nations?

2 What is the role of the United Nations today?

Great American Documents

The United Nations Charter

On January 1, 1942, 26 nations signed the United Nations Declaration, which set up a wartime alliance. President Franklin Roosevelt, concerned about maintaining such an alliance after the war, ordered the United States State Department to develop a plan for a permanent international organization.

Think About It

As you read the following excerpt, think about the role the United Nations has played in the world.

Creating the Charter

In 1945 representatives of China, the United States, Great Britain, and the Soviet Union, met in Washington, D.C., to discuss the creation of the new United Nations. Over a period of 4 months, they worked on a constitution, or charter, for the new world organization. Later, delegates from 50 nations met in San Francisco to adopt the charter. The United Nations officially came into being on October 24, 1945.

The Preamble to the Charter

We the peoples of the United Nations, determined to save succeeding generations from the scourge of war, which twice in our lifetime has brought untold sorrow to mankind, and to reaffirm faith in fundamental human rights, in the dignity and worth of the human person, in the equal rights of men and women and of nations large and small, and to establish conditions under which justice and a respect for the obligations arising from treaties and other sources of international law can be maintained, and to promote social progress and better standards of life in larger freedom, and for these ends to practice tolerance and live together in peace with one another as good neighbors, and to unite our strength to maintain international peace and security, and to ensure, by the acceptance of principles and the institution of methods, that armed force shall not be used, save in the common interest, and to employ international machinery for the promotion of the economic and social advancement of all peoples, have resolved to combine our efforts to accomplish these aims.

Accordingly, our respective Governments, through [our] representatives . . . have agreed to the present Charter of the United Nations and do hereby establish an international organization to be known as the United Nations.

The charter states that UN membership is open to all "peace-loving states." Today nearly 200 nations belong to the United Nations.

INTERPRETING SOURCES

1 What was the purpose of the original United Nations Declaration?

2 How does the preamble of the United Nations Charter compare with the preamble of the United States Constitution?

SECTION 3

United States Interests Abroad

American foreign policy today faces a number of challenges around the world. The end of the cold war has brought an increase in ethnic conflicts in some areas and raised the potential for more outbreaks of regional warfare. **Nuclear proliferation,** the growth and spread of nuclear weapons, remains an ever-present danger. Human rights abuses threaten the well-being of millions of people around the globe. Increased economic competition tests the limits of international cooperation. The United States must deal with these and other challenges when considering its interests in various world regions.

Europe

After World War II, the NATO alliance played a major role in protecting Western Europe from Soviet aggression. With the collapse of the Soviet Union, NATO members, including the United States, are now considering their post–cold war role.

Changes in NATO

In the United States, some people argue that American participation in NATO is no longer necessary. Others, however, support continued participation because NATO membership provides an opportunity for cooperation between European countries and the United States. Although the United States continues to support NATO, it is bringing home many of the American troops stationed in Europe.

In recent years a number of eastern European countries have requested to join NATO. In 1994 NATO responded with a plan called the Partnership for

International Cooperation American volunteers teach eastern European citizens about Western procedures. *What are some of the challenges facing American foreign policy?*

Peace that links participating eastern European nations to NATO. The agreement allows these nations limited participation in NATO military activities and peacekeeping missions.

Problems in Eastern Europe

The collapse of communism in the early 1990s led to dramatic changes in eastern Europe. American foreign policy in the region is now focused on helping Russia and eastern European nations develop strong capitalist economies and stable democratic governments. The United States has provided financial aid and sent experts to advise these nations on economic policy and democratic procedures. Along with other Western nations, the United States has also signed trade agreements with these countries.

One factor that has hindered political and economic progress in eastern Europe is the rise of old ethnic hatreds and rivalries. The most obvious example was the war in Bosnia, which pitted Muslim Bosnians against Christian Serbs. The war represented a serious threat to the stability of the region until the Dayton agreement, signed in 1995, helped to restore peace. NATO sent peacekeepers to the nation, but ethnic tensions remained high.

The Middle East and Africa

The Middle East and Africa represent two very different challenges for American foreign policy. In the Middle East, the primary goal has been to end the Arab-Israeli conflict and bring peace to the region. In Africa the goals have been to encourage the growth of democracy and improve the lives of the people.

The Middle East

The Arab-Israeli conflict has been a source of tension in the Middle East since 1948, when the nation of Israel was

DID YOU KNOW?

The Name Game

Countries sometimes change their names, and new countries are formed. As a result, even the most recently published maps and atlases may be out of date. For example, Belarus became an independent state in 1991, when the Soviet Union broke apart. In 1993 Czechoslovakia split into two nations—the Czech Republic and Slovakia.

Here are some countries that have changed their names and other new countries that have formed.

Zaire, 1971 (Belgian Congo)
Sri Lanka, 1972 (Ceylon)
Benin, 1975 (Dahomey)
Zimbabwe, 1980 (Rhodesia)
Belize, 1981 (British Honduras)
Burkina Faso, 1984 (Upper Volta)
Myanmar, 1989 (Burma)
Azerbaijan, established 1991
Croatia, established 1991

Belize

Gulf of Mexico

MEXICO

BELIZE

GUATEMALA

HONDURAS

PACIFIC OCEAN

EL SALVADOR

NICARAGUA

Changing names

formed. For decades American Presidents have tried to create a peace process to end Arab-Israeli tensions. The first step came in 1979, when President Jimmy Carter persuaded Egypt and Israel to sign a peace treaty. In May 1994 Israel and the Palestine Liberation Organization (PLO) signed an agreement that granted Palestinians self-rule in areas occupied by Israel. In October 1994, President Bill Clinton helped Israel and Jordan negotiate a peace treaty ending hostilities between them.

Despite the initial success of the Arab-Israeli peace process, the Middle East has not grown more secure. One source of tension is the rise of Islamic fundamentalism, a conservative religious movement that aims to replace **secular,** or nonreligious, governments with Islamic rule. Fundamentalists control Iran, and they pose a serious threat to stability in Egypt, Algeria, and other Arab countries.

South Africa

Until recently a majority of South Africa's population was denied many basic rights, including the right to vote. The nation followed a policy called **apartheid,** a government plan of racial segregation and discrimination against the country's black population. Under apartheid a small white minority ran the country.

Apartheid divided South Africa for many years. The ruling minority resisted any change, despite trade sanctions and political pressure from other nations. Change finally came in 1991, when South African President F. W. de Klerk announced plans to abolish all apartheid laws. In April 1994, South Africa held its first elections open to all South Africans. Nelson Mandela, a popular black leader held as a political prisoner for many

End of Apartheid   Nelson Mandela and F. W. de Klerk joined hands to celebrate the results of South Africa's 1994 elections.   *What was significant about this election?*

years, was elected president. The process continued with the ratification of a new constitution in 1996.

Other Areas of Africa

Crises in Liberia, Somalia, and Rwanda have commanded the attention of the world in recent years. All three countries have been embroiled in civil wars. The United States sent troops to Somalia in an effort to get food to starving people. It also took part in UN efforts to monitor human rights abuses in Rwanda.

Throughout the rest of Africa, the United States has kept a lower profile. It has watched from the sidelines as many African nations have moved toward democracy. The future is uncertain, however. Change may also bring increased ethnic tensions that could erupt as they did in Liberia, Somalia, and Rwanda.

Haitian Turmoil Haitian refugees detained at Guantanamo Bay hoped to be allowed to enter the United States. *What caused the Haitians to flee their home?*

Latin America and the Caribbean

The United States has always had a special relationship with nations in Latin America and the Caribbean. Even during our country's most isolationist periods, the United States maintained strong ties in the region. It often became involved in the internal affairs of Caribbean and Central American nations, following an **interventionist** policy.

In recent years immigration has been a source of conflict between the United States and countries south of its border. The wealth and opportunities of the United States have attracted millions of immigrants from the poorer countries of Latin America. Many people in the United States are now calling for stricter immigration laws to reduce the number of immigrants.

Changing Trade Policies

Another source of tension is economic competition. In some cases competition has led to tariffs and other trade barriers that have hindered economic cooperation. Passage of the North American Free Trade Agreement (NAFTA) in 1993 has helped open the market with Mexico. Chile signed the agreement in 1994, and it may be expanded to include other Latin American countries at a later date.

Change in trade policy reflects an important development throughout Latin America—its nations are becoming increasingly democratic. In Brazil, Chile, and a number of other countries, dictatorships and military rule have given way to elected civilian governments. With greater democracy has come greater stability.

Cuba and Haiti

Two Caribbean countries—Cuba and Haiti—have raised special concerns. The United States has considered Cuba a threat to national security since 1959, when Fidel Castro established a communist dictatorship there. This threat has declined since the collapse of the Soviet Union, Cuba's major ally and source of financial support. Cuba now suffers from severe shortages of food and other products, and the country seems on the verge of collapse. The United States continues to maintain a trade embargo against Cuba, and relations between the two countries remain tense.

The United States has a long history in Haiti. Between 1915 and 1934, the United States occupied Haiti because of political turmoil and violence there. In the years since, Haiti has struggled with poverty and dictatorship.

Relations With China China's communist government has introduced some economic reforms, but human rights abuses continue. *What reforms has China introduced to improve its economy?*

In December 1990, Jean-Bertrand Aristide was elected president of Haiti. Nine months later Haitian military leaders ousted the president and expelled him from the country. A period of military dictatorship followed. During this period many Haitian refugees fled to the United States.

In July 1994, the UN authorized an invasion of Haiti by a multinational force led by the United States. Faced with the threat of invasion, the Haitian military leaders agreed to step down and let Aristide resume office. As part of the agreement, thousands of American troops landed in Haiti in September 1994 to monitor the transition. The Americans turned over the peacekeeping duties to UN forces in March 1995.

In December 1995, Aristide's former prime minister, Rene Preval, was elected president. When Preval took office in 1996, he became the first democratically elected Haitian president to succeed another democratically elected president.

Asia and the Pacific Rim

Asia is another area of special interest to American foreign policy. It contains powerful communist nations that still pose a threat to world peace. It also contains some of the strongest and most rapidly growing economies in the world.

China

China, the most populous nation in the world, remains a communist dictatorship. Its Communist party denies citizens basic political rights, but it no longer tries to regulate the entire economy. Since the mid-1980s, China has passed economic reforms designed to improve its economy and form ties with noncommunist nations. It now encourages foreign investment and allows some Chinese citizens to experiment with capitalism.

China remains a totalitarian state, however. In 1989 army troops crushed pro-democracy demonstrations in the capital city of Beijing. Human rights abuses continue. China also maintains its nuclear capability, and it sells weapons and missiles to countries such as Iran.

In the past the United States linked trade with China to human rights reform. Yet China offers an enormous market for American goods. In 1994 President Clinton announced that trade with China would be on a most-favored-nation basis. The United States would encourage trade despite continued abuses. Then in 1995 President Clinton threatened to impose trade sanctions on China because of a dispute over unauthorized Chinese copies of American products. China finally agreed to introduce reforms. Relations between the two countries will be difficult, however, until the political situation in China stabilizes.

North Korea

Communism also persists in North Korea. This country presents another potential danger. For many years it has been isolated from most of the world, and it is very unpredictable. One recent cause for alarm was North Korea's efforts to develop nuclear weapons. Because of its militant communist government and its history, North Korea remains a threat to the stability of the region.

Vietnam

Vietnam is familiar to Americans because of our nation's experience in the Vietnam War. Although still a communist country, Vietnam has started to reform its economy and open its borders to foreign trade and investment. In 1994 the United States ended its 19-year trade embargo of Vietnam because of the government's cooperation in returning the remains of American soldiers killed in the war.

Economic Success Stories

The Asian nations that border the Pacific Ocean, the so-called Pacific Rim nations, include some of the world's most rapidly growing economies. Thirty years ago South Korea, Taiwan, and Singapore were still developing nations. Even Japan was considered a secondary economic power. Today these nations are the powerhouses of the Pacific, and they are strong economic competitors to the United States.

Trade barriers these nations and the United States erected have hindered completely free and open trade. In recent years, however, the Pacific Rim nations have begun working with the United States and other nations to reduce or eliminate trade tariffs and other economic barriers to promote free trade and stimulate global economic cooperation.

★ SECTION 3 REVIEW ★

UNDERSTANDING VOCABULARY
Define nuclear proliferation, secular, apartheid, interventionist.

REVIEWING OBJECTIVES
1 How have recent events in Europe affected the United States?

2 What are some of the sources of tension in the Middle East and Africa?

3 What interests does the United States have in Latin America and the Caribbean?

4 What major challenges does the United States face in Asia and the Pacific Rim?

How to Read a Natural Resource Map

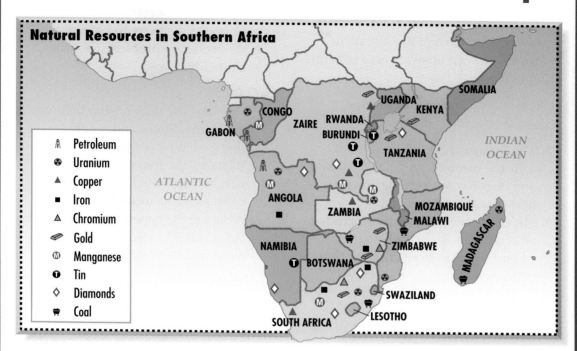

Natural Resources in Southern Africa

Key:
- Petroleum
- Uranium
- Copper
- Iron
- Chromium
- Gold
- Manganese
- Tin
- Diamonds
- Coal

M aps that provide information on a specific topic are called special-purpose maps. They may show the population density in a region, how people use the land, or where natural resources are located.

What This Map Shows

A natural resource map shows the location of materials—such as petroleum, minerals, and trees—that people take from the earth to use for manufacturing and other needs. The map on this page indicates where major mineral and petroleum resources are located in the southern part of the African continent. The map key explains what mineral each symbol on the map represents. Use the map and key to answer the questions that follow.

CITIZENSHIP IN ACTION

1 Which country has the greatest concentration of different kinds of minerals? What kinds of minerals are found there?

2 How many nations have deposits of iron?

3 Do the nations of southern Africa have petroleum resources? How do you know?

4 Which mineral seems to be most scarce? Which minerals are the most plentiful in this part of the world?

5 How might a natural resource map be used to draw conclusions about relations between countries?

Identifying Key Terms

Choose the vocabulary term that best completes each of the sentences below. Write your answers on a separate sheet of paper.

embargo   isolationism   diplomacy
apartheid   secular   disarmament

1. The President hoped to arrive at a solution through _____, by talking and negotiating with the other nation's leader.
2. Efforts to solve the conflict included an economic _____, which prevented any supplies from crossing the nation's borders.
3. By trying to avoid any entanglements with other countries, the nation was following a policy of _____.
4. At one time the United States imposed trade sanctions on South Africa because of its policy of _____.
5. One aim of the conservative religious movement known as Islamic fundamentalism is to replace _____ governments.
6. Negotiations were underway to reduce the number of nuclear weapons and to bring about complete _____.

Reviewing the Main Ideas

SECTION 1
1. How can foreign policy be carried out through trade measures?
2. How has the arms control issue changed since the 1970s?

SECTION 2
3. What actions can the UN Security Council take to try to keep peace?
4. What current problems face the United Nations?

SECTION 3
5. How has the relationship between the United States and South Africa changed in recent years?
6. What are the major sources of tension between the United States and Latin America today?
7. What are the benefits and disadvantages of the United States policy toward trade with China?

Critical Thinking

SECTION 1
1. **Developing a Point of View** Do you think the United States should continue to help Russia? Explain why or why not.

SECTION 2
2. **Evaluating Information** What do you think is the most important role of the United Nations in the world today? Why?

SECTION 3
3. **Analyzing Information** How do you think the United States should deal with regional conflicts in other parts of the world?

Reinforcing Citizenship Skills

In an atlas, locate maps that show the natural resources available in European countries. List the countries and their major resources. Write an opinion on how you think the location of these resources might affect relations among the nations in this part of the world. Present your report to the class.

Cooperative Learning

Some people have criticized the United Nations because they feel that small nations, which contribute little financial support, have too much power in the organization. Other people argue that power in the United Nations should not be related to the amount a nation can contribute. In groups of four, prepare arguments, pro or con, for debating the following statement: The United States should reduce its financial support to the UN.

Focusing on Your Community

Interview several members of your community, including relatives and neighbors, to find out their views on United States foreign policy. Find out how they feel about United States policy toward one particular nation, such as Russia, China, Haiti, Cuba, or Bosnia. Prepare an oral report to present to the class.

Technology Activity

Using a Word Processor

Use sources in your school or public library or search the Internet to learn about current American relations with any country you choose. If you use the Internet, you may wish to use the following key words to focus your search: **state department, foreign relations, White House.** Use a word processor to write a report about what you learn.

Analyzing Visuals

The United Nations has often been required to act as a peacekeeper in conflicts around the world. Study the political cartoon below, which illustrates the UN's role in the conflict in Bosnia. Then answer the questions that follow.

1. What does the UN tank represent?
2. What has the tank fired at the Serbs?
3. What does the UN's form of ammunition suggest about its ability to force both sides to keep the peace?
4. What do you think would be the result of the UN's effort?

THE UN FIRES BACK AT THE SERBS

An Interdependent World

CIVIC PARTICIPATION

We live in an interdependent world. Vast international communication and transportation networks link people and nations around the globe.

Contact a local business or organization that is connected in some way with other nations. Perhaps it has branch offices in other countries or sponsors activities there. Find out about these international connections and how they have affected the business or organization.

Working in Your Community

Next ask family members and neighbors about ways in which your community is connected to other parts of the world. Prepare a short fact sheet on the international connections of your community and give it to your local library. ■

Your Civics Journal

As you study this chapter, pay attention to world events. Make a list in your civics journal of the ways in which international developments can affect your life. Next to each entry, note what you, as an individual, can do about these developments.

Earth Day celebration ➤

The Global Economy and Environment

FOCUS

TERMS TO KNOW

interdependence, protectionism, free trade, acid rain, greenhouse effect, conservation, nonrenewable resource, renewable resource

OBJECTIVES

- Discuss some of the characteristics of global **economic development and trade.**

- Explain how nations are interdependent in regard to environmental **pollution and conservation.**

- Identify and describe several major **world health** problems.

Today every country depends on other countries for some of the things it needs to survive. The United States depends on Saudi Arabia and other countries for oil. Russia depends on the United States and other countries for agricultural products. The relationship among nations in which they depend on one another for products, services, and raw materials is called **interdependence.**

Economic Development and Trade

Intense competition and economic cooperation characterize today's global, interdependent economy. A country's economic success depends a great deal on how it deals with this competition and how it cooperates with other nations.

Economic Development

Although the economies and interests of the world's developed and developing nations are quite different, they are interdependent. The prosperous industrial nations depend on developing nations for raw materials such as iron ore, nickel, and zinc and for crops such as sugarcane and rice. The poorer, developing nations of the world depend on industrial nations for manufactured goods such as cars, computers, and machinery.

Global Interdependence

Global interdependence has been a major factor in the economic success of some developing nations. During the

Interdependence   Industrialized nations depend on developing nations for crops such as rice.   *For what do developing nations depend on industrial nations?*

International Cooperation Leaders of the world's major industrialized nations attend regular summits to discuss trade and economic matters. *What are some problems associated with international trade?*

past 30 years, for example, international trade has given a big boost to the economies of South Korea, Taiwan, and Singapore. The British colony of Hong Kong has also been successful in developing its economy. In 1997 Hong Kong became part of China. The Chinese government has said that it will allow Hong Kong to continue operating a capitalist economy.

Many industrial nations try to help developing nations improve their economies through foreign aid and technical assistance. American businesses help by investing money to build factories, which provide jobs and training. United States citizens help developing nations by serving as volunteers to teach important skills such as modern methods of farming.

Global Trade

The most important aspect of economic interdependence is global trade. Trade involves both competition and cooperation. Nations compete for markets for their products. They also cooperate to make trade beneficial for everyone involved.

Global trade has many advantages. Businesses can make greater profits by selling to a large world market. Increased competition among businesses worldwide may result in lower prices for consumers and a greater range of products from which they can choose.

Global trade can also lead to problems. Competition can cost some workers their jobs, and businesses may lose money to foreign competitors. Furthermore, if a country buys more products than it sells in the world market, it has a trade deficit, which may damage its economy.

Nations often try to reduce trade deficits and economic competition by placing tariffs on foreign goods. The policy of erecting tariff barriers is called **protectionism.** Protectionist policies often harm the economies of nations and the global economy. They may cause price increases, making consumers pay more for products. They may also lead to trade wars, in which nations set up greater trade barriers and try to block more products from entering the country. Trade wars can create serious tensions between nations.

Trade Agreements

Many countries now support a policy of **free trade** that aims to eliminate tariffs and other economic barriers. The North American Free Trade Agreement (NAFTA), which took effect in January 1994, will gradually abolish all trade barriers between the United States, Mexico, and Canada. An even more ambitious trade agreement is the General Agreement on Tariffs and Trade (GATT). This agreement, involving more than 150 nations, created the World Trade Organization (WTO) that will work to reduce tariffs among all members and eliminate quotas on imported goods.

Pollution and Conservation

The world is not only economically interdependent. It is also environmentally interdependent. When one country pollutes its environment, the effects often extend far beyond its borders.

Pollution

Although pollution is found in all parts of the world, some of the worst situations are in countries that tried to industrialize rapidly. In Russia and the nations of eastern Europe, for example, efforts to industrialize without concern for the environment have caused severe pollution. In developing nations, lack of adequate sanitation or other pollution controls has often resulted in serious problems.

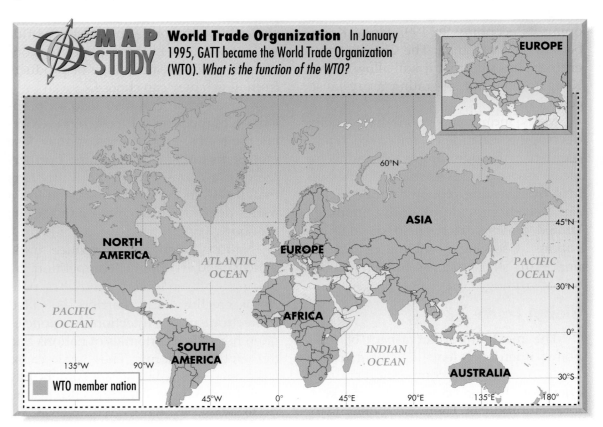

MAP STUDY

World Trade Organization In January 1995, GATT became the World Trade Organization (WTO). *What is the function of the WTO?*

EUROPE

WTO member nation

Careers

Customs Inspector

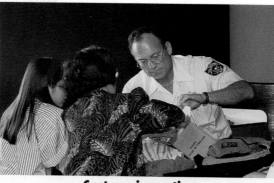

Customs inspection

When traveling to other countries, you have to pass through "customs." Customs inspectors are responsible for enforcing laws that regulate the flow of goods into a country.

Duties

The United States Customs Service employs thousands of customs inspectors. Much of their work is done behind the scenes, where they process applications for goods entering the country and inspect shipments that arrive. Customs inspectors also work in public. They examine the belongings of travelers entering the United States to look for prohibited items such as narcotics, animals, and plants. Customs inspectors also check travelers' purchases. If the value of the goods exceeds a certain amount, the traveler must pay a duty, or tax.

Education

Customs inspectors must be high school graduates and have some further education or law enforcement experience. It is useful for customs workers to know a foreign language and to take courses in business and law. To become a customs inspector, an applicant must pass a civil service test. Customs workers may be stationed at any port or point of entry along the United States border or at any international airport within the United States.

School to WORK

Write to or e-mail the United States Customs Service to learn what types of jobs they have available as well as the qualifications required. Use the information you receive to create a help wanted bulletin board. If possible, illustrate the bulletin board.

The effects of water and air pollution extend far from the source. Oil from a damaged tanker spreads along the coastline, killing fish and wildlife. A chemical called sulfur dioxide released by coal-burning factories is carried hundreds of miles through the air. The sulfur dioxide mixes with water vapor and later falls to earth as **acid rain.** Thus sulfur dioxide from factories in the Midwest may fall as acid rain in Canada, damaging forests and raising the acid level in hundreds of Canadian lakes. The higher acid level of the water kills many fish. The United States and Canada have formed a joint commission to explore solutions to the acid rain problem.

The Greenhouse Effect

The burning of coal and oil also contributes to the **greenhouse effect,** a gradual warming of the atmosphere. When burned, these products release carbon

Conserving Resources   New England's once-thriving fishing industry is now paying the price for overfishing.   *What are some of the benefits of conserving resources?*

dioxide and other gases into the atmosphere. As these gases build, the effect is like that of a greenhouse, allowing the sun's heat to enter the atmosphere but preventing it from escaping.

The destruction of forests contributes to the greenhouse effect because trees absorb carbon dioxide. Trees are the earth's natural protection against carbon dioxide buildup. As millions of acres of forest—particularly in Latin America—are cut down each year, this natural protection is lost. Up to now the greenhouse effect has caused only minor problems. Experts disagree over whether global warming is a temporary or a long-term trend.

Conservation

To help the environment, countries must work to end pollution within their own borders. They must also work with other nations to solve pollution problems that extend beyond national borders. An important way of controlling pollution is through **conservation,** or efforts to limit the use of resources that cause pollution.

These resources are classified as nonrenewable or renewable. **Nonrenewable resources,** such as oil and minerals, are resources that are gone forever once they are used. **Renewable resources,** such as trees and fish, are resources that grow back or renew themselves. Renewable resources can become scarce if they are used too rapidly. One of the world's richest fishing grounds, in the Atlantic Ocean, has a shortage of some species of fish because too many have been removed. As a result, the fishing industry in New England is on the verge of collapse.

Results of Conservation

Conserving resources will help ensure that they are available when they are needed. Conservation can also help lessen the impact of pollution. Conserving gasoline cuts back on the amount of gases that pollute the atmosphere. Conserving forests slows global warming by leaving more trees to absorb carbon dioxide.

Some people criticize conservation efforts, claiming that they slow economic growth by making resources unavailable. Others argue that a lack of conservation may produce short-term economic benefits but result in long-term problems. Not dealing with air pollution, for example, may lead to changes in climate, destruction of forests and lakes, and more health problems as people breathe polluted air.

Global Environment

In recent years many nations have become increasingly concerned about the global environment. In 1992 a major conference on the environment was held in

Rio de Janeiro, Brazil. This Earth Summit brought together representatives from 178 nations, who discussed ways of protecting the environment. Leaders signed treaties, pledging to safeguard the diversity of animal and plant species and to halt global warming. Although the environment has already been damaged, further damage may be prevented if nations remain willing to cooperate.

World Health

The issue of world health is related to both the global economy and the environment because poverty and pollution affect people's health. Poor countries often lack adequate food, which results in hunger and malnutrition. They may also lack adequate sanitation, which can lead to the spread of disease. Both air and water pollution can contribute to illness.

Hunger

The most pressing health problem of developing nations is hunger. More than 1 billion people, many of them in developing nations, do not receive enough food. An estimated 15 million people, mostly children, die of hunger or hunger-related causes each year. As world population continues to grow, hunger will become an even greater problem for many nations.

Developed nations have worked hard to end world hunger. The United States and other countries have contributed billions of dollars' worth of food to developing countries. They have also contributed billions more in financial aid. Private organizations, such as Oxfam America, also raise millions of dollars each year for hunger relief.

Green Revolution   Improved farming techniques have helped farmers in developing nations grow more crops.   *What are some other achievements of the Green Revolution?*

Green Revolution

Much of this financial aid is spent on research. In the 1960s and 1970s, scientists developed better seeds and new fertilizers. These products, along with improved farming techniques, began the "Green Revolution," which enabled farmers in many developing nations to grow more and better crops. The Green Revolution had some success, but it did not end world hunger. Many developing nations could not afford new supplies and equipment. Others lacked adequate water to support modern farming methods. Population growth also outstripped the ability of many nations to meet their food needs even though they were using new crops and techniques.

A lack of food is not the only factor that contributes to hunger. Some countries lack transportation to get food from farms to markets. Droughts and floods

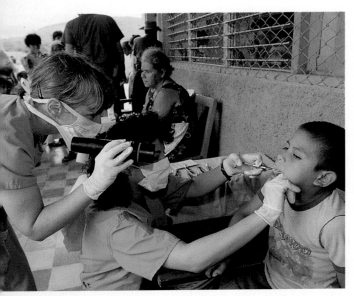

Health Infectious diseases are still major killers in many developing countries. *What factors contribute to the spread of these diseases?*

can wipe out food supplies. Political problems, such as civil wars, can also interfere with raising crops and distributing food.

Disease

Disease is a major health problem in all countries. Most developed nations, with their advanced medical care and "wonder drugs," have curbed many infectious diseases. In many developing nations, however, cholera, typhus, and other infectious diseases can erupt quickly and kill millions of people. These countries lack adequate medical care, and their poverty leads to malnutrition, unsanitary conditions, and other factors that contribute to disease.

In recent years new health dangers have emerged. In the early 1980s, the AIDS epidemic began. AIDS is a viral disease that destroys the body's immune system. By 1994 about 14 million people worldwide were infected with HIV, the virus that causes AIDS. So far, medical science has been unable to find a cure.

Some experts think that new diseases may be emerging because of changes in the environment. As people destroy tropical forests, they may release diseases that have remained hidden within animal populations. Some of these diseases can spread to people. The greatest danger is that such diseases could spread rapidly around the globe. Modern transportation allows disease to spread more quickly and to a wider area.

Fortunately, modern medicine has reduced the impact of many diseases. In 1994, for example, an outbreak of pneumonic plague in India was brought under control before it could reach epidemic proportions. The challenge is to find new medicines and techniques to fight diseases, both the old ones that still threaten human life and the new ones that may emerge in the future.

★ SECTION 1 REVIEW ★

UNDERSTANDING VOCABULARY
Define interdependence, protectionism, free trade, acid rain, greenhouse effect, conservation, nonrenewable resource, renewable resource.

REVIEWING OBJECTIVES

1 What are some of the characteristics of global economic development and trade?

2 In what ways are nations interdependent in regard to environmental pollution and conservation?

3 What are several major world health problems?

Using a Database

Adatabase can help you to organize information in a way that is most useful for you.

Learning the Skill

An electronic database is a collection of facts that has been stored in files on a computer. Information is organized in different fields. For example, one field might be the years in which an event takes place. Another field could be made up of the types of events. You can create your own database to best reflect your needs. When your database has been set up, you can tell the computer to search and retrieve information and display it on the screen.

Practicing the Skill

To build a database about environmental protection, follow these steps:

- Decide what you want to include. For example, do you want to include important events and influential people? Should you include dates when important legislation was enacted? Should you include specific statistics?

- Follow instructions in your computer program to set up fields. Then enter each item of data in its assigned field. Take as much time as you need to complete this step. Inaccurately placed information will be difficult to retrieve.

- Determine how you want to organize the facts in the database.

Keep in mind that you want this information to be more useful to you. You want to make it as easy to use as possible.

- Follow the instructions in your computer program to sequence the information in order of importance.

- Check a reliable source to verify that you have all the information you need and that it is correct. You may add, delete, or change information. It will be easier, however, if you begin with as much information in your database as possible.

Balancing Accounts

APPLYING THE SKILL

Build a database to support a search for information about the greenhouse effect. Write a brief paragraph describing how your database is set up.

The Global Community

The world is so large and its challenges so complex that many people believe individuals cannot make a difference. When a flood in Bangladesh drowns several hundred thousand people, other people are sorry. When rain forests are destroyed, people may feel regret. When a government tortures its citizens, people get angry. These same people, however, often think they can do nothing about these situations.

Yet people can make a difference. Although the world is led by governments, it is made up of individuals. By themselves, individuals may seem weak, but they have imagination and energy. They can see problems and decide to do something about them.

Solving Environmental Problems

The environment is one area in which individuals can make a difference. As an individual, you can help preserve the environment by using resources wisely and avoiding waste. Recycle paper, cardboard, glass, aluminum, and plastic. Turn off lights and appliances when you are not using them. Open windows instead of using an air conditioner. Buy products made of recycled material and products in reusable containers.

You can also help by staying informed about environmental issues and expressing your opinions to local, state, or national leaders and to those responsible for environmental problems. Finally, you can volunteer your time to help improve the environment. Most communities have local organizations devoted to

Individuals Making a Difference

Many people volunteer their time and energy to help improve their community environment. *What are some actions an individual can take to help preserve the environment?*

AMOUNT OF TRASH GENERATED PER PERSON PER DAY IN THE U.S.

2.65 pounds — 1960
3.58 pounds — 1986
4.00 pounds — 2000*

* projected by the Environmental Protection Agency

the environment. Join an organization and help with its activities. Volunteer groups can help clean up dump sites, set up recycling centers, and educate others about environmental issues.

A popular environmental slogan is, "Think globally; act locally." The point of this is that, by doing something on a local level, you will also be helping the global environment.

Safeguarding Human Rights

Human rights is a continuing concern of the United States. Throughout its history, our nation has struggled to preserve human rights both here and around the world.

One important human rights issue is the plight of refugees. During this century millions of people have fled their homelands because of war, persecution, famine, or natural disaster. These refugees are at the mercy of their host nation. They are often forced to live in crowded refugee camps, where life can be extremely harsh.

The stream of refugees fleeing their homelands continues today. In 1994 ethnic strife in the African nation of Rwanda caused millions to flee the country. In Europe many fled war-torn Bosnia when war began there in 1992. In both of these countries, many people fled because of the fear of **genocide,** the mass killing of an entire group of people. The crisis in Rwanda began as a genocidal attack of one ethnic group against another. In Bosnia thousands of Bosnian Muslims were massacred under a policy of "ethnic cleansing."

Another human rights issue is the persecution of individuals or groups who hold different ideas and beliefs from the people in power. Sometimes those in power persecute people of a different racial or ethnic background.

The Healing Power of Rain Forests

Nearly half of all medicines prescribed in this country come from plants, animals, and microorganisms found in the environment. In searching for new drugs, many pharmaceutical companies are focusing on tropical rain forests. Scientists estimate that a staggering 30 to 50 million species of living things remain to be discovered in the world, many of them in the rain forests. No one knows what new wonder drugs these might produce.

Several pharmaceutical companies now provide funds to governments and private organizations in countries such as Costa Rica that have large rain forests. This money is used for rain forest research. In return, the pharmaceutical companies receive plant and animal samples they can screen for medicinal value.

Pharmaceutical companies stand to reap huge profits from these new medicines. A welcome consequence is that the world's rain forests may be preserved for their healing potential rather than being destroyed for lumber, ranches, and farmland.

Rain forest research

Campaigning for Human Rights   American citizens can influence the outcome of events around the world.   *How can they do this?*

The United States and many other nations are concerned about these human rights issues, and they use foreign policy, trade, and other means to try to deal with the problems. As an individual, you can help by speaking out on human rights issues and contributing to organizations that are devoted to human rights. Let your elected leaders know your opinions, and encourage them to sponsor human rights initiatives. You can also safeguard human rights by respecting others in your own community and by speaking out against violence and hatred toward others.

Participating in World Affairs

Before you can do anything to change the world, you must become familiar with the world and the events that happen in it. The best way to do this is to read newspapers and magazines and watch TV news reports. If you have a home computer, it can also connect you to information about the world.

Learning About the World

If you really want to understand world affairs, you must also learn how people in other countries think and feel. To do this, you can read translations of articles and books by foreign writers, study a foreign language so that you can read foreign newspapers and magazines, and make an effort to meet and talk with people from different backgrounds. You might also be able to travel to other countries or talk to people who have done so.

As an individual, you can help relieve poverty, hunger, and disease throughout the world by contributing time or money to charitable organizations, such as the

Multicultural Awareness Studying a foreign language is a stepping-stone toward understanding another culture. *Why is it important to learn about people in other countries?*

International Red Cross and the United Nations Children's Fund (UNICEF), which send medicine and food that help save human lives.

Participating Through the Political Process

Your greatest power to change the world, however, lies in your rights as an American citizen. Your voice, through your elected representatives, can affect world affairs. You can campaign and vote for candidates whose views you support. You can write to your representatives and express your ideas and opinions. You can join a political party or other political organization and work together with citizens who share your ideas. One day you may even decide to run for office yourself.

The United States is a powerful and respected nation, and the decisions of its leaders affect the lives of people throughout the world. As a citizen of the United States, your decisions also affect the lives of all people.

★ SECTION 2 REVIEW ★

UNDERSTANDING VOCABULARY
Define genocide.

REVIEWING OBJECTIVES

1 What are three things individuals can do to help solve environmental problems?

2 What can individuals do to help safeguard human rights?

3 What can individuals do to assume a greater role in participating in world affairs?

Identifying Key Terms

Choose the vocabulary term that best completes each of the sentences below. Write your answers on a separate sheet of paper.

renewable resource   greenhouse effect
free trade   protectionism
nonrenewable resource   conservation

1. The President's belief in _____ caused him to oppose tariffs.
2. Some scientists are concerned about global warming brought on by the _____.
3. The country had a policy of _____, with high trade tariffs.
4. Trees are an example of a(n) _____, which can be replenished with careful management.
5. Minerals are an example of a(n) _____, which cannot be restored once it is gone.
6. The use of resources that cause pollution can be limited through _____.

Reviewing the Main Ideas

SECTION 1

1. In what ways are industrial and developing nations interdependent?
2. How can protectionist trade policies harm the economies of nations and the global economy?
3. What are the possible consequences of acid rain?

SECTION 2

4. What can individuals do to help preserve the environment?
5. How do their rights as citizens give Americans the power to change the world?

Critical Thinking

SECTION 1

1. **Evaluating Information**   What do you think are the best approaches to solving environmental problems and preventing further destruction of the earth's environment?

SECTION 2

2. **Analyzing Information**   Why is it important for individual citizens to become involved in world issues?

Reinforcing Citizenship Skills

Study a recent issue of a local or national newspaper. Read through the lead article on the front page. Then write down the byline and the dateline and a summary of what the article is about. Answer the questions Who, What, When, Where, Why, and How. Share your summary with the class.

Cooperative Learning

With three other students, choose an environmental problem such as water pollution or forest destruction. Collect as many facts and figures as you can about this problem. Identify important sources of information and groups that are working to solve this particular problem. Present your findings to the class.

Focusing on Your Community

What opportunities exist in your community for individual involvement on issues? For example, does your community have a recycling program? Are

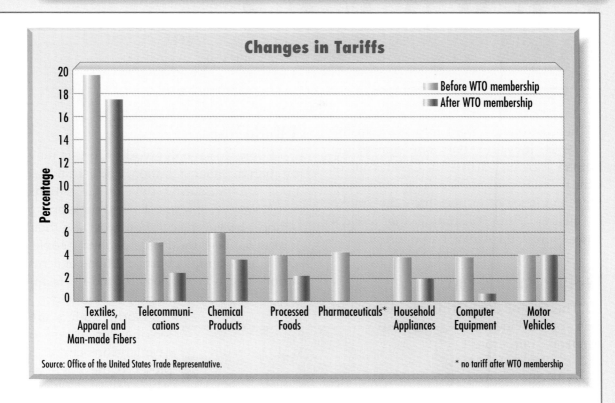

Changes in Tariffs

Source: Office of the United States Trade Representative.

* no tariff after WTO membership

there any community groups working to reduce or prevent environmental pollution? Are there any groups working to reduce world hunger? Find out what you might do to assist in these efforts. Report your findings to the class.

Technology Activity

Using E-Mail
Search the Internet to find the e-mail address of a local television station or newspaper. You may wish to use the following key words to focus your search: **newspapers, television call letters.** Then select a world event or issue that you recorded in your civics journal. Expand on your ideas by

sending electronic mail to a local newspaper or television station. Describe the event or issue, discuss how it can affect people's lives, and explain what you think individuals can do.

Analyzing Visuals

The General Agreement on Tariffs and Trade created the World Trade Organization (WTO). Study the graph above, which shows changes in tariffs for WTO members. Then answer the questions.

1. What is the average proposed tariff reduction on various products?
2. Which products would experience the greatest tariff reductions?
3. For which products would the tariff reductions be the smallest?

CLOSEUP
SAVING THE FORESTS

When astronauts went into space in the 1960s, they saw only one sign of the human race on earth—the Great Wall of China. Today astronauts can see other, startling, evidence of human life—the smoke of gigantic fires consuming the world's largest forest, the Amazon rain forest.

The Importance of Forests

The fate of the world may depend in part on saving the Amazon rain forest and other forests around the world. The use of such fuels as oil and coal is greatly increasing the amount of carbon dioxide in the atmosphere. This carbon dioxide is a major contributor to the greenhouse effect, a gradual warming of the earth's tempera-

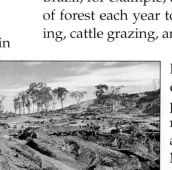

Rain forest destruction

tures. Forests help reduce the greenhouse effect by absorbing carbon dioxide from the air.

There are other reasons to save the world's forests as well. When forests and their habitats are destroyed, many species of plants and animals become extinct. Destroying forests can also cause or worsen natural disasters such as floods and droughts.

A World Issue

Efforts to save the world's forests may pit nation against nation. Industrial nations are pressuring developing nations to preserve virgin forests. The developing nations, however, feel they must use their forests to meet the needs of their people. Brazil, for example, burns millions of acres of forest each year to create land for farming, cattle grazing, and new settlements.

World leaders are looking for ways to ease tensions and also preserve the environment. The World Bank and the International Monetary Fund have instituted programs to reward developing nations that conserve forests and penalize those that do not. World leaders now recognize that these problems cross international borders and affect all of the world's people.

CLOSEUP REVIEW

1 Why is the Amazon rain forest so valuable to the world?

2 What are some ways that governments can save forests?

Multimedia Activities

Surfing the "Net"

The United Nations

The United Nations (UN) has close to 200 member nations working together to promote peace. To find out more information about the UN look on the Internet.

Getting There

Follow the steps below to find out information about the United Nations.

1. Go to your favorite search engine.
2. Type in the phrase *United Nations*. Following this phrase, enter words like those below to focus your search:

information	general
history	facts

The search engine should provide you with a number of links to follow. Links are pointers to different sites on the Internet and commonly appear as blue underlined words.

What to Do When You Are There

1. Click on the links to navigate through the pages of information.
2. Using a word processor, create a fact sheet of answers to the following questions:
   - What does the UN logo symbolize? When was the UN officially established?
   - What is the main purpose of the United Nations? Why was it originally created?
   - Who are the five permanent members of the Security Council? Why have there been demands to reform the Security Council?
3. Present your findings to the class.

Focus on Government

Global Interdependence

The world today includes many different economic and political systems. Because of the technological revolution these systems are becoming increasingly interdependent. The **Focus on Government** programs referenced below help explain these systems and their interdependence.

Side 3, Chapter 56
Lecture Launcher:
Comparing Systems of Government

Setting Up the Video

Using a bar code reader or an electronic keypad, work with a group of your classmates to view these video segments of the videodisc **Focus on Government:**

Side 3, Chapter 57
Lecture Launcher:
Comparing Economic Systems

Side 3, Chapter 58
Lecture Launcher:
Our Interdependent World

Hands-On Activity

Look through magazines to find advertisements for products that you use. Clip the advertisements and do research on the products to find out how and where they are made. Construct a bulletin board display featuring the advertisements and the information you have learned about the production process.

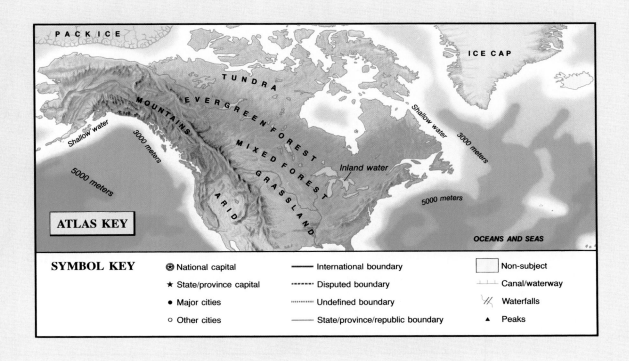

ATLAS KEY

SYMBOL KEY

- ⊕ National capital
- ★ State/province capital
- ● Major cities
- ○ Other cities

———— International boundary
-------- Disputed boundary
·········· Undefined boundary
———— State/province/republic boundary

☐ Non-subject
⊢⊢⊢ Canal/waterway
Waterfalls
▲ Peaks

UNITED STATES

- ◉ National capital
- ★ State capital
- ● Major city
- ○ Other city
- ─── International boundary
- ─── State boundary

| 0 | 150 | 300 Miles |
| 0 | 150 | 300 Kilometers |

Projection: Albers Equal Area

The United States   577

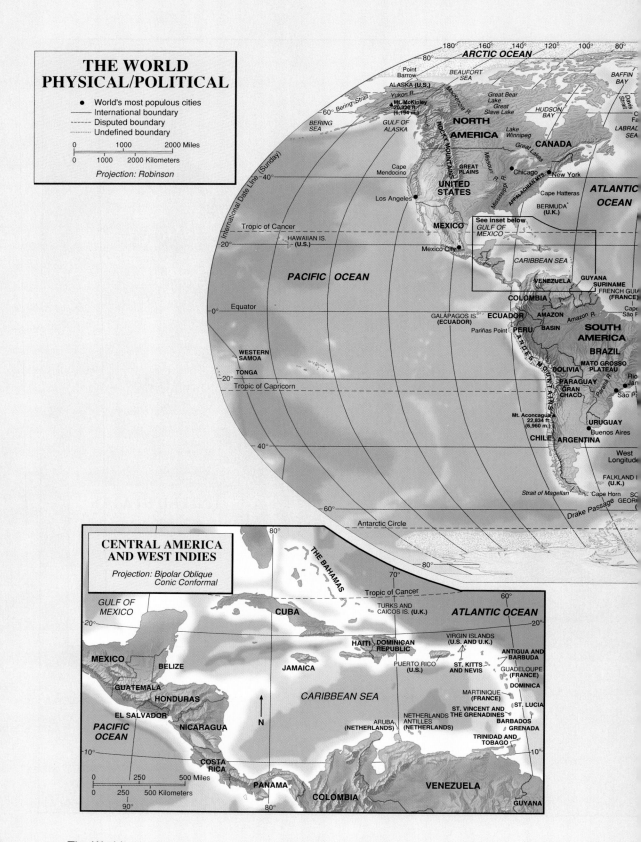

THE WORLD
PHYSICAL/POLITICAL

- ● World's most populous cities
- ⎯ International boundary
- ⎯ ⎯ Disputed boundary
- ⋯⋯ Undefined boundary

| 0 | 1000 | 2000 Miles |
| 0 | 1000 | 2000 Kilometers |

Projection: Robinson

180° 160° 140° 120° 100° 80°

ARCTIC OCEAN

BEAUFORT SEA

Point Barrow

ALASKA (U.S.)

Yukon R.

Mt. McKinley 20,320 ft. (6,194 m.)

Bering Strait

BERING SEA

GULF OF ALASKA

Cape Mendocino

Los Angeles

HAWAIIAN IS. (U.S.)

PACIFIC OCEAN

WESTERN SAMOA

TONGA

Mackenzie R.

Great Bear Lake

Great Slave Lake

NORTH AMERICA

ROCKY MOUNTAINS

Lake Winnipeg

Great Lakes

CANADA

HUDSON BAY

BAFFIN BAY

Davis Strait

LABRADOR SEA

GREAT PLAINS

UNITED STATES

Missouri R.

Mississippi R.

Chicago

New York

APPALACHIAN MTS.

Cape Hatteras

ATLANTIC OCEAN

BERMUDA (U.K.)

MEXICO

Mexico City

See inset below

GULF OF MEXICO

CARIBBEAN SEA

VENEZUELA

COLOMBIA

GUYANA

SURINAME

FRENCH GUIANA (FRANCE)

GALÁPAGOS IS. (ECUADOR)

ECUADOR

AMAZON

Amazon R.

Cape São R.

Pariñas Point

PERU

BASIN

SOUTH AMERICA

BRAZIL

BOLIVIA

MATO GROSSO PLATEAU

Paraná R.

Rio de Jan

São Pa

PARAGUAY

GRAN CHACO

Mt. Aconcagua 22,834 ft. (6,960 m.)

URUGUAY

Buenos Aires

CHILE

ARGENTINA

West Longitude

FALKLAND I (U.K.)

Strait of Magellan

Cape Horn

SC GEOR

Drake Passage

International Date Line (Sunday)

Tropic of Cancer

Equator

Tropic of Capricorn

80° 60° 40° 20° 0° 20° 40° 60°

Antarctic Circle

CENTRAL AMERICA AND WEST INDIES

Projection: Bipolar Oblique Conic Conformal

GULF OF MEXICO

MEXICO

BELIZE

GUATEMALA

HONDURAS

EL SALVADOR

NICARAGUA

PACIFIC OCEAN

COSTA RICA

PANAMA

COLOMBIA

THE BAHAMAS

CUBA

JAMAICA

HAITI

DOMINICAN REPUBLIC

TURKS AND CAICOS IS. (U.K.)

Tropic of Cancer

ATLANTIC OCEAN

VIRGIN ISLANDS (U.S. AND U.K.)

PUERTO RICO (U.S.)

ST. KITTS AND NEVIS

ANTIGUA AND BARBUDA

GUADELOUPE (FRANCE)

DOMINICA

MARTINIQUE (FRANCE)

ST. LUCIA

ST. VINCENT AND THE GRENADINES

CARIBBEAN SEA

ARUBA (NETHERLANDS)

NETHERLANDS ANTILLES (NETHERLANDS)

BARBADOS

GRENADA

TRINIDAD AND TOBAGO

VENEZUELA

GUYANA

N

| 0 | 250 | 500 Miles |
| 0 | 250 | 500 Kilometers |

90° 80° 70° 60°

20° 10°

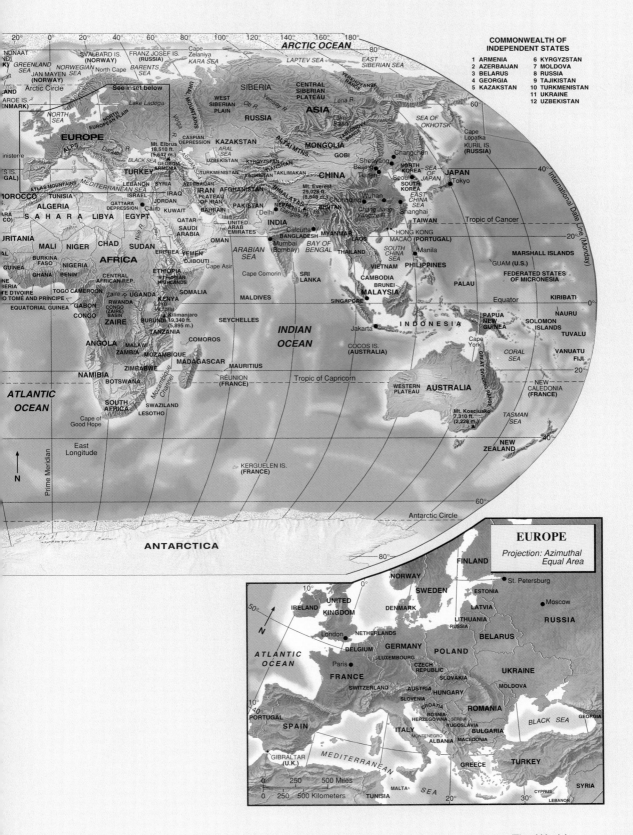

ARCTIC OCEAN

COMMONWEALTH OF
INDEPENDENT STATES

1	ARMENIA	6	KYRGYZSTAN
2	AZERBAIJAN	7	MOLDOVA
3	BELARUS	8	RUSSIA
4	GEORGIA	9	TAJIKISTAN
5	KAZAKSTAN	10	TURKMENISTAN
		11	UKRAINE
		12	UZBEKISTAN

EUROPE

Projection: Azimuthal
Equal Area

Consumer Prices, 1985–1995

Consumer prices rose more than 50 percent between 1985 and 1995.

*Base years 1982–1984 = 100

Source: *Economic Report of the President, 1995;* Department of Labor, Bureau of Labor Stastistics.

National Debt Per Capita, 1989–1996

The national debt per capita has reached almost $20,000.

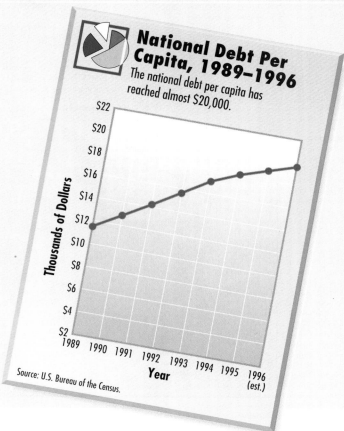

Source: U.S. Bureau of the Census.

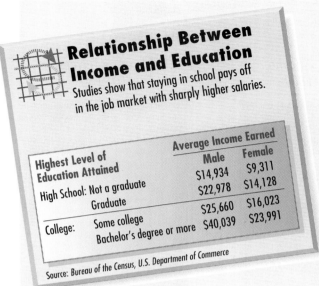

Relationship Between Income and Education

Studies show that staying in school pays off in the job market with sharply higher salaries.

Highest Level of Education Attained		Average Income Earned	
		Male	Female
High School:	Not a graduate	$14,934	$9,311
	Graduate	$22,978	$14,128
College:	Some college	$25,660	$16,023
	Bachelor's degree or more	$40,039	$23,991

Source: Bureau of the Census, U.S. Department of Commerce

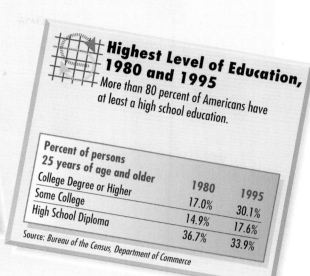

Highest Level of Education, 1980 and 1995

More than 80 percent of Americans have at least a high school education.

Percent of persons 25 years of age and older	1980	1995
College Degree or Higher	17.0%	30.1%
Some College	14.9%	17.6%
High School Diploma	36.7%	33.9%

Source: Bureau of the Census, Department of Commerce

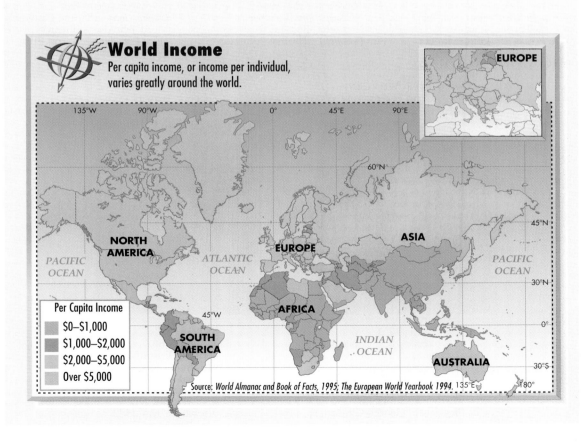

World Income

Per capita income, or income per individual, varies greatly around the world.

EUROPE

NORTH AMERICA
PACIFIC OCEAN
ATLANTIC OCEAN
EUROPE
ASIA
PACIFIC OCEAN
AFRICA
SOUTH AMERICA
INDIAN OCEAN
AUSTRALIA

Per Capita Income
- $0–$1,000
- $1,000–$2,000
- $2,000–$5,000
- Over $5,000

Source: World Almanac and Book of Facts, 1995; The European World Yearbook 1994.

PRESIDENTS OF THE UNITED STATES

1 *George Washington*
1789-1797

Born: 1732
Died: 1799
Born in: Virginia
Elected from: Virginia
Age when elected: 57
Occupations: Planter, Soldier
Party: None
Vice President: John Adams

2 *John Adams*
1797-1801

Born: 1735
Died: 1826
Born in: Massachusetts
Elected from: Massachusetts
Age when elected: 61
Occupation: Lawyer
Party: Federalist
Vice President: Thomas Jefferson

3 *Thomas Jefferson*
1801-1809

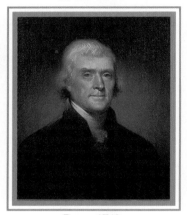

Born: 1743
Died: 1826
Born in: Virginia
Elected from: Virginia
Age when elected: 57
Occupations: Planter, Lawyer
Party: Republican**
Vice Presidents: Aaron Burr,
George Clinton

4 *James Madison*
1809-1817

Born: 1751
Died: 1836
Born in: Virginia
Elected from: Virginia
Age when elected: 57
Occupation: Politician
Party: Republican**
Vice Presidents: George Clinton,
Elbridge Gerry

5 *James Monroe*
1817-1825

Born: 1758
Died: 1831
Born in: Virginia
Elected from: Virginia
Age when elected: 58
Occupations: Politician, Lawyer
Party: Republican**
Vice President: Daniel D.
Tompkins

***The Republican party during this period developed into today's
Democratic party. Today's Republican party originated in 1854.*

PRESIDENTS OF THE UNITED STATES

6 John Quincy Adams
1825-1829

Born: 1767
Died: 1848
Born in: Massachusetts
Elected from: Massachusetts
Age when elected: 57
Occupation: Lawyer
Party: Republican**
Vice President: John C. Calhoun

7 Andrew Jackson
1829-1837

Born: 1767
Died: 1845
Born in: South Carolina
Elected from: Tennessee
Age when elected: 61
Occupation: Lawyer
Party: Democratic
Vice Presidents: John C. Calhoun,
Martin Van Buren

8 Martin Van Buren
1837-1841

Born: 1782
Died: 1862
Born in: New York
Elected from: New York
Age when elected: 54
Occupation: Lawyer
Party: Democratic
Vice President: Richard M.
Johnson

9 William H. Harrison
1841

Born: 1773
Died: 1841
Born in: Virginia
Elected from: Ohio
Age when elected: 68
Occupation: Soldier
Party: Whig
Vice President: John Tyler

10 John Tyler
1841-1845

Born: 1790
Died: 1862
Born in: Virginia
Elected as V. P. from: Virginia
Assumed presidency upon Harrison's death
Age when became President: 51
Occupation: Lawyer
Party: Whig
Vice President: None

PRESIDENTS OF THE UNITED STATES

11 James K. Polk
1845-1849

Born: 1795
Died: 1849
Born in: North Carolina
Elected from: Tennessee
Age when elected: 49
Occupation: Lawyer
Party: Democratic
Vice President: George M.
Dallas

12 Zachary Taylor
1849-1850

Born: 1784
Died: 1850
Born in: Virginia
Elected from: Louisiana
Age when elected: 64
Occupation: Soldier
Party: Whig
Vice President: Millard Fillmore

13 Millard Fillmore
1850-1853

Born: 1800
Died: 1874
Born in: New York
Elected as V.P. from: New York
Assumed presidency upon Taylor's death
Age when became President: 50
Occupation: Lawyer
Party: Whig
Vice President: None

14 Franklin Pierce
1853-1857

Born: 1804
Died: 1869
Born in: New Hampshire
Elected from: New Hampshire
Age when elected: 48
Occupation: Lawyer
Party: Democratic
Vice President: William R. King

15 James Buchanan
1857-1861

Born: 1791
Died: 1868
Born in: Pennsylvania
Elected from: Pennsylvania
Age when elected: 65
Occupation: Lawyer
Party: Democratic
Vice President: John C.
Breckinridge

16 Abraham Lincoln
1861-1865

Born: 1809
Died: 1865
Born in: Kentucky
Elected from: Illinois
Age when elected: 52
Occupation: Lawyer
Party: Republican
Vice Presidents: Hannibal
Hamlin, Andrew Johnson

17 Andrew Johnson
1865-1869

Born: 1808
Died: 1875
Born in: North Carolina
Elected as V.P. from: Tennessee
Assumed presidency upon Lincoln's death
Age when became President: 56
Occupations: Tailor, Politician
Party: Republican
Vice President: None

18 Ulysses S. Grant
1869-1877

Born: 1822
Died: 1885
Born in: Ohio
Elected from: Illinois
Age when elected: 46
Occupations: Farmer, Soldier
Party: Republican
Vice Presidents: Schuyler
Colfax, Henry Wilson

19 Rutherford B. Hayes
1877-1881

Born: 1822
Died: 1893
Born in: Ohio
Elected from: Ohio
Age when elected: 54
Occupation: Lawyer
Party: Republican
Vice President: William A.
Wheeler

20 James A. Garfield
1881

Born: 1831
Died: 1881
Born in: Ohio
Elected from: Ohio
Age when elected: 49
Occupations: Lawyer, Politician
Party: Republican
Vice President: Chester A. Arthur

PRESIDENTS OF THE UNITED STATES

21 Chester A. Arthur
1881-1885

Born: 1830
Died: 1886
Born in: Vermont
Elected as V.P. from: New York
Assumed presidency upon Garfield's death
Age when became President: 50
Occupation: Lawyer
Party: Republican
Vice President: None

22, 24 Grover Cleveland
1885-1889 1893-1897

Born: 1837
Died: 1908
Born in: New Jersey
Elected from: New York
Age when elected: 47; 55
Occupation: Lawyer
Party: Democratic
Vice Presidents: Thomas A. Hendricks, Adlai E. Stevenson

23 Benjamin Harrison
1889-1893

Born: 1833
Died: 1901
Born in: Ohio
Elected from: Indiana
Age when elected: 55
Occupation: Lawyer
Party: Republican
Vice President: Levi P. Morton

25 William McKinley
1897-1901

Born: 1843
Died: 1901
Born in: Ohio
Elected from: Ohio
Age when elected: 54
Occupation: Lawyer
Party: Republican
Vice Presidents: Garret Hobart, Theodore Roosevelt

26 Theodore Roosevelt
1901-1909

Born: 1858
Died: 1919
Born in: New York
Elected as V.P. from: New York
Assumed presidency upon McKinley's death
Age when became President: 42
Occupations: Author, Politician
Party: Republican
Vice President: Charles W. Fairbanks

PRESIDENTS OF THE UNITED STATES

27 *William H. Taft*
1909-1913

Born: 1857
Died: 1930
Born in: Ohio
Elected from: Ohio
Age when elected: 51
Occupation: Lawyer
Party: Republican
Vice President: James S. Sherman

28 *Woodrow Wilson*
1913-1921

Born: 1856
Died: 1924
Born in: Virginia
Elected from: New Jersey
Age when elected: 56
Occupation: College Professor
Party: Democratic
Vice President: Thomas R.
Marshall

29 *Warren G. Harding*
1921-1923

Born: 1865
Died: 1923
Born in: Ohio
Elected from: Ohio
Age when elected: 55
Occupations: Newspaper Editor,
Publisher
Party: Republican
Vice President: Calvin Coolidge

30 *Calvin Coolidge*
1923-1929

Born: 1872
Died: 1933
Born in: Vermont
Elected as V.P. from: Massachusetts
Assumed presidency upon Harding's death
Age when became President: 51
Occupation: Lawyer
Party: Republican
Vice President: Charles G. Dawes

31 *Herbert C. Hoover*
1929-1933

Born: 1874
Died: 1964
Born in: Iowa
Elected from: California
Age when elected: 54
Occupation: Geologist
Party: Republican
Vice President: Charles Curtis

PRESIDENTS OF THE UNITED STATES

32 Franklin D. Roosevelt
1933-1945

Born: 1882
Died: 1945
Born in: New York
Elected from: New York
Age when elected: 51
Occupation: Lawyer
Party: Democratic
Vice Presidents: John N. Garner,
Henry A. Wallace, Harry S Truman

33 Harry S Truman
1945-1953

Born: 1884
Died: 1972
Born in: Missouri
Elected as V.P. from: Missouri
Assumed presidency upon Roosevelt's death
Age when became President: 60
Occupation: Businessman
Party: Democratic
Vice President: Alben W. Barkley

34 Dwight D. Eisenhower
1953-1961

Born: 1890
Died: 1969
Born in: Texas
Elected from: New York
Age when elected: 62
Occupation: Soldier
Party: Republican
Vice President: Richard M.
Nixon

35 John F. Kennedy
1961-1963

Born: 1917
Died: 1963
Born in: Massachusetts
Elected from: Massachusetts
Age when elected: 43
Occupations: Author, Politician
Party: Democratic
Vice President: Lyndon B. Johnson

36 Lyndon B. Johnson
1963-1969

Born: 1908
Died: 1973
Born in: Texas
Elected as V.P. from: Texas
Assumed presidency upon Kennedy's death
Age when became President: 55
Occupations: Teacher, Politician
Party: Democratic
Vice President: Hubert H. Humphrey

37 Richard M. Nixon
1969-1974

Born: 1913
Died: 1994
Born in: California
Elected from: New York
Age when elected: 56
Occupations: Lawyer, Politician
Party: Republican
Vice Presidents: Spiro T.
Agnew, Gerald R. Ford

38 Gerald R. Ford
1974-1977

Born: 1913
Born in: Nebraska
Appointed by Nixon as V.P. upon
Agnew's resignation; assumed
presidency upon Nixon's resignation
Age when became President: 61
Occupations: Lawyer, Politician
Party: Republican
Vice President: Nelson A. Rockefeller

39 Jimmy Carter
1977-1981

Born: 1924
Born in: Georgia
Elected from: Georgia
Age when elected: 52
Occupations: Businessman,
Politician
Party: Democratic
Vice President: Walter F.
Mondale

40 Ronald Reagan
1981-1989

Born: 1911
Born in: Illinois
Elected from: California
Age when elected: 69
Occupations: Actor, Politician
Party: Republican
Vice President: George H.W. Bush

41 George H.W. Bush
1989-1993

Born: 1924
Born in: Massachusetts
Elected from: Texas
Age when elected: 64
Occupations: Businessman,
Politician
Party: Republican
Vice President: J. Danforth Quayle

42 William J. Clinton
1993-

Born: 1946
Born in: Arkansas
Elected from: Arkansas
Age when elected: 46
Occupations: Lawyer, Politician
Party: Democratic
Vice President: Albert Gore, Jr.

Most of the Presidents are portrayed in this section by their official White House portrait.

UNITED STATES FACTS

The Fifty States The number in parentheses is the order in which each state was admitted to the Union. For the original 13 states, this is the order in which each state approved the Constitution. Population figures are based on Census Bureau projections for 2000.

Alabama (22)
Admitted to the Union: 1819
Capital: Montgomery
Population: 4,451,000
State Bird: Yellowhammer
State Flower: Camellia
Yellowhammer State

Alaska (49)
Admitted to the Union: 1959
Capital: Juneau
Population: 653,000
State Bird: Willow ptarmigan
State Flower: Forget-me-not
The Last Frontier

Arizona (48)
Admitted to the Union: 1912
Capital: Phoenix
Population: 4,798,000
State Bird: Cactus wren
State Flower: Flower of saguaro cactus
Grand Canyon State

Arkansas (25)
Admitted to the Union: 1836
Capital: Little Rock
Population: 2,631,000
State Bird: Mockingbird
State Flower: Apple blossom
Land of Opportunity

California (31)
Admitted to the Union: 1850
Capital: Sacramento
Population: 32,521,000
State Bird: California valley quail
State Flower: Golden poppy
Golden State

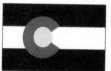

Colorado (38)
Admitted to the Union: 1876
Capital: Denver
Population: 4,168,000
State Bird: Lark bunting
State Flower: Rocky Mountain columbine
Centennial State

Connecticut (5)
Admitted to the Union: 1788
Capital: Hartford
Population: 3,284,000
State Bird: American Robin
State Flower: Mountain laurel
Nutmeg State

Delaware (1)
Admitted to the Union: 1787
Capital: Dover
Population: 768,000
State Bird: Blue Hen chicken
State Flower: Peach blossom
First State

Florida (27)
Admitted to the Union: 1845
Capital: Tallahassee
Population: 15,233,000
State Bird: Mockingbird
State Flower: Orange blossom
Sunshine State

Georgia (4)
Admitted to the Union: 1788
Capital: Atlanta
Population: 7,875,000
State Bird: Brown thrasher
State Flower: Cherokee rose
Peach State

Hawaii (50)
Admitted to the Union: 1959
Capital: Honolulu
Population: 1,257,000
State Bird: Nene
State Flower: Hibiscus (yellow)
Aloha State

Idaho (43)
Admitted to the Union: 1890
Capital: Boise
Population: 1,347,000
State Bird: Mountain bluebird
State Flower: Syringa
Gem State

UNITED STATES FACTS

Illinois (21)
Admitted to the Union: 1818
Capital: Springfield
Population: 12,051,000
State Bird: Cardinal
State Flower: Violet
Prairie State

Indiana (19)
Admitted to the Union: 1816
Capital: Indianapolis
Population: 6,045,000
State Bird: Cardinal
State Flower: Peony
Hoosier State

Iowa (29)
Admitted to the Union: 1846
Capital: Des Moines
Population: 2,900,000
State Bird: Eastern goldfinch
State Flower: Wild rose
Hawkeye State

Kansas (34)
Admitted to the Union: 1861
Capital: Topeka
Population: 2,668,000
State Bird: Western meadowlark
State Flower: Sunflower
Sunflower State

Kentucky (15)
Admitted to the Union: 1792
Capital: Frankfort
Population: 3,995,000
State Bird: Kentucky cardinal
State Flower: Goldenrod
Bluegrass State

Louisiana (18)
Admitted to the Union: 1812
Capital: Baton Rouge
Population: 4,425,000
State Bird: Pelican
State Flower: Magnolia
Pelican State

Maine (23)
Admitted to the Union: 1820
Capital: Augusta
Population: 1,259,000
State Bird: Chickadee
State Flower: White pine cone and tassel
Pine Tree State

Maryland (7)
Admitted to the Union: 1788
Capital: Annapolis
Population: 5,275,000
State Bird: Baltimore oriole
State Flower: Black-eyed Susan
Free State

Massachuetts (6)
Admitted to the Union: 1788
Capital: Boston
Population: 6,199,000
State Bird: Chickadee
State Flower: Mayflower
Bay State

Michigan (26)
Admitted to the Union: 1837
Capital: Lansing
Population: 9,679,000
State Bird: Robin
State Flower: Apple blossom
Wolverine State

Minnesota (32)
Admitted to the Union: 1858
Capital: St. Paul
Population: 4,830,000
State Bird: Common loon
State Flower: Showy lady slipper
North Star State

Mississippi (20)
Admitted to the Union: 1817
Capital: Jackson
Population: 2,816,000
State Bird: Mockingbird
State Flower: Flower of evergreen magnolia
Magnolia State

Missouri (24)
Admitted to the Union: 1821
Capital: Jefferson City
Population: 5,540,000
State Bird: Bluebird
State Flower: Hawthorn
Show Me State

Montana (41)
Admitted to the Union: 1889
Capital: Helena
Population: 950,000
State Bird: Western meadowlark
State Flower: Bitterroot
Treasure State

UNITED STATES FACTS

Nebraska (37)
Admitted to the Union: 1867
Capital: Lincoln
Population: 1,705,000
State Bird: Western meadowlark
State Flower: Goldenrod
Cornhusker State

North Carolina (12)
Admitted to the Union: 1789
Capital: Raleigh
Population: 7,777,000
State Bird: Cardinal
State Flower: Dogwood
Tar Heel State

Nevada (36)
Admitted to the Union: 1864
Capital: Carson City
Population: 1,871,000
State Bird: Mountain bluebird
State Flower: Sagebrush
Sagebrush State

North Dakota (39)
Admitted to the Union: 1889
Capital: Bismarck
Population: 662,000
State Bird: Western meadowlark
State Flower: Wild prairie rose
Sioux State

New Hampshire (9)
Admitted to the Union: 1788
Capital: Concord
Population: 1,224,000
State Bird: Purple finch
State Flower: Purple lilac
Granite State

Ohio (17)
Admitted to the Union: 1803
Capital: Columbus
Population: 11,319,000
State Bird: Cardinal
State Flower: Scarlet carnation
Buckeye State

New Jersey (3)
Admitted to the Union: 1787
Capital: Trenton
Population: 8,178,000
State Bird: Eastern goldfinch
State Flower: Purple violet
Garden State

Oklahoma (46)
Admitted to the Union: 1907
Capital: Oklahoma City
Population: 3,373,000
State Bird: Scissor-tailed fly-catcher
State Flower: Mistletoe
Sooner State

New Mexico (47)
Admitted to the Union: 1912
Capital: Santa Fe
Population: 1,860,000
State Bird: Roadrunner
State Flower: Yucca
Land of Enchantment

Oregon (33)
Admitted to the Union: 1859
Capital: Salem
Population: 3,397,000
State Bird: Western meadowlark
State Flower: Oregon grape
Beaver State

New York (11)
Admitted to the Union: 1788
Capital: Albany
Population: 18,146,000
State Bird: Bluebird
State Flower: Rose
Empire State

Pennsylvania (2)
Admitted to the Union: 1787
Capital: Harrisburg
Population: 12,202,000
State Bird: Ruffed grouse
State Flower: Mountain laurel
Keystone State

Rhode Island (13)
Admitted to the Union: 1790
Capital: Providence
Population: 998,000
State Bird: Rhode Island Red
State Flower: Violet
Ocean State

Vermont (14)
Admitted to the Union: 1791
Capital: Montpelier
Population: 617,000
State Bird: Hermit thrush
State Flower: Red clover
Green Mountain State

South Carolina (8)
Admitted to the Union: 1788
Capital: Columbia
Population: 3,858,000
State Bird: Carolina wren
State Flower: Carolina yellow
jessamine
Palmetto State

Virginia (10)
Admitted to the Union: 1788
Capital: Richmond
Population: 6,997,000
State Bird: Cardinal
State Flower: American dog-
wood
Old Dominion

South Dakota (40)
Admitted to the Union: 1889
Capital: Pierre
Population: 777,000
State Bird: Ringnecked pheasant
State Flower: American
pasqueflower
Coyote State

Washington (42)
Admitted to the Union: 1889
Capital: Olympia
Population: 5,858,000
State Bird: Willow goldfinch
State Flower: Coast rhododen-
dron
Evergreen State

Tennessee (16)
Admitted to the Union: 1796
Capital: Nashville
Population: 5,657,000
State Bird: Mockingbird
State Flower: Iris
Volunteer State

West Virginia (35)
Admitted to the Union: 1863
Capital: Charleston
Population: 1,841,000
State Bird: Cardinal
State Flower: Rhododendron
Mountain State

Texas (28)
Admitted to the Union: 1845
Capital: Austin
Population: 20,119,000
State Bird: Mockingbird
State Flower: Bluebonnet
Lone Star State

Wisconsin (30)
Admitted to the Union: 1848
Capital: Madison
Population: 5,326,000
State Bird: Robin
State Flower: Wood violet
Badger State

Utah (45)
Admitted to the Union: 1896
Capital: Salt Lake City
Population: 2,207,000
State Bird: Seagull
State Flower: Sego lily
Beehive State

Wyoming (44)
Admitted to the Union: 1890
Capital: Cheyenne
Population: 525,000
State Bird: Meadowlark
State Flower: Indian paintbrush
Equality State

The District of Columbia and various territories of the United States also have flags.

District of Columbia
Population: 523,000
Bird: Wood thrush
Flower: American beauty rose

Territories

American Samoa
Capital: Pago Pago
Population: 52,860*
Flower: Paogo
Date of Acquisition: 1899

Puerto Rico
Capital: San Juan
Population: 3,522,037*
Bird: Reinita
Flower: Maga
Date of Acquisition: 1898

Guam
Capital: Agaña
Population: 133,152*
Bird: Fruit dove
Flower: Bougainvillea
Date of Acquisition: 1898

Virgin Islands
Capital: Charlotte Amalie
Population: 101,809*
Bird: Yellow breast
Flower: Yellow elder or
      yellow trumpet
Date of Acquisition: 1917

Northern Marianas
Population: 48,581*
Date of Acquisition: 1947

*1993 Census Bureau estimates

A

accountable having to explain one's actions to the voters (p. 161)

acid rain rain containing sulfur dioxide, which destroys forests and pollutes water (p. 561)

acquittal a vote of not guilty (p. 408)

administration officials who help the President plan and carry out policy (p. 251)

adversary the opposing side in a dispute (p. 298)

affirmative action programs to help minority groups and women gain access to jobs and opportunities (p. 130)

alien a person who lives in a country but is not a citizen of that country (p. 11)

alliance a formal agreement or union among nations (p. 538)

ambassador an official representative of a country's government (p. 243)

amend to change (p. 42)

amendment any change in the Constitution (p. 92)

amnesty a pardon granted to members of a group who have broken the law (p. 248)

Anti-Federalist a person who opposed the Constitution before 1789 (p. 61)

apartheid a government plan of racial segregation and discrimination against a portion of the population (p. 549)

apathy a lack of interest (p. 170)

appellate jurisdiction the authority to review cases from lower district courts or from federal regulatory agencies (p. 288)

apportionment the distribution of legislative seats according to population (p. 320)

appropriations funds reserved for a specific use (p. 224)

arbitration settling a dispute by agreeing to accept a third party's decision (p. 457)

arraignment a hearing in which a suspect is charged and pleads guilty or not guilty (p. 406)

B

bail money paid to the court by an accused person to guarantee that he or she will appear for trial (p. 104)

balanced budget a budget in which expenditures do not exceed revenues (p. 479)

bankruptcy a legal statement that one cannot pay one's debts (p. 496)

bench trial a trial by a judge (p. 386)

beneficiary the person named to receive money in an insurance policy (p. 498)

bias a one-sided or slanted point of view (p. 193)

bicameral having two legislative houses (p. 212)

bill of attainder a law that punishes a person accused of a crime without a fair hearing in court (p. 383)

bond a note from the government or a corporation promising to repay money with interest by a certain date (p. 357)

boycott a refusal to buy goods or use services as a means of protest (p. 37)

brief a written argument prepared by an attorney (p. 297)

budget a plan for managing and spending money (p. 476)

bureaucracy a government or other organization with many different departments and complex rules and procedures (p. 242)

business cycle the ups and downs of the economy (p. 444)

by-election a special election to replace a member of Parliament in Great Britain (p. 513)

C

cabinet a group of presidential advisers made up of the heads of the executive departments, the Vice President, and other officials (p. 236)

campaign an organized effort to gather support for a candidate (p. 154)

candidate a person seeking an elected government office (p. 144)

canvassing going through neighborhoods asking for votes or taking public opinion polls (p. 176)

capital goods the buildings and machines needed to make goods and to provide services (p. 425)

capitalism an economic system in which individuals put their money into a business in hopes of making a profit (p. 431)

caucus a meeting of political party members to conduct party business (p. 172)

censure a legislature's formal disapproval of one of its members (p. 217)

census a process for counting a nation's population (p. 17)

certificate of deposit a savings account in which money deposited for a certain period earns a fixed rate of interest (p. 494)

charter a plan of government (p. 330)

checks and balances a system in which each branch of government is able to limit the power of the other branches (p. 65)

circuit the area of jurisdiction of a federal court of appeals (p. 288)

citizen a member of a community with a government and laws (p. 4)

civics the study of citizenship and government (p. 4)

civil case a case in which one party takes legal action against another party (p. 282)

civil law law concerned with disputes between people or between the government and its citizens (p. 390)

civil rights the rights of a citizen (p. 129)

civil servant a government employee (p. 277)

closed shop a business that hires only union members (p. 456)

cloture a procedure used in the Senate to limit debate on a bill (p. 229)

coalition a political alliance with another party or parties (p. 147)

cold war a conflict between nations involving a clash of ideas (p. 518)

collateral property used as a guarantee that a loan will be repaid (p. 461)

collective bargaining negotiations between business owners and labor unions about conditions and terms of employment (p. 455)

collective security political and military alliances formed to protect member nations from aggression by other nations (p. 539)

colonists members of a colony; those who settle in a new place (p. 32)

colony a group of people in one place who are ruled by the government of another place (p. 32)

command economy an economy in which the government controls the means of production and makes all economic decisions (p. 430)

common law a system of law that is based on precedent (p. 30)

common stock a share of a corporation that pays its owner a dividend if the corporation makes a profit (p. 438)

community a group of people who share the same interests and concerns (p. 137)

commute to reduce a criminal sentence (p. 316)

compact an agreement, or contract, made among a group of people (p. 33)

complaint a formal notice that a lawsuit is being brought (p. 399)

compromise an agreement in which each side agrees to give up something to get something more important (p. 59)

concurrent jurisdiction shared authority of courts to hear and decide a case (p. 284)

concurrent powers the powers shared by the national and state governments (p. 89)

concurring opinion an opinion written by a justice who supports the majority decision but has different reasons (p. 299)

confederation a group of individuals or states that band together for a common purpose (p. 42)

conference committee a joint committee of Congress consisting of members of the House and the Senate to work on the details of a proposed law (p. 220)

conglomerate a company formed by a merger of companies that supply different goods and services (p. 451)

congress a formal meeting at which representatives discuss matters of common concern (p. 38)

consensus a general agreement (p. 525)

conservation protection of public lands and natural resources (pp. 265, 562)

constituency the people in a particular election district (p. 513)

constituent a person from a legislator's district (p. 214)

constitutional monarchy a government that has a monarch who serves as the symbolic head of state (p. 512)

consul an official who heads a consulate (p. 260)

consulate a government office in a foreign country that protects the interests of its citizens (p. 260)

consumer a person who buys and uses products (p. 423)

contempt of court a charge of obstructing or interfering with the judicial process (p. 385)

contract a formal agreement between two or more parties (p. 391)

cooperative an organization formed to share business costs or to buy and sell goods at the lowest possible price (p. 439)

corporation a large business that has many owners (p. 436)

coup an attempt to overthrow a government (p. 518)

court of appeals a federal court that hears only cases on appeal from lower district courts or from federal agencies (p. 288)

court-martial a trial before a panel of military officers (p. 289)

criminal case a case in which a person is accused of breaking the law (p. 282)

cross-examination the process of questioning a witness at a trial or hearing to check or discredit the testimony (p. 407)

D

deduction money for items such as medical expenses that is subtracted from income before taxes are paid (p. 470)

defendant a person who is accused of a crime or is being sued (p. 391)

deficit an excess of government expenses over revenues (p. 479)

delegate a representative to a meeting (p. 38)

demand the amount of a good or service that consumers are willing to buy (p. 423)

democracy a government in which citizens hold the power to rule and to make the laws (p. 7)

deport to expel from the country (p. 12)

depression a severe economic recession (p. 445)

deregulation the removal of government regulations or control (p. 452)

devaluation a lowering of the value of a nation's currency in relation to other currencies (p. 531)

developed nation a country with a strong industrial economy (p. 545)

developing nation a country that is struggling to build an industrial economy and to meet the basic needs of the people (p. 544)

dictatorship a government controlled by one person or a small group of people (p. 6)

diplomacy the process of conducting relations with foreign governments (p. 538)

disarmament the reduction of arms (p. 540)

discrimination unfair and less equal treatment of a particular group (p. 129)

dissenting opinion the written statement of a judge who disagrees with the majority decision (p. 299)

district court the lowest level of the federal court system (p. 285)

dividend a share of the profit paid to the stockholders of a corporation (p. 438)

division of labor a method of production in which each worker does just one part of the job (p. 426)

docket a schedule of cases to be heard by a court of law (p. 297)

domestic relating to matters within a country (p. 252)

double jeopardy putting a person on trial again for a crime of which he or she was acquitted (p. 103)

draft to call up people for military service (p. 132)

due process of law procedures established by law and guaranteed by the Constitution (p. 103)

duties the things we are required to do (p. 131)

E

Electoral College a group of people who elect the President and the Vice President (p. 60)

electoral vote votes cast by members of the Electoral College (p. 181)

electorate the people who are eligible to vote in an election (p. 169)

embargo the act of prohibiting the shipment of goods into or out of a country (p. 539)

embassy a government office, headed by an ambassador, set up in a foreign nation (p. 260)

eminent domain the right of the government to take private property for public use (p. 103)

entrepreneur a person who starts a new business (p. 426)

enumerated powers the powers of the federal government specifically mentioned in the Constitution (p. 89)

environment the surroundings of a person or community (p. 138)

ex post facto law a law that would allow a person to be punished for an action that was not against the law when the action took place (p. 383)

excise tax a tax on certain products (p. 472)

exclusive jurisdiction the authority of courts to hear and decide cases (p. 284)

executive having the power to carry out laws (p. 65)

executive agency an independent agency responsible for dealing with specialized areas of government (p. 271)

executive agreement an agreement between the President and the leader of another country (p. 244)

executive order a rule the President issues that has the force of law (p. 242)

exemption the amount of money subtracted from income for each person before determining taxes (p. 469)

exit poll a survey taken at polling places of how people voted (p. 180)

expenditures money spent by a government (p. 476)

export to sell goods to other countries (p. 60)

expressed powers congressional powers specifically stated in the Constitution (p. 223)

expulsion forcing a member of Congress accused of a serious crime to resign (p. 216)

extradition returning a suspected criminal to the state where the crime was committed (p. 312)

F

faction a small group within a political party (p. 526)

federalism the system in which the power to govern is shared between the national government and the states (p. 308)

Federalist a person who supported the Constitution and a strong national government before 1789 (p. 61)

federal system a political system in which the power is shared between a national government and the states (p. 56)

felony a serious crime such as robbery or murder (p. 324)

filibuster a tactic for defeating a bill in the Senate by talking until the bill's sponsor withdraws it (p. 229)

fiscal policy the way the government taxes citizens and spends money (p. 446)

fixed expenses expenses that are the same from month to month (p. 487)

flexible expenses expenses that vary from month to month (p. 487)

foreign aid money, military assistance, food, or other supplies given to help other countries (p. 538)

foreign policy a government's plan for dealing with other nations (pp. 260, 536)

franking privilege the right of members of Congress to send work-related mail without paying postage (p. 216)

fraud taking property by dishonest means or by misrepresentation (p. 402)

fraudulent making false claims (p. 502)

free enterprise an economic system in which individuals are free to own businesses, and competition helps determine prices (p. 432)

free trade a policy that aims to eliminate tariffs and other economic barriers among nations (p. 560)

G

genocide the systematic killing of a group of people (p. 567)

gerrymandering dividing a state into odd-shaped election districts for political reasons (p. 214)

glasnost the policy of "openness" introduced in the former Soviet Union by Mikhail Gorbachev (p. 518)

government the power or authority that rules a country (p. 4)

government corporation a business owned and operated by the government that provides services to the public (p. 273)

grand jury a group of citizens that decides whether there is sufficient evidence to accuse someone of a crime (p. 385)

grant-in-aid federal funds given to a state or local government for a specific purpose (p. 480)

grassroots beginning with the people (p. 160)

greenhouse effect the gradual warming of the atmosphere caused by a buildup of carbon dioxide and other gases (p. 561)

gross domestic product (GDP) the total value in dollars of all the final goods and services produced within the nation in a year (p. 447)

gross income the total amount of money a business or individual makes (p. 426)

H

home rule the power granted by state legislatures to cities to manage their own affairs (p. 343)

hung jury a jury that cannot agree on a verdict (p. 408)

I

immigrant a person who comes to a country with the intention of living there permanently (p. 11)

immunity legal protection against prosecution (p. 216)

impartial not favoring any particular side (p. 193)

impeach to accuse a government official of wrongdoing (p. 224)

implied powers congressional powers not stated specifically in the Constitution but suggested by the Constitution's necessary and proper clause (p. 94)

income tax a tax on the money an individual or business earns (p. 469)

incorporate to receive a charter from the state to form a corporation (p. 437)

independence self-reliance and freedom from outside control (p. 38)

indict to formally accuse a person of a crime (p. 102)

inferior court a lower court (p. 282)

inflation a general rise in the prices of goods and services (p. 448)

infrastructure a community's system of roads, bridges, water, and sewers (p. 354)

initiative procedure by which citizens can propose laws through the use of a petition (p. 182)

injunction a court order commanding a person or group to stop a certain action (p. 399)

insurance a type of investment that protects a policyholder against unpredictable loss, illness, or injury (p. 497)

interdependence the reliance of countries on one another for products, services, and raw materials (p. 558)

interest a fee paid for the use of money (p. 460)

interest group people with a similar point of view who work together to promote that point of view (p. 189)

internationalism the idea that individual nations promote common aims through membership in an international organization (p. 543)

interpret to decide the meaning of (p. 42)

interventionist becoming involved in the internal affairs of another country (p. 550)

investment the purchase of something that is expected to increase in value (p. 494)

isolationism a policy of avoiding alliances and remaining neutral in international disputes (p. 539)

J

joint committee a committee that includes members of both houses of Congress (p. 220)

judicial having the power to decide how laws should be applied in individual cases (p. 65)

judicial review the power of the Supreme Court to review federal and state laws and decide whether they are in accord with the Constitution (p. 292)

jurisdiction the authority to hear and decide a case in a court of law (p. 283)

jurisprudence the study of the law (p. 379)

justice of the peace a judge in a local court who hears minor cases (p. 323)

juvenile a person not yet legally an adult (p. 410)

juvenile delinquent a child or teenager who commits a serious crime or repeatedly breaks the law (p. 410)

L

labor union an organization of workers that tries to improve the working conditions and wages of its members (p. 454)

laissez-faire an economic approach in which government does not interfere with business (p. 450)

landfill a site for burying waste (p. 367)

larceny the unlawful taking of property (p. 402)

lawsuit a legal action in which a person sues to collect damages for some harm that is done (p. 391)

legislative having the power to make laws (p. 65)

legislature a group of people who make laws for a state or country (p. 28)

liability insurance insurance that protects property owners against injuries that occur on their property (p. 498)

libel the criminal act of printing lies about other people (p. 109)

limited liability the risk of losing only a limited sum because ownership is shared by many people (p. 438)

line-item veto the option to approve certain parts of a bill and to veto others (p. 320)

literacy test a test to prove that a voter can read, write, and understand public issues (p. 169)

lobby to try to persuade government officials to support the goals of a special-interest group (p. 201)

lobbyist a person who tries to persuade government officials to support a particular group or position (p. 201)

M

magistrate an official in a district court who issues court orders and determines whether cases should be brought to trial (p. 287)

magistrate court a local court that handles minor cases (p. 323)

majority more than half (p. 147)

majority leader the leader of the majority party in each house of Congress (p. 219)

majority opinion a statement explaining the majority view in a case in which the justices are divided (p. 299)

mandatory sentence the punishment required by law for a certain crime (p. 404)

market economy an economy in which individuals make economic decisions according to the principle of supply and demand (p. 431)

marketing getting goods to consumers who want them (p. 427)

marshal a district court official who arrests suspects, delivers defendants to court, and serves subpoenas (p. 287)

mass media sources of news information that are widely distributed, including television, radio, newspapers, and magazines (p. 189)

master plan a document submitted by a planning commission that states community goals and how to achieve them (p. 355)

mayor the chief executive of a city government (p. 343)

mayoralty the office of a mayor (p. 530)

mediation a way of settling disputes in which a third party listens to both sides and then suggests a solution (p. 457)

medicaid government-funded health insurance for people with low incomes (p. 499)

medicare government-funded health insurance for people age 65 and older (p. 499)

member-at-large a representative of a city council who is elected by the entire city (p. 343)

mercantilism the theory that a country should sell more goods to other countries than it buys (p. 36)

merger a joining of two or more companies to form a larger one (p. 450)

merit system the practice of giving government jobs to those who are most qualified (p. 276)

metropolitan area a city and its suburbs (p. 346)

migration a mass movement of people from one area to another (p. 22)

minority leader the leader of the minority party in each house of Congress (p. 219)

misdemeanor a relatively minor crime (p. 323)

mixed economy an economy that includes both private ownership and government guidance and regulation (p. 432)

monetary policy the way the government regulates the amount of money in circulation (p. 446)

monopoly the control of the supply of a good or service by one company or by a small group of people (p. 450)

N

national debt the total amount the government owes on money it has borrowed (p. 479)

national security the ability to keep the country safe from attack or harm (p. 536)

naturalization the process by which resident aliens become citizens (p. 14)

nominate to choose a candidate to run for political office (p. 153)

nonpartisan not involving political parties (p. 163)

nonprofit organization an organization that exists to provide goods or services, not to make a profit (p. 439)

nonrenewable resource a resource, such as petroleum, that is gone forever once it is used (p. 562)

nuclear proliferation the growth and spread of nuclear weapons (p. 547)

O

offender a person who breaks the law (p. 410)

oligarchy a system of government in which a small group of people hold power (p. 524)

open shop a business or factory where workers can choose whether or not to join a union (p. 456)

ordinance a law, usually of a city or county (p. 331)

original jurisdiction the authority of a court to be the first to hear a case (p. 285)

override to defeat a veto on a bill (p. 65)

P

PAC Political Action Committee; an organization established to raise money to support an issue or candidate (p. 177)

pardon a declaration of forgiveness and freedom from punishment (p. 248)

Parliament the British legislature (p. 28)

parliamentary government a government in which the elected representatives of the legislative body have both legislative and executive power (p. 512)

parole an early release from prison (p. 316)

partnership a business owned by two or more people (p. 436)

party whip a Republican or Democrat in each house of Congress who tries to persuade party members to vote together on issues (p. 219)

passport an official document that identifies a traveler as a citizen of a particular country (p. 260)

patronage giving jobs or special favors to loyal party members (p. 154)

penal code the criminal laws of a state (p. 402)

perestroika Mikhail Gorbachev's plan to reform the political and economic structure of the former Soviet Union (p. 518)

petition a formal request for government action (p. 109)

petit jury a jury that hears trials (p. 386)

pigeonhole to set a congressional bill aside in committee without considering it (p. 228)

plaintiff a person or party filing a lawsuit (p. 391)

plank an item of a political party's platform (p. 157)

platform a political party's statement of its goals and positions on public issues (p. 157)

plea bargain an agreement to plead guilty to a crime in exchange for a reduced sentence (p. 325)

plurality the largest number of votes or seats in a legislature (p. 147)

pocket veto the President's power to kill a bill, if Congress is not in session, by not signing it for 10 days (p. 231)

political machine a strong party organization that can control political appointments and deliver votes (p. 156)

polling place a place where votes are cast (p. 179)

pollster a person who takes polls, or samples, of public opinion (p. 190)

poll tax a sum of money paid in exchange for the right to vote (p. 114)

popular sovereignty the idea that people should have the right to rule themselves (p. 87)

popular vote votes cast directly by the people (p. 181)

Preamble the introduction to the United States Constitution (p. 63)

precedent a ruling that is used as the basis for a judicial decision in a later, similar case (p. 30)

precinct a geographic area that contains a specific number of voters (p. 155)

preferred stock stock that earns a fixed amount each year the corporation makes a profit (p. 438)

premium a payment made to an insurance company for coverage (p. 497)

president *pro tempore* a senior member of the majority party who presides over the Senate in the absence of the Vice President (p. 219)

primary election an election in which party members choose candidates to run for office (p. 173)

principal the original amount of money that was borrowed and on which interest is paid (p. 495)

priorities the goals a community considers most important (p. 355)

privatization the selling of state-owned companies to private entrepreneurs (p. 531)

profit the income that remains after a business has paid its expenses, taxes, and other costs (p. 426)

progressive tax a tax in which people who earn more money pay more taxes (p. 468)

propaganda techniques used to promote a particular person or idea (p. 175)

property tax a tax based on the value of a person's property (p. 471)

proposition a petition asking for a new law (p. 182)

prosecution the state's side of the proceedings in a criminal trial (p. 407)

protectionism the use of tariffs or other barriers to protect a nation's industries (p. 559)

public pertaining to the people in a community, or for the use of all (p. 137)

public opinion the attitudes of a large group of people on a particular issue or person (p. 188)

public policy a government policy (p. 352)

Q

quota a specific limit on the number of persons allowed to enter a country (p. 19)

R

ratify to vote approval of (p. 42)

recall an election in which voters can remove a public official from office (p. 183)

recession a slowdown in economic activity (p. 445)

recycling the reusing of old materials to make new ones (p. 367)

red tape inefficiency caused by too many rules and regulations (p. 274)

referendum an election in which voters can approve or reject a local or state law (p. 183)

refugee a person who flees his or her homeland because of war, famine, or political oppression (p. 20)

regressive tax a tax in which all people pay the same amount (p. 468)

regulatory commission an independent agency that protects the public by controlling certain types of businesses and industries (p. 272)

remand to return a case to a lower court for a new trial (p. 288)

renewable resource a resource that grows back or renews itself (p. 562)

repeal to cancel a law (p. 37)

repossess to take back property bought on credit because of nonpayment (p. 496)

representative democracy a government that consists of representatives elected by the citizens (p. 7)

reprieve an order to delay carrying out a sentence or court order (p. 248)

reserved powers the powers the Constitution gives to the states (p. 89)

resources the materials, people, and money available to a community (pp. 355, 422)

responsibilities obligations people fulfill voluntarily (p. 131)

revenue the money governments receive from taxes and other sources (p. 466)

roll-call vote a procedure in which each person is called upon to announce his or her vote (p. 229)

S

sales tax a tax placed on the sale of goods (p. 471)

search warrant a legal document that allows law enforcement officials to search a suspect's home for evidence (p. 102)

secular nonreligious (p. 549)

segregation separation of people because of race or ethnic origin (p. 130)

select committee a temporary committee of Congress formed to deal with a particular issue (p. 220)

seniority system a system that gives the most desirable committee assignments to members of Congress who have served the longest (p. 221)

session the period of time when Congress meets (p. 217)

shadow cabinet the leaders of the opposition party in Great Britain who follow the activities of the government's cabinet members and are ready to take over, should the government fall (p. 515)

slander the criminal act of lying about another person to harm that person's reputation (p. 108)

social security federal insurance, financed by a special tax, that provides benefits for people who are retired (p. 498)

sole proprietorship a business that one person owns (p. 435)

sovereignty the supreme power to govern (p. 524)

speaker of the house the leader of the House of Representatives, chosen by the majority party (p. 219)

special district a unit of government set up to deal with a single issue or to provide a single service (p. 340)

split ticket the practice of voting for candidates of different parties in an election (p. 180)

spoils system the practice of giving jobs as a reward for party loyalty (p. 276)

standard of living the quality of people's lives determined by the goods and services they have and their leisure time (p. 448)

standing committee a permanent committee of Congress that focuses on a particular area (p. 219)

standing vote a method of voting in which people stand to support or oppose a measure under consideration (p. 229)

stare decisis the practice of using earlier judicial rulings as a basis for deciding cases (p. 380)

stock a share of ownership in a company (p. 437)

stockholder a person who buys shares of ownership in a corporation (p. 437)

straight ticket the practice of voting for all the candidates of one political party (p. 180)

strike a refusal to work until an employer meets certain conditions (p. 455)

subcommittee a group within a standing committee of Congress that handles special problems (p. 220)

subpoena a court order requiring a person to appear in court (p. 287)

suffrage the right to vote (p. 113)

suit the formal complaint to the court in a legal action (p. 283)

suit of equity a special kind of lawsuit that seeks fair treatment in a situation where there is no existing law (p. 398)

summons a notice directing someone to appear in court to answer a complaint or a charge (p. 405)

supply the amount of a good or service available to consumers (p. 423)

supremacy clause a section of the Constitution stating that national law has higher authority than state law (p. 89)

T

tariff an import tax designed to protect a nation's industries from foreign competition (p. 473)

tax return a form a taxpayer submits to the government, reporting income and listing deductions (p. 469)

taxable income the amount of money that remains after subtracting a taxpayer's exemptions and deductions (p. 470)

testimony the statements a witness makes under oath (p. 407)

third party a minor political party in the United States that challenges the two major parties (p. 150)

toleration respect and acceptance of people of a different race, religion, or lifestyle (p. 135)

totalitarian characterized by government control of most aspects of life (p. 517)

town meeting a gathering of local citizens to discuss and vote on important issues (p. 33)

township a division of a county that has its own government (p. 336)

trade deficit the amount by which a country's spending on imports exceeds the amount received from exports (p. 527)

trade sanction an effort to punish a nation by imposing certain trade barriers (p. 539)

traditional economy an economy in which people supply the goods they need by methods passed down through the generations (p. 429)

treason an act that endangers one's country or gives assistance to its enemies (p. 108)

treaty a formal agreement between two or more countries (p. 243)

trust several separate companies that are run by one board of directors (p. 450)

U

unconstitutional in conflict with the Constitution (p. 292)

underemployment work that does not use a person's skills to the fullest (p. 531)

unicameral having a one-house legislature (p. 319)

unit price the price per ounce or other standard unit of measurement (p. 490)

urban renewal rebuilding old neighborhoods in cities (p. 360)

user fee a charge for the use of a service or product (p. 340)

V

vandalism the deliberate destruction of property (p. 402)

veto to reject a bill (p. 65)

visa a permit that allows a person to remain in a foreign country for a certain length of time (p. 260)

voice vote a method of voting in which those who support a measure say yea and those opposed say nay (p. 229)

voluntarism the tradition of unpaid community service (p. 362)

W

ward a voting district within a city (p. 343)

welfare the health, prosperity, and happiness of a person or community (p. 138)

wholesaler a business that buys goods from a manufacturer and then sells those goods to retailers (p. 427)

writ of certiorari a written order directing a lower court to send its records on a case to the Supreme Court for review (p. 298)

writ of habeas corpus a court order guaranteeing a person who is arrested the right to appear before a judge in a court of law (p. 382)

Z

zoning board a commission set up by a local government to decide where houses, stores, factories, and offices may be built (p. 356)

PhotoEdit; **345** Terry Ashe/Gamma Liaison; **346** Reuters/Bettmann; **347, 350–351** B. Daemmrich/The Image Works; **352** M. Granitsas/The Image Works; **353** McLaughlin/The Image Works; **354** Bob Daemmrich; **355** David Young-Wolff/PhotoEdit; **357** Paul Conklin/PhotoEdit; **358** Bob Daemmrich/Stock Boston; **359** Reuters/Bettmann; **360** Bob Daemmrich/Stock Boston; **361** Bob Daemmrich/The Image Works; **362** Bob Daemmrich; **363** Tony Freeman/PhotoEdit; **364** Photri, Inc.; **367** W. Biedel, M.D./Photri, Inc.; **368** Owen Franken/Stock Boston; **369** Charles Feil/Stock Boston; **372** Gary Braasch/Woodfin Camp; **374–375** John Barr/Gamma-Liaison; **376–377** Arnold & Brown; **378** Photri, Inc.; **379** Stuart Franklin/Magnum Photos, Inc.; **380** Ron Slenzak/West Light; **382** Llewellyn/Uniphoto; **383** Michael Newman/PhotoEdit; **384** Shirley Gazin/The Image Works; **386** John Neubauer; **387, 388** Tony Freeman/PhotoEdit; **389** UPI/Bettmann; **390** James Shaffer/PhotoEdit; **392** John Dewaele/Stock Boston; **393** Ron Chapple/FPG International; **396–397** Arnold & Brown; **398** David Young-Wolff/PhotoEdit; **399** John Neubauer; **400** PBJ Pictures/Gamma-Liaison; **401** Crandall/The Image Works; **403** Richard Pasley/Stock Boston; **405** Daemmrich/The Image Works; **406** Arnold & Brown; **408** Jim Pickerell/Stock Boston; **409** Jeff Greenberg/PhotoEdit; **410** Llewellyn/Uniphoto; **411** John Harrington/Black Star; **413** Michael Newman/PhotoEdit; **416** UPI/Bettmann; **418–419** KS Studio; **420–421** Mary Kate Denny/PhotoEdit; **422, 423** Michael Newman/PhotoEdit; **425** Jeffrey Sylvester/FPG International; **426** Photri, Inc.; **427** David Young-Wolff/PhotoEdit; **428** Dennis MacDonald/PhotoEdit; **429, 431** Paul Conklin/PhotoEdit; **432** David Young-Wolff/PhotoEdit; **433** Tony Freeman/PhotoEdit; **434** Arnold & Brown; **435** M. Antman/The Image Works; **436** Ron Coppock/Gamma-Liaison; **437** Courtesy of Alvarado Construction, Inc.; **438** D. Wray/The Image Works; **439** J. Sohm/The Image Works; **442–443** B. Daemmrich/The Image Works; **444** David Wells/The Image Works; **446** The Bettmann Archive; **447** Photri, Inc.; **449** Lee Snider/The Image Works; **450** Culver Pictures, Inc. **451** Laima Druskis/Stock Boston; **542** Bob Daemmrich; **453** Jim Pickerell/West Light; **454** Culver Pictures, Inc. **455** Dale & Marian Zimmerman/Animals Animals; **456** Chris Young/Black Star; **459** Michael Newman/PhotoEdit; **463** © Mike Thompson, *The State Journal-Register*, Copley News Service; **464–465** Terry Qing/FPG International; **466** North Wind Picture Archives; **467, 468** B. Daemmrich/The Image Works; **469** Michael Newman/PhotoEdit; **471** David Young-Wolff/PhotoEdit; **472** Michelle Bridwell/PhotoEdit; **473** Randa Bishop/Uniphoto; **474** Bob Daemmrich; **476** NASA; **477** Baroah/Uniphoto; **479** Daniel Nichols/Gamma-Liaison; **481** Paul Conklin/PhotoEdit; **484–485** KS Studio; **486** B. Daemmrich/The Image Works; **488** Llewellyn/Uniphoto; **490** Michael Newman/PhotoEdit (l); Arnold & Brown (r); **491** Willie L. Hill, Jr./Stock Boston; **493** Michael Krasowitz/FPG International; **495** Richard Pasley/Viesti Associates, Inc.; **496** Bob Daemmrich; **497** Fritz Hoffmann/JB Pictures; **498** Gary A. Conner/PhotoEdit; **499** Fritz Hoffmann/JB Pictures; **500** Arnold & Brown; **501** Roger Sandler/Uniphoto; **502** John Neubauer; **503** Roger B. Bean/Council of Better Business Bureaus, Inc. **506** Bob Daemmrich; **508–509** Erik Freeland/Matrix; **510–511** Rex USA Ltd.; **512** Topham-PA/The Image Works; **514** Jose Caldeira/Black Star; **516** Rex USA Ltd.; **517, 518** Photri, Inc.; **520** Reuters/Bettmann; **521** Jeff Greenberg/PhotoEdit; **524, 525** Fujifotos/The Image Works; **526** Jose Caldeira/Black Star; **527** Dennis Brack/Black Star; **528** Michael Newman/PhotoEdit; **529** Courtesy of Camard de Disputados; **530** Stephen Ferry/Gamma-Liaison; **531** Mark Hume/Black Star; **534–535** Joe Viesti; **536, 537** Reuters/Bettmann; **539** Fred Ward/Black Star; **540** Rick Freedman/Black Star; **542** John Nordell/JB Pictures; **543** Lisa Quinones/Black Star; **545** James Mason/Black Star; **547** Paul Conklin/Uniphoto; **549** Reuters/Bettmann; **550** Wesley Bocxe/JB Pictures; **551** Jeff Greenberg/PhotoEdit; **555** © 1994 Michael Ramirez, Memphis Commercial Appeal/*USA Today*/Copley News Service; **556–557** Mark Reinstein/Uniphoto; **558** D. H. Hessell/Stock Boston; **559** Keisuke Mizumoto/JB Pictures; **561** Phil McCarten/PhotoEdit; **562** Susan Van Etten/PhotoEdit; **563** Scott Rutherford/Black Star; **564** Bob Daemmrich; **565** Mary Kate Denny/PhotoEdit; **566** Robert Brenner/PhotoEdit; **567** PhotoEdit; **568** Robert Brenner/PhotoEdit; **569** Paul S. Conklin; **572** John Maier/JB Pictures; **574** Jim Barber; **582–589** White House Historical Society; **590–594** Glencoe file.